Wind Over Sand

Wind Over Sand

THE DIPLOMACY OF
FRANKLIN ROOSEVELT

Frederick W. Marks III

THE UNIVERSITY OF GEORGIA PRESS
Athens and London

© 1988 by the University of Georgia Press
Athens, Georgia 30602
All rights reserved

Designed by Sandra Strother Hudson
Set in 10 on 13 Trump Mediaeval
by the Composing Room of Michigan
Printed and bound by Thomson-Shore

The paper in this book meets the guidelines
for permanence and durability of the Committee on
Production Guidelines for Book Longevity of the
Council on Library Resources.

Printed in the United States of America

92 91 90 89 88   5 4 3 2 1

Library of Congress Cataloging in Publication Data

Marks, Frederick W.
Wind over sand.

Bibliography: p.
Includes index.
1. United States—Foreign relations—1933–1945.
2. Roosevelt, Franklin D. (Franklin Delano), 1882–1945.
I. Title.
E806.M38   1987   973.917′.092′4   86–24976
ISBN 0-8203-0929-X (alk. paper)

British Library Cataloging in Publication Data available

To Sylvia

Contents

Preface

*To judge rightly of the present we must oppose it to the
past; for all judgment is comparative. . . . If we act only for
ourselves, to neglect the study of history is not prudent; if
we are entrusted with the care of others it is not just.*

SAMUEL JOHNSON, *Rasselas*

T HE following chapters will have
served their purpose if they succeed in exposing but a small portion of
the immense body of myth which has come to cling to the record of
New Deal diplomacy. Winston Churchill once remarked of Stalin that
he was a riddle wrapped in mystery inside an enigma. So, too, in the
case of Franklin Roosevelt. His ability to shroud motivation and conceal the inner spring of executive action has given rise to one misconception after another. While it is the nature of diplomacy to operate
behind closed doors, this is particularly true of the era 1933–45.

In dealing with someone as elusive as FDR, whose record has
prompted an endless stream of inquiry, the need is for research at once
deep enough and broad enough to yield a series of interconnected
monographs. Manuscript collections, many of them previously untapped, in France, England, Scotland, and Canada, not to mention the
United States, all produced one or another link in the following chain
of argument.[1] Indeed, it was only from such a diverse fund of information that one could begin to construct a vehicle capable of accom-
modating the full range of Roosevelt's foreign policy. To have approached the problem in any other way would have been like trying to
piece together a giant jigsaw puzzle without indication of overall color
scheme. Patterns indistinguishable on the basis of archival work covering a limited period would often become clear as one moved forward or
backward in point of time. Likewise, presidential tactics which appeared vague on the basis of research conducted in one particular for-

eign capital began to crystallize when placed alongside situations observable elsewhere.

Although there is insufficient room at the outset to allude to all the findings of an extended research effort, it may be useful, by way of introduction, to touch upon a few of the more salient points. To cite one example, historians and political scientists have pictured FDR as preoccupied with economic concerns during his first year in office—so much so that he could find little room for diplomatic maneuver.[2] I will argue, in light of fresh evidence, that he was exceedingly active on the diplomatic front, and with far less success than one would be inclined to assume. This applies not only to the first Hundred Days, as treated in Chapter 1, but also to the prewar period as a whole. It will thus be seen that by repeatedly fumbling the ball during his initial term, he contributed in no small measure to the extreme isolationist sentiment which later tied his hands against Nazi Germany.

Chapter 2 seeks to demonstrate that the United States never sought genuine accommodation with Japan. Roosevelt's policy appears to have been one of equivocation or, to put it another way, "no war, no peace." This, in turn, aroused false hope on the part of Tokyo, leading in the end to tragic consequences. Misrepresentation, ambivalence, and prevarication were common elements on Roosevelt's side of the equation from the beginning. Most readers will be familiar with the American case against Japan. It is deeply etched on the national psyche, having been rehearsed in countless books, documentaries, and war trials. What is important is that Tokyo, finding itself on the losing side of the war, never attempted to reply in kind. Naturally, this places a serious obstacle in the path of anyone seeking a genuinely balanced view of history. What I have attempted to do, therefore, is to outline Tokyo's case for involvement in Manchuria in the kind of scope and detail required if one is to understand the major elements of the Japanese position. Chapter 2 also treats a succession of signal events, including Roosevelt's famed Quarantine Address and the much neglected Brussels Conference of 1937. Here, as elsewhere, the search is for criteria upon which to evaluate presidential performance. We are left with the profile of a sharply divided administration, one which yielded, little by little over the years, to Roosevelt's pro-Chinese sentiment. What is perhaps most striking in this respect is that events of 1934 prove to be on an almost perfect parallel with those of 1941.

The third chapter, which focuses directly upon the final break be-

tween Tokyo and Washington, is an extension of themes developed earlier. Together with the previous chapter, it singles out a number of key
phases, many of them hitherto ignored, in the eight-year period of talks
carried on between the United States and Japan. Again, the stress is on
American duplicity, as exemplified by Roosevelt's role in the funeral of
Ambassador Hiroshi Saito. One will observe that the Hull-Nomura
talks, far from reflecting positive effort on the part of the administration, proceeded from a determination to avoid anything approaching
meaningful negotiation. Similarly, where the Maryknoll missioners,
Bishop James E. Walsh and Reverend James M. Drought, have traditionally been depicted as well-meaning amateurs who jeopardized
America's chance for a compromise peace, they are shown in this context to be quite different. The talks themselves are developed within a
historical framework which invites comparison with earlier rounds of
negotiation, all of them equally barren, equally lacking in commitment,
and equally overlooked.[3] In addition, I shall argue that FDR gave Britain
the equivalent of a secret military guarantee to protect its possessions in
the Far East and that he did so long before the date generally accepted.[4]

Roosevelt's double life, as crusader for democratic values and covert
agent of appeasement, is the theme of Chapter 4. Among the incidents
making their monographic debut are Samuel Fuller's succession of trips
to Berlin; visits by Sumner Welles and William C. Bullitt to transatlantic capitals in September and November of 1937; Hugh Wilson's talks in
Prague during August of 1938; Ambassador Joseph P. Kennedy's role in
last-minute negotiations leading to Munich; and Colonel Truman
Smith's discussion of Czech partition with his Polish colleague in Berlin
(Smith was U.S. military attaché in Germany).[5] Added to these events
are James D. Mooney's missions to Berlin; Roosevelt's effort to win a
lion's share of the credit for Munich; and the Welles mission of early
1940, which is stripped of pretense and reduced to its essential function
as an outgrowth of FDR's seven-year exercise in appeasement.

A number of auxiliary myths are felled in the process. It will become
clear, for instance, that the movement for American rearmament was
blocked not by isolationist forces, as is widely assumed, but by the
White House. Rejecting the advice of nearly all his counselors, FDR
refused to carry the case for rearmament until opinion polls showed him
lagging well behind Congress and the public. All at once, he became a
consistent advocate of Allied resistance to Germany. At the same time,
presidential promises made to France, Britain, and Poland without con-

gressional authorization proved impossible to fulfill, and Hitler's Third
Reich was led to view Western policy as a colossal bluff built upon a
militarily defunct United States.

Chapter 5 opens with an analysis of Roosevelt's relationship with two
embattled generalissimos, Joseph Stalin and Chiang Kai-shek, both of
whom were destined to play a pivotal role in the postwar world. As with
other topics, a broad body of factual evidence is adduced with an eye to
testing conventional interpretation. To this is added a scholarly appraisal, the first to date, of Roosevelt's reputation as a world leader.
Nearly every facet of his image overseas, including the celebrated relationship with Churchill, has been subjected to careful scrutiny. Moreover, since Roosevelt's Good Neighbor Policy is so often cited as a showcase in the diplomatic field, and with references which tend on the
whole to be less than conclusive, an effort is made in a separate chapter
to develop objective standards for measuring America's standing
throughout the hemisphere.

Finally, in the concluding essay, my aim has been to analyze presidential proclivities and thought processes as they influenced the making of
American foreign policy over a twelve-year span. Perhaps I am more
optimistic than I have any right to be about the possibility of penetrating
Roosevelt's labyrinthine mind on the basis of discernible patterns. But I
believe it significant, among other things, that parochialism, which
characterized the outlook of the nation generally, was also a powerful
force in the White House—and with all the limitations inherent in any
type of mindset. Here again, much of the ground to be covered is relatively uncharted.

The task of extricating riddle from mystery and mystery from enigma
has not been an easy one, nor is it by any means complete. Truth is
seldom hard and fast. In this case, especially, there is much work still to
be done. Nevertheless, those who persist in believing that it is possible
to learn from history and that one may benefit from a systematic study
of the past will find their faith strengthened, and I venture to hope that
whatever modest beginning is made in this volume will help to illumine
the path for future scholars.

Special thanks are extended to the staff of the Franklin D. Roosevelt
and Herbert H. Hoover presidential libraries for supplying sheaves of
documentation on frequent request; also to the late Reverend James
Logue, M.M., director of Maryknoll Archives. Father Logue enabled me

to tap correspondence essential for my analysis of the Hull-Nomura talks. I wish to thank Thomas B. Lee, director of American Studies at Tamkang University, Republic of China, for his help in obtaining a valuable collection of documentary material relating to the Sino-Japanese War during my research trip to Taipei. I also wish to express my thanks to B. S. Benedikz, head of special collections at Birmingham University (England), for pointing the way to various productive pockets of research. In addition, I should like to mention the following: James Ritchie, keeper of manuscripts at the National Library of Scotland, who made it possible to retrieve important documents in storage; Marion M. Stewart, archivist at Churchill College, Cambridge, who smoothed my access to a trove of material relating to the 1930s; and Sarita Lady Vansittart, who graciously granted permission to inspect her husband's papers. Janine Bourdin and Marie-Geneviève Chevignard of the Fondation Nationale des Sciences Politiques were most helpful in making the Daladier Papers available; Peter De Lottinville, archivist of the Canadian Prime Ministers Archives, directed me to the heart of Ottawa's valuable collections; and Julian Wolff, commissionaire of the Baker Street Irregulars, granted me an extraordinary interview.

I am indebted as well to a number of universities for permission to use their archives: in particular, to Princeton, Yale, and Harvard; also to Georgetown, the University of Delaware, Columbia University (Oral History Collection as well as Archives), Oxford, Cambridge, and Queens University (Kingston, Ontario). Nor would it do to close out this list of acknowledgment without expressing my sincere appreciation for courtesies extended by the Manuscript Division of the Library of Congress; the French Foreign Ministry (Quai d'Orsay); the French National Archives; the British National Library; the Scottish Record Office; and the Public Record Office at Kew, England.

Portions of certain chapters, along with occasional quotations, have been included by permission of the *Pacific Historical Review;* the *Historical Journal* of England; *Presidential Studies Quarterly;* the *South Atlantic Quarterly;* the Houghton Library, Harvard University; Princeton University Library; the University of Delaware Library; the Hoover Institution; the Master, Fellows and Scholars of Churchill College in the University of Cambridge; the trustees of the National Library of Scotland; the syndics of Cambridge University Library; Birmingham University Library; Yale University Library; the British Library Board;

the Public Archives of Canada; the Earl of Halifax; the Marquis of Lothian; and the executors of the estate of the late Sir Alexander Cadogan.

Many are the colleagues whose work has furnished a valued point of departure as well as a deep fund of knowledge upon which I have drawn freely and at times almost unconsciously. They are too numerous to mention except by way of notes. But among those who read *Wind over Sand* in the formative stage are Bradford Perkins, Walter O. Forster, and Thomas R. Maddux. Each of them offered useful advice, volunteering views which on occasion differed refreshingly from my own. Tadashi Aruga, T. Inoue, and Takeo Iguchi offered valuble assistance in refining specific sections relating to Japan. And last, but by no means least, my wife, Sylvia Ann, has helped far beyond anything in the power of poor words to express.

Wind Over Sand

Introduction

WHAT manner of man, Franklin Delano Roosevelt? What manner of statesman? Like a colossus, he bestrode American history for twelve tumultuous years. Sphinxlike, he continues to baffle each succeeding generation of historians. To some, he appears to have been an internationalist turned isolationist, to others an internationalist who merely made timely concessions to the isolationist bloc.[1] The leading analyst of his mind cannot be certain whether initially he favored or opposed the idea of a United Nations.[2] Whether he was for or against the fateful Munich Conference of 1938 leads to still another quandary.[3] One writer calls him a "practical idealist," another an "idealistic realist."[4] Most would agree that he possessed both qualities, but since one does not preclude the other, how much of his well-known domestic realism carried over into the field of foreign policy? How were his ideals manifested? What motive or set of motives prompted him to call for a quarantine of aggressor nations in 1937? How successful was the Good Neighbor Policy? And how does one define success? How far did he go to involve his country in the war against Germany, and to what degree did he induce the lightning attack on Pearl Harbor?[5] These are but a few of the many questions to which this volume is addressed.

Diplomatic historians have run the gamut. Charles Tansill devoted hundreds of pages to building a case for Roosevelt's devious side just as others of like persuasion have maintained that his exposure of the Pacific fleet was deliberate. Some among the early revisionists concentrated on the administration's illiberal policy regarding Spain and France.[6] Many rested their case on the arguable assumption that the Axis posed no long-term threat to the United States.[7] Most concentrated on one or two stock themes. Not a few made dubious use of the evidence or forfeited credibility by referring to the president as "Uncle Sap" or "the Savior." Charles Beard, whose concern stemmed mainly from what he considered wrongful diversion of the nation's energy from domestic reform to war, was not overly concerned with the nuts and bolts of diplomacy.[8] At the other end of the spectrum are Joseph Alsop and Robert Kintner, who, in *American White Paper* (1940), examined events leading to World War II solely from the slant of the White House. Alsop wrote Eleanor Roosevelt, his wife's cousin, that he was "deeply in accord with the President's foreign policy" and wished to write an account of his role in events leading to the German invasion of Poland to dispel "idiotic misapprehensions." Anything intended for publication, he promised, would be properly cleared.[9]

Traces of the white paper mentality remain.[10] One collection of essays on the origin of the war with Japan finds fault with everything and everyone except Roosevelt.[11] In other accounts, Japan's case is conspicuous for its absence, and the core of the problem is located in a trinity of supporting players, Admiral Nomura, Father Drought, and Bishop Walsh.[12] Wittingly or unwittingly, the term "United States" has been used as a substitute for the name Roosevelt where the context would appear compromising.[13]

Frequently, FDR's problems are traced to events or persons beyond his control. It is said that the 1930s was a decade of exceptional turbulence, as indeed it was. The isolationist thesis is then invoked to explain everything from Roosevelt's acquiescence in storm-cellar neutrality to his position regarding the wartime capture of Berlin and Prague. When unfortunate military decisions are not attributed to his zealous immersion in the role of commander in chief intent upon saving lives, they are often imputed to a desire on the part of the American people to "bring the boys home."[14] It has even been suggested that one of the most consummate political tacticians of all time could not control his own bureaucratic apparatus. Whether it is the promise of a battleship to Stalin, the effort to block France's return to Indochina, or an alleged desire to sustain negotiations with Japan in 1941, noble instincts are shown sinking willy-nilly beneath the weight of executive departments.[15] One may well wonder at times if there really was a man named Roosevelt.[16] Senator Key Pittman of Nevada presents a favorite target in the halls of Congress, just as the ambassadorial trio of Joseph Kennedy, William Bullitt, and Joseph Davies serves as a conductor in the field.[17] Apologists are also fond of citing Secretary of State Cordell

Hull.[18] Criticism aimed squarely at the president is apt to be sand-wiched outlaw-wise between a laudatory introduction and an unwar-ranted conclusion.[19]

For some time, a movement has been under way to render more dis-passionate accounts. Where Professor Harry Elmer Barnes could once complain of academic whitewashing and historical blackout, the New Deal is rapidly becoming three-dimensional.[20] No longer are historians content to explain Roosevelt's failure on neutrality reform by suggest-ing that he did not want to stir antipathy at home or reveal to the world the strength of the isolationists.[21] Since 1945, there has been a growing awareness of the extent of his deference to public opinion. More and more questions have been raised about the strength of his leadership.[22] The Marxist theory that he is best understood in terms of a drive to make the world safe for American capitalism has sparked extensive debate.[23]

At the same time, there are remarkable gaps in the literature. Given the bulk of the source material available, and hence the opportunity to examine virtually every episode in depth, it is surprising how little has been written on the diplomacy of the Hundred Days, so vital for under-standing all that came after. There is no book on the Brussels Con-ference, no rigorous analysis of the ill-fated Hull-Nomura talks. The meaning of the Welles mission to Europe in 1940 remains opaque.[24] Many questions go begging. How acute was the presidential vision? To the degree that events on the Continent were beyond his control, how effective was he in wielding the influence at his command? How suc-cessfully did he take the lead in the Western Hemisphere? How many initiatives did he launch and how many of these bore fruit? How many appeals did he make and how many were heeded? How many invita-tions did he extend to leaders of foreign countries and how many were accepted? How was he regarded by those foreign officials who knew him best? One may legitimately ask whether he had viable alter-natives. How many in either political party offered sound advice? Did he tailor power to policy? Did he grasp alien attitudes and points of view? Given the levers at his disposal prior to Japan's attack on Pearl Harbor, did he enhance the reputation of the United States? Did he establish the credibility of his office?

Because the following essays were written with these and other such queries in mind, the aim has been to organize the discussion along conceptual as well as chronological lines. As indicated above, much of the facual evidence presented here appears for the first time. Nevertheless, the emphasis throughout has been on establishing norms for analysis and exploring new lines of development.

One reason why the quest for certainty has proven so engagingly inconclusive in the past is that a great many primary sources have been lost, destroyed, or deliberately withheld from public view. The war trials atmosphere that still pervades the postwar era can hardly be expected to ensure candid reporting. In Japan, such figures as Shigenori Tōgō, Mamoru Shigemitsu, and Nobutaka Ike have written pro-American accounts of their native land, and the diplomatic silence extends to friends as well as erstwhile enemies. [25] Nations allied with the United States during the war continue to rely on Washington for aid. Thus, when Chin-tung Liang tapped Nationalist Chinese archives to publish his revealing study of Stilwell in China—it achieved instant best-seller status in Taiwan, going through five printings in three months—he barely scratched the surface of potential sources.[26] Similarly, when Lord Templewood (Samuel Hoare) published a description of his experience as head of the British mission in Madrid, he portrayed Alexander Weddell, his American counterpart, as charming and blamed Weddell's difficulties with Spanish Foreign Minister Ramón Serrano Suñer on the latter. All of this must be read against a background of unpublished utterance in which Hoare accused Weddell of being "completely incompetent" and prone to "gaffes."[27] It is interesting to note that the greater the time span following Roosevelt's death, the more trenchant the criticism. Churchill wrote first, then de Gaulle, then Eden. Each became a trifle bolder, with Eden's second volume more sharply worded than the first.[28]

It is customary, of course, even under normal circumstances, for governments to publish their documents selectively, and the period under review is no exception. Working at the National Archives, one quickly became accustomed to seeing stamps and memoranda signifying that the papers in hand had been cleared for inspection. One of the best examples of British removal of sensitive material is a section of the minutes of the Churchill War Cabinet.[29] Nothing could be more commonplace than the disappearance of records outlining an exchange between Secretary of the Treasury Henry Morgenthau, Jr. and French agents in which a means was sought to circumvent American neutrality law.[30] If there is no transcript of a crucial Roosevelt phone call to Premier Daladier, it is again to be expected.[31] FDR asked the French never to divulge his position on the Brussels Conference much the way Sumner Welles told British Ambassador Sir Ronald Lindsay to burn evidence relating to American operation of a provocative naval patrol.[32] We do not have the full text of Welles's talk with German leaders in 1940, only scraps. Likewise, when one tries to locate the record of an important interview between roving ambassador Norman Davis and Prime Minister Ramsay MacDonald, one finds only a note in the published documents to the effect that the minutes of the interview are inexplicably missing.[33] Searching for the German reaction to Roosevelt's discussion of possible helium sales to Berlin, one must be content with a truncated version ending in ellipses.[34]

Further complicating the work of the scholar is the fact that good-sized portions of private manuscript collections have been impounded. This applies to everything from drafts of books by Joseph Davies (on file at the Library of Congress) to Churchill's papers, which will not be available until ten years after the completion of his official biography. The papers of Léon Blum and Joseph Paul-Boncour, held respectively by the French Fondation Nationale des Sciences Politiques and the French Archives Nationales, contain little more than newspaper clippings and speech manuscripts for the period. What makes it doubly difficult is the way materials are sometimes doctored for publication. When the Dutch minister to Japan warned of a possible descent by the Japanese on Guam, American Ambassador Joseph Grew commented in his diary, "I do not think such an insane step is likely." In *Ten Years*, however, Grew added the word "now," making himself appear more prescient.[35] Occasionally, deletions may change the whole tone of a memoir as in the case of the Forrestal diaries and sections of the Davies diary included in *Mission to Moscow*. Ambassador Breckinridge Long's impolitic comments on *Mein Kampf* have been omitted in his published diary just as important parts of a Bullitt cable were shielded from publication by the State Department.[36] Most disquieting of all is to find certain parts of a manuscript collection unaccountably missing. While the research for this work was in process, key letters exchanged by Roosevelt and his British friend Arthur Murray (Lord Elibank) were absent from the Elibank Papers. Sections in the Grew diary for August 1941 had been scissored out. Many pages of the Long diary at the Library of Congress were missing (one was razored away).[37]

Another obvious difficulty in dealing with any twelve-year period of modern history is the sheer size of the documentation. The *Foreign*

Relations series alone runs to approximately one hundred thick tomes. This is especially awesome when the proverbial needle in the haystack turns out to be missing. The best sampling and selection techniques will never be proof against official censorship. Yet in treating a figure as enigmatic as FDR, one who held his cards so close to his chest, they are vital. There is a compelling need to see his presidency whole. Even if there were a great many more monographs to throw light on critical episodes, the curious student would still be obliged to comb through piles of print covering the entire period. As previously suggested, he would still have to range over many geographical boundaries to identify patterns which furnish a clue to Roosevelt's modus operandi. To cite one example, Sumner Welles's trip to Europe in 1940 cannot be properly evaluated unless it is seen as the culmination of many other missions including two by Samuel Fuller, one by Welles himself, and separate trips by American envoys William Bullitt, Hugh Wilson, William R. Davis, and James D. Mooney. Ambassador Long's suggestions to Mussolini in 1935, classed by Roosevelt as unauthorized, turn out to be one of a series of diplomatic initiatives made under similar circumstances. To cite a third instance, when Roosevelt aides blamed Admiral Nomura in 1941 for misunderstanding the American diplomatic position on account of a faulty command of English, the accusation bears a striking resemblance to other situations involving similar charges on the part of the administration.[38] Hull's talks with Nomura can be fully understood only within the context of earlier exchanges between Grew and Nomura, Francis B. Sayre and Hachiro Arita, Grew and Arita.

Still another challenge in evaluating the record of the New Deal is that one must conjure with a figure so heavily laden with emotional freight. Since 1933, Roosevelt has been the object of special fondness and hate. In fact, his personality reveals more of the gnarled than the straight; there are enough twists and turns within one psyche to fascinate any would-be biographer. Clowning antics, a sarcastic tongue, mimicry, and a magnificent smile were all part of the act, and the act was the man. His puckish response to reporter Arthur Krock when asked why he could not meet confidentially with European leaders at sea near the Azores was typical: "I would find Bob Allen, Drew Pearson, Paul Mellon, and Walter Winchell appearing, pencil in hand from the mouth of a sea-going whale!" Not many could resist the charm of his stories or the seemingly inexhaustible fund of anecdote from whence they came. Blandishments followed, one upon another, tempting the strong and overwhelming the weak. Reporters marveled at the range of a memory that could absorb almost any event of consequence at the local, state, national, or international level. Few rivaled him in sidestepping an awkward question or firing off one of his own.[39]

He was supremely gifted with the ability to speak in language intelligible to the average man. Dictatorship, as he once said, was a system for sheep, and "we still intend to do our own thinking!" Well did he know how to stoke America's smoldering resentment against Hitler: "The experience of the past two years has proven beyond doubt that no nation can appease the Nazis. No man can tame a tiger into a kitten by stroking it. There can be no appeasement with ruthlessness. There can be no reasoning with an incendiary bomb. We know that a nation can have peace with the Nazis only at the price of total surrender."[40] It was on the rostrum that he excelled, his head thrown back and eyes atwinkle behind spotless pince-nez, cigarette holder tilted at a jaunty angle. After refining multiple drafts of an address and preparing its delivery for near perfect timing and cadence, his vibrant voice could rouse the dullest of hearts. To this day, Roosevelt's speeches still breathe much of their original fire when read flat down on the printed page. Although critics have tried to take the bloom off the flower by stressing the help he received from a pool of talented writers, his mastery of style is evident even in diplomatic dispatches where he would insert corrections to eliminate an occasional arch phrase or touch of arrogance.[41] Such was his diction that Professor Lloyd James, linguistic adviser to the BBC, proposed it as a standard for the English-speaking world.[42]

What is paradoxical about Roosevelt's strength is that the very virtues and skills which made him so formidable as a domestic politician were not necessarily of use in diplomacy; indeed, they may have served to create a false sense of security. One must take care not to mistake the personality for the man. Although he cut a big figure at home, this could not guarantee his effectiveness in the give and take of diplomatic exchange. International relations require a different set of credentials. A winner of elections may lose the peace. The same charm and humanitarian instinct which count for so much in American democratic practice do not of necessity carry weight abroad. Stalin never much cared whether Roosevelt appeared cheerful or morose. What mattered was the second front. A man who could be spellbinding on American radio or before a joint session of Congress had no such hold on the constituency of another country. And while American reporters might be flattered by his informal manner or impressed by the quickness of his repartee, foreign observers looked more to substance. A man who could dangle patronage to advantage before the nose of an American congressman had nothing comparable to offer under the intense gaze of a Winston Churchill or Charles de Gaulle. The leaders of independent nations were his equal in bargaining power as no individual senator or congressman could ever be.

Even the phrase "New Deal diplomacy," though useful, is something of a misnomer. It was not for any failure in diplomacy that the opposition lost its mandate in 1932, and Roosevelt knew it. Republicans, having taken the lead in sponsoring worldwide disarmament, had maintained a fair amount of momentum in the years since the Washington Naval Conference. Secretary of State Charles Evans Hughes had been so successful, in fact, in arranging a diplomatic solution for the Far East that he caused most journalists to discard their vision of war with Japan as inevitable. Roosevelt himself published an article at the time urging Americans to "trust Japan." The irony is that when President Coolidge announced naval exercises geared to the defense of Pearl Harbor, FDR echoed the national mood in an editorial written for the *Macon Daily Telegraph*: "It is hardly tactful for the American Government to give . . . the impression . . . that we are trying to find out how easy or how difficult it would be for the Japanese Navy to occupy Hawaii." Few Japanese officials took the trouble in those days to read Franklin Roosevelt's editorials, but had they done so, they would have found a very mixed bag, for he took care to balance his counsel of trust with an equally popular caveat: "Californians have properly objected [to Japanese immigration] on the sound basic ground that . . . the mingling of Asiatic blood with European or American blood produces, in nine cases out of ten, the most unfortunate results." This, needless to say, was the logic which produced the discriminatory Immigration Act of 1924.[43]

If Coolidge identified his administration with a campaign to outlaw war, Herbert Hoover prompted disengagement of American forces from Latin America and engineered the policy of the Good Neighbor. His secretary of state, Henry L. Stimson, took the lead in championing a policy of nonrecognition with regard to Japanese advances in the Far East. Publicly, in an open letter to the Senate Foreign Relations Committee, Stimson condemned Japan for its "aggression" and refused to recognize the new state of Manchukuo. Privately, he suggested that Tokyo was in the hands of militarists and that economic sanctions would bring her to heel. Roosevelt made a point not only of consulting Stimson in January 1933 but of supporting his Far East policy in a special press release. In short, he accepted the basic assumptions of the outgoing administration with reference to the Far East as well as other areas of the world.[44]

And what of Theodore Roosevelt and Woodrow Wilson? No treatment of the diplomatic context would be complete without touching on the way FDR was influenced by the great Progressive leaders of his youth. He invoked them, copied them, and kept their example continually in mind even as he piloted the ship of state with a compass uniquely his own. The first Roosevelt was bound to make an indelible impression on the second, if for no other reason than that he was a fifth cousin who happened to live in the White House. His visit to the Harvard campus while FDR was editor of the *Crimson* provided the latter with an unprecedented scoop, and it was Theodore who gave niece Eleanor away when she married Franklin. Many are the ways in which the two Roosevelts resembled one another. If someone were to ask which president loved ornithology and the navy, took boxing lessons as a young man, and possessed an ebullient personality with a great store of animal energy; if it were added that said person cultivated members of the British Embassy while serving as assistant secretary of the navy and took a hunting trip to the marshes of Louisiana after losing an important political campaign; if, in addition, one knew that the man in question loved to hike strenuously, to play "hare and hounds" with his children and neighbors, and to scale cliffs; if, finally, one were told that he was elected governor of New York before reaching the White House, one might feel confident in naming T.R. The correct answer, however, would be Franklin Roosevelt. FDR rented a home from T.R.'s sister while in Washington and sounded like him in most of his early statements on war and preparedness.[45]

The second Roosevelt not only attempted to follow the first into the presidency through the rear door of the vice-presidency; he tried to imitate a number of his diplomatic devices, attaching the phrase "gentlemen's agreement" to various understandings and recruiting a London *Times* correspondent to deliver a stern warning to Whitehall. His use of British military attaché Arthur Murray as a confidential link with the British government resembled the way T.R. had used another military attaché, Arthur Lee.[46] Like his namesake, FDR loved to call royalty by their first names and do away with the ceremony connected with traditional diplomacy. Both loved to talk affairs of state while at play, one in the swimming pool, the other on the tennis court.[47] Both grappled with the problems of how to prevent war from convulsing Europe, and each tried to end hostilities in the Orient. They were also presented with similar opportunities to act as peacemaker in the Western Hemisphere. The chill wind of isolationist sentiment was as much a factor in 1905 as it was in 1935, yet both Roosevelts succeeded in charting an interventionist course. Although FDR criticized T.R. for overreaching executive prerogative in the anthracite coal strike and Panamanian Revolution, the two presidents were strong executives who found a way to make their will prevail over Congress and the people.[48] One can easily mistake FDR for T.R. when listening to the former discuss his Destroyers for Bases agreement: "If I had done that [consult Congress], the subject would still be in the tender care of the Committees."[49]

Such examples could be multiplied, but there is another side to the coin. If the similarity between the two Roosevelts was great, so too was the dissimilarity. One saw the world in terms of a balance of power and stressed the need for military preparedness. The other did not. It is FDR's lack of any coherent strategy in the field of foreign policy which forms a prominent theme in each of the following seven chapters. Both Roosevelts emerged from an unusually cosmopolitan background, yet with a marked difference, as will be seen in Chapter 7. The second Roosevelt had no Jules Jusserand upon whom to rely for international perspective. There was no Kaneko or Strachey during the 1930s, no Sternburg; nor were there any foreign faces in Hull's game of croquet.[50]

In practice, it was Wilson, not T.R., who made the most enduring impression on FDR. Whether one thinks of 1917 or 1937, there is the same difficulty with the press in Paris, the same view of Berlin and Tokyo. Wilson viewed Germany as a land controlled by militarists, almost by definition hostile to democratic countries. He also believed firmly that Japan, as the "Prussia of the Far East," would be inimical to the West if ever it gained control of the Chinese mainland. "Yellow Peril" thinking intensified as the country faced successive war scares with Japan. Assistant Secretary of the Navy Franklin Roosevelt, faced with a belligerent Japanese reaction to California's Alien Land Act, drew up a plan for war in 1913. Corregidor gunners were ordered to man their posts day and night. Manila Bay fairly bristled with mines. Journalist William Randolph Hearst forecast a Japanese invasion of the United States, and when the guns of August 1914 finally fell silent, Secretary of the Navy Josephus Daniels, assisted by FDR, took steps to secure the nation's Pacific flank.[51]

All through this period, Roosevelt served a president who was closely associated with the missionary movement in China, one who expected great things from the twin leaven of democracy and Christianity. As Wilson told his cabinet, he felt "keenly the desire to help China." Of the two Oriental experts who accompanied him to Versailles, one, Stanley K. Hornbeck, went on to become the most influential of Roosevelt's advisers on the Far East. Significantly, in the case of both Wilson and the second Roosevelt, American policy fell between two stools. Wilson opposed Japan's Twenty-One Demands on China yet allowed Secretary of State Robert Lansing to sign an agreement with Viscount Ishii making the American defense of Chinese sovereignty nominal at best. Almost single-handedly, he maneuvered to defeat Tokyo in its campaign for a treaty clause upholding racial equality. Nonetheless, he acquiesced in the continued occupation of Shantung and for this was nailed to the Senate wall by Henry Cabot Lodge, who subscribed as much as anyone to the notion of Japan as malevolent warmonger. Wilson was also troubled by Japanese occupation of Siberia and sent seven thousand marines to Vladivostok as an earnest of his concern. Japan, in no mood to heed the gesture of a discredited president, boosted the size of its occupation force tenfold until the United States withdrew, leaving the Russian bear to lick its cubs into shape. British leaders, just as skeptical in 1919 of America's ability to defend China as they would be in 1939, were equally ready to concede Tokyo a place on the mainland in return for a quid pro quo. Colonel House persisted in his role as dissenter on Far Eastern policy, but where Wilson brushed his advice aside, Roosevelt listened to him until he died, albeit with only one ear.[52]

Like Wilson, FDR asserted the universal validity of the democratic ideal, but unlike him he possessed neither the mind of a philosopher nor the soul of a prophet. Wilson was prepared to give his life for the League. FDR wavered. The second Roosevelt did not wish to repeat the mistakes of an older generation. Wilson, in his opinion, had not warned Germany often enough prior to her invasion of Belgium. Neither had he made enough personal contact with Allied leaders during the war. At the same time, Whitehall had been permitted to monopolize Middle Eastern oil and shut American business out of North Africa. Remembering that certain advisers had resigned over Wilson's so-called "Shantung sellout" and that such opponents as William Borah used it to inflict defeat, he confided to Halifax that he, too, might be confronted someday with a "Battalion of Death" unless proper steps were taken. Perhaps this is one reason why he paid such rapt attention to opinion polls and brought Republican spokesmen into cabinet decisions and postwar planning as well as into his drive for American membership in the International Labor Organization (ILO). Full-scale belligerency fell to the lot of both men, and as neither one ventured to lead the country into the fray precipitately, but only after repeated sinkings of American vessels, it was fitting that Mrs. Wilson should have accompanied Mrs. Roosevelt to Capitol Hill on the day FDR delivered his war message.[53]

1. The Hundred Days

Wᴴᴇɴ William L. Langer and S. Everett Gleason published their magisterial two-volume account of New Deal diplomacy more than three decades ago, they chose as their starting point the year 1937 and said virtually nothing about FDR's first Hundred Days. Ever since, Roosevelt's Quarantine Address has been regarded as the opening gun in a campaign for American involvement overseas. The presumption is that try as he might to educate Americans to their responsibility during his first term, a wall of isolationist sentiment sealed off every avenue of approach. While it is generally granted that he mismanaged the London Economic Conference, he is thought to have been handicapped by severe pressure resulting from the economic crisis at home. Not until events in Germany and the Far East began to impinge directly on the mind of the average citizen, one is given to understand, did he find room for maneuver. Only then, through a process of advance and retreat, and with the aid of numerous trial balloons, could he awaken America to the twofold danger of isolation and neutrality. Such is the standard interpretation.[1]

In point of fact, one does not have to go as far as 1937 to observe Roosevelt in full diplomatic panoply. From the moment he first took office, and even before, he embraced the role of world leader with a relish rarely surpassed. As we shall see, he was more active as a statesman during this initial period, and less successfully active, than at any other time prior to the attack on Pearl Harbor. Very quickly he revealed nearly every trait and pattern that would characterize his stewardship over the next decade. Just as the Hundred Days proved crucial in the enactment of domestic legislation, placing FDR's personal stamp on the face of social reform, so did it prove decisive in setting the course of diplomacy.

There can be no doubt of the urgency of the panic that rocked Wall Street in 1929 and all but guaranteed President Hoover's defeat. Financial chaos was indisputably the first business of the New Deal. By 1933, unemployment stood at 15 million. Five thousand banks had failed and $9 billion in liquid assets were gone. Steel plants operated at 12 percent capacity, and one hundred thousand Americans applied for jobs in the Soviet Union. Natives of the Cameroons in West Africa sent New York City $3.77 for relief of the "starving." Radical leaders Huey Long, Father Coughlin, and Dr. Townsend each had a following. There were violent farm strikes and communist-led demonstrations. In 1932, a "bonus army" of seventeen thousand angry former servicemen encamped near the White House.

At the same time, the combined vote of the Communist and Socialist parties in the election of 1932 came to a trifling 3 percent. The Democratic Platform Committee drafted a conservative document, and the prime concern of delegates to both party conventions in 1932 was liquor. "Here we are," wrote John Dewey, "in the midst of the greatest crisis since the Civil War, and the only thing the two national parties seem to want to debate is booze." During the campaign, Roosevelt assailed Hoover for radical social measures and prodigal spending, for wanting to center control of everything in Washington. At Sioux City, Iowa, he accused his opposition of being "the greatest spending administration in peace times in all our history. It is an administration that has piled bureau on bureau, commission on commission." In Pittsburgh, he said, "I regard reduction in federal spending as one of the most important issues of the campaign." And when Britain's Stanley Baldwin visited the United States in the fall of 1933 between terms as prime minister, he noted "little evidence of what we should call a revolutionary spirit, even amongst the unemployed."[2] There is little to show that this was not so a year before. The domestic situation may have been serious, but it does not support the common view that Roosevelt was compelled to move slowly in foreign affairs. Although it may be theoretically true, as one scholar puts it, that the crisis at home made foreign relations a secondary concern, we shall see that this is not how things worked out in practice.[3]

Where failure in foreign policy has not been attributed to financial chaos, it is often said to flow from lack of executive interest. Charles Beard ascribed the president's "intense concentration on his domestic program" in 1933 to a "break with internationalism." Another critic wrote that "concern for domestic reform probably determined the President's action" because "he had not yet become a firm believer in collective security."[4]

Such interpretations, tempting as they may be, do not square with the record. Few presidents have plunged into office so primed for diplomatic action and with such insistence upon serving as their own secretary of state. FDR demanded direct reports from principal envoys and took it upon himself to correspond with a long list of individuals including William Dodd, William Bullitt, Breckinridge Long, Francis Biddle, Josephus Daniels, Robert Bingham, Leland Harrison, Lincoln MacVeagh, and Colonel Edward M. House. Prior to election, he sounded world leaders on the possibility of a preinaugural trip to Europe. He invited his English friend Liberal party leader Arthur Murray to visit him at Hyde Park, and when Murray declined, he hosted Lord Astor of Cliveden. Before inauguration, he sent Bullitt on two important overseas missions, one in November and another in January. On taking the oath of office, he threw Norman Davis into conference with Ramsay MacDonald, John Simon, Stanley Baldwin, Neville Chamberlain, Joseph Paul-Boncour, Edouard Daladier, Edouard Herriot, Léon Blum, Konstantin von Neurath, and Adolf Hitler—all in the first two weeks of April. Davis then returned to Europe in May and September for further talks.[5]

Well in advance of inauguration, Roosevelt saw to it that presidential advisers Raymond Moley and Rexford Tugwell stationed themselves at the State Department to assure a smooth, speedy change of administration. In addition, he invited dozens of foreign leaders to Washington for face-to-face talks. Whereas the custom for presidents and prime ministers had been to see foreign envoys only rarely, he made it a regular practice. As president-elect, he met at least once with Canadian Minister William Herridge, twice with British Ambassador Sir Ronald Lindsay, and four times with French Ambassador Paul Claudel, all on business. He also held diplomatic policy meetings with Moley, Tugwell, Davis, and Bullitt and issued an unsolicited public statement on Far East policy during the interregnum.[6]

Within a hundred days of taking office, he sent a representative to Geneva to sit as a silent observer on the League Advisory Committee. And to this list of preinaugural working interviews, he added four with Lindsay; seven with the French ambassador; two with Italian Ambassador Augusto Rosso (to discuss a démarche in the direction of Japan);

one with German Ambassador Friedrich von Prittwitz (to request, among other things, an immediate visit from Foreign Minister von Neurath); and one with Prittwitz's successor, Hans Luther. He conferred with Chinese finance minister T. V. Soong and issued a joint statement. He held four meetings with Japanese envoy Viscount Kikujiro Ishii covering every topic of mutual concern. He made openings on his calendar for Yosuke Matsuoka, as well as Admiral Osani Nagano (most likely), and he still found time to see Takashi Komatsu and Admiral Nomura. If these sessions were not sufficiently taxing, he invited eleven heads of state and missions from forty-two nations, including members of the Petite Entente, to meet in Washington to concert plans for the upcoming London Economic Conference. Covering a vast range of subjects in both afternoon and evening sessions, he bargained intensively and personally with British Prime Minister Ramsay MacDonald (21–26 April) as well as with Edouard Herriot, former premier of France (23–28 April). Hitler, who refused two of his invitations for a meeting, also refused to send Foreign Minister von Neurath and declined to receive Colonel House as a special presidential envoy. He did, however, send Reichsbank President Hjalmar Schacht, who held extensive conferences with the president on 6, 8, 10, and 12 May.[7]

The parade of diplomats that began with MacDonald's arrival on 21 April did not abate until after the arrival of the last special mission, that of Chile on 3 June. Others whom Roosevelt received for official talks included the finance ministers of Italy, Mexico, and Chile, as well as leading personages from Argentina and Brazil. He conducted talks with the prime minister of New Zealand, the president of Panama, top officials of the Philippines and many other countries, including the prime minister of Canada, who stayed at the White House. Mrs. Roosevelt handled the social arrangements and, after experiencing at first hand the unprecedented nature of her husband's program, was impelled to comment on the "almost unbelievable number of guests."[8]

Roosevelt, who personally carried the burden of all these talks, was pictured in *Time* magazine seated with envoys on a special black leather couch reported to have magical properties of conciliation: "The couch's deep easy pitch not only relaxes the body but loosens the tongue to friendly informal talk. If the World Economic Conference opening in London, June 12, proves a success, it will be due in no small measure to last week's discussions between President Roosevelt and his distinguished visitors on this White House couch." *Time* also ascribed the breaking of a logjam in disarmament talks at Geneva to "the friendly, smiling face of Franklin D. Roosevelt." So comfortable did FDR feel at center stage that he formulated instructions for his ill-fated delegation to London without consulting State. On 16 May, he took it upon himself in a way few leaders of any country have done to address a message of instruction to the heads of fifty-four governments and to the people of the entire world. One diplomat observed that the closest precedent he could recall was a papal message of 1917. When Hitler responded with an unexpectedly mild-mannered address to the Reichstag, Roosevelt leapt to the conclusion that he had averted a German attack on her neighbors.[9]

It is generally assumed, and wrongly so, that diplomatic responsibilities were thrust upon FDR earlier than he would have wished.[10] Far from fending off the call of duty, he sought to enlarge the sphere of his responsibility and accelerate the pace of negotiation. MacDonald would have preferred to send a second-level functionary to Washington to discuss trade, currency, and debts, but Roosevelt insisted on seeing the prime minister in person and adding disarmament to their agenda. Where MacDonald wanted to postpone Anglo-American talks until April or May to give the president a chance to lay some groundwork, Roosevelt wished to play host immediately after inauguration. He wanted the World Economic Conference, scheduled for July, to open on 1 May. Most astonishing, he told Lord Astor in November of 1932 that he would not mind if the site of the gathering were transferred from London to Washington. After prolonged effort to have the conference meet in America, he expressed hope that it might reconvene in Washington should it fail in London.[11] His delegation fought to chair one of the two major committees—Downing Street wanted them both to go to minor powers—and if MacDonald felt the conference should take its time and deliberate for perhaps half a year, Roosevelt preferred a wind-up in two months. Similarly, he wished to handle negotiations with the Soviet Union on a personal level, and at the most rapid clip, even as he urged that the Seventh International Conference of American States be held on schedule in preference to postponement as suggested by many Latin American leaders.[12]

In the midst of all this intense presidential activity, Secretary of State Hull began, as he ended, an anomalous figurehead whose day-to-day knowledge of White House planning left a wondrous lot to be desired. He had no part in the announcement of Roosevelt's decision to extend a sizable loan to China. Nor was he informed that British economic adviser Sir Frederick Leith-Ross would remain in Washington after MacDonald's departure to engage in talks with Raymond Moley and Lewis Douglas. Ambassador Lindsay had to tell him. Never having been consulted on the makeup of the delegation he was expected to lead to London, he must have squinted in pure amazement as Roosevelt reversed himself on policies decided well in advance and to which his delegation had already given strong support.[13] From the beginning, it was clear who would be making American foreign policy.

Another common misconception obscuring the significance of the Hundred Days is the belief that Roosevelt's options were severely limited by a combination of pacifism and isolationist sentiment.[14] At the University of Pittsburgh 350 students protested the choice of U.S. Army Chief of Staff Douglas MacArthur as commencement speaker in 1932. They were arrested for doing so, however, and compelled to take an oath of allegiance to the American Constitution. If a student opinion poll in 1932 showed 72 percent opposed to serving in the armed forces, with 50 percent opposed even in the event of an attack on the United States, and if campus rallies in 1934 sometimes featured professors denouncing military service and urging students to take the Oxford Pledge, this did not represent the mood of the country at large. Newspaper czars Hearst and Howard came out for greater preparedness in 1933, and George Gallup stated two years later that opinion was "overwhelmingly in favor of building up our defenses." Ninety percent of the people wanted to increase the size of the air force.[15]

Hiram Johnson and William Borah, veterans whose verbal fusillades had done much to unhorse Wilson, still had lances to break. Nevertheless, there is no basis for assuming that Roosevelt faced the kind of sentiment that confronted someone like a Churchill. The obstacles in America appear to have been far from insuperable. William Appleman Williams and Richard Leopold have pointed out that the decade of the 1920s was not nearly as isolationist as supposed, and the same assessment could be applied to the first half of the 1930s. In 1926, there were more than a thousand organizations in the United States for the study of international relations. The percentage of Americans traveling abroad was steadily on the rise. Three presidents during the 1920s favored American membership in the World Court, and *Time* urged American cooperation with the League to expel Japan from China. FDR told an audience in 1932 that the nation was solidly against League membership, yet a referendum on this question in eleven Massachusetts towns showed twenty-six thousand in favor and only fifteen thousand opposed. In 1934, Scottish author John Buchan visited the United States and concluded that "the Irish trouble so far as America is concerned is out of the way." Powerful isolationist tracts by Seldes, Engelbrecht, and Millis came out in 1934 and 1935, and by mid-decade the strength of isolationist forces in the press and Congress seems to have grown considerably. Nonetheless, public reaction to the Quarantine Address of 1937 has been found to be more supportive than originally supposed; the Ludlow Amendment was something of an anomaly which went down to defeat in 1938, if only by twenty votes; and two years later, British Ambassador Lord Halifax found the Midwest surprisingly free of isolationism.[16]

A recent study has shown that midwestern magazines and newspapers had no isolationist leanings until well into the mid-1930s, and this would seem to be true of the media as a whole.[17] Few believed in the "sanctity" of Versailles or harbored strong feelings on the subject of Manchuria. Thus there was ample room for accommodation with Germany and Japan, as well as for an approach similar to Stimson's, depending on the will of the White House. At the same time, both party platforms endorsed membership in the World Court in 1932, and Senate majority leader Joseph Robinson advised Roosevelt to request action from a sympathetic committee. Instead, the president opted for postponement, which tended to cast doubt on his own position.[18]

With proper handling, arms embargo legislation permitting discrimination between an aggressor and its victim seemed likely to win congressional approval. A bill such as Roosevelt wanted had been favorably received by the Senate during the last weeks of the Seventy-second Congress even though final passage was blocked by a motion to reconsider. In addition, the new House had given its assent by a margin of 253 to 19. Such legislation was endorsed by Idaho's powerful senator, William Borah. Although President Hoover had given it forthright backing in a message of 10 January 1933, Roosevelt prejudiced its chances by making contradictory statements and at one point agreeing to renounce the very power he sought. Within a space of four weeks, he reversed himself *no less than four times*. By contrast with Hoover, who had submitted two special messages, he drafted a single statement but decided not to send it lest, in so doing, he appear to accord it undue importance. Letters addressed by Secretary Hull to committee chairmen were recalled after reaching their destination because it was thought that they stated the case for presidential discretion too harshly and might arouse antagonism. The under secretary of state agreed to testify before a House committee, then canceled his appearance, while Hull declined to testify before the Senate Foreign Relations Committee and sent Joseph Green, his specialist on arms control, to act as mouthpiece. Green mistakenly raised the specter of Japan blockading American goods on their way to China, and in the end an indecisive president refused to fight Senator Hiram Johnson's disabling amendment eliminating presidential discretion. The bill was tabled.[19]

Isolationism in the mid to late 1930s might have been less of a problem for Roosevelt had he not done so much to foster its growth. In two books, *Looking Forward* (1933) and *On Our Way* (1934), he came out directly *against* American entry into the League. During 1934, he made isolationism and noninterference in European affairs a theme of one public statement after another. Obviously satisfied with the way things were going by late 1935, he wrote Ambassador Harrison in Bucharest: "I find things progressing well over here and our neutrality stand is almost universally popular."[20] By this time, he had asked Congress to grant the Nye Committee a generous budget, opened executive files to committee members, and found praise for the senator from North Dakota. Instead of vetoing the ensuing neutrality acts, he lent presidential authority to their cosmetic appeal, telling an audience just before the Democratic National Convention of 1936, "We are not going to get tangled up."[21]

His initial inability to establish rapport with Congress on matters relating to foreign policy can also be traced to the figure of William C. Bullitt. Bullitt assumed an immediate behind-the-scenes role during the Hundred Days, and his subsequent influence as a key diplomatic aide to the president spanned the decade. Leaving the United States on 19 November 1932, with letters of introduction from the president-elect and orders to discuss every major issue, he returned four weeks later, having conferred with Prime Minister MacDonald, Premier Herriot of France, various Italian officials, and a dozen or more Germans. FDR received Bullitt's final report on 27 December and was pleased enough to send him back to Europe on 15 January for a second round of talks. As the president-elect's special envoy, Bullitt spent the weekend of the twenty-first with MacDonald at Chequers and passed a working day with the prime minister before going on to Paris. At this point, he was reported acting without President Hoover's authorization. Worse still, it was said that he had offered to cancel 80 percent of Britain's debt to the United States without demanding anything in return. This was taken as an affront to congressional opinion as well as a violation of the Logan Act, which provided for a fine of $5,000 and up to three years in prison for any individual negotiating on behalf of the United States without official sanction. On 2 February, Senator Arthur Robinson of Indiana branded Bullitt "an undercover agent" who was "preaching the doctrine of cancellation." Robinson demanded a State Department investigation leading to arrest and prosecution. Senator Otis Glenn of Illinois took an equally jaundiced view, while one headline glared: "SENATOR DEMANDS BULLITT ARREST AS FAKE ENVOY." Two other senators, David Reed of Pennsylvania and James Lewis of Illinois, spoke critically of the way Roosevelt appeared to be ignoring Congress in the manner of a Wilson; whereupon FDR, about to leave on an eleven-day fishing cruise, pledged to keep the appropriate House and Senate committees informed and to conduct the debt negotiations personally.[22]

Roosevelt's first contact with Congress on a matter pertaining to diplomacy was thus a damaging one. By undermining confidence in the executive and disinclining Congress to relinquish discretionary power, it set an inauspicious tone for the future. It also revealed the president-elect's more devious side. In answer to reporters' questions and a query from Ambassador Lindsay, he denied any connection with Bullitt.[23] Lindsay described him in a report to the British Foreign Office as "shamefaced." Congressional criticism cooled, but there had been good reason for it, and if one assumes that first impressions are lasting, Roosevelt was laying up trouble for himself.[24]

With this background in mind, we may proceed to examine three of the better-known issues of the Hundred Days: namely, Roosevelt's management of the American delegation to the London Economic Conference, his effort to collect debts owed by Europeans, and his approach to Latin America.

The London Economic Conference is of special interest since it involved the president personally in a variety of ways and placed his reputation directly on the line. It was his debut in international affairs, and in selecting his delegation he sought to avoid Wilson's supposed mistake of taking with him to Paris too few influential members of Congress. In attendance were Key Pittman and Samuel McReynolds, chairmen of the two congressional committees on foreign affairs.

Chief among the aims of the conference was a major departure in the area of currency reform. By provision of the Paris peace settlement, a Bank for International Settlements had been organized for the steady interchangeability of currencies. This was something which would have made economic opportunity more equally available around the world. Promotion of greater equality of trade conditions, including removal of trade barriers, was another benefit promised at Versailles but never realized. Those who went to London were concerned about this issue also. But the main concentration was directed at currency owing to the fact that the Bank for International Settlements had served as little more than bait to induce German acceptance of an unsound reparation program. Nations had no more permitted the Bank to influence their currency policies than they had allowed proper functioning on the part of the League of Nations, the Mandates Commission, or the World Court. The Economic Conference marked a belated effort to mitigate a general postwar failure along the lines of trade and finance. As we shall see, the United States insisted upon its right to solve its own particular problems in its own particular way. Roosevelt hoped that by revaluing gold and silver he might produce a rise in domestic commodity prices which would in turn reduce the burden of America's internal debt and stimulate internal production. This would, of course, further disrupt currency relationships between nations and create new obstacles to the international sharing of economic opportunity. Yet America insisted on its right, thereby frustrating the wider objective of the Conference. Its collapse afforded final proof that nations, acting on their own, would repudiate a sense of social solidarity and operate on the principle of *sauve qui peut.*

Returning now to London in the year 1933, problems seemed to multiply on the American side almost at once. Hazy presidential instructions opened the door to intradelegation feuding—Senator James Couzens of Michigan spoke against lower tariffs while McReynolds pinpointed reduction in duties as the key to recovery. Bullitt described Hull as in a state of "complete collapse" and Mrs. Hull as having "literally wept all night." To his chagrin, the secretary of state made the mistake of signing a paper on his way to Windsor which he thought was merely a list of proposed topics for discussion. Mimeographed and circulated as the "American Plan," it specified a 10 percent reduction in tariffs; but when taken up by the Economic Commission, Senator Pittman declared that it did not represent the thinking of his fellow delegates. The Dutch committee chairman could not believe what he heard, yet Pittman turned out to be correct. Roosevelt declined to seek congressional authorization for tariff reduction, upsetting one of the main props upon which Hull had built his strategy.[25]

On the one hand, FDR promised to work for an international gold standard and the stabilization of currency, both important goals of the conference—as many as six statements to this effect came out under his name. On the other hand, he failed to follow through. Once his chosen experts, George Harrison, Oliver Sprague, and James Warburg, had definitely committed him to temporary stabilization, he went on to repudiate the very document they had signed. When this, in turn, elicited widespread disgust, he dispatched Raymond Moley to London. Moley succeeded in calming troubled waters by returning slightly to the original, more liberal, American position. No sooner had he done so, however, to the evident satisfaction of all, than the stock market began to fall and he found himself the victim of yet another presidential repudiation. Roosevelt's bombshell message of 3 July, dubbed by the British a "sin against the Moley Ghost," extinguished any hope that might have lingered in Europe for meaningful American cooperation. On 22 June, delegate James Cox, governor of Ohio, had cabled FDR: "If you love us at all don't give us another week like this one." It was the end of the road for Cox and his fellow Americans. Despite a written statement to George V that "the Conference must establish order in place of the present chaos by a stabilization of currencies," Roosevelt refused to support any plan to restore international banking to the basis of fixed currencies attached to gold.[26]

The message of 3 July, which lectured Europe on the virtue of economy and the need for a balanced budget, drew scathing criticism from every quarter of the foreign press.[27] No one could have predicted that by 1939 Washington would be operating on its seventh unbalanced budget, but Britain's *Spectator* lamented the "disastrous uncertainty which besets negotiations with the United States at all times." King George V was indignant and Stanley Baldwin so exercised that he refused to attend a dinner given by the prime minister because he saw the name of Roosevelt's son James on the guest list. Neville Chamberlain, all at once, developed something of a loathing for Americans. When MacDonald asked him to give an "appreciation" of the Roosevelt policy to fellow cabinet members who could not understand it, he had a jolly time representing Yanks as a "barbarous tribe" and Roosevelt as "a medicine

man whose superiority over other medicine men consisted in an astonishing agility with which when one kind of mumbo jumbo failed, he
provided another."[28]

British feelings were nothing alongside the towering rage of the
French, who had engaged the Americans in a bitter squabble over who
would chair the prestigious Monetary Conference. Hull let it be known
that his group had been promised the chairmanship before sailing,
whereupon Finance Minister Georges Bonnet retorted that "with Washington committed to devaluation we cannot have an American as monetary chairman." Governor Cox parried: "With Paris committed to debt
repudiation, we cannot have a Frenchman." Not until Cox had assured
fellow delegates of the soundness of his views on currency stabilization
did France withdraw her opposition. But hardly had he done so than his
position underwent a total change by order of the White House. Thereafter, the French lobbied for adjournment, something especially repugnant to the United States because it had assumed the primary
responsibility. Bonnet at one point claimed to have lined up forty out
of sixty-four delegates for immediate dismissal. Seeking, in addition, a
resolution censuring FDR, he agreed to desist only when Bullitt threatened to reveal Bonnet's earlier rejection of a Roosevelt stabilization proposal. As it was, President Albert Lebrun was quoted as saying that for
the Americans "to speak of tariff adjustments while moneys are vari-
able is pure Utopia!" Parisian newspapers poured out their ridicule.[29]

As mentioned above, it can be argued that FDR was merely responding to the national interest when he decided to raise prices and devalue
the dollar in disregard of repercussions elsewhere. The American Index
of Production had moved steadily upward, from 59 in March to 100 by
July (the highest it had been in 1929 was 125). The stock market had
reacted positively in April and May to enactment of such nationalistic
measures as the Agricultural Adjustment Act (AAA) and National Recovery Act (NRA), which could function properly only in a highly pro-
tected market. The economy, in other words, seemed to be recovering on
the impetus of New Deal measures designed to insulate it from international competition. Depreciation of the dollar had the effect of impos-
ing an indirect tariff of 69 percent on imports. Furthermore, a large
majority of congressmen passionately desired inflation. This included
spokesmen for debtors, who saw it as the only way to avoid taxation
slavery, and farmers, a third of America, who saw in it some hope for
restoring the value of their property and raising farm prices high enough

to ensure a tolerable standard of living. It can also be argued that Roosevelt was reacting to British and French refusal to do more to liquidate their own debts. He may have hoped that all nations would support public works by means of loans, thus driving foreign prices up and pegging the American dollar on a par with other currencies.[30]

Whatever the merits of the case, the behavior of the American delegation appeared farcical to the rest of the world and set an unfortunate tone at home. Senator Pittman went on a drinking spree as soon as he boarded ship and became drunk on several occasions following his arrival in London, once reportedly with Winston Churchill. He took pleasure in shooting out London street lamps with a silver pistol and chased an uncooperative colleague down a corridor of Claridge's with his bowie knife.[31] All that seemed to interest him besides liquid refreshment was an international agreement for the coinage of silver. Ironically, such an agreement proved to be the only real fruit of the conference.

Half of Roosevelt's delegates threw away their invitations to dine with the Fishmongers' Company since they had no idea that it was one of London's richest guilds and would be serving them on gold plate at a meal given by special request of His Majesty's Government. At the same time, American wives forced themselves on the king and queen by objecting to a palace reception that had been scheduled for delegates only. Mrs. Couzens followed her introduction to the royal couple by telling reporters, "They are real people," and Senator Couzens spoke out on such a wide variety of topics that the British filed a complaint with Bullitt, executive officer of the American delegation: one did not release one's ideas to the press; one submitted them to the conference. Anything else was certain to cause resentment and obstruct progress. Bullitt does not appear to have given much thought to such matters. His name was already mud for having complained to MacDonald's secretary about a reference to debts in the prime minister's opening speech. MacDonald insisted the criticism should have come to him directly from Hull.[32]

A favorite target for local pundits was the retired businessman Ralph W. Morrison of Texas. Never without a cigar, he would smoke placidly in front of signs bearing the message "prière de ne pas fumer," and when the name of Eduard Beneš, the famous Czech foreign minister, came up, he asked, "Who is Beneš?" McReynolds, who violated the rule of confidentiality more than anyone else, improved upon the occasion of a formal speech to denounce the Republican party. Like Morrison, he rarely opened his mouth, and when reporters asked him why, his stock answer was that he was playing a waiting game. "Waiting Game" McReynolds, as he came to be known, allowed his daughter to be interviewed on radio about her presentation at court and to divulge particulars never before made public and never intended to be. But his most egregious act was to take to the air in a transatlantic broadcast and complain about the hostility of the British and Continental press. "I want to say," he told home listeners, "that no delegation to an international conference ever met as fierce a barrage of criticism as that which practically all the British and French have levelled at us . . . I need not tell an American audience that these stories [about the American delegation] were as unfounded as they were malicious."[33]

McReynolds's lesson in parochialism was echoed by an angry Roosevelt, who publicly intimated that he was finished with Europe and would now devote all his attention to South America.[34] A few weeks earlier, with Paris irate over inflation of the dollar at the expense of the franc, he had charged the French news media with gross distortion of his policies. Now he scolded the French for being so "awfully upsettable" that "no human being can tell from one day to another what the Chamber of Deputies is going to do." On 5 August, he imprinted McReynolds's message indelibly upon the American consciousness. With a disgruntled Hull standing by his side before a battery of reporters and poking fun at the British custom of taking an annual vacation in August ("they leave promptly on August 12 and shoot grouse"), he explained that the failure of the Economic Conference had been due to "the Continental and London press. It was rotten, absolutely rotten and they gave us a dirty deal. . . . The whole press just ganged us. . . . The French press is owned by anybody that will buy it." Hull added, "I have never been accustomed to a really bad press but I did get a good dose of it over there." Asked if he was glad to be home, he replied, "Yes." And to the question "You will appreciate us now, Mr. Secretary?" he responded, "It was an impossible situation." Those in the audience, doubtless sensing the popularity of Hull's theme, pursued it for several minutes more before asking, "What did you think of the Conference?" "It was very interesting," Hull replied. Whereupon, Roosevelt interjected, "How did you like your first view of New York Harbor?" This produced a ripple of laughter, and the interview ended.[35]

A second element of Roosevelt's style that fed the isolationist impulse was his deliberate failure to persuade Britain, France, and other countries to pay their debt to the United States. During the 1930s, he never ceased to apply nominal pressure in this direction. Yet the pressure was no more than nominal, and the issue continued to rankle as much at home as it did abroad. The question of debts was injected into the campaign of 1936; indeed, we find Bernard Baruch proposing that Whitehall pay £10 million in less than four years, to which Churchill replied that £7 million with additional time to pay seemed more realistic.[36] Roosevelt's debt initiative is interesting less for its futility than for the tactics employed and the difference between what he appeared to be doing and what actually transpired behind the scenes. Here, as elsewhere, it is the basic pattern that claims our attention. France, having defaulted in December of 1932, continued to default, refusing to make even partial payment in June and December of 1933. At the same time, the British, who paid on schedule in 1932, made only token payments in June and December of the following year and then lapsed. All of which came as a definite disappointment to Congress and the American people, especially as the example set by France and Britain was followed by every other European debtor save Finland.

There were two schools of thought on the matter. According to Hoover and Stimson, French and British willingness to cancel 90 percent of Germany's war reparations called for similar enlightened generosity on the part of the United States. The debt might be substantially reduced if payment came in the form of cash, or it might be paid by increasing purchases of American goods. At the very least, Europe was entitled to a moratorium of several years to allow for the Depression. Europeans naturally agreed. They insisted that the outcome of the Lausanne Conference was conditional. It depended upon a positive response from Congress, and they would not cancel one another's debts unless they received like consideration from the United States. The American Senate, on the other hand, reflected the more popular view, which regarded payment as a moral duty and refused to grant more than a year's reprieve from December of 1931 with the express proviso that there would be no reduction.[37]

It is well-nigh impossible to establish Roosevelt's own position on the question since he expressed himself in a variety of ways depending upon who happened to be listening. Temperamentally, he seems to have stood on the side of cancellation in spite of the advice given him by Moley, Berle, and Tugwell. In an article written several months before his 1929 return to public office, he made light of Europe's obligations and denigrated Coolidge's hard line as "one of the many causes for the dislike in which we are held among the peoples as well as the governments of Europe." Sara Roosevelt, who encouraged her son's natural inclination toward liberality, served as a type of mediatrix. Concerns felt by French and British leaders and confided to her at garden teas were promptly relayed to the White House. A certain reluctance to bargain earnestly on such matters is reflected in FDR's handling of Soviet Foreign Commissar Maxim Litvinov. The two initialed a "gentlemen's agreement" on 15 November whereby the Soviet Union was to pay no less than $75 million on its debt to the United States. Litvinov was to "advise" his government to offer $100 million, and FDR stated his belief that Congress would accept no less than $150 million. Litvinov was also to remain in Washington for additional talks with Bullitt and Treasury Secretary Morgenthau in which it was assumed they would work out a settlement somewhere in the vicinity of $75 million to $150 million. Before anything had been agreed in writing, however, Roosevelt yielded gratis the very thing the Soviet Union desired most: namely, diplomatic recognition. It goes without saying that the United States thereafter realized little on its claims.[38]

The Kremlin had taken Roosevelt's measure. Litvinov was instructed to negotiate with him in preference to any of his subordinates, and Roosevelt *volunteered* to confirm that any stipulation regarding debt payment was designed primarily to appease the American electorate. Litvinov immediately cabled Stalin: "He is ready to agree that it is completely impossible to settle the question about claims but [merely] wants to consider the possibility of agreement on some in principle."[39]

Since Roosevelt was nothing if not responsive to public opinion, there soon developed a dichotomy between personal feeling and public statement, between what he said to foreign envoys privately and what he told his countrymen. This is a theme which carries over into American dealings on a variety of other matters; indeed, it figures in the entire fabric of New Deal foreign policy. Nowhere, though, is it more evident than here. During the 1932 campaign, as well as in his book *Looking Forward*, FDR inveighed against cancellation. Likewise in 1934, he joined the general outcry against default by supporting and helping draft the Johnson Debt Default Act, which barred the granting of loans to nations in default. On the other hand, in order to save face for Britain, he opined that she could avoid the Johnson penalty by virtue of her token payments (this despite a contrary ruling by his attorney general).[40] Striking one pose before Congress, he revealed an altogether different side in off-the-record conversations with the French and British. Many weeks before inauguration, as early as January 1933, he offered London a reduction of interest on the foreign debt to 4 percent, in addition to an interest-free moratorium of up to three years, perhaps longer. To the British cabinet, this suggested the possibility of a moratorium "so long that the American public would forget what was to be paid." And well it might have been, for while Bullitt conferred with Whitehall, Roosevelt told Ambassador Lindsay that the British had *no moral or legal obligation* to pay anything and that he would not hold them responsible! He also suggested cancellation of all interest and a term of up to sixty-two years for payment of the principal, adding that he had no objection to a moratorium if Congress could be brought to agree. He felt it best, he said, to keep debts in the background, and he would not try to bargain by linking them to other areas of mutual interest. Envoy Norman Davis told MacDonald in London at the end of March that in view of world economic conditions all the United States could do about the debt was to ask for it; if the prime minister would agree to come to the United States for talks with Roosevelt, he could expect that the president would ask Congress for authority to grant Britain another moratorium and reduce the required payment by executive fiat. Roosevelt was no less obliging in the case of the French. To Ambassador Claudel, he suggested that Hoover had behaved badly when he equated nonpayment with default.[41]

As the European position hardened and it became clear that congressional sentiment would not budge, FDR eased the path of default by suggesting to the British that they offer an insignificant fraction of the sum owed and call it a token payment. He would then declare it a valid alternative to default. This made good copy in the House of Commons, which gave several cheers for the prime minister. When the White House countenanced another token payment in October, Chancellor of the Exchequer Chamberlain marveled at "how quietly it was accepted," and by June of 1934 he could tell his cabinet, with evident pride, "Well, we have defaulted on the American Debt and not a dog has barked." Washington did indeed remain quiet. *News-Week* described American policy as "listening without limitation," and the expedient of the token payment, first proposed by Roosevelt in May, was adopted by other debtor nations with only one exception: French officials announced blandly that they were obliged to "defer" payment.[42]

Although an American note termed the Italian offer "unsubstantial" and Moley gave French Ambassador André de Laboulaye a dressing down with the aid of a vocabulary acquired during his Ohio boyhood, what counted was the attitude of the White House. Britain claimed a budget surplus in 1934, as against Washington's deficit, and Roosevelt encouraged her to cease all payment. According to Lindsay, the president "could see perfectly well that the natural course for H.M.G. to take now must be to discontinue payments. . . . He quite understood that H.M.G. must send in a note about the situation. . . . He said he would really like to draft it for himself . . . and he actually recommended that H.M.G. should state in their note that in order to remove social injustice the burden of the British Empire must be lightened and that for some years to come the first charge on any surplus achieved ought to be reduction of burden of taxation." So that Whitehall might present its case to the American people with maximum effect, Roosevelt further advised that it give figures of the British national debt and facts respecting taxation, the latter to be characterized as the heaviest taxation known to history: "The surplus realized this year should be referred to as result of unparalleled sacrifices. Resulting situation should be described as one of 'social injustice' to the people." According to Lindsay, Roosevelt repeated the need to emphasize social injustice and suggested that the British note would best meet with American approval if it were put not in diplomatic language "but in as simple a style as possible so as to be comprehensible to ordinary people."[43]

In effect, the winner of the 1932 election was conspiring against the popular will and doing so as regards both Germany and Britain. It is worth recalling that citizens of the United States had made sizable loans to Berlin during the 1920s. Many of these obligations were still outstanding in 1933. Hjalmar Schacht tells in his *Autobiography* of going to Roosevelt's office on 6 May 1933 and stating that Germany would soon be obliged to cease payment of the interest on the American loans: "Hull grew nervous. Luther fidgeted in his chair. I myself expected an indignant outburst on the part of the President. To our astonishment, there was nothing of the sort. Roosevelt gave his thigh a resounding smack and exclaimed with a laugh: Serves the Wall Street bankers right!" The next day, Hull handed Schacht an envelope containing a curt note from the president stating that he had been shocked by Schacht's attitude toward debts the previous day. But this did not faze Hitler's envoy, who recalled that "the President had not experienced any shock until twenty-four hours had elapsed." On 8 May, Schacht boldly announced that his country would cease payment on its debt. Publicly, Roosevelt expressed outrage. Privately, however, he was less upset than embarrassed that repudiation should come only two days after Schacht's White House call, giving color to reports that he had connived at it. He soon sent an ambassador to Berlin who sympathized openly with the German position on finance. This was Professor William Dodd of the University of Chicago, who believed that if the Reich had to buy three times as much in America as it sold, it could ill afford to honor its obligations. Instead of making a forceful case on behalf of American bondholders, Dodd held von Neurath's hand. Even when Hull categorically ordered him to read the Wilhelmstrasse a strong protest, he delivered it to the German authorities unread and departed after a pro forma visit of ten minutes. Berlin could not have been more gratified nor American financiers less so.[44]

Many presidential advisers, including Norman Davis, felt that if FDR was going to waive foreign obligations, he should bargain for something in return, either tariff reduction, market access, currency reform, or disarmament. This view was shared by Hoover, Stimson, Borah, and President A. L. Lowell of Harvard University. British emissaries Lord Astor and Lord Lothian apparently anticipated such a tactic, and Roosevelt did toy with it throughout the year. After using the hope of a moratorium to lure MacDonald to Washington, he hinted that he might give way on the debt issue in return for reduction of British trade barriers. Such linkage would have been eminently appropriate given the abnormal conditions of finance prevailing at the time. Nevertheless, he changed his mind several times in a matter of days and never pursued any one plan with vigor or consistency.[45]

The issue was thus left to fester. Congressional pressure dwindled but never entirely ceased during the seven years preceding the voting of Lend-Lease. After Bullitt's preinaugural offer of a downward revision of the interest to 4 percent, Roosevelt notified Lindsay that he would waive *all* interest. Early in 1934, Chicago lawyer Sam Levinson worked closely with Borah and the State Department on an offer which envisaged still greater cancellation: 60 percent of the capital in addition to interest. Although such offers fell on barren soil, Roosevelt kept the issue alive, apparently in deference to popular sentiment. Hull reminded Italy that the money she spent on arms could be better spent on debt service. U.S. Ambassador to France Jesse Straus approached the

Quai d'Orsay several times between 1934 and 1936, once with an offer to settle for 2 percent of the interest over a term of 150 years. In 1938, Herriot promised that if returned to office in France, he would pay off the French debt in toto. FDR discouraged Britain's desire to reopen the war debt question in early 1937, although the subject was revived later in the year during a conference between presidential adviser Bernard Baruch and Winston Churchill. As late as 1939, British chargé Victor Mallet was called to Morgenthau's office at a late nocturnal hour and kept waiting in a large room with a table on which were inscribed all the debts owed to the United States since World War I. When Roosevelt's treasury secretary apologized for the delay, Mallet replied that he did not mind except for being confined in "the Chamber of Horrors!" During the calm preceding the outbreak of war, George V came to the United States and discussed the possibility of resuming partial payment. He feared that under the terms of the Johnson Act his people could not apply for a loan. To his relief, Roosevelt assured him that payment of partial sums would only rouse Congress to demand more. France's foreign office, after making similar offers in 1939, received a similar reply.[46]

In sum, there was much about the Roosevelt style which might have caused members of Congress to have second thoughts about executive prerogative. Bullitt's preinaugural trip to Europe is perhaps the best example, though certainly not the only one. Apart from any isolationist sentiment that may or may not have existed at the time, FDR's initial position on German bonds and the European debt can only be described as deceptive, and it is with this rather unpleasant experience in mind that he began to shift his attention from Europe to Latin America.

He is justly famous for "baptizing" the Good Neighbor Policy. The phrase itself dates back nearly a hundred years to the Treaty of Guadalupe Hidalgo, but it gained powerful credence in keynote speeches delivered during the Hundred Days. By means of a joint statement with President-elect Arnulfo Arias of Panama, FDR assured the people of the Isthmus that his most sympathetic consideration would be given to the removal of their just grievances. At Montevideo in December, Hull pledged a policy of nonintervention in the most unequivocal language to date.[47] Such gestures, however, do not tell the whole story.

Having failed in every effort to control the course of world events, Roosevelt set about to bring hemispheric politics into greater conformity with American practice, most notably in the case of Cuba. Stimson had been at pains to emphasize that as long as the United States kept hands off there was no danger of an uprising against President Gerardo Machado of the kind which would necessitate intervention. According to Hoover's secretary of state, American lives were safe, American property secure, and Machado firmly in control with a nonpolitical army. The Pearl of the Antilles had always been resistant to outside control, though never more so than in 1933. Nonetheless, Sumner Welles and a number of American academic experts traveled to Havana to revamp the local constitution and introduce American-style electoral reform. Hoping to unseat Machado in favor of a less repressive leader, they coaxed, cajoled, and threatened. Eventually, Machado agreed to grant civil liberties on a much broader scale coupled with amnesty for political prisoners arrested since 1927. Roosevelt was not satisfied, however, and with power of life and death over the native economy, he intimated publicly that Cubans should rid themselves of their president in the name of democracy. When Machado fled, his place was taken by Welles's hand-picked successor, Manuel Cespedes. Cespedes, popular as Cuban ambassador to the United States from 1914 to 1922, continued for all practical purposes to function in his former capacity. He received three visits from Welles the day before he announced his cabinet, and on 19 August Welles reported that he was "daily being requested for decisions on all matters."[48]

Welles's influence proved to be the undoing of Cespedes. Popular resistance mounted in the name of freedom, and by September Cuba's president found himself unable to function. A radical professor by the name of Ramón Grau St. Martín, less desirable from the American standpoint even than Machado, assumed power; Welles then cabled the White House for a military demonstration, and Roosevelt dispatched twenty-four war vessels. One battleship dropped anchor in Havana Harbor on the very spot off Moro Castle where the U.S.S. *Maine* had been sunk in 1898. In addition to this visible display of American military might, FDR wielded the bludgeon of nonrecognition. Availing himself of the media, he tried to discredit the Cuban president by portraying him as "sitting there in the presidential palace . . . [having] his local army with him, which consists of about fifteen hundred men and a bunch of students." Welles reported disquieting news on 3 October. Ninety-four Cuban officers, soldiers, and civilians had been killed in civil strife and more than two hundred wounded. "Respect for us is diminishing," he noted. In December, with Grau St. Martín still in place, he conceded defeat and withdrew ignominiously. By January of 1934, Cuba was reeling from the installation of its fourth government in ten months, one which functioned under the leadership of Fulgencio Batista, an army officer whose rule would prove to be quite as absolute in the long run as that of Machado. Roosevelt's public attitude, in concert with his refusal to grant recognition (he would bestow it upon Grau St. Martín's successor in five days), could only be decisive against a backdrop of American warships and an attractive package of promises conferred upon the new government: abrogation of the Platt Amendment, a favorable new trade treaty, and immediate shipments of food. Grau St. Martín, who described Yankee imperialism in its latest guise as "intervention by inertia," rapidly lost control—as he put it, "because Washington willed it."[49]

Events elsewhere in the hemisphere during 1933 did not appear much more promising. The press of Rio de Janeiro, traditionally friendly, began to adhere to the more critical line of the French news agency, Havas. By December, the reputation of the United States was anything but enviable in Haiti, Nicaragua, and El Salvador. In Puerto Rico, Roosevelt had installed a new governor who made a poor showing. Robert Gore legalized cockfighting and insisted that all appointees submit undated letters of resignation. Angry students out on strike presented him with a manual of manners; both of his houses were planted with bombs; and there was talk of an attempt to poison him. In January of 1934 he resigned, telling reporters, "That's just what you expect in those countries down there." A few weeks earlier, the American delegation to the inter-American congress at Montevideo had met with a frigid reception. Huge billboard signs shouted "Down with Hull!" and Welles was exposed to withering criticism from the Cuban group. Angel Giraudy, Havana's chief delegate, had no taste for Hull's flowery compliments. Rising from his seat and shaking his fist at the startled assembly, he shouted, "In the name of freedom and right I proclaim that the United States is intervening in Cuba by not allowing her a free government! If it is not intervention to surround our island with warships and to impose upon us a government we do not want, there has never been any intervention in the Americas!" Roosevelt's proposal for a world nonaggression pact the previous May had been interpreted as an effort to upstage Argentina's foreign minister, Carlos Saavedra Lamas, who was proposing an antiwar pact of his own. By October, the dapper Argentine, with black mustache, high stiff collar, and imperious manner, had won endorsement from six of the leading Latin American republics. Consequently, at Montevideo, he was able to present Hull with an actual treaty awaiting the secretary's signature. The American had little choice but to sign, yet in so doing he committed his government to a sweeping pledge of nonintervention. Pressure for such a pledge had been building for a number of years under Republican leadership, and Roosevelt, for his part, made a virtue of necessity, persuading press and people alike that Montevideo had been a victory for his Good Neighbor Policy.[50]

One might add that there were many moments during the Hundred Days when opportunities for constructive statesmanship were simply lost. From Rome came the idea of a Four Power Pact aimed at erasing some of the stigma connected with Versailles and granting Germany concessions on Danzig, colonies, and the Polish Corridor. Such a pact would have reflected Germany's resurgent power and called for reassurance of peaceful intent. Five times during the Hundred Days Italy sought American endorsement for the effect this was expected to have on Britain and France. Breckinridge Long, American ambassador in Rome, solicited Roosevelt's support, as did Ray Atherton and Norman Davis. But it was not forthcoming. FDR would no sooner express sympathy in face-to-face talks with German officials than he would encourage the French to reject compromise.[51] A watered-down agreement was signed in early June, and Roosevelt, faced now with a fait accompli, gave lukewarm approval. But the pact ended stillborn. It was never ratified. Some would argue that appeasement was tried from 1933 to 1939 and found wanting. Concessions offered at the point of a gun, however, are not likely to succeed. It will never be known what course German history might have taken under less adverse circumstances. What is certain is that the failure of Mussolini's plan owed something to the president of the United States.

Roosevelt was establishing a clear pattern of partisanship. He strove sedulously, even before taking office, to marshal support for economic sanctions against Tokyo. Thus, by the time the Land of the Rising Sun parted company with the League on 27 March, he had gone far to disqualify himself for the role of mediator in disputes affecting the Far East. Likewise, in the case of Europe. His first move was to tip the delicate balance of MacDonald's disarmament plan away from Germany. Publicly, he pledged support while, beneath the table, he encouraged Paris to insist on changes involving inspection of sample weapons, all of which proved unacceptable to Berlin.[52] On one hand, he promised Norman Davis that "if you pull off disarmament they will bury you in Arlington when you die if that is any comfort to you now." On the other, he balked at Davis's counsel to press France for instant reduction of her arsenal. In Paris, Ambassador Straus encouraged officials at the Quai d'Orsay *not* to disarm, and when Davis queried Roosevelt by transatlantic telephone: "You do agree with me that we should try to avoid any united front [against Germany]?" Roosevelt at first agreed, then disagreed: "Yes," he answered, "but at the same time, we must not be in a position of breaking up the solidarity."[53] Long backed Davis in recommending greater leniency toward Germany, but the president would consider only minor concessions as face-savers.[54] Inevitably, the British plan met with rejection. MacDonald's fall from power in 1935 stemmed from a wide variety of causes, but one of these was Roosevelt's refusal to cooperate on disarmament and world trade.[55] Subsequently, Hitler would withdraw from the League and boycott the Geneva Disarmament Conference. German cooperation on a workable scheme of arms control might have been problematical in the long run, but if it stood any chance at all of realization, FDR's tactics militated strongly against it.

One may search the annals of American diplomacy and not find a year to compare with 1933 as a graveyard of ill-conceived plans and shattered promises. To the degree that international leadership depends upon credibility, Roosevelt had gone about as far as one could go to take himself out of the running. Among the implied conditions for MacDonald's visit in April had been FDR's promise to go to Congress for authority to strike a generous bargain on debts. As we have seen, this never came to pass. In another instance, he lined up French and German support for a British return to the gold standard, only to take the United States itself off gold. He said in a radio address, and again in his message to fifty-four heads of state, that he would contribute to stabilization of the world economy by pegging the value of the dollar to other currencies. Still, he did not follow through. After hinting to foreign officials that he might travel to Europe during the interregnum, he decided to remain at home. He was again in character when, after allowing Norman Davis to commit the United States to cooperate with potential League action against an aggressor, he reneged on his promise in the face of legislative resistance. Davis's pledge was conditioned upon a disarmament agreement, yet any value it may have had vanished altogether when FDR permitted Senator Johnson to kill the enabling legislation pending in Congress. We have already observed how he permitted Hull to assure Europe of a more liberal American trade policy while declining to sponsor it in Congress.[56] By 16 June, every positive measure possessing a direct international bearing had been either shelved or dropped.

Insofar as world leadership hinges on the mounting of successful initiatives, Roosevelt fell equally short of the mark. His involvement in a move by Rome to sound Tokyo on the possibility of great power mediation in the Far East fell flat.[57] Washington's proposal for a tariff truce was spurned by France, causing all other truces negotiated by Hull to unravel between November and the end of the year.[58] A treaty with Canada for joint development of the St. Lawrence Waterway suffered a similar rebuff in May despite the support of the previous administration and Roosevelt's record of fighting for it while governor.[59] Proposals filed at Geneva for a world nonaggression pact and a new definition of aggression met with silence or worse. None were adopted. Even his successful campaign to gain recognition of the Soviet Union ended in anticlimax. He encouraged Senator Claude Swanson to open a national discussion; he then interviewed Colonel Hugh Cooper, a distinguished engineer engaged in building a dam on the Dnieper River; finally, he collected a large store of pertinent information and set up a channel of communication with Moscow during the London Economic Conference.[60] One thing he did not do, and which proved critical, as we have already noted, was to heed a warning by Robert Kelley, chief of the State Department's Division of Eastern European Affairs, that such questions as debts and espionage should be settled on paper prior to recognition, and this failure proved crucial. Not a single one of the short-range goals upon which recognition had been predicated was ever realized, including the prospect of greatly enhanced commerce. Trade between the countries did not increase nearly as much as anticipated, and the Export-Import Bank, designed mainly to promote trade with Moscow, was eventually diverted to the benefit of other countries. Meanwhile, Bullitt, originally a friend of the Kremlin, became one of its most outspoken foes, all of this within the space of two years.[61]

Roosevelt's message in the spring of 1933 to fifty-four heads of state presents still another example of diplomatic misadventure. Coolly received by the foreign press, it became a source of special irritation to Berlin. Germany did not appreciate being arraigned for wanting an increase in arms beyond the level allowed by a treaty that was binding only upon her. The implication that she alone lusted for additional territory pleased her even less. The British could not fail to wonder why FDR had addressed himself to the king rather than the prime minister. But beyond this, Roosevelt's message wrought confusion. Its unqualified definition of aggression as armed incursion beyond one's boundary left Downing Street in limbo regarding England's military presence in Africa and Asia. Then, too, the call for elimination of "offensive" as opposed to "defensive" weapons was thought by the British Chiefs of Staff to rest on a dubious distinction. By December of 1933, Roosevelt was far removed from the halcyon days of the "black leather couch" and "smiling face" portrayed by *Time* magazine. Senator Pittman's Silver Convention faced a hostile hearing in the Senate and had to be enacted by executive fiat.[62]

What is perhaps most telling, amid all these difficulties, is the manner in which the president bore himself. Never one to dwell upon the negative, he held his head high, and on 4 July, the day European leaders accused him of blasting their best hopes, he hosted a festive soirée for the French and British ambassadors. So, too, at his year-end reception for the diplomatic corps. Breasting a sea of reverses, he seized upon the occasion to do cheerful violence to protocol. First names were heard on the receiving line in lieu of the formal Coolidge handshake or Hoover's "How do you do," and the procession was made to revolve clockwise rather than counterclockwise.[63] The only doubtful sign of the evening came when the host chose to retire early, leaving his wife to watch others dance.

Few could have guessed how accurately Roosevelt's early retirement foreshadowed American withdrawal from the international scene. It was only a matter of days before he would suggest in his annual message that "the United States can not take part in political arrangements in Europe." Bullitt, who assured him that "your present policy of keeping out of this [European] mess now and hereafter is the only one consistent with the interests of the United States," reported from Paris that the arrival of the American ambassador at the Quai d'Orsay was causing the same feeling as might be caused by the arrival of the Dalai Lama— perfect neutrality and unbiased benevolence. FDR shot back approvingly: "Dear Bill Buddha . . . what a mess it all is! You, too, seem pessimistic, and I think you are right . . . I gather that no European capital in the present confusion cares a continental damn what the United States thinks or does."[64] Europe, he felt, was unwise in its attitude toward the United States.

By December of 1933, American foreign policy had shifted to a more isolationist stance than anything seen since the late nineteenth century.[65] McReynolds's broadcast, FDR's own press conference of 5 August, and his early retirement from the ambassadorial soirée were so many parts of the whole. This was an administration which, intentionally or not, reinforced parochial attitudes, helping thereby to fashion the isolationist juggernaut of later fame. If Roosevelt's first year as president, in particular the Hundred Days, did not absolutely determine the shape of the decade, it was a harbinger of things to come, a microcosm containing nearly all the elements of presidential style soon to become familiar. Only Far Eastern policy, so highly charged for the future, defies instant analysis. It took longer than a hundred days for the relationship with Japan to crystallize. Yet here, too, the themes were set and the motifs fixed, if not by December of 1933, then surely by the end of 1934.

2. Roosevelt v. Japan

TODAY, when the Soviet Union routinely occupies neighboring territory under cover of the Brezhnev Doctrine, it is important to recall why democratic leaders reacted so violently when Japanese troops returned to mainland China in 1931. For nearly two decades following World War I, there existed a compelling treaty structure, one which involved the United States on the theoretical if not the practical level. There was, at the same time, a moral mandate embodied in the League of Nations. This served to freeze international boundaries even as firm hope persisted for the eventual liberation of subject peoples everywhere. Empires might have succeeded for the moment in withstanding increased pressure for change, but so far as Hoover and Stimson were concerned, they had no claim on the future and there were to be no further occupations or annexations. Roosevelt, in particular, clung to the Wilsonian ideal of self-determination.

Equally to the point is a sense for Tokyo's unique outlook. Whenever Japan's case for involvement in Manchuria is presented, it is likely to be in the form of caricature. This chapter will therefore begin by laying out a body of data, some of it familiar, much of it unfamiliar, with an eye to the need for greater balance and objectivity.

The first item for consideration may be simply stated: Japan, unlike the United States, was a conspicuously dependent nation. In the years after 1905, she had come to rely upon Manchuria as an absorptive blanket for her burgeoning population and intensive capital development. The exchange of raw materials for finished goods benefited both sides at a time when the door to British, French, and Dutch preserves remained firmly shut. Equally important, Manchuria was the only place in the world available for emigration from Japan at a time when her census registered an increase of 30 million in thirty years. From Manchuria came 50 percent of her food and pig iron, and while a full third of Manchuria's coal crossed the Yellow Sea to Japan, several billion yen and some one hundred thousand persons traveled in the opposite direction. It is no exaggeration to say that Manchuria was more closely linked with Tokyo than with Peking. More than half the population of Dairen was Japanese by 1930, and because Tokyo depended so heavily upon the mainland, she could not tolerate the kind of treatment Mexico had meted out to American businessmen. Forty percent of her exports were subject to Chinese boycott, and in any trade war between an industrial and agricultural society no one doubted which of the two would be the more vulnerable.[1]

In strategic-military terms, Tokyo feared the long arm of Moscow. Two wars and two hundred thousand lives had gone to halt Russian penetration of Manchuria and Korea, yet the danger lingered. In 1912, Czar Nicholas II had drawn the Mongols into an agreement recognizing Russian hegemony, and by 1931 Outer Mongolia had been sovietized.[2] During the next few years, as the Kremlin infiltrated Sinkiang Province and made a dramatic industrial recovery, the Red Army began to expand. Plans were laid to double-track the Trans-Siberian Railway. Stalin projected a munitions plant and other installations in the East at the same time that he poured troops and supplies into sensitive border areas.[3] China, meanwhile, was sunk in chaos, a vast power vacuum into which Soviet leaders were presumed ready to move as soon as opportunity beckoned. Japan had profited from Russian weakness to consolidate her influence in South Manchuria under agreements based on the so-called Twenty-One Demands. But when she took Shantung from Germany and occupied Siberia, outcries from the West persuaded her to withdraw, and Russia immediately mounted a new campaign for ascendancy.

Moscow's principal aim was to gain control of the Kuomintang (KMT), ruling body of the Nationalist party. Adolphe Joffe and Mikhail Borodin were sent to mold it along anti-imperialist and communist lines, and they achieved a large measure of success. With Russian help the Whampoa Military Academy was founded. Chiang Kai-shek, its future head, went to Moscow for training, and every Chinese division acquired a Soviet adviser. Russian leaders made political capital in 1924 by giving up their right to a Boxer indemnity and renouncing extraterritoriality. Then, after Sun Yat-sen died, Borodin helped en-

gineer the coup that brought Chiang to power, and Bolshevik General
Blücher drew up his grand plan to eliminate Chinese warlords and curb
Japanese aliens. Soldiers marched behind plainclothes propagandists
who handed out literature extolling Sun and Lenin. Even though
Chiang repudiated communism, shucked off Soviet control, and married a Christian, Japanese qualms persisted. Red China went underground, retreating to Hunan and Kiangsi provinces, but when Nationalists clashed with Russian forces between 1929 and 1931 they
were badly beaten. Communist leader Mao Tse-tung, after setting up a
Chinese-style Soviet republic in Kiangsi Province, rallied fellow communists to march eight thousand miles to the safety of Yenan. Chiang
controlled no more than eight out of twenty-four Chinese provinces,
and thereafter communist armies gradually gained in strength under
the influence and funding of Moscow. By December of 1941, Russian
credits to the Chinese came within a hair's breadth of equaling the
total outlay of all Western countries combined.[4] This is a fact worth
remembering.

Throughout the period under consideration, Japan laid claim to a
Monroe Doctrine of its own, while the United States never ceased to
deny it on the ground that Tokyo, unlike Washington, aimed at political and economic control. On the other hand, when the situation is
viewed from the perspective of the Japanese foreign office (the
Gaimusho), Washington exercised de facto control over a large portion
of hemispheric commerce, giving it an effective voice in politics. By
comparison with Tokyo, it was considerably less dependent on foreign
trade and, with its naval base at Guantanamo Bay, much less threatened militarily. Latin America depended heavily on trade with the
North, but the United States enjoyed virtual self-sufficiency. Washington, in other words, seemed to exercise preponderance without
need, whereas in the Orient it was the exact opposite which obtained.
There, Great Britain, as much as any nation, dominated China's economy in the 1920s and 1930s, and this made no sense to Tokyo, whose
ties with China constituted 24 percent of her overall trade as compared
with only 1.6 percent for London. Japan had sunk 82 percent of its
foreign investment capital into China and Manchuria as opposed to
only 6 percent for Britain.[5]

As regards morality, the picture might have been somewhat different
if, in addition to Russian, British, and Japanese rivalry, there had existed
some immediate prospect of Chinese control. Moreover, if Japan's proc-

lamation of a Greater East Asia Co-Prosperity Sphere lacked something in the way of legitimacy and legal foundation, Tokyo could recall that American pretensions at the time of John Quincy Adams had elicited nothing but incredulous scorn. On the same side of the ledger, China tended increasingly during the 1920s to exploit the restraint exercised by Japanese Foreign Minister Baron Shidehara.[6] Incidents multiplied, some minor, some less so. American naval vessels were attacked thirty-seven times within a few months in 1927 by Chinese troops. The Gaimusho, for its part, counted three hundred cases pending against China by 1937.[7]

The main source of complaint, other than chaos and boycotts, was that China aimed at destruction of Japan's vital interest in the South Manchurian Railway by constructing parallel lines and a new terminus threatening Dairen. In theory, Japanese nationals were entitled to lease land inside and outside the railway zone in Manchuria. Yet in practice, Chinese officials made it hard to do so. An ordinance passed in 1929 by the Mukden government barred the sale and lease of land to aliens even though the right to buy and lease was secured by the Sino-Japanese treaty and notes of 1915. Although the Chinese claimed that various agreements with Japan had been signed under duress and were therefore null and void, not all observers could agree. It is instructive to note that two American ambassadors, both of them stationed in China, not to mention Washington's envoys to Tokyo, sided with Japan. John Van Antwerp MacMurray and Nelson T. Johnson both testified to China's impotence and turpitude. Both felt Japan's position strong enough on moral as well as military grounds to warrant a hands-off policy on the part of the United States. Johnson vacillated in his judgment and changed course when it became expedient, but MacMurray wrote a brilliant book-length memorandum in 1935 which apportioned most of the blame to China. Even Ambassador Joseph Grew, a Stimson appointee and no friend to Japan's military solution, admitted that China had shirked elementary obligations and failed to rectify "chaotic conditions in Manchuria."[8]

Japan took matters into her own hands in 1931 when she encouraged Manchuria to assert a claim to formal nationhood under the name of Manchukuo. Tokyo was not deterred by the League's Lytton Commission, which held Manchuria to be "unalterably Chinese," for this could be true only in the most literal sense. Manchuria's identification with China proper had never been closer historically than the bond between

England and Ireland, except that no Irish invaders ever ruled England as the Manchus did China. It was to keep "barbarians" such as the Manchus out of China that the Great Wall had been completed in 204 B.C. Manchus breached the wall in 1644 to bring an end to the glittering Ming dynasty, and for the next three hundred years (1644–1912) they ruled China. The Chinese were subsequently forbidden to emigrate to Manchuria, which, though now a part of the Chinese empire, remained semiautonomous. It would continue to remain so after the revolution. During the 1920s, warlord Chang Tso-lin flew a five-barred flag rather than the white sun of China. Retaining his own ministries and collecting his own taxes, he paid no revenue to China. Occasionally, he fought Kuomintang forces to ensure that Peking would exercise power only in the realm of foreign relations, and this arrangement continued under his son, Chang Hsueh-liang. Only when the latter showed signs of joining Chiang and Mao to appropriate Japanese property did Tokyo step in to secure the area from Chinese dominion. In a certain sense, then, Japanese intervention resembled French aid to the American Revolution. Manchurians and Americans had both been accustomed to a large measure of independence before achieving it in name. Symbolically, Pu-yi, first emperor of Manchukuo, had been the last emperor of China.[9]

John Hay, architect of the Open Door policy, had accepted Manchuria as beyond the domain of the Chinese empire in the same way that Theodore Roosevelt stressed its importance to Japan and spoke approvingly of a Japanese Monroe Doctrine. And because Manchuria had never been a fully integrated part of China, Japan made it clear when she signed the Nine-Power Treaty that she had no intention of applying its precepts to Manchuria or Inner Mongolia.[10]

Ethnically, it is true, Manchuria was Chinese. Nevertheless, twenty-one out of twenty-eight Sino-Manchurian families had settled there before 1885, and those who came later assimilated quickly, happy for a chance to escape the turbulence of their native land. Here, then, is another similarity between 1937 and 1776. Most Americans were British by descent, just as most Manchukuans were Chinese, yet this did not diminish their native patriotism. In neither case was blood the determining factor. New arrivals from China would fight alongside native Manchus and 750,000 Japanese residents with limited support from Tokyo. Indeed, separatist sentiment could be observed even in the province of Jehol (just north of the wall and not a part of Manchukuo as originally defined). In one of the first messages that Hull received as secretary of state, Ambassador Johnson informed him that Japan had widened the area it controlled *with the cooperation and goodwill of local residents:* "Chinese population of Jehol, hostile to Tang Yu-lin [a Chinese general], aided and welcomed Japanese attack on him." The American consul general at Tientsin added that Chinese regular troops, as well as a number of Chinese officials, were said to have gone over to the side of insurgent forces during the campaign. Understandably, Ambassador Grew, who was stationed in Tokyo, assumed the existence of a genuine separatist movement in North China apart from any aid rendered by Japan.[11]

The residents of Manchuria, forced to choose between an economically inviting Japanese hegemony and the kind of Russian or Chinese occupation which they had resisted for centuries, naturally chose the former. Nor were they disappointed. The new government wrought instant miracles in the realm of taxation, currency, and justice. Foreigners acquired the right to own property; bandits bowed to the law; graft all but disappeared; roadbuilding and other public works flourished. In short, what the Lytton Commission declared impossible had come to pass. By 1934, Grew could report that Manchukuans were living "with a considerable degree of contentment," and North China, if subjected to disturbances, might well unite with Manchukuo "without force of arms." Chinese Vice-Minister for Foreign Affairs Tang Yu-jen admitted that Japan had no need to send troops into North China to induce separation; it needed only to "supply arms to discontented elements." A month later, Johnson cabled that the northern provinces no longer had any real connection with Nanking, Chiang's capital, and that if fighting developed, it would pit Chinese against Chinese. Maryknoll Bishop James E. Walsh noted on a trip to the Far East in November 1938 that "peaceful Manchukuo is not such a misnomer as many tend to believe."[12]

This, in a nutshell, was the view held by Tokyo. It was also the view reflected in firsthand reports received by the State Department and White House during 1933 and 1934. Based on the evidence, it is hard to refute. But for a variety of reasons it did not strike home at the time, and the consequences of such misunderstanding were vast. One fear persistently voiced in Washington related to the future of American business. When Japanese leaders cited the war and Roosevelt's unneutral support for China as the source of most of the difficulty encountered by American firms in Manchukuo, skeptics refused to listen. Tokyo had no way of proving that she would not some day slam the Open Door and that monopolies set up to serve the need of the Japanese army would not be maintained in the aftermath of a peace treaty. There can be no doubt that American businessmen were gradually being squeezed out of certain areas by Japanese competition, whether as a natural result of Japan's proximity and entrepreneurial skill or of less tangible political factors. On the other hand, not a few agreed with Frank Williams, the American commercial attaché in Tokyo, who believed that American capital would have considerable opportunity once the war ended. Many American businessmen in China actually favored Japanese suzerainty as reflected in the 1935 report of the National Foreign Trade Council. What is remarkable is that despite Japan's inherent ability to undercut prices on many American lines of merchandise, despite the fact that most residents of Manchukuo's chief port were Japanese, and even though the United States gave moral and financial support to a country with which Japan was at war, American trade with Manchukuo actually tripled in the period 1932 to 1940. The war turns out to have been a crucial factor just as Tokyo said it would be. The outbreak of hostilities in 1931 hampered American trade substantially, but when peace returned the following year, it settled back to a healthy rhythm. The years 1932 to 1936 were good ones, and the period immediately thereafter was beginning to give promise of a dramatic increase when renewal of all-out hostilities commenced in 1937. Even so, the Open Door was not in serious jeopardy until mid-1938, and American exports to China were not affected in either 1938 or 1939.[13]

Had economic considerations been paramount, it is by no means certain that the United States would have sided with China. Forty-eight percent of U.S. exports to the Far East and 21 percent of all imports were to or from Japan, and the Nipponese, who bought more from the United States than from any other country (yielding only to Canada and Britain as America's premier customer), found their best customer in America. All in all, the United States had twice as much capital invested in Japan as in China and three times as much trade, along with a favorable trade balance.[14] What strikes the student of history is that here, as in other situations involving war and peace, trade statistics were not the decisive element. Every American village and town knew by 1933 that Japan had defied the League and run afoul of world opinion. Manchukuo's declaration of independence in 1932 was followed by Japanese firebombing of Shanghai and a bloody amphibious invasion that not only claimed an enormous number of civilian lives but impinged on American interests. Furthermore, the Chinese behaved like a company of heroes, sacrificing more men against greater odds than French forces had done at Verdun.

The editor of the *Atlantic Monthly* remonstrated to Britain's Lord Lothian that Americans were getting "a very crude impression of Japanese recalcitrancy." Lothian concurred, finding Americans as a whole disturbingly uninformed on the Far East. London's *Contemporary Review* estimated that the United States was biased about ten to one in favor of China. After the Lytton Report called for Tokyo's withdrawal, prompting Japan to withdraw from the League, China had paid its dues, long overdue, and Russia, just as piously, had joined. Less clearly etched on the American mind was the story of Chinese outrages, admitted by Lytton, and the history of Manchurian separation from China, which the Lytton Commission went on record as wishing to preserve. Glimmerings of the Japanese view there were. Roy Howard, head of the Scripps Howard chain of twelve hundred newspapers, visited Japan in the summer of 1933 and published a positive report. Roosevelt, he suggested, should recognize Manchukuo and liberalize immigration policy to remove the stigma attached to Japanese nationals. The United States would also be wise to build its fleet on the theory that power, not logic, was the prime determinant in international relations. Media czar William Randolph Hearst came out with a similar view. At the same time, there were powerful voices in opposition. *Time* magazine refused absolutely to credit Tokyo with any success, even in the business of suppressing Manchurian bandits, and when the Roosevelt administration opted for a policy of inertia, the Howards and Hearsts were heard no more.[15]

Cultural ties played a role as well. For twenty-five years after the Revolution of 1911, Americans held considerable sway over certain sectors of Chinese life. From every pulpit came the message that China aspired to democracy and a knowledge of the Christian God. Sun had been raised in Honolulu. And was it not natural that the world's oldest republic should feel a kinship with the world's youngest? In 1938, Generalissimo and Mme Chiang, both practicing Christians, announced the lifting of the traditional ban on teaching Christianity in the schools. There were three times as many American missionaries in China as there were in Japan with three times as much investment in schools and churches. In addition, if the term "missionary" can be stretched to include close relatives of missionaries as well as Americans teaching school in China, it encompassed some of the most influential leaders of opinion: Congressman Walter Judd, publisher Henry Luce, writer Pearl Buck, and two chiefs of the Department of State's Far Eastern Division, E. T. Williams (1914–18) and Stanley K. Hornbeck. American investors ranged from the YMCA to the Ivy League. Peking, Yenching, and Tsing Hwa universities, as well as the large Peking Union Medical School, had all been founded with Rockefeller funds. American administrative boards controlled Nanking University, Ginling College for women in Nanking, Shanghai University, and American University near Foochow City; nor does this take account of Chinese universities in Canton, Chengtu, and Tsinian and a great many middle schools and hospitals. The national universities were heavily staffed by scholars who had studied in America. Hu-Shih and Chiang Mon-lin, two stars of the Chinese literary renaissance, studied under Professor John Dewey of Columbia University, who traveled to China in 1923 to help develop a national education scheme. Mme Chiang, along with her brother, T. V. Soong, and her brother-in-law H. H. Kung, graduated from Wellesley, Harvard, and Yale respectively. St. John's University in Shanghai, under the presidency of an American, Dr. Hawks Pott, turned out a steady stream of social and political leaders; and for a short while Chinese universities had "credits," "semesters," "campuses," "programs," and "recitations."[16]

It was nearly inevitable that this Americanization of China would beget a corresponding Chinafication of Washington. Although Hull's views must be discounted since he played a secondary, if not tertiary, role in the shaping of Far Eastern policy, it is safe to say that he never showed the slightest sign of understanding, or even of wanting to understand, Japan's dilemma. Closest to the president stood Treasury Secretary Morgenthau, who dismissed Japan's grievances out of hand and vouched for the efficacy of economic sanctions down to the eve of Pearl Harbor. Meanwhile, Under Secretary of State Welles, who entered Morgenthau's camp in 1938, served as a bridge between the State Department and the White House. As such, he had to be more guarded in his assessment, especially since the chief of the Western European Division, J. Pierrepont Moffat (Grew's son-in-law), took a relatively tolerant view of Japanese moves and favored a hands-off policy. According to Moffat, American interests did not warrant the risk of war. Even if Japan were defeated, her place would only be taken by the Soviet Union. Leaning toward Morgenthau and eventually prevailing in the competition for Roosevelt's ear was Stanley K. Hornbeck, chief of the Far Eastern Division at State. After earning his doctorate from the University of Wisconsin and teaching for five years in China and Manchuria, he had gone to Harvard as a professor and then to Versailles as one of Wilson's advisers. Fluently self-assured, he once replied to the accusation of being anti-Japanese by observing that this was "a good deal like saying that parents and teachers . . . are partial in favor of good boys and biased against bad boys . . . Chinese delinquencies are comparatively petty and for the most part those of inefficiency and ineptitude." As for his advice on how Tokyo might best be contained, he told Roosevelt to act in such a way that "nature may be allowed to take its course." The "flood tide" of Japanese expansion would come and the "ebb" would follow.[17]

Hornbeck left his post in late 1937, but only to become an intimate adviser to Roosevelt, and his replacement, Maxwell Hamilton, never departed substantially from the line laid down from above. Hamilton had served as a consular officer in China. This left only five influential individuals whose stand on the Far East coincided with that of Moffat: William Bullitt, Hugh Wilson, Colonel House, Joseph Grew, and Francis B. Sayre.[18] Since Bullitt and Wilson were kept on for their expertise in European affairs, the burden of providing advice fell upon House, Grew, and Sayre.

Few figures could be as dissimilar as Grew and House. While one kept a voluminous "diary" intended for official eyes, the other nursed a passion for anonymity, going out of his way to conceal his role during the Hundred Days and staying almost entirely out of sight down to his death in 1938. Of the two, House remains the more obscure as a presidential adviser even though he probably exercised greater influence. As elder statesman of the Democratic party, he had a voice in Roosevelt's appointments and corresponded not only with the president but with Long in Rome, Straus in Paris, Cudahy in Warsaw, and Dodd in Berlin. He heard regularly from Bingham in London; indeed, he helped him hold his job in 1936 and 1937.[19] Roosevelt introduced House to members of the diplomatic corps, included him in the discussion of sensitive issues, and in 1935 wrote him, "I do wish we had someone to fulfill the splendid missions which you carried out in Europe before we got into the war— but there is only one you and I know of no other."[20] House introduced FDR to Arthur Murray and received such visitors as Lord Lothian, Austen Chamberlain, and George Lansbury. Among the Japanese guests whom he entertained were Yosuke Matsuoka; Count Kabayama, close friend of both emperor and prime minister; Shigeru Yoshida, minister to Great Britain; and Prince Konoye along with his college-age son. He also heard from Count Makino, lord keeper of the privy seal, father-in-law to Yoshida, and an old friend from Paris Peace Conference days.[21] In short, House acted as Japan's main channel to the White House, passing on ideas and delivering letters.[22] Nor did his lobbying end here. He granted interviews to Japanese journalists and availed himself of the American press to publish his views on the Far East at the suggestion of the Japanese ambassador. In January of 1938, he was quoted in Tokyo newspapers as having said without rancor that Japan was "determined to gain hegemony over Asia."[23]

House's counsel was far from decisive. He could not compete with Hornbeck, and his power base shrank somewhat at the end of six months with the dismissal of protégé Raymond Moley. Postmaster General James Farley spoke of him as a remote figure who received no more than the outward signs of respect owing to a distinguished career in the past. This judgment, however, would appear to be well shy of the truth. Once, in 1936, when George Messersmith happened to be in New York between posts as minister to Austria and assistant secretary of state, he received a phone call from House asking if he would care to stop by for a chat. Though he could think of no good reason to answer a summons by House, he not only made the visit but submitted to an hour and a half of probing questions on the European scene. Then came the punch: Roosevelt wished to nominate him as ambassador to the Soviet Union and would he accept? A surprised Messersmith hastened to explain that his wife could not abide Russia, and on this note the interview ended. Later, checking with friends who knew both House and Roosevelt, Messersmith learned that the aging colonel retained more influence than he had thought.[24]

If House was not "Roosevelt's strategic adviser," as one of his biographers has claimed, neither was he inactive. Had he been only one member of a larger group seeking to steer Roosevelt toward a more conciliatory course in the Pacific, he would be well worth mentioning, for the balance of advice between those favoring conciliation and those preferring coercion appeared quite even at first. It is interesting to note that soon after House died in 1938, Roosevelt shifted to economic sanctions. By the same token, in 1939, another of House's nominees, Assistant Secretary of State Sayre, was transferred from his seat of power in Washington to serve as high commissioner to the Philippines. Finally, a year later, the last bastion of House power, J. Pierrepont Moffat, was detached from the State Department to head Roosevelt's embassy in Ottawa.

By contrast with the silence one encounters with respect to House, it is difficult to read any work on the period without finding continual reference to Ambassador Grew. He is portrayed as the voice of reason, a believer in meeting Japan halfway. Although he did not speak Japanese, he had spent ten years in Tokyo and was married to a woman who not only spoke the language but had passed her childhood in Japan and could trace her lineage to Commodore Matthew C. Perry, a local idol. Grew worked long hours, demanding as much of himself as he did of his staff, and through his unusually gracious manner and bearing he gained en-trée to the highest circles of Japanese society. It was Grew who coun-seled delay in 1939, when Roosevelt began to move toward economic warfare, and he is well remembered for his advocacy of a Pacific summit meeting in 1941. Such a conference, he felt, could break the diplomatic logjam and enable Premier Konoye to carry Japan on a program of mili-tary retrenchment.

Like Nelson Johnson, Grew was unusual in being a Republican who continued to serve under Roosevelt, and he soon acquired a reputation for being furious with any American who ventured to criticize the ad-ministration. Both he and FDR had served on the Harvard *Crimson*. Each had an uncle in the China trade. Each played poker and devoured detective stories. And with their mutual faith in the power of personal ties and creation of a climate of trust, they preferred facts to ideas, regarded Europe as in a "mess," and felt the United States should keep its distance. Grew expressed instant or near-instant agreement with many other views of the Roosevelt entourage. These included opposi-tion to any form of tangible cooperation with Britain, unwillingness to tolerate any increase in the Japanese naval ratio, and an opinion of the Japanese that can only be described as cliché. With his professional future still in question, Grew wrote Hull in 1933 that the Japanese were "war loving," "aggressive," "unscrupulous," and potentially "menac-ing." In 1934, he advocated a policy of economic sanctions certain to please Hornbeck and reported that the Japanese were out to conquer the world, with Guam included as a potential target on their list.[25]

Far more than is realized, Grew's views were in a state of constant flux. One moment, he would praise Japanese courtesy, while the next, he would describe it as a veneer masking deceit. In one place he stated that

Japan was in the grip of an elite and unrepresentative group of militarists; in another, he suggested the country was united, with all groups agreed on basic aims. In still a third communication, he espoused both points of view at once. In 1936, he preferred a policy of accommodation, but by 1938 his mood had shifted, along with administration plans, to the negative. With each turn of the White House weathervane, Grew made a turn of his own. From the initial letter to Roosevelt, in which he recalled their common background of Groton and Harvard, to his letter of 14 December 1941, in which he wrote, "Dear Frank . . . you are playing a masterly hand in foreign affairs," his response to the exigencies remained constant. It also suited his ambassadorial taste to purchase a Scottie dog resembling Fala, the famed White House terrier.[26]

Returning, however, to the balance of opinion on Far Eastern questions, one cannot avoid the president himself. Aside from the stricter, more authoritarian cast of Japanese society, which could scarcely have been congenial to a man with his political leanings, FDR never had an opportunity to know the Japanese as he did the Chinese. During his childhood, he made frequent visits to Algonac, home of his beloved grandfather Delano, who had spent thirty-three years in China as a private merchant and United States consular representative. Algonac resembled Hyde Park in its landscape as well as furnishings, which included a Buddhist bell, Chinese trees and shrubs, and paintings of the Delanos by a Chinese artist friend. Roosevelt's mother, Sara, who lived in Macao before her marriage, had collected stamps from Hong Kong and Peking, which eventually formed the nucleus of her son's rich collection. Then, too, other Delano relatives not only built the first Chinese telegraph and established the first regular steamship service on the Yangtze but brought back the first treaties between Peking and Washington. Three aunts could speak firsthand of a proud people who chafed under Japanese occupation, Aunt Annie having lived in China for five years, Aunt Doe for thirty, and Aunt Dora, one of Sara's closest friends, for thirty-five.[27]

So far as one can tell, Roosevelt never experienced any feeling toward Japan other than revulsion. He liked to recall that in his grandfather's time, "European and American traders regarded Chinese employees as essentially honest, whereas . . . Japanese employees were not so rated." From Groton, he reported to his parents that a guest speaker had run down the "poor Chinamen" a little too much and thought too much of the Japanese. Later, on his honeymoon cruise, he conversed with several

"Japs" but found to his displeasure that he was giving more information than he received. Foreigners who conferred with him during the Hundred Days made it a point to note that Japan was his great "preoccupation." And this should not be surprising. The sum of his wisdom, as expressed in an interview with Stimson, came down to a story about a Japanese student at Harvard who had allegedly told him of Japan's plans for the conquest of Hawaii, Australia, and New Zealand. From the start of his presidency, he determined to keep Japan from increasing her naval strength relative to the United States and refused to associate himself with liberal criticism of racist features in the immigration law. Just as he pressed Britain and France to renew their preinaugural pledges of opposition to the floating of Japanese loans, pledges given to Bullitt, he instructed Davis to engineer an Anglo-American embargo on arms to Tokyo.[28]

Naturally, none of this entered the ear of Japanese visitors who sat upon the "black leather couch." Roosevelt was about to follow a zigzag course based upon fluctuations of opinion at home and abroad. Grew intimated to the Gaimusho that although the United States would continue to pay lip service to the Stimson Doctrine, the two countries could agree to disagree. Roosevelt, too, sounded reassuring at first. He discussed the Far East with Colonel House and on 31 March 1933, flying in the face of Stimson's advice, opened the executive mansion to Yosuke Matsuoka. Matsuoka had just led his delegation out of the League and was telling reporters that American naval units in the Pacific posed a threat to his country, yet FDR described his talk with the Japanese envoy as "very friendly" and permitted him to broadcast a farewell message to the American people. A cascade of protest letters fell upon the White House, but the president still held out official hope for rapprochement. After meeting four times with Viscount Ishii between 24 and 27 May, the most he would do to even the balance was to issue a statement with T. V. Soong on behalf of peace with China, one that could be taken with a grain of salt as it was completely pious.[29] Four days after the last of the Roosevelt-Ishii conferences, Peking signed the Tangku Truce, which granted Japan a legal basis for stationing troops north of the Great Wall. This truce was often cited as a charter for future Japanese encroachment notwithstanding Roosevelt's announcement of a $50 million credit to China. Chiang would have to wait four years for another financial fillip.

According to press accounts of his talks with Ishii, FDR endorsed the idea of a Japanese-American arbitration treaty; he also entertained the

idea of a nonaggression pact and encouraged the prospect of a commercial treaty. At the same time, the White House issued puzzling denials.
Tokyo insisted that Ishii had received broad assurances from Roosevelt,
but such assurances were disavowed by Hull during talks in London.[30]
Roosevelt himself gave the impression of being unconcerned. He permitted the commander in chief of the Asiatic Fleet to visit Tokyo and
accept a cordial greeting. In addition, Prince Iyesato Tokugawa, former
president of the House of Peers, met no objection from Washington
when he embarked upon a goodwill voyage to the United States and
spoke in a radio braodcast of "our friendly feeling toward America."
Contributing to the atmospherics, Japanese Finance Minister Takahashi
issued a statement defending America's part in the London Economic
Conference. And in October, Hornbeck discussed an arbitration treaty
with Ambassador Katsuji Debuchi, with Ishii quoted on his return to
Japan as being much in favor of it. The White House then lapsed into
Delphic silence until November, when it suddenly announced plans for
recognition of the Soviet Union. This was chilling news to Tokyo, however much it may have been offset by the announcement that America's
Pacific Fleet, after three years in the Pacific, would soon steam eastward.
And to add to the mystery, it became known that Roosevelt intended
to go to Hawaii during the summer of 1934, presumably to hold talks
with Japanese leaders. This, surely, could be taken as a sign of encouragement.[31]

FDR now authorized a reprinting of his friendly 1923 article "Shall
We Trust Japan?" and made a point of conferring with Clark Howell, an
old friend and editor of the *Atlanta Constitution*. For his help in the
campaign of 1932, Howell had been offered a variety of ambassadorial
posts, and because of his interest in Japan he retained influential contact with leaders of opinion on both sides of the Pacific. The purpose of
his Thanksgiving visit with Roosevelt at Warm Springs, Georgia, and
subsequent train ride to Atlanta at the side of the president was to
present Japan's case and test the temperature for negotiation. It could
be assumed that he would relay whatever he heard to Tokyo, and what
he heard turned out to be highly significant: the president would not
only receive the offer of a nonaggression pact from Japan, he would
welcome it. Two months later, Howell informed Roosevelt that the
State Department, Hornbeck in particular, was biased against Japan.
According to Howell, the White House should therefore deal with a
special envoy from Tokyo in the person of fellow Harvard alumnus

Otohiko ("Otto") Matsukata. The president replied that he would be "delighted" and set the Department of State busily to work drafting a nonaggression pact.[32]

Tokyo, understandably optimistic when one of Hornbeck's hard-line speeches was airily dismissed by Grew, decided to turn the eightieth anniversary of the Perry treaty into a diplomatic tour de force. On 26 January 1934, the Pacific Club of Tokyo, of which FDR was honorary president, tendered him an invitation to visit Japan en route to or from Hawaii. Well-known figures such as Admiral Ryozo Asano began to embark on goodwill missions to the United States. On 1 March, a transpacific radio program was produced in Tokyo featuring concilia-tory speeches by Viscount Ishii and Ambassador Grew, along with the reassuring voice of Japan's new ambassador, Hiroshi Saito, and that of former American envoy to Japan Roland Morris. Grew's remarks on friendship were published and, since it now seemed likely that Mat-sukata and Saito would be able to clinch a general settlement, it was said that, as a crowning touch, the highest noble of the land, Prince Konoye, would visit the United States after consulting with his prime minister and cabinet.[33]

Few observers were as realistic as France's ambassador to Japan, who remarked that the Gaimusho was pressing its suit in such fashion as to lose prestige, if not dignity. Roosevelt, who, as we shall see, was allow-ing expectation to rise far above the level of intended satisfaction, received Matsukata cordially on two separate occasions and signed the Tydings-McDuffie Act signaling an obvious American retreat from the Far East. Hull followed up by writing a warm letter to the U.S. Cham-ber of Commerce commending the Perry celebrations and by impli-cation encouraging Foreign Minister Koki Hirota to suggest additional means of strengthening ties of friendship. Thus, Chinese leaders looked on in stupefied fashion since there was nothing as yet to indi-cate that Roosevelt would deny Matsukata's request for a third visit or that the nonaggression pact discussed with Howell would perish under Hornbeck's pointed pen (it was later offered in the harmless form of an arrangement to include China and the Soviet Union).[34]

Similar ambivalence marks the manner in which Roosevelt dealt with the Amau Declaration. On 17 April, Eliji Amau, spokesman for the Japanese foreign office, warned all foreigners to stay clear of China, which he described as a region of special importance and responsibility for Japan. While the League continued to channel substantial aid to

Chiang with the backing of the United States, American aircraft and flying instructors poured into China, and Colonel Jouett, formerly of the United States Air Force, graduated hundreds of Chinese air cadets from the academy he helped to found. Increasingly, Japan's vulnerable urban population lived in fear of American bombs, while Washington was accused of building air bases in areas of China which posed an immediate threat.[35] Roosevelt's response to Amau was at once milder than Ambassador Johnson would have wished yet firmer than suggested by Hamilton. Making straight for the middle, as was his custom, he expressed frank disapproval in an *aide-memoire* while conveying an air of tolerance to the press. Hull, for his part, urged reporters to refrain from writing stories antagonistic to Tokyo and counseled Grew to emphasize the "good neighbor" side of American diplomacy. In this sense, American reaction to Amau proved to be more forebearing than that of the British. On 22 and 23 April, despite remarks by the chief of the Japanese navy widely interpreted as an attack on the American navy, one hundred ships of the Pacific Fleet transited Panama en route to New York. Even more indicative of American tolerance, nothing was said or done to deny reports that FDR planned to rendezvous with Japan's prime minister in Honolulu. On 17 April, the day that Amau spoke, such a plan was announced by the Agence Economique et Financiere as having been confirmed by Tokyo, and anticipation was permitted to mount during the coming weeks.[36]

When the equalizer arrived, it came in the form of a series of shocks administered face to face. Hull met Ambassador Saito three times in private, once at the latter's office and twice at his own apartment. The ambassador renewed his plea for a doctrine of two spheres whereby the United States would keep hands off the western Pacific in return for a guarantee of the Open Door and a pledge of Chinese territorial integrity. Hull not only rejected the proposals; he went on to suggest, none too subtly, that two thousand bombers could now fly from many of the capitals of western Europe to London, blow that city off the map, and return. Because the United States made no secret of constructing air bases on the Aleutian Islands, as well as aiding the Chinese in similar construction of their own, there could be no doubt as to what Hull, and therefore the president, had in mind. Roosevelt congratulated Hull for his "magnificent position," and Secretary of the Navy Claude Swanson blustered that if Japan did not accept a continuation of her inferior naval ratio, the United States would respond in kind.[37]

Swanson's threat drew a swift rejoinder from the Japanese press, and the *Washington Post* criticized the administration for "drifting into naval rivalry." Once again, the president reversed course—or so it appeared. On 8 June, he received Konoye at the White House and, according to his visitor, said he would welcome a meeting with Hirota and other Japanese officials if the talks could be set for Hawaii along the route of his summer cruise. At this juncture, Japanese newspapers seized upon the conference idea, referring to a Roosevelt-Hirota meeting in Hawaii as not only desirable but probable, and Hirota declared that if invited to Honolulu he might accept. Just as Konoye's presence in America reflected Japanese trust in Roosevelt's word, surely the fact that the Gaimusho permitted reports of a summit conference to be broadcast implied confidence that such an event would materialize. Suddenly, however, the White House veered off, insisting that if Tokyo did not drop the idea at once, Roosevelt would have to issue a public denial—his cruise was solely for rest and relaxation.[38] And so it went in the classic pattern of all that transpired between Washington and Tokyo down to the morning of 7 December 1941.

Almost certainly, Roosevelt made an offer similar, if not identical, to the one described by Konoye. He had been invited to visit Japan not only by the Pacific Club but also by the Pan Pacific Association (most likely, also, by Prince Iyesato Tokugawa, one of the foremost Japanese princes and a ranking member of the last Shogunate family). Although there is no definite proof that he intended to go the full distance, he did plan to hold a conclave at Hawaii to discuss the Far East, and he expected to be joined in this conference by Grew and Bullitt.[39] It is also clear that Ambassador Saito, who accompanied Prince Konoye to the White House, was asked by the president when he expected to sail for Tokyo. Roosevelt suggested that Japanese and American officials might arrive in Hawaii at about the same time. Indeed, FDR admitted as much to Assistant Secretary Phillips when confronted with the awkward fact that newspapers in Tokyo, Geneva, and London were speaking of a summit parley between himself and the leadership of Japan.[40] How much of the offer as reported by the media was intimated, how much explicit, and how much misunderstood may never be known. What is important is that Roosevelt created the impression of an honest offer without actually giving one and proceeded to rub salt into an open wound. Great must have been the consternation in Tokyo when reports circulated to the effect that Japan had renewed its offer of a bilateral nonaggression pact. According to Reuters News Agency, the proposal had been rejected by Senator Key Pittman. Tokyo feigned surprise that any such arrangement should be thought necessary between two friendly countries. Nevertheless, no small amount of damage had been done, and Roosevelt did little to ease the pain. On the contrary, after reaching Honolulu, he alluded publicly to American air bases in the Aleutians and American support for Chinese airpower; he then went on to praise the efficiency of the Pacific Fleet, due to return to its base at Pearl Harbor. Such remarks were labeled "insolent" by General Kunishige Tanaka, president of Japan's retired military officers' society.[41] In August, the president gave a tea for Prince and Princess Kaya, relatives of the emperor, but this gracious event represented only the afterglow of a dead flame.[42]

Once again, the French embassy in Tokyo furnished an accurate reading: the affair smacked of "genuine deception, if not a certain humiliation."[43] Prince Konoye's fall from power a few months before Pearl Harbor was dramatically paralleled by the downfall of the Saito government on 4 July 1934.[44] In both instances, as we shall see, Roosevelt held out hopes which he had no intention of satisfying, and in each case, American rhetoric, along with American action, was perceived as inflammatory. A dangerous current arose in the Orient which swept rapidly across the Pacific. Tokyo's new government announced its intent to abrogate the London Naval Agreement of 1930, which bound it to the inferior naval ratio of seven to ten, and Finance Minister Korekiyo Takahashi criticized the New Deal for shortening the work week: "What any nation needs now is more work, not less."[45] Japan was beginning to take off the gloves. As part of what can only be described as a dress rehearsal for 1941, the vicar general of Maryknoll, Reverend James M. Drought, lodged two complaints: one with the president of the American Foreign Policy Association to the effect that American opinion appeared biased against Japan; a second with the Department of State urging that more thoughtful consideration be given to Japanese-American détente in the form of naval parity, reciprocal commercial treaties, and a nonaggression pact. In 1934, as in 1941, important Japanese proposals were sidetracked while the United States made unfathomable gestures. On 19 June, just after the Hull-Saito talks had ended in stalemate, Congress approved the Silver Purchase Act, which Roosevelt had recommended and which sent the Chinese economy into a nose dive. A week later, Hornbeck offered Saito a new consular convention.[46]

It was not only that Roosevelt turned aside substantive compromise as a consequence of having little intellectual or moral commitment to a specific strategy. He went a step further in barring the way to others. Britain and the Soviet Union were both prepared to recognize Manchukuo and sign a nonaggression pact with Japan, but they refrained from doing so out of fear of giving offense to those in high places along the Potomac.[47] When FDR heard of British efforts in the summer of 1934, he let it be known that if they were "even suspected of preferring to play with Japan to playing with us," the United States would go over their head and appeal to Canada and the Dominions. England's first concern being Germany—her desertion of the League, rearmament, and pressure on Austria—she naturally wished to minimize friction in the Far East. Roosevelt's answer was to ask her to build up her naval base at Singapore while counting on America to shoulder responsibility in adjacent areas. He would even help to contain Hitler, he promised, in return for British moral support in the Far East. As reported by France's ambassador in London, the American government had promised to do all it could, in consonance with public opinion, to have the country join to the maximum degree in a system of Anglo-French guarantees. Ambassador Bingham was saying that it should not be impossible for the United States to "participate in rigorous economic sanctions which would isolate Germany completely and condemn her to a precarious situation should she violate her agreements."[48]

One other characteristic of Roosevelt's approach to Tokyo that appeared quite early in the game was his refusal to negotiate confidentially at the highest level. Japanese newspaper correspondent K. K. Kawakami informed his government that the only sure way to influence FDR was through direct personal contact. He and Viscount Ishii, who held a similar view, must have been impressed by the example of China's T. V. Soong going straight to the president and winning generous aid without recourse to Hull. As a result, Tokyo dispatched no less than nine goodwill envoys to America in the years 1933–34, including Prince Tokugawa, whom Under Secretary Phillips recognized as the foremost living Japanese. But the question remained: would Roosevelt receive these emissaries in good faith and negotiate *confidentially* at the *highest* level? The answer was a disappointing one, for although

Phillips advised FDR to see Tokugawa, although Hornbeck urged him to receive Admiral Nagano, vice-chief of the Naval General Staff, and although Roosevelt himself encouraged Tokyo to send Admiral Asano (who, like Matsukata, was a Harvard graduate), neither Phillips nor Roosevelt nor anyone else on top favored the kind of secret communication between Tokyo and the White House which the mission of such prominent goodwill envoys implied. Thus did the gentlemen from Japan arrive, one by one, only to be led over a carpet of thickly tufted words. Asano must have been astonished when his contact with Roosevelt amounted only to an hour-long tea in the presence of the president's wife. By the time an editorial appeared in the *Japanese Advertiser* suggesting that Tokyo was risking humiliation by overdoing its goodwill policy, the damage had been done.[49]

Roosevelt closed out the year 1934 with a final burst of contradiction. On the one hand, he sent Bullitt to Tokyo for a friendly ten-day visit and told Morgenthau that China had not changed very much in fifty years; it was still the mecca of "those people whom I have called money changers in the temple. . . . It is better to hasten the crisis in China—to compel the Chinese people more and more to stand on their own feet." On the other hand, he publicly excoriated Japan for her refusal to endorse the naval status quo. Colonel House, taken aback by the crudity of this tactic, objected to language that could "easily have been avoided by simply confining ourselves to the proposal that in the future, the Japanese might build what they liked, we reserving the same right and feeling certain that the friendship between the two countries was so close that it would be understood that there was no intention to compete." Because Japan sought parity, in part to assuage national pride, in part because anything else caused a "certain country" to look on her with contempt, Whitehall proposed a face-saving extension of the seven-to-ten ratio. London and Washington would agree to yield parity while having it tacitly understood that Japan would hold herself in check. Norman Davis, who represented the United States in these naval limitation talks, liked the scheme; Admiral Isoroku Yamamoto, head of the Japanese delegation, also spoke warmly of compromise. And there were important precedents. Hoover, for example, had permitted Japan to go from a six-to-ten balance on all ships to seven-to-ten in minor categories and parity in submarines. The United States had also agreed in 1930 to delay completion of her heavy cruisers until after 1936 and to forego the desire for twenty-one 8-inch cruisers, settling for eighteen in return for a compensatory increase in 6-inch ships. Roosevelt, however, would not hear of extra cruisers for Britain and flatly ruled out Japan's insistence on equal status among the powers.[50]

Lord Lothian suggested that the United States should tailor policy to power and vice versa. While making judicious concessions to Japan, Roosevelt would be well advised to shore up America's fortifications and naval presence in the Pacific. Significantly, nearly every one of the president's advisers concurred on this basic point. Grew urged Roosevelt to build his navy to the 1930 treaty limit if he wished to avoid a Pax Japonica. Hornbeck called for a fleet "so strong that no other country will think seriously of attacking." And Hull offered to help by jogging Congress for the necessary funds. But the president fell silent. Instead of accepting Britain's offer of a contractual agreement to resist Japanese expansion, FDR rested content with recognition of Russia and told Lothian that "we should have to rely on the fact that our ideals and interests [in Britain and the United States] were fundamentally the same." Lothian spoke for a good many when he said, "I doubt whether this is enough."[51] It was *not* enough. Neither here nor anywhere else along the tortuous path leading to Pearl Harbor did FDR demonstrate a capacity to coordinate military and political factors in the interest of shaping a coherent and consistent foreign policy.

During the next four or five years, Roosevelt's policy became, if anything, more amorphous. He continued to stand in the way of a comprehensive settlement yet showed signs of softening. In outward appearance, if not in fact, his position changed appreciably. When Manchukuo won a measure of recognition by purchasing Russia's shares in the Chinese Eastern Railroad and by persuading Britain to send a trade mission, he was inclined to move his embassy from Peking to Nanking so that it would be easier for him to withdraw American garrisons at Tientsin and Peking and hence concede a greater degree of Japanese control. John Van Antwerp MacMurray bolstered Tokyo's position further by penning his celebrated memorandum, courtesy of the State Department, and Secretary of War George H. Dern sailed to Tokyo for a cordial reception.[52]

Meanwhile, Japanese inroads into North China were passing almost unnoticed. A slight hike in the tariff on Japanese goods and a "cotton" loan to Chiang seemed to be as far as the White House was willing to go. American members of the Olympic Committee voted for Tokyo as host to the 1940 games, and when the Japanese ambassador to the Court of St. James's took the trouble to express his appreciation to U.S. envoy Robert Bingham, the latter assured him that there was "no anti-Japanese feeling in the United States normally except on the fringe of the western coast." Foreign Minister Hachiro Arita could honestly say, as he did in August of 1936, that relations with the United States were going "very well." They were indeed going well in the eye of the casual beholder. Roosevelt informed President Quezon that he would welcome an earlier date for Filipino independence, and later in the year, the cabinet heard him outline a plan for neutralizing all but a few major possessions in the Pacific. Since this proposal could be construed as consonant with the two spheres principle proposed by Saito in 1934, its significance lies less in the realm of practicality—it was vetoed by the chancelleries of Europe as well as by the State Department—than in the evidence it affords of American willingness to retrench militarily while appearing to trust Japan.[53]

Even Tokyo's decision to launch full-scale war against China in July of 1937 and its murderous attack on American and British gunboats the following December did not immediately alter the thrust of American policy. FDR's reaction to the outbreak of hostilities can only be described as supine, setting the stage for his weak response to Germany's challenge a year later. Why, he wanted to know, had American troops not been withdrawn from Peking and Tientsin as the White House had directed? It vexed him to think that his original judgment in this matter had been overridden. On 5 September, he announced that any citizen of the United States who wished to remain in China would have to do so at his own risk. When Admirals Yarnell and Leahy requested additional cruisers to protect American nationals against illegal search, he refused to send them. Instead, he halted nineteen American bombers on their way to China and prohibited merchantmen in government employ from carrying war matériel to China or Japan. Private ships were warned to proceed at their own risk, and Ambassador Johnson took shelter aboard an American gunboat, an act for which he was roundly condemned as doyen of the diplomatic corps. In October, after flirting with a "quarantine" of Japan, Roosevelt reversed course completely. Maxwell Hamilton brought out an official study on the feasibility of economic sanctions leaning heavily to the pessimistic side. Sanctions, Hamilton warned, would come too late; furthermore, the United States would have to take the lead and would inevitably wind up bearing the brunt. Adding that public opinion was negative in this regard, he indicated in conclusion that a more "constructive" program would be needed to eliminate the cause of Japanese aggression. Totally antithetical to the idea of quarantine, this is the approach that actually characterized American policy before 1937 and for some time thereafter. Hamilton was promoted, and the president refused to approve anything but "minor restrictive measures" which would have to be "decided upon by other powers."[54]

While delegates to the Brussels Conference (3–24 November) were thundering against Japanese aggression at U.S. instigation, Roosevelt proceeded to extend a friendly hand beneath the table. To draw the sting from Davis's rhetoric and limit German diplomatic gains in the Far East, he sounded Tokyo on the idea of an American role similar to that played by Theodore Roosevelt at Portsmouth. This would have meant obtaining peace terms from China and Japan, announcing receipt of both declarations simultaneously, and introducing the adversaries as an impartial broker. When Eugene Dooman, Grew's chargé, conveyed FDR's offer "unofficially" to Sejiro Yoshizawa, director of the American Bureau of the Japanese Foreign Office, Tokyo was delighted. All parties, including the Chinese and British, proved anxious to invoke the example of T.R. Great, then, must have been Yoshizawa's amazement when, in the act of accepting Dooman's proposal of 15 November, he received an inscrutable rejoinder from FDR: Tokyo must not expect Washington to legitimize Japanese aggression. Undeterred, the Gaimusho took advantage of what seemed a heaven-sent opportunity to throw Roosevelt on the defensive and fend off a condemnatory resolution at Brussels. Was the United States, it demanded to know, behind the conference? Was it attempting to take the lead in humiliating Nippon? To all such questions, Dooman and Grew (who saw Hirota on 16 November) returned a polite no.[55] Roosevelt, amiable as ever, consented to see Otohiko Matsukata, who was returning as a goodwill envoy in the company of his brother Kojiro. After the brothers failed to appear, he granted them a second opportunity, then entertained Prince Konoye's son on his way to attend classes at Princeton.[56] "It afforded me great pleasure," he wrote Konoye, "to welcome on November 9 your son, Fumitaka, and to receive from him your letter of September 15. I was impressed by his address and bearing . . . I take it as a compliment to our country that his education is being entrusted to American institutions. I also wish to express my appreciation of your cordial personal greetings and of your message of friendship . . . I heartily reciprocate your sentiments."[57]

Four days after the last of the Brussels sessions, when Kojiro Matsukata told Assistant Secretary Hugh Wilson that Dooman's proposal deserved serious consideration, Washington behaved according to what was rapidly becoming the custom. Grew introduced Hirota to the sympathetic MacMurray; Roosevelt invited Matsukata to meet with members of his family, but nothing further happened.[58]

It was at this point that Japanese aerial gunners targeted American and British gunboats on the Yangtze River. Neville Chamberlain, who was as perplexed as anyone else in the face of Roosevelt's inexplicable behavior, nevertheless hoped that Washington would at last join in a show of force. "It is always best and safest to count on the Americans for nothing but words," he wrote, "but at this moment they are nearer to 'doing something' than I have ever known them and I can't altogether repress hopes!" With a death toll of three and dozens wounded, the *Panay* became the first American ship ever lost to enemy aircraft, and there could be little doubt of Japanese intent. Crew members had submitted to on-board inspection the day of the attack; they had draped five-by-nine-foot flags over the vessel's awning and sides; the weather was clear. The only thing Chamberlain does not appear to have reckoned with was the inert state of American public opinion and, once again, the peculiar coloration of Roosevelt's diplomatic style. The isolationist Ludlow Amendment was about to come to a close vote in the wake of much disillusionment following upon Brussels, and FDR must have known that his countrymen could well recall incidents in the past which had been the fault of China. On 14 August, for example, there had been a shocking series of Chinese assaults on the International Settlement at Shanghai. Among the many hundreds of civilian fatalities was one Frank Rawlinson, who happened to be the best-known American in China at the time. Chinese fliers had then gone on the rampage a second time, killing two more Americans, injuring twenty-six others, and scoring several hits on the American flagship *Augusta* along with the merchantman *President Hoover*. In 1927, American naval vessels had been attacked thirty-seven times within several months by Chinese troops, and Washington had been sufficiently exercised by outbursts of Chinese xenophobia to bombard the city of Nanking. Public sentiment in 1937 ran seven to three in favor of a withdrawal of American citizens from China as against the possibility of confrontation with Japan.[59]

Hill anticipated Britain's request for a joint protest and hastened to forward a unilateral American demand for apology, even before reports of the survivors had been received. Roosevelt, for his part, turned aside any idea of an Anglo-American naval demonstration, choosing instead to propose economic sanctions, which London again rejected in the absence of American military commitment. He also revived his idea of a blockade of Japan after the next "grave outrage." As outlined to Ambassador Lindsay, such an operation would interdict Japanese trade south and east of a line drawn from Hong Kong or Singapore through the Philippines to Alaska. Presumably, it would bring Japan to her knees in eighteen months without war. Lindsay, nonplussed, cabled the Foreign Office that these were the utterances of "a harebrained statesman" in his "worst inspirational mood." As was generally the case, those closest to FDR seem to have been divided on the issue with the result that he sent Captain Ingersoll to London for secret naval talks while disabusing Britain of any hope for united action in the near future. The most the United States proved willing to do was advance the date slightly on naval exercises already planned for Hawaii and send several cruisers on a goodwill visit to Singapore. In the meantime, FDR put the best possible face on a Japanese apology, speaking in his Christmas message of the need for international goodwill, and Ambassador Grew arrived at Hirota's home suitably wreathed in smiles.[60]

One question remains. There are few speeches in the twentieth century that have provoked as much controversy as Roosevelt's Quarantine Address of 5 October, which, in conjunction with its almost instant repudiation (6 October), laid the groundwork for the ensuing debacle at Brussels. Almost to a man, foreign commentators placed it in the context of domestic politics. They referred to the president's defeat on court-packing, as well as the summer's disquieting economic recession and the embarrassing attention being given to the Ku Klux Klan affiliation of Roosevelt's Supreme Court nominee, Hugo Black. According to British chargé Victor Mallet, FDR was attempting to draw a red herring across a Black trail. To be sure, Mallet's view has a ring of truth though one does not have far to go for an explanation in the realm of foreign policy. How, one must wonder, was Roosevelt to escape the consequences of an ignominious China policy if not by sounding boldly decisive? How else was he to rebut charges of knuckling under to Hitler in his recent decision to fire Ambassador Dodd? Welles had assured the German ambassador on 1 October that Dodd's recall was imminent, and FDR, after urging Americans to leave China and appearing for the moment to defend Ambassador Johnson's feckless flight to the shelter of a U.S. gunboat, seemed to favor disengagement by the navy as well. Admiral Yarnell complained from the China station on 22 September that a withdrawal of the fleet would bring "great discredit" upon his service and that American nationals not in direct danger should not be expected to abandon their livelihood.[61]

There is, of course, the possibility that Roosevelt had some specific plan in mind when he used the word "quarantine." This is a consideration we shall take up presently. The president may also have overestimated the power of words, a theory that will form part of the concluding analysis in Chapter 7. Most likely, however, he was responding on 5 October to a broad combination of stimuli which included an insistent clamor of voices from abroad.

It is well to bear in mind that the White House had come under intense pressure from London, Geneva, and other foreign capitals to do something constructive. Prior to the renewal of Sino-Japanese hostilities, when Whitehall called upon Roosevelt to join in applying leverage on Japan and China to settle their differences peacefully, he had been averse. Later, after fighting broke out, he offered his good offices at least three times, only to be rebuffed.[62] During July, August, and September, London and Paris pressed him repeatedly to participate in a joint offer of good offices or a show of naval strength. Indications are that *he rejected no less than ten British appeals during the period July through November,* and before the end of the year the figure would rise to a dozen or more.[63] As a practical politician he did not relish the prospect of making common cause with Downing Street, and so he replied that he would prefer to act in concert with other peace-loving nations. He would consider a move to obtain League condemnation; if necessary, he would join in economic sanctions. In July, he told Clark Eichelberger of the League of Nations Association that he wanted to propose an economic blockade of aggressors, and when Ambassador Bingham sounded the British on a boycott of Japanese trade, he assured them that the president's hands would not be tied by the Neutrality Act. Foreign Secretary Anthony Eden agreed in principle to economic sanctions but only on condition that Roosevelt pledge military aid in case of war. Significantly, Roosevelt was not prepared as yet to offer such a commitment.[64] Still, London persisted. Stimson, in his book *The Far Eastern Crisis* (1936), had made a compelling case for Anglo-American sanctions, and Interior Secretary Harold Ickes heard the president say in September that aggressor states should be isolated by having their trade links cut.[65] Thus it was that at the very time the State Department was preparing to draft a fresh reply to Whitehall on this very question, FDR sounded the tocsin in Chicago.[66]

By October, Britain's foreign secretary was coming under heavy pressure. Eden's ambassador to China had been shot, and the archbishop of Canterbury was scheduling a mass protest rally for Royal Albert Hall on 5 October.[67] What better salve for popular indignation than official recourse to the League? And was it not a byword among diplomats that the shortest road to Washington lay through Geneva? Had Assistant Secretary of State Hugh Wilson not indicated that the United States would welcome League action? Had Roosevelt not discussed such a course with Josephus Daniels during the previous summer just before Daniels's departure for Europe?[68] And had Wilson not written Norman Davis on 24 September that he wished the League would move toward a nine-power conference? The only question in Wilson's mind was how to bring such a meeting about "without becoming a spearhead in this movement and having responsibility for making proposals. . . . We have avoided initiating through this entire thing."[69]

The nub of the problem for Downing Street was that while Roosevelt might inspire the League to take action along economic lines, he would refuse any military guarantee and thus would take credit for proposing sanctions England could not endorse.[70] It was, in effect, a dead-end street, and so it would remain until the fall of 1940, although no one could know this at the time. Hope sprang eternal in Europe, pressure on Roosevelt continued to mount, and he must have felt an almost irresistible urge to cooperate, not only for the reasons mentioned above but also because he loved to lead and could see plainly that events on the international level were passing him by. He had tried to mastermind a solution to the problem of German revanchist goals, but it was Prime Minister Chamberlain who took the lead. Lord Halifax was due to visit Hitler in November, and the French planned to send a high-level delegation to London.[71] Italian submarine attacks on neutral shipping had been eliminated without U.S. involvement by collective action on the part of the major powers meeting at Noyen.[72] On 1 September, Bernard Baruch was perfectly in earnest when he confided to British officials that Roosevelt wanted a share of the leadership in Europe and that, in return, he was prepared to offer support for British policy in the Far East along with trade concessions and a liberal debt settlement.[73] By now, Roosevelt knew that if he wished to lead, or even give the appearance of leading, he must do so through the League. In sum, Geneva provided a handle for all parties concerned. To Roosevelt, it furnished a means of sharing the limelight; to Europeans, it offered hope that Washington might at last be induced to make a firm military commitment. And so, when the French, Belgians, British, and Chinese all requested a sign that Washington was prepared to offer meaningful cooperation under the terms of the Nine-Power Treaty, the president gave such a sign.[74]

On 5 October, while in Chicago en route home from a political tour of the West, he warned: "The epidemic of world lawlessness is spreading . . . and when an epidemic of physical disease starts to spread, the community approves and joins in a quarantine of the patients in order to protect the health of the community against the spread of the disease." Such words were not only arresting; they were marvelously well timed. Observers at Geneva knew that the League stood on the verge of ordering some form of concrete action against Japan. Two weeks earlier, a delegate from the United States had begun to sit as a silent member of the Advisory Committee. Roosevelt had also accepted a seat on the subcommittee dealing with Pacific affairs. Australia and Britain had introduced resolutions calling for a nine-power conference, and China was hoping to win support for a resolution aimed at containing aggression through collective economic measures. Roosevelt's words, cabled to Geneva six hours ahead of delivery, struck home at precisely the right moment. China's resolution won the day, and on 6 October the League Council invited the signatories of the Nine-Power Treaty to convene a special conference (Brussels).[75]

Clever timing had long been a hallmark of the Roosevelt style. On 16 May 1933, he had appealed to the leaders of the world just before Hitler was scheduled to address the Reichstag. Germany had thus appeared to act in response to an American initiative. Two years later, with the Ethiopian crisis at white heat, he proclaimed his "moral embargo" on the very eve of League action. In 1937, he again succeeded in grasping the mantle of leadership, nimbly avoiding isolationist charges of being a tail to the League kite. In both 1935 and 1937, his aim was the same:

to avoid risk by remaining in the company of four, five, or six prominent governments.[76]

Unfortunately, it must also be recorded that on 5 October 1937, as on
4 October 1935, FDR encouraged the League to embark upon a program
which, in view of the underlying American position, had no real
chance of success.[77] This was dramatically underscored when Roosevelt, speaking before klieg lights to an eager group of reporters on the
following day, 6 October, refused to allow that the word "quarantine"
implied a policy of coercion. His speech, he insisted, might even add up
to "an expansion of neutrality." To Ernest Lindley, who questioned him
rather sharply on the point, he replied insouciantly, "Put on your
thinking cap, Ernest." Ever since, a host of historians has put on the
thinking cap, and taken it off again, without forming any reasonable
consensus. Some have argued that FDR did not really back down since
he had never settled upon a definite course of action. Few, however,
would deny that he gave the impression of retreat.[78] In any case, one
thing is certain. Real or imagined, his volte-face demoralized interventionist forces everywhere. Almost immediately, the American press
swung from a posture of neutrality to one of doubt, and by 10 October,
Hearst felt the time had come to launch an antiquarantine campaign.
American opinion began to lean seven to three in favor of nonintervention, and France and Britain were bound to be mightily disappointed by
what they took to be a false start.[79] An open coffin lay waiting for the
Brussels Conference.

Given the history of Roosevelt's refusal to buttress sanctionist measures with military muscle, British statesmen could not be expected
to take the Chicago speech seriously once doubt began to arise as to
Roosevelt's intent. Eden dismissed it with a few perfunctory words
to his constituents and when asked about it in Parliament replied
offhandedly that he had already dealt with the matter. Roosevelt wrote
his friend Murray that he had hoped for "a little more unselfish spine
in your foreign office!" But in British eyes, the spine that needed stiffening was the president's own. When Chargé Mallet asked Welles on 12
October to tell him what was contemplated under the rubric of "quarantine," Welles replied that Roosevelt had nothing particular in mind.
Two days later, Mallet returned to the chargé only to be informed by
the under secretary that if His Majesty's government did not know
what the word "quarantine" meant, it certainly should: the president
was not likely to be "unaware of what he intended to state in an ad-

dress of that high importance." Mallet promptly changed his tune at this point, assuring Welles that "of course, the British Government had no misconception." On 19 October, when Eden tried to elicit a more precise meaning from the American embassy in London, Bingham simply told him that any attempt "to pin the United States down to a specific statement as to how far it would go and precisely what the President meant . . . was objectionable and damaging." Several weeks later, a fourth British probe directed at Welles produced the observation that "contingencies" such as the need for military force "were remote and should not be considered at this time."[80]

There can be little doubt that FDR was considering a wide range of options. But just how serious he was about implementation or how expert at following an idea to its logical conclusion is another matter. To Cardinal Mundelein, he had broached the possibility of diplomatic ostracism, which would involve severance of ordinary communications with Japan. Only the possibility. He was also partial to the idea of a world conference for the promotion of disarmament, free trade, and reform of the Versailles settlement. Only three days after the Quarantine Address, work began on the Welles Plan; likewise, with varying degrees of enthusiasm, the president considered a league of armed neutrals, collective neutrality as outlined by the American delegation at Buenos Aires, and the possibility of prevailing upon nations to close their ports to Japan and refuse financial assistance. Last but not least, he gave some thought to a naval blockade as suggested to Lindsay during the *Panay* and *Ladybird* crises. Twenty-five years earlier, serving as assistant secretary of the navy and faced with a similar war scare in the Pacific, Roosevelt's instinct had pointed in the same direction. The glamour inherent in this notion of blockade seems never to have faded. During the summer of 1937, he pored over nautical maps and ordered a report on the history of blockades, all with the approval of his chief of naval operations, Admiral William Leahy. Three years later, Secretary of the Navy Frank Knox would tell Fleet Commander Admiral James O. Richardson that the president wanted to blockade Japan in case of an attack on the Burma Road. Just as Richardson reported the fleet ill prepared in 1940 for such an operation, most American and British strategists gave the plan short shrift in 1937. Hull and Welles discouraged it, while Bullitt wrote FDR in disgust: "I never believed you were about to mount a white charger." None of this ever became clear to Chamberlain, but it helps to explain Roosevelt's retraction on 6 October.[81]

As regards public response to the speech, historians have been of two minds. Roosevelt himself wrote that reaction seemed as good as could be expected. Hull, on the other hand, referred to it as politically disabling. In reality, both appraisals were probably correct, allowing for Roosevelt's unique style of operation. Editorial comment and White House mail sided substantially with the president. Church groups and organized labor stood solidly behind him, too. However, a small segment of the press, including the *Chicago Tribune* and the *Wall Street Journal*, voiced disapproval. Hugh Johnson, a former White House aide and Scripps-Howard columnist, took up the cudgels, as did six major peace societies. Leading members of Congress, including the powerful senators Gerald Nye of North Dakota, Arthur Vandenberg of Michigan, William Borah of Idaho, and Hiram Johnson of California, growled audibly; there was even talk of impeachment.[82] In short, the response was mixed, and to a consensus politician, one who rarely flew in the face of vocal minority opinion, this alone would have been sufficient to give pause.

Roosevelt's turnabout can also be viewed as part of a familiar syndrome. Whenever he moved against tolerable opposition, he did so by degrees. Each advance into enemy terrain was followed by a calculated retreat. In 1933, for instance, he requested discretionary power to impose trade sanctions, but when faced with vociferous dissent from a handful of senators, he canceled the drive only to resume it at a later date. The same holds true for his campaign to persuade the Military Affairs Committee that America's frontier was on the Rhine. One is also reminded of his "unlimited national emergency" speech of 27 May 1941, which he took back at a press conference the next day despite telegrams running 95 percent in its favor. Implying the need for convoys, he insisted that American supplies must reach Britain: "It can be done; it must be done; it will be done." Nonetheless, within hours, under heated interrogation, he announced that there would be no convoying and no request for revision of the neutrality law after all. Neither Harry Hopkins, his intimate adviser, nor anyone else could fathom it. Other examples can be found, but suffice it to say there was a chameleon quality about Roosevelt, which, if it be accounted one of his more potent weapons, was also an abiding weakness.[83]

All things considered, the fact that FDR delivered the Quarantine Address when he did and with all its attendant circumstances should come as no surprise. There were a great many reasons for his doing so and only one powerful factor militating against. Had he known the damage that could come as a result of championing an impractical scheme and throwing American weight behind a plan he was not prepared to execute, he might have acted differently and avoided the unseemly spectacle of an international conference with nowhere to go.

Those who suspected that the president would regard the Brussels Conference as a mere sounding board to agitate world opinion had their worst fears confirmed. Chief American delegate Norman Davis not only prevailed upon a reluctant Eden to join in proposing peace plans which he knew would most likely be rejected by Tokyo; he insisted on sending Japan a second public invitation to attend the conference, again with the outcome a foregone conclusion. French Foreign Minister Yvon Delbos suggested that one invitation and one refusal were enough, but Davis was not to be denied; a second invitation went out only to be spurned as rapidly as the first. Instructed to seize upon any opportunity to discredit Japan in the eyes of the world, he told reporters that in dealing with a bully, one had to be firm; the United States was "prepared to uphold law and order with its entire fleet." As may be imagined, this created something of a sensation, but when approached by the French and British for reassurance that his country was indeed prepared to fight should sanctions lead to war, Davis declined. Such waffling prompted Sir Robert Clive to deplore the diplomacy of homiletics and Saburo Kurusu, Japanese ambassador to Belgium, to assert that such tactics would simply open the door to German inroads. Still, as the conference drew to a close, Davis continued to score verbal points. From the few delegates who remained, he wrung a strongly worded declaration of adjournment, and had he had his way, the conference would have sent Tokyo an embarrassing list of questions.[84]

What is surprising is that the Brussels conclave lasted as long as it did. On opening day, eight out of ten delegations, already in a mood of sullen gloom, wished to go home. Eden longed to return to London, while Delbos, along with Belgium's Paul Henri Spaak, favored immediate adjournment. Delbos, Roosevelt's most outspoken critic, may have had an inkling of Washington's sub-rosa feelers to Japan. In any case, he wanted no keynote speeches and accepted the American preference grudgingly. Davis's hollow rhetoric met with exposure at the hands of the same French editors who had panned Roosevelt during the London Economic Conference of 1933. Press correspondents, for lack of anything better to do, reportedly bribed a streetwalker to accost Eden as he emerged from one of the meetings.[85]

Caprice seemed by far the most consistent feature of American leadership. Before sailing for Europe, Davis had gone to Hyde Park and he thought he knew what was expected. Nevertheless, Secretary Hull disallowed his opening speech at the last moment, forcing him to postpone and revise it. After encouraging delegates to expect an imminent move by Roosevelt to achieve revision of the Neutrality Act, something which never came to pass, Davis wound up proposing a whole series of measures which the White House repudiated. They included nonrecognition, a ban on loans to Japan, a boycott of Japanese exports, revision of the Neutrality Act, the arming of China, and concerted American, British, and French fleet action in the Pacific. Just as Davis was beginning to take the wraps off Roosevelt's program, the Hearst papers erupted, and Hull cabled that "none of the measures envisaged should be proposed by the United States." On direct appeal to Washington, Davis found that the president had indeed undergone a change. Stunned, he could only tell Hull: "I bow before your judgment." Eden then wanted to know, since there would be no backing from the White House, what use there could possibly be in asking the conference to use the sort of language FDR had in mind. Davis could give no answer. "For a whole minute," Eden recalled, "his brain ceased to function."[86]

Compounding the performance of Roosevelt's chief envoy was an embarrassing interchange between the president and Jules Henry, France's chargé d'affaires in Washington. Roosevelt had the temerity to suggest that Frenchmen were behaving like "scared rabbits" in yielding to Japanese demands for a shutdown of Chiang's supply route through Indochina. When Henry asked him how Paris could be expected to resist Tokyo without a concrete offer of American support, the president replied, rather grandly, that French fears of Japan were exaggerated. Moral considerations should come first, and "was it not understood in France that a Japanese attack on Hong Kong, Indochina or the Netherlands Indies would be regarded in the same way as an attack on the Philippines?" Referring specifically to an attack on French Indochina, Roosevelt assured Henry that "our common interests" would then be "threatened" and "we would have to defend them together" ("dans cette éventualité, nos intérêts communs seraient menacés et nous aurions à les défendre ensemble").[87]

Davis, queried on what the president had meant to say, replied that it was too early to tell just how the United States might react. When the French produced Henry's report of the conversation, Davis explained that in a democracy it was impossible to make advance commitments. Bullitt was then asked to clarify who spoke for the United States, Davis or the White House, and when he requested instruction from the State Department, Under Secretary Welles cabled that Roosevelt had merely told Henry that acts of aggression would have worldwide repercussions which would obviously affect the United States but that war was such a remote contingency he did not think it should be discussed. In no case had the president given any impression "directly or indirectly as to the possible extension of . . . the American fleet." To add to the confusion, Welles gave Henry a pledge almost as strongly worded as the one Henry had reported receiving from Roosevelt: "If the possessions of the powers in the Far East were the object of a Japanese attack, there would result a world situation to which the United States would not be able to remain indifferent."[88]

France was not reassured. She could not afford the luxury of relying upon words in place of action. And so China lost two lifelines, one through Indochina, another through the Portuguese port of Macao. An angry Premier Chautemps felt the need to unburden himself to Bullitt:

> Look here . . . what I cannot understand is that you Americans from time to time talk as if you really intended to act in the international sphere when you have no intention of acting in any way that can be effective . . . I should infinitely rather have him [FDR] say nothing than make speeches, like his speech in Chicago, which aroused immense hopes when there is no possibility that in the state of American opinion and the state of mind of the Senate he can follow up such speeches by action. Such a policy on the part of the United States merely leads the dictatorships to believe that the democracies are full of words but are unwilling to back their words by force, and force is the only thing that counts today in the world.

Henry showed more understanding. He had known Roosevelt since World War I and, as he informed Delbos, "It happens sometimes that the President, whose impulsive temperament you recognize, expresses himself in terms which exceed his thought . . . he gives the impression occasionally of wanting to transform into action certain intentions that he holds one moment but which he is forced to abandon thereafter . . . I recall several examples: the economic conference; the debts; the project for a meeting of heads of state, etc."[89]

Regardless of explanation, the Brussels meeting ended the way it began, as an exercise in futility. A candid Kurusu told American reporters that the Roosevelt administration could not stand behind Davis without congressional support, and since this was something he did not have, Davis would be instructed to "close down with some more resounding phrases." China's delegate, Wellington Koo, did not hesitate to say that his people felt betrayed; the United States, unlike Britain, had not acted the part of a true friend. As for Delbos, who had never reconciled himself to the idea of a world conference without American military commitment, he refused to join in drafting the concluding statement. Finally, Italy's chief delegate echoed Mussolini's impression of the London Economic Conference four years earlier, insisting that Brussels had been "entirely superfluous from the beginning." The delegates drifted away, one by one, until Davis was left virtually alone on the last day, trying as best he could to put a positive face on what had taken place. It made a poignant picture, this lonely figure from Tennessee, who had served his country as assistant secretary and under secretary of state, who had never been highly regarded by Europeans (Chamberlain called him "detestable"), now about to return home to direct the Red Cross. Davis was not the only one, however, to suffer from the pall cast by Brussels. Anthony Eden, Robert Vansittart (Britain's permanent under-secretary), and Yvon Delbos all found themselves out of office within a few months.[90]

Another effect of the Brussels Conference may be measured in terms of shifting national allegiance. The Japanese quickly began to show signs of resenting France's presence in Hainan and the Paracel Islands. Thus Tokyo now called upon Berlin to monitor her talks with China. Even before the conference ended, Italy, having acted as custodian for Japanese interests, joined the Anti-Comintern Pact, which put an end to German isolation and set in motion a movement foreshadowing the Tripartite Pact of 1940. Furthermore, coinciding with this growth of German prestige, one could detect a corresponding decline in respect for the United States. During the scramble to apportion blame for what had happened in Belgium, most leaders pointed an accusatory finger at Washington.[91] Having indicted France for cowardice in Indochina, Roosevelt could only appear inconsistent when he resisted Anglo-French pleas for military backing.[92] He suffered further loss of face owing to the fact that Eden had told the House of Commons that American leaders were responsible for choosing Brussels as a site. Technically, this was true; Britain preferred the Hague.[93] But the London and Tokyo press latched onto it as proof of American responsibility for conference results. By the time Eden explained himself, few cared to listen. American delegates spent a good deal of their time disowning responsibility, both for the conference and for its impending failure.[94]

What, then, is to be said regarding the larger picture? Before carrying our discussion of American-Japanese relations into the watershed period 1938–40, there are certain fixtures of the diplomatic scene worth noting. One theme which spans a full range of events from 1933 to 1941 is that of diplomatic dualism, the discrepancy between what Roosevelt said and what he thought, between what he promised to do and what in fact he did. It was not unusual for him to pursue contrary lines of policy simultaneously and to alternate between several lines of strategy. Although there were two schools of thought on Far Eastern policy, both within the State Department and within his immediate circle, FDR's personal leaning was toward China, and this served to nullify any positive move made by American officials in the direction of Japan. At the same time, he was neither prepared nor anxious to become actively committed to either side, at least initially. When pressure from Europe mounted for concerted action against Tokyo, he refused to go beyond rhetoric, and his harsh-sounding words meant little when accompanied by subtle, behind-the-scenes gestures of friendship. Beyond this, there was the public image he chose to cultivate, which, by contrast with his equivocal diplomatic posture, never varied. To the people at home, he was always an uncompromising foe of autocracy and aggression.

In the next chapter, we shall have occasion to observe how presidential rhetoric assumed a force of its own. It would not be long before Congress would press for forthright action, perhaps as Roosevelt had always known it would. Capitol Hill would vote economic sanctions that proved to be too stringent for British or French approval in the absence of a definite American military commitment. And so it was that FDR found himself out of step. By late 1940, it was the United States which was taking the lead against Japan, though never without a strong and debilitating undercurrent of domestic dissent.

3. Saito's Ashes

SUCH traits as ambivalence and prevarication, which by 1938 had become a regular feature of presidential policy, invited the Japanese to pursue a counterpolicy of divide and conquer. This carried with it the long-term risk of war. But Otohiko Matsukata, stressing his country's love for America, along with its alleged antipathy to Britain, sounded the State Department a second time on Dooman's tender of good offices. Welles, Grew, and Wilson all took refuge in bland generalization regarding the terms of the Nine-Power Treaty, but Colonel House was quoted by *Nichi Nichi* as saying that Far Eastern problems should be settled without outside interference.[1] Three American cruisers sailed for Singapore even as American garrisons withdrew from North China. Tokyo thus remained in a state of limbo, unable to divine what meaning, if any, could be found within such a welter of contradiction. In December, after Premier Konoye had proclaimed a Greater East Asia Co-Prosperity Sphere and called for a "new order" of economic cooperation and joint defense against communism, Roosevelt opted for a $25 million loan to China. Two months later, however, in a novel display of friendly feeling for Japan, Mrs. Roosevelt made an unprecedented personal call on Mrs. Saito. Even Roosevelt's final decision to grant a generous loan to China appears to have been something of a compromise. Morgenthau gave it strong support and Hornbeck welcomed it as the first move in a "diplomatic war plan" to include denunciation of treaties, repeal of the Neutrality Code, retaliatory tariffs, embargoes, and fleet movements. In the opposite camp, as usual, stood Secretary Hull, representing a powerful group within the State Department that was adamantly opposed to the loan. What happened is that while Hull was away on a visit to Lima, Peru, Acting Secretary Welles offered Morgenthau his backing in return for Treasury Department acquiescence in a plan for Cuban economic recovery, and predictably the president "split the difference" by adopting the loan without reference to Hornbeck's "war plan."[2]

This may have seemed a small step at the time. Yet Roosevelt's decision to support Morgenthau, however incrementally, marked a signal development. In effect, the White House was now taking steps aimed at controlling external events not by the traditional balancing of power against power but by a gradual tightening of America's purse strings. Economic sanctions, sans military commitment, had long been a staple of New Deal thought (more of this in the concluding chapter), and this time the president would not allow the coolness of Downing Street to dissuade him. After Chancellor of the Exchequer Sir John Simon rejected Morgenthau's proposal in December 1937 for an Anglo-American freeze on Japanese assets, the treasury chief was authorized to set up a department of economic warfare, and it is from this crucial intersection that the entire future of American Far East policy may be plotted.[3]

Public opinion, congressional sentiment, and best-selling books were all in agreement—so much so that if one were not certain of the president's mind, it might seem that he acted less out of conviction than out of a desire to keep pace with the times. Freda Utley had argued in her best-selling *Japan's Feet of Clay* (1937) that sanctions would not lead to war, and while AFL and CIO conventions voted to boycott Japanese imports, six hundred delegates of the American Student Union at Vassar participated in a mass burning of silk stockings. It was a movement popularized by such journalists as Edgar Mowrer and John Gunther, who held that Japan was "running amuck." As a result, Roosevelt was prepared by the summer of 1938 to make his fateful call for a "moral embargo" on aircraft sales and the extension of credit to Japan. With the passage of time, American companies would refuse to fill Japanese orders, Du Pont would decide not to supply munitions to either side, and a cry would arise in Congress for additional measures to divorce the American economy from Japan's war. With opinion polls showing 75 percent favoring an arms embargo and 66 percent a boycott of Japanese goods, a majority of the Foreign Relations Committee led by Senator Pittman would set out to persuade the administration to abrogate its commercial treaty with Japan and clamp an embargo on all trade.[4]

Journalist Walter Lippmann, speaking from hindsight, lamented that "the administration, which knew better, acquiesced in this utterly un-statesmanlike policy of challenging Japan in Asia while we were forbidden to support the allies in Europe." Whether the White House really knew better is a moot point. There can be no question, however, that Roosevelt set his face like flint against any meaningful form of compromise. If, by Breckinridge Long's estimate, Hornbeck was conducting his own private war against Japan, the same could be said of the administration generally. The idea that Nature should be left to take its course underwent slow metamorphosis in the years 1938–40. White House counselor R. Walton Moore and John Carter Vincent at State, not to mention Hull, Welles, and others, were all agreed that Nature needed a prod; the nation must act. Such dissenters as Moffat, Wilson, and Bullitt no longer had Roosevelt's ear, and Grew, though still inclined to a policy of noninterference, thought better when his son-in-law Moffat warned that such views were out of joint. Sanctions now had the support of Congress and people alike, and Roosevelt contributed all he could to a tide that would soon carry him to the point of hard steel. In two years, Gallup polls would show 80 percent in favor of an embargo. Assistant Secretary of State Adolf A. Berle would soon be noting in his diary that "the plan is to go on gently turning the economic screws. . . . Our policy is to keep up a continuing pressure until they stop their foolishness in China." Hornbeck admitted that Japan, "under the urge of certain shallow-minded" military people, might shake hands with Germany and Italy. So be it, for if Japan ever gained the upper hand in China she would be free to carry out aggression in other areas, which might prove fatal to the British and Russian position vis-à-vis Hitler.[5] As war clouds gathered over Europe in 1939, Roosevelt's refusal to meet Tokyo halfway troubled London and Paris exceedingly, for on each occasion when he seemed to be about to reconsider, there would come an unaccountable stiffening.

Perhaps the most dramatic instance of the two stools policy relates to the death of Hiroshi Saito, Japan's ambassador to the United States. As the youngest head of mission in Japanese history, age alone would have endeared him to an administration proud of its youthful vigor. With the sprightly air of a college freshman, he promised complete candor and refused to attend the exclusive preview of a film he himself had produced on grounds that it would be accepting special privilege. After twenty-eight years in America, he reputedly knew the difference between a Texas leaguer and an infield hit. People marveled at his impeccable command of slang. Reports circulated of his yen for scotch whiskey. He even played poker with presidential secretary Marvin McIntyre. Although his proposal for a nonaggression pact won few converts, he inaugurated a period of greatly lessened tension. Indeed, such was his charm that when he died in February of 1939, after an ambassadorial term of five years, the House of Representatives voted unanimously to enter an obituary in the *Congressional Record.*[6]

This was the setting in which FDR, on 1 March, decided to carry out a State Department recommendation that Saito's ashes be returned to Japan in a large funeral urn aboard an American battle cruiser. The Gaimusho had shown similar consideration on the death of American ambassador Edgar Bancroft; but Bancroft, unlike Saito, had died in harness. FDR made his decision on the heels of Japanese occupation of Hainan Island and went ahead despite Tokyo's bold announcement on 31 March that it intended to occupy the Spratly Islands. Besides being claimed by France, the Spratlys were well within striking range of the Philippines, Borneo, Vietnam, and Singapore. Grew was not exaggerating, therefore, when he called Roosevelt's gesture an act of "unprecedented courtesy, honor, respect, and friendship."[7]

With one voice, Tokyo hailed it as a graceful act, a sign of America's desire to restore good relations. It was discussed in the House of Peers. Every metropolitan paper but one gave it an editorial. On 19 March, in a transpacific broadcast, Vice-Minister for Foreign Affairs Setsuzō Sawada thanked Americans for a rare mark of kindness to Saito's widowed mother, consoling her for the loss of her last remaining child: "Surely this is a reflection of the tender regard in which your President holds his own mother." A few days later, the United Press predicted that the crew of the battle cruiser *Astoria*, led by Captain Turner, would be given the greatest reception ever accorded a visiting naval delegation. Scores of entertainments were planned. Gifts for officers and men accumulated at the embassy. One Osaka merchant presented Grew with twenty pearl necklaces for senior officers' wives.[8]

Suddenly, in the midst of this happy scene, came a veritable bolt from the blue. Washington ordered Grew not to accept any unusual entertainments or gifts. Naturally, the ambassador was mortified. Without being consulted, he was bidden to ask a highly intelligent and sensitive people to curb its generosity. He could only remind Hull that the *Astoria* was expected to remain nine days in Japan and it was too late to cancel any of the major events scheduled, which included radio broadcasts and dinners to be given in the captain's honor by the embassy, the Japanese Foreign Office, and the Navy Ministry. After a prolonged silence, Hull relented. Turner might accept framed silk embroidered pictures of marine subjects for his wardroom and warrant officers' messes because these items had already been accepted on his behalf by Grew. But the embassy was to insist absolutely on return of the twenty pearl necklaces, along with other gifts. Grew tried to save the situation by indicating that Turner should be allowed to decide whether to accept or reject individual gifts, but this time Hull remained obdurate. All gifts must be returned at once. Accordingly, a notice appeared in the *Japanese Advertiser* saying that the United States would return all the commemorative dolls and swords that had been arriving at the embassy since 1 April. In addition, a monster public meeting to have been held at Meiji Stadium was diverted by request of the ambassador to more sober surroundings at a university theater.[9]

What is remarkable is that, despite all restrictions handed down from on high, nothing could dampen the festive spirit. A play about Saito's ambassadorship opened in Tokyo, with portions of the script rendered in English, and Grew fought gamely to stave off further interference. When reminded by Hull that the *Astoria* should not stay in port longer than three days, he remonstrated that the earliest date he could tactfully suggest for its departure was 23 April, a full week after arrival and the day of the Yasukuni Shrine festival. Informed by the Gaimusho that even this minor curtailment of schedule would likely give offense, he promptly agreed to a full ten days of activities as originally planned, and Hull said nothing.[10]

At this juncture, like the proverbial writing on the wall, came Roosevelt's second sign of contradiction. A day or two before the arrival of Saito's remains, and under considerable Anglo-French pressure to protest Tokyo's latest claim, he announced that the American fleet would return to the Pacific and engage in maneuvers at Hawaii! Hull likewise instructed Ambassador Grew to do all he could to discourage the Japanese from sending a warship to San Francisco and New York as an expression of thanks.[11] Captain Turner remained until 26 April, during which time his officers were lavishly feted and showered with attention, including an audience with the emperor. But one day after the *Astoria* weighed anchor, Senator Pittman, whose utterances were generally taken to reflect the view of the White House, made the comedy complete by introducing a resolution allowing the president to cut all trade with Japan. Saito must have turned in his urn.

The British were not particularly gratified, either. That Roosevelt should go ahead with the *Astoria* visit despite Japan's earlier seizure of Hainan and her recent declaration of intent to occupy other key islands was an object lesson not easily forgotten. Much as Prime Minister Chamberlain desired American support on the European Continent and wished to facilitate repeal of the Neutrality Act, he could not consider drastic sanctions without American naval commitment, and so his only hope of breaking the impasse with Tokyo, as it seemed, was to extend recognition both to Manchukuo and to the newly organized pro-Japanese, anti-Chiang government of Chinese President Wang Ching-wei.[12] On 8 July, Roosevelt appeared open to such an arrangement when he asked Premier Kiichirō Hiranuma to exert himself on behalf of peace in Europe. Sir Robert Craigie, the British ambassador to Japan, issued a "formula" two weeks later in concert with Foreign Minister Arita by which Britain agreed to recognize Japanese hegemony in the areas of China controlled by her military. But it was not to be. Any chance of compromise in the Far East was dashed on 26 July, when Roosevelt denounced the Japanese-American Treaty of Commerce, assuring its termination in six months. Even after European guns began to flash, he insisted with great adamance that British troops remain on station in China. Small numbers stayed on in Peking and Tientsin, with a larger body at Shanghai, as the British continued to feel the need, in Halifax's words, of "keeping in step" with the United States. At the same time, FDR ignored all requests from Whitehall and the Quai d'Orsay for guarantees of contingency aid in the Far East. Hitler posed an obvious threat, but the most Roosevelt would do was to send more ships and planes to the Pacific and hold naval maneuvers near Honolulu.[13]

Grew, meanwhile, began the year with considerable hope for rapprochement. On his desk lay Whitney Griswold's *Far Eastern Policy* and MacMurray's memorandum of over one hundred pages. Both works made a powerful case for Japan, with the latter carrying special weight because its author had served as secretary of legation in Peking (1913–17), counselor of embassy in Tokyo (1917–19), chief of the Division of Far Eastern Affairs (1919–24), and minister to China (1925–29). MacMurray's record included additional experience as chief of the Division of Near Eastern Affairs, assistant secretary of state, director of the Johns Hopkins School of International Relations, and, since 1933, minister to the Baltic states. Although he sympathized with China's dream of self-determination, he reasoned that the only immediate alternative to a Japanese presence on the mainland was the presence of Russia. What impressed him most was, first of all, Moscow's capacity to absorb Korea; second, Japan's vital ties with China and Manchukuo; and third, China's willful violation of treaties. Americans, he felt, had not been prudent in brushing aside Japan's complaints of treaty violation in 1928, and the Japanese felt "quite naturally and strongly" that "justice was on their side." Unlike most observers, MacMurray realized that Western assumptions were not readily transferable. If East and West could differ on the proper relationship between man and woman, a phrase like "equality of commercial opportunity" might also be susceptible to more than one interpretation.[14]

Armed with the views of Griswold and MacMurray, Grew paid a visit to Washington during the summer of 1939. In two fruitless sessions with Roosevelt he tried to show that economic sanctions would not work and might lead to war. The president would not listen; if anything, his attitude seemed to harden as he spoke of sending more forces to the Pacific and intercepting the Japanese when they moved south. Talk then turned to the holding of military maneuvers in Hawaiian waters, and before Grew could return to Tokyo, Roosevelt denounced the Japanese-American Treaty of Commerce. That Grew's presence in Washington should coincide with such a dread blow did not escape the *Japan Times:* "The unkindest cut of all came from the hand of an American whom we always believed to be our best friend."[15]

Instead of resigning out of an understandable sense of betrayal, Grew traveled to Chicago and other cities and delivered a set speech bearing the unmistakable mark of the White House. He did not ignore the Japanese side of the question altogether, but his positive statements, including a complimentary reference to MacMurray, were tucked away in the middle of his text while he rang all the conventional changes on Tokyo's alleged lust for expansion. Like the good soldier that he was, he began with reference to the "rape of Nanking" and the "massacre of undefending populations." The Japanese military caste, he suggested, had "outdone the Huns in barbarity" and put a blot on the imperial escutcheon that could never be erased. The *Panay* incident had been intentional, and American indignation at Nipponese leaders was "fully justified." In closing, he admitted that not all Japanese, not even all of the army, supported a policy of aggression. Japanese gentlemen were as fine as any in the world. Yet the implication was clear. While residing in Tokyo, he recalled, he had to be accompanied everywhere by detectives. Clearly, Japanese gentlemen were not in the saddle.[16]

On returning to his post, he commenced talks with the new liberal government of Premier Nobuyuki Abe and Foreign Minister Kichisaburo Nomura. Personally, he still preferred a modus vivendi featuring renewal of the commercial treaty in return for the redress of specific grievances. He also continued to warn the White House that economic sanctions would not succeed. Publicly, however, he hewed to the condemnatory line laid down by FDR. With Japanese closure of the Yangtze River a special cause of irritation and hundreds of unsettled cases involving American life and property still pending, he delivered a hard-hitting formal address. He was determined, as he put it, to let Tokyo hear it "straight from the horse's mouth," and the American press was quick to award him plaudits for "bare-knuckle" diplomacy. On 4 November, engaging Foreign Minister Nomura in the first of a series of four talks, be again sought publicity and, once more, the press granted him generous coverage, making it look to all the world as if he had threatened Tokyo with refusal to renew the commercial treaty. One can only marvel that Premier Abe managed to survive such treatment as long as he did. In Tokyo's inner council, commanding voices were urging a political berth with Hitler. Army chief Seishirō Itagaki, who had recommended such a course the previous spring only to meet with determined resistance from navy chief Mitsumasa Yonai, was again voted down and Abe managed to ward off political challengers for many weeks by insisting that he would succeed in restoring the commercial treaty.[17]

In his initial conference with Nomura, Grew asked for an end to the bombing of American enclaves, settlement of a list of outstanding claims, and the opening of the Yangtze River to Western commerce. Subsequently, he noted a cessation of bombings and indignities, with investigations begun, solatiums paid, properties evacuated, and many, if not most, of the American claims settled. However, when it became obvious at the second meeting (not held until 4 December) that Grew lacked authorization to negotiate a new trade treaty, the harassment of Americans resumed. Grew chafed at instructions which confined him to vacuous statements to the effect that Japanese concessions had not gone far enough. He felt totally helpless as there was nothing further to do. When he made an urgent request for greater flexibility, it was denied, and Nomura was never able to ascertain what Roosevelt would require in return for renewal of the treaty. On 18 December, the foreign minister indicated that his government was prepared to reopen the Yangtze and forego all the military advantages attached to closure. This, certainly, was a major concession, and while it might not be wholly satisfactory, Matsukata vouched for the support of the army and indicated that if it were accepted in a constructive spirit, Japan would "double its efforts to effect a lasting rapprochement." No matter. On 22 December, Grew informed Nomura that there would be no renewal of the treaty, only trade on an ad hoc basis. Bitterly disappointed, Abe and Nomura could no longer bear the strain and resigned.[18]

By this time, Tokyo had recognized Wang Ching-wei's mainland regime. Grew agreed with the British and French that Wang stood a good chance of survival, especially with continued Japanese backing, for he was neither a quisling nor a puppet. This was also the view of a number of senators, including Vandenberg. Nonetheless, Roosevelt denounced Wang as a stooge, even as he encouraged the new Yonai-Arita ministry to send unofficial envoys to Washington, a Mr. X and Mr. Y. As if to draw the curtain further over the face of reality, he sent Francis B. Sayre to Tokyo for confidential talks. Having completed six years as assistant secretary of state, Sayre was holding down the post of high commissioner to the Philippines in a sort of diplomatic exile that may have reflected his tendency to see Japanese policy through Japanese eyes. After maintaining contact with MacMurray, House, and a brilliant Wall Street lawyer by the name of John Foster Dulles, he suddenly appears on center stage as spokesman for the president.[19]

The dialogue between Sayre and Foreign Minister Arita was no chance encounter, whatever it may have seemed in its barren aftermath. Sayre had corresponded with the president and obtained specific instructions. He was also in close touch with Roosevelt's ambassador to China, Nelson T. Johnson, having forwarded one of the latter's recent letters to the White House. "I hope," Roosevelt wrote, "you will be able to take a little holiday in Japan and talk things over with Grew . . . and if he [Ambassador Johnson] is able to get say to Saigon, you might run over there and see him." He was to allow "several months" between prospective trips to Japan and China and arrange to be in Washington during July.[20]

Once in Tokyo, Sayre met the emperor and conferred with Arita on 1, 2, 3, and 6 May. Grew attended the first of these sessions, the one confined to ceremonial and Philippine matters. Subsequently, Sayre initiated discussion of a Pacific nonaggression pact and proposed that Japan join China in requesting American mediation. When Arita suggested that Roosevelt might propose direct talks between the two sides, Sayre countered with the idea that Chinese and Japanese representatives could meet at Manila or perhaps Hong Kong, implying American or British good offices. Arita, however, had no sooner agreed to send a military officer to Hong Kong for face-to-face talks with the Chinese, assuming that Sayre would pledge his "good offices," than Undersecretary Welles cabled that the talks were compromising America's position vis-à-vis China. Sayre then reverted to the standard American defense of Chinese policy. Arita declared testily that under these circumstances it would perhaps be better for him to "withdraw the more or less formal reply which he had made and to forget the whole matter." Sayre did not disagree, and the talks ended.[21]

Amid a flurry of press speculation, Roosevelt tried to cover his trail by labeling the Sayre initiative "unauthorized." Sayre echoed the administration line, saying that his proposals had been "personal" rather than official. It is nevertheless abundantly clear that, as in similar situations involving William Bullitt (1933) and Breckinridge Long (1935), the men in the field had Roosevelt's support in all but name. Furthermore, whether intended or not, FDR had aroused another set of false hopes, something which Hull deplored. Sayre's own disappointment is implicit in the advice he tendered Roosevelt on 16 May: Japan, he wrote, was weary of fighting and if given "compensations in North China"—in other words, if permitted to "retire gracefully"—she would not be averse to doing so. "The way lies open now . . . to extend American good offices or mediation." Roosevelt, as one might expect, had no intention of offering compensation, and Sayre did not return home as planned. Grew, meanwhile, could think of nothing better than to adopt Hornbeck's original assumption of time being on the side of the United States "if we allow Nature to take its course." In this, he proved woefully mistaken. Hitler's string of victories in the spring and summer engendered in even the most conservative Japanese what Foreign Minister Shigenori Tōgō has described as a fear of "missing the bus."[22]

During the summer of 1940, Ambassador Grew struck up another series of talks, this time with Arita, in the hope of reviving Sayre's proposal for a Pacific nonaggression pact. Although the American position was dictated, as heretofore, by an administration which refused to put anything in definite terms, Grew's initiative, which began on 10 June, gained unexpected impetus on 6 July when Roosevelt endorsed the concept of three Monroe Doctrines, one for the Western Hemisphere, one for Europe, and another for Asia. Speaking at Hyde Park through press secretary Steve Early, he outlined his vision of a system whereby the nations of each area would decide collectively on the form of leadership desired. As quoted by the *New York Times*, the idea was to "let all of them settle their disputes in Asia and Europe. . . . There is an absence of intention on the part of this government . . . to interfere in any territorial problems in Europe or Asia. . . . In the case of French Indo-China we think the disposition should be decided among the Asiatic countries." There could be only one inference: Germany should organize the European bloc, Japan the Asian.

This pronouncement drew instant fire from the liberal press, as well as from China proper, and again, as expected, Roosevelt spun quickly around. By 11 July, Grew and Arita were no longer talking, and in another two weeks Roosevelt would clamp a partial trade embargo on Tokyo, one which affected such items as aviation motor fuel, lubricants, and high-grade melting scrap. In Japan, the newly installed government of Prince Konoye and his foreign minister, Yosuke Matsuoka, would soon be extending serious feelers to Rome and Berlin.[23]

By this time, France and the Netherlands were no longer operating as independent nations, and a colonial vacuum had developed in Southeast Asia which the Gaimusho perceived as a standing invitation to Britain and the United States. Tokyo believed further in a natural right to leadership in the area by virtue of ability, geographical proximity, and racial affinity. Negotiations were therefore begun with Vichy for a Japanese military presence in northern Indochina. French field officers were not unwilling to resist, as it developed, but they could do so only with the moral, diplomatic, and, if need be, military backing of the United States, and FDR's stance remained noncommittal. After his prior refusal to join in a protest against the seizure of Hainan Island or to offer France support for the holding of the Spratly Islands, he was still in the act of making overtures to Tokyo. The notion of a Monroe Doctrine for Asia had touched off a paroxysm of disbelief in Paris, and Japan now set out to occupy northern Indochina. This Japanese "preempting" of Indochina in time of war was, of course, no more than

Russia had done in Finland during time of peace. Roosevelt might condemn it as an act of aggression, but Japanese leaders could point to Allied occupation of Iceland, Curaçao, and Aruba. They had to assume that they might need military bases in Indochina for an invasion of Singapore should London force them to fight on a second front. Furthermore, only by control of Indochina could they interdict the heavy supply of war matériel going to China, where a million of their best troops had been mired since 1937. Next to Hong Kong, there was no lifeline more valuable to Chiang Kai-shek than French Indochina.[24]

China's future seemed especially doubtful on 27 September 1940, the day the Tripartite Pact was signed, for Prime Minister Winston Churchill had turned aside Roosevelt's call for a reopening of the Burma Road. Washington derived two-thirds of its tungsten as well as other vital raw materials from China via the Burma Road so that for industrial reasons, not to mention a desire to keep Chiang alive, the White House desired British cooperation. One thing, and only one thing, however, could move Churchill to change his mind. Twice in June he had offered to keep the road open on condition that FDR pledge military support in the event of a Japanese attack.[25] America, he suggested, should send a permanent squadron to Singapore. When the president demurred, the prime minister made a second suggestion. Washington should notify Tokyo that "any attempt to change the status quo in the Far East or Pacific" would not be tolerated.[26] Again, Roosevelt refused. It cannot be too much emphasized that Churchill would not agree to stringent economic sanctions, with their attendant risk of war, or to an equally risky reopening of the Burma Road, unless an American fleet stood behind him, its decks cleared for action. Otherwise, he insisted, he would have to make his peace with Tokyo. On 14 July, for the last time, he made it clear that without definite assurance of American military muscle in reserve, the Burma Road would close. And close it did.[27] So stung was the administration by this pinching off of Chiang's lifeline that Hornbeck suggested outright retaliation—against London—if necessary.[28] This, however, is not the route the president chose.

What Roosevelt did, if the following hypothesis is borne out, was to make the kind of offer Churchill demanded—the equivalent of a formal military guarantee to come to Britain's aid in order to prevent capitulation to Japan's New Order.[29] One would never guess from Halifax's correspondence, or even from the minutes of the British War Cabinet, that such a commitment came this early. On the other hand, it is unlikely that the entire British cabinet was privy to all that transpired between Roosevelt and Churchill. Even if this were so, we shall have occasion to see that censors did their work on the War Cabinet minutes. In addition, it is important to recall that we are dealing here with five British desiderata: (1) a *secret* American military commitment to stand behind Britain in defense of her Far East possessions; (2) a *public* declaration of such purpose; (3) a *warning to Japan* of such purpose; (4) a secret pledge to stand behind other territories such as Thailand and the Dutch East Indies; and (5) a *public* pledge of such support.[30]

As we shall observe, the third of these demands was satisfied by February 1941, the second not until the very eve of Pearl Harbor, while the first was granted in a variety of ways by 8 October 1940, before the announcement that the Burma Road would reopen.

Downing Street was merely reiterating a position that Britain and France had staked out since the early 1930s.[31] When, in late 1937, it was feared that resumption of war in China would tempt Tokyo to expand southward into the Dutch Indies, as well as the Philippines and a number of possessions flying the Union Jack, a British consul general told the Foreign Office, "We must do our very best to get the U.S. government interested in a policy which would guarantee the present territorial status quo in the Malayan archipelago and Philippine Islands; also British Malaya and Hong Kong."[32] FDR could not very well have forgotten, either, that when the French asked for an American military guarantee at Brussels and he had declined to go beyond words, an irate Premier Chautemps had shut down Chiang's supply route through Indochina.

When Hitler absorbed what remained of Czechoslovakia in the spring of 1939, European statesmen shaped their policy toward Germany on the basis of the kind of help they expected to receive from the United States in the Far East. That they were unwilling to face the prospect of a two-front war without active American participation was something that French leaders made patently clear. On 12 May, American naval units set a hopeful precedent when they landed alongside French and British forces at Kulangsu, China. Two hundred Japanese troops, having landed earlier, were claiming authority over the local international settlement; but when thus confronted with a three-power show of unity, they backed down. In June of 1939, the French naval attaché in Tokyo noted confidently that in case of a German-

Japanese combination, France was counting on the weight of the American fleet. Paris still believed that Japan could and should be weaned away from the Axis, but every eventuality had to be weighed. As usual, neither Britain nor France was interested in economic sanctions against Tokyo until the United States had given a firm indication of military commitment in case of war. That they followed the American lead in this most sensitive of areas is a fair indication that by June of 1939 all doubt of Roosevelt's ultimate intent had been removed. As early as 30 January 1939, Lord Lothian had written Canadian Prime Minister W. L. Mackenzie King that Washington was ready to say that it would participate in any war pitting democracies against dictatorships and would fight, if necessary, for the defense of Australia and New Zealand.[33]

By late April 1940, Secretary Hull and Norman Davis were confirming that their government was prepared to defend British interests in the Pacific. Roosevelt reinforced this promise the following month when he told Mackenzie King that should France fall and Britain come under heavy aerial attack, the United States would not sit idly by. It would open its ports to the Royal Navy for refitting and provisioning and do its best to build up Singapore and Halifax. Furthermore, according to Mackenzie King, "Its fleet would hold the Pacific and especially defend Australia and New Zealand against Japanese and other attacks. As soon thereafter as grounds could be found to justify direct and active American participation (and neither Mr. Roosevelt nor Mr. Hull believes that this would be more than a very few weeks), the United States would participate in a stringent blockade of the Continent." Since Canada's chief executive acted as an important channel of communication between the White House and Downing Street, his diary is eminently worth quoting. An entry for 27 September reads, "The United States will not allow Japan to get control of Asia and the Pacific."[34]

Many other signs point in the same direction. Father Drought remembered that Roosevelt had thwarted an Anglo-Japanese understanding based on the reopening of the Yangtze Valley to British trade *in September 1940*.[35] On 14 September, the day after Congress agreed to a military draft, Assistant Secretary of State Breckinridge Long recorded in his diary that, according to what he had heard, Roosevelt had decided to go all out to protect British possessions in the Far East. In his opinion, this would mean war: "I now understand that it has been discussed as a matter of high policy that the administration has made up its mind to deal very firmly with Japan and that no steps will be spared and that those steps may lead to war."[36] The signing of the Tripartite Pact on 27 September did not create an Allied bond. Rather, a bond already in place was noticeably strengthened. Washington announced that China would receive a $25 million loan, followed within a month by the announcement of an additional $25 million, and it is clear that by 2 October, Churchill had obtained sufficient assurance of an American guarantee to decide in favor of reopening the Burma Road. Asked by dubious colleagues if it would be such a good idea to have America at war in the Pacific when her aid was so sorely needed in the Atlantic, his answer was a resounding yes. If anything, he wanted to go a step further and extract a *public* pledge from Roosevelt stating that the United States, in conjunction with the British, Dutch, and Dominions, would guarantee the status quo in the South Pacific.[37] On 4 October, Roosevelt conversed with House Speaker Sam Rayburn of Texas and Representative John W. McCormack of Massachusetts. He spoke in sharp terms about the relationship between Washington and Tokyo: although Japan might regard any aid to its enemies as a casus belli, the United States was prepared to act. Four days later, Roosevelt told his associates, "This country is ready to pull the trigger if the Japs do anything. I mean we won't stand any nonsense."[38]

The question naturally arises as to what, if any, additional quid pro quo Roosevelt received for throwing American military support to Britain in the Far East. Here again, the diary of Mackenzie King is instructive, for it indicates that the United States obtained something far beyond a mere opening of the Burma Road. There is reference to a Canadian cabinet poll taken during the first week of October on whether Ottawa should join London in standing by Washington in case of a Japanese attack against U.S. possessions.[39] How the members of the cabinet voted is unclear, but London's position stands out in bold relief.

One can go further. During the first week of October, British ambassadors reported what seemed to be an important new commitment on the part of the United States, although they were not clear about its precise terms. It is unlikely that they were referring to the Destroyers for Bases program, which was now more than a month old. FDR had just called up the entire naval reserve and was rushing supplies, ammunition, and an anti-aircraft regiment to the Philippines. Moreover, in a move nearly always associated with war, he had ordered all Americans out of the Far East. On 7 October, the British War Cabinet was informed that the American navy wanted to know how fully Singapore could be made available to U.S. vessels in case Japan retaliated for the reopening of the Burma Road (effective 17 October) or threatened the Dutch East Indies. Churchill is reported to have been immensely pleased as he considered this a capital development coming in the train of the Tripartite Pact. We do not know all the details of what Roosevelt offered, or how Churchill and his cabinet reacted, owing to the fact that a critical section of cabinet minutes is missing. But it is evident that the word was "go." On 8 October, Britain announced what Churchill had decided a week earlier—namely that the Burma Road would reopen on 17 October.[40]

The extent of the American commitment is further confirmed by another set of facts. FDR wanted immediate Anglo-American staff talks, and he wanted them in Singapore, as well as in Washington and London. Furthermore, Admiral James O. Richardson, commander of the U.S. Pacific Fleet, was apprised by Navy Secretary Frank Knox on 10 October that in the event of an attack on the Burma Road, Roosevelt wished to deploy American naval units to blockade Japan by means of two lines of ships, one running from the Philippines to Hawaii, the other from Samoa to the Dutch East Indies. Richardson, who had lunched with the president several months earlier and found him "fully determined to put the United States into the war," balked at this latest plan and informed Knox that the navy was ill prepared. He told FDR to his face that senior naval leaders did not have confidence in the civilian leadership of the United States. Within a short space of time, he would be fired.[41]

A variety of subtle indications mark the fall of 1940 as a decisive turning point in American policy toward Japan. In mid-October, Foreign Secretary Lord Halifax wrote his friend Victor Hope, Marquis of Linlithgow: "For the first time in the last two years the Americans have shown their teeth to some purpose." *Time* magazine observed that an attack on the Dutch Indies might draw the United States into combat and claimed that the navy would rather confront Japan sooner than later (quite untrue). Hull refused to reassure the American people, as he had done in the past, that their sons would not be sent to fight in a foreign war. Although Roosevelt gave such assurance several times in the heat of his campaign for a third term, Hull later noted that "knowing the situation and the dangers as I did, I refused."[42]

Nor is it insignificant that by December 1940, Ambassador Grew had executed a complete about-face. In the past, he had regarded commercial warfare as an incitement to war. Now, he wrote FDR from his post in Tokyo: "Japan has become openly and unashamedly one of the predatory nations . . . which aims to wreck about everything that the United States stands for. . . . We are bound to have a showdown some day . . . I am profoundly thankful that . . . you are piloting the old ship of state."[43]

With this assessment Francis B. Sayre took pointed exception. As U.S. high commissioner to the Philippines and recently special envoy to Tokyo, where, as we have seen, he held confidential talks with Foreign Minister Arita, he agreed with Long that decisions were being taken that would "suck" the country into war. Just before the arrival of a British military mission in Washington, he warned the White House that aid to Britain must be given "without ourselves entering the war." Sayre's opinion notwithstanding, on 29 December the president delivered his hard-hitting Arsenal of Democracy Address in which he labeled Japan a direct threat to the United States. Sayre received this revealing explanation from the Oval Office two days later:

> On one side are aligned Japan, Germany and Italy, and on the other side, China, Great Britain and the United States. . . . If Japan, moving further southward, should gain possession of the region of the Netherlands East Indies and the Malay Peninsula, would not the chances of Germany's defeating Great Britain be increased and the chances of England's winning be decreased thereby? . . . Would we be rendering every assistance possible to Great Britain were we to give our attention wholly and exclusively to the problems of the immediate defense of the British Isles and of Britain's control of the Atlantic? . . . They live by importing goods from all parts of the world.

Obviously, there were two schools of thought on the question of how best to prevent Japan from hobbling the war effort against Hitler. Some believed in compromise, others did not; and FDR, who belonged to the latter school, began to withhold more and more exports on the pretext of stockpiling for national security. Sayre later wrote that for all practical purposes Roosevelt had decided on war by 31 December 1940. From then on, it was only a matter of time. His phraseology is worth recalling: "Whether ourselves to take the initiative by declaration of war and attack or whether to await further the turn of events and a possible attack upon ourselves, as finally came at Pearl Harbor, was a profoundly difficult and momentous decision." Just how accurate

Sayre's memory was after seventeen years and how much he knew of Roosevelt's inner mind is not easy to tell. But his recollection dovetails neatly with Long's sense of the situation.[44]

A conference on Pacific relations held on 7 December at Princeton, exactly one year to the day before Pearl Harbor, furnishes another gloss on the drift of informed opinion. Aviator Charles Lindbergh, who attended along with others, could not but comment on how many seemed to take it for granted that "the most desirable course of action for this country was that which would be of greatest aid to England, whether or not it involved us in war!" Discussion centered on whether war with Japan would help or hinder Great Britain and what steps short of war would involve the United States most quickly. It was agreed that while the American people would not endorse a flat declaration of war, they would support incremental steps *leading* to war: "I kept wanting to remind them that we were in *America* and *not* in England," exclaimed Lindbergh, "that our primary concern was the future of *America* and not that of the British Empire."[45]

Additional evidence of a shift in American policy is implicit in the administration's behavior during February 1941. With Lend-Lease legislation safely secured, FDR delivered an ultimatum to Tokyo through the person of Eugene Dooman, second in command of the American embassy. On 14 February, Japanese Vice-Minister for Foreign Affairs Chuichi Ohashi remarked to Dooman: "Do you mean to say that if Japan were to attack Singapore there would be war with the United States?" Dooman replied with precisely the argument that FDR had impressed upon Sayre only six weeks before: "It would be absurd to suppose that the American people, while pouring munitions into Britain, would look with complacency upon the cutting of communications between Britain and British dominions and colonies overseas. If, therefore, Japan or any other nation were to prejudice the safety of those communications, either by direct action or by placing herself in a position to menace those communications, she would have to expect to come into conflict with the United States." Later in the conversation, Dooman reminded his listener that a "major preoccupation" of the United States was "to assist England to stand against German assault" and that Japan "cannot substantially alter the *status quo* in Southeast Asia" without "incurring the risk of a very serious situation." These were strong words in the parlance of diplomacy, and they seem to have made their mark. Grew recalled that Australian Minister

Sir John Latham, having seen Ohashi a few minutes after the session with Dooman, had found him "greatly agitated and distrait [sic]."[46]

There is little room for guesswork as to the authenticity of Dooman's ultimatum. It was immediately relayed to Washington and never thereafter repudiated. Twelve days later, Grew gave it emphatic confirmation at the foreign minister level. On 26 February, the American ambassador cabled Hull for permission to tell Foreign Minister Matsuoka that "the statements made by Mr. Dooman to Mr. Ohashi were made with my prior knowledge and have my full approval." We do not have Hull's reply, but we may assume that it was positive, for the next day, 27 February, Grew cabled Hull a second time: "Yesterday, I told Matsuoka that I entirely concurred in and approved of all that Dooman had said to Ohashi on 14 February."[47]

When Langer and Gleason published *The Undeclared War* (1953), they were in possession of all pertinent data relating to Dooman. But without benefit of additional facts adding up to a more convincing general context, they appear to have been psychologically incapable of grasping the truth. They were correct in attaching little weight to Grew's testimony before a congressional committee in late 1945. It was not to be expected that a former ambassador, especially one in Grew's position, would willingly accuse himself—and the administration—of having forced Japan's hand. Thus, the dualism of his response. He could not recall having received any instruction from the State Department in this connection ("not to my recollection"); he denied that Dooman's ultimatum was "necessarily from official sources," and he tried to play down the choice of language. Langer and Gleason also pointed out that at no time did FDR or any of his advisers ever disavow either Dooman's ultimatum or Grew's confirmation. At the same time, they could not square what transpired in Tokyo with "the spineless program being discussed in Washington."[48] FDR did, of course, see Ambassador Kichisaburo Nomura on the same day that Dooman saw Ohashi, and while one interview bristled with tension, the other turned out to be relatively cordial. One must remember, however, that these were standard tactics for a man who, in one-to-one contact, tended to avoid anything verging on the disagreeable. To borrow an expression from another student of the subject, Roosevelt had a way of "leading with someone else's chin."[49]

As 1941 dawned, the Gaimusho found itself in control of most of China's coastal area, most of her populace, and the bulk of her slender industrial apparatus. At the same time, even though Chiang had re-treated to the remote reaches of Chungking, his Nationalist armies gave no sign of surrender, and because Washington was their principal under-writer, Tokyo still hoped to engage the United States in serious talks leading to a mutually acceptable compromise. Roosevelt, appearing in-terested as always, received Admiral Nomura in March as a special ambassador from Premier Konoye.[50] Another round of talks would en-able the White House to satisfy all shades of opinion. Isolationists and pacifists could be encouraged to look for genuine accommodation while hard-liners could be assured that the talks were merely intended to give Tokyo a graceful means of retreat. They would be accompanied by ever-increasing economic pressure.

For some time, Japan had invited the aid of the Catholic Church as an intermediary, and it now enlisted the service of two Maryknoll priests: Bishop James E. Walsh, superior general of Maryknoll, the Catholic Missionary Society of America, and his vicar general or treasurer, the Reverend James M. Drought. After visiting Tokyo in late 1940 and con-veying to Japanese leaders a sense of what terms they felt Washington might be willing to accept, they went to Roosevelt with an outline of what they thought Japan might be persuaded to offer. Two additional representatives came to the United States to serve as liaison between Washington and the Japanese cabinet. The first of these, Tadao Wikawa, headed Japan's largest banking group and, with the rank of minister plenipotentiary, remained in touch with Premier Konoye by private code. Related by blood or marriage to former premier Reijirō Wakatsuki, as well as to the head of the Domei News Agency, he had risen from the rank of finance commissioner in New York to become minister of fi-nance and then to draft Japan's foreign exchange law. Colonel Hideo Iwakuro, who arrived a few weeks after Wikawa, bore the unassuming title of military attaché and did not speak English, but he could negoti-ate in French or German and was assistant to General Akira Mutō, chief of the powerful Military Affairs Bureau of the War Department. Accord-ing to Grew, Iwakuro was exceedingly influential in military circles and had the complete confidence of the Japanese secretary of war.[51]

Initially, Drought served as a bridge between Wikawa, whom he saw directly, and Roosevelt, whom he reached through Postmaster General Frank Walker. When Iwakuro entered the picture, Nomura was not far behind, and it was out of this group that there emerged Drought's cele-brated Draft Understanding of 16 April. Among its prominent features were the following: the United States was to recognize Manchukuo, allow greater scope for Japanese immigration, and support demands for British withdrawal from Hong Kong and Singapore; Japan would withdraw from China in recognition of that country's independence and territorial integrity; she would also refrain from exacting any war indemnity and would endorse the doctrine of the Open Door, to be more precisely defined at a later date. Chiang Kai-shek and his rival, Wang Ch'ing-wei, were to merge their governments, and both Japan and the United States were to oppose the transfer of any territory in the Far East, including the Philippines. Secretary of State Hull agreed to accept the Draft Understanding as "a basis for the institution of negotiations" with the exception of its clauses on immigration, Hong Kong, and Singapore and with the further proviso that Japan would assent to four general principles for which the United States had long contended: namely, the territorial integrity and sovereignty of all nations, noninterference in the internal affairs of other nations, equality of commercial opportunity, and nondisturbance of the Pacific status quo except by peaceful measures.[52]

Once the Hull-Nomura talks began in earnest, Drought made seventeen visits to Washington, ranging in duration from several days to several weeks, and before he was finished he had spent most of May, September, and November on the Potomac.[53] Bishop Walsh, who personally delivered two of Konoye's messages to the president, kept a close watch on the Japanese side. He passed two months with Wikawa during summer and fall at various locations in the vicinity of Tokyo. At the request of Dooman, he also transmitted many messages from the Gaimusho to the State Department with an eye to narrowing differences which seemed to bar the way to a final settlement.[54]

The major issues in dispute may be reduced to four: American economic opportunity in China and Manchukuo; allowance for Japanese troops to remain in China as a barrier against communist inroads and for the shielding of Manchukuo; Japan's neutrality in the event of American entry into the European war; and American recognition of Manchukuo. The last of the four was accepted by both parties as an automatic part of any peace agreement, and Japan proved willing to concede everything regarding the first and third points.[55] She had never ceased to promise that once the war ended in China, America would be given ample economic opportunity, and before the talks ended she proved willing to set this down on paper. As for the Axis, Tokyo was technically bound to fight if and when the United States should enter the war, but the language of the Tripartite Pact was such that she could interpret it loosely. This she promised to do in return for tolerance of her stake in North China and Manchukuo. On 21 November, she offered to put such an interpretation of the pact in writing, which, considering the premium she placed upon "face," was a momentous concession. No one can be certain that she would have honored this promise or any other, but the likelihood is great. This, at any rate, was the opinion of Downing Street, and the prospect seemed real enough to cause considerable concern on the part of high German officials.[56] There is no compelling evidence to the contrary.

Troops proved to be the sticking point. Yet even here the Japanese took the position by late May that they would be willing to withdraw up to 90 percent of their occupation force within two years and restrict the remainder to specified zones in North China. Hull dashed any hope of compromise by insisting upon a *one*-year withdrawal of *all* forces with the suggestion that Chiang or an international commission be given the task of halting communist penetration. On 13 September, Japan went a step farther by offering to withdraw the remaining 10 percent after "a certain period." Hull, however, stood firm on immediate withdrawal of all troops. This might have been the last word, but it was bruited that Konoye would accept a Chinese police corps in North China under Japanese officers and might agree to a specific withdrawal date if Roosevelt would attend a Pacific summit conference as originally anticipated. Many, including Walsh and Grew, believed that if Konoye went to Hawaii as the first premier ever to leave his country on an official visit, he would deliver what he promised.[57]

What is extraordinary is that the Japanese were willing to go as far as they did when the history of the American side from the start had been one of backing and filling. Professor Paul Schroeder has demonstrated that as Nomura offered more and more in the way of concessions, Hull offered less and less, until Japan finally moved into southern Indochina, providing Roosevelt with an excuse for further stalling and justifying American imposition of a lethal de facto oil embargo beginning 24 July. Hull had been the first to back away from the Draft Understanding on stipulations involving immigration and British withdrawal from Hong Kong and Singapore. This, in turn, invited similar retreat on the part of Nomura, who immediately became vague on the question of the Axis and stationing of troops. Thereafter, Hull initiated each mutual departure from the expected basis for agreement.[58]

Typically, Hull insisted on 16 May that Nomura return to the Draft Understanding while he himself drew even farther away from it. In the early rounds of negotiation, he focused on the issue of troops; but when Japan promised to withdraw most of its forces in two years, he shifted to the question of unity in Japanese politics and argued about whether the government of Prince Konoye was actually in a position to honor its promises. When this point was answered acceptably, he moved on to economics until Japan offered to do in China exactly what the United States was doing in South America. Seemingly satisfied on this point, he then agreed to the Draft Understanding substantially intact, only to return to the troop issue even as he admitted in private the need for Japan to station forces in the north. Each time the Japanese offered a concession, he raised the ante. On 7 July, he introduced a demand for public rejection of the Axis Pact, which the United States had promised as early as January it would not do. Finally, on 8 October, after Tokyo indicated that even the question of troops in North China might be negotiable, Hull took the extreme position that he would not sign any agreement until Tokyo proved its seriousness by withdrawing some of its troops in advance. Drought, maddened by White House tactics, called them "contemptible."[59]

It is generally assumed that the president was sincere in his approach to Japan.[60] Yet why, if he was bargaining in good faith, was Drought brought to complain on 7 July: "We have now gone three and a half months without offering any official counter-statement"? If Roosevelt had been serious, why did he encourage the idea of a summit meeting on 17 August and again on the twenty-eighth only to retreat from it? On the seventeenth, having just returned from his meeting with Churchill at Argentia, he suggested that Nomura consider a specific date, 15 October. On 28 August, he backed away from Hawaii as a site, naming Juneau, Alaska, as more convenient. He was still "keenly interested," he told Nomura, "in having three or four days with Prince Konoye." In the meantime, press leaks had begun to cause Foreign Minister Teijirō Toyoda acute embarrassment. His country had extended an unprecedented invitation without receiving the courtesy of an answer, and he urgently requested announcement of a definite meeting date such as 20 September. Inexplicably, Roosevelt now came to a dead halt.

There would be no meeting, he told Nomura, until major principles had been settled. On the following day, 4 September, he announced the closing of the Panama Canal to Japanese shipping.[61] Toyoda and Konoye were thus left dangling.

Nor is this the full story. Why, one must ask, did FDR allow his subordinates to offer the idea of a modus vivendi on 18–19 November only to fall back on generalities two days after the Japanese indicated their acceptance and advanced a specific proposal? It is true that Japan's offer of 20 November included an unsatisfactory proviso that the United States halt all aid to China (must cease all measures "prejudicial" to "peace between Japan and China"). But instead of objecting, Hull chose to add two requirements of his own: that Japan vacate *all* of Indochina instead of just the southern portion and that she receive only enough oil to meet her *civilian* requirements.[62]

Why, one may also wonder, did Roosevelt interpret the Japanese advance into southern Indochina beginning 2 July solely as an act of aggression? It placed Tokyo in a better position to threaten Singapore and Manila, but it also helped to secure her food supply at a time when Britain had sealed off an alternate source of rice in Burma. Maxwell Hamilton, chief of the Far Eastern Division at State, viewed the advance as basically defensive in light of anticipated intensification of American and British economic pressure. Two weeks earlier, Washington had instituted a new phase of trade restriction affecting East Coast and Gulf ports. Japan, in short, had her back to the wall. She envisaged bloodshed.[63]

Why, finally, did Hull confine himself to such vague terminology? Why did he use the term "Indochina" several times when he plainly meant only the southern half of Indochina, and why did it take him ten months to indicate that complete and immediate troop withdrawal from all of China was a sine qua non? The proposal he submitted on 31 May was nebulous with respect to both the Axis Pact and troops remaining in North China. Three and a half months later, when Nomura finally agreed to consider a time limit on troops remaining in North China, Roosevelt ordered Hull to return to general principles and "reemphasize my hope for a meeting [with Konoye]." Nomura was stunned when presented on 2 October with another spate of generalities. Accused of stalling, it was at this point that Roosevelt countered with his radical insistence on *prior* withdrawal of troops as a token of good faith.[64]

The reader will recall that beginning on 24 July, FDR acquiesced in the imposition of a total oil embargo against Tokyo. Again, if one were so disposed, one could raise the question of *why*, as American action left the Japanese with no logical middle ground between abject surrender on the diplomatic front (with resulting economic, military, and strategic difficulties linked with national dishonor) and a direct attack on the United States.[65]

It is ironic that Japan should be the nation whose good faith was called into question when neither Hull nor presidential adviser Stanley Hornbeck nor Roosevelt himself ever regarded the Drought-Walsh initiative as anything but a ploy. From the outset, Hornbeck and Hull advised against serious negotiation, and when Roosevelt told Churchill in August that he felt he could "baby" the Japanese along for another thirty days, this is just what he meant. It is what he had been doing since the fall of 1939; indeed, his strategy became so obvious at times as to be almost comic.[66] Although Japan presented important new proposals on 9 April, Hull used subsequent sessions with Nomura to concentrate less on specifics and more on general questions such as democracy versus the inherent evil of Hitlerian Germany.[67] Again and again, he cited America's exemplary conduct in Latin America without acknowledging the glaring differences that separated one hemisphere from another. Repeatedly, he arraigned Nazism and propounded the advantages of free trade.[68] By June, therefore, the dialogue was reduced to trivia, and Hull folded his tent for a six-week summer vacation. Nomura sought him out at the Greenbrier resort in West Virginia, only to be told that he was unavailable on a doctor's excuse.[69]

Long-suffering Bishop Walsh confessed to being "a little mortified" by the administration's foot-dragging. "If the thing is finally done," he wrote, "it will not be due to their good management." On 7 November, we may observe Hull holding forth on the virtues of the Pan-American system. A week later, he is to be heard maintaining the preposterous fiction that talks with Nomura had not yet got beyond the "exploratory" stage. Contributing to the carnival atmosphere was a simultaneous series of parallel talks. Grew had been conversing with Toyoda; Welles had fallen to squabbling over minor points with Minister-Counselor Kaname Wakasugi; Roosevelt had been seeing Nomura at frequent intervals; while both Eugene Dooman and Joseph W. Ballantine (a Japanese-speaking Foreign Service officer on special assignment in Washington) had entered into an exchange with their opposite numbers. Nor does this include conferences between Hamilton and Wikawa.[70]

The coup de grace came on 26 November, when Hull presented Tokyo with a set of demands totally divorced from the context of the past six months and calling for Japanese withdrawal from Manchukuo.

Any student who has attempted to thread his way through the record of these talks will not be surprised that a task force of Japanese carriers was soon on its way to Hawaii. Even if Hull never admitted, as he did, along with Under Secretary of State Welles, to a deliberate policy of stalling, the record reveals numerous devices employed since the fall of 1939 to cover the face of American intransigence.[71]

As spring blossomed into summer and summer gave way to fall in 1941, Tokyo had less reason than ever to surrender. Hitler, in full control of nearly all western Europe, had expelled Britain from Greece and Libya, Tobruk excepted, and gone on to throttle Russia. Never had Japanese proponents of the Axis been stronger. In August, an attempt was made on the life of former premier Kiichirō Hiranuma, principal diplomatic adviser to the emperor, and he barely escaped. In September, a bullet passed within inches of the premier himself. Grew took to carrying a revolver.[72]

Some historians have pinned the blame on Nomura, stressing his relative inexperience and echoing Hull's charge that the admiral did not possess an adequate command of English: "I frequently doubted whether he understood the points I was making."[73] But why, then, did Hull continue to negotiate with a person who demonstrated such difficulty with communication? Many have accepted Hull's thesis that Nomura erred in presenting the Draft Understanding to Tokyo as an American proposal when it was merely a paper drawn by Drought, which Hull had agreed to accept "as a basis for starting conversations" and subject to four principles for which the United States had long contended.[74]

In point of fact, Drought's Draft Understanding of 16 April was nothing if not an American proposal. It had been drawn on the initiative of American clergymen in collaboration with the president of the United States and his advisers. The Japanese had made it perfectly clear to Drought, and through Drought to Roosevelt, that they were sending a plenipotentiary and that FDR was expected to designate his own representative to work with Wikawa and hammer out an agreement. The Japanese government would approve said agreement in due time, and the president would call a conference to seal the compact before the eyes of the world.[75] Wikawa's presence in Washington, in fact the whole idea of a Draft Understanding, with emphasis on the word "understanding," was intended by Tokyo to assure agreement with the United States before the tendering of a formal proposal. As Drought put it to Joseph Ballantine, Hamilton's assistant, "The Japanese would want some intimation that the Japanese proposals would be substantially acceptable to this [the U.S.] government." If America accepted unofficially, the Japanese cabinet would give formal endorsement, hopefully before Foreign Minister Matsuoka returned from a trip to Berlin and Moscow. The pro-Axis Matsuoka would then be faced with a fait accompli.[76] Walker warned Hull on 17 March that "Prince Konoye, Count Arima and Marquis Kido [Lord Keeper of the Privy Seal] are endangering their lives by these negotiations. Obviously, they will not confide in the Japanese embassy at Washington until they are certain of substantial agreement with the two persons" (Wikawa and Iwakuro).[77] The next day, Walker again warned Hull that the Japanese wanted either "substantial change introduced or substantial approval given" to the Draft Understanding "so that Tokyo can immediately instruct its Embassy to submit the Draft officially upon which both governments can announce an 'Agreement in Principle.'" The idea was so crucial to Walker that he mentioned it a third time to Hull. It was therefore a warrantable expectation on Japan's part that when Hull authorized Nomura to submit the Draft Understanding to Tokyo as "a basis for the institution of negotiations," it constituted a morally binding agreement, and not at all what Hull later claimed.[78]

Originally, when asked by Nomura if the United States could approve the Draft, Hull replied encouragingly that some points would need modification or elimination, but he could see "no good reason why ways could not be found to reach a fairly satisfactory settlement of all the essential questions presented." Drought referred to this wording when on 12 May he recalled "our assurance that there will be no substantial modifications in the proposed 'understanding,'" and it is why Nomura told his superiors that Hull had agreed "in general." Here was anything but a misunderstanding based on language barriers. According to Walker, Hull actually assured Nomura that there would be no substantial modifications, and according to Konoye, Hull accepted Japan's second tentative plan (the Draft Understanding) as a basis for discussion, which amounts to the same thing.[79]

One reason why Hull's initial response to the Draft Understanding was so misleading is that there was a difference between what he initially said and what he had been told to say. On 7 March, Hornbeck, who believed there was no use negotiating with men whose word could not be trusted, informed him that although Roosevelt wanted him to engage in talks with Nomura, he must be reserved and keep the ambassador guessing; the United States was in no hurry. In April, he was instructed to remain as vague as possible and confine his talk to generalities such as the desirability of trade liberalization or the merits of the Declaration of Lima. If asked whether he could accept the Draft Understanding, he was to say it could be "a starting point for discussion." In other words, Roosevelt and Hornbeck wished to remain noncommittal while giving the impression of interest. Hull was advised to state that if Tokyo approved the Draft, he would study it "sympathetically" and "feel optimistic that on the basis of mutual good will our differences can be adjusted."

Needless to say, in the language of diplomacy, where "no" may be interpreted to mean "maybe" and "maybe" is generally taken to mean "yes," differences resolvable in an atmosphere of goodwill cannot be very substantial. Inadvertently, Hull ended by promising a good deal more than his instructions permitted. For the phrase "starting point" he substituted the word "basis," which carries an entirely different meaning. On 10 June, Hornbeck reined him in with a reminder that he had succeeded in bringing himself "to a negotiation . . . no matter how it may otherwise be technically described." Almost as if an invisible wire had tightened about his neck, Hull now ceased to direct his attention to substantive matters. By 20 June, the Japanese leadership was protesting that he seemed more interested in silk purchases or a bus line franchise than in the major points at issue. Drought agreed, telling Walker that "it makes us look perfectly ridiculous."[80]

Another stock criticism of Nomura is that he did not let Tokyo know immediately of Hull's insistence on four general principles as a condition for considering the Draft Understanding. Such an omission pales, however, against the backdrop of the summer's talks. Japan could have paid lip service to Hull's principles. But from the beginning, it was specifics that counted. Even if Nomura had been less than proficient in English—and this may be doubted in view of his former residence in Britain and the United States, not to mention his 1939 talks with Grew—and even if there had been a genuine misunderstanding as to the nature of the Draft Understanding, these issues alone could never have been decisive. One or two mistakes on Nomura's part do not ex-

plain Hull's stalling. Nor do they account for his flight from speci-
ficity. Any failure in communication was due to ignorance of another
kind. Roosevelt misunderstood Japan's relationship with China even
as he misunderstood the aims of the Soviet Union. Conversely, Japanese leaders never seem to have entirely grasped the true nature of
Roosevelt.

Some have shifted the blame to Walsh and Drought, claiming that
they were meddlesome amateurs who exaggerated on both sides the
concessions each was willing to make. Admittedly, the "Preliminary
Draft of an 'Agreement in Principle,'" which Drought first circulated
to Hull via Walker on 17 March, implied the withdrawal of all Japanese
troops when it provided for China's absolute independence. It also stip-
ulated that Japan would sever all trade ties with Germany and withhold
shipments to countries trading with Germany. Neither of these provisions appeared in the Draft Understanding of 16 April. But neither did
there appear the earlier provisions for a Japanese Monroe Doctrine and
a dividing of the Pacific into two zones of naval influence. In any case,
it was the latter document which Hull accepted as a "basis" for discussion, not the former.[81]

While the priests were not professional diplomats, neither were they
"self-appointed" in the sense often implied. They were chosen by Japan
and accepted by Roosevelt. Their mission was self-starting only insofar
as a telegram from publisher-philanthropist Robert Cuddihy to former
Vice-Minister of Foreign Affairs Setsuzō Sawada got the ball rolling.
Letters of introduction from Lewis Straus helped keep it in motion.
Before leaving Tokyo in December of 1940, the priests had conferred
with Foreign Minister Matsuoka on two occasions and helped him
draft a speech to the America-Japan Society. Although their meeting
with the premier was canceled at the last minute, they called on General Mutō. They met the Japanese vice-minister for foreign affairs and
were introduced to Prince Saionji's grandson, head of the Domei News
Agency. They also saw Wikawa and called on Tarō Terasaki, chief of
the American desk at the Japanese Foreign Ministry. Several times they
visited their old friend Sawada, who had recently held a position comparable to that of Welles in the United States. Nothing was left to
chance. It is especially significant that once they had the confidence of
the Japanese, the Roosevelt administration welcomed them as an important channel of negotiation. Hull asked Drought to remain on tap in
Washington, and Walsh was requested by the American embassy in

Tokyo to serve as a go-between. The bishop made frequent visits to the embassy in the fall and stayed in touch with Grew through Dooman. Roosevelt himself encouraged the priests and thanked them for their help.[82]

Drought, who is said to have been an "innocent abroad" and "as wrong about Japan as any person could be," had worked as a young missionary in China and written a Hakka grammar that later became a standard text.[83] As treasurer of a great religious society with large interests in Japan, he also had ample opportunity for diplomatic contact. Typical was a letter he addressed to Ambassador Kensuke Horinouchi objecting to the 1939 bombing of a Maryknoll center in China. He knew how careful the Japanese had been to protect noncombatants, he said, and was keenly aware of why their people were at war; sensitive to the larger issues, he had consistently tried to represent the Japanese viewpoint to the American people. Nevertheless, this latest incident, in which a Maryknoll father had been wounded, might be misconstrued: "Our relations must be conducted with frankness and on a basis of honorable self-respect, and I am sure that I should be wanting in both, and unworthy of your esteem were I to fail to invoke your particular consideration to the injuries suffered by our Father and the property losses sustained by our Society."[84]

Walsh, one of six men to found the first American Catholic mission in China, had lived in that country for eighteen years. After acquiring a fair command of Chinese calligraphy, he had found time to write several books on subjects related to China, including *Observations in the Orient* and *The Young Ones* (stories about Chinese children). Among his published works, which included several plays and innumerable articles, was a biography of Father McShane containing a section on Oriental psychology.[85]

Together, Walsh and Drought articulated the Japanese outlook more accurately than anyone at the highest echelons of State. With a healthy respect for the Eastern mind, they could appreciate Japan's insistence upon secrecy as well as the grave risk of assassination her leaders were running.[86] As Walsh remarked in 1940, "We deal in the Orient with superior civilizations, with essentially good people; with fine sensibilities." Drought explained the futility of Hull's preaching in a single sentence: "Orientals put a different value on speech than we do." Far better than any of Roosevelt's other advisers, he understood Japan's fear of communism and her usefulness as a potential makeweight against

Russia. He was also aware that American cooperation might be parlayed into Japanese support in the struggle against Hitler.[87]

Unique in the annals of American diplomacy, Drought composed lengthy memoranda detailing problems and outlining solutions from Japan's point of view. Using the term "our" to mean "Japanese," he laid out Tokyo's best approach to the United States in line with American psychology. Japan would be well advised, he argued, to compare her desire for a friendly government in China to Woodrow Wilson's preference for Carranza over Huerta in Mexico; she should borrow from the corpus of Pan-American thought to describe her Pan-Asian League; she should continue to claim her own version of a Monroe Doctrine for the Far East. If the Maryknoller had his way, Matsuoka would also have tried to dispel lingering fear of a Japanese deal with the Axis by broadcasting to the American people on Christmas Eve 1940.[88] He foresaw the appeal that a Pacific summit conference would have for Roosevelt and assured Japanese leaders that even if such a meeting proved only moderately successful it could do nothing but good as it would "break down the present tension and permit Japan to consolidate her position, *with or without American approbation.*"[89] This, perhaps as much as anything else, explains why Roosevelt withheld his consent. Realizing the need for different nations to have different systems of government, Drought considered a cosmopolitan outlook so vital for peace that he included in his "Preliminary Draft of an 'Agreement in Principle' between the United States and Japan" the following: "The governments of the United States and of Japan recognize that the diversity of cultural and consequent [sic] political and social forms prevailing among advanced nations [is] . . . inescapable. . . . Only a perverted will can distort as an incitement to conflict . . . this natural diversity which, when properly appreciated and encouraged, is one of nature's gifts for creative human and international progress. . . . Among nations the political form of constitution . . . [is a] private domestic concern." He has been accused of being pro-Japanese and "going over" to Tokyo. In fact, he was one of a handful of diplomats capable of seeing things as they really were.[90]

Had more people seen what the Maryknoll missioners saw, the diplomatic climate might have been somewhat different. As it was, the Hull-Nomura talks entered their final phase with Drought and Walsh receding into the background, their place taken by men sworn to fight. Unknown to Roosevelt, a mammoth task force was girding for action at an island base far to the north of Honshu. Six carriers with 423 planes, 2 battleships, 2 heavy cruisers, 11 destroyers, 28 submarines, and 8 tankers were practicing for the most successful surprise attack in modern naval history. The president's attention was effectively diverted from this engine of destruction when Tokyo dispatched a highly visible armada south toward the Philippines on 25 November. The northern-based fleet steamed eastward undetected along a northerly route far removed from conventional traffic. Traveling by night without light and burning a specially refined fuel to minimize smoke, it left behind no telltale evidence, not even refuse. Unwieldy tankers, losing their way in the darkness like so many sheep, were rounded up in the morning by destroyers; dangerous feats of refueling were accomplished on a tempestuous sea.

U.S. cryptographers had of course cracked the Japanese diplomatic code by now, and FDR was fully aware of the imminence of war. One intercept made it clear that 25 November was to be the last day for signing an agreement. Another indicated a decision by Tokyo to extend the life of the talks to the twenty-ninth; after that, things were "automatically going to happen." Still another product of the so-called "Magic" system revealed that Japanese diplomats had been instructed to return home after destroying their files. Knowing, as American officials did, that five Japanese divisions were already seaborne south of Formosa and en route to an unknown destination, they naturally concentrated on the mounting threat to Singapore, the Netherlands East Indies, and Manila.

On 27 November, a warning went out from Washington to all American bases in the Pacific: "Attack imminent." Nothing further was known. Virtually no one dreamed Japan capable of striking an outpost as remotely situated as Pearl Harbor. So it was that Commander Giles E. Short prepared for sabotage. On 6 December, Roosevelt received a final intercept which removed all doubt as to the immediacy of the impending threat; yet he was in no hurry to publicize it lest some over-zealous serviceman fire the first shot and jeopardize his chance to unite a bitterly divided nation. It was a precaution not taken in vain. According to Commander Itaya, leader of the Japanese attack group, "Pearl Harbor was asleep in the morning mist. . . . Calm and serene inside the harbor . . . important ships of the Pacific fleet were strung out and anchored two by two." They were perfect targets. By 7:55 A.M. the entire base was engulfed in panic as sailors raced to man their anti-aircraft guns and loudspeakers carried the voice of Rear Admiral Bellinger: "AIR RAID PEARL HARBOR, THIS IS NO DRILL."

Inasmuch as Tokyo struck without warning—Nomura did not deliver his declaration of war until twenty minutes after the fact—FDR declared 7 December a day that would "live in infamy." Ever since, it has been associated in the popular mind with an element of murderous deceit. Nevertheless, if there was treachery, one must conclude that it was not the Japanese who led their adversary on, not they who broke their word, nor they who slapped their interlocutors in the face. Hull not only arranged to snub Nomura when he came calling in West Virginia. Similar presumption led him to make an unprecedented demand for a change in the Tokyo cabinet. Yoshie Saito, adviser to the foreign minister, protested strenuously at the Thirty-eighth Imperial Liaison Conference held on 10 July: "Hull's 'Oral Statement' contains especially outrageous language. For instance, it says . . . 'there are differences of opinion within the Japanese government. . . . We cannot make an agreement with a Japanese government of that kind.' . . . His attitude is one of contempt for Japan. I have been in the foreign service for a long time. This language is not the kind one would use toward a country of equal standing; it expresses an attitude one would take toward a protectorate or a possession. These words are inexcusable." The foreign minister concurred: "Hull's statement is outrageous. Never has such a thing occurred since Japan opened diplomatic relations with other countries . . . I was truly amazed that he [Nomura] would listen without protest to a demand that Japan, a great world power, change her cabinet." It seems to have been Hull's insulting manner that stung the most: "The United States did nothing about our proposal for forty days." At the Imperial Conference of 1 December, it was said that Roosevelt had not only refused to make a single concession; he had added new demands. He wanted a complete and unconditional withdrawal from China, the withdrawal of recognition of Nanking, and reduction of the Tripartite Pact to a dead letter. This, according to Premier Hideki Tōjō, "belittled the dignity of our Empire." Even the distinguished Hara Yoshimichi, president of the Privy Council, a man who continued to argue against war with the United States, was brought to admit before his colleagues on that same day: "The United States is being utterly conceited, obstinate, and disrespectful."[91]

None of the above need be taken to mean that Roosevelt lacked a valid reason for refusing compromise. It can be argued that if Konoye's troops had been permitted to march out of China under the flag of victory, they might have gone into action elsewhere, and to the serious detriment of America. Roosevelt himself seems to have been of this persuasion, even though many at the time, including British leaders, disagreed. War with Japan was the last thing Whitehall wanted. When Prime Minister Churchill told his people in February 1942 that he had toiled unremittingly for American belligerency, he was referring primarily to the Atlantic theater. British leaders may have preferred war in the Far East to American neutrality, but they generally disapproved of Roosevelt's take-it-or-leave-it attitude.[92] As late as 18 October 1941, the Foreign Office took the position in cables to Lord Lothian, its newly appointed ambassador to Washington, that Britain had been willing to follow the American policy of maximum economic pressure, but "we should still prefer if possible to keep Japan out of the world conflict and to detach her from the Axis."[93] Churchill did object to the Japanese version of a modus vivendi under consideration in late November, but this was because it called for a break in the supply line to China, not because it held out hope for a compromise. All agreed that the Chinese coolie must not be deserted as long as he continued to hold down large numbers of Japanese, but though no one wanted a subservient China, the fear was that Washington was not giving Tokyo sufficient opportunity to distance itself from the Axis.

On this point, good men may disagree. The crux of the issue is that FDR's methods at their best frustrated the normal process of communication. At their worst, they violated common canons of courtesy, not to mention fair play. So devious was he on occasion, and so adroit in concealing the true nature of the Hull-Nomura talks, that individuals on each side of the bargaining table have ever since been saddled with a burden of blame which is in no way theirs. Here again, British opinion is worthy of note. Informed observers at the Court of St. James's never accepted the notion of Japan's attack as a stab in the back. Oliver Lyttelton, minister of production and a leading member of Churchill's War Cabinet, told the American Chamber of Commerce that the United States had not been driven to war by Tokyo but rather had challenged her to the point where she felt compelled to stand and fight. Lord Halifax, who replaced Lothian as ambassador at Washington, concurred with Lyttelton, noting that this was an idea Americans seemed unable to grasp.[94] Indeed, Halifax and Lyttelton were face to face with an attitude which even the passage of forty years has done little to alter.

Before proceeding to a discussion of American diplomacy as it affected the national rivalries of Europe, there are several additional observations to be made about events surrounding Pearl Harbor. First, it seems clear that Roosevelt's own attitude toward the war, and toward war in general, was tinged with fatalism. At the age of sixteen, he had written his parents that war with Spain "seems to be nearer and more probable now, and we can only hope that Spain will do the wise thing and *back down completely.*" Eighteen years later, as assistant secretary of the navy, he predicted that "the Mexican situation is going through one of its periodically peaceful revivals, but the pendulum will swing back to intervention in a week or a month or a year. I don't care much which as *it is sure to come* and at least Army and Navy are gaining by every hour's delay" (italics added in both quotations). Such casualness on the part of an assistant secretary proved doubly significant coming from a president. FDR began his first term in office by telling advisers Moley and Tugwell that war with Japan might just as well come sooner as later. This was an extraordinarily bellicose thing to say in 1933, and the idea seems to have been contagious. By 1937, Admiral Leahy was recording in his diary that "a major war between the Occident and the Orient must be faced at some time either now or in the future." A year later, the feeling was such that Assistant Secretary of State Hamilton felt it necessary to draw a distinction between himself and other White House advisers: "I am not one of those who believes that war between the United States and Japan is inevitable." Roosevelt and his intimates reverted again and again to the idea of inexorability. Arthur Krock gained the impression that the president was looking ahead to "the war he thought he could not avoid." FDR's son James, as well as Congressman Sol Bloom, confirmed this assessment some years later when they recalled that after the surrender of France, the White House considered American belligerency a foregone conclusion. Certainly this was an assumption shared by Secretary of War Stimson, Secretary of the Navy Knox, and Chief of Staff Marshall in January of 1941, when Anglo-American staff talks got under way.[95]

Not that any of the above should be taken to suggest that Roosevelt was a warmonger. He was far too complicated for any such easy system of classification. Yet, while he may not have desired war for its own sake,

it flowed from many of his thoughts and actions. Never much of a believer in preparedness after the death of Theodore Roosevelt, he repeatedly blocked the road to American rearmament. While Japan added
rapidly to her naval establishment and neared the limits set by the
Treaty of Washington, he told reporters, "There isn't any cloud on the
horizon at the present time."[96] Not until 1936 did he speak out on
foreign policy and then only to warn against the horrors of war, saying
that it was his goal to reach treaty strength by 1942. Although naval
building increased during 1937 so that the nation was soon spending
twice what it had spent five years earlier, the defense structure, measured in relative terms, was allowed to atrophy. Only in late 1938 and
early 1939 did the president really begin to move. But the pace was still
so slow that the strength of the nation vis-à-vis other world powers
continued to decline. The year Roosevelt first sought a hemispheric
defense program, 1938, was also the year that Germany's chargé in
Washington reported incredulously, "Still no military preparations
whatever in the United States." In 1939, the U.S. Army ranked nineteenth in the world—behind Portugal and ahead of Bulgaria. In percentage of population under arms it ranked forty-fifth. It stood at less
than 70 percent of the peacetime strength authorized by Congress and
less than 25 percent in terms of combat readiness. General John J. Pershing considered America in a "lamentable" state.[97]

For another two years, public opinion continued to outstrip presidential leadership in this area. Although Roosevelt paid lip service to an air
program, he suppressed Stettinius's defense recommendations. Thus,
when France collapsed in the summer of 1940 and Britain and Germany put thousands of planes into the air, the United States stood
nearly defenseless with a bare minimum of 53 modern bombers and
187 modern pursuit planes. The White House has been commended for
"pushing through" a draft bill during an election year, but it should
also be pointed out that polls showed 59 percent of the people in favor
of a draft law in June, 69 percent in July. Roosevelt waited until 2 August to support a bill jointly sponsored by a Republican and an anti–
New Deal Democrat. Americans, in other words, wanted to spend
more on guns than FDR was willing to request, while Congress appropriated more for defense than he was ready to spend. When he branded
the two-ocean navy an "outmoded conception" and requested a billion
dollars for army and navy combined, Congress kept itself in emergency

session and insisted on a two-ocean navy with $5 billion in defense spending.[98]

Roosevelt could have taken a Navy Department request for three battleships and petitioned Congress for six, knowing full well that he could count on no more than half this number, but he pared down the original order from three to two. As a result, he obtained only one. A typical case concerns the reinforcement of naval bases. Pressure to fortify United States possessions in the Pacific during the spring of 1938 came, not from the Oval Office, but from the Hill. Congress instructed Charles Edison, FDR's unenthusiastic secretary of the navy, to commission a strategic survey, and Edison, after gathering the pertinent data (Report of the Hepburn Board), recommended the revamping of twenty-five bases at a cost of $326 million. Roosevelt's Bureau of the Budget cut the figure to twelve bases at $94 million, and the president reduced it further to $65 million. Although Guam was designated by navy men as urgently in need of an air and submarine base, Roosevelt requested a paltry $5 million. In January, when Tokyo voiced objection to U.S. plans for Guam, he told the press that he did not intend to submit any specific plan for immediate approval. Under pressure from reporters, he then denied ever having supported a $5 million appropriation in the first place. Finally, after being brought to admit that he had indeed endorsed such a sum, he went on to explain that the money would not be used for fortification. The upshot was that Congress found no difficulty in rejecting the item altogether and Guam was never dredged to provide for larger ships. Hopkins's biographer Robert Sherwood has termed this an act of "puerile self-delusion." Even so, it was not nearly as detrimental to rearmament as were a series of other presidential actions. On 13 May 1938, FDR wrote Daniel Bell, acting director of the budget: "The increase of 9900 men for the navy can be cut by nearly 4,000—in other words, I think the total increase for the Navy of 6,000 men is enough. In regard to increase of Marine Corps by 4,000 men, I suggest that this figure be cut—1,000 men."[99]

Closely allied to the question of bases and recruitment was the situation in the Philippines, which had never been satisfactory from a strategic point of view. After Manila rejected the Hawes-Cutting Independence Act of January 1933, Roosevelt recommended substitute legislation duly approved in the form of the Tydings-McDuffie Act. He then announced that the United States would probably give up all its Phil-

ippine bases when it yielded civil jurisdiction. Some feared that this
would send the wrong signal to Tokyo. There was also the problem of
power. Both the commanding general of the Philippine Department
and the commander in chief of the Asiatic Fleet addressed a letter to
Washington saying in effect that the United States must either increase
the size of its military base or pull out.[100] Observers in both Britain
and Australia agreed, but Roosevelt hewed to a middle course. As zero
hour approached, the defenses of Corregidor were little different from
what they had been in 1922 before the advent of airpower. In addition,
FDR clamped an oil embargo on Japan over the objection of army and
navy men, who knew this would deny them their most valuable commodity, time. Incredibly, as bombs fell on Manila in December 1941,
American ships were actually carrying troops away from the scene of
action rather than to it. In extending the draft, Congress had required
the discharge of all selective service men over the age of twenty-four
and FDR was accordingly in the process of deactivating eighteen National Guard divisions.[101]

It can be shown that Roosevelt failed to make effective use of even
the limited forces at his disposal. In 1934, when difficult talks were
under way with Tokyo, he withdrew his fleet from the Pacific. When
talks broke down, Grew commented on how uncooperative the Japanese had been in contrast with their attitude toward Russia, which
had bolstered its Far Eastern defenses and was demonstrating a willingness to use them. Japan no longer thought of seizing Vladivostok and
was willing to pay a substantial price to acquire the Chinese Eastern
Railway. Anti-Soviet propaganda had decreased markedly, while anti-
Americanism was on the rise:

> When our naval supply ship *Gold Star* came to Kobe lately, there were
> sneering references to the fighting qualities of a navy which permitted the
> presence of women on one of its vessels. . . . a recent editorial (*Fukuoka
> Nichi Nichi*) stated: "Intimidatory diplomacy can only be applied to nego-
> tiations with a weaker power. America may apply such a policy to the
> Central or South American countries but she cannot do so to Japan."
> Would such statements appear if American naval preparedness was a rec-
> ognized fact in Japan?[102]

This was not the only instance in which power and diplomacy gave
the appearance of being out of harness. In June of 1938, only six
months after the *Panay* outrage, and in spite of the probability of additional insult, Roosevelt ordered his naval units out of the Pacific and

into the Atlantic. Japan subsequently occupied Hainan Island and went on to announce annexation of the Spratly Island group. When he did decide to send the fleet back to the Pacific, he stationed it at Pearl Harbor, once again against the advice of ranking military officers. Just as Admiral Harold R. Stark had objected to his policy of separating small units from the battle fleet and having them pop up at spots like Australia—Stark felt it undermined American credibility—Admiral Richardson now insisted that the fleet would be a more powerful and convincing weapon if stationed on the West Coast instead of at Pearl Harbor. Hawaii lacked facilities to maintain it in a state of battle readiness, and one could not expect to bluff the Japanese. As we have already seen, Richardson was relieved of his command thirteen months into a tour of duty normally lasting twenty-four.[103]

America's later decision to separate about 40 percent of the Pacific Fleet from the main body and transfer it to the Atlantic in May 1941, just as negotiations between Nomura and Hull were thought to be reaching a critical stage, dumbfounded the British and shocked many closer to home. Years ago, Theodore Roosevelt had warned against any division of the battle fleet, and this was still the consensus of presidential advisers. Hull agreed that all major units should remain in the Pacific; Stimson, Stark, and Knox preferred to have the entire fleet in the Atlantic.[104] Either way, the fleet should not be divided. FDR's response was typical of his tendency in situations involving divided counsel. He compromised, and in so doing committed an irreparable blunder. Japan, perceiving the United States as overextended on two fronts, felt it could deliver a sudden blow that would send Washington reeling. As Admiral Nagano told an imperial conference on 5 November 1941, "The combined force of Great Britain and the United States has weak points. We are, therefore, confident of victory. We can destroy their fleet if they want a decisive battle."[105]

None of this would necessarily have been decisive had Roosevelt's mode of thought and action not aroused feelings of contempt. He had difficulty viewing any move on the part of Japan as anything but a step along the road to world conquest, and nearly all his statements referring to Japan were provocative, especially after 1937. When Assistant Secretary of State Pierrepont Moffat heard what the president had said in Chicago, he warned that such words would "drive us much further than we wish to go."[106] The effect was to kindle animosity on both sides of the Pacific and narrow the parameters of peace.

Given time and the democratic process, fighting words stimulated a demand for action. Congress and leaders of American opinion joined the chorus, and Roosevelt was forced to move from token measures to the brink. In February and April of 1941, he extended unneutral aid to China in the amount of $100 million. Subsequently, on 6 May, China qualified for equally unneutral outlays of Lend-Lease. Early in the year, American volunteers, soon to be known as the Fourteenth American Airforce or the Flying Tigers, began to fly for China under the direction of Claire Chennault. While more and more planes and fliers embarked for China, General Douglas MacArthur built a powerful striking force on Japan's southern flank in the Philippines. After the arrival of a small squadron of B-17 bombers in the spring, larger squadrons followed, with plans to send Super Flying Fortresses with a fifteen-hundred-mile operating radius and a capacity to reach either Osaka at full bombing strength or Tokyo partially loaded. In November, the *Washington Post* enumerated just how many planes Roosevelt had stationed in the Philippines, how many more would be there by December, and how many after six weeks. Air bases in Siberia, as well as possible operations in Indochina and Malaysia, were mentioned, and Roosevelt's assemblage of bombers was touted as the greatest in the history of the world.[107] Thus did the press convert a form of military insurance into an incendiary threat without a flickering of disapproval from the White House.

Weeks passed, the Hull-Nomura talks ground on, and American provocation accelerated. Not content to cut Tokyo's vital oil line, Roosevelt sent heavy tankers to within a few miles of Japanese territorial waters en route to the Soviet port of Vladivostok. Although Tokyo warned him that this would be considered an unfriendly act, it was allowed to proceed, and for good measure Secretary of the Interior Ickes fired a verbal fusillade at the Japanese, again with Roosevelt's blessing. As the emperor's navy began to move southward in early December, the president ordered three small armed vessels into the path of the oncoming fleet.[108] His intention may or may not have been to ensure American involvement before Japan could strike a knockout blow against the British. In any case, Churchill happened to be dining with American envoys Winant and Harriman when news of the Pearl Harbor attack arrived in London, and as he remembered it, "One might almost have thought they had been delivered from a long pain."[109]

In retrospect, it is interesting to imagine what might have happened had Western leaders approached the Orient with less smugness and complacency. In 1909, Wallace Irwin published *Letters of a Japanese Schoolboy* in which he depicted a thirty-five-year-old Japanese male who spoke pidgin English and was buck-toothed, smiling, courteous, and crafty. Thirty years later, Americans still perceived the Japanese as quaint little people devoted to cherry blossoms and Mount Fuji. Breckinridge Long recorded in his diary: "Hull believes in fighting [Japan]" and has told columnist Anne McCormick that it "would only be a naval war anyway." In the same vein, it was a truism to Hornbeck that "no oriental nation has today the perspective and the outlook of the more advanced Occidental nations, and Japan is no exception. . . . The Japanese state is still essentially feudal." Were the Nipponese not, after all, a race of copiers? *Time,* referring to them as "little yellow men," dismissed their 1940 austerity campaign as a matter of geisha girls being deprived of permanent waves; Premier Konoye was described as a "finicking hypochondriac" who spent each Sunday seated in lotus form; and the editors went out of their way to assure American readers that a naval blockade of Japan would quickly bring her to her senses— she was running scared. Half of Tokyo's homes were "built of wood and paper," and the populace was already feeling the pinch of "economic strangulation."[110]

This was the feeling which U.S. Commodore Glynn had carried with him to Tokyo almost a hundred years earlier: America "could convert their selfish government into a liberal republic in a short time." For a half dozen decades or more, such a conversion seemed well on the way to fulfillment. Grew told American audiences in 1939 that when the United States spoke, Japan listened. According to Stimson, it had been "historically shown that when the United States indicates by clear language and bold actions that she intends to carry out a clear and affirmative policy in the Far East, Japan will yield."[111]

Roosevelt, who felt the Japanese suffered from underdeveloped skulls, interested himself in a new method of genetic crossbreeding. Doubtless, too, he accepted his friend Arthur Murray's image of a people given to "truculence, impudence, trickery, swollen headedness, and brutality." Above all, he did not regard the Japanese people as formidable. A year after entering the White House, he was already describing his policy as one of babying them along. Hull and Stimson advised him that there could be no future in settling with Japan since China was the ultimate power in the Far East. He therefore rejected compromise, assuming all along that he could tighten the bit in Tokyo's mouth by means of economic coercion. The same summit conference that he so earnestly sought with Hitler and Mussolini was a conference which he spurned in connection with Konoye. In 1933, he told Stimson with honest conviction that trade sanctions would force Japan out of Manchuria. Likewise, in 1938, he cited figures on Tokyo's sinking gold reserve to assure the British that a moral embargo would bring Nippon to account.[112]

Given the failure of one economic measure after another, it is remarkable how few persons perceived war as a logical outcome of escalation. On this point, Senator Burton Wheeler of Montana was as confirmed in his thinking as was John Leighton Stuart, president of Yenching University. Maxwell Hamilton filed his lengthy report on sanctions in 1937 without including a single allusion to war, and Hornbeck never saw any binding tie between the oil embargo and all-out hostility (he later admitted his error). Roosevelt was surprised to find that the Nazi-Soviet Pact had no immediate impact on Japanese policy, but he never allowed this to influence his basic style of thinking. He continued to feel in October 1940, as he had felt the year before, that he could intimidate the Japanese by moving his fleet to Hawaii. And no amount of explanation on the part of Admiral Richardson could sway him. The fleet would simply blockade Japan or intercept a thrust against the Indies. As for Pearl Harbor, Marshall and Knox regarded it as well-nigh impregnable. Few believed Tokyo capable of dropping torpedoes in shallow harbor water. Nor was it expected that a way might be found to make bombers so fuel-efficient that they could fly fully loaded from Formosa to Clark Air Force Base in Manila. It was truly unimaginable that within a matter of days a torpedo would sink two of Britain's greatest prizes, the *Prince of Wales* and the *Repulse*, or that Singapore would be overrun from the one direction in which her guns could not be fired.[113] And so the war came.

Whether Roosevelt could have reached a viable settlement with Japan during an eight-year interval will probably never be known because he never made a determined effort to do so. It is curious, though, to reflect on what such a story may reveal about a president's intellectual power, his character, and his sensitivity. Precisely why did he resist every diplomatic initiative on the part of Tokyo? Can he be regarded as a fatalist or simply as unalterable in his opposition to Japan by 1935? And to what degree did he feel compelled to weigh impulses of conciliation and firmness against fluctuations in American public opinion? These are questions almost impossible to resolve with finality on the basis of the data presented thus far. The hope, however, is that additional light may be brought to bear upon them by examining the American approach to Europe during a similar period and under a similar set of circumstances.

4. From the Potomac to the Rhine

BEFORE surveying the broad spectrum of people and events which helped to shape American policy toward Europe, it may be helpful to pause for a moment and scan a map of the world as it appeared to Germany and Italy in the aftermath of World War I. As a prelude to the main line of argument, we may then go on to examine FDR's personal attitude toward several of the leading European protagonists.

It is important to recall that few observers in Britain, France, or the United States were prepared to defend the justice of the status quo as defined by the Treaty of Versailles.[1] Why, it was asked, should Germany remain disarmed when her neighbors refused to reduce their weaponry in accord with Woodrow Wilson's Fourth Point and defeated powers such as Hungary built up their stock in open violation of the treaty?[2] When Germany surrendered to the Allies, she had assumed that Wilson's peace program would be realized substantially intact.[3] It never was. In violation of Wilson's Fifth Point, and on the basis of self-serving allegations against German colonial administration, Berlin had been summarily stripped of all her colonies, four of which were in Africa: Togo, the Cameroons, Southwest Africa, and East Africa. In the Pacific, she lost New Guinea and Samoa; in Asia, Kiaochow, one of the most prosperous and progressive of colonial administrations. Together, the confiscated area had a population of 24.5 million.[4]

Memel was taken and given to Lithuania in 1923 despite local pleas for a plebiscite, despite an ethnically German and German-speaking population, and in spite of the fact that the surrounding area was bilingual and 90 percent Protestant. Furthermore, when Lithuanian rule resulted in discrimination against the minority, local appeals to the League Council generally failed.

Czechoslovakia represented another anomaly with its mixture of 3.25 million Germans, 2.25 million Slovaks, half a million Hungarians, half a million Ruthenians, 800,000 Poles and 7.5 million Czechs. Slovaks and Sudeten Germans had been transferred to the new state not only against their will but against the considered judgment of Secretary of State Lansing.[5] Berlin suffered special humiliation in this case, although Warsaw and Budapest were also outraged at the loss of their nationals. Persons of German ancestry who had once staffed the best regiments of the Austrian army were seldom admitted to the Czechoslovak tank corps or air force. In addition, neither they nor their Slovak compatriots could count on receiving justice in their native tongue. Chronic job shortages affected them twice as severely as other elements of the population; they received less in unemployment relief; local elections were arbitrarily suspended for periods of five or six years; and their constabulary was manned by Czechs. Predictably, when the Munich Conference caused Beneš to resign, Slovaks banded together and struck for autonomy, forcing the state to add a hyphen to its name (Czecho-Slovakia). Then, as Czech troops attempted to move against the Slovak government, Slovakia declared its independence. Hitler granted instant recognition, and Emil Hacha, who had succeeded Beneš, was now ready to throw himself into the arms of Germany. To be sure, he had little choice, but this was not an altogether unnatural alliance. The Slovaks of Bohemia had belonged to the Holy Roman Empire and German Confederation during the years 1815–66; and thereafter they had been linked with Austria until 1918. To many, therefore, a vote for Hitler was equivalent to a vote for the fatherland. Polish and Hungarian minorities returned just as readily to their former connection. And most leaders of the time, including those of Great Britain, could find little fault with Hitler's position. On 15 March 1939, the day Slovak officials asked for German protection, Chamberlain stated plainly in the House of Commons that he no longer regarded Britain's guarantee of Czech independence as binding because of "internal disruption."[6]

Another unnatural situation created by Versailles resulted from the award of German-speaking areas to Poland so that Warsaw might acquire a corridor to the sea. This drew criticism from a wide range of opinion. It perplexed international lawyers; it displeased Pierre Laval and Georges Clemenceau; and it ran counter to the instinct of British statesmen Churchill, David Lloyd George, Lord Cecil, Herbert Asquith, and Lord Halifax. Among the questioning voices were a good many from the United States. When Hitler invaded Poland, William C. Dennis, president of Earlham College, was speaking for not a few when he described the attack as an attempt to settle a "legitimate grievance." Hitler had offered a settlement that appeared fair and reasonable. Danzig, 95 percent German and under Nazi rule, was suffering from the competition of neighboring seaport Gdynia, recently built by Poland. Under Berlin's terms, it would return to Germany, along with two rail lines and an autobahn, all cutting across the Polish Corridor, while Warsaw would retain a rail line and highway as well as a free port in Danzig territory.[7]

Turning for a moment to Italy's case for investing Ethiopia, we see a dictator again making demands that were difficult for the Western world, in good conscience, to deny. Few European leaders perceived Mussolini as acting immorally when, after failing to obtain satisfaction from the League over the Walwal border incident, he took justice into his own hands. Ethiopia was anything but an upright member of the family of nations. As a slaveowning, slave-trading state that habitually foraged across its border for human plunder, it had reduced the population of adjacent Riffa from five hundred thousand to twenty thousand. It made raids not only into British Kenya, but also into Italian Eritrea and Somaliland, and after conquering Somalia and Sidamo it had become a menace to the Sudan and French Somaliland as well. Addis Ababa had not carried out the terms of its treaty of 1928 with Rome nor had it fulfilled its obligations as a member of the League. Aggression against defenseless neighbors and long-standing failure to pay League dues, not to mention its sale of slaves to Arabia in violation of another promise to the League, made it an unlikely plaintiff before the bar of world opinion.[8]

The principal question for each of the powers concerned was therefore one of strategy. London and Paris, committed to a defense of their respective positions in Africa, regarded Rome as a Johnny-come-lately. Yet over the years, they had struck bargains allowing Italy virtually unlimited sway in Ethiopia save for control of Lake Tsana, source of an important tributary to the Nile. London encouraged Rome to occupy Marsowa and approved an Italian protectorate negotiated with Emperor

Menelik. This ended unforgettably when Menelik tore up the treaty and inflicted savage retribution on Italian troops at the Battle of Adowa. Nevertheless, Italy refused to withdraw, and when France entered the picture in 1906, a third sphere of influence came into existence. By secret treaty signed in 1915, Italy obtained land claimed by Ethiopia along the border of Eritrea and Somaliland, with other nations to receive compensation elsewhere. But, in fact, the agreement was never kept. France and Britain engrossed large portions of German Africa, while Italy came away with considerably less.[9] In 1925, Rome agreed that London would control Lake Tsana in exchange for Italian dominance over southern and western Ethiopia preparatory to the forging of a rail link between Eritrea and Somaliland. Ten years later, France formally acquiesced in this arrangement in return for a covert promise of Italian backing against Germany. And by then, the London *Times* was contending that the League should invoke Article 19 to allow Italy greater scope in her own back yard, in particular a mandate or protectorate over Ethiopia.[10]

As is known, Haile Selassie made a skillful appeal to world opinion, leaving Rome in an awkward position, in effect unable to make good on its understanding with London and Paris. Mussolini, however, because of France's obvious interest in barring him from further expansion and Britain's desire to avoid an Italian wedge between the Sudan and British Somaliland, could accuse both countries of a double standard in their support of League sanctions. His argument fell on receptive ears. Churchill, for one, refused steadfastly to condemn Italy on moral grounds, and the Court of St. James's proved amazingly flexible in its willingness to strike a deal. In America, Congressman Emmanuel Celler of Brooklyn and Joseph Kennedy, chairman of the Securities and Exchange Commission, were not alone in reserving their most trenchant criticism for the French and British. It was at this point that Ambassador Long, aware that Mussolini was receiving "bad press," offered his "unofficial" plan providing for Italian acquisition of the Abyssinian lowlands, in addition to part of West Mia and the upland area extending as far as Addis Ababa. In short, the issue was widely regarded as one of expediency even though Roosevelt and Hull hewed publicly to their definition of morality and took comfort in the widespread belief that Italy's chances of military victory were slender.[11]

There is no reason to believe, incidentally, that FDR ever attempted to understand, much less sympathize with, German or Italian points of view. On the contrary, he seems to have harbored little admiration or respect for any of the European powers, Britain and France included. Indeed, the feeling was mutual, especially in the case of France.

If any group of people took pleasure in exposing the inherent weakness of Roosevelt's approach to world affairs, it was the French. Paris never troubled to apologize, as did London, for her failure to service the war debt. And if French officials annoyed Stimson with their rigid stance on naval ratios, they positively mortified the president by declaiming against his delegation at London and Brussels. Chamberlain is perhaps the one most frequently quoted as a critic of Roosevelt's propensity to rely upon words. However, it was the French who held him most strictly to account. No one lectured him as they did for misleading a chargé d'affaires in 1937. Nor, as we shall see, is there any parallel to the way in which Foreign Minister Georges Bonnet tore away the mask worn by Ambassador Bullitt at Pointe de Grave.[12]

Bittersweet ran the course of Franco-American relations throughout the entire period 1933–45. FDR might break with Republicans on the issue of debt default; he might incline to Paris on the armament question; he might intercede personally to prevent high duties on French wines. Still, the altercations were many and long. At the London Economic Conference, French delegation chairman Bonnet was said by Bullitt to be about "as cooperative as a rattlesnake." For months, Ambassador André de Laboulaye was persona non grata at the White House, and Roosevelt did not dispatch the customary presidential salute on Lafayette-Marne Day. Then, quite suddenly, as the autumn leaves began to fall, he invited Laboulaye to an intimate soirée and passed word that he hoped to teach Americans to drink less whiskey and more wine. By February 1934, the ambassador could suggest that no president since Washington had been more inclined "to favor France and what she stands for."[13]

The dominant strain in Roosevelt's thought is far from clear. Some felt that he entertained a certain sympathy for France while others were inclined to doubt it. We have only a handful of clues. But it would not be unfair to say that from youth to maturity he looked upon the darker side of *la mission civilisatrice*. Certainly, as the 1930s witnessed a bewildering succession of French ministries, one following the other like so many turns of a revolving door, any esteem he may have felt for the country of Vergennes seems to have vanished. He needed no reminder that Germany had marched into Austria at a time when France was

without a government. Nor can the Franco-American trade and stabilization agreements of 1936 be seen as specially indicative since 1936
was an election year. During the same period, French labor unrest became chronic, giving birth to the four-day week. There were riots, violent work stoppages, and a general sense of moral rot. When friends
urged Marshal Pétain to return to national politics from his post as
ambassador to Spain, he is said to have replied, "What would I do in
Paris? I have no mistress!"[14]

In letters to the White House, Ambassador Jesse Straus emphasized
France's intellectual and spiritual decay, as well as "rotten" business
conditions and a tax collection system which Roosevelt had already
taken to task in an editorial in 1925. The same old hacks continued in
the same time-honored posts, and the Chamber of Deputies was said to
resemble a disorderly nursery school. Labor Secretary Frances Perkins
returned from a transatlantic tour convinced that every Frenchman
hated every other Frenchman. Such impressions were more the rule
than the exception. Whether one spoke with Raymond Moley, Joseph
Davies, or Breckinridge Long, one heard the same story. Roosevelt
agreed with Chamberlain, who liked to say that France was "not able to
keep a secret more than half an hour, nor a government for more than
nine months." After burning his fingers on an offer to waive all interest
on the French debt, he never doubted that the Quai d'Orsay leaked like a
sieve. In 1937 he made sure that copies of his Quarantine Address
reached London and Geneva in advance of Paris. And if, in the eyes of
Morgenthau, France was the sick man of Europe, a fourth-rate power,
there was at least one member of the Foreign Service who viewed it as
"our great enemy in Europe." Roosevelt took special umbrage at the
treatment meted out to him by French newspapermen. Unlike the British, who never permitted anything to appear in public print without one
eye cocked across the Atlantic, the French criticized whenever and
whomever they pleased, and their opinion influenced neighboring countries. It was to be expected, for example, that the French delegate on the
Lytton Commission would be the one to speak out on behalf of Tokyo.
Britain showed as much willingness as any other country to recognize
Japanese gains in China, but with an important difference: publicly,
Lord Lytton always sided with Peking—and Stimson.[15]

Frenchmen may have made less of an effort to soft-pedal areas of
disagreement because they felt less dependent upon American naval
power. Whatever the reason, Roosevelt classed them as prima donnas,

applying the term indiscriminately to Bonnet, Giraud, Darlan, and de Gaulle. Bullitt warned him that he would dislike Bonnet when the latter came to Washington as head of the French mission, and there is little reason to doubt that he did. Bonnet's successor, Count René de Saint-Quentin, displeased him equally, and his recall was immediately requested. When Paris fell under the shadow of the Nazi war machine, Churchill, in the company of Premier Reynaud, begged FDR to declare that America would enter the war to save an ally or, at the very least, announce a policy of all aid short of troops. Instead, he refused even to let Reynaud make public the assurance that he was doing all in his power to supply the Allies with matériel. De Gaulle never forgot his visit to Reynaud on 10 June during the government's death struggle. Finding Bullitt there, he supposed that the ambassador was bringing encouragement for the future. "But no! He had come to say good-bye." Nothing could erase the impression "that the United States no longer had much use for France." Bullitt refused to accompany the government when it moved west, although a number of military experts, including de Gaulle, pronounced it defensible in its new location. A short while later, when Anthony Biddle (Bullitt's successor) submitted a formal report on the causes of the French surrender, he laid stress on moral deficiencies. Nowhere can one find a single reference to the prowess of Hitler's army.[16]

Very different was the tenor of America's relationship with England. The British not only made a relatively strong recovery from the Depression but demonstrated political stability and a high civic tone. Presidential advisers House, Dodd, and Stimson all favored some tie with Whitehall as a counterweight to German resurgence, and the prospect seemed fairly bright. Senate majority leader Joe Robinson volunteered his support in 1934 for an entente, and Downing Street extended a friendly hand.[17]

Roosevelt refused to be pressured, however. Within recent memory, William Hale Thompson had won election as mayor of Chicago by attacking school texts for their alleged pro-British bias. Senator Borah was throwing off anti-British alarums as regularly as a clock, and there was the matter of the unpaid war debt which heightened America's traditional aversion to "pulling British chestnuts out of the fire." Every British lecturer who traversed the country had the same question flung in his face (debts were later cited as justification for demanding British bases in the West Indies). In addition, two books reinforced the popular feeling against England: Whitney Griswold's *Far Eastern Policy of the United States* (1938) and Margaret Halsey's *With Malice toward Some* (1939). FDR thus took care to maintain a safe distance between himself and the Thames. When Austen Chamberlain knocked on the White House door in 1935, he found it tightly shut. Another British spokesman, Ambassador Halifax, faced rotten eggs on a trip to Detroit in November of 1941, when militant women calling themselves "American Mothers" raised placards inscribed "Remember the Burning of the Capitol." (Asked for his reaction, he replied imperturbably, "My feeling was one of envy that people have eggs and tomatoes to throw about. In England they are very scarce.") Finally, while Roosevelt was on the political tight wire between Destroyers for Bases and Lend-Lease, it had been Ambassador Lothian's great misfortune to be quoted as saying, "Well, boys, Britain's broke; it's your money we want." This remark earned him a swift reprimand from both sides of the Atlantic, and within weeks he fell victim to a fatal malady.[18]

As regards Roosevelt's personal opinion of England, he was not without a chip on his shoulder. As a boy at Groton, he had read the *Illustrated London News,* but at Harvard he was to be found heading a movement for Boer relief. On various trips to Great Britain, he came to know such friends of his parents as Sir Hugh Cholmeley, Henry Edwards, Lord Revelstoke, and the Duke of Rutland. At the same time, his comments on British society tended to be as critical as those of his wife: the English did not introduce people; their women made themselves up to look artificial; they displayed negative traits of selfishness, crabbedness, and arrogance. He once told Willkie that the English, as a group, were foxy and had to be dealt with in kind. Felix Frankfurter knew his man when he wrote FDR from London that he did not suppose his feeling about the local citizenry was "any warmer than yours."[19]

Whitehall touched a sensitive nerve early in the president's first term by suggesting that he send Treasury Secretary Morgenthau incognito to the Canadian border to hold talks with British finance counselor Leith-Ross. By way of reprisal, Morgenthau was pleased to report that when he received Sir Frederick Phillips, permanent under-secretary of the exchequer, he sat silently with his guest until the latter "broke down and talked first." Assistant Secretary of State Berle, invited to a British embassy dinner, took offense when the hostess spoke of being "out here" (in Washington). Six times, he countered by refer-

ring to being "out in London" until "finally the truth began to dawn."
He then informed the assembly of guests that they should not say "out
here" when they were in an American capital. According to his diary,
he continued to make himself disagreeable for the remainder of the
dinner. Nor was he alone. Eleanor Roosevelt had few positive things to
say about the Astors, who hosted her at Cliveden, and her backhanded
compliments to the queen bespeak a volume. Similarly, it was an obviously nervous president and first lady who entertained the royal couple at Hyde Park in 1939. Servants dropped trays of china and crystal,
while Roosevelt himself sat down on a set of glassware in the act of
pulling himself out of his swimming pool. At best, the relationship
was not an easy one.[20]

FDR's closest friend among representatives of the Court of St.
James's was Arthur Murray, whom he had known casually during World
War I. Murray had been active in British intelligence as well as parliamentary secretary to Sir Edward Grey. In 1936 and again in 1938,
Roosevelt hosted him, along with his attractive wife, Faith, for extended stays at the White House and Hyde Park.[21] But for the most
part, Anglo-American relations lacked substance and continuity. In
1933, Prime Minister MacDonald purred satisfaction at "two or three
days of friendly, pleasant conversations" in Washington. Within a matter of months, however, the spell was broken by unilateral action on
the part of Roosevelt, action that Permanent Under-Secretary Vansittart termed "nauseatingly disloyal." In 1934, several senators went so
far as to accuse the king of putting improper pressure on Poland to
award arms contracts to a British firm. Although Senator Nye dis-
claimed intent to give offense, his committee continued to release information embarrassing to the crown, action that seemed all the more
heinous because it presupposed the president's cooperation. Other irri-
tants included the Factor Case, the Persian Gulf Reservation, and
American opposition to increased tonnage for the Royal Navy. Whitehall killed an American proposal for arms control, and Roosevelt stood
in the way of British overtures to Tokyo.[22]

Though the White House made it clear that it placed a premium on
negotiation of a trade treaty with London, Downing Street demurred
since it had little to gain from the opening of imperial coffers. By 1936,
however, with FDR reasonably certain to win a second term, some agreement was seen as necessary to predispose the United States to pull its
weight against Germany. Chamberlain, as chancellor of the exchequer,

refused to consider a high-level conference with the president, but he did agree to send Murray with the understanding that, in return for trade benefits, U.S. neutrality laws would either be revised or circumvented and Britain would be able to tap American industrial power in time of war. Murray's trip paved the way for a follow-up visit in early 1937 by Walter Runciman, president of the British Board of Trade. Although Roosevelt insisted that America play host to a world conference on trade liberalization and arms reduction in contrast to Chamberlain's prefer- ence for a different approach, this preliminary period of testing soon passed, and especially after Munich progress on the trade pact came rapidly. Murray returned to the United States in October 1938, and the treaty was signed a month later. As expected, Britain made most of the concessions, although the number of tariffs reduced was less on her side than on that of the United States.[23]

By this time, the British were determined to do all they could to put their best foot forward. Eden, out of office, paid Roosevelt a call in December, and in June of 1939 the king and queen arrived, recalling a similar royal progress to France in 1903, one which helped to make possible the Entente Cordiale. The queen charmed all who turned out to see her, and Chamberlain felt the time was now ripe to send a larger number of lecturers to America to present the British point of view. One official suggested giving the United States a copy of the Magna Carta; another felt Britain might shake its reputation for effeteness by finding room on its embassy staff for a muscular soccer star (a "thirteen stone Rugger Blue"). Inasmuch as Roosevelt, on each of Murray's visits, had championed unrestricted Jewish access to Palestine, along with a trans-Jordan state for the Arabs, Churchill in turn stressed the need to concili-ate American Jewry. Above all, there was the feeling that whatever was done should be done subtly for, as Ambassador Lindsay had observed, Americans were best educated by their president, and Roosevelt's ad-ministration was "a horse that will run best when the spur is not used."[24]

A good deal of calculated give and take entered the picture. Hull asked Eden's advice on how to predispose American opinion, and Roosevelt selected Joseph Kennedy to replace Bingham in London. Bingham had earned a reputation for being more pro-British than any American am-bassador since Walter Hines Page, and a way had to be found to placate Irish sentiment. lt was thus that the Kennedy appointment, in conjunc-tion with Myron Taylor's mission to the Vatican, seemed to strike just the right chord. No particular harm was done, either, when Roosevelt engaged in some well-publicized scrapping with the Court of St. James's over the ownership of Canton and Enderbury islands, Pacific specks valued mainly for their potential as commercial airline bases. After threats and counterthreats, followed by the landing of "settlers" by both Britain and the United States, a plan for dual supervision was adopted in time for a gracious toast by FDR in the presence of King George VI.[25]

Undoubtedly, the Canton-Enderbury dispute represented more than a smoke screen for rapprochement. Roosevelt generally drove a hard bargain in his talks with Downing Street. At this juncture, he would like to have seen London turn back a number of former German colonies, and when this did not happen, he was delighted to take over British bases in the Caribbean. Later he cheerfully carried off South African gold deposits for "safe-keeping" and strove to strengthen the position of American oil companies against British competition. In essence this was the same FDR who, after failing to grasp the mantle of world leadership in 1933 and again in 1936–37, and who, after again coming up short on issues related to Palestine and the foreign debt, felt little compunction about undercutting imperial influence in India, Greece, and Italy. He even tried to appropriate Sherlock Holmes, Britain's celebrated detective figure, naming his secret service quarters at Shangri-La "Baker Street" and maintaining that Holmes's personal traits were characteristically American. According to Roosevelt's theory, the most famous sleuth in the world had most likely grown up in the American underworld before making a clean start in London.[26]

If, in reviewing FDR's relationship with Britain and France, one may conclude that there was no special warmth or understanding, this applies equally in the case of Germany, though with a curious added contrast between personal feeling and rhetoric on the one hand and diplomatic reality on the other. As a boy, he had mimicked the German accent and referred to Germans seated at the dinner table as swine, a habit borrowed from his Teutophobe parents. Traveling in Europe on official business during World War I, and finding German prisoners of war unintelligent looking, he had scorned them for atrocities, and repeated what he heard the king of England say: "In all my life I have never seen a German gentleman."[27] Time and again, he would find occasion to denigrate the land of Bismarck and to reiterate his impression of its sheeplike character.[28]

Beginning with presidential spokesman Joe Robinson's tongue-lashing of the Hitler regime, events on the surface indicated that Ger-man-American relations could well be summed up in Hull's phrase "criminations and recriminations." Roosevelt delayed several months in appointing an ambassador to Berlin (Hitler returned the compliment by delaying Dodd's reception); he refused to support the Four Power Pact; and Dodd led a boycott of the Nazi Party Congress at Nuremberg. Both president and secretary of state boasted of keeping Reichsbank Presi-dent Schacht standing while they pretended to be looking for papers (Dodd was later repaid in kind). FDR liked to parrot Schacht's heavy accent and tell about how Ambassador Hans Dieckhoff was received by Hull and Welles in stony silence in the aftermath of Anschluss. Over and over, he excoriated Germany for her form of government. In his book *On Our Way*, published in 1934, he blamed Berlin for the failure of disarmament, and this was mild alongside the ridicule he injected into press conferences. Hitler's secret service, he told reporters, was being followed by Goebbels's secret service, which was being followed by the Reichswehr's secret service, which was being followed by the Gestapo. One of his favorite stories was about how Germans were furiously at work building bomb shelters simply because they had been informed by their government that the French and Americans were doing it. The record reveals that in 1934 he tried to encourage a democratic entente composed of France and Britain just as he envisioned the need for pre-ventive war to nip German economic recovery in the bud. The follow-ing year, he proposed an economic blockade of Berlin to be enforced by troops. One notes also that he sent no greeting to Hitler on the German national holiday, calling instead for a moral embargo on arms.[29]

Throughout the years 1933–39, Morgenthau was encouraged to carry on what Hull termed a "personal war" against the Third Reich. Re-strictive economic measures, which began in 1935 with the withdrawal of most-favored-nation status, mounted with every German action that drew unfavorable comment in America. Remilitarization of the Rhine-land met with the levying of countervailing duties, Anschluss with refusal to deliver helium already purchased, Kristallnacht (the smashing of Jewish shop windows) with a 25 percent increase in comprehensive countervailing duty, the absorption of Czechoslovakia with still another restriction. Except for a brief respite in 1937, American economic repri-sals grew ever sharper until by March of 1939 they had reached the stage of virtually unrestricted economic warfare.[30]

Needless to say, the anti-Christian and anti-Semitic tone of Nazi

Germany aroused such universal revulsion in the United States that Roosevelt's public stance answered the call of politics as well as personal feeling. At the same time, rhetoric and trade restrictions do not represent the sum and substance of one nation's relationship with another. As we shall see, the gap between appearance and reality can be very wide indeed.

It is no exaggeration to say that, with the exception of the Four Power Pact, the keynote of Roosevelt's approach to Hitler beginning in 1933 was appeasement. Even before inauguration, he tried to persuade Ambassador Lindsay of the need for "political resettlement" to include compensated retrocession of the Polish Corridor to Germany. "I expressed liveliest alarm," reported the Scotsman, and "I think we shall hear no more about it." Lindsay proved to be mistaken, however. The president made no objection when Norman Davis held that "political appeasement" would be needed to arrange a lasting peace. On the contrary, he sent him posthaste to German officials, including the fuehrer himself, and tried to arrange tête-à-têtes of his own, first with Hitler and then with Foreign Minister von Neurath. He also tried, as we have seen, to gain entrée at the Wilhelmstrasse for Colonel House, though again without success. When Schacht came to Washington in May, Roosevelt reportedly told him that Hitler was the right man for Germany and that no one else could inspire such confidence.[31]

Although Dodd is remembered for his scathing criticism of the Nazi regime, his initial position was anything but firm. One of his first efforts was aimed at dampening the effect of anti-Nazi demonstrations in the United States. When a mock trial of "Civilization against Hitlerism" was held at Madison Square Garden, he moved to prevent a similar event from taking place in Chicago. This he did in return for Hitler's promise not to sponsor propaganda in the United States or jail his own citizens for more than twenty-four hours without warrant. On the issue of the German debt, as it affected American bondholders, he took a surprisingly soft line, voicing animus against his fellow citizens and sympathizing with von Neurath on the question of Germany's trade deficit. The United States was at least partially to blame, he conceded, on account of the Republican-sponsored Smoot-Hawley tariff. Similarly, after Hull framed a strong protest on German default and ordered it read aloud, he delivered it perfunctorily, turning on his heel in ten minutes. In the words of State Secretary von Bülow, Dodd appeared to act "with a bad conscience." Thereafter, he indulged in open criticism of Morgenthau and the president for anti-German trade legislation.[32]

It was not until the advent of the 1936 election that Dodd became stridently anti-Nazi—and then only to find himself completely isolated. Home on a prolonged leave of absence in the spring and summer, he was denied access to the president. Meanwhile, Counselor Mayer opened negotiations for a new commercial treaty behind his back in Berlin, and German leaders learned that he was becoming so unpopular at home that he would soon be recalled. No sooner had he taken leave of his post the following summer than American chargé Prentiss Gilbert saw fit to discard the embassy practice of boycotting Hitler's Nuremberg Congress. Dodd filed an angry complaint with the State Department; but the complaint leaked and Hull proceeded to defend Gilbert at a press conference. Gilbert, as if to confirm the underlying attitude of the administration, then raised his flag in honor of a visit by Mussolini to Berlin, the only nonfascist representative in the city to do so. Dodd, for his part, continued to speak out fearlessly against powers whose aim was to "destroy democracies everywhere." Such statements meant little, however, for when Germany demanded apologies Hull gave them. According to the secretary of state, Dodd could be safely ignored. He had gone "somewhat insane" on the subject of Jeffersonian democracy. Intelligent people regarded racial and religious animosity as a matter of "temporary abnormality," and it was best to think of the German people as in "the days of Schiller and Goethe." On 14 January 1938, Hull assured Dieckhoff further that Dodd "does not in his utterances represent the views of this government." Welles made no attempt to disguise his view of the professor as "incomprehensible," and FDR warned everyone to discount Dodd's prejudice against Hitler. Although Roosevelt encouraged Dodd to return to his post, he was summarily fired the moment he reached Berlin.[33]

Dodd's disgrace was but the culmination of a long series of events beginning in 1935, when Senator Borah emerged from a luncheon with the president to tell reporters that German rearmament was not likely to lead to war. The Versailles Treaty, in his opinion, stood in serious need of revision. Moreover, Hitler could not be blamed for his repudiation of the war guilt clause or territorial provisions. FDR told reporters that the senator had "an extremely interesting mind," and within two months, James Clement Dunn, chief of the Division of Western European Affairs, was on his way to Germany seeking contacts. In September of 1935, Roosevelt asked Samuel Fuller, an old business friend with powerful ties, to go to Berlin and ascertain Hitler's price for a comprehensive peace settlement. Two years earlier, Fuller had apprised the White House of Schacht's long list of accusations against German Jewry. Now he met Schacht at the American embassy, and after entertaining a demand for the return of German colonies, currency stabilization, and a new trade treaty with the United States, he journeyed to London for talks with Prime Minister Baldwin and Foreign Secretary Sir Samuel Hoare. As it developed, the British were not interested.[34]

When German troops entered the Rhineland on 7 March of the following year, Dodd and Mayer filed a formal protest, but the White House remained deafeningly silent amid French pleas for condemnation. Mrs. Roosevelt went so far as to write an editorial condoning the occupation. Two weeks later, after a speech by John Foster Dulles calling for revision of the Versailles Treaty, the State Department opened a new decimal file significantly labeled "World Program." Roosevelt had decided to seek liberalized world trade and multilateral disarmament at a conference to be held in the United States (or, less preferably, abroad) during 1936. As part of the arrangement, he would promise to cancel war debts and reduce the American tariff. Fuller therefore returned to Germany to advocate, among other things, a British scheme for long-term leases in Africa, which would be offered in lieu of outright return of colonies. Following talks with Hitler and Schacht, of which Dodd remained ignorant, Fuller again crossed the Channel to see "personages of great importance." Once more, Britain's foreign secretary held aloof, though this was rather to be expected. Ambassador Bingham had already made known Roosevelt's desire to sponsor a disarmament conference and been advised that the time was not ripe.[35]

Roosevelt's basic strategy during the interval 1935–37 is vividly reflected in the thoughts and words of his lieutenants. Davis, who advocated a secret understanding between the United States, Britain, and Germany, urged his British friends to sit down with Hitler and arrive at "a really constructive settlement." Likewise Bullitt, incensed at the danger of international communism, expressed himself in favor of Franco-German rapprochement and, after lengthy talks with Roosevelt at Warm Springs, returned to his embassy in Paris determined to strengthen Hitler's hand against Stalin and pressure the French into talks with their traditional enemy.[36] The year 1936 was also one in which General Motors Vice President James D. Mooney made his first recorded appearance on the diplomatic scene as a luncheon guest at the American embassy in London. Mooney would soon take Fuller's place and conduct another secret mission to Germany on behalf of the president. This was also the year in which John Cudahy, American ambassador to Poland, wrote Roosevelt that Germany should be compensated for shutting down her arms industry and that this should be in the form of a "dramatic stroke for the enhancement of German world prestige." Roosevelt replied: "Your conclusions go along very largely with mine." Anxious to convince Germany that he would seek the return of her colonies if she would back a world conference on trade and disarmament, FDR had Dodd put the American proposal directly. In the meantime, Cudahy reported on how difficult Poland was making it for German residents of Upper Silesia (they faced confiscatory taxation and loss of jobs).[37]

Although the president and his secretary of state continued to feel that arms and economics were interrelated and should therefore be addressed at the same time, they were open to suggestion. Morgenthau, who favored a conference on arms alone, was permitted to approach Britain independently, but when Whitehall answered in the negative, FDR began to concentrate on the economic and legal side of the question. He also shifted from proposing Washington as a conference site to the idea of arranging a meeting at sea. Arthur Krock was encouraged to float a trial balloon in the *New York Times* hinting that the president might ask leaders of six or seven countries to attend a round-table convention in the Azores. The idea proved unpopular and was soon disowned by the administration with Roosevelt returning to his original proposal for a summit meeting in the capital. At the same time, he began to consider the possibility of a gathering of major powers to revise the Versailles Treaty and strip the League of its power to resort to sanctions.[38]

Stalemate flowed from a confluence of irreconcilables. Germany would not attend any meeting without assurance of tangible gain, and since concessions to Berlin would fall most heavily upon London, Chamberlain began to dig in his heels.[39] Individual Britons such as George Lansbury and Arthur Salter might encourage FDR to lead the way toward more equitable access to the world's markets and raw materials; but it was quite another matter to get action from Downing Street. Foreign Secretary Samuel Hoare imitated Hull in speaking of

"Have-Not" nations. Still, when the time came, British leaders stood in Roosevelt's way, insisting upon Anglo-American consultation while engaging Berlin in separate talks. By January of 1937, there were rumors of an impending cut in Britain's tariff. International consortiums, it was bruited, might also be encouraged to develop parts of Africa. Germany would receive the Cameroons outright, while other colonies, with the exception of French North Africa and British South Africa, would go into some kind of common pot. To Hitler, of course, this was hardly an inducement. Membership in consortiums held little attraction per se, and he could not accept the idea of the League controlling his access to raw materials. Would the British, he asked, turn over their portion of New Guinea if the Dutch volunteered to do likewise? Schacht reminded the treaty powers of FDR's promise on debts as well as trade and agreed with the president on the need for a new, more flexible organ of world cooperation.[40]

In the end, talk remained talk. If Paris promised substantial cooperation on the colonial issue, London refused. Salmon O. Levinson, a Chicago lawyer, fancied that England might seize upon the coronation of a new king in 1937 as a convenient pretext for change. After discussing the possibility with Hull and Roosevelt, he sailed for England, only to find upon arrival that Eden could not be reached. In the meantime, Chamberlain resorted to yet another delaying tactic, the delegation of Belgian premier Paul Van Zeeland to serve as a roving ambassador charged with testing the climate for Roosevelt's world conference.[41]

FDR, who never ceased to pursue Hitler, kept insisting that Britain take the lead in offering economic concessions sufficiently attractive to make war seem disadvantageous. Thus, when Schacht published an article in *Foreign Affairs* (January 1937) presenting the case for German claims, Dodd told the fuehrer that he thought it an able piece. Joseph Davies made two visits to Berlin for confidential talks, one in January, the other in June; and after the United States joined the International Committee on the Problem of Access to Raw Materials, Germany began singing the president's praises. According to Schacht, Roosevelt had become one of the world's great statesmen.[42]

In September, Under Secretary Welles traveled to various European capitals exclusive of Berlin and returned to argue that the United States should support Hitler's demand for colonies as well as "European adjustments." Only with a satisfied Reich, went the argument, could one settle with Italy. This was the logic of the so-called Welles Plan, submitted to Roosevelt on 6 October, just as Dodd was about to be dismissed. Emphasizing the injustice of Versailles and the need to adjust access to raw materials, it left little doubt of Roosevelt's basic orientation. Whatever doubt there may have been evaporated altogether when Ambassador Bullitt completed Welles's itinerary in mid-November. If important concessions could not be wrung from England, perhaps they might be found elsewhere. Skeptical about the chance of winning Hitler without cutting into Czech and Polish boundaries, Roosevelt sent Bullitt to Warsaw and Berlin. Several days of talks followed, including five conferences with Foreign Minister Josef Beck centering on what concessions the Poles might make and what Warsaw might gain at the expense of Prague. Beck described Czechoslovakia as a French satellite in central Europe and recalled that there were three hundred thousand Poles in the district of Teschen alone. While a sympathetic Bullitt had himself photographed marching beside German Luftwaffe Chief Hermann Göring in a Warsaw parade, Baruch was in Paris speaking with the Polish ambassador about the state of Poland's economy and the danger facing Polish Jews.⁴³

On reaching Germany, Bullitt plunged into talks with von Neurath, Schacht, and Göring. He was consulted by the latter on steps preparatory to German annexation of the Sudetenland, and the French ambassador in Berlin quoted him as saying that the time was ripe for Paris to talk seriously with Hitler. Foreign Secretary Halifax's visit would not suffice, according to the American; concessions must be made to bring about European unity. Schacht and Göring agreed that the Polish Corridor might stand if a way could be found to bridge it and unite Danzig with East Prussia. In addition, Hitler would not require the return of German East and Southwest Africa if he could count on receiving compensation elsewhere, as, for example, in the Belgian or Portuguese empire. Göring made a special point of deploring the state of German-American relations. With some states, he pointed out, Germany had good relations, with others bad relations, but with the United States no relations. Trade between the two countries was ceasing to have any importance. Bullitt was given to understand that Hitler had no designs on Alsace and would conclude an offensive and defensive treaty with France the moment his colonial demands were met. At this juncture, an exultant Welles congratulated Bullitt, "I wish to the good Lord that during the past years we had been getting this type of information from Germany," and Ambassador Dieckhoff, who had been in regular touch with Roosevelt, was assured that the Quarantine Address did not apply to Germany.[44]

It is hard to avoid the conclusion that Roosevelt thought he saw a way to steal the lead from Paris and London. Halifax's conferences with Hitler, Göring, and Goebbels in the fall of 1937 had gone well enough for him to declare on his return to England: "Now that the door has been opened, it will remain open." Lord Cecil, whose proclivity for meeting Nazi demands was well known, had won a Nobel Peace Prize, and Halifax's trip to Berlin inspired a similar excursion on the part of French Foreign Minister Delbos, who went to Whitehall in the company of Premier Chautemps. One did not have to be clairvoyant to perceive that the democracies were about to close with the dictatorships.[45] FDR simply wanted to be on deck.

One should not be unduly disconcerted, at this stage, by the direction of New Deal policy, however much it may have belied official rhetoric. Hoover, Stimson, Dulles, Wilson, and Borah all endorsed similar goals, though with perhaps a different choice of tactics. There was, moreover, a large company of Democrats in basic agreement: House, Bullitt, Davies, Bingham, Long, Biddle, Welles, Kirk, Moffat, Feis, and Frankfurter.[46] Davis had been arguing for appeasement of the Nazi regime since 1933, while Berle, along with other liberals, continued well into 1938 to favor a Greater Germany alongside a reconstituted Austro-Hungarian Empire. To this roster may be added the names of British leaders Lloyd George, Winston Churchill, and Viscount Samuel, not to mention Léon Blum of France. With the London *Times* patently soft in its line and Walter Lippmann proposing changes in July 1938 at the expense of Czechoslovakia, FDR was, as always, au courant. What is surprising is not so much his basic underlying policy as the appearance he managed to convey of checking dictators at every turn. Prominent on the record is a string of presidential speeches between 1935 and 1937, all of which decried autocracy and aggression, followed by the Evian Conference on aid for refugees in 1938. When Ambassador Kennedy made a speech that smacked of appeasement, Arthur Krock was instantly reassured by the White House that it implied no shift in America's basic position.[47]

Joseph Kennedy's appointment to the Court of St. James's may be described as something of a double coup. Not only did Roosevelt alleviate Irish opposition to Anglo-American rapprochement; he landed an articulate spokesman for compromise on a spot regarded as crucial. One may assume that Kennedy, who wished to give Germany a free hand in the Balkans, lost no time pressing for economic concessions at the expense of England. Symbolically, his appointment was announced the same day as that of like-minded Hugh Wilson, who took Dodd's place in Berlin at the recommendation of Bullitt. London, for its part, proceeded to make an equally logical choice of envoys. Both Lothian and his successor, Lord Halifax, had conferred with Hitler, and though the former may have been tapped for his personal rapport with the president as well as the compatibility of their views on free trade and India, his strong advocacy of concessions to Hitler qualified him all the more. Certainly, the fact that he favored retrocession of Memel, the Corridor, and Danzig (especially after the Polish construction of rival port Gdynia) did not disqualify him.[48] The year of Czechoslovakia's mortal wounding, 1938, was thus the year of Kennedy, Wilson, and Lothian, all three chosen by or for FDR.

On 11 January, Roosevelt sounded Britain on the Welles Plan, which by then had undergone three revisions.[49] Welles's solution was twofold. It called first for a conference of representative neutrals to frame new principles of international law. These would include guaranteed access to raw materials; methods by which international agreements might be "pacifically revised"; and the removal of "inequities . . . reached at the termination of the great war." Second, there was to be a convention of major powers in Washington to implement recommendations and orchestrate disarmament. To Chamberlain, bent upon cutting his losses by direct negotiation with Hitler and Mussolini, this idea could not have been very attractive. Roosevelt was proposing arms reduction, something problematical in the extreme, and he was doing so when the British had just begun to mount a credible military program. Most officials in London shuddered at the prospect of returning to Versailles. To some, the plan appeared vague, to others "fatuous," to still others a "preposterous effusion" that would invite disdain. Chamberlain therefore declined. To be sure, FDR could not have placed much confidence in his own proposal, for after Foreign Secretary Eden persuaded the prime minister to reconsider and Chamberlain flashed a green light on 20 January, Welles's scheme was postponed five times *by the White House*—thrice before Eden resigned, twice after, and the last time (13 March) indefinitely. Bullitt's letter of 20 January, addressed to the president, may suggest some of the reasoning: "I remember talking over with you the idea that you might call a world conference in Washington to discuss international law. I feel now that, while such a conference would be acceptable to American public opinion, it would seem an escape from reality to the rest of the world. It would be as if in the palmiest days of Al Capone you had summoned a national conference of psychoanalysts to Washington to discuss the psychological causes of crime."[50]

Roosevelt's uncertainty did nothing to alter the course of French and British policy, nor is there anything to indicate that he really cared. A Welles memorandum dated 1 February pledged the United States to contribute to "world appeasement of a major character," and the under secretary told French chargé Henry that Eden's resignation opened the door to a more realistic policy. Norman Davis advised Lord Astor along similar lines: it was "most important for Germany and England to get together" as long as it did not involve "too much sacrifice of other peoples. . . . Unfortunately there is a great prejudice in this country against Germany." Breckinridge Long, incidentally, had just finished reading *Mein Kampf*, noting that it was "eloquent in opposition to . . . exponents of communism and chaos." This was the same man who shortly became assistant secretary of state and took charge of Jewish refugee immigration. It should also be noted that Roosevelt's friend Lothian was reading *Mein Kampf* with similar approval, regretting only that in England no more than a third of the book could be obtained in published form. Given the prevalence of such feeling, one could expect almost anything—except firmness. Bullitt advised Roosevelt that there was no way of saving Czechoslovakia so long as Russia refused to raise a hand, and in February the American ambassador to Prague took the astounding position that the Czechs had nothing to fear from Germany.[51]

One practical way Roosevelt could contribute to appeasement was to approve de jure recognition of Italian rule over Ethiopia. On 22 January, he let it be known through Welles that though he would regard recognition as a bitter pill, it was one he wished to have Britain and the United States swallow together. When Lindsay asked for a statement in unequivocal terms, Welles responded that the president considered Britain "entirely right." At this point, the administration temporized, insisting that FDR had never meant to express an opinion about right versus wrong. Welles would say only that his chief viewed the British decision as "wise." Ten days before the actual signing of the Anglo-Italian Treaty, William Phillips, who succeeded Long in Rome, had introduced Italian officials to the British diplomatic community in such a way as to restore the two sides to speaking terms after a long hiatus, and Roosevelt further risked his liberal reputation by proclaiming "sympathetic interest" in the treaty once signed. French Ambassador Saint-Quentin interpreted "sympathetic interest" to mean American moral support and advised the Quai d'Orsay that Britain had pocketed such support several days in advance. He noted, too, that all this occurred during Hull's absence from Washington when Welles, an open supporter of Chamberlain's policies, was in ad hoc charge at State.[52]

As usual, FDR contrived to display one side of his political nature to foreigners while presenting quite another to voters at home. For the record, he refused to recognize Italy's conquest of Ethiopia (Mussolini, also for the record, ceased speaking to Phillips). Nevertheless, he discretely assured Rome that if the United States were to host a world peace conference, Mussolini could expect "a reasonable adjustment of the concessions to which he felt Italy was entitled." Toward the end of 1938, Welles held lengthy talks with the French on how they might satisfy Italy's appetite for expansion. Again, one should not be surprised. In 1935, when the duce had first moved decisively against Haile Selassie, we have seen how Long offered American support for an arrangement that would have compromised Roosevelt's definition of international morality. After clearing it with the White House and hearing from Hull that it sounded "extremely interesting," Long had presented it to Mussolini. As we know, nothing came of it, and Hull wrote him that he was glad he had offered the plan in his "private capacity"; it was "important that no impression be created that such proposals are under consideration by this government."[53]

The gap between appearance and reality widened in March, one week after Germany's absorption of Austria. Saint-Quentin spoke with Roosevelt at the White House and reported that the president, sporting yellow shoes ("souliers jaunes"), had said that Czechoslovakia would not be able to resist German pressure without British and Russian aid. Since, in the president's opinion, such aid would not be forthcoming, France had no alternative besides rapprochement with Germany. By this time, Paris had begun to stiffen with respect to German designs on central Europe—accounting, perhaps, for Saint-Quentin's reference to yellow shoes. According to the ambassador, the State Department was in full accord with the White House in regarding Czech acquiescence as "inévitables dans un avenir très proche" (inevitable in the very near future). American newspapers continued to depict France as a psychological invalid, and Bullitt met quietly with Bonnet to urge that France lower Prague's expectations.[54]

Perhaps the most striking thing about Roosevelt's posture in March, April, and May of 1938 is the transformation that it underwent in June. Suddenly, as if to fall in with the new mood of Paris, he swung like a pendulum. All at once, he was praising France for backing Czechoslovakia against a country that understood "only force." Making like a boxer, he said to Saint-Quentin, "This is how one must speak to them." France had no choice, he said, but to "risk war" with a nation which, if unchecked, would go from one conquest to another. "If France goes down," he added, "quite obviously we shall go down with her" ("si la France sombraient, bien évidemment, nous sombrerions avec elle"). Saint-Quentin recalled that these words "were spoken with an air of deep conviction." By this time, Assistant Secretary Messersmith and his group at State were as one with Stimson Republicans in condemning Anschluss. *Foreign Affairs* began to wage an all-out campaign against revision of the Versailles settlement; interventionist sentiment rose rapidly; and Roosevelt, with one eye fixed on the barometer of opinion, began to voice threats, both in Canada and the United States, of American aid in a war against Germany.[55]

There were the standard elements of contradiction. Kennedy sought out German ambassador Herbert von Dirksen in London and assured him that he supported not only Germany's racial policy but also her economic goals in eastern and southeastern Europe. Roosevelt, Kennedy insisted, was not anti-German; he simply never saw honest reports from those who had been to Germany. He himself would like nothing better than to visit Berlin to express support for the German position on colonies. Two weeks before the Munich Conference, Roosevelt's envoy actually requested a conference with the fuehrer.[56]

In the meantime, the most authoritative American voice in Berlin, that of Ambassador Hugh Wilson, was criticizing Beneš for duplicity and delaying tactics. Wilson went on to suggest that a democratic defense of Czech borders was unrealistic. During the first week of August he gave force to his words by flying to Warsaw and Prague in a Messerschmitt fighter on loan from the German air force. While in Prague, he attended a British luncheon honoring Runciman, saw President Beneš for an hour and a quarter, then met with Foreign Minister Kamil Krofta. In no uncertain terms he told Beneš not to count on backing from the United States since interventionist sentiment existed only along the Atlantic coast. Such, unfortunately, were the facts of life, and Czechoslovakia would be wise to soothe Germany by scrapping her defensive pact with Russia. This meant surrendering those areas of the Sudetenland where, by Beneš' own admission, German minorities were the object of shabby treatment. In short, Wilson's goal appears to have been the same as Bullitt's. Each sought to compose Poland's differences with Germany by seeing to it that both nations shared in the spoliation of Czechoslovakia. Colonel Truman Smith, U.S. military attaché in Berlin, would presently be discussing with his Polish colleague which portions of Czechoslovakia, excluding those already awarded to Germany, were to go to Hungary, which to Poland (the assumption being that Slovakia would become independent).[57]

Just how difficult it was for Roosevelt to operate on two levels, one rhetorical, the other practical, may be inferred from Franco-American reaction to an address given by Ambassador Bullitt at Pointe de Grave, burial site of Americans fallen in World War I. The date was 4 September. Foreign Minister Bonnet, who shared the platform and knew that everything the American would say had been expressly authorized by Roosevelt at the request of the Quai d'Orsay, listened intently: "If war were to break out in Europe," said the ambassador, "no one could rule out the possibility of American involvement" ("si la guerre éclatait en Europe, personne ne pourrait déclarer ou prédire si oui ou non les Etats-Unis seraient entraînés dans une telle guerre"). These were fighting words, of course, with the result that Roosevelt's isolationist critics were brought immediately to full cry—and Roosevelt himself to rapid retreat. To the disgust of French observers, Bullitt was soon instructed to say that his remarks had been misinterpreted. The president went on record as saying that it was 100 percent incorrect to associate the United States with Britain and France. At which point Paris hardly knew where to turn. Bonnet later argued that dead silence from the United States would have been less damaging than Roosevelt's intermittent backing for the defense of Czech borders. France might in that case have chosen to support Beneš on her own. But to have gained a promise of American support, to have cited its value in debate with French appeasers, and then to have it withdrawn was utterly self-defeating. Still fresh in the memory of the foreign minister was a moving transatlantic radio appeal he had made on 4 July, and which had brought a glowing tribute from the White House.[58]

Adding to the disillusionment was a visit by French Senator Robert Thoumyre to the White House on 1 September. Roosevelt had told Thoumyre in strict confidence that Paris could count on Washington for everything but troops and loans; France and Britain had enough credit; and money would not be a problem—the United States would honor its commitments. Naturally, this was taken as confirmation of what the president had been saying on and off for months to other Frenchmen including Bonnet, Saint-Quentin, and de Tessan, French undersecretary for foreign affairs: namely, that in case of war with Germany, ways could and would be found to evade the Neutrality Act; the United States would not remain on the sidelines as she had done in 1914–17. FDR had sent similar messages to Britain through Canadian Governor General Lord Tweedsmuir, as well as via Ambassador Lindsay to Prime Minister Chamberlain. Whitehall was of one mind with the Quai d'Orsay in regarding FDR's authorization of the Bullitt speech as a "great help" and indicative that the United States would be "fully with us."[59]

It was for this reason that London and Paris were confounded when Roosevelt, in answer to domestic criticism, returned to the language of appeasement. Most Americans, in the absence of strong executive leadership, were content and even pleased when their president whiplashed the dictators rhetorically, just as they would have looked askance at movement in the direction of accommodation.

Bullitt now began to say that the chance of American entry into a war with Germany must be liberally discounted since there would be no way to negate the Neutrality Act. Welles sailed to Europe to warn the French in person that as American opinion was 80 percent opposed to intervention, France, in time of war, would not even receive planes that had been ordered in May and for which it had already paid. Senator Pittman, regarded by the French as close to the president ("une grande autorité"), blasted all hope of collaboration in a speech given on 17 September, and although Morgenthau continued to confer secretly with French treasury agents on how to evade various provisions of the Neutrality Code, Roosevelt began to position himself carefully to share in the credit for Munich. The moment it became clear that England sought to satisfy Hitler at Czechoslovakia's expense, Kennedy and Chamberlain commenced confidential talks. The ambassador saw the prime minister on 17 and 19 September, twice in a single day. He spoke with Cadogan on 21, 23, and 24 September. On the twenty-fourth, he phoned Hull to report: "Halifax will call me when they finish the conference . . . we have been working until three or four o'clock in the morning." More meetings with Halifax followed, and on the twenty-seventh he cabled Welles, "There was a cabinet meeting at nine and that is what kept me so long." The next day, after being rung up by Chamberlain, he informed Hull that Hitler's reply had been received and read in Parliament. At long last, with everyone obviously relieved, he could get six hours of sleep, something he had not had for seven days.[60]

Roosevelt's only regret was that he had not assumed a more prominent role in the Munich settlement. Bullitt had told him that if an impasse ever developed on the matter of the German minority in Czechoslovakia, he should call the principal powers to a Hague conference attended by American representatives and recommend a Czech plebiscite, which would appease Germany while saving face for France. During the third week of September, he told White House guest Léon Jouhaux, president of the French labor organization, that although he could not summon a conference, he was prepared to participate in one if called by France or England. When this startling proposal found its way to the press, threatening political damage to the White House, Hull accused Jouhaux of failure to comprehend: "In the first place, the President of no country gives out important official information in that manner to an individual citizen and, in the second place, unless Mr. Jouhaux thoroughly understands English, it would be well to verify his version of the conversation before repeating it." As in similar situations involving Konoye and Nomura, Jouhaux more than likely understood perfectly well. It is no coincidence that at about the time of the interview in question, Roosevelt saw Lindsay and told him—he realized he would be impeached, he said, if word got out—that he would be the first to cheer if French and British pressure on Czechoslovakia bore fruit; should the Western powers call a frontiers conference he would attend in person as long as it was not held in Europe. A week later, still seeking Hitler's favor, he considered making public a statement offering his good offices for revision of the Versailles Treaty.[61]

Ultimately, Roosevelt never achieved the status he sought as architect of Munich. Although he issued an appeal for peace as prescribed by Bullitt and followed through on the idea of appealing for a conference of "all the nations directly interested" at "some neutral spot," the final conference was held in unneutral Germany. In addition, Czechoslovakia, the most interested of all parties, was not invited. No American representative attended; there was no plebiscite; and, to Roosevelt's dismay, Chamberlain's appeal reached the dictators before his own. Daladier and Chamberlain commended him for his instrumentality and Morgenthau tried to smooth his ruffled feathers over the phone: "I want to be the first to congratulate you." This, of course, was not the accolade he sought, and when he discovered that Phillips had been away from Rome, delaying delivery of a presidential message to the duce by nineteen hours, he dispatched a stinging reprimand. Phillips, offering to resign on the spot, argued lamely that the Italian foreign ministry, if not the duce, knew that such a message had arrived before British ambassador Lord Perth made his decisive call. Fortunately for the American ambassador, FDR relented and reassured his envoy that misunderstandings with the press were clearing up except with "cads like Arthur Krock"; he was "not a bit upset over the final result."[62]

Just how resigned Roosevelt really was is open to question. American opinion continued to run 60 percent in favor of Munich, and Krock was duly reminded that the president had been anything but a passive spectator, having tried to avert war by inviting Hitler to a meeting at sea (Krock later learned that FDR's invitation had been delivered to Foreign Minister Joachim von Ribbentrop by the young Hohenzollern prince Louis Ferdinand, who had stayed at the White House).[63] Saint-Quentin was issued a time chart containing data clearly intended to document the case for Roosevelt's importance. Similarly, Hugh Wilson was directed to make thorough inquiry into the exact sequence of events leading to Hitler's decision. As it developed, the fuehrer, like the duce, had acted without immediate reference to Washington. FDR's gestures had, in other words, come after the event. He had cabled Chamberlain "Good Man" as the latter set out to return to Germany on Hitler's terms, much as he had applauded him on the aftermath: "We in the United States rejoice with you and with the world at large." In another belated sequence, Bullitt rushed to Bonnet's apartment in Paris with tears in his eyes and flowers under his arm, while Wilson, the same day, inspected a German factory in the company of Lindbergh and flew back to Berlin in a big four-motor Condor Focke Wulf doing elaborate dips and turns. That evening, a great dinner was given for Lindbergh at the American embassy at which Göring presented America's aviation ace with the Service Cross of the Order of the German Eagle with Star. It is true that about a month later, following the violence of Kristallnacht,

Wilson was recalled from Berlin, but this was effected without forceful protest.[64]

Needless to say, world opinion soon transmuted Munich into a symbol of capitulation, and the president could be genuinely grateful that he had not jockeyed more successfully for a major share of the credit. With new currents in the air, he could fashion a new policy, which, in fact, is what he proceeded to do, incrementally and with all requisite skill, though not with absolute finality until many months after the outbreak of war. On the one hand, he instigated a sweeping verbal attack on Munich by surrogates such as Baruch and Ickes. Baruch, who published an article in *Current History*, appeared before the Senate Foreign Relations Committee, while Ickes's speech "Esau, the Hairy Man" so enraged the Germans that they spoke of breaking off relations. On the other hand, Roosevelt refused four requests from the Polish ambassador for a face-to-face conference, and as late as 28 January 1939, Welles addressed the New York Bar Association to denounce the Versailles Treaty as an unjust structure whose provisions for amendment had never been properly utilized. Meanwhile, FDR managed handily to keep the confidence of the interventionists by engaging in secret negotiations aimed at making a dead letter of the neutrality legislation. As soon as Morgenthau finished with French treasury officials, he entertained Arthur Murray at Hyde Park for a week-long discussion on how he might furnish Britain with war matériel. Downing Street wanted to know which minerals and aircraft parts would be forthcoming from the United States because new plants had to be designed with this in mind. How did he expect to supply "partly finished basic materials" for twenty to thirty thousand planes? Would he include plates for wings, castings for engines, cylinder blocks, and spark plugs? Would it be realistic to count on some form of Canadian-American aircraft production?[65]

As the new year wore on and the winds of opinion began to shift once again, both at home and abroad, Roosevelt returned foursquare to the theme of rapid American involvement in a war pitting democracies against dictatorships. He also, after Germany's swift incorporation of Memel and Prague, renewed his call for containment: the British must stand for the status quo in Poland; they must guarantee Romania and Greece. Saint-Quentin heard from Hull that Americans were now extremely anxious to help Paris, as each new act of German aggression affected the security of the United States. The president spoke optimistically of revising the Neutrality Law and asking the dictators to state their intentions before the entire world. France, then, was again encouraged to stake her future on American credibility.[66]

The reader will recall dealing at length in Chapter 3 with the kind of assurances offered to London and Paris in connection with the Far East. Here, it will be seen that Roosevelt went far along the same path in his campaign to strengthen democratic resolve against Germany. At a press conference on 14 April, he strongly implied that American involvement in any European conflict of significant scale would be inevitable. And so it seemed. France, after agreeing to fight for the Versailles frontier, was promised advanced models of American aircraft. In the meantime, Polish diplomats, both in Washington and Warsaw, were steeled to intransigence on questions affecting Danzig and the Corridor. Bullitt told them the United States would be in the war, if not immediately, then surely at the finish. In May, Roosevelt assured Beneš there was no question the United States intended to enter World War II, and Bullitt repeated this to British colleagues in Paris: the United States would join the war "almost immediately." Still again, in talks with London *Times* correspondent Arthur Willert, FDR minimized the importance of the Johnson Debt Default Act, painting a picture of the American fleet patrolling the eastern Atlantic and Mediterranean with limitless opportunities for a shooting incident. Willert thus gained the distinct impression that Roosevelt "would not be sorry to see the United States in the war" and would "even help to bring . . . about" the necessary circumstances.

Evidence of this same sense of a U.S. commitment can be found in North America as well. Canada's governor general had held this belief since 1937. "The general view," said Tweedsmuir, "is that they would be in the next day." It was a common opinion. Former First Lord of the British Admiralty Duff Cooper concluded after coming to America in early 1939 that, in spite of isolationist sentiment, the United States would pitch into the fray "within three weeks." FDR's promise of material aid was seen as enough in itself to ensure U.S. entry: "Half-in will soon mean all-in." To George VI, who stopped at Hyde Park in June, the president spoke of taking over British bases and having the American navy range as far as a thousand miles in search of enemy submarines to sink. The United States, he volunteered, would be at war with the first bombing of London.[67]

France was receiving similar assurances. As noted in the previous chapter, the French naval attaché in Tokyo predicted on 1 June 1939 that although the United States had delayed its entry into World War I, it "will participate in World War II immediately after the opening of hostilities." The same theme appears several weeks later in dispatches from the French embassy in London, just as it was implied a few months earlier in Foreign Minister Bonnet's confident statement to the Chamber of Deputies. Bonnet later testified that Bullitt had done everything in his power to persuade France to enter the war.[68]

Had Roosevelt studied to precipitate a war in Europe, he could hardly have been more effective, for he succeeded in simultaneously encouraging both sides to hold fast. At the same time that his tactics prompted Chamberlain and Daladier to adhere to a hard line in public, Hitler and Mussolini came to scorn him for his supposed callowness. German and Italian leaders could see neither principled opposition to their goals nor mobilization of American power. True it is that in his Annual Message of 1939 he called for large defense increases. But this came several years too late. An uneasy Arnold Toynbee had written in his 1937 *Survey of International Affairs* (1:52) that "the United States was lazily playing with a fraction of her immeasurable strength." Yet this was a state of affairs that would continue. Berlin's impression was identical to Tokyo's: America's armed forces were not battle ready, and their commander in chief was unwilling to confront isolationists in Congress. The rest of the world could scarcely believe its eyes when, in February of 1939, Congress appropriated the almost ridiculous sum of $500 million for defense. The Russians, the French, and the Chinese all remonstrated adamantly, and when the president told Mussolini a year later that America might double its shipment of planes to the Allies if Italy decided to enter the war, the duce remarked pointedly that the United States was shipping only 150 aircraft a month.[69]

Without doubt, Germany was the country most tempted by American weakness. Nye's neutrality legislation, to which Roosevelt had so handsomely contributed, gave the Wilhelmstrasse great confidence. Only once was there a flurry of concern in Berlin and that was early in 1936 when Congressman McReynolds proposed a new form of neutrality based on discrimination between aggressor and victim.[70] McReynolds's proposal soon died, however, and German leaders could feel all the more secure when Roosevelt, after being quoted as saying that the American frontier was on the Rhine, wheeled about and labeled the quotation a "deliberate lie." It was a foregone conclusion that America would not fight, and if she did, there would be nothing to fear. In late 1939, several months after the outbreak of war, Roosevelt obtained a revision of the Neutrality Law permitting trade with belligerents, but this was on a strictly cash-and-carry basis and with presidential assurances that the act would not be used to augment executive power. Hence, when an ad appeared in American papers on 10 June 1940, "Stop Hitler Now," Propaganda Chief Joseph Goebbels shot back, "Stop Hitler? With What?" Later that summer, the minister of propaganda conceded that the United States might enter the war the following winter, but "such a step would be of very little importance." According to von Ribbentrop, the United States "could not wage war militarily at all"—its policy was a "great big bluff." Hitler told his generals that Roosevelt's armament program would not become effective until 1945. The president's claims in the area of potential rearmament struck him as "lies pure and simple." When State Security Chief Walter Schellenberg spoke to Göring on one occasion of the possibility that America might project its power onto the Continent, Göring told him to see a psychiatrist.[71]

Roosevelt's neglect of military power was especially damaging when it appeared in conjunction with bravura. Just as Hull had threatened Japan with two thousand American bombers and Italy had been informed of Washington's "extreme misgivings" regarding her involvement in Ethiopia, Mussolini was repeatedly confronted with what he perceived as empty threats of American participation in a European war.[72] In similar vein, FDR requested on 14 April 1939 that Germany promise not to attack a specified list of thirty-one countries. To Italian leaders, this "Thirty-one Nations Address" was thought to be "the most incredible document in the whole history of diplomacy." Mussolini dismissed it with a few cutting words, vowing not to be moved by "convivial vociferations or Messiah-like messages." Meanwhile, the fuehrer, after obtaining notes from each of the allegedly threatened nations that they harbored no such fear, used the message as a springboard for what William Shirer has called "the most brilliant oration he ever gave."[73]

Roosevelt's last-minute appeal for flexibility on the part of Poland did nothing to restore an already depleted stock of credibility. Ambassador Biddle, long in favor of concessions to Germany, had spoken in Danzig at a time when Chamberlain was exhorting Roosevelt to apply additional pressure on Warsaw. Following conversations with the chairman of the Danzig Foreign Relations Committee, Biddle handed Beck a White

House plea for compromise. Came the terse reply: "Poland would have to resist a threat to her vital interests and principles."[74]

In the absence of American power and reputation, one way of fencing German ambition would have been to encourage a partnership between Britain, France, and the Soviet Union. Roosevelt, however, refused resolutely to make such an appeal. Positive remarks to the British just before Munich were offset by what he told the French at the time. Likewise, suggestions to the French in late May of 1939 were belied by what he uttered in conversations with George VI at Hyde Park. Britain's monarch found him "definitely anti-Russian."[75] For a brief interval, Paul-Boncour and Bonnet had given serious thought to a Franco-Soviet alliance. Chamberlain, too, with the enthusiastic backing of Churchill, Lloyd George, and the British chiefs of staff, made overtures to Moscow in the last weeks of peace (the Strang mission). It was too little, too late, however. Whether or not outspoken support from Washington would have made any appreciable difference is debatable. The fact is that such support was not forthcoming. Professionals at the American embassy in Moscow felt sufficient revulsion at the Stalinist trials (1936–38) to clamor for a reduced diplomatic presence at the American embassy. George Kennan and Loy Henderson could never understand, much less tolerate, what they perceived as a denial of human rights, and when the former suggested that Davies be let go without replacement, his wish was granted. Stalin soon reciprocated by appointing an ultra-hard-liner to Washington, the unpopular Constantin Oumansky. Meanwhile, FDR tried unsuccessfully to exclude Russian representation at Brussels. Early in 1939, he encouraged the fiercely anti-Soviet Ukrainian associations of Europe and America to establish a diplomatic bureau in Washington for the maintenance of official ties linking the United States with champions of an independent Ukraine. Several weeks after the outbreak of war in 1939, Welles told Saint-Quentin that the Chinese had more to fear from Moscow than they did from Tokyo.[76]

Admittedly, Roosevelt's options were somewhat circumscribed. It would have required strong leadership to reverse the common tendency to equate communism with Nazism as twin evils. Noninterventionists such as Hoover and Lindbergh, who wished to shun Moscow for a variety of reasons, were apt to warn of "the effect of Asia on European civilization." Hoover in particular never deviated from his anti-

Soviet line and would have been delighted to tar Roosevelt with the brush of communism.⁷⁷ Perhaps for this reason, as much as any other, Washington affected an indifference bordering on hostility and others were encouraged to do the same. Ambassador Joseph Davies left his embassy in Moscow on 11 June 1938, and it was not until 11 August 1939 that a successor presented his credentials. This was a mere twelve days before the signing of the Russo-German nonaggression pact.

War followed almost as a logical consequence—along with peace sentiment. No sooner had Poland collapsed under the weight of German and Russian armor than doves began to make themselves heard across the Continent. Hitler, secure behind the Siegfried Line, showed himself eager to disavow hostile intent, while Roosevelt heard from the American embassy in London that he might be of service in arranging a settlement. Accordingly, on 15 September, he summoned William Davis, a businessman formerly involved in the sale of Mexican oil to Germany. Two of Davis's associates, Messrs. Smith and Reber, were also in Washington at the time. Reber, an official of Texas Oil, had participated in prewar conversations between Norman Davis and British officials, and the record shows that Bingham invited him to an embassy dinner in honor of Eleanor Roosevelt and the Astors. Whether Roosevelt actually conferred with Reber is unclear, though he did see Smith. In any event, Davis proved to be the president's chosen instrument. After being instructed to take soundings in Rome and Berlin, he began a series of talks with Göring (1, 2, and 3 October). Hitler's second in command suggested a conference between Germany, Britain, and France to be held in Washington and indicated that it was time for the White House to inform Berlin of its peace terms and how it proposed to mediate. Germany, he said, would accept a new Polish state as well as an independent Czechoslovakia.⁷⁸

Outright French and British rejection of Hitler's peace overture of 6 October seems to have put FDR off, although Davis returned to confer with State Department officials and was beginning to draw British agents into the act when a Swiss leak threatened to expose the nature of his activity. As a result, Hull felt it necessary to disavow any connection between him and the White House, and there is nothing to indicate that he ever served the president again.⁷⁹

All along, Roosevelt was receiving encouragement from Belgium, Finland, and the Soviet Union, as well as from Bishop Berggrav of Norway. *Tass*, the official Soviet news agency, reported five American sen-

ators in favor of compromise. The Low Countries were offering to mediate with backing from the Scandinavian bloc, while Clark Eichel-
burger, editor of the *League of Nations Chronicle,* and Columbia University Professor James Shotwell had inaugurated a weekly radio program on behalf of peace. All that remained was for Schacht, Alexander
Kirk (American chargé in Berlin), and later Averell Harriman to indicate that Hitler's peace appeals of 19 September, 6 October, and 24
October were genuine. Roosevelt already knew that he could count on
the moral support of the Vatican along with the Quai d'Orsay, and
France was more than willing to review the question of colonies, not to
mention Danzig, the Sudetenland, and the Corridor. Even in England,
where war sentiment lodged most strongly, the conservative government had come under heavy fire by December. George Bernard Shaw,
Lloyd George, and others were starting to roll out the verbal artillery.[80]

As mentioned earlier, the man recruited by FDR to take up the skein
of negotiation where Davis left off was James Mooney. After speaking
with Göring for two and a half hours in October, Mooney reported to
the American embassy and set out for London to confer with Ambassador Kennedy and Bill Bullitt (the latter by telephone). During December and January, he took counsel with the president and insisted,
much as Davis had done, that Hitler would make sizable concessions,
including an independent Poland, an autonomous Czechoslovakia
with new frontiers, and possibly a reconstituted German regime without Goebbels and von Ribbentrop.[81]

Mooney's next mission to Europe is of exceptional interest for two
reasons: first, because it runs parallel to segments of the Welles mission; second, because it throws light on obscure aspects of the American peace plan. Roosevelt, as it turns out, sought to appear as friendly
as possible to the Germans. He wanted it said, for example, that he had
spent a fair amount of his youth in Germany, having attended elementary school there, and further, that the Germans were free to have
whatever form of government they desired—that was "their affair." In
addition, Mooney was to let it be known that FDR wished to act as
"moderator," a term he preferred to "mediator" because it was commonly used at American town meetings. Berlin might satisfy its colonial aspiration by developing central tropical Africa instead of its former colonies, but with the right to colonies reaffirmed (Göring accepted this idea, adding that there was no reason to undermine the
stabilizing influence of the British Empire). As anticipated, disarma-

ment and liberalized world trade were brought forward as a substitute for "extreme" political demands which could not be met, and Roosevelt went further to promise contributions to the German economy, including tariff reduction and a "free gift" of American gold. Finally, it was suggested that Hitler might raise his popularity rating in the United States by bringing an end to the Russo-Finnish War.[82]

Mooney not only set the pattern for Welles by beginning and ending his talks in Rome; his three and a half weeks in Germany coincided precisely with Welles's visit. He went into conference with von Ribbentrop on 29 February, one day before Welles, and with Hitler and Göring on 4 and 7 March, in each case a few days after. He thus not only paved the way for Welles but attempted to clinch what the under secretary had set in motion. His was the first word and the last—until trouble arose from an unexpected quarter.[83] Although his detailed reports from Rome were forwarded to Washington by naval intelligence, their confidentiality was in some way impaired, and the State Department, true to form, denied any link between him and the White House.[84] Mooney was thus forced into retirement in much the same manner as Davis.

Before pondering Welles's overtures, it should be said that there were four basic facets of the Roosevelt peace strategy: first, a sustained effort to separate Mussolini from the Axis by holding out choice imperial inducements; second, a campaign to pry meaningful concessions from Britain; third, an attempt to organize various neutral blocs, including Scandinavia, the Low Countries, and Latin America, in such a way as to induce them to draw up principles of peace that would satisfy Berlin and focus world opinion on London. Finally, Roosevelt hoped to enlist leaders of three major religious faiths, the Roman Catholic, the Greek Orthodox, and Islam.[85] Of the four aims, only the first and second, entrusted to Welles, came anywhere near fruition. The under secretary, who by coincidence not only shared a godmother with Mrs. Roosevelt but also attended the same schools as FDR and served as an usher at the president's wedding, came closer to being a presidential counselor than perhaps anyone else with the exception of Morgenthau. Possessed of unusual savoir faire, including a fluent command of French and Spanish, he had served as the youngest division chief in history.

Some have doubted that Welles could ever have aimed at serious compromise in light of America's well-known animus against Germany.[86] The fuehrer tried to save face by claiming that the president was only stalling to delay a German spring offensive. Roosevelt, in turn, felt obliged to keep his cards close to his chest in deference to Chamberlain. Assistant Secretary Long, Secretary of Agriculture Henry Wallace, and French Ambassador Saint-Quentin were all told that there was no thought of bargaining with Hitler. Consequently, a number of observers attributed the Welles mission to domestic politics in an election year. Robert Murphy, in Paris, suspected as much, as did Mussolini and other foreign leaders. In Chile, American ambassador Claude Bowers formulated still another theory: if Germany were to collapse, the United States wanted to "be ready with some sort of scheme of economic rehabilitation for Europe generally . . . to prevent Germany from succumbing to Bolshevism." Then there was Welles himself, who, after the failure of his mission, gave the impression that he had been merely an envoy testing the European climate. Understandably eager to avoid charges of appeasement, he printed attacks on the dictators that were so labored and *ad hominem* as to border on the ludicrous: Mussolini carried himself with "elephantine" motion and sat at the bargaining table with eyes closed; von Ribbentrop appeared haggard; Göring's hands resembled the paws of a badger, and so forth.[87]

When all is said and done, however, the weight of evidence points overwhelmingly to authentic effort on the part of Welles. Apart from what is suggested by the Davis and Mooney missions, given Roosevelt's attempt to wrap them in secrecy, one cannot forget what Welles said and did during the preceding three years. There is his trip to Europe in 1937 and the probes undertaken by Fuller, Bullitt, and Wilson. We have the record, too, of Roosevelt's obeisance to public opinion. Americans looked favorably upon appeasement as late as the spring of 1940. With one poll showing 58 percent in favor of a peace conference involving Germany, Senator Pittman called for a thirty-day armistice and referred to Hitler as a genius. Roosevelt welcomed the Nazi president of the German Red Cross and, along with Hull, held conferences with former chancellor Heinrich Brüning and a member of the German foreign service by the name of Adam von Trott. As von Trott and Brüning both opposed Nazi designs (von Trott, a Rhodes scholar and lineal descendant of America's first chief justice, John Jay, was hanged by Hitler in 1944), such conferences may have been a screen for Roosevelt's willingness to work with Hitler—or they may have aimed at breaking the diplomatic logjam. German moderates apparently felt they were influential enough to exert pressure on behalf of a compromise peace plan.[88] In any case, the implication is clear.

If Welles lacked conviction in 1940, he certainly managed to conceal it from the Court of St. James's where his trip created rank consternation. British intelligence showed Roosevelt to be dangerously in earnest, and his desire to make peace with Hitler was viewed in London as *both* a "dirty trick" to secure reelection *and* a "crime against common sense." It would stir antiwar sentiment and raise false hopes. Offers of mediation tendered by Denmark, Sweden, and the Vatican were already providing more than enough ammunition for the British peace movement. Foreign Secretary Halifax thought Welles naive but at the same time not atypical of what one should have to expect from America. He dared not say this publicly, of course; one could not afford to offend the president "by appearing to assume either his duplicity or his stupidity." But Prime Minister Chamberlain reacted with "white hot anger" to Welles's proposal that Hitler remain in power, and Vansittart thought it shocking that Britain should be asked to cede Gibraltar to Italy. How could the president propose a revised Czech state without Moravia? How could he maintain that French peace terms were too harsh? Roosevelt's answer was simple. Difficult adjustments would be offset by relief in the area of trade and disarmament, the latter to be backed by an international peace-keeping air force. Washington would contribute its share in the field of finance and volunteer to inspect the dismantling of armament and weapons plants.[89]

According to Welles, Chamberlain and Halifax "laughed" at his proposals and subjected him to a comical seminar in which members of the War Cabinet, led by the foreign secretary, held forth on a series of unrelated topics. Sir John Anderson, minister for civilian defense, who had not spoken a word during the session, took Welles by the arm and said, "Please do not for an instant believe that most of us agree with the opinions you have heard expressed tonight. I can assure you we do not." Pain turned to astonishment as Churchill unburdened himself of an hour and fifty minutes of oratory "brilliant and always effective, interlarded with considerable wit." It should be said that Welles stood his ground; but so, too, did Chamberlain, who agreed only that Danzig might return to Germany along with German-speaking parts of Poland and that Hitler might be granted free immigration, trade, and investment in Africa from heartland to horn. Had Welles been less in earnest, his reputation might not have suffered so severely. *Punch*, on 6 March, showed a caricature of an individual surrounded by smoke, holding an American flag in one hand and a wand in the other and saying, "My name is John Washington Welles—I'm a dealer in magic and spells."[90]

The sincerity of the under secretary's professed intent was accepted wherever he went. Hitler had long sought American mediation, and Welles was known for his criticism of the Versailles settlement. Ulrich von Hassell, distinguished veteran of the German diplomatic corps, agreed with the British that Roosevelt aimed at both reelection and a peace settlement. Thus, when Welles arrived in Germany on the heels of Mooney, he was able to deal seriously and at length. Von Ribbentrop saw him on 1 March, Hitler and Göring on 2 March, Göring a second time on 4 March. The last of these conferences lasted three hours and twenty minutes. By special request he also held talks with Hitler's aide, Rudolf Hess, and with Reichsbank President Hjalmar Schacht. Although Hitler insisted on a Monroe Doctrine for eastern and central Europe, in addition to colonial restoration, this did not discourage the American envoy, who told Göring on his departure that he wanted to keep in close touch. To Dieckhoff, he said he expected his mission would succeed, and to State Secretary Ernst von Weizsäcker he confided that Roosevelt could be counted upon to resume the initiative after his (Welles's) return to Washington.[91]

France took the White House just as seriously. But in contrast to British ridicule and German satisfaction, she expressed outrage. Only a few, including Treasury Secretary Paul Reynaud, preferred FDR's plasticity to Churchill's steel. Most resented the undermining of their position and the strengthening of "defeatists" such as Bonnet. Welles was known in Paris not only for his proximity to Roosevelt but also for a set of isolationist views which led him to prefer the spread of Nazism in Europe to any major risk of American involvement. It was not easy to forget that on the morning after Munich, while Roosevelt was congratulating Beneš for refusing to be drawn into a war in which he would have been "crushed," Welles had told the French of his optimism that Munich would pave the way for further concessions to Hitler, including a retrocession of former German colonies held by France.[92] In any case, Welles engaged in extensive talks with Daladier and left the impression that Roosevelt was not only resigned to German control of central and eastern Europe but supremely confident in Mussolini. No amount of praise for the duce would suffice.[93]

Welles's first and last stop was Rome, in keeping with a strategy of seeking to detach Italy from the Axis, and the ground there had been well laid. FDR had assured Mussolini's ambassador that in any peace conference hosted by the United States, the duce could expect reasonable satisfaction. Roosevelt had also lunched with Cardinal Mundelein in late 1937, thus clearing the way for an episcopal trip to Italy, where the cardinal was warmly received by Foreign Minister Ciano.[94] In line with this approach, Welles sailed for Europe in the company of Myron Taylor, special envoy to the Vatican. Mussolini had not dealt with an American official for two years due to Roosevelt's position on Ethiopia, and an Italian-American treaty of commerce, already signed and sealed, had perished ad interim. Now there were elaborate floral decorations at railway stations and a private car to take Welles from Naples to Rome. He was able to return the compliment by presenting a written note from president to duce: "I still hope to meet you some day soon." When Mussolini disregarded the invitation to a meeting at the Azores, Welles repeated it on his return to Rome after visiting Berlin, Paris, and London. He also brought pleasant news. Although the administration was still undecided as to whether it could recognize Italian rule over Ethiopia—to do so would imply willingness to recognize Manchukuo (which every other nation in the world had done, including the Soviet Union)—it did intend to seek a generous congressional appropriation for American participation in the Rome Exposition planned for 1942.[95]

As might have been foreseen, Mussolini turned out to be more interested in Gibraltar, Tunis, and Djibouti, or a share in Suez, than he was in world fairs or in meeting Roosevelt face to face. Disarmament and free trade ranked relatively low on his list of national priorities. Nor did he forget German aspirations in central Europe, which he insisted must take precedence over all else. Welles seems to have grasped the importance of this consideration. Nonetheless, when he phoned Roosevelt for permission to discuss territorial issues, the answer was no.[96] Just as the White House hedged in its approach to the Vatican by stopping short of full diplomatic recognition and sending an Episcopalian with Quaker leanings, its public position on European political questions remained vague. It was comparatively easy for Berlin to quash Roosevelt's initiative when von Ribbentrop came to Rome and Hitler met Mussolini at the Brenner Pass.

Interestingly enough, American overtures continued despite Mussolini's indifference to a personal meeting. The president granted a unilateral concession when he lifted the countervailing duty on some of Italy's most valued silk exports—notwithstanding German conquest of Denmark and Norway and Bullitt's impression that Washington was showing too much velvet and not enough iron. At about the same time, in response to a suggestion by Welles and Taylor, he dropped all derogatory reference to dictatorship in his speeches.[97] On 10 April, in a dramatic reversal of all he had been saying since he took office, he stressed that the United States enjoyed friendly relations with many countries under authoritarian rule and that the manner in which other people chose to be governed was not the proper concern of Pennsylvania Avenue.

Taylor, after sounding British envoys, concluded that Italy must be granted some or all of her territorial demands. At the same time, he assured the president that he need not be concerned about any "lack of caution" in the handling of "these delicate matters." At this juncture, Lord Lothian advised Roosevelt on how to draft an inquiry respecting terms for Italian neutrality. Mussolini must be assured that the Allies "were prepared to consider all reasonable Italian claims" and that any agreement with regard to them would "come into force as soon as the war was ended." The United States, in other words, would lend moral support by acting as recorder and monitor of a pact between Rome, London, and Paris. The French went so far as to speak of an American "guarantee." On 26 May, Roosevelt cabled Mussolini that he stood ready to "communicate" Italian desiderata to France and Britain. Paris and London were prepared to give "assurance" that such a compact "would be faithfully executed by them at the end of the war and that those governments would welcome Italian participation at any eventual peace conference with a status equal to that of the belligerents." The sole requirement on Italy's side would be for Mussolini to assure Roosevelt that the secret covenant satisfied all Italian claims necessary for the guarantee of Italian neutrality.[98]

Italy's response was crisp and immediate. She planned to enter the war in a matter of weeks, if not days: "It will happen soon," Ciano declared. Again, an American proposal had arrived too late. This was the third rejection of as many Roosevelt offers within a month; yet the president resolved to make still another démarche, this time threatening to supply the Allies with aid and, if need be, troops. Mussolini again came to the point: he had decided on war and preferred not to receive any further pressure from the United States.[99]

Two days after the Dunkirk evacuation, with Belgium and the Netherlands firmly under German control and the Battle of France a day old, Roosevelt again returned to the charge, suggesting that Europe, as well as Asia, might operate on the principle of the Monroe Doctrine. When Admiral Horthy of Hungary had championed such a scheme in the form of three leagues, each to be headquartered in Geneva, *Time* had called it as "improbable as a Hungarian opera." Now, with reporters still unaware of any clandestine links between Lafayette Square and Berlin, the editorial page of the *New York Times* exploded. But the excitement did not last. Almost as suddenly as the Hyde Park oracle had spoken, it fell silent. Roosevelt hastened to issue a "clarification." He was even inclined to support another French offer of concessions to Italy. This time, however, he sided with Hull. On 10 June, Italy's notification to France that she would enter the war within hours precluded further effort on the part of the United States. Lord Lothian would extend feelers to Berlin as late as September, but FDR's address to the graduating class of the University of Virginia on the day that Italy invaded France inaugurated a new phase of American policy. "The hand that held the dagger," he intoned, "has struck it into the back of its neighbor!"[100]

On hindsight, Roosevelt's use of stiletto imagery would seem to have been less than accurate as it implied an attribution of virtue to American foreign policy which was hardly deserved. White House strategists may not have deployed shock troops in the manner of a Mussolini, but they dealt lethally enough in the language of diplomacy. The Welles mission was entirely consistent with what FDR had been saying and doing behind closed doors since at least the mid-1930s. Indeed, it may be viewed as the culmination of a series of feelers that had their origin in the president's initial ambivalence and reached their zenith over a year earlier at the time of Munich. Beginning with preinaugural statements and running like a leitmotif through the work of Fuller, Bullitt, and Wilson, then of Davis, Mooney, and Welles, is the theme of appeasement. This becomes all the more apparent in light of Dodd's humiliation at the hands of the White House, Kennedy's firsthand connection with Munich, and Roosevelt's own effort to claim a lion's share of the credit.

To the degree, therefore, that blame may be assessed for the ultimate failure of Allied strategy, the United States must accept its fair share. Too many spans linked the chancelleries of Europe with Lafayette Square to allow the position of one Western capital to be set apart from that of the others. FDR, in particular, was intimately involved in the patronage of Nazi Germany, more so than anyone has perhaps imagined. Throughout the decade, he managed to cover nearly every track that ran between Washington and Berlin. In the popular eye, he remained what he had always been: an uncompromising foe of dictatorship. But such policy carried with it important elements of weakness as well as strength. In the end, there was a price to be paid for ambivalence, and it remains for history to decide whether, in this case, the price proved exorbitant.

The remainder of the story is too well known to require more than the broadest of brush strokes. Holland collapsed in five days, and Belgium's leaders, who had foregone preparedness in order to avoid giving offense, raised the white flag in a single week. While France could hardly conceive of the velocity of the panzer thrust across her border, Britain sent what reinforcement she felt she could spare. It was not enough. An expeditionary force of 338,000 managed to avoid capture, but enemy troops soon entered the heart of Gaul. Having outflanked the Maginot Line and penetrated the Ardennes Forest, Nazi units approached Paris.

With one eye fixed across the Atlantic, Churchill assured a packed House of Commons: "Wars are not won by evacuations . . . we shall fight on the landing-grounds, we shall fight in the fields and in the streets, we shall fight in the hills; we shall never surrender, and even if . . . this island . . . were subjugated and starving, then our Empire beyond the seas, armed and guarded by the British Fleet, would carry on the struggle until in God's good time, the New World, with all its power and might, steps forth to the rescue and liberation of the Old." Here was the rub. Would the New World in fact step forth to the rescue of the Old? Roosevelt returned a cryptic answer: America "could not at once go to war."[101]

On the twenty-second, Marshal Pétain signed an armistice which caused FDR to regard American belligerency as merely a matter of time. Again, Churchill appealed to the Commons—and to the New World: "The Battle of France is over. I expect that the Battle of Britain is about to begin. . . . If we fail, then the whole world, including the

United States, including all that we have known and cared for, will sink into the abyss of a new Dark Age. . . . Let us therefore brace ourselves to our duties, and so bear ourselves that, if the British Empire and its Commonwealth last for a thousand years, men will say, 'This was their finest hour.' "[102] As Hitler gathered his amphibious invasion force in the dockyards of northern France, England stood desperately alone. Clouds of planes, sometimes as many as fourteen hundred, seventeen hundred, or eighteen hundred at a time, darkened the skies over London, Birmingham, and Coventry. Submarine wolf packs took such a dread toll of Allied shipping that half of all who served in the British merchant marine were forced to pay with their lives.

The gravity of the situation was underscored by another battle, one being waged between William Allen White's Committee to Defend America by Aiding the Allies and Charles Lindbergh's America First Committee. It was a conflict which raged over many a dining room table between Maine and California as friends became enemies and enemies friends. But although the outcome in this instance might have appeared doubtful, England could be counted fortunate in at least one important respect. Roosevelt found himself exempt from much of the pressure of a normal election campaign since Republicans had chosen Wendell Willkie, a candidate whose views on foreign policy coincided largely with his own. With Willkie's tacit consent, he could and did abandon all pretense to lawful neutrality. In rapid succession came Destroyers for Bases, executive endorsement of the Burke-Wadsworth selective service training bill (the first peacetime draft in American history), the secret guarantee of British possessions in the Far East, and Lend-Lease. Each of these commitments fell far short of long-standing promise. Nevertheless, they drew upon all of the president's considerable skill in domestic political maneuver, and at least the direction of American policy was no longer in doubt. Roosevelt easily vanquished opponents of the destroyer deal, stressing the value of the Caribbean and Canadian bases and the urgency of their acquisition for American home defense. To many, his transfer of vessels, artfully described as "on their last legs," appeared to be little more than an afterthought and therefore unobjectionable. The administration proceeded to announce formation of a Joint Canadian-American Defense Board and, in line with Churchill's lead, opened confidential contact with Moscow (via presidential aide Harry Hopkins). It moved just as consummately to educate American public opinion, in particular Roman Catholic opinion, to the utility of Soviet-American cooperation. Finally, in Lend-Lease, it devised a marvelous stratagem, brilliantly executed, to meet Britain's pressing need for credit. Like a number of other key phrases coined by FDR, this one was deliberately deceptive, aimed at achieving a larger purpose. The act, having little to do with loans or leases, was styled with a felicity bound to attract the support of patriots everywhere: House Resolution 1776.

All of these moves pointed unquestionably in a single direction—toward American belligerency. To be sure, there is nothing to indicate that FDR initially desired war with Germany any more than he did with Japan. On the other hand, one is struck by the same sense of inevitability, one might almost say abandon, in his general approach. Early in his first term, Morgenthau heard him say that war with Germany was "a very strong possibility," and if it came, the United States "could not afford to let Britain go down." In like vein, he hinted to Ambassador Phillips in September 1938 that he considered another war inescapable and that if ever the American system of government were threatened by a coalition of European dictators, "we might wade in with everything we have to give." When such a coalition came to pass, he acted precisely as he said he would, playing on the popular fear that Hitler planned to invade the United States through Latin America. Months before the first of Hitler's divisions entered Poland, 60 percent of the American people feared a German attack in the event that Britain were to go down with France. At the same time, many United States officials, including Breckinridge Long, anticipated a possible Nazi take-over of the British fleet.[103]

From the opening gun of September 1939, therefore, Roosevelt acted to maximize American involvement. Six days after declaring neutrality (on 5 September), he invited Britain's first lord of the admiralty, Winston Churchill, to enter into confidential correspondence. He then instituted a naval patrol that tracked Nazi merchantmen and reported their positions to the Royal Navy. By April of 1941, Erwin Rommel's Afrika Korps had recaptured all of Cyrenaica; Yugoslavia had been overrun; the Greek army had surrendered; and German paratroopers were about to carry out their successful assault on British positions in Crete. FDR now confided to Bullitt that American entry was certain, even though it had to await the "incident" he was "confident that the Germans would give us." Furthermore, had it not been for an anti-convoy resolution introduced in Congress at the end of March, he would have ordered the navy to attack German ships on sight. Failing this, the best he could do was to extend the boundaries of the security zone within which his destroyers did their tracking. By executive agreement, he assumed an informal protectorate over Greenland, and as commander in chief, he ordered sizable units of the Pacific Fleet into the Atlantic (two destroyer squadrons, three battleships, and one carrier).[104]

When the hoped-for incident failed to materialize—the sinking of the American freighter *Robin Moor* on 21 May did not provide a clear enough case—American troops were dispatched to take Britain's place in Iceland, formerly an independent kingdom with personal ties to Denmark. Admiral Stark called this "practically an act of war," and Roosevelt assured Lord Halifax that the "whole thing would now boil up very quickly." American patrols already ranged as far east as twenty-five degrees longitude, a line midway between Africa and Brazil, and this was bent to include Iceland. Next came Roosevelt's order for the navy to convoy *all* ships to Iceland, including vessels of foreign registry. Isolationists raised such a storm that he felt obliged to retrench temporarily, but German chargé Hans Thomsen wrote the Wilhelmstrasse in early July that according to reliable sources in America and secret reports from abroad, FDR had reaffirmed his determination to provoke war with Germany. A single naval incident was all he felt he needed. Secretary of War Henry Stimson, who favored an immediate war message, tried to explain Roosevelt's policy of watchful waiting by analogy with Lincoln: "The vacillations and the pulling back and forth, trying to make the Confederates fire the first shot. Well, that is what apparently the President is trying to do here."[105]

Should war develop in the Far East, American plans called for "offensive" action against Germany so as to follow a "Europe-first" strategy.[106] Japan, however, was no more willing than Germany to issue a direct challenge.

By August of 1941, the British felt sufficiently confident of Washington's help in the Atlantic to begin assembling a separate fleet in the Mediterranean. Thus it was that they hoped to mount a North African campaign and fill the vacuum created in the Far East by Roosevelt's naval transfers. To a man, they believed American entry to be imminent. Lord Beaverbrook, visiting the president before the Argentia Conference, concluded that "the whole administration were in favor of going to war." Halifax felt sure that however much Roosevelt seemed to trail public opinion, he was looking more than ever for an incident on which to hang the case for intervention; he would "drift" into war. Churchill, who made it bluntly plain at Argentia that Britain could not win without America, reported FDR "obviously determined" to come in:

> The President had been extremely anxious about the Bill for further appropriations for Lend-Lease which had only passed with a very narrow majority. Clearly he was skating on pretty thin ice in his relations with Congress, which, however, he did not regard as truly representative of the country. If he were to put the issue of peace and war to Congress, they should debate it for months. The President had said that he would wage war, but not declare it, and that he would become more and more provocative. If the Germans did not like it they could attack. . . . Everything was to be done to force an incident.

When he warned the president that Britain might sue for peace if Russia collapsed or if, by the spring of 1942, the United States continued to stand out, Roosevelt again "made it clear that he would look for an 'incident' which would justify him in opening hostilities." He also promised to occupy Portugal's Azore Islands if and when Britain moved to seize the Canaries.[107]

On 4 September, the United States destroyer *Greer* was fired upon by a German U-boat. FDR made as much of the incident as he possibly could at the time, offering to send *American* vessels manned by *American* crews into British home ports for the transshipment of twenty thousand British troops to war zones in North Africa. Downing Street accepted this sensational offer without delay and began making the necessary arrangements, only to meet with another ninety-degree turn in White House policy. Roosevelt told Churchill that he regretted having to go back on his transshipment offer, but on second thought he felt the plan would jeopardize his drive for revision of the Neutrality Law. Britain could have the transports if it supplied its *own* crews or it might have them with American crews if it agreed to pack its twenty thousand men off to Halifax for embarkation from there to North Africa. Churchill chose the latter alternative. But, chafing under what he must surely have regarded as indecisive American leadership, he chose the House of Commons on 30 September as the forum for a rare public criticism of the White House: "Nothing is more dangerous in wartime than to live in the temperamental atmosphere of a Gallup poll, always feeling one's pulse and taking one's temperature."[108]

One week after the attack on the *Greer*, Roosevelt delivered a fireside chat in which he described Nazi submarines as the "rattlesnakes" of the Atlantic. What he did not say was that the *Greer* had been tracking its quarry for three hours and signaling its position to British destroyers. According to German accounts, the American skipper actually fired first with antisubmarine shells. Facts notwithstanding, Roosevelt ordered the navy to adopt a shoot-on-sight policy and went to Congress for power to deploy armed merchant ships in combat zones. There followed a wave of sinkings, and when the U.S. destroyer *Kearney* was torpedoed with a loss of eleven lives in the same month that witnessed five sinkings of American merchantmen, he told a Navy Day audience, "The shooting has started. And history has recorded who fired the first shot. . . . Our ships have been sunk and our sailors have been killed. I say that we do not propose to take this lying down." Using a fraudulent map to document German designs on Latin America, he charged Berlin with dividing South America into "five vassal states," one of them Panama. He claimed also to be in possession of a secret Nazi document showing that Hitler aimed to abolish religion and confiscate the property of all churches. "We Americans have cleared our decks and taken our battle stations. We stand ready."[109] The date was 27 October, exactly six weeks minus one day before Japan's attack on Pearl Harbor.

Most scholars would agree that Roosevelt could have done a good deal more than he did to combat isolationist sentiment, especially during his initial term of office.[110] As suggested in Chapter 1, he appears to have been more responsible than anyone else for the backward progress of public opinion from 1933 to 1939. Some may be inclined to think that he should have moved more boldly even in later years (1940–41) to align his countrymen with the policy of France and Britain—or, from another perspective, that he might have striven more resolutely to resist interventionist pressure. Naturally, these are questions that hinge to some extent upon one's reading of domestic trends. All too often, the period lends itself to sweeping judgment based on hindsight and a slender thread of evidence. There are, however, many instances in which the factual basis is perfectly adequate to draw fairly clear-cut conclusions. In the eyes of Roosevelt and certain of his advisers, it may have been a happy fact that the United States could stand aloof from Europe's broils, content to rely upon the combined strength of Britain and France as a buffer against Axis aggression. But this does not excuse him from shirking preparedness, nor will it do to credit the

White House with a coherent and consistent foreign policy when in fact none existed.

One is bound to be troubled by the president's apparent drifting, by his lack of any clearly defined strategy, and by his refusal to raise American military potential to a level commensurate with the nation's natural influence. His continual shifting and trimming to accommodate moods of public opinion, both at home and abroad, coupled with his inability to separate just from unjust demands on the part of revanchist states, served to disqualify him for useful service as a mediator. There is, in addition, his failure to appreciate the potential of Soviet Russia as part of a viable diplomatic and military fence around Germany. Above all, the abiding need for vision in a chief executive constitutes an underlying theme in each of the separate chapters of this book. Vision, or the absence thereof, lies at the root of every major decision, and not surprisingly, it is to this most elemental of considerations that we must now turn if we are to speak of American diplomacy during World War II.

5. Roosevelt as World Leader

IT will not be the aim of this chapter to render an exhaustive account of American diplomacy during World War II. To do so would be to enter upon a myriad of intricacies connected with coalition warfare and to cover each of the great Allied decisions as, for example, Operation TORCH and unconditional surrender. Such an objective would take us far beyond the confines of a single chapter without necessarily adding to what is already known about Franklin Roosevelt. What manner of man, what manner of statesman? Such were the questions raised at the outset of the narrative, and as such they will remain central to our quest. We shall therefore concentrate on that portion of the story which has most to contribute to an understanding of how FDR dealt with two giants of the Eastern scene, Joseph Stalin and Chiang Kai-shek, along with two of the more prescient leaders of the West, Winston Churchill and Charles de Gaulle. By way of conclusion, and again with an eye to breaking new ground, we shall offer an extended analysis of Roosevelt's reputation worldwide.

Before proceeding to specifics, it is sobering to recall that it took the United States several years and hundreds of thousands of fatalities to emerge on the winning side of World War II, this in conjunction with a dynamic Britain and two of the world's most populous nations. America's friends and allies, as well as her adversaries, were compelled to sacrifice the best of their people in a slaughter of bestial intensity and on a scale unprecedented in all the pages of recorded history. In addition to six million Jews who perished during the war, the list of deaths includes scores of millions of Russians, Germans, Poles, Chinese, Japanese, Hungarians, French, British, and others. The estimated death toll is in the neighborhood of forty to fifty million. But equally somber, especially for the long run, is the fact that officials in Washington labored under an entirely erroneous view of the world and of what that world was about to become.

According to Roosevelt's personal estimate, a large share of Russia's suspicion and hostility, as directed against the West, could be explained in terms of the past. Naked geographically and under attack since the rise of the Huns in the fourth century, she had been obliged to defend herself against countless invaders. Kiev, laid waste in 1240, was ravaged a hundred times thereafter. In 1571, the Tartars captured Moscow and set it afire, killing 800,000 and deporting 130,000. In 1606, Moscow fell to a Polish army. Five years later, it was burned by the Swedes. Napoleon arrived in 1812. Czarist Russia collapsed under German hammer blows in 1917 and was forced by treaty to yield large areas of land. Then, from 1918 to 1921, a million and a half foreign troops fought to dictate the course of Russian history, including a Greek force numbering 200,000. All of this occurred before Hitler.

None of the above is to be gainsaid. At the same time, Roosevelt would have done well to bear in mind his own analogy: that one cannot stroke a tiger into a kitten. The smiles, jests, and territorial concessions which he felt would be disarming served merely to whet Russia's appetite for more. They did not alter the way a great power sought to do business. Neither did they alter the kind of business it sought to do.

There were weaknesses at nearly every point along the line of Roosevelt's thought. If he felt that Russia could be made amenable, he also assumed that Britain would remain America's chief commercial rival and that postwar France would be unable to raise a finger. Especially did he bank on the idea that China would survive the war as a strong and viable nation. According to much of the advice he received at the time, there were no real communists in China and Chiang's domestic feuding came down to a simple matter of personalities.[1] By knocking heads together, by pressing Chiang for social democratic reform and insisting on coalition government, China would coalesce and find herself. Needless to say, on each of these counts Churchill knew Roosevelt to be mistaken, but there was no way the English leader could prevail upon his opposite number. When the truth finally began to dawn in Washington, pundits were to speak of a "Cold War." But again, London knew differently. America's Cold War was nothing but a continuation of Britain's age-old struggle to contain the power of the czars. International life had changed but little.

Stalin, whose name means steel, was nothing if not worldly wise. The only thing he had in common with FDR was a scourge of physical illness that left his face pock-marked and one arm several inches shorter than the other. Far removed from the sheltered groves of Dutchess County, New York, he had endured a drunken father's beatings. As a revolutionary verging on the criminal, he had taken a pseudonym, "Koba," which to the people of his native Georgia meant Robin Hood, and he went on to brave the censure of polite society. Having survived a brutal power struggle and achieved mastery in a world of Oriental intrigue, he knew how to dissemble. He could make men crawl. Thus when Roosevelt approached him in 1933 seeking his friendship, he instinctively held back. A decade later, he announced himself the champion of religious liberty and dissolved the Comintern, giving credence to liberal theories of communist evolution. At Teheran, where butter would not melt in his mouth, he expressed a preference for Paasikivi as Finnish president even though the latter was a democrat rather than a communist. The Red Army, he insisted, would return home with a new ideology, and the USSR would then chart a postwar course between communism and capitalism. There would be private ownership, he assured Roosevelt, along with freedom of worship. The time had come, he added, to change the name of the Soviet Union back to Russia. And no sooner were these words spoken than the Soviet ambassador was reported at a Washington banquet going by the title of "Russian Ambassador."[2] This was Stalin.

As for the outstanding questions central to any study of World War II, there are several which may be succinctly stated. First, did Roosevelt, during the Big Three Conference at Teheran in late November of 1943, have to offer so much in return for Moscow's continued support against Germany and her pledge to join the war against Japan? In addition to promising Stalin a second military front in Europe, Roosevelt acquiesced in a Soviet protectorate over Mongolia, against Chiang's wishes, as well as Soviet acquisition of the Kurile Islands and the southern half of Sakhalin Island. He violated another solemn engagement to Chiang Kai-shek at the same conference when he bestowed his official blessing upon the internationalization of Dairen and the cession of Port Arthur to the Soviet Union as a naval base on long-term lease. Dairen and Port Arthur were among China's most vital ports. Finally, he agreed unilaterally, again in violation of the spirit of his understanding with Chiang, to a half-interest for Russia in the operation of Manchurian railways, with Soviet interests throughout the area to be recognized as "preeminent." Other questions follow along a similar line. During the Big Three Conference at Yalta in February 1945, Roosevelt obtained a modicum of Soviet cooperation regarding the structure of the United Nations. In return, he threw American support to the communist-sponsored Lublin government of Poland, broadened to include various noncommunist elements, but communist nevertheless. Was this a wise bargain? Did the president have to reject, out of hand, Churchill's plea for practical safeguards to ensure the outcome of "free elections" as promised for eastern Europe? And did he have to side with Stalin against Churchill on miscellaneous questions regarding reparations, industry, and labor in postwar Germany?

Few will deny that there were many tactics Roosevelt might have used to contain communist expansion in eastern Europe and the Far East, although how successful they would have been will continue to be a matter for speculation. Some have argued that Russia's postwar gains were inevitable and even morally justifiable given her enormous sacrifice in human life, estimated at twenty million (approximately ten times the figure for all the rest of the Allied forces). To be sure, there is an element of truth in this argument. Few things in history are inevitable, and Stalin did carry weight at the conference table. The specter of a separate peace between Russia and Germany could never be laid. Moreover, Stalin proved masterful in the use of veiled threats. No Western leader was ever permitted to forget that Moscow had engaged 270 German divisions as compared with only 90 for Washington and London combined. Roosevelt needed Stalin's cooperation and he needed it badly since his goal was to win the war at minimum cost to his country while securing the unconditional surrender of Germany and Japan. Nevertheless, had he operated on a different set of assumptions, his strategy and prospects would also have been different. The crux of the issue is simple: *he never grasped the need* for an alternative approach. He believed that the Soviet Union would exhaust itself against Germany and, in association with a cooperative West, evolve gradually toward capitalism and democracy. The Russian empire was too cumbersome, he felt, to absorb additional territory, and he was convinced that by charming Stalin he could lead him gently along the path to postwar unity. "I think I can personally handle Stalin better than either your Foreign Office or my State Department," he confided to Churchill. "Stalin hates the guts of all your top people. He thinks he likes me better, and I hope he will continue to do so."[3]

Had FDR glimpsed the true contours of power in a world aborning, he might have given more support to Mao Tse-tung or backed Chiang with less reserve. It was his to decide which would be more important in negotiating with Stalin, the United Nations charter or the composition of eastern European government. He might have accepted de Gaulle's advice that Polish interests dictated an Anglo-American demand for access to Baltic ports in return for Soviet access to terminals in the North Sea. Furthermore, had he assumed, as Eden and the Red Chinese did, that Russia had a natural interest in entering the war against Japan, he might have yielded far less in exchange. Never was he the absolute prisoner of events.[4]

On the one hand, Stalin derived powerful leverage from his option to grant or withhold aid against Japan. Atomic warfare, still in the experimental stage, offered little assurance of instantaneous surrender, particularly given the depth of Japanese commitment, and Roosevelt's military advisers were as one in stressing the importance of Moscow's aid. On the other hand, it is clear that Roosevelt gave away much of his hand in a game whose rules he did not comprehend. He did not have to *volunteer* to hand over such prizes as Dairen and the Kurile Islands. He need not have offered Stalin a free gift of Allied merchant vessels, along with captured enemy warships. Admiral King said he could not believe the Allies were in a position to demand Italian men of war, yet the president insisted on letting the USSR have one-third of these vessels as a token of goodwill. Ultimately, Stalin was granted one battleship, one cruiser, and eight destroyers. Britain supplied thirteen warships from the Royal Navy, and the United States turned over one of its cruisers, the USS *Milwaukee*. Roosevelt also volunteered to make part of the Anglo-American merchant fleet available to Stalin after the war.[5]

Possibilities abound. FDR might have baited his line with the promise of a credit or loan for Soviet postwar rehabilitation, as recommended by Harriman and Morgenthau. He might have been more stringent on conditions for the continuation of Lend-Lease. He did not have to announce his intention of withdrawing from Europe at the end of the war, particularly when a contrary policy had the support of public opinion, as well as of powerful political leaders and top military advisers. By the fall of

1944, the Joint Chiefs of Staff had reversed their opposition to an occupation policy, and Senators Vandenberg and White were agreed that stationing American occupation forces in Germany for a prolonged period would "not be at all difficult"; there would be "less difficulty . . . on this point than on almost any other" because it could be done by volunteers, of whom there would be many. There was no reason why Roosevelt had to rule out American spy activity in Russia, just as it fell within his province to file a much stronger protest on the Soviet takeover of Romania. In addition, his armies might have rolled on into Berlin and Prague as Churchill advised. At Teheran, he allowed Stalin to persuade him to put less effort into an underbelly invasion of Europe and more into the battle for France. Again, the decision can scarcely have been predetermined since it was FDR, not an Englishman, who in late 1943 proposed a landing at the head of the Adriatic, followed by a thrust to the east in conjunction with Soviet forces. General Eisenhower did not object at the time, and neither Churchill nor anyone else assumed that the underbelly approach would preclude a cross-Channel invasion, always the darling of American strategists. To lengthen the list of alternatives, Roosevelt might have sided with Churchill on the value of Germany and France as potential makeweights against Soviet power. He might have bargained on questions affecting the partition of Germany, the sum of reparations to be exacted, or the question of a fair trial for prisoners of war.[6]

Above all, he might have given the Polish government in exile more of an opportunity to survive. When Russian armies were about to enter Warsaw and pro-Western underground forces rose to attack retreating Nazi units, Stalin ordered his troops to halt on the Vistula River. There they stayed until German gunners had all but annihilated the prospective leadership of a democratic Poland. Churchill proposed an airlift to relieve the embattled patriots, but Stalin refused to permit American or British planes to land at nearby airfields. When Churchill insisted that Roosevelt go ahead with or without Soviet permission, the president could not be budged. He declined even to write Stalin a note of protest. As it happened, a detailed American plan for the United Nations was under consideration at Dumbarton Oaks, and what FDR wanted was Soviet support on voting procedure along with assembly membership and location of the organization in New York City. This, rather than Poland, was the apple of his eye. Hopkins put it bluntly when he said, "We cannot take a chance of having that bitched up."[7] In essence this

was the American position. But it was to no avail. A crafty Stalin withheld his assurances even as he swallowed Warsaw. Cooperation on the
United Nations would still be his to grant or withhold when it came
time to muster support for the Soviet-sponsored Lublin government.

At Teheran, in November of 1943, FDR sat silent when he was not
actively undermining the case for Polish territorial integrity. Later, Averell Harriman, who at the time was serving as American ambassador to
the Soviet Union, would assure Poland's foreign minister that FDR had
not agreed to any revision of prewar Polish boundaries. In fact, the president had told Stalin that he had no objection to a new frontier for Poland
because he was interested in the Poles and Balts for only one reason:
their impact on the election campaign of 1944. According to the
official record of the Teheran Conference:

> He [Roosevelt] said personally he agreed with the view of Marshal Stalin as
> to the necessity of the restoration of a Polish state but would like to see the
> Eastern border moved further to the west and the Western border moved to
> the River Oder. He hoped, however, that the Marshal would understand that
> for political reasons outlined above, he could not participate in any decision
> here in Teheran or even next winter on this subject . . . the President went
> on to say that there were a number of persons of Lithuanian, Latvian, and
> Estonian origin, in that order, in the United States. He said he fully realized
> the three Baltic Republics had in history and again more recently been a
> part of Russia and added jokingly that when the Soviet armies reoccupied
> these areas, he did not intend to go to war with the Soviet Union on this
> point.[8]

None of this is to suggest that Churchill, in contrast with Roosevelt,
was exactly unswerving in his support for the Poles. One could not
expect someone in the position of British prime minister to be as much
concerned over the future of Warsaw as he would be over that of Cal-
cutta, Hong Kong, Athens, or even Paris. Full well did he know that
Soviet support at the bargaining table might prove invaluable in a test
of wills with Roosevelt. Some have gone so far as to suggest that
Churchill traded on the future of Poland for that of France. One sus-
pects, however, that the problem went deeper. Doubtless, he shared
something of the attitude of Permanent Under-Secretary of State Sir
Alec Cadogan, in whose eyes the Polish people were "suicidal" and to
whom Mikolajczyk seemed "unconstructive—like all Poles." At the
Moscow Conference of 1944, the king's first minister exchanged Polish
jokes with Stalin and intimated that his country took less interest in

the status of Poland than in that of other parts of the world. The previous year, when the Soviet leader proposed at Teheran to move Polish borders westward, Churchill signified his assent by moving three match sticks across the table. He also found it opportune, at both Teheran and Yalta, to criticize the Polish national character.[9]

Nevertheless, if the Polish people were ever represented in the counsels of the Big Three, they found their voice in Winston Churchill rather than in Franklin Roosevelt. Ultimately, the difference between London and Washington came down to a question of diplomatic judgment. Churchill concluded that while it might be futile to contest the Polish boundary issue, one must nevertheless fight for a pro-Western government in Warsaw. Roosevelt, on the other hand, demonstrated scant concern about the future of Poland because he never shared Churchill's suspicion of the Soviet Union. Churchill insisted on a total scrapping of the Lublin puppet government; FDR was content with a broadening. The former urged strong representations against Lublin while the latter sent weak ones accompanied by a slur against the London Poles. Where Churchill wanted to insist on Western observers, Roosevelt again demurred. When Mikolajczyk asked that Western troops be sent to Poland to prevent Russian reprisals, Roosevelt not only declined to send troops but proposed a political cease-fire, which could only help Russia. Churchill nudged him to intervene personally, but he preferred to let the ambassadors handle it. Exasperated, the prime minister opened fire: "Poland has lost her frontier. Is she now to lose her freedom? . . . We are in the presence of a great failure." Roosevelt, who diagnosed the problem as one of semantics, could not even be brought to the point of prodding Stalin.[10]

Perhaps it is suggestive that Roosevelt never appointed an ambassador to the London Poles once Biddle resigned in the aftermath of Teheran. Before this, he sided with Stalin on the hotly contested question of responsibility for the Katyn Forest Massacre, telling him that the London Poles must learn to act "with more common sense." After Teheran, from 1 December 1943 until August 1945, the United States continued in the same posture, with Roosevelt counseling Mikolajczyk to trust Stalin and pressing him to replace anti-Soviet cabinet members with neutrals or communist sympathizers. Secretly, he sent two pro-Soviet American Poles to Moscow against the advice of Hull and Stettinius, and in the months after Teheran he rejected two requests by Mikolajczyk and four by Ambassador Jan Ciechanowski for a personal meeting. When he did see the Polish prime minister in June of 1944, he promised he would help him establish his claim to Lvov, Tarnopol, and the oil fields of eastern Galicia. In truth, Poland might well have done without such help as it consisted in Roosevelt's telling Stalin that Polish demands were not to be regarded as demands but merely as suggestions for Soviet consideration. Mikolajczyk promptly resigned.[11]

Without question, Stalin held a strong hand. His armies were on the ground. Nevertheless, nothing about the shape of postwar Polish politics had been foreordained. There was more than empty pride in Mikolajczyk's charge that "we were sacrificed by our allies." Nowhere was it written that twenty thousand pro-Western Polish patriots had to die in the Warsaw Uprising. Roosevelt did not have to boost Soviet hopes at Teheran by conceding that Polish affairs were "of special concern" to Stalin. Nor did he have to remain silent when Churchill depicted Poles as the type of people who would never be satisfied. He need not have repeated to Stalin at Yalta what he had already told him, that his only interest in Poland was to appear "in some way involved with the question of freedom of elections." And he did not have to characterize Poles as a "quarrelsome people not only at home but also abroad." By stressing that his principal interest lay in six million Polish-American voters and alleging that in some years there had not really been any Polish government, he was sinking saber teeth into the future of eastern Europe. It is strange to read the minutes of the plenary meetings at Yalta and to discover that Stalin, of all people, was the only one to volunteer anything complimentary on the subject of Poland or its people.[12]

FDR made Stalin's work relatively easy. In the face of American willingness to grant unconditional Lend-Lease, Stalin responded with condescension: he was "willing to accept" it.[13] When Admiral William H. Standley, Roosevelt's ambassador to Moscow, spoke out against unconditional aid, the president dismissed him with a curt reminder that his mission had but one purpose: "full and friendly cooperation" with the Soviet Union. Again and again, Roosevelt described himself as "deeply appreciative" and "thrilled" at Soviet cooperation, and eventually the United States would succeed in shipping some four hundred thousand trucks, two million tons of petroleum products, four million tons of food, two thousand locomotives, and ten thousand flatcars, along with vast quantities of clothing. All to the Soviet Union.[14]

When roving envoy Joseph Davies journeyed to Moscow to convey a

Norman Davis with FDR at Campobello, June 1933. Davis, formerly under secretary of state and during the 1930s one of Roosevelt's roving envoys, represented the United States at various international conferences, including those held at London (1935) and Brussels (1937).
(Franklin D. Roosevelt Library.)

William Bullitt, ambassador to the Soviet Union (1933–36) and to France (1936–40), executive officer of the U.S. delegation to the London Economic Conference (1933), and roving presidential envoy on special missions to Europe and the Far East. Of all U.S. diplomats in the field, he was probably closest to Roosevelt and therefore the most influential.
(Franklin D. Roosevelt Library.)

Neville Chamberlain, British chancellor of the exchequer (1931–37) and prime minister (1937–40). Long a symbol of appeasement, Chamberlain is generally pictured waving an umbrella on the aftermath of the Munich Conference and proclaiming "Peace in our time." He is likewise quoted as saying it is always best and safest to count on the Americans for "nothing but words." (Franklin D. Roosevelt Library.)

Prince Konoye, Japanese premier (1937–39 and 1940–41). Konoye concluded the Axis pact with Germany and Italy as well as a non-aggression agreement with the Soviet Union. In 1941, he offered to meet Roosevelt face-to-face to arrange a compromise peace in the Far East, but Roosevelt declined. (Franklin D. Roosevelt Library.)

FDR with Dr. Carlos Saavedra Lamas, 30 November 1936, Buenos Aires. As Argentina's minister for foreign affairs (1932–38), Saavedra Lamas served as president of the League of Nations Assembly (1936) and chaired the Buenos Aires Conference of 1935 that ended the long Chaco War. In 1936 he was awarded the Nobel Peace Prize. (Franklin D. Roosevelt Library.)

Sumner Welles (center) with Mrs. Gordon Crawford and the rector of St. Paul's Church, Mt. Vernon, 6 December 1941. Welles, ambassador to Cuba (1933) and under secretary of state (1933–43), was perhaps the most powerful of all Roosevelt's diplomatic advisers. (Franklin D. Roosevelt Library.)

T. V. Soong with FDR in Washington. Soong, brother-in-law of Sun Yat-sen and Chiang Kai-shek, served as China's minister of finance (1927–33) and foreign minister (1942–45). In 1936 he founded the Bank of China. (Franklin D. Roosevelt Library.)

Generalissimo and Mme Chiang Kai-shek with FDR and Churchill, Cairo Conference, 25 November 1943. Roosevelt gave Chiang his solemn promise, subsequently broken, that China would regain complete control of Manchuria, including the key ports of Dairen and Port Arthur. (United States Army Signal Corps.)

Seated, from left to right, at the Quebec Conference of 1943: Anthony Eden, FDR, Princess Alice, and Churchill. Standing, from the left: the Earl of Athlone, Governor General of Canada; Prime Minister W. L. Mackenzie King; Alexander Cadogan; and Brendan Bracken. Among other things, the First Quebec Conference reaffirmed 1 May 1944 as the target date for OVERLORD (the Normandy invasion). (Franklin D. Roosevelt Library.)

General Joseph ("Vinegar Joe") Stilwell, center of the table, at the Cairo Conference, 1943. Stilwell, Chiang's chief of staff in the China war theater and commander of all American forces in the China-Burma theater, acted as Roosevelt's leading representative in China during the crucial period 1942–44. (United States Army Signal Corps.)

Harry Hopkins and Averell Harriman at Teheran, 2 December 1943. Hopkins was FDR's Lend-Lease administrator as well as his personal envoy to Russia and Britain. Harriman served as American ambassador to the Soviet Union (1943–46). (Franklin D. Roosevelt Library.)

Secretary of State Cordell Hull (center), Director of War Mobilization James Byrnes and FDR, 17 December 1943. Father of the Reciprocal Trade Agreement program and a specialist in Latin American affairs, Hull served longer than any other secretary of state (1933–45) and in 1945 was awarded the Nobel Peace Prize. (Franklin D. Roosevelt Library.)

FDR with Stanislaw Mikolajczyk, 14 June 1944. Polish prime minister in exile from 1943 to 1944, Mikolajczyk resigned when he failed to obtain firm backing from the president of the United States.
(Franklin D. Roosevelt Library.)

General de Gaulle on a visit to the United States, 6 July 1944. After founding the Free French Movement in 1940 and spearheading French resistance groups around the world, de Gaulle led his side to victory in 1945 with the aid of Allied armies and in spite of Roosevelt's determined opposition. (National Archives.)

Molotov and Stalin at the Yalta Conference, 1945. Many controversial questions relating to the postwar world were decided at Yalta, including the future of Germany and Eastern Europe, Soviet influence in China, and the founding of the United Nations. Stalin was *de facto* leader of the Soviet Union from 1924 to 1953, and Molotov served brilliantly as Soviet foreign commissar from 1936 to 1956. (United States Army Signal Corps.)

King Ibn Saud and FDR in conference (with General Eisenhower and Admiral Leahy looking on) at Great Bitter Lake, Suez. FDR sought King Saud's support for American oil investments as well as the creation of a Jewish state in Palestine. Saud gave qualified approval to plans for oil development; but to the cause of Zionism, he turned a deaf ear.
(United States Army Signal Corps.)

presidential apology for Standley's behavior, Stalin listened in stony silence, doodling on a piece of paper. Davies then appealed for a personal meeting between the Soviet and American chiefs and, denigrating Churchill, reassured his listener that there would be no American objection to a new Polish border as long as it was postponed so as not to inflame American opinion before the next election.[15]

There is probably no better example of how one-sided the Washington-Moscow relationship had become by 1945 than the sporadic negotiations which took place for a summit conference. Roosevelt began importuning Stalin for such a conference as early as April 1942. Standley suggested a conference between the two leaders in Alaskan or Siberian waters. Churchill then sounded the Kremlin on a top-level Soviet-American meeting in Iceland. Davies was thus delivering the president's third invitation in May of 1943 when he approached Stalin for a parley à deux in Fairbanks, Alaska, during July or August. The Soviet leader accepted this time, only to renege when he found Roosevelt not delivering on his promise of a second European front. In September of 1943, Roosevelt tried a fourth time. Stalin again refused, awaiting the moment of maximum psychological advantage, when German troops would be expelled from Russia and his own armies would stand ready to "liberate" Poland. In the meantime, it was agreed that the foreign ministers of France, Britain, the United States, and the Soviet Union might hold a preparatory conference and discuss the location of a future summit. Churchill wanted the meeting held in London since he had gone to Moscow the previous year; Stalin, just as decidedly, preferred Moscow. Roosevelt suggested Casablanca, Tunis, or Sicily as a compromise, but Stalin held firm and the president acquiesced—that is, until Churchill convinced him that such an arrangement would involve loss of British face. He then wrote Stalin that the question of location must be reopened because Moscow was too distant for an ailing Hull. What is important is that in the end Roosevelt sent Hull anyway.[16]

The tone of the correspondence is as arresting as its content. In discussing the site for a summit meeting, Churchill proposed London or Scapa Flow, whereas Stalin expressed a preference for Teheran. To break the impasse, Roosevelt let it be known that he could not go as far as Teheran since he had to stay in close touch with Congress. Instead, he proposed four locations in the same general vicinity. Stalin promised to consult his colleagues but then informed Roosevelt that Molotov and members of the Politburo preferred Teheran for its telegraphic connection with the war front. Roosevelt replied, "I am deeply disappointed . . . it is impossible for me to go." He explained that he needed to stay within convenient range of his legislature in order to sign bills that had to be returned to Washington within a specified number of days as required by "a constitutional government more than one hundred and fifty years old." Members of the cabinet and leaders of Congress were adamant, he pleaded. Then came a fairly apt summation of the Soviet-American relationship as it had evolved over a lengthy period: "*I am begging you*" not to "fail me in this crisis" (italics added). To emphasize the sense of urgency, Hull delivered the president's appeal in person and told Stalin to his face that he was the kind of leader who appeared in history only once every hundred or two hundred years.[17]

Stalin withstood the flattery. "I cannot but take into account the circumstances which you say prevent you from going to Teheran," he replied in a letter to Roosevelt. "It is for you alone, of course, to decide whether you can go there. . . . As far as I am concerned there is no city more suitable." Molotov, he added, would be free to go anywhere as a substitute. At this point, Roosevelt, extremely eager as always for a personal encounter, informed Stalin that he had discovered a way of communicating with Congress: if he heard of the need to sign a bill, he would fly out of Teheran as the bill was being delivered from Washington and execute the signing in Tunis: "I have therefore decided to go to Teheran and this makes me especially happy." In a subsequent letter, the president asked Stalin's advice on where to stay once his party reached the Iranian capital, and Stalin suggested that he stay at the heavily guarded Soviet embassy, promising, "I shall be at your service." After the meeting, he wrote Roosevelt that he was glad to have been able to "render" him a service.[18]

On meeting Stalin, Roosevelt was the first to speak: "I'm glad to see you. I have tried for a long time to bring this about." There were numerous jokes at Churchill's expense; indeed, FDR refused to meet individually with the Briton the way he did with the Russian. He took delight, he said, in welcoming the Soviets as a new member of the international family circle. Later, on his return home, he assured the American people that judging from his talks with Marshal Stalin, they would "get along very well with him and the Russian people—very well indeed."[19] It was a lesson similar to McReynolds's lesson of 1933, one not quickly unlearned, especially when FDR drove it deeper into the national consciousness as part of his Third Inaugural Address a month later: "We have learned the simple truth, as Emerson said, that 'the only way to have a friend is to be one.' "[20]

By the end of the year, Stalin had extended his power beyond anything dreamed of by the czars and given Americans a succession of lessons in the art of statecraft. To Hopkins, he termed it a mistake to believe that just because a state was small, it was necessarily innocent. To Davies, who hoped that a top-level meeting between Soviet and American leaders would resolve all outstanding problems, Stalin replied that he was not so sure. Litvinov instructed Ambassador Bullitt in like manner: there was no such thing as "really friendly" relations between nations. When FDR took the liberty of calling Stalin "Uncle Joe," the reaction proved unexpectedly frigid. Always, it seemed, one man spoke as teacher while the other listened as pupil. On one occasion, when Roosevelt suggested that India needed reform from the bottom up, Stalin remarked that in a land with so many tiers of culture and no interchange between the castes, this would invite revolutionary chaos. The Soviet chairman also favored restoration of the monarchy in Yugoslavia. On another occasion, when Roosevelt called Hitler mad, Stalin again corrected him, pointing out that whatever one might think of Hitler's methods or his level of cultural and political sophistication, there was no ground for judging him mentally unbalanced. Only a very able man could have succeeded in unifying the German people. Finally, as if to make the picture complete, FDR advocated a peace imposed by "four policemen" only to be reminded by the Soviet leader of the feelings of smaller nations. Realistically, Stalin predicted that China, one of the prospective four, would not be powerful enough in the aftermath of the war to assume such responsibility.[21]

Of Roosevelt's relationship with Chiang Kai-shek there is only one thing to be said. It was nearly the reverse of what has been observed in the case of Stalin. FDR made practically no effort to assuage Chiang's fears or to cater to him personally. In the epic battle for China, he extended remarkably little material or moral aid, and such sacrifices as were made by the United States tended to undermine Chiang politically. Intentionally or not, great blows were leveled against the prestige of Nationalist China as Roosevelt broke one promise after another.

FDR liked to recall the way China's first lady pounded the White House bridge table to underscore her country's need for aid. What escaped him, however, was the reason for such insistence. The president's personal representative in China, General Joseph "Vinegar Joe" Stilwell, regretted that "we fail in *all* our commitments and blithely tell him [Chiang] to just carry on, old top." In fact, Roosevelt broke virtually every important promise made to Chiang between the time of Pearl Harbor and his death in April 1945. He shipped less than 10 percent of the aid pledged. He went back on his commitment to assist Chiang's Burma campaign with an amphibious invasion. At various times, supplies earmarked for Chungking were diverted without consultation. Scores of bombers and transports, once the entire U.S. Tenth Air Force in India, were rerouted to bypass China after the United States had given its word. Roosevelt pledged a loan of a billion dollars which was never delivered. And more than once, he promised increased tonnage to be flown from India over the Himalayan Hump. In almost every instance, such tonnage failed to eventuate.[22]

Only the whipcord of public insult can compare with this array of broken promises as a factor in Chiang's ultimate defeat on the mainland, at least insofar as Roosevelt's role is concerned. Much has been made of American willingness to relinquish the privileged status of extraterritoriality by a treaty signed on 11 January 1943. Eleven months later, Congress repealed the Chinese Exclusion Act, making it possible for 105 Chinese to immigrate to the United States each year. And to this must be added Secretary Hull's success in obtaining Stalin's consent to include China in the Four Nation Declaration. Yet such concessions proved minor when placed alongside the many humiliations Chungking had to endure. It would have cost Roosevelt little to have greeted the Chinese leader when his plane landed in Cairo. Barred from the Atlantic Conference of 1941, China took no part in major Allied planning groups such as the Joint Chiefs of Staff and the Munitions Board, to name two of the more prestigious ones. Membership on the Pacific War Council, thrown to Chiang as a sop, was no substitute for genuine collegiality, an idea Roosevelt seems never to have entertained.[23] Gandhi's jibe about British and American racial prejudice appeared all too apt when it turned out that Chinese representatives received no invitation to help plan the Burma campaign in which their finest divisions were expected to fight. Chiang merely received word from Roosevelt at Quebec apprising him of what "the Prime Minister and I have just decided."[24]

Chiang felt humiliated when Roosevelt failed to inform him of developments as they broke during the Casablanca Conference of late January 1943. He was likewise prevented from sending an official representative to the Teheran and Yalta conferences, where the fate of a vital portion of his realm would be settled. During the Dumbarton Oaks Conference, in which questions of world organization were hammered out on a multi-lateral basis, Stalin convinced Roosevelt to hold two separate sessions: one for Britain, America, and the Soviet Union; another, of secondary importance, to include Britain, America, and China. For Chiang to be given only a week's notice before the ill-fated Doolittle raid, then to have Washington go ahead with it over his strenuous objection, con-stituted a stunning indignity. Although bombing hits were made on Tokyo for the first time, all sixteen of Doolittle's aircraft were diverted from their targets or forced to make crash landings, which brought the Japanese down like hornets on any Chinese who dared to succor the pilots. As Chungking had warned, Japan was able to discover and destroy the intended landing fields, and Chiang had to abandon his dream of bombing Japan from Chinese bases. All American B-24s were sent to Egypt. In a similar incident, Vice-President Henry Wallace's trip to Chungking became known to Chiang through a press leak. Overall, things were not good. Nationalist China reaped a mere one half of one percent of all Lend-Lease aid, and this came with strings attached to conciliate the Chinese communists.[25]

Even if Chiang had managed to survive such treatment, he would still have had to withstand the kind of diplomatic punishment meted out to him and his country behind his back, something already mentioned but worth repeating. After solemnly promising at Cairo that China would recover all of Manchuria, including the ports of Dairen and Port Arthur, which together held the key to surrounding industrial areas, Roosevelt went on at Teheran to say that he thought Dairen should be converted to an open port subject to Soviet "preeminent interests." When Stalin replied that Chiang might object, Roosevelt would not hear of it. So, too, in the case of Port Arthur, which went to the Soviet navy on a ninety-nine-year lease. Chiang may have been reassured at Cairo on the return of Outer Mongolia to China, but again, FDR made no effort to follow through at the conference table. Finally, Yalta undercut Chiang's best chance for operational control of Manchuria by awarding Stalin a prime stake in the railways. Though it can be argued that America was pursuing a Europe-first strategy and that the Soviets, who demanded even more than they received, would have been in position to take for themselves what Roosevelt freely offered, this is rather to miss the point. Chiang regarded the issue as one of face; and Roosevelt, not content to underwrite Stalin's "preeminent interest" in an area that he had championed through the 1930s as the exclusive preserve of China, even to the point of war with Japan, now laid the blame for civil war upon Chiang personally. The fault, he told Stalin, "lay more with the Kuomintang."[26] Here was the ultimate slap.

There is evidence that Roosevelt, after suggesting to Stilwell at Cairo that an intransigent Chiang ought to be eliminated "once and for all," ordered a contingency plan drawn for Chiang's assassination. Needless to say, no such plan ever went into effect. But the very idea of coalition government, as prescribed by American officials, posed a lethal threat. No one knew this better than Chiang, who forecast for Chungking the same fate as Warsaw and Belgrade. Yet it was one thing for Chiang to know something, another for him to act upon it in the face of unreasoning American influence. FDR not only instructed Patrick J. Hurley to obtain "a working agreement between the generalissimo and the North China forces," he also refused American aid for use against Mao, suggested that the American military establish a mission in Yenan (communist headquarters), and sent American envoys by way of Moscow. Wallace initiated a U.S. intelligence mission to Yenan and, along with Hurley, breathed new life into Red China by going to Mao's personal suite. Subsequently, Hurley stood for photographs beside Chou En-lai while communist forces reaped a harvest of Lend-Lease medical supplies and Stilwell continued to press Chungking relentlessly for concessions to the Left.[27]

Admittedly, Roosevelt was not without justification for leaning toward coalition government, although the wisdom of such intense pressure as was ultimately brought to bear amid the exigencies of wartime is arguable. Reports filed by State Department officials, many of them firsthand, bore witness to widespread corruption in the ranks of the Kuomintang. It was widely believed that Chiang held only marginal control over portions of the Nationalist army. Furthermore, few Americans were willing to excuse such alleged KMT faults as venality and inefficiency (never ascribed to Chiang personally) notwithstanding the foreign and domestic war that Chiang's government had been obliged to wage since 1937 and 1927 respectively. Roosevelt's officials, with scant concern for the difficulty of embarking upon social reform in a boiling caldron, tended to see the extremity of the situation as warranting extreme measures. Then, too, Chiang's problems appeared all the more damning alongside traits commonly associated with his commu-

nist opposition: honesty, cohesiveness, democracy, liberality, progressive reform, and a sworn determination to fight. Above all, China's
armies were not thought to be doing their best on the military front.
Chiang's preoccupation with the communist menace and his Fabian
strategy in the contest with Tokyo were neither understood nor approved by American observers. In short, Chiang was regarded by many
in the United States as having lost his Mandate from Heaven, and it
was to Mao Tse-tung that the future seemed of right to belong.[28]

One must bear in mind, of course, that Roosevelt's perception of
what constituted reality in China was conditioned by the perspicacity
of his envoys. Which gives rise to still another question. What were the
qualifications of those chosen by Roosevelt to represent American interests in Chungking? One of them, Clarence Gauss, American ambassador from 1941 to 1944, proved unpopular with the Chinese, while
another, Donald Nelson, former chairman of the War Production
Board, was seeking release from embarrassing political coils at the
time of his appointment. Roosevelt thought nothing of tapping Willkie, Wallace, and Hurley, all during an election year. Wallace's trip, it
should be added, was timed in such a way as to remove him from the
councils of the Democratic Convention and allow Roosevelt to dispose
of him in favor of Harry Truman. Although it is true that the vice
president was mildly familiar with things Chinese, Morgenthau described the cabinet meeting at which his trip was discussed as "a fiasco" in which the president was terribly misinformed. On arrival in
China, Wallace sought to convince Chiang of the genuine patriotism of
American communists until his host politely but firmly reminded him
that Chinese communists, unlike their brethren in America, were
counting on an immediate seizure of power.[29]

As for Hurley, who replaced Gauss and was known to certain Kuomintang officials as the "Second Big Wind," suffice it to say that he once
referred to the first lady of China as "Madame Shek" and to Chiang
himself as "Mr. Shek." His way of impressing Yenan leaders was to let
out with a Choctaw Indian war whoop. He was perfectly capable of
tongue-lashing Foreign Minister T. V. Soong in front of other Chinese
officials just as he lost his temper with General Wedemeyer's chief of
staff at a cocktail party. To a man who admired Yenan's open shops and
free exchange of money, the "so-called Communists" were simply striv-
ing for government of the people, by the people, and for the people;
indeed, "the only difference between Oklahoma Republicans and the

Chinese Communists" was that "the Oklahoma Republicans" were "not armed." Gauss's immediate predecessor, Nelson Johnson, came somewhat closer to the truth when he remarked that the Red Chinese were "no more democratic than Trotsky or Stalin."[30] Johnson, though, did not have the ear of the White House.

Typical of the flights of fancy to which Americans were prone was an observation by Congressman Walter Judd: "We are nearer to the Chinese in our basic beliefs, our basic emphasis on the rights of the individual, and in our basic personal habits of democracy than we are to most of the countries of Europe." Such thinking was more the rule than the exception, particularly on the part of those closest to FDR. Owen Lattimore, presidential adviser to Chiang in 1941 and a famed sinologist, predicted that China would emerge as one of the world's great democracies. Lattimore did as much as anyone to promote the myth of Chinese individualism, once describing Chungking as a "genuinely democratic democracy." Another White House aide, Lauchlin Currie, who visited Chungking in 1942, ostensibly to untangle Chinese finances, sided with Chiang on the issue of native administration of Lend-Lease as well as on Stilwell's removal. Yet he continued to view local politics through the prism of American lenses. Coalition government, the release of political prisoners, a free press, radical agrarian reform, increased taxation of landlords, and other "small steps in the direction of democracy" were typical elements in a typically parochial prescription. Currie prodded Chiang to take a liberal into his cabinet and applauded the institution of popularly elected advisory councils on the local level.[31]

Naturally, in considering Roosevelt's choice of envoys, none can compare in importance with Joseph Stilwell. As the president's personal representative and commander of Allied forces in the China theater, the general could point to a number of positive points in his background, including ten years of service in China, first as language officer, then as military attaché and regimental commander. Having lived with native Chinese as a construction foreman and studied Chinese on the university level, he knew more about the language and customs of China than perhaps any other senior military officer. Just as significant as credentials, however, "Vinegar Joe" suffered from an almost total lack of diplomacy. Tact and a healthy admixture of savoir faire are qualities one might expect on the part of any individual entrusted with control over China's supply of Lend-Lease, indeed of anyone serving as chief of Allied staff to Chiang himself and managing Allied operations involving the joint use of British, Chinese, and American troops.[32] Such qualities, however, were conspicuous for their absence. Three times during the prewar period, Stilwell would doubtless have been fired from his staff position at Fort Benning had it not been for the intercession of George Marshall. Similarly, there were at least three occasions when he might have been relieved of his duties in China at the request of the British and Chinese had it not been for this same individual's loyal support. As coordinator of the Anglo-American war effort in his theater, he could not get along with the British, whom he described as "damn snotty" in their short pants and swagger sticks. Admiral Mountbatten figures in his diary as "Glamour Boy," and FDR earns sobriquets such as "unimpressive," "a lot of wind," and "old softy." Peeved by Roosevelt's patronizing tone at Cairo, he reacted with characteristic petulance: "F.D.R. calls me 'Joe' the double xx-ing bastard." Much of his language is too crude to bear repetition.[33]

Roosevelt felt it necessary to chide Stilwell for public use of the appellation "Peanut" in snide reference to Chiang, and Marshall warned him several times to drop his wisecracking. Essentially heedless and biased in his view of the Chinese, he misunderstood Chiang's New Life Movement with its stress on punctuality, good posture, cleanliness, and neatness. It seemed to him quaint to ask people to refrain from spitting watermelon seeds or to exhort them to kill more rats. Nor could he ever come to terms with the Oriental insistence on face. Without hesitation, he spoke critically of Chinese officers to their face and lectured Soong on the need for wartime sacrifice.[34]

Repeatedly, Stilwell defied Chiang's orders, rejoicing at reports of provincial insurrection and using his authority over Lend-Lease to press for coalition with Yenan. When the generalissimo wrote in his files "does not know discipline," he knew whereof he spoke. Professor Chin-tung Liang mentions five cases of insubordination on Stilwell's part within a hundred days, 23 December 1943 to 7 April 1944. At the Trident Conference, in broad daylight before Roosevelt and Churchill, Stilwell branded Chiang a fool. He then returned to Chungking and repeated the accusation at Chinese military headquarters. Perhaps it is more than a little ironic that after forcing the first Burma campaign on an unwilling Chiang and sustaining sharp reverses, he proceeded to demand the execution of several of Chiang's high-ranking officers, including two generals, on the charge that they had been recalcitrant.[35]

Last of all, it should be said that if much of the friction between general and generalissimo stemmed from clashing personalities or differences in perception of the communist menace, there was an equally serious breach when it came to tactics and strategy. Chiang wished to concentrate his limited resources on China proper, where the Japanese were driving ahead with all the awesome power of a modern military machine. This is where the bulk of his domestic opposition lay and where the political future of his regime would most likely be decided. Stilwell, on the other hand, wanted to force Tokyo out of Burma and restore Chinese access to the sea. To do so, he was willing to gamble with Chiang's best divisions. Furthermore, Chiang favored a defensive style of combat, whereas Stilwell exhorted his Chinese lieutenants to risk all. Chiang emphasized the excellence of Japanese communications and the difficult terrain. Even with the aid of an amphibious assault, he knew that as one who stood to lose far more on the offensive than on the defensive he would need to outnumber the Japanese by a sizable margin. It was thus with much foreboding that he turned over his finest armies, the Fifth and Sixth, in June of 1942—something which amazed even Stilwell—only to see them tortured on a rack of malnutrition, overexposure, and frontal assault. If Japan lost twelve hundred men and suffered three thousand casualties, Chiang lost more than ten thousand. In this way, Stilwell drained off Chiang's best-trained and best-equipped reserves, and the generalissimo, who asked for his recall, refused ever again to deal with him on a confidential basis.

Through all of this, Roosevelt informed his cabinet that he took "great satisfaction" in Stilwell's handling of the situation, and Marshall continued to send warm personal greetings. The upshot is that Stilwell survived to argue for a second Burma offensive, one which proved just as unrewarding as the first in terms of practical gain. Japan's grip on Burma was broken at Myitchina, but the building of the Ledo Road over a mountainous stretch of 271 kilometers took two years, yielding in the end a mere six thousand tons per month and falling rapidly into disuse. As far as the generalissimo was concerned, his view of Roosevelt's representative remained much as it had been from the outset:

> If Stilwell were only unable to cooperate with me personally, that would be one thing. But his character and attitude are deeply prejudiced against the Chinese as a whole. He still perceives us as a backward country. Not

only does he insult us but he goes further and embarrasses us. Worst of all, he is a man who goes back on his word. . . . After he came here, the morale of our troops was undermined. . . . [He] believes that China has no good fighting men and he does not believe that we can win. . . . If we do not do something about it, I think the situation will be grave.[36]

Chiang found himself at bay. Owing to American policy, he was not at liberty to campaign against domestic enemies; neither could he defend himself adequately against front-line drives from the sea. Japanese campaigns in the summer of 1944 stretched his forces thin along a line drawn from Peking to Hankow, thence to Canton. He mounted a powerful counterattack when Changsha fell and held Hengyang for more than forty days of heavy siege. Yet in his greatest moment of need, Stilwell refused Lend-Lease and waved aside every entreaty for aid. Colonel Claire Chennault accused his fellow American of withholding vital supplies and deliberately neglecting Chiang's needs in order to gain command of all Chinese forces. And not without cause. When Japanese troops advanced to Kweilin and Liuchow and Chiang's warlord enemy, Li Chi-chen, began maneuvering to undermine Nationalist authority in eight southwestern provinces, Stilwell shook the dust from his feet and flew to New Delhi. Again, Chiang demanded his recall; but Roosevelt, instead of removing him as promised on more than one occasion, tried to promote him to the command of all Chinese armies. An extraordinary presidential order was handed to the generalissimo in the presence of Stilwell—so extraordinary, in fact, that the latter was inspired to compose some doggerel in honor of the occasion: "F.D.R. has finally spoken plain words . . . I handed this bundle of paprika to the Peanut and then sank back with a sigh. The harpoon hit the little bugger right in the solar plexus, and went right through him."[37]

As is known, Chiang ultimately forced Stilwell's ouster. Roosevelt had little choice. Still, the whole episode ran against Roosevelt's political grain and likely contributed to the final erosion of American support for Nationalist survival. It would appear that Stilwell, along with many of his State Department aides, had developed a high regard for Chinese communism as early as 1937. "Vinegar Joe" was convinced that Mao knew how to lead a guerrilla movement, and before leaving China in 1944 he paid a courtesy call on General Chu Teh, commander of Mao's Eighth Route Army.[38] Roosevelt partook of the same sentiment. He could not believe, any more than Stilwell, that there were "real" communists in China. Moscow denied it, and influential figures in both State and Treasury departments had affixed the innocuous label of "agrarian reformers" to Chiang's opposition.[39] Letters addressed to the White House in the late 1930s by Evans Carlson, a roving marine officer, laid the initial groundwork by emphasizing actual but misleading features of the Red regime such as its friendliness to Western observers. At the same time, Roosevelt was constantly reminded of the more temperamental, inefficient, and corrupt aspects of Kuomintang leadership. It is no wonder that he came to regard Chiang as unsympathetic to the plight of the masses.[40] Professors Griswold of Yale and Fairbank of Harvard were comparing Chiang's government to a fascist dictatorship. Meanwhile, Roosevelt and his advisers took offense at what they judged to be un-American behavior on the part of the Chiangs.[41] Finally, the president, along with Stilwell, clung to the notion, as seen above, that Chiang's armies did not fight well against Japan and would fare much better if they could only mend their fences at home.[42]

Such ideas were to remain *de rigeur* for a good many years. A State Department White Paper issued in the fall of 1949, after Chiang's retreat to Formosa, devoted more than a thousand pages to the case against Chiang, stressing faults and failures and especially the ways in which his organization refused to democratize on the U.S. model. Not once in a thousand pages was the reader given any reason to suspect that Roosevelt or any of his envoys might have been remiss in any way or that they might ever have jeopardized Chiang's chance for survival. A similar presumption characterized the Wallace Report, read into the record of the first session of the Eighty-second Congress, and another well-known report, the Davies Memorandum, issued on 6 January 1945, argued that Chiang was obviously fighting a losing battle so that the United States had no realistic alternative but to throw in its lot with Mao. This has been the line taken by most American scholars ever since.[43]

Just as one encounters repeated reference to Chiang's alleged unwillingness to fight, much is predicated upon his declaration of satisfaction with the Sino-Soviet Treaty of August 1945.[44] On paper, the document provided for withdrawal of Soviet forces from Manchuria within three months, noninterference in Chinese internal affairs, and the awarding of Soviet political support to Chiang. Optimists hailed it as a victory for the Kuomintang since Soviet troops had already shouldered their way into Manchuria and assumed a position from which they could aid the Red Chinese as never before. To argue, however, that Chungking officials genuinely approved of what Roosevelt had done behind their back at Yalta is to fly in the face of abundant evidence to the contrary. Even Mao and company could scarcely believe it when they learned of America's covert action. Chargé Walter Robertson recalled later that his trip along with Hurley in June 1945 to inform Chiang of the terms of Yalta had been a "humiliating experience" made all the worse in light of subsequent American pressure for the Sino-Soviet "friendship" pact, something which sent a "blush of shame" up the top of Robertson's neck. Foreign Minister T. V. Soong refused point-blank to sign the treaty, and when forced by Washington to choose between signing and resignation, he chose the latter. According to Hurley's recollection, Roosevelt himself harbored second thoughts, and this is confirmed by an attempt on the part of the State Department to alter the terms of Yalta after the fact.[45] For months after FDR's return from the Crimea, the wording of the text remained secret. On 6 March, Soong was denied a meeting with the president, and it was not until June that his government learned (accidentally) the actual terms of agreement. Before this, when Soong asked Acting Secretary of State Grew the meaning of the phrase "preeminent Soviet interests," he was told that the United States could not be certain of its meaning and that he should consult Stalin. In vain did an anxious Chiang suggest that Britain, the United States, and the Soviet Union act as joint guarantors with particular attention to sections regarding Manchuria, Sakhalin, and the Kurile Islands. In vain did he hope that Port Arthur might become a naval base jointly administered by China and the Big Three. Truman refused this or any other means of softening the impact of Yalta, and it was only then that Chungking, with nowhere else to turn, accepted the face-saving treaty of August, which was proclaimed by the New York Times "a victory for peace as great as any scored on the battlefield."[46] How easily the Soviets violated it, and with what effect, is scarcely in need of retelling.

Some have suggested that Roosevelt should not be faulted for misreading the situation in China since his view jibed with that of the more experienced British.[47] This, however, does not square with the facts. When Ambassador Johnson was relieved by Roosevelt in 1941 and replaced by Gauss, Chungking looked increasingly to General Sir Adrian Carton de Wiart, Churchill's personal representative on the scene, as well as to the regular British ambassador, Sir Horace Seymour. London did what amounts to the opposite of Washington by transferring Seymour's predecessor, Sir Archibald Kerr, to Moscow, where his political sympathies were not as likely to be wasted. Like most British observers, Seymour realized the folly of coalition government and guessed correctly that the more Roosevelt insisted upon it, the more Chiang would be driven into the hands of extremists and the more intransigent the communists would become.[48] Men such as G. P. Hudson of the Foreign Office not only rejected any application of the word "democracy" in the Western sense to things Oriental; they saw very clearly that one could not ride two horses in China any more than one could do so in Yugoslavia or Greece. Yenan would gravitate toward Moscow, and if the United States did not throw its full weight to Chiang, it risked serious consequences; Red China would be no more pro-American than Tito was pro-British. Eden, as may be seen, viewed the situation similarly. "I was much impressed by Chiang," he noted: "His strength is that of the steel blade. Madame [Chiang] surprised me. She was friendly, a trifle queenly perhaps. Obviously used to getting her own way, but an industrious and earnest interpreter and neither sprightly nor touchy as I had been led to expect. I liked them both, Chiang particularly, and I should like to know them better."

Churchill's foreign secretary regarded the Yalta accord as discreditable and advised Downing Street not to sign it. Churchill, for his part, considered Chiang to be as fine a leader as the West was likely to see. The prime minister was not by any means a sentimental admirer of the Chinese. He could see little use in touting Chiang as one of the Big Four, and he viewed Roosevelt's estimate of Chinese influence in the postwar era as highly inflated. Nonetheless, he quite agreed with Eden and Hudson on the essentials of the political situation, and he came away from Cairo impressed with Chiang's "calm, reserved, and efficient personality."[49]

One last observation may be in order before going on to examine Roosevelt's status and standing in various regions of the world, Great Britain included. Churchill had to deal with a civil war in Greece comparable in many respects to that in China, and it may well be that if he had acted as FDR did, Athens would have capitulated to communist guerrillas. The Greek equivalent of the Red Chinese were the EAM and ELAS groups demanding an end to monarchy and clamoring for coalition with the pro-Western government led by M. Papandreou. Both were Moscow-fed, and Roosevelt acted predictably in urging Churchill to yield to the "inevitable." What is noteworthy is the kind of answer returned by the prime minister:

> We are an old ally of Greece. We had 40,000 casualties in trying to defend Greece against Hitler, not counting Crete. The Greek King and the Greek Government have placed themselves under our protection.
>
> It would be quite easy for me, on the general principle of slithering to the left, which is so popular in foreign policy, to let things rip when the King of Greece would probably be forced to abdicate and EAM would work a reign of terror in Greece. . . . The only way I can prevent this is by persuading the Russians to quit boosting EAM and ramming it forward with all their force.

Where the president handed over the keys to Manchuria and invited a Soviet voice in Chinese politics, the prime minister negotiated a spheres-of-influence agreement with Stalin whereby Greece fell strictly within Britain's orbit. Stalin proved true to his word, and although Churchill pressured Papandreou to allow a handful of leftists into his cabinet in return for their promise of loyal cooperation, this was merely an expedient. What mattered was that British troops entered Athens as soon as the Germans pulled out, and when EAM-ELAS forces began to engage Papandreou's men in combat, Churchill threw in additional army units as needed and spurned any form of substantive political compromise while the life of the Greek government was at stake.[50]

December of 1944 brought events to a climax. EAM-ELAS units fought hand-to-hand up and down the streets of Athens, and several established British papers, in concert with the American press, began to protest intervention on the ground that it thwarted free expression of the Greek will. Thus it was that Churchill found himself before a jeering House of Commons in a situation not unlike others that rang down through the crowded years of a brilliant career. He could go one of two ways, but as had been true so often in the past, he chose to meet the challenge head-on. "Democracy," he exclaimed, "is no harlot to be picked up in the street by a man with a tommy gun": "We are told that because we do not allow gangs of heavily armed guerrillas to descend from the mountains and install themselves, with all the bloody terror and vigour of which they are capable, in power in great capitals, we are traitors to democracy. I repulse that claim." In the end, the government won a vote of confidence by the impressive margin of 279–30. Even the

White House sent congratulations. At the same time, to satisfy "informed" opinion at home, Roosevelt continued to undercut Churchill and Papandreou through statements released by Secretary of State Edward R. Stettinius, Jr. Churchill therefore renewed his appeal to the president on 14 December: "You will realize how very serious it would be if we withdrew, as we easily could, and the result was a frightful massacre, and an extreme Left Wing regime under Communist inspiration installed itself, as it would, in Athens. . . . The fact that you are supposed to be against us, in accordance with the last sentence of Stettinius' press release, has added, as I feared, to our difficulties and burdens." Hopkins replied to the prime minister two days later: American public opinion was "deteriorating rapidly," and the president might have to issue a statement on the need for a free world. Still, Churchill refused to give ground, even in the face of criticism from Field Marshal Alexander and the British ambassador to Greece. There must be no peace without victory, he insisted. To Alexander, he wrote in no uncertain language that "the political field in the present circumstances can only be entered by the gate of success." Not until 26 December, with the military situation in Athens well in hand, did he agree on a regency to take the place of the Greek monarch, stipulating, however, that there were to be no communist sympathizers in the Papandreou cabinet.[51]

What Churchill proved was that "inevitability" may on occasion be forced to give way to vision and courage. In the wake of the Yalta Conference and with Chiang's future clouded by the ink of the Crimea, Britain's prime minister entered Athens in an open car. Thin lines of kilted Greek soldiers stood between him and an enormous, boisterous crowd of well-wishers. In the evening, fifty thousand persons gathered expectantly in Constitution Square to hear him speak impromptu. And what they heard were the words of a steadfast ally: "Freedom and prosperity and happiness are dear to all nations of the British Commonwealth and Empire. We who have been associated with you in the very long struggle for Greek liberty will march with you till we reach the end of the dark valley, and we will march with you till we reach the broad highlands of justice and peace."[52]

Granted, Greece and China cannot be equated in every respect. One of them, in addition to being more accessible geographically than the other, appeared vital to Britain's lifeline through the Mediterranean. Nevertheless, the parallel is sufficiently clear to reveal a notable difference in diplomatic style. FDR seems to have been convinced that he had only two choices in China: either he must compel Chiang to embrace thoroughgoing democratic reform, albeit in the crucible of civil and foreign war, or he must write him off. Ultimately, of course, he did neither. His peculiar blend of action and inaction undermined Chiang even as it fell short of providing the basis for a positive relationship with Mao.

At this point, one cannot resist speculating on what the results might have been if Churchill had administered Allied aid to Chungking and Roosevelt had directed the Western movement in Athens. Most likely, Churchill would have instructed Gauss and Stilwell in much the same way he did Leeper and Scobie: "This is no time to dabble in Greek politics or to imagine that Greek politicians of varying shades can affect the situation. You should not worry about Greek Government compositions. The matter is one of life and death. . . . Firmness and sobriety are what are needed now, and not eager embraces while the real quarrel is unsettled." Had Churchill occupied the White House, he might have addressed Congress in words akin to those he spoke in Parliament: "How is the word 'democracy' to be interpreted? My idea of it is that the plain, humble, common man, just the ordinary man who keeps a wife and family . . . is the foundation of democracy. . . . I feel quite differently about a swindle democracy, a democracy which calls itself democracy because it is Left Wing. It takes all sorts to make democracy, not only Left Wing, or even Communist. I do not allow a party or a body to call themselves democrats because they are stretching farther and farther into the most extreme forms of revolution."[53]

Churchill's view of Chiang, so diametrically different from that of Roosevelt, raises the question of what the two English-speaking leaders thought of one another. Both, certainly, were charming, anecdotal, and persuasive. Admiral King once remarked that if the king's first minister had asked him for a favorite watch, he would gladly have surrendered it. The same may be said of the man from Hyde Park. Both lost their fathers at an early age (as did Stalin, Hitler, and Chiang). Roosevelt, who started out as a Republican at Harvard, entered politics as a Democrat, while Churchill began as a Conservative and, after shifting to Labour, returned to his original party. "Anyone can rat," he jested, "but it takes some ingenuity to rerat!" Having held more cabinet posts than any other prime minister in history, he reached the pinnacle of power

with a rapier-sharp mind, the product of forty years of debate and repartee in the House of Commons. With a fine sense for history in the
making, he recognized Munich instantly as "a disaster of the first mag-
nitude" and took the true measure of de Gaulle. He had never been
under any illusion with respect to Chungking, Yenan, Versailles, Moscow, or Weimar.[54]

Many have assumed that there was a friendly, if not affectionate,
relationship between Downing Street and the White House. Historians
have also taken note of the surface camaraderie that existed to the degree that both sides stood to benefit. Nor can one forget FDR's playful
cable to Churchill about "how much fun" it was to be in the same
decade with him. At the same time, beneath all the gaiety and merri-
ment lay a hard substratum of distrust.

As eighth cousins once removed, they seem to have gotten along
well enough when they first met in Washington during World War I.
Subsequently, however, their paths and views began to diverge.
Churchill's political position began to slip just as Roosevelt was regain-
ing a foothold in public life. During the 1930s, the Briton cried in the
wilderness for the kind of defense program which neither FDR nor
Baldwin was willing to grant. One of a handful of Europeans to praise
Roosevelt's performance at the London Economic Conference, he also
published a statement on the futility of the New Deal. In 1937, he took
aim against FDR's court-packing campaign and predicted results "profoundly harmful." He then pooh-poohed the Quarantine Address and in
the following year delivered a transatlantic broadcast that the White
House considered less than helpful in its ongoing effort to break down
isolationist sentiment. Subsequently, in 1939, he criticized Roosevelt's
Thirty-one Nations Address for its "tactless phrases." At this juncture,
the president appears to have been understandably annoyed at Churchill's outspoken opposition as well as a bit fearful of the Englishman's
political prospects. On the one hand, Murray assured him that "not
much attention need be paid to any movement led by Winston." Bullitt, too, had it from the British ambassador in Paris that Churchill was
regarded as criminally foolish for his anti-appeasement crusade. But
could one be certain? FDR consequently went out of his way to sound
negative when George VI mentioned Churchill as a possible successor
to Chamberlain. Twice, the president passed word to Mackenzie King
that Churchill drank too much and was "tight most of the time." This,
of course, was only the first of many sour notes in an often troubled

partnership. In years to come, Downing Street would be incensed whenever Roosevelt associated himself with the forces of revolt in India. Conversely, the tenacity with which the prime minister clung to empire led Roosevelt to poke fun at "Winnie" for his "mid-Victorian" imperial "obsessions." Presidential assistant William Hassett described Churchill as having "everything except vision," and Roosevelt's wife, who could never abide the Englishman's "argumentative" ways, accused him of being an emotional, if not intellectual, reactionary who wearied the president with his drinking and night-owl habits.[55]

As Sherwood suggests, White House aides feared constantly that their man might be upstaged by his more colorful colleague. Lord Moran, Churchill's private physician, observed once that things were not at all what they appeared to be. The two men did not get on at all well at Yalta. In fact, spitefulness and angry exchanges left their mark on the entire last year of their acquaintance. Roosevelt's jealous pique has been noted by individuals as far apart on the ideological spectrum as Oliver Lyttelton and Joseph Goebbels, and there is the judgment of FDR's good friend Messersmith: "The relation between them . . . was not quite the easy one which is generally supposed. Both Roosevelt and Churchill wanted their way."[56]

It is interesting to note certain differences of character which separated the protagonists. Of the four mottoes that ring out from Churchill's history of World War II ("In War: Resolution. In Defeat: Defiance. In Victory: Magnanimity. In Peace: Goodwill."), it is the third that most clearly distinguishes one man from the other. As painter, philosopher, savant, and wit, there were few individuals or groups to which Churchill's understanding and sympathy did not extend in one form or another.[57] Hence the unfortunate General Gamelin was "a patriotic, well meaning man," one "skilled in his profession," who had his own "tale to tell." Whatever Churchill may have thought of Rommel, he could remember him as a "daring and skillful opponent . . . a great general." And there is the sterling piece of juxtaposition in which Stalin goes down as a "callous," "crafty," and "ill-informed giant."[58]

Roosevelt, too, preached magnanimity and understanding, but he did not always practice it. It was not out of character for him to speak of castration for the Germans, sterilization for Puerto Ricans, and a frying pan for Burma's people to "stew in their own juice."[59] Perhaps the wartime issue that sets off British and American leadership most graphically in this respect relates to the question of trial for German prisoners of war. In Stalin's mind, summary execution was a convenient means of eliminating opposition. Having tested it to dispose of Polish officers as well as balky Soviet generals, he anticipated it would again prove serviceable in dealing with the Germans. This pleased FDR. Early in 1943, during one of Eden's visits to Washington, it became evident that Hull and Roosevelt wanted war criminals shot without trial. Later, when Hull flew to the foreign ministers' meeting in Moscow, FDR sent him a British proposal for treatment of Nazi officers and soldiers accused of atrocities. Where Russia wanted "stern, swift justice," the British had decided to hold out for the observance of legal form, but Hull sided with Stalin when he addressed the assembly of delegates. If he had his way, Hull vowed, he "would take Hitler and Mussolini and Tojo and their archaccomplices and bring them before a drumhead court-martial. And at sunrise on the following day there would occur an historic incident." This invoked such "loud exclamations of approval" from the Soviet delegation that it broke up the conference momentarily.

Thus when Stalin spoke at Teheran on behalf of automatic execution of fifty thousand German officers, he knew he could count on American support. Churchill, unwilling to be cowed, adopted the role of challenger as he was to do at Moscow and later at Yalta, and Roosevelt's contribution was equally predictable. He encouraged Stalin. He and his son Elliott proposed banquet toasts seconding the marshal until Churchill stalked indignantly out of the hall. At Yalta, FDR recalled Stalin's "joke" at Teheran and said he hoped for the same toast again, even though Churchill had written him a few months earlier that he had prevailed upon the Kremlin to take an "unexpectedly ultra respectable line" on war criminals: no execution without trial. Von Papen was correct when he wrote that it was Churchill, not Roosevelt, who had fought for the principle of war trials.[60]

One need not be judgmental. Roosevelt and his English cousin each bore the mark of an entirely different past. If Castlereagh had opted to restore France after Napoleon's defeat, such an example could be invoked at a later date in deciding the fate of Nazi Germany. Because Churchill represented a nation that had striven for generations to contain czarist Russia, it was less easy for him to assume, as FDR did, that the Soviet Union would automatically break down in the aftermath of war owing to its ethnic and linguistic divisions.[61] Eleanor Roosevelt recalled that Churchill would often try to explain to her husband the danger inherent in Soviet growth, but never with success. Walter Lippmann wrote two books extolling the Soviets and *Time* twice made Stalin its cover man of the year, but the British press and public knew better. This is one reason why Churchill could argue for more lenient treatment of Germany and speak of the need for a balance of power. It explains why, on two occasions during April of 1945, he pressed for an Allied occupation of Berlin. It is also the reason why he warned FDR to leave no doubt with the Soviet Union regarding Western intentions in Iran. Needless to say, the Englishman was fully capable of holding his own in the wartime exchange of letters with Stalin. Twice, he rejected Soviet demands for a second front though German armies were on the verge of total victory, and once, when Stalin insisted upon more aid to compensate for a larger loss of human life, Churchill blazed back: "Your reproaches leave me cold." Could Stalin not recall that Russia had allowed Britain to fight on alone for two agonizing years against Hitler?[62]

Churchill represented a nation well taught by its professors and journalists to appreciate foreign points of view. As early as 1929 the archbishop of York came out with a repudiation of the Versailles guilt clause, and it may be that the case against the treaty was better understood in London than anywhere else outside of Germany. On this score, there were few Americans who could match an Asquith, a Henderson, or a Lloyd George. The Foreign Office, like the State Department, tended to be pro-Chinese, reflecting the competition between Britain and Japan for control of the Chinese economy. Still, many top leaders acknowledged the existence of two sides in the Far Eastern dispute, recognizing that Manchuria, never genuinely a part of China, had become a vast asylum for brigands. Just as Sir John Simon was capable of pointing out weaknesses in the Lytton Report, Neville Chamberlain could admit that for British trade there was as much to gain as to lose from Japanese hegemony over China. The point is not that Simon and Chamberlain were representative of all groups within their country but rather that they lacked counterparts of equal stature in America. What American consul general stationed in China ever appreciated Chiang as British Consul General Harding did? Harding is here describing a visit made by the generalissimo to a remote province in 1933: "Even if for the time being no change in the methods of provincial administration is made, Chiang's visit will not have been made in vain. His openly expressed hostility to some of the distinctive features of life here (opium, corrupt administration, domestic slavery). His charming friendliness with all whom he meets, whatever their rank . . . his friendliness to foreigners and, in particular, his having asked me to accompany him on two expeditions have greatly struck very many inhabitants of this backward province."[63]

If Britain was not the world's most cosmopolitan country, her intellectuals were at least aware of possible shortcomings. British periodicals of the 1930s were laced with data reflecting the opinion of Berlin and Tokyo. As the *Fortnightly Review* explained: "The problem of security presses upon the Continental peoples with an urgency which we in this country cannot appreciate." The same journal carried articles on Iraq, India, the Commonwealth, the United States, and "the Russian Mentality," along with pieces titled "The Red Scourge in China" and "Prejudice against Japan." Its readers could make no mistake: Chinese communism was real; the Manchukuan government contained some of the ablest and most highly respected of its citizenry; China had defaulted on Japanese loans; Russian influence constituted a definite threat; North China had never till 1928 submitted to southern domination; and the provinces of Szechuan and Yunnan had been de facto independent even in the 1930s. A similar discussion can be found in other periodicals as, for example, the *London Morning Post*, which confronted the problem of reader bias head-on: "Too many people on this side of the world, unfortunately, try to judge the East by our own standards. . . . If we could only accept the Japanese as moderns who are not necessarily the worse for being different from ourselves, we should avoid many misunderstandings."[64]

In light of the subtle difference in outlook that set Britain apart from the United States, it is remarkable that the leaders of the two English-speaking peoples harmonized as well as they did, remarkable too that they chose to meet with one another on more than a dozen different occasions. One possible reason for such apparent harmony is the fact that Roosevelt was willing to put himself under Churchill's tutelage, at least initially. This is what infuriated Stilwell and caught the attention of leaders in other countries.[65] Anyone who reads the Roosevelt-Churchill correspondence is immediately struck by the latter's role as initiator. A sample list of Allied decisions prompted by Churchill would include the Atlantic naval patrol, aid to Russia, Destroyers for Bases, occupation of Iceland, preparations to occupy the Azores, Colonel Donovan's publicity mission to London, the decision to hold fast in the Middle East, and the idea of a Giraud–de Gaulle coalition.[66] Roosevelt even adopted Churchill's model of an executive map room.[67]

How, then, did one man establish such an ascendancy over the other? Did Britain need America any less than America needed Britain? Was it perhaps the Englishman's access to a superb intelligence network? Was it his proximity to Allied governments in exile or his nation's prior declaration of war? Might it have been his unique mastery of things military? This descendant of the first Duke of Marlborough had dreamed from the days of his toy soldier collection of becoming a general. In 1915, after a term of four years as first lord of the admiralty, he actually resigned to command troops in the defense of Antwerp. Thereafter, having read all of the standard books on war, he could boast of having added twenty-five of his own. The two lives that he wanted most to write, though he never did, were those of Napoleon and Julius Caesar.

It is easy to forget that until late in the year 1943, when American preponderance first began to tell in a material way, Great Britain bore the brunt of the Western effort against Hitler. The British, by comparison with the Americans, not only lost four times as many wounded and killed, they also put between two and three times as many men into Italy. They had by far the largest armies in the Mediterranean, and although Churchill deemed it politic to accept an American commander during the assault on North Africa, one only recently promoted from the rank of colonel, nearly all the naval equipment and roughly half the airpower were British. American newspapers, running true to form, rarely mentioned British, Australian, or New Zealander contributions, prompting Eden to remark, a trifle caustically, that "Americans have a much exaggerated conception of the military contribution they are making in this war. They lie freely about this e.g. figures of percentages of forces for Overlord or their share of sunken U-boats and we are too polite."[68]

Something else which stands out in stark relief is Churchill's persistent and calculated effort to cultivate Roosevelt. Few battles fought among friends can compare with this one fought by an Englishman for the patronage of an American. Beginning with his assumption of the title "Naval Person" in his correspondence with the president, thereby emphasizing their common naval background (it became "Former Naval Person" when he became prime minister), he took elaborate care to present himself in the best possible light. After signing the Destroyers for Bases Agreement, he imitated Roosevelt's custom of handing out pens; later, he thanked the president for sponsoring Lend-Lease in words the president had already quoted to him. One has the distinct impression that his plea, "Give us the tools and we will finish the job," was less a conviction than an astute turn of phrase aimed at sheltering his American "friend" from isolationist critics. As a guest at the White House, he wheeled the president to the elevator and indulged the American preference for informality by wearing blue denim overalls. Ambassador Halifax reported happily, "Winston has been working like a beaver here, and doing a grand job. He got on the most intimate terms with the President, who visits him in his bedroom at any hour and, as Winston says, is the only head of state whom he, Winston, has ever received in the nude!" Churchill knew what he was about. He made certain that Roosevelt received full credit for the idea of a landing in North Africa and refrained studiously from crossing him. Once, when he ventured to suggest a presidential "preoccupation" with domestic considerations, Roosevelt took sudden offense. "I am sure," came the reply from Pennsylvania Avenue, that "we do not admit preoccupation with anything but the war." Churchill remained perfectly calm and merely doffed his hat: "Let me withdraw at once the word 'preoccupation' . . . and substitute the word 'trials.' "[69] As for the prickly question of Indochina, he sidestepped Roosevelt altogether and dealt with officers in the State Department who saw things more along the line of de Gaulle.[70]

Although Churchill never relished the need to play Sir Walter Raleigh to Roosevelt's Queen Elizabeth, there was little else he could do. Besides, his strategy paid off handsomely. Had it not been for Roosevelt's offer to divert three hundred Sherman tanks after the calamitous fall of Tobruk in June of 1942 and his sending an additional hundred mobile guns on the fastest craft afloat, the Mediterranean theater might well have folded and along with it the British government. As Churchill stated in his memoirs, tongue firmly in cheek, "a friend in need is a friend indeed."[71]

FDR proved no mean friend by this definition. He instituted an unneutral Atlantic patrol, shipped destroyers, engineered passage of Lend-Lease, and courted war with Germany and Japan. One day in the fall of 1944, he promised the princely sum of $6.5 billion in postwar aid, and Churchill, who recalled that he had to "stand up and beg" for it "like

Fala," thanked the president with tears in his eyes.[72] In return, he endorsed the Morgenthau Plan and Yalta accords, much against his better judgment.[73] When de Gaulle chose to assert his independence in dealing with Roosevelt, Churchill would ask him impatiently if he understood "how much we all depended on American aid and good will" and "why should he always try to offend these powerful Governments without whose help he could not live." De Gaulle's choice was simply out of range for the man who wrote FDR in March of 1945: "Our friendship is the rock on which I build for the future of the world."[74] In sum, the key to the Roosevelt-Churchill relationship was pinpointed by Churchill himself when he made the following candid admission: "My own relations with him had been most carefully fostered by me."[75]

Having come this far in our analysis, we are free to go a step further and address the knotty question of what Winston Churchill really thought of his distant cousin, Franklin Roosevelt. In Churchill's widely read war memoirs, America's chief executive appears noble, far-seeing, and valiant; he is a man of knowledge and experience who possessed "commanding gifts." Each of the six volumes, moreover, contains at least one special term of endearment. It may also be recalled that Churchill was selected by Parliament to deliver a fitting eulogy on the death of FDR and that on this particular occasion the president was lauded for his upright and generous disposition: he was a man of "clear vision and vigour upon perplexing and complicated matters," in fact "the greatest American friend we have ever known" and "the greatest champion of freedom who has ever brought help and comfort from the New World to the Old."[76]

Such encomiums must, of course, be evaluated within the context of their immediate background as well as against a body of countervailing evidence. Even if it were not apparent that Churchill leaned heavily upon his American connection, there are other grounds for questioning the genuineness of his regard for Roosevelt. Nearly all his praise is contained in the memoirs, which, according to Halifax, were askew in certain places and designed to make a record. Maurice Ashley, after four years as Churchill's research assistant, commented on his employer's "extraordinary gift for irony." And surely there is more than a touch of sarcasm in Churchill's offhand comment that Lend-Lease increased British supplies by about 20 percent so that "we were actually able to wage war as if we were a nation of fifty-eight millions instead of forty-eight."[77] Britain, in other words, sacrificed the flower of her youth while Washington stood by and furnished ammunition. In like vein, nothing could be more devastatingly suggestive than Churchill's choice of an epithet for Lend-Lease when he pronounced it "the most unsordid act." He alone could have given such verisimilitude to a token vote of thanks. The record did not show it at the time, indeed it is no more than faintly visible today, but Churchill was woefully angry, disappointed, and let down by America's two-and-a-half-year refusal to come into the war.

Additional terms such as "evil" and "wicked" were most often code words signifying a departure from conventional wisdom. Thus when one reads that Argentina, one of Britain's most valued trading partners, chose "to dally with evil," one can be fairly certain the author is speaking with tongue in cheek. Of another of FDR's antagonists, Churchill says, "It is fashionable at the present time to dwell on the vices of General Franco, and I am, therefore, glad to place on record this testimony to the duplicity and ingratitude of his dealings with Hitler and Mussolini. I shall presently record even greater services which these evil qualities in General Franco rendered to the Allied cause." The prime minister had no love for Hitler, yet one cannot fail to detect a perverse note of respect when he calls him a "bad man." It is likewise as an ardent defender of the British imperial record in India that he must be read when he indicts Japan for "torturing China by her wicked invasions and subjugations." His contempt for America's China policy is barely concealed in the remark that "although the Generalissimo and his wife are now regarded as wicked and corrupt reactionaries by many of their former admirers, I am glad to keep this [photograph of Churchill, FDR, and Chiang] as a souvenir." Neither is he endorsing the presidential standard when he reflects on American behavior toward India: "States which have no overseas colonies or possessions are capable of rising to moods of great elevation and detachment about the affairs of those who have."[78]

Eden stated flatly that Churchill "had to play the courtier" and that if he had ever aired his real opinion he would have described the president as a charming country gentleman without any businesslike method for dealing with serious situations. In de Gaulle's judgment, Churchill "bitterly resented" the "tone of supremacy" which FDR adopted toward him, while the prime minister's physician relates that his patient was most reticent when it came to criticizing Roosevelt. Nowhere is it recorded that Churchill ever uttered a word of praise in private. On the contrary, Lord Coleraine, who saw him shortly after the news of Roosevelt's death, remembered that he seemed "remarkably unmoved."[79]

Another means of gauging Churchill's opinion is to note the phrasing of his tribute to other world leaders. He never, for instance, uses the word "respect" in reference to FDR as he does in referring to such individuals as Prime Minister Curtin of Australia. He never expresses "admiration," as in the case of de Gaulle, who struck him as the personification of a great nation. Eisenhower is hailed as "broad-minded," "practical," and a person of "cool selflessness," Marshall as a statesman with a "penetrating and commanding view of the whole scene." Masaryk is called "great," Beneš a "master of administration and diplomacy," and Smuts a man with "breadth of vision." One will search in vain, however, for anything comparable regarding Roosevelt. For every word of praise, Churchill appends a criticism: Roosevelt failed to prepare his country for war; he did not know how to delegate authority; he "drifted to and fro in argument." He was "prejudiced" against de Gaulle. When reminiscing about his visit to Hyde Park in June of 1942, one of the few things Churchill chose to mention was Roosevelt's invitation to him to feel his biceps. By contrast, one finds an entirely different tone in descriptions of Stalin, who was perceived as a shrewd adversary worthy of great respect. Without hesitation, he described the Georgian as "profound" and "wise," terms not to be found in any reference to Roosevelt. Once, he stated frankly that Stalin was "more prescient and possessed of a truer sense of values than the President."[80]

When a newspaper correspondent found occasion to resent the prime minister's "fawning attitude" toward Roosevelt and confronted him with his phrase about being a "loyal lieutenant" of the president's, Churchill made no answer. But Richard Law, a British official reputed for his specialized knowledge of America, replied that it would be good policy to treat Americans in general as a father treats his undergraduate son.[81]

Basing one's estimate solely upon confidential correspondence, it is clear that Roosevelt did not impress the British with his choice of envoys. John Winant, wartime representative to the Court of St. James's, is perhaps an exception, being regarded by Eden as "the best American ambassador we have had here since Page." But Winant's predecessors left behind an unenviable reputation. Bingham made little impression, positive or negative, while Kennedy became the object of blistering resentment the moment he adopted a defeatist attitude toward the war.

Bill Bullitt, who came as close as anyone to being on intimate terms with his chief, was thought to be overly impressed by atmospherics. Sir Eric Phipps, head of the British mission in France, dubbed him a "light weight," and Eden remarked in 1936 that "nobody, not even Lady Astor, now takes Mr. Bullitt seriously." Norman Davis, who met British leaders more frequently than any other American, was portrayed in a Foreign Office bulletin as "excitable, apt to be suspicious without cause, and rather a bore." Other Americans on the diplomatic scene who labored in other vineyards, among them Dodd and Hurley, came in for a similar drubbing.[82]

In the opinion of the proverbial man on the street in England, few could fail to appreciate Roosevelt's eloquent profession of solidarity and friendship, his condemnation of dictators, and the way he swung American industry behind the war effort. Great numbers rushed to subscribe to a memorial erected in his honor in Grosvenor Square—so many, in fact, that within six days, 150,000 persons had pledged the required sum.

Nor was FDR altogether lacking in admirers among high society. Some, including the Earl of Crawford, viewed America's president with reservation, never knowing quite what to make of him yet confident that his policy would redound to the benefit of England. Ramsay MacDonald, at first very fond of him, experienced a change of sentiment by late 1936. George VI made some very gracious comments. By his account, Roosevelt was not only "very great" but a "staunch friend" who, with "superb courage and vision," risked his all to help Britain in a seemingly hopeless struggle. Altogether, the king's portrait was a flattering one in which FDR "led, cajoled, and ordered" Americans into giving their help, "educating them to the realization that this was no war in the old-fashioned sense but a fundamental struggle to the death between the forces of good and evil." Reference was made to Roosevelt's subtlety, agility of mind, and blinding charm, as well as to his ironclad determination, verging on ruthlessness, and uncanny understanding of American public opinion "by means of an almost feminine intuition." Other British leaders with equally positive things to report include Lord Cecil, who came away from Washington convinced of the president's warmth and decency, not to mention his courage and his brilliance as a conversationalist. According to historian G. M. Trevelyan, this president of the United States who received an honorary degree from Oxford University was "better as a human being than any statesman I know of except Lincoln and our own dear Sir Edward." Frank Milner, a friend of Lothian's, after being warned before meeting Roosevelt in 1933 to be on guard against a man whose tongue would be held constantly in cheek, went on to record his impression of "a real humanitarian whose inner nobility suffuses his whole personality with spiritual sunshine."[83]

None of these witnesses, including George VI, had the opportunity to know Roosevelt well. One meeting, at most several, was the extent of their acquaintance. The same is true of Lord Beaverbrook, who once referred to FDR as "the foremost figure thrown up in many generations, perhaps in countless years."[84]

More valuable by far was the testimony given by long-term ambassadors Lindsay (1933–39) and Halifax (1940–45), also by such officials as Chamberlain, Eden, Vansittart, and Cadogan, all of whom dealt directly with Roosevelt for extended periods on day-to-day matters of business. Here the verdict was far from enthusiastic. For some reason, Chamberlain and Baldwin seem to have conceived an aggravated dislike of Americans beginning in 1933. Vansittart, who served as chief diplomatic adviser before Cadogan and who knew Roosevelt in person as well as by transatlantic cable, thought him "more astute than wise." Although most British leaders threw their support to FDR in 1940, this was less a tribute to him than a vote against an unknown Republican in whom they hesitated to place their trust. Even more, it was a vote for American entry into the war, something in which London was not to be disappointed. Most officials stressed Roosevelt's misplaced reliance upon disarmament and economic panaceas. The Hundred Days had left a bitter taste, and when the president invited George VI to pay a visit in 1937, the king could not find time. Invitations to Chamberlain and Eden the same year met with a similar rebuff. As we have noted, the Welles Plan was regarded as simply another presidential bid to participate in the adjustment of European disputes, a role for which FDR was thought to be singularly ill-suited. At the same time, Whitehall became increasingly convinced of the need to ensure American aid in case of war. Much that London did from 1938 on is therefore attributable to a single motive. When Roosevelt's successful bid for reelection elicited a chorus of congratulation from London and other foreign capitals, *Time* observed tartly, "London editors mostly wrote as though their words were intended not so much for the British reader as for the possible good they might do when cabled overseas and read by President Roosevelt and his fellow citizens." There was, as well, the fear that Alf Landon, if elected, might press in earnest for a resumption of debt payments.[85]

Notable is the absence of positive comment in confidential correspondence. The emphasis falls almost exclusively upon the negative. Walter Runciman tells of visiting the White House in 1937 and being asked by Roosevelt if he would like to see "how we do business over here." He was then kept sitting for several hours while the president "summoned lieutenants and gave orders . . . exactly in the manner of a staccato hero." Many perceived him as a man with dictatorial tendencies in the sense that he surrounded himself with pygmies and delighted in gathering all the reins of power into his own hands. Similarly, he was often taken to task for a knee-jerk deference to public opinion. Neither did it escape the notice of Lothian, or indeed most foreign observers, that he subordinated foreign policy to the exigencies of domestic politics.[86] During one trying period, King George may have aimed a two-edged compliment at the president for this very reason: "I have been so struck by the way you have led public opinion by allowing it to get ahead of you." Chamberlain, in like vein, pointing out how FDR was apt to blame his delinquencies on Capitol Hill, suggested a colorful analogy: "Congress (and in particular the Senate)," he lamented, "are the Mr. Jorkins of American representatives."[87]

The London and Brussels debacles, together with Roosevelt's retraction of his Quarantine Address and his inchoate plan for a naval blockade of Japan, lowered the standing of the United States still further and contributed to the common estimate of its president as "amateurish." This view applied not only to economics, as stressed by Lindsay, but to all matters connected with foreign policy.[88] Chamberlain's well-known objection to the rodomontade that crossed the Atlantic was shared by persons as diversely situated as Foreign Secretary Hoare, Lord Moran, Maurice Hankey, and the Washington correspondent of the London *Times*.[89] Eden, who claimed to like Americans, pronounced Roosevelt charming but superficial; and if "amateurish" was Cadogan's favorite description, Eden spoke about presidential jealousy of rivals and the "cheerful fecklessness" with which FDR appeared willing to pronounce on the future of foreign nations. Neither Cadogan nor Eden ever referred to him as fair-minded, witty, astute, or clever. Such praise was reserved for others. Nor was this atypical. Eden admitted to liking Mikolajczyk and having "the most sincere admiration" for de Gaulle, but where Roosevelt was concerned, observers were left to draw their own conclusion.[90]

Paradoxically, it was an arch Tory, Lord Halifax, who registered one of the more balanced judgments, one not unmixed with sympathy. He held no special brief for Americans; indeed, they impressed him as indiscreet, impractical, and emotional. He was not especially charmed, either, by having to eat lunch off a corner of FDR's desk and listen to stories about the way Calvin Coolidge was supposed to have marked the White House cheese to see if the servants were eating any on the sly. Like other visitors, he noted the haphazard nature of Roosevelt's administration, and this left him cold. "I don't think the President ties up awfully well," he once said. Attempts to gather information in Washington reminded him of "a disorderly day's rabbit shooting. . . . Nothing comes out where you expect and you are much discouraged. And then, suddenly, something emerges . . . at the far end of the field." At the same time, this canny master of hounds was not given to snap judgments. While he faulted FDR for letting public opinion lead him by the nose, he was also capable of seeing that the president employed indirect methods of guidance. There can be no doubt that Halifax had a good eye for the positive side, although in the final analysis the famous presidential aura came to seem "faintly synthetic" with a distinct "whiff of the faux bonhomme." Roosevelt was nothing if not an astute politician, but in Halifax's mind this could also be a "fatal gift of manipulation bestowed by a bad fairy."[91]

British opinion is worth considering because it reflects opinion in other areas of the world where the evidence tends to be more fragmentary and less accessible. The farther one travels along the road to the Orient, the more restricted the record. It is not easy to decipher the mind of the Kremlin or the Forbidden City. One can only surmise that if Roosevelt's relationship with Stalin and Chiang is any indication, his prestige in China and the Soviet Union could not have been very high. The Yugoslav leader Milovan Djilas recalls Stalin as having said that Churchill was the type who would reach into one's pocket for a single kopeck, whereas Roosevelt dipped his hand in only for larger coins. Given the Oriental respect for hard bargaining, this can be taken in more ways than one. There is, too, the issue of presidential authority. Stalin could not believe that Roosevelt would promise him a battleship built in American shipyards and then fail to deliver it. To Davies, he marveled: if the president of the United States wants a battleship built, how can army and navy technicians stop it? Russian leaders in general tended to point out the disparity between word and deed.[92]

The Soviet boss ignored Roosevelt's appeals in connection with the Lublin government and wondered aloud how a chief executive could blame public opinion for his own inability to act. Was a true leader not one who educated people and commanded their support? Curiously, for all their quarreling, the British and Russian chiefs got along quite well. Stalin invited Churchill to his home, and, after some sharp exchanges that ended in a resolution to defend mutual interests, the two men enjoyed a convivial time together. Precisely how Roosevelt impressed the average Soviet leader may never be known, but Nikita Khrushchev, successor to Stalin, may furnish a clue, both in what he includes and in what he does not include in his memoirs. There is the remark that Roosevelt "always treated us with such understanding"; also that Ambassador Harriman "conducted policies that were very much to our liking." What he does not affirm is that he and his colleagues ever felt respect for Roosevelt. John Foster Dulles, secretary of state under Eisenhower, was a "worthy" adversary, one who "always kept us on our toes to match wits with him"; de Gaulle "walked straight and tall" and "earned our respect as an intelligent military leader . . . [he was] a subtle politician." Dulles's chief, President Eisenhower, is singled out for his modesty, common sense, and experience. But though FDR does not come off as poorly as certain other Americans, he never rises above the level of benefactor to Moscow. Hungary's statesman Admiral Horthy maintained that Roosevelt's "mistakes" and "unlimited policy of appeasement" towards Stalin led finally to "the destruction of self-determination in Central Europe."[93]

Where Chiang Kai-shek and Prince Konoye are concerned, one must assume that Roosevelt's reputation bore some relation to the series of pirouettes and broken promises associated with his name. After he had encouraged and then scotched Japanese overtures for a nonaggression pact in 1934, his ambassador reported from Tokyo that it would take years and no small outlay "before the Japanese will take at face value the representations of the U.S. government. . . . From the Japanese standpoint, nothing is more disastrous to prestige than failure to act on a statement of intention." Could opinion along the Tokaido have been any more positive after the return of Saito's ashes or during the mock negotiations of 1941? Kurusu commented at Brussels about "resounding phrases." Matsuoka, the most Americanized of Japanese statesmen, regarded Roosevelt as a demagogue and warmonger. And why, one might wish to know, did Shigemitsu, in his detailed treatise on Japanese politics and diplomacy of the 1930s, fail to mention Roosevelt's name until page 213?[94]

Ordinarily, one might be inclined to disregard the opinion of Hitler and Mussolini, who viewed the president as ignorant, parochial, and noisy. What is less easy to ignore is their perception of him as essentially harmless.[95] The reader will recall that his Thirty-one Nations Address of 1939, which even the Vatican scored for its lack of tact and good sense, not only triggered ridicule at both ends of the Axis but afforded Hitler his excuse for going to the Reichstag and subjecting the president to a devastating cross-examination in absentia. Hitler had not always held the United States in low esteem. Never an admirer of democracy and always pessimistic about America's racial mix, he nonetheless felt the United States would someday be a vital force because of its imperial restraint, its natural inventiveness, and other qualities. Gradually, after 1933, his respect diminished as Roosevelt engaged in sermonizing, launched an unsuccessful attack on unemployment and national indebtedness, and turned finally, in Hitler's opinion, to warmongering.[96]

The idea that Roosevelt was bellicose and deserved "chief blame" for the war found currency not only with Hitler, Goebbels, and von Ribbentrop but with more moderate German politicians as well. Hans Dieckhoff, ambassador to the United States from 1937 to 1941, was convinced that by virtue of his "unique frivolity" and "meddling in European affairs" Roosevelt bore a "great" responsibility for the outbreak and prolongation of World War II. Dieckhoff was von Ribbentrop's brother-in-law and one of Hitler's early favorites, but he was also a liberal, not particularly trusted by main-line Nazis and one of the few Germans in whom Dodd felt he could confide. We also have the opinion of von Hassell, the Weimar diplomat who refused to obey von Ribbentrop and left the foreign service in 1937. As an opponent of the Nazis and eventually a conspirator, he was executed by Hitler in September 1944. A man of broad experience and equally broad views, he had served in China, Italy, Spain, Denmark, and Yugoslavia. While in Italy, he had become a good friend of the Phillipses. Yet he, too, no less than Dieckhoff, perceived the president as bellicose for insisting upon the inevitability of a clash between democracies and dictatorships.[97]

It is interesting to observe that although Hitler had every reason to despise Stalin, his criticism of the Georgian was mingled with praise.

He admired him immensely, and if he found in him a beast, it was a "beast on the grand scale . . . one of the most extraordinary figures in history." Stalin, he liked to say, "must command our unconditional respect." Von Ribbentrop, too, commended Stalin for his restraint, clarity of thought, firmness, and wisdom, qualities never attributed to Roosevelt. Although the Germans recognized in FDR what they called an experienced mass psychologist, he seemed dictatorial to them, as to others, and they expressed alarm at his suspected imperialist bent. Mainly, however, they could not abide his self-appointed role as schoolmistress of the world. Schacht, more liberal than most German spokesmen, called him "highly intelligent" in his *Autobiography*, but elsewhere he had little to say on his behalf and still less for Hull.[98]

Canada, the country with which FDR enjoyed his best relationship, happens also to be the one to which he granted the most lucrative trade concessions. Ambassador Herridge may have voiced a common complaint in 1935 that the United States was untrustworthy, but Roosevelt eventually delivered a generous treaty to Ottawa and on reelection could count Mackenzie King and Governor General Lord Tweedsmuir among his best "friends." Tweedsmuir, who criticized FDR for petty jealousy toward potential rivals and incoherence in the area of administration, nevertheless praised him for his vitality, leadership, and the fecundity of his ideas. He was much impressed by the president's kindness, along with his skill as a mass persuader. Prime Minister W. L. Mackenzie King, who had been a personal friend of Roosevelt's since 1910, shared with him many ideas on the subject of world organization. During the seven years before Pearl Harbor, FDR entertained his fellow Harvard alumnus, either at Hyde Park or in Washington, on the average of once a year. And just as Tweedsmuir claimed that the president's Quarantine Address was "the culmination of a long conspiracy between us (this must be kept secret!)," Mackenzie King liked to reminisce about his own role as collaborator in American plans for a world economic conference as well as the Destroyers for Bases deal and the Atlantic Charter meeting of 1941. Canada's chief executive helped to bring pressure on Whitehall and various dominion leaders to lower their trade barriers, make concessions to Germany, and agree to a liberal trade treaty with the United States. Equally important, he acted as a confidential channel through which Roosevelt passed secret messages to Westminster and Berchdesgarden. While on a visit to Hitler in 1937, the Canadian assured his German host that Berlin need not doubt the friendly disposition of the United States in the event that plans should be drawn to ensure the future of world peace.[99]

French opinion of New Deal leadership was closer to the British than to the Canadian view. There are today in Paris a boulevard and a metro station named after Franklin Roosevelt. It is also true that Frenchmen who relied as much as did Churchill and Mackenzie King on the American connection were as one in pronouncing favorably. Included in this number were Blum, Herriot, Claudel, and Jean Monnet. Monnet, in particular, described Roosevelt as a man of universal vision, for whom freedom was "indivisible." Those who found fault with Roosevelt, however, and there were many, stressed his weakness as a leader. It was felt that he did not pull his weight on the vital issue of neutrality and that he held out more hope than was prudent. Jules Henry, the one who perhaps knew him best, felt, as we have seen, that in this sense he was "impulsive." Georges Bonnet, who served as both foreign minister and ambassador to the United States, acknowledged his brilliance, questioning ability, and mobility of mind but also offered a good deal of oblique criticism. At the same time, Havas, France's news agency, was frequently anti-American.[100]

Strange as it may seem, de Gaulle, least powerful among the Allied war leaders, was the only one to put a dent in Roosevelt's liberal reputation. He alone had the temerity to brook the president's displeasure. Among the more dramatic scenes of the period is one in which Roosevelt received Gaullist envoys Adrien Tixier and André Philip just after he had extended recognition to the North African administration of Nazi collaborator Admiral Darlan. Shaking their fingers at the president, they are said to have subjected him to a political tongue-lashing of the kind to which he, of all men, was most sensitive.[101] On another occasion, de Gaulle protested publicly against the American refusal to allow him, a French leader, to land on French territory in North Africa.[102]

De Gaulle, the most articulate and widely published of all French critics, was aware of the glitter, subtlety, and kingfisher rapidity of Roosevelt's mind, but he could not dismiss his nemesis without trenchant comment, and the feeling was mutual. Neither Roosevelt nor Hull appreciated Cassandras as a rule. Especially did they feel uncomfortable in the presence of men who found it within themselves to question the universal utility of democracy.[103] Hull accused de Gaulle of "fascist and dictatorial tendencies" and, if Stimson is to be believed, the secretary rambled into incoherence every time the subject arose.[104] William Hassett could recall nothing of de Gaulle's arrival at the White House in 1944 except that the general stepped from his automobile with an air of arrogance and strode into the Diplomatic Reception Room with a "Cyrano de Bergerac nose" high in the air. Evidently, this was also Roosevelt's view. Churchill was struck by the way he brought up the issue of de Gaulle every day to the point of fixation. Naturally, de Gaulle's view of Roosevelt was affected by Roosevelt's attitude toward him as head of the Free French, and from the very outset there could be no doubt what this attitude would be. With cool calculation, FDR sidestepped recognition of de Gaulle by installing General Henri Giraud as administrator of French North Africa and promising him sufficient equipment to field an army of three hundred thousand men. Fortunately for de Gaulle, this promise, like so many of Roosevelt's others, fell by the wayside. Arms shipped from America proved to be second-rate by comparison with those Churchill was delivering to de Gaulle, and from this time onward Giraud's days were numbered.[105]

In the meantime, Roosevelt engaged in a number of bureaucratic maneuvers aimed at protecting Giraud. Once, he refused to let de Gaulle's agent fly from the United States to French Guiana to organize a new government; only Giraud's men received clearance. Later, when a Gaullist tried to fly to London, his plane was grounded by American authorities in Trinidad. None of these ploys proved successful in the long run, of course, because Roosevelt also insisted that Giraud broaden his government, thereby forcing him to take in elements loyal to de Gaulle. Moreover, when Churchill suggested that Giraud and de Gaulle be recognized as co-leaders of the French Committee, the United States concurred, opening the door to a coup by de Gaulle. Roosevelt did invite Giraud to the White House after Gaullist forces captured Dakar, but such attention availed little. Less than a week after Giraud's return to North Africa, he was effectively excluded from power.[106]

Until the time of his death, the president continued to be nettlesome, promising restoration of the French empire yet undermining it at every turn. He tried to dictate the administration of French North Africa; he descended upon the French outpost of Casablanca; he even summoned French leaders to meet on their own territory. Whenever de Gaulle resolved to resist one or another threat to the integrity of the French empire, Roosevelt would call him an egoist. Despite clear signs that de Gaulle had won the allegiance of virtually every resistance movement in metropolitan France, Roosevelt persisted in picturing him as a reluctant bride married off to Giraud in a shotgun wedding at Casablanca. According to Roosevelt's version of the story, de Gaulle also suffered from delusions of grandeur in which he likened himself to Joan of Arc and Clemenceau. Washington therefore continued to withhold recognition, claiming that to do otherwise would be to grant de Gaulle a white horse upon which he might ride to victory over the will of the French people. American planes dropped millions of leaflets over the French countryside urging citizens to suspend political judgment and await a plebiscite. Frenchmen, in other words, were asked to heed the president of the United States in preference to one of their own who had staked his life and honor on the cause of a free France.[107]

Only when Eisenhower reported widespread enthusiasm for the Gaullist party in every department of France, including Paris, did FDR bow to the inevitable, and then only to set himself rigidly against any shoring up of French influence worldwide. Not surprisingly, it was an Englishman rather than an American who marched beaming down the Champs Elysées on Armistice Day 1944, side by side with de Gaulle to the cheers of hundreds of thousands.

Roosevelt's reputation in France was also affected by his refusal to answer French pleas for wartime cooperation in Indochina. Although Hull encouraged the French commander in Tonkin to draw out his talks with Tokyo, the United States declined to stage a naval demonstration and refused to deliver 120 fighter aircraft for which Paris had already paid. While French border forts came under intense fire and their defenders fought to the last cartridge, Roosevelt busied himself with Lend-Lease for England. The Japanese, determined to crush every vestige of local resistance, bombed Hanoi and killed or massacred two hundred French officers, along with four thousand soldiers. Finally, when French partisans renewed their resistance in late 1944 and early 1945, American OSS officers supported indigenous forces hostile to Paris (the Vietminh) and did nothing to obtain the release of de Gaulle's minister for the armed forces. FDR signed a death warrant for thousands when he ordered General Wedemeyer to hold back on U.S. aid. French generals were arrested at the dinner table, and French women and children were used as human shields to storm the redoubt at Ha-Giang. At Fort Brière de l'Isle, an entire garrison was machine-gunned to death while singing the *Marseillaise*. When Japanese officers tried to induce Lang-Son to surrender by ordering Governors Lemonnier and

Auphelle to go to the wall of the fortress and urge capitulation, both men refused and were beheaded. American Colonel Claire Chennault, who abhorred the idea of leaving gallant Frenchmen to be slaughtered in the jungle but was "forced officially to ignore their plight," took the initiative to send a small quantity of men and supplies. It was not enough. The last word Sabattier received from the doomed garrison at Lang-Son was, "Where are the Americans?"[108]

Where *were* the Americans? Roosevelt was devising a scheme to prevent the arrival of French troops: Japan was to be disarmed north of the sixteenth parallel by the Chinese and south of it by the British. He was likewise engrossed in plans to reduce France to the status of a minor power. This once-proud nation would be required to submit to disarmament and bid adieu to its colonial possessions while all its citizens over the age of forty or involved in the Vichy regime would be barred from public office.[109] Roosevelt's plan seemed particularly cruel because France had lost so many of her youth in World War 1. The number of adult males in the age group twenty to fifty was abnormally small. Relatively few children had been born during the period after 1914, and by 1939 the death rate had begun to exceed the birth rate.

For a brief interval, from about 1945 to 1949, France exulted in her liberation, and the average man, who knew little about diplomacy, was inclined to associate his deliverance with the name Roosevelt. Two popular books were written on the topic of New Deal foreign policy, both of them highly simplistic but positive in tone.[110]

As time passed, however, and eastern Europe slipped irrevocably into the orbit of Moscovy, as the French position in Indochina grew increasingly precarious, and as Roosevelt's role became more and more apparent, his reputation suffered a corresponding decline. A new crop of histories began to spring up, the most scholarly of which, almost without exception, offered a harshly negative verdict. The general impression was that America's leadership had been ignorant, arrogant, and naive. FDR was perceived as a benevolent dictator who ruled with refinement and noblesse oblige amid the trappings of democracy yet who nevertheless ruled, and ruled more absolutely than Stalin. One interpretation concluded that "his ignorance of the conditions of foreign countries, of the traditions and reasons for their politics was profound." By other accounts, he tolerated only those pliable enough to cater to his vanity. More than one French author lashed out at his "double standard" of morality as, for example, when he expressed indignation at the al-

leged misery of the Moroccan masses without admitting a similar condition in Puerto Rico. He had pushed Burma and Morocco along a pre-
mature road to independence while saying nothing of Moscow's
dependents, the Kirzhizes, Kurds, Ukrainians, and others. He was said
to be blind to the danger of the political Left and biased against Poland, a
Catholic and Slavic country. In still other reviews of the administration,
it was pointed out that he built his policy on a false theory of the
primacy of economics, seeking to assure the peace of the world by assuring its prosperity. Then, too, he had provoked Japan into an attack on
Pearl Harbor and committed egregious blunders at Lividia Palace. Yalta
was not taken to be an accident connected with the president's failing
health but rather "the culmination of a mischievous policy pursued
through thick and thin in the face of solemn and repeated warnings": the
Soviet Union learned in early 1945 that America could be seduced by
words, and it was a lesson from which she was to derive great benefit.
Finally, as regards Roosevelt's treatment of de Gaulle and the country
de Gaulle represented, this was attributable to America's "puberté
politique."[111]

De Gaulle himself harbored as much resentment over America's turn-
coat policy on Indochina as he did over Roosevelt's charges of mega-
lomania. By 1944, Republican presidential nominee Wendell Willkie
could tell his audiences without exaggeration that "the name of the
United States is now greeted with silence at meetings of Frenchmen."
To the general and his confreres, it was FDR who held his nose high in
the air, issuing "Messiah-like messages" and engaging in a grand effort
to play "Savior" to the world. Roosevelt was too much the "star per-
former," overly "touchy as to the roles that fell to other actors." And if
FDR accused the Quai d'Orsay of betraying confidences, de Gaulle returned such criticism in spades.[112]

In conclusion, Roosevelt's overseas reputation is not what it has appeared. We have dealt with reactions in a comparatively small group of
countries, but the story elsewhere does not vary appreciably. Characteristically, Roosevelt let it be known that he thought the Spanish "indo-
lent by nature," and in the fall of 1941, Hull seized upon the departure of
Spain's envoy to deliver a blunt homily, which began: "In all the relations of this government with the most ignorant and backward governments in the world." Foreign Minister Ramón Serrano Suñer scarcely
mentions FDR in his memoirs except to compare him unfavorably with
Churchill. The latter appears as a grand competitor and person of im-

mense human warmth, whereas Roosevelt is portrayed as an opportunist who wished to enter the war and who later made Stalin's task a great deal easier. Serrano Suñer had no more reason to admire Stalin than he did Churchill, yet he speaks of the Russian as astute, energetic, and a "genius." Likewise, Israel's leader David Ben-Gurion praised contemporary figures such as de Gaulle and Churchill for their wisdom and astuteness while dismissing FDR as a "lofty humanitarian." The verdict extends even to India, where native officials had looked hopefully to Washington for a short while during the war. But as soon as Gandhi and company realized the White House would not hesitate to trade on the future of their country, the American reputation in New Delhi plummeted.[113]

A number of individuals, including Australian Prime Minister Robert Menzies, marveled at the way Roosevelt, after singling Hitler out as a threat to world freedom, acted with imagination and persistence to convert strict neutrality into benevolent neutrality and thence into all aid short of war. On balance, however, the respect that Roosevelt might have earned as president of the United States simply did not materialize. Nothing is more misleading than the eulogies that poured from foreign chancelleries in 1945, when few failed to see the benefit, if not the necessity, of cultivating the party of Roosevelt.[114] Within two years, veteran diplomat George Kennan would be moved to declare that world opinion toward the United States was "at worst hostile and at best resentful."[115] Thoughtful Americans might well have wondered at the time, reading Kennan's dour appraisal, how their nation's standing could have fallen off so precipitately. But the more one sees of FDR, in particular his image in the eyes of the world, the more one is inclined to take Kennan at his word. America's reputation did not fall suddenly, however. It had been in semi-eclipse for more than a decade.

6. The
Good Neighbor Policy:
Image and Reality

 ANY would argue that Roosevelt made up for American weakness in Europe and the Far East by inaugurating a new and better era in hemispheric relations. Immediately after World War II, the Good Neighbor Policy became the focus of a number of scholarly evaluations, nearly all of them positive. By one account, "there was throughout Latin America greater trust in the United States in December, 1941, than there had been at any time in the past . . . as much as could have been expected." According to another, the expropriation of American oil properties in Mexico was a "relatively small price" to pay for "winning the friendship and esteem of the Mexican nation, and all of Latin America." A third writer concluded that Roosevelt "was more highly esteemed throughout Latin America than any foreigner who had ever lived." More recently, New Deal policy has been labeled "the golden age of Pan American cooperation."[1]

Repeatedly, FDR cited his own record of peaceful coexistence with neighboring countries as an example to other nations. We have seen how Secretary Hull expatiated on the subject in conversations with Saito and Nomura, and the record shows similar emphasis in talks held with German envoys. Roosevelt informed Ambassador Dodd in Berlin that a conference scheduled for Buenos Aires in 1936 would set a salutary example for Germany and Italy if news of its proceedings could filter down through the media to the people of these countries. To quote the German ambassador, the policy of the Good Neighbor had become America's "showpiece."[2]

Roosevelt wove this theme into his inaugural address and repeated it a few weeks later on Pan American Day. The United States, he promised, was determined to eliminate every form of military intervention in the Western Hemisphere and accord its neighbors the autonomy to which they were entitled. Within months, Cuba regained some of the power it had yielded in the form of the Platt Amendment, and American forces took advance leave of Haiti. From then on, Washington strove sedulously, and for the most part successfully, to adhere to its original intention, and the effort did not go unheralded. Few scenes in the history of presidential experience can equal FDR's visit to Rio de Janeiro, Buenos Aires, and Montevideo in December 1936. No foreigner had ever been greeted with such tumultuous acclaim. He was hailed by Argentina's press as "the shepherd of democracy," and his oratory was continually interrupted with applause. Hundreds of thousands of spectators turned out on a specially declared holiday to wave and cheer America's chief executive in the company of their own president, while mounted police rode at the crowds with sabers drawn. Vice President Wallace, who visited Chile in 1943, received a welcome which, again, turned out to be the warmest ever accorded a visiting dignitary. Finally, Cordell Hull won the Nobel Peace Prize in 1945 and, after retirement, became the recipient of Peru's highest decoration.[3]

Doubtless, these were brilliant moments, all of them reflecting genuine credit on the administration. But whether they furnish an accurate key to Roosevelt's reputation and standing south of the Rio Grande is another question, one that merits more than passing attention. How much authentic respect did Roosevelt inspire in Latin America? And at what cost? These are queries worth pursuing, and we shall begin with four case studies: Brazil, Mexico, Bolivia, and Argentina. Two of these nations have been described as "friendly" toward the United States, another as neutral, and a fourth as openly hostile. Together, therefore, they comprise a fairly accurate sampling of how American policy worked in practice.

Brazil was one of roughly half a dozen Latin American countries to grant FDR the right to establish military bases on its home soil and, with the exception of Mexico, the only country south of the border to send troops to fight alongside the Allies. It would be no exaggeration to say that from the time of Theodore Roosevelt, when traditional ties between London and Rio de Janeiro were altered to run more nearly between Rio and Washington, Brazil had been among the friendliest of

South American republics. T.R. and his secretary of state, Elihu Root, marveled at the glowing tribute awaiting them when they arrived in Rio; American naval officers en route around the world in 1908 met a similar reception. Brazil welcomed a resident American naval mission long before 1933, and because of the complementary nature of her export trade, she became one of three South American countries to sign a reciprocal trade treaty with Washington during the 1930s.[4]

At the same time, one need not assume that all was wine and roses. This friendliest of countries granted the United States no base rights until repeated German sinkings of her merchant vessels within five hundred miles of her coast outraged the national honor. Over the years, Washington was obliged to purchase cooperation at an unusually high price. By 1936, German trade had made such inroads in Rio that Berlin could boast of tripling its exports and standing first on the list of foreign suppliers. Roosevelt countered by extending a $27 million credit to the Bank of Brazil. But only by threat of tariff retaliation and the promise of a $60 million loan did he succeed in persuading Brazil's foreign office, the Itamaraty, to cancel a large coffee deal with Germany. Later, in March of 1939, with Berlin still in control of a substantial portion of Brazilian railways, he extended a $20 million credit and $50 million loan, followed by $45 million for a steel mill. Foreign Minister Oswaldo Aranha spent the first two months of 1940 in Washington, and when he left, he carried away promises of an additional $19 million in credit plus $50 million in gold, not to mention generous offers of technical assistance. Altogether, Roosevelt's commitment was rumored to be in excess of $120 million. By April, the United States Export-Import Bank was preparing to loan Brazil an additional $6 million and by September $20 million more. After this came still another infusion of $25 million on loan. In 1941, presidential aide Lowell Mellett, traveling through Latin America, could describe only one nation south of the border as truly "friendly." This was Brazil. Even so, it is well to remember that President Vargas had not lost his taste for the Nazi trade connection and Aranha was a self-admitted expert in the art of selling cooperation. One knowledgeable observer concluded that the Brazilian people respected the United States less in 1944 than they had twenty-five years earlier.[5]

One does not have to be a Marxist to appreciate the intimate connection between trade and aid, on one hand, and "friendship" on the other. Wallace remarked in 1942 that the American technical mission to Bra-

zil had increased considerably as a result of Brazil's declaration. Ultimately, the Itamaraty netted $154 million in Lend-Lease not only to
equip its army, navy, and air force but also to construct a new steel
complex, shipyards, airplane plants, and a more diversified economy. In
addition to special status for its exports, the United States obtained
temporary use of thirty military installations covering twenty thousand acres, and a Brazilian expeditionary force fought in Italy with the
United States Fifth Army beginning in the summer of 1944. FDR was
heartily cheered when his picture appeared on movie screens in Rio.[6]
Yet how great a role his highly lauded nonintervention policy played is
debatable, especially when the case of other less friendly nations is
considered.

Roosevelt became the first American president to go to Mexico on
official business, and it was to Mexico City that he sent one of his
closest confidants, Josephus Daniels, under whom he had served as
assistant secretary of the navy. Letters from White House to embassy
invariably began "Dear Chief," those going in the other direction "Dear
Franklin," as Daniels dispensed with the custom of clearing his
speeches with the State Department. Like many of Roosevelt's appointees, he did not feel comfortable with the native language. Typically, too, he did not hesitate to impose American custom or to run
counter to the Latin American sense of punctilio by instructing his
staff to dispense with spats, mufflers, canes, and the like. In fact, one of
the skits staged at the embassy actually featured a fop in formal attire
paired off against a casually dressed Uncle Sam. Daniels was an ambassador who chose the golden rule as his guide in handling American
claims and allowed himself to be governed by professions of altruism
on the old Chamizal border dispute as well as in other issues connected
with the course of the Rio and Colorado rivers.[7]

Always popular, he sat with cordial smile and ready applause through
any number of speeches, which he could not understand because they
were in Spanish, including presentations denouncing *imperialismo
Yanqui*. He believed in letting the Mexicans "take down their hair," as it
were. After several years, when the question arose as to whether American oil companies should be required to raise wages paid to native workers above the Mexican standard, Daniels naturally sided with Mexico,
and it was this issue that provided President Lázaro Cárdenas with a
pretext for announcing the expropriation of American property in
March of 1938. Hull's response to the action against Standard Oil, firm

though moderate, came in the form of a note marked for oral delivery to the Mexican foreign minister. It demanded payment of "present effective value to the owners from whom the properties are taken" and expressed American concern and apprehension. Daniels, after reading it as instructed, advised the Mexican government to disregard it (consider it "not received"). He then contented himself with Cárdenas's vague reassurances of compensation notwithstanding angry criticism from Hull and the American press.[8]

Roosevelt's reaction to the gravest crisis of its kind in memory was to issue a statement sympathetic to Mexico and warn American companies that they were entitled only to damages totaling actual investment less depreciation. In other words, they could not claim prospective profits. Mexico, naturally, was only claiming the right to reap greater rewards from its own resources and this was not, by any means, the first airing of such an issue. Oil had been an explosive issue at the time of Woodrow Wilson as well as under President Coolidge. Roosevelt's decision, however, dealt a staggering blow to the oil companies, British as well as American, since they would most likely never have risked their investment in the first place without assurance that profitless ventures and losses resulting from local instability would be outweighed by equity in the subsoil value of productive wells and properties. Roosevelt recommended arbitration, but this implied a yielding on substance. The awards would never have equaled the value of the property leased nor would they have been paid because Mexico simply could not raise the money. For a brief moment, when American silver policy changed in 1938, it appeared that Roosevelt might be having second thoughts—but not for long. Treasury Secretary Morgenthau gave a special dinner honoring the Mexican finance minister and further embarrassed Hull by buying more Mexican silver than ever at prices above the world market. In 1941, with the shadow of war fast approaching and Mexican cooperation at a premium, Roosevelt accepted $24 million in compensation, amounting to about 5 percent of the sum demanded by Standard Oil. All along, he continued to make it clear that he would not support claims for subsoil property (oil not yet pumped) and would concentrate instead on what he termed the more legitimate grievance of American landowners whose real estate holdings had been seized along with company oil.[9]

An irate Secretary Hull, ostensibly at cross-purposes with the White House, stated the position of the American companies when he pro-

tested: "Daniels is down there taking sides with the Mexican government" giving "the impression that they can go right ahead and flaunt
everything in our face." To Norman Davis it seemed that the Good
Neighbor Policy would have to be rephrased so as not to "surrender
everything we had." Expropriation without substantial reimbursement
set off a fuse that ran in several different directions at once. Not since
the introduction of the Smoot-Hawley tariff in 1931 had commercial
exchange between the two countries reached such a low, and to the
degree that creditors were regarded as criminals in Mexico, their
chance for justice would be that much slimmer in Venezuela and Iran.
One British observer felt that expropriation on the "American" pattern
would undermine international morality. Cárdenas did appeal to other
Latin American countries to follow Mexico's example of defying "foreign imperialists," and the supreme courts of Bolivia and Uruguay
would soon uphold compensated expropriation of American and British companies. Chile warned Anglo-American oil firms that they were
next on the list. Venezuelans under General Isaias Medina Angarita
held out the threat of nationalization to force American oil companies
to pay higher royalties and taxes. And in 1944, it was learned that Colombia was about to cancel Standard Oil concessions in Barranca
Bermejo.[10]

Despite a liberal policy, there is next to nothing to indicate that the
United States earned more than the usual modicum of respect in Mexico. In actuality, New Deal approaches may even have been counterproductive. President Cárdenas, who came to power in 1934, turned
out to be far more radical than his predecessors, preaching "Mexico for
the Mexicans." Within three years, traditional anti-Americanism, coupled with a severe economic crisis and strong Axis gains, had become
enough of a problem for Morgenthau to warn that fascist states threatened to control Mexico "inside a year." During the summer of 1939,
both the American embassy and the American School in Mexico City
were attacked by a mob led by Joel F. Torres, a leader of the Cantina
Society. The United States had become the target of leftist groups, right-
ist groups, indeed all social classes, and its name was reviled by the
Acción Nacional, a party of the upper classes. It was cursed by the
Sinarquista, the party of peasants and underdogs, which took its cue
from youth, intelligence, and culture. In fact, so widespread was the
revulsion that gentlemen bankers such as Manuel Gomez Morín, first
chairman of the board of the Government Bank of Mexico, could find

common cause with labor leaders in their jaundiced view of Franklin Roosevelt's America.[11]

By 1941, a powerful Nazi party claimed large segments of the population and was attacking the United States in eighteen well-distributed weekly publications. German was heard on the streets, in cafés, bars, and nightclubs. German drinking songs rang out at Liverpool 123 and the Reforma Bar, punctuated by lusty shouts of "Death to the Jew Roosevelt." Things had not changed significantly in the twenty-five years since 1917, when Germany offered American territory in exchange for an alliance (the Zimmerman Incident). Some Mexicans were confident enough that their position vis-à-vis the United States would improve with a German victory that the Nazi chargé d'affaires in Washington reported on 4 May 1940 that "the Mexican government is prepared to afford every kind of clandestine support for Germany." Later in the year, when Vice President Wallace made a visit to Mexico, he implicitly recognized the truth of this observation, marveling at the "whale of a lot of fifth column activity" in Mexico.[12]

The Communist party of Mexico persisted in its attacks on FDR even after Russia entered the war, which is not without irony, for after granting recognition to the USSR in 1933, Roosevelt had urged Mexico to mend its relationship with Moscow. Under an arrangement sponsored by the United States, the Mexican minister in Washington worked out many of the details with Litvinov which led to later agreement, and when Leon Trotsky moved to Mexico in 1937, the year before Cárdenas expropriated American oil properties, he was amazed at the cordial nature of his reception and the degree to which the country leaned leftward. A presidential train awaited him upon arrival, and he lived in comfort for two years as guest of the brilliant artist Diego Rivera, one of the founders of the Mexican Communist party. Recalling that it was from the large Soviet compound in Mexico City that Ambassador Oumansky worked to enlarge Russian influence elsewhere in the hemisphere, notably in Cuba, it is significant that when Vice President Wallace toured Latin America in 1943, he spoke on behalf of unity between the Slavic and Latin peoples. There was very little difference, he maintained, between Christianity and communism. Secretary of State Stettinius carried the same message to Rio in February 1945, when he assured President Getulio Vargas that the Soviets were too preoccupied at home to spread communism abroad; Brazil should feel free to accord Moscow its long-awaited diplomatic recognition.[13]

Wallace could converse in Spanish. He also loved Mexican folk music. He read Latin American books, lobbied strenuously for aid to the region, and held regular Spanish-speaking luncheons in Washington. With a specialization in agricultural research, he could appreciate one of Latin America's central concerns and reach out to people on every social level. This, however, does not seem to have been enough to win him a friendly reception when he visited Mexico in 1940. Although the crowds he met were generally well-disposed and he received a standing ovation at President Avila Camacho's inauguration, there is a less positive side to the story. On his arrival at the capital, an ugly mob was demonstrating outside the American embassy. Roosevelt had sided with Camacho, a Roman Catholic and one of two leading contenders for the presidency in a disputed election, and as Wallace had come to represent the United States at Camacho's installation, partisans demonstrated fearlessly against Yankee interference. "Viva Almazan!" they chanted, "Down with the Gringos" and "Death to Wallace!" The United States naval attaché, standing outside the embassy, was cracked over the head with a blackjack, and someone threw a punch at the American military attaché, Lieutenant Colonel Gordon McCoy (McCoy struck back and flattened his assailant). Wallace, meanwhile, was kept under heavy security and assigned one of Mexico's top generals as a personal aide. Twenty thousand soldiers stood guard in the capital city, and when it came time for him to leave the country, he was obliged to do so by stealth because of the rumor that an attempt would be made on his life. After giving out that he would depart by train instead of by car, as originally planned, he left secretly by plane.[14]

Mexican officials, who refused to allow a single American military base on their soil despite repeated requests, found that they could deny Roosevelt with impunity. In return for a promise of goodwill and other vague formulas, Washington signed a treaty authorizing a $40 million loan and $300 million in credits. The bulk of the American oil claim went out the window by means of a face-saving expedient, and Mexico received an additional $18 million in Lend-Lease military equipment for which it paid a third of the normal price. In spite of this, Mexico did not declare war on Germany until May 1942, and then only after two of its tankers were sunk. When one of these, the *Potrero de Llano*, went down off the coast of Florida, it was rumored that the sinking was an American plot to push Mexico into the war, and Roosevelt's name was hissed in Mexican theaters. Betty Kirk, a reporter for the *Washington Post* and

Christian Science Monitor on special assignment to Mexico, reported that "loyal Mexican friends came to me to report that from old aristo-crats to the Indians in the plaza, the anti-*gringo* hatred included at least 90% of the people and that there was open talk of overthrowing the government" for having sold out to Roosevelt. Most Mexicans not con-nected with leftist organizations or employed by the government voted against the declaration of war. As it was, the total Mexican contribution, in terms of combat troops, consisted of a solitary air squadron sent to the Philippines. Mexico, the only Latin American country besides Brazil to send combat troops, suffered a death toll of eight.[15]

Before extending the discussion to a broader consideration of Latin American attitudes, there are two other countries, Bolivia and Argen-tina, which have a special claim to attention. Both are conceded to have been something less than friendly to the United States, with Bolivia achieving distinction as the first country to announce expropriation of American oil property in March 1937. As happened in Mexico, Roose-velt's ambassador to La Paz paved the way by insisting that American companies have recourse to local justice.[16] Three years earlier, FDR had instituted an "impartial" arms embargo against both sides in the Chaco War, involving Bolivia and Paraguay. But of the two belligerents, Bolivia suffered more because she had relied more heavily upon United States arms shipments. In this case, Roosevelt was responding to a public outcry caused by the discovery of ads taken by five American arms firms in a Bolivian newspaper. At the same time, the United States resisted Argentine pressure to curb Bolivia in the peace talks, and Roosevelt continued with an even hand despite the initial Bolivian action against Standard Oil. It is against this background that the Bolivian Supreme Court upheld expropriation and President Germán Busch adopted total-itarian rule at home and friendship with the Axis abroad. In exchange for substantial German aid in the construction of an oil refinery and pipeline across the Gran Chaco, he contracted with Berlin to export $15 million of Bolivian products, mostly oil. Washington responded by re-fusing to buy Bolivian tin or to grant loans and technical assistance, but by 1942, with the United States at war, Roosevelt did what he could to steer La Paz away from the Axis, taking nearly all of her tin, tungsten, and rubber; $25 million was promised to develop Bolivian agriculture, industry, mining, and roads; $5.5 million was earmarked for oil develop-ment; $2 million for currency stabilization, road building, and railway rolling stock. Unhappily for the new president, Enrique Peñaranda del

Castillo, Roosevelt did not follow through. Thus when Wallace came to pay his respects in 1943, the reception proved lukewarm. During one of his speeches at City Hall, a member of the audience jumped up and shouted, "The Vice-President has spoken, but he has spoken of nothing for Bolivia."[17]

Peñaranda's days were numbered. Accused of selling tin to the United States at an arbitrarily low price, he was replaced by Major Gualberto Vallarroel, who drew his support from students, radicals, and segments of the middle class. Vallarroel was a popular choice who imposed press censorship and formed a cabinet loaded with Nazi sympathizers. When Axis propaganda spread, Roosevelt threatened to halt metal purchases and reverted to nonrecognition, a policy he had foresworn as unwarranted interference in the internal affairs of a neighbor. At this point, Vallarroel responded with a series of empty gestures. Several cabinet members were dropped, and after the government instituted a crackdown on overt Axis activity, the United States resumed relations. The situation never really changed, however. La Paz continued to gravitate to the Right. Expropriation proceedings against German owners quickly ended, censorship returned, and Bolivia was as dictatorial and fascist as ever. One opinion poll taken in 1944 showed at least half the populace harboring strong resentment against Washington.[18]

Argentina, with a population of only 14 million, as compared with Brazil's 40 million, ranked second in population among the nations of South America, but it admitted no rival in wealth, culture, or efficiency.[19] Like Finland, it continued to pay its debts throughout the Depression, which was particularly remarkable since it produced commodities such as grain and beef that competed with North American farmers on the world market. Under Coolidge and Hoover, the traditional Argentine sense of independence had deepened as economic rivalry between Washington and Buenos Aires manifested itself increasingly in the field of hemispheric politics. It was under the leadership of FDR, however, that relations sank to their lowest ebb in a century and a half.[20]

At first, Roosevelt gave personal attention to the fostering of better trade ties and went out of his way to confer with the Argentine ambassador, along with various technical experts. When Hull arrived in Montevideo in 1933, he made it a point to pay the first call on Latin delegation chairmen, one of whom was Carlos Saavedra Lamas. This brilliant and punctilious "minister of foreign affairs and worship" must have been puzzled by Hull's desire to set aside protocol. His wife received flowers from the American secretary, and Roosevelt, after yielding to his insistence on holding the next inter-American convocation in Buenos Aires, supported him for the Nobel Peace Prize. This, despite a State Department tradition of never backing foreigners. FDR even offered to delay the 1936 conference until the Argentine completed a round of duties as president of the League Assembly in Geneva. Hull, who praised Saavedra Lamas lavishly during the conferences of 1933 and 1936, advised Roosevelt to lay on his compliments with a steam shovel. Roosevelt's aides agreed; flattery was the thing.[21]

It soon became apparent, however, that mere words could not satisfy Argentina's desire for access to North American markets. Local officials were especially sensitive to laws which discriminated against their meat on sanitary grounds. In 1935, Roosevelt negotiated a treaty providing for the admission of Argentine mutton in modest quantities, but the treaty languished in the Senate. The following year, he again promised at Buenos Aires that he would work for Senate approval, and a grateful people loaded his ship with lamb, bacon, and beef as an earnest of their trust. Nevertheless, with opposition anticipated from congressional lobbies, FDR did not bestir himself. The year 1937 turned out to be inauspicious for the passage of New Deal legislation. Eventually, he made a show of ordering the State Department to go ahead with its campaign for treaty approval but failed to furnish the personal support needed to win. Instead, he tried to buy Argentine cooperation by offering aid so generous that Assistant Secretary Berle considered it politically risky.[22]

Mellett, after sounding Latin American leaders in January of 1941, told Roosevelt that trade was what mattered; if the president could not deliver on the proposed treaty or honor subsequent pledges, he should at least provide Buenos Aires with something tangible as a face-saver. Hull, for his part, made an urgent appeal for presidential clout in the treaty battle. Still, Roosevelt would not move. On the twentieth of the month, Wallace muffed his first chance as vice president to break a tie vote in the Senate. An amendment to a bill that would have allowed naval purchases of Argentine meat was being considered, and he was busy entertaining guests in the Senate dining room. The Argentine Chamber of Deputies, thoroughly incensed, not only voted to reject $110 million worth of American loans and credits over the objection of

President-elect Ramon Castillo; it vetoed a proposal for joint military staff conversations and, having accused Washington of rapacious designs, went on to refuse permission for American bases on Argentine soil. Uruguay refused a similar request under the influence of her southern neighbor.[23]

One other issue rankled in the Argentine breast. Brazil had been on the verge in 1936 of purchasing ten American cruisers of the *Omaha* class. Shrill protest from the Casa Rosada caused the White House to back down, but Roosevelt promised Rio six American destroyers on lease and offered to help her build a first-class fleet of her own. She was to receive American naval plans, technical advice, and financial aid with the proviso that materials would be purchased in the United States. When word of this agreement spread, the Women's International League for Peace and Freedom landed a sheaf of protest mail on the front portico of the White House. This did not faze the administration in the least, however. Hull and Welles led reporters to believe that there was no such agreement, and Roosevelt went ahead with his promise to assist Brazil in its shipbuilding.[24]

In August of 1937, when the president applied to Congress for permission to lease decommissioned destroyers to any American nation for training purposes, *La Prensa* of Buenos Aires branded the scheme an affront to the idea of the Good Neighbor. Britain then followed suit, questioning its legality under the recent London Naval Treaty. Saavedra Lamas, meanwhile, spoke of Roosevelt's threat to involve the hemisphere in an arms race and upset the delicate balance of power. Before a group of reporters, the Argentine jibed that it should come as no surprise if Hull appeared uncertain regarding the proposed deal's compatibility with the London Naval Treaty; this had occurred to Argentina, too. Roosevelt must take care, he warned, not to violate American law in the form of the 1937 Neutrality Act. On the very day that these words were spoken (12 August), the Senate Foreign Relations Committee handed Roosevelt a second defeat, voting four to two not to refer his leasing proposal to the floor. This time, it was the turn of the Itamaraty to express consternation. Rio buzzed with talk of betrayal. One influential paper, *O Jornal*, commented that this was "the most unfortunate page in Brazilian history . . . [it had been] badly begun, negotiated in worse fashion, and ended by being horribly managed." Hull told reporters he was holding the leasing resolution "in abeyance," but for all intents and purposes this was the end of it. Brazil ordered its six destroyers from England.[25]

As the United States edged closer to war in 1941, Argentina inched closer to the side of the Axis. Traditionally bound to Europe by virtue of intellectual, political, cultural, and economic ties, she was now more impressed than ever by Hitler's military prowess and so began to demand a more "natural" form of Pan Americanism, one without subservience. Roosevelt could find no leverage in the offer of a lucrative new trade treaty; nor was he able, after Pearl Harbor, to prevail by resort to economic sanction. Neither the freezing of Argentine assets, nor the refusal of export licenses, nor even an embargo on the reception of Argentine ships in American ports seemed able to advance his cause one whit. Loan agreements were canceled. Military aid ceased. Finally, in the summer of 1944, the State Department broke diplomatic relations and persuaded Britain to do likewise. Grudgingly, Buenos Aires severed relations with the Axis early in 1944, but Roosevelt still could not extract a declaration of war. When President Pedro Ramírez showed signs of yielding, his days in office were numbered. Resigning for reasons of "ill health," he left the Casa Rosada to General Edelmiro Farrell who, backed by War Minister Juan Perón, swung even farther to the Right.[26]

Roosevelt, unwilling to admit that he had been worsted, encouraged a buildup of Brazilian armed forces along the Argentine border and excluded Argentina from United Nations planning conferences. When an international session on food and agriculture convened at Hot Springs in 1943, Buenos Aires did not appear on the list of countries invited. The following year, he tried to keep her from membership in the world body but was forced to acquiesce in return for vague promises of democratic reform. On 9 April 1945, several days before his death and in exchange for Argentina's declaration of war on a dead Axis, Roosevelt recognized the Farrell-Perón government. Rarely have two American governments indulged in such recrimination or fought one another to such an absolute standstill over so long a period of time.[27]

Turning, however, to a more general overview of opinion in the Americas, it seems clear that despite radical expansion in the use of foreign aid, the United States made little headway in cementing genuinely positive ties. As war was about to break out in 1939, U.S. Treasury Research Director Harry Dexter White felt impelled to write Morgenthau: "Our progress in bringing Latin America into the United

States orbit has yielded negligible results in the past six months . . . with Franco's victory in Spain, the strength of the aggressor nations in Latin America has greatly increased." Barring a shift toward greater amounts of aid, White continued, Latin America would "succumb." German chargé Thomsen could not have been more in accord. "In spite of all the optimism, externally displayed, regarding South America's loyal friendship [with the United States]," he assured the Wilhelm-strasse, "there are no illusions here as to the reliability of the new friends." The point was further confirmed by Breckinridge Long on his return from a fact-finding mission to Latin America. From what he had been able to gather, Brazil, Uruguay, and Argentina had all but fallen under the influence of Germany and Italy. He therefore recommended that the United States extend more aid, underwrite the purchase of more Latin American products, and enlarge the Export-Import Bank.

Other countries that leaned toward the Axis in 1939, after having basked for six years in the golden sun of New Deal generosity, included Bolivia, Peru, and Chile. Historian Claude Bowers peered from embassy windows in Santiago during 1940 and could not overlook the "manifest hostility to the United States in numerous quarters." A $16 million credit for industrialization helped to promote cooperation, and additional American money was soon on its way for the defense of the Straits of Magellan. Nevertheless, Chile refused to break with Hitler or even to ratify the Act of Havana until after General Eisenhower's impressive landing in North Africa.[28]

By 1942, Long's recommendation had been adopted in toto. Prior to 1939, American aid remained relatively modest. The Export-Import Bank operated under a ceiling of $100 million imposed by Congress, and though most of its capital flowed to Latin America, the administration did not lend to full capacity. Roosevelt now began "shooting the works," to borrow Adolf Berle's phrase. Throwing his weight behind an inter-American currency to be called the unitam, he obtained authorization for Export-Import Bank loans of up to $700 million. In October 1940, he played host to twenty Latin American military chiefs and promised a generous supply of American military hardware at bargain prices. Before long, the United States had signed Lend-Lease agreements with nearly every nation south of the border except Panama and furnished $263 million in military supplies and equipment, including aircraft and naval vessels.[29]

Senator Hugh Butler of Nebraska rocked the country when, after returning from a visit to Latin American capitals in 1943, he charged that the Good Neighbor Policy had cost the United States $6 billion in three years and with very meager results:

> Our policy toward Latin America, which began as Good-neighbor-ism, has . . . become "rich-uncle-ism." . . . [It] surpasses anything known in the long history of handouts. . . . We are not winning the friendly collaboration of the peoples of Latin America. We are trying to buy it. . . . We are hated . . . for upsetting their economy. . . . Local employers of capital cities in South America are antagonized by spending measures which force them to meet new wage scales—or lose their employees. . . . South Americans, in the main, care little for United States solicitude. The well-to-do and the cultured groups consider us soft and regard us as easy marks. Other groups resent, even pridefully scorn, our "uplift" gestures. Few respect us. . . . They fear our influence. They balk at our propaganda. . . . They bite the hand that's feeding them. . . . [There] are direct grants, grants disguised as loans, real loans, which may or may not be repaid with . . . interest, subsidies, lines of credit, premium prices paid for Latin American products we need, purchases of Latin American products we do not need or want, but which we buy because they need the market; sales of our products below cost, advisory services, grants to our allies to enable them to buy Latin American products, administrative costs, stabilization loans, and so on. Such expenditures are made by Government departments and bureaus, by special government agencies, by Government corporations and their subsidiaries and the subsidiaries of those subsidiaries and by the special banks or corporations, Government or private, American or Latin American, financed largely or entirely by one or more of these agencies, bureaus, corporations, or corporation subsidiaries. . . . How well will our relations with Latin America stand the shock of the morning after, when we have finally decided to abandon this open-handed largesse? For this nonsense will stop, of course, when we run out of money. . . . Just how much good will do we generate in Latin America by attempting to force them to make over their social forms and economic systems?

Butler made a point of noting that in the case of a single country, Cuba, Export-Import Bank authorizations had totaled $40 million by 1943, of which nothing had been repaid. Huge military bases had been built and promised to Havana for after the war. And how could a New Deal for Latin America be justified in such extravagant terms inasmuch as the region was not a major factor in the war? Should America not have been more concerned about winning the goodwill of countries such as Sweden, Turkey, Portugal, India, and China?[30] In sum, Butler raised three important questions: Was the United States obliged to purchase the goodwill of Latin America on account of enlightened self-interest? If so, at what cost? And was the lavish scale of the Roosevelt program not corrupting Latin American economies, giving rise to unrealistic expectations and creating a dangerous dependency on future American support?

Allowing for exaggeration in the figure of $6 billion (which appeared in the *Reader's Digest* as well as the *Congressional Record*) and for Butler's affiliation with the Republican party on the eve of an election, the United States was still spending a princely sum considering that it exercised indisputable control over hemispheric sea lanes. Millions were given in matching grants; millions more were awarded gratis. Even after the tide turned in 1944, Roosevelt shipped an additional five hundred thousand books, films, maps, pamphlets, and charts, along with a host of movie stars, athletes, musicians, and writers. As one critic observed, "Sometimes people prefer to do things themselves, even badly, rather than have others do for them in their behalf." In the construction of the Pan-American Highway, the president of one of the participating countries refused to allow American officials to pay higher than standard wages. Nor was this an isolated case.[31]

Some idea of the corrupting power of the United States dollar may be gleaned from the realization that Washington's annual budget was *nearly eight times* the annual budget of all twenty states of Latin America combined. In many cases, the aid proffered to a given country within a period of a few years equaled its entire annual outlay, and the decision to accept or reject it lay within the province of relatively few. In Bowers's words, "One man could write his name on a document and break relations with the Axis overnight, without consulting any Congress, without consulting public opinion—and only, I'm afraid, after they had gotten assurance as to how much money they'd get from Lend-Lease. Then there would be loud applause on the part of the American press." John Campbell White, American ambassador to Haiti, explained how President Stenio Vincent was influenced in his choice of a successor: "It was known that we were prepared to spend a certain amount of money in Haiti. The Haitians were naturally interested in getting that. I was eventually able to give a broad hint to President Vincent [who was presumed able to handpick his successor] in regard to Lescot's candidacy which I presume had its effect. Lescot was duly elected. He was very friendly to the United States. . . . Of course, he knew on which side his bread was buttered."[32] Lescot had been serving as Haiti's minister to the United States, and some might argue that, as in the case of Cuba's Cespedes, he continued to do so as president.

As early as November of 1936, *Time,* still friendly to the administration, referred to Roosevelt as "Santa Claus," and two years later, the president was roasted at a Gridiron dinner for sending delegates to a conference in Lima, where they would "show their good will by coming home without their shirts." A figure impersonating Hull described the hemispheric defense plan as "fifty-fifty, we give, they take." The *Worcester Telegram* attacked Wallace for acting the part of a "Gringo Santa Claus" when he toured Latin America in 1943, and *Time* referred to the administration aid program as diplomatic butter.[33]

The point that requires emphasis here is that Roosevelt engaged in an unparalleled and futile effort to purchase goodwill. Brazilian Foreign Minister Aranha is reported to have said during his profitable trip to Washington in 1939: "I shall propose that we erect a statue to Herr Hitler. For it is Hitler who at last succeeded in drawing the attention of the United States to Brazil."[34]

Ministers of other countries became equally dexterous in conjuring up ties with the Axis (real or imaginary) to extract additional aid from a worried White House.[35] In 1937, the government-managed press of Costa Rica berated Washington for having more funds at its disposal than it was willing to admit; Costa Rican natives had the distinct impression that supplementary projects could and should be funded by the United States. Thus American Ambassador William H. Hornibrook insisted that Roosevelt's reputation had come to depend upon the delivery of further largesse. Likewise, when Wallace arrived in Panama in 1943, he was immediately reminded of the military facilities that had been made available and asked why certain aid projects authorized by Roosevelt had not materialized. Where, it was asked, were the funds promised by the Rockefeller Committee for an inter-American university? Nelson Rockefeller denied that such a promise had ever been made but hastened to confirm that his country might be willing to help establish a public health school. Every nation south of the border except El Salvador, which had recognized Manchukuo, benefited from Washington's distress. For Peru, it was a $10 million loan extended in 1940 after the replacement of an anti-American president.[36] Haiti reaped $5.5 million in road construction funds, as well as $6 million for an abortive project to develop rubber. Panama received the promise of an improved sewage system. Other Central American countries were enabled to spend hundreds of thousands of dollars to complete segments of the Inter-American Highway.[37]

Despite all this largesse, it is not clear that American popularity increased commensurately. Colombia, one of the most economically dependent of all Latin American countries and traditionally one of the friendliest, notwithstanding Washington's role in Panamanian independence (1903), proved to be no different from its neighbors under the stimulus of the New Deal. Hull pressed Bogotá for a reciprocal trade agreement which favored U.S. economic interests overwhelmingly and made few, if any, substantial concessions. Colombia acquiesced only because she eventually ran out of delaying tactics and feared American retaliation against her coffee. But she was under no illusion. Newspapers such as *El Espectador* referred to the treaty as a "contract of slavery." The American legation had to be guarded by two dozen police, and as late as November 1942, Colombia remained solidly pro-Nazi. Ambassador Spruille Braden could not help noting that the foreign minister practically kissed Axis envoys good-bye.[38]

Economic dependency became one of the principal targets for native criticism. Chile's delegate to an agricultural conference in Mexico City objected that too many things were centered in Washington; there was too much preponderance on the part of the United States. But nowhere was such feeling more pronounced than in the Pearl of the Antilles. Although Roosevelt's second Export-Import Bank had the effect of propping up Cuba's new government, Havana shortly became the scene of a murderous attack on the American ambassador. American money poured into Fulgencio Batista's development projects, and loans flowed freely to finance Cuban purchases of American silver. In 1934, moreover, the bank granted two silver loans, followed in subsequent years by five more. Roosevelt also abrogated the Platt Amendment and signed lucrative trade agreements liberalizing the American quota on Cuban sugar by 25 percent. Nonetheless, it is apparent that anti-American sentiment actually increased in Cuba during this period. Jefferson Caffery, head of the American mission in Havana from 1934 to 1937, dispatched doleful reports about economic hardship and terrorist activity. Braden, who served as ambassador from 1942 to 1945, could not move about Havana without being followed by an official machine-gun squad. He voiced constant complaints of corruption and forecast a dark future for American influence. Cuba, supinely dependent upon the United States, was at the same time doing all it could to obstruct the war effort. There was "increasing abuse of American interests and individuals," and leftist influence was on the rise. Cuba became the first Latin American nation to recognize the Soviet Union. A Marxist school was founded in Santiago (Oriente Province). And the Communist party, with two members in the Cuban cabinet, demonstrated remarkable discipline. On Pan American Day 1943, Mexico's ambassador to Havana chose as his theme "the increasing and potentially menacing shadow of the 'giant of the North.' " Might the rationing of goods, he wondered, not be a forerunner of the "rationing of our liberties?"[39]

While Venezuela remained a good friend and Colombia granted base rights after receiving a $12 million loan, other countries acted more along the lines of Cuba. The situation in Puerto Rico remained highly charged, especially during the period 1936–39, with a rash of assassinations accompanying feverish agitation for independence. Virulently anti-American neofascism flourished, and some leaders even looked to a Japanese victory for their deliverance. Despite aid to rehabilitate Ecuador's war-ravaged El Oro Province, Quito resented Roosevelt's failure to deliver significant quantities of Lend-Lease. An opinion poll in 1944 showed respondents well-disposed toward Roosevelt, but the populace changed its mind at reports of North American designs on the Galápagos Islands. Uruguay, one of three countries reported by Long to have been under Axis influence in 1939, denied Roosevelt's request for military bases in 1940 even though it accepted a gift of approximately $7.5 million in aid. Deep-seated anti-American sentiment smoldered through the war and beyond. As for Peru, which in 1943 extended such a hearty welcome to Vice President Wallace—ten thousand cavalrymen met him at the airport and fifty thousand schoolchildren formed a "V" for victory—it cannot be said that Lima was entirely well disposed either. Peruvians voted Hull their highest award after the war, but a poll of public opinion in 1944 showed 60 percent of the people harboring deep suspicion toward the United States. Peru received the highest level of Lend-Lease of any of the northern Andean countries. Yet, according to Dora Mayer de Zulen, one of its leading feminists and civic workers, "the man in the street, or let us say the public, likens the Good Neighbor Policy to a white glove put on by the big brother to hide . . . greedy claws."[40]

Finally, there is Panama, which, in relative terms, benefited from

American liberality as much as any other Latin American nation. FDR assured its people that "sympathetic consideration would be given to the removal of their just grievances," and the Hull-Alfaro Treaty, signed in 1936, gave such consideration. Stipulating an end to the American protectorate, it recognized Panama's right to a larger share of Canal Zone revenue; it also promised increased annuities based on canal tolls amounting to almost 80 percent and recognized a joint defense commitment. Although Roosevelt refused to press for instant Senate approval, he did promise aid for highway construction during a visit to Panama. In mid-1939 came the hoped-for ratification. But instead of reaping goodwill, FDR had to shield himself from invective. A new president, Arnulfo Arias, Harvard-educated and a physician by profession, began his term with a radio address criticizing American Canal Zone commanders for illegal occupation of proposed defense sites. In return for bases, he demanded the enormous sum of $25 million plus $30 million in annual rent. Refusing long-term base rights at any price, he damned Yanqui imperialism up and down the countryside, accusing the United States of niggardly behavior. Anti-Americanism subsided momentarily when, on a visit to his Cuban eye doctor in October of 1941, Arias was overthrown. Even so, the new regime balked at granting base rights until after the bombing of Pearl Harbor, something historians Langer and Gleason have described as "a sad commentary on the limitations of Pan-American solidarity when the need arose to translate high sounding words into concrete measures of action."[41] Given Roosevelt's brand of rhetoric and the high expectations thereby generated for better-than-usual treatment, Panama shared in sentiments common to the area. She was likely to construe benefits as mere compensation for past instances of intervention, and in this case there was not only the added desire for income commensurate with a transisthmian canal but also some resentment at American efforts to transform the country into a defense site.

Roosevelt paid dearly for his version of the Good Neighbor Policy when all factors are weighed. In addition to direct aid and discarded rights of intervention, an accurate expense tally would have to include losses suffered by American companies and individuals on transactions involving oil, land, and bonds.[42] Within a few months of Bolivia's expropriation, Ecuador resorted to similar action in less direct form. The South American Development Company, a United States concern which controlled various mining properties, had been losing money for years when in 1937 it began to make a profit and Quito slapped a confiscatory tax on its property that was as arbitrary as it was discriminatory. One must also take into account British losses, in excess of American, even though London obtained a proportionately larger recompense. Other European countries lost out, too, and the many agencies and committees established to administer various and sundry programs were costly.[43] One of these ran through an annual operating budget of $8 million.[44] Not to be overlooked, either, is the cost of "gunboat diplomacy." Roosevelt may have succeeded to some extent in substituting the power of finance for the power of the military. Nevertheless, powerful units of the South Atlantic Fleet continued to enter the mouth of the River Plata as a matter of course. Six bombers touched down at Rio de Janeiro in 1939 to celebrate the founding of the Brazilian Republic, and when Uruguay began an investigation of Nazi activity in 1940, it produced a "good will visit" to Montevideo of two United States cruisers. Roosevelt thought nothing of sending six B-17 Flying Fortresses over Buenos Aires to demonstrate his support for Roberto Ortiz just as he sent a cruiser to signal American reluctance to recognize Farrell.[45]

Not least in any reckoning of New Deal expenditure was the price paid in terms of leadership. Careful to avoid any move that might jeopardize his reputation as friend to all and enemy to none, Roosevelt confined his intervention in hemispheric disputes to bland expressions of goodwill.[46] Such an approach has been characterized by one leading historian of the period as "solicitude in anarchy."[47] Earlier in the century, the United States had used its influence to reconcile Guatemala and El Salvador, Nicaragua and Honduras. It had taken the lead in resolving the Tacna-Arica controversy, a dispute of fifty years' standing between Chile and Peru, which terminated in 1929 with the signing of the Treaty of Santiago. Beginning in 1933, however, the tone and shape of American diplomacy changed considerably. Not once did the United States venture to propose a substantive solution, yielding in every case to the lead of others. During his first two years in office, FDR transferred American responsibility for two inter-American quarrels to the League of Nations, and thereafter Hull sought in vain to orchestrate an effective form of Pan-American mediation.[48]

All three hemispheric wars of the period were settled without reference to the White House, in itself a striking indication. Two of these were in progress when Roosevelt took office and one, Marañon, began

during his tenure. In the case of the Chaco conflict, involving Bolivia
and Paraguay and costing one hundred thousand lives, Saavedra Lamas
spearheaded a peace initiative which bore fruit after three years of talks
in Buenos Aires. By then, both sides had exhausted themselves, and
Roosevelt, having abdicated his chairmanship of a neutral commission
dating from the days of President Hoover, was in no position to claim
credit. He also reversed Stimson's policy of resistance to intrusion by
the League in inter-American disputes. The paradox is that despite all
such precautions, Bolivia still found reason to decry American action
(or lack thereof) and, as mentioned above, La Paz set Mexico City an
example by expropriating American oil property. As regards the Letitia
boundary dispute, it was internal dynamics rather than action by the
United States or any other American state that brought an end to the
bloodshed. In the Marañon conflict, Ecuador and Peru asked permission to come to Washington for bilateral talks with the understanding
that if they should fail, Roosevelt would himself hand down an award.
Come they did in 1936; but when difficulties ensued, Roosevelt inexplicably declined to commit himself and ended up with a diplomatic
fiasco. In 1941, Lima drove Quito out of watershed rivers and laid claim
to a sizable area of the western Amazon. With Peruvian forces occupy-
ing the main Ecuadorian port of Guayaquil, Quito agreed in 1942 to a
border recommended by Argentina, Brazil, Chile, and the United
States. Later, when the war ended, Ecuadorian nationalists denounced
the border treaty, setting the stage for renewed bloodshed. The persistence of inter-American hostility during the New Deal era was extremely unfortunate, prompting one of the foremost students of the
subject to conclude that North American influence for hemispheric
peace reached an all-time low under Roosevelt.[49]

Inter-American conferences held between 1933 and 1942 bear dubious witness to the quality of United States leadership. Montevideo in
1933 and Lima in 1938 were regularly scheduled international conferences of American states, the seventh and eighth in a series held
at five-year intervals. Another, Buenos Aires, was a special inter-
American conference convened at Roosevelt's request in 1936 to consider steps for the maintenance of *world* peace. Three others, Panama
in 1939, Havana in 1940, and Rio de Janeiro in 1942, brought American
foreign ministers together in consonance with a provision adopted at
Lima in 1938. Each of the latter three came after a notable crisis: the

outbreak of fighting in 1939, the fall of France in 1940, and American belligerency in the case of Rio.

Remarkable in nearly every instance is the extent to which Roosevelt failed to consummate his plans. In 1933 at Montevideo, despite an offer of $5 million for hemispheric transportation and communication, Saavedra Lamas defeated an American peace initiative and, in so doing, managed to commit Washington to a seemingly unequivocal pledge of nonintervention in Latin American affairs. Roosevelt's offer of aid was rejected. Three years later, at the very moment that FDR was being hailed in Argentina, Mexican legislators voted to expropriate American oil and Cárdenas was reported ready to sign the enabling decree.[50] At Buenos Aires, Washington once again held out an attractive financial inducement, this time in the form of a proposed convention for the promotion of inter-American cultural affairs, which promised to draw heavily on United States funds. But once more, a Roosevelt blueprint for hemispheric cooperation was shunted aside. Hull, who sponsored a plan to deal with hemispheric war by means of provisions contained in the United States Neutrality Code, also asked Latin American nations to pledge joint action against extrahemispheric war in the form of an embargo on war supplies or trade in general. In the end, his plan went down to defeat in favor of a hollow compromise. There was to be no organ for consultation, no clearly defined purpose, no enforcement machinery, and no obligation to accept the verdict of consultation. Saavedra Lamas, who claimed the American proposal conflicted with duties owed the League, exchanged sharp words with Hull and, in spite of his position as host of the conference, chose not to see the departing secretary off. The Lima Conference of 1938 came close to achieving what Hull had hoped to do at Buenos Aires, but it produced a resolution to consult on the foreign minister level rather than an actual treaty specifying concrete emergency measures. Hull failed to unite the Western Hemisphere militarily, and delegates were not impressed by his undisguised attempt to stir resentment against the Axis while ignoring communist propaganda. Argentine foreign minister and chief delegate Ramón Castillo boycotted most of the meetings and succeeded in forcing Hull to recede substantially from his original position.[51]

The Panama Conference, which convened in 1939 after the outbreak of war, proved a pleasant exception to the rule. Washington won backing for a "safety zone" stretching three hundred to a thousand miles off the coast of the Americas within which the belligerent powers were forbidden to commit hostile acts. Although the plan was frowned upon by Hull as unenforceable and no European power took it seriously, it supplied the United States Navy with a pretext for tracking Axis vessels and radioing their position to the British.[52]

In July of 1940, following the defeat of France, came the Havana Conference. FDR had just pronounced against transfer of colonies from one European power to another, and he sought hemispheric support. In the event, nine Latin American nations refused to include foreign ministers in their delegations and when Buenos Aires managed to steer the discussion away from transfer and on to the issue of self-determination, delegates cast the United States in the role of imperialist. The Act of Havana did stipulate that American states acting as a group, and in urgent cases singly, would take possession of any territory threatened by a non-American power. This act multilateralized the no-transfer principle of the Monroe Doctrine even as it manifested a gratifying deference to the United States. But Hull never obtained approval of a Pan-American trusteeship over threatened colonies. To his regret, the resulting unanimity was at best nominal, and he anticipated serious trouble if Britain were ever to fall. Havana, supposedly the most successful of the conferences, also had a close connection with American finance. On its eve, FDR petitioned Congress for an increase in Export-Import Bank lending authority from $200 million to $700 million.[53]

The last of the convocations was held at Rio in the wake of Pearl Harbor, and though the administration knew that it could not persuade every delegation to declare war on the Axis, it did hope for an across-the-board break in diplomatic relations. Argentina, as usual, stood in the way, joined this time by Chile. Hull, who did not attend, found fault with the final compromise, and Berle agreed that it was a defeat for America's allies, as well as for Washington.[54]

In sum, it cannot be said that the series of hemispheric convocations beginning with Montevideo in 1933 and ending with Rio in 1942 offers a vindication of New Deal policy. By almost any reckoning, the conferences must be accounted a mixed bag, even allowing for unparalleled concomitant challenges such as worldwide capitalist depression, unexpected success on the part of Soviet communism, and any number of remarkable gains on the side of the Axis.

Some observers, looking elsewhere for proof of New Deal persuasiveness, have professed to find it in the record of Latin American wartime cooperation. Lord Halifax, for instance, judged Roosevelt's policy a success on the ground that a fair number of Latin American countries allowed American troops on their soil, which he felt would not have been possible during World War I. Sumner Welles, too, emphasized that fewer countries remained technically neutral during World War II than in the preceding war. By Welles's count, the people of the hemisphere were friendlier to the United States than ever before.[55]

The problem in this case is that neither Welles nor Halifax allowed for the force of dissimilar circumstance. During World War I, President Woodrow Wilson began by urging neutrality in thought as well as deed, whereas Roosevelt tilted dramatically to one side and issued a clarion call for total opposition to the Axis. Secondly, Kaiser Wilhelm was not attempting to exterminate racial and religious minorities. In spite of this, and despite Germany's customary appeal to neighbors south of the border, *no less than eight Latin American countries entered World War I as belligerents.* Five others sided with the Allied cause as non-belligerents, and only seven remained neutral. None fought on the side of Germany, which is all the more remarkable when one considers that American marines had bloodied the soil of Haiti, as well as the Dominican Republic, and invaded Mexico by land and sea. In addition to Wilson's crimson record of intervention, there existed no Export-Import Bank in 1917 and no Lend-Lease. Furthermore, the duration of American belligerency in the first war amounted to only half of what it proved to be in the second. One president, Wilson, with less time to win converts, persuaded four times as many countries to throw in their lot with the United States in the opening months of hostilities. It seemed possible for a short while during World War II that Germany might wrest control of Britain's powerful navy, but the prospect faded quickly, and by the end of 1943, the Axis had lost much of its glitter. Within a year, it shone hardly at all. Nonetheless, if all Latin American nations had declared war by the spring of 1945, only a half dozen had offered military facilities.[56] One could perhaps argue that the Good Neighbor Policy, as executed by FDR, prevented significant aid from going to Hitler. More likely, however, the reason was America's virtually unchallenged naval supremacy in the Western Hemisphere.

Early in the century, a British diplomat concluded that the United States had come to possess a special "moral authority" in Latin America. Such a claim would have been difficult to sustain by 1939. Hull did not prevail upon a single neighboring nation to welcome Jewish refugees in significant numbers, hardly surprising in view of the example set by Washington. Between 1933 and 1945, the United States made a concerted effort to achieve the codification of hemispheric law, again without success. Men such as Welles, who expected reasonable reimbursement for expropriated American oil property were, of course, disappointed. Mexico would not even consent to go to arbitration under the Inter-American Arbitration Treaty of 1929. Politics swallowed the law. Then again, the Inter-American Highway, which Roosevelt hoped to complete, remained unfinished, with 2,000 miles of road usable in dry weather only, 1,200 miles of bullock cart trails, and 186 miles of hopeless tangle between Panama City and Colombia. In 1947, a special War Investigating Committee concluded that New Deal projects had been "hastily" conceived and "unbusinesslike" in execution; 347 miles of the highway had been completed at a cost of $36 million as compared with an anticipated 905 miles to be built for an estimated $14.5 million.[57]

Even the Reciprocal Trade Program, so loudly acclaimed by New Deal apologists as a mark of success, has been found wanting. What Latin America needed was a barter arrangement with countries capable of taking its raw materials. The one thing it did not need was free trade as advocated by Hull. As late as 1939, only three South American countries had entered a reciprocal trade agreement with the United States (Brazil, Colombia, and Ecuador), and Brazil appears to have done so for political reasons. It is, of course, true that Secretary Hull's program was hampered by powerful opposition from George Peek, special adviser to the president on foreign trade. Peek, who was far more barter-minded than Hull, headed two special government banks to promote the export trade and a new trade organization. American policy was therefore beset by confusion and overlapping jurisdiction until Peek resigned in 1935. On balance, the Reciprocal Trade Program did improve the ratio of U.S. exports to Latin America as compared with imports. It also boosted the relative U.S. share of all exports to Latin America. The economies of Latin America were thus more closely integrated with that of North America. And this, in turn, laid the foundation for a free trade philosophy that was to govern American thinking on international commerce for the next four decades (by 1947, the United States had signed twenty-nine reciprocity agreements and set the stage for GATT—General Agreement on Tariffs and Trade). However, in the very act of strengthening the financial position of his own country, Hull was rendering other nations more subservient. Moreover, neither the secretary nor the president was notably courageous in dealing with the domestic pressure that militated against such equalizing concessions as would have been accepted as liberal and fair by the leaders of Latin America.[58]

It has been shown that Roosevelt's trade campaign actually harmed countries such as Cuba by curbing diversification. Continued reliance upon the export of sugar and tobacco meant continued reliance upon the United States. Welles acknowledged as much when he mused on the situation awaiting his successor in Havana: "Caffery unquestionably will obtain all of the needed influence immediately after his arrival, but it will be an influence exerted behind the scenes and not apparent to the public." This also explains why Argentina rejected American aid and why Chile turned down a technical education agreement. Santiago's nationalist faction feared that it, too, would become subservient. When rocks were thrown through Ambassador Bowers's windows in the aftermath of the war, he could not be sure whether to blame Nazis, communists, or the rising tide of young patriots disaffected by Roosevelt's unique brand of dollar diplomacy. European analysts were under no illusion. If the French ambassador had spoken in 1938 of an unprecedented American imperialism thinly disguised by flattery ("impérialisme qui se dissimule mal sous des compliments immérités aux républiques soeurs"), it was because Latin America had become dependent upon the United States to a degree hitherto unknown. If, in the eyes of the British, FDR's Good Neighbor Policy appeared "dominating and patronizing," it was because in London's view a new and subtler form of imperial control had merely replaced an older one, and at considerable expense to the American taxpayer.[59]

If there is any one common denominator linking Latin American opinion of the New Deal with views found elsewhere, it lies in the notion of Washington as a threat. This, in turn, may help to explain the clarity and incisiveness of foreign vision when it comes to an appraisal of the Good Neighbor Policy. Among the papers of French Premier Daladier is a collection of handwritten notes concerning a book entitled *Der Masslose Kontinent*. Written by the popular German author Giselher Wirsing and published in French translation in 1942, it includes a chapter on America's "politique impérialiste." Admittedly, such a concern had deep roots in the past. Foreigners had begun to voice concern over the need to contain the United States as early as the signing of the Treaty of Paris in 1783. Still, the fact remains that Roosevelt did not dispel any of this residual suspicion. If anything, it increased. We have noted various instances of this in our brief survey of Latin American sentiment, but the concern was worldwide, which brings us full circle to some of the conclusions found in the previous chapter. Whether one reads *Izvestia* in 1934 or Japanese newspapers on the eve of the war, American greed serves as a constant theme. If one does not wish to credit French historians of the postwar period, one may read similar Spanish expressions of anxiety for the future of Cape Verde and the Canary Islands. Always, Roosevelt comes across to the reader as an imperialist in disguise, all the more dangerous for his outward repudiation of expansionist goals.[60]

But to return to the subject at hand, it may be said that, apart from the element of increased dependency, Roosevelt added surprisingly little to the policy laid down by his Republican predecessors. The phrase "Good Neighbor" had already been heard on the lips of Elihu Root, Charles Evans Hughes, and Herbert Hoover. Nonintervention was also a well-established Republican policy, along with the Inter-American Highway program inaugurated in 1924. Hoover, after embarking on a ten-week goodwill tour of Latin America as president-elect, made public the Clark Memorandum, which, by implication, questioned the right of the United States to act as hemispheric policeman even where chronic wrongdoing or disorder might invite foreign intervention. The first president to visit South America and participate in an inter-American conference was Calvin Coolidge, who attended the Sixth International Conference of American States at Havana in 1928. Moreover, as noted above, FDR produced no peace initiative to match the resolution of the Tacna-Arica controversy entrusted for arbitration to Coolidge and settled by Hoover, nor was there anything after 1932 to match Chief Justice Hughes's arbitration of a boundary dispute between Guatemala and Honduras. The one thing dear to Republicans that FDR did relinquish was the right of American oil companies to claim equity in subsoil property. This was the so-called "positive acts" principle, affirmed by Mexico in the early 1920s and reaffirmed at the urging of Coolidge's popular ambassador, Dwight Morrow.[61]

Aside from the enormous outlays of foreign aid which FDR introduced, including a modest cultural exchange program directed by Nelson Rockefeller, and aside from a more equitable canal treaty with

Panama and the first official vice presidential visit to Latin America, the main modification associated with New Deal policy was a sweeping nonintervention pledge given at Montevideo and Buenos Aires. Even here, previous presidents had traversed much of the same ground, foreswearing intervention on behalf of economic interests. American marines left Cuba in 1922, the Dominican Republic in 1924, Nicaragua in 1925 (only to return and leave again under Hoover), and they were scheduled for withdrawal from Haiti when Roosevelt came to power. Hoover, on taking the presidential oath, had announced that the United States would not intervene by force to uphold any contract between an individual or corporation and a Latin American government. Instead, he advised recourse to local courts and arbitral panels and between 1929 and 1933 did not intervene militarily in a single Latin American revolt. Needless to say, when FDR sought to intercede for Mexican Catholics beset by a powerful anticlerical administration, he was pursuing the same mediatory line followed by Hoover. And when he adopted a nationalistic trade policy wrapped in the rhetoric of free trade (with all due respect for Hull's idealism), he was again merely imitating the type of policy which had produced earlier red flags such as the Fordney-McCumber tariff of 1922, the Argentine meat embargo of 1927, and the Smoot-Hawley tariff of 1931.[62]

FDR did strive, on occasion, to foster the impression that Latin America counted. Pan American Day was celebrated more widely in American schools. Ministries were raised to the embassy level. Latin American leaders were treated more or less as equals and accorded prestigious treatment during their visits to Washington.[63]

At the same time, one cannot overlook Roosevelt's strain of insensitivity. Addressing newsmen in 1940 on the subject of Latin Americans, he observed smugly: "They think they are just as good as we are, and many of them are." Later in the war, he ignored the record of Brazilian troops fighting in the front rank of Allied forces near Bologna. Only when Rio remonstrated was an attempt made to assure adequate press coverage. During the Hundred Days, he tried to formulate plans for world peace and stability without consulting Latin American leaders, and when it came time to devise a frame of world government, Latin Americans were again excluded. Brazil's presence at Dumbarton Oaks was sorely missed, and certain American republics were threatened with exclusion from the United Nations unless they declared war on the Axis. Such warnings aroused feelings of acute resentment, especially when they appeared in the press. Nor did the discomfort end here. This is the same Roosevelt who, while on tour in Latin America, spent a fair amount of time exhorting host countries to remodel their governments in the image and likeness of the United States. Ironically, he suggested to an audience in Buenos Aires that war could be prevented "by strengthening the processes of constitutional democratic government"—ironic because Argentina had not been involved in a single foreign war for well over fifty years, whereas the United States had entered two and was headed for a third. Never does one observe Roosevelt identifying those features of a foreign culture worth emulating. Shortly after his 1936 visit to Latin America, Peru spoke for its sister republics when it stated through official organs and over the airwaves that Washington had been "impertinent": "We cannot tolerate the imposition of the zeal of others to make us seem to be what we are not." Political institutions cherished by descendants of Spanish colonizers would not be suited to the descendants of the Jamestown settlement.[64]

Secretary of State Stettinius admitted candidly that relations with Latin America had deteriorated steadily during World War II, reaching their nadir in February 1945, when southern capitals protested their exclusion from postwar planning and confessed to a fear of great power condominium. He was not prepared, however, for the stiff opposition which confronted his delegation to Mexico City's Inter-American Conference on Problems of War and Peace. Buenos Aires attracted far more sympathy than anticipated, and, after being plagued with this contentious issue from start to finish, Stettinius modified his position considerably. Many questions proved difficult to answer. Would the United States, for example, tolerate Latin American tariffs? Would it promise to continue its wartime import of Latin American produce? Concessions were made in each of these areas to put the best face possible on a trying situation. Yet this did not prevent Latin American delegates at a future conference, one held at San Francisco, from again throwing the United States on the defensive.[65]

With all of his success in putting the United States on the road to social reform, FDR lacked one of the qualities most highly prized in Latin America: the strength of the caudillo. To a people who admired firmness and consistency, he sent gifts. One Peruvian critic referred to the new brand of American aid in resolving hemispheric disputes as "sweet reasonableness" and "aristotelian logic." So passive was Washington at the time of the Chaco Peace Conference in 1936 that Chile's Nieto del Rio told American delegate Spruille Braden that "the United States must demonstrate its authority and the fact that a strong hand of control still exists." When Mexico threatened to confiscate large oil holdings with Roosevelt's apparent approval, an official in the Brazilian foreign office voiced disbelief: "I have often wondered why such a great power as the United States has not just sent an army into Mexico." *El Plata* of Montevideo reflected similar concern when it noted Roosevelt's lack of control over his own Congress in the area of foreign affairs. Major presidential commitments such as the Argentine trade treaty and lease of cruisers to Brazil were lost as a result of senatorial resistance. And not only did Roosevelt prove incapable or unwilling to influence Congress on vital issues of international import, he did nothing to prevent Senator Nye from giving voice to revelations that shook Latin American officialdom to its core. The vice president of Electric Boat Company quoted Nye as saying that "the real foundation of all South American business is graft." Nye, who offered proof in the case of Bolivia, went so far as to implicate the son of Argentina's president. Allusion was also made to corruption in other countries, one of which, Chile, suspended all arms purchases in the United States. Argentina considered suing for damages in United States courts, and Peru did bring suit after court-martialing one of its military commanders.[66]

Roosevelt's reputation gained nothing from his repeated castigation of dictatorship. Had he not bowed to Stalin? Had he not courted the autocrat of Turkey and invited Cuban strong man Fulgencio Batista to attend Armistice Day ceremonies at Arlington National Cemetery and review an honor guard at West Point? Brazil, which received the lion's share of American aid, was known to have the tightest press censorship in Latin America. And had not President Vargas, absolute in all but name, perpetuated himself in office by extending his four-year term indefinitely pending a plebiscite? Roosevelt's list of hemispheric protégés reads like a roster of despots. It is headed by Rafael Trujillo of the Dominican Republic and Anastasio Somoza of Nicaragua. When Somoza (who got along so famously with FDR that his people began calling him "El Yanqui") came to Washington in 1939, he was met by thirty tanks drawn up before Union Station. Rank upon rank of American soldiers snapped to attention; large crowds gathered on a specially extended federal luncheon break to greet him; and on the receiving line, along with the president and his wife, were to be found Vice

President and Mrs. Garner and Chief Justice Hughes. All of Somoza's expenses from New Orleans to the World's Fair in New York were prepaid, and he was invited to appear before Congress. Appropriately enough, he urged an American-built canal across Nicaragua and presented FDR with a table showing T.R. and the Panama Canal.[67]

What, then, are we to conclude? One recent essay on Roosevelt's Good Neighbor Policy maintains that it was "a new chapter in an old story"—the effort by United States leaders "to build an 'American System'" under the leadership of the United States of North America and "shaped in its ideological mold." As compared with what came before, the author sees a new and expanded dollar diplomacy, which may have produced "a more serious deterioration in inter-American relations than did the old gunboat diplomacy." He also discerns a far greater emphasis on public relations and image building. It is noted that Roosevelt used every inter-American conference from 1936 on to produce a document stating that the nations of the hemisphere supported the foreign policy of the United States. In most cases, the agreements were worded to secure unified support because the appearance of unity was as important to United States officials as the policies agreed upon.[68] On balance, this estimate seems fair.

Bishop Walsh, who visited Latin America in 1942 and had an opportunity to study conditions in Peru, Colombia, and Panama, as well as seven other countries, concluded that 90 percent of the American nationals residing in these lands were cordially disliked, with U.S. embassy staffs heading the list. "The bulk of our people cannot be esteemed," he maintained, "because they are not known, they do not mix with the people, they do not like or understand them, they are not interested in them, not polite to them, pay no attention to their customs, do not learn the language and cannot speak to them."[69] In much the same way, career diplomat Hugh Wilson, canvassing the political climate of Brazil in 1946, came away "shocked" at the "disrepute" into which his countrymen had fallen: "The Brazilians, usually so discreet, are quite plain-spoken about our behavior. They all look upon Berle [appointed by FDR in January 1945 to head the American mission] as brilliant—but slightly loony. He had a weekly press conference at which he held forth outrageously on internal affairs and laid down the law as to what Brazilian women should do. His wife went about the country lecturing the Brazilian women. . . . She promoted a movement on birth control and in spite of being told plainly that this was profoundly shocking in a Catholic country she persisted." Because American policy had been one of "shovelling millions and hundreds of millions into the country with promises of more" and assurances that unlimited giving was a moral duty, he predicted it would be difficult to bring Brazilians back to the idea that cooperation was a two-way street.[70]

It would be next to impossible, in so brief a compass, to explore all of the elements which together made up the North-South picture. What we have tried to do, therefore, on a limited scale, is to suggest some of the more neglected aspects of Roosevelt's Good Neighbor Policy and to narrow the gap somewhat between image and reality. To be sure, hemispheric nationalism and radicalism had been mounting since at least the time of Woodrow Wilson, if not earlier. Anti-Americanism was therefore nothing new. Countries in and around the Caribbean had, until recently, also felt the sting of actual occupation by United States marines. In the case of Nicaragua, a rebel leader had arisen who managed to elude capture by these same marines for years on end. Clearly Roosevelt did not inherit any Garden of Eden. But neither, by objective criteria, did he reap in proportion to what he sowed. Considering that he instituted a level of aid far beyond what succeeding administrations could realistically maintain, the results were frequently counterproductive. Foreign officials proved marvelously adept at using real or imagined ties with the Axis as a lever to draw down American wealth. This, of course, was but a foretaste of skills employed later, on the aftermath of the war, when, instead of the Axis connection, potential links with Soviet Russia became the chief bargaining counter.

For a country that spent munificent sums overseas, the United States realized few of its goals, not only in relation to minor issues such as completion of the Inter-American Highway and codification of hemispheric law but also with regard to the Reciprocal Trade Agreement Program and the record of Latin American wartime cooperation. This is especially plain when Roosevelt's record is set alongside that of Woodrow Wilson, who achieved greater satisfaction more quickly and without recourse to foreign aid. In most cases, if not all, Washington failed to acquire the right to build bases; it failed to achieve an immediate break in relations between Latin America and the Axis. It also failed to obtain declarations of war as rapidly as it would have wished and received little in the way of troop commitment. Few of the hemispheric conferences held between 1933 and 1945 yielded results that can be termed gratifying in light of the high level of expectation.

Even more striking, perhaps, is the abdication of America's traditional role as mediator in disputes south of the border. Unlike Theodore Roosevelt, FDR was never cited for special commendation at an inter-American congress; he failed to gain broad support among Latin American leaders for the Nobel Peace Prize. If public opinion polls and reports filed by on-site observers are any indication, the president failed even to win a healthy measure of respect. In the main, we have relied upon the impression of figures within the administration or, if not within the administration, then within the Democratic party— such officials as Lowell Mellett, Secretary of State Stettinius, Henry Wallace, Breckinridge Long, Harry Dexter White, Spruille Braden, Henry Morgenthau, Jr., and Bishop Walsh. But whether one accepts the testimony of an American official, a Chilean delegate to Mexico City, or that of a Mexican ambassador to Cuba, there is little deviation from the theme of Latin American suspicion.

All too often, FDR displayed a bland insensitivity to foreign culture. His neglect of Latin American opinion in 1933 and 1945 when planning international reform, added to his vocal insistence on the superiority of North American social and political systems, may be described as a form of cultural imperialism. Nor, as we shall see, was he altogether free of territorial designs. Even if he had been, his renunciation of physical intimidation, after an initial bitter experience with Cuba, gave way to subtler and more insidious forms of control stemming from the attractive power of money. This alone, apart from any reference to the encouragement he gave to communist activity in Latin America, should help to explain why certain areas were so receptive to Soviet overtures in the immediate postwar period.

7. Beneath the Wind

WE come, finally, to the question of what circumstance, or set of circumstances, could possibly account for such an uneven performance in the diplomatic arena. How, apart from the realm of actual policy, are we to explain the fact that Roosevelt won so little esteem in the eyes of foreign statesmen? Was he not among the most urbane of presidents? And did he not stretch himself to the limit of endurance in meeting and establishing rapport with leaders of other countries? By now, the reader is well aware that we have been engaged since the opening page of the narrative in a process of reevaluation; yet one of the greatest misconceptions of all has been permitted to stand. This is the notion that FDR's style on the international level was more than usually cosmopolitan. Before identifying some of the key intellectual underpinnings which shaped the American approach to world affairs from 1933 to 1945, we must examine a side of Roosevelt the man which is rarely, if ever, considered.

No one would deny that FDR traveled a great deal, both before and during his presidency. By the time he reached the age of fourteen, he had made eight trips to Europe and studied under French, German, and Swiss governesses.[1] As is widely recognized, however, travel can produce more than one effect. Depending upon an individual's receptivity and ability to reflect, it may either broaden one's horizon or reinforce native prejudice. Roosevelt, it would appear, fell into the latter category. His attitude toward Germans and Italians tended to be patronizing, not to say provincial. One day, while in Germany, he was arrested no less than four times: for stealing cherries, for pushing his bicycle through the waiting room of a railway station, for running over a goose on the open road, and for bicycling in Strasbourg after sunset. Years later, while at a German health resort, he and his wife noticed signs requesting guests to make as little noise as possible. Eleanor seems to have taken personal offense at "all kinds of strange rules and regulations. . . . In consequence we always slam the doors. . . . Franklin is not even allowed to light a cigarette after dinner on the piazza! I think we may be thrown out before Sunday." It is this type of experience, this kind of reaction to life in a foreign land, which turns out to be not atypical. It is of a piece with the way FDR's son John responded to a suggestion by one of Mussolini's aides that the president visit the duce. As recorded by an approving father, he "very properly suggested that Mussolini might well pay a visit to the President. . . . Johnny told him with complete politeness that the United States had three times the population and ten times the resources of Italy, and that the whole of Italy would fit comfortably into the State of Texas."[2]

FDR has been called a cosmopolite, but to the degree that this may be true, he was eclipsed by most of the foreign leaders with whom he had to deal. While the handsome young lad from Hyde Park was pasting foreign issues into his mother's stamp album, Blenheim's scion, eight years older, was thrilling to action as a cavalryman in India. Within a brief stretch, Churchill would fight on three continents: with the Malakind Field Force in northwest India, with Kitchener against the Mahdi in the Sudan, and against the Boers of South Africa. American on his mother's side of the family, he went to Cuba in 1895 and attached himself as a reporter to the losing side of the civil war. De Gaulle knew what it was like to fight in the armed forces of one foreign country, Poland, and to write a book about the social and political life of another, Germany (one of his volumes attracted a greater audience outside his native country than within). Chiang, who drew upon the academic tradition of three countries, studied in Japan and Russia, married the graduate of an American college, and embraced a Western religion. Stalin began by steeping himself in the kaleidoscopic variety of Soviet folk culture and, as agent for his party, attending international congresses in London and Stockholm. He toured Tammerfors, Cracow, and Vienna.[3]

Roosevelt's linguistic skill, as well as his willingness to support international causes, cannot be gainsaid. In addition to reading and understanding a certain amount of Spanish, he could converse in German and was known to speak fluent French. Hiking through the mountains of Haiti, a country whose constitution he claimed to have written, he experienced little difficulty with the native tongue; in fact, he prided himself on his ability to engage in profanity *en français.* As the son of a mother who had resided in China, France, and Germany (Sara Roosevelt also possessed an excellent command of French and German with a smattering of Italian), it was perfectly in character for him to help found the Woodrow Wilson Foundation and take an active part in launching the Walter Hines Page School of International Relations. As a natural extension of his upbringing, he felt comfortable promoting worldwide study of diplomacy on the college level and supporting the creation of an award for the best peace plan, the Bok Award.[4]

To this degree, he was an internationalist. But language skills, foreign contacts, and sympathy with international causes do not guarantee a cosmopolitan outlook, nor are they necessarily productive of sensitivity to foreign culture. Roosevelt was most himself when burlesquing foreign envoys for their failure to speak perfect English. Invariably, he felt pity for the "poor Old World," not respect. In an address to Congress in 1935, he contrasted "our own peaceful and neighborly attitude" with Europe's petty jealousies and passions, its strivings for armament and power. The need was for a new and more practical form of representative government. Failure to agree on disarmament, he felt, was a sad commentary on "what we like to think of as a modern and excellent civilization." But his fellow countrymen could take comfort, he assured them, in knowing that all of this was entirely the fault of Europe; the position of the United States was "unassailable."[5]

The squire of Hyde Park was without question a man of varied interests, one who did not object, on occasion, to borrowing from an alien culture. Canadian immigration policy struck him as a fine example for the United States, and he encouraged Hopkins to search the statute books of Europe for precedents upon which to base social policy. He was capable, too, of chastising American travelers for "making fun of the local people" in Mallorca.[6]

Nonetheless, for all such instances, one can cite multiple cases of bumptious insularity. To a Chicago audience in 1935 he expressed the fervent wish that other nations would "stop their . . . international quarrels and squabbles, and take a leaf out of the notebook of the United States." It was all rather uncomplicated. Germany's reoccupation of the Rhineland was merely a "disgusting spectacle," Russia's move into Finland was "rape" pure and simple, and Italy's invasion of Ethiopia must be the work of an armed bandit. The separate states of India and the nations of Europe would do well to adopt the confederation system, which had been tried in America during the period 1781–88 (unsuccessfully); and because the United States had experienced only one civil war, which ended in a form of harmony unimaginable in other regions of the world, he assumed that fratricidal conflict in Greece, China, or elsewhere amounted to a form of pettiness. He was quite sure that Tito sparred with Mihailovic just the way de Gaulle did with Giraud.[7]

Disinclined toward Slavs and Spaniards, he lumped Asians together and misread their most basic cultural impulses. We learn in one of his messages to Churchill that he "never liked Burma or the Burmese." Repeatedly, he threatened to send his diplomatic black sheep to Siam. Despite Bangkok's tradition of independence over a period of several centuries, he reckoned that ancient country in need of a United Nations trusteeship, doubtless as punishment for its collaboration with Japan.[8] Of the Vietnamese, he had little to say except that they must be peaceful and unwarlike on account of their small physical stature. Unaware or unconcerned about ramifications of "face," he told Tokyo's envoy that the Japanese were a "chauvinistic" people and assumed that because his letters to Chiang were rewritten by Chinese aides before being presented to the generalissimo they were not registering. Hull, in like manner, assumed incorrectly that Tokyo's desire to keep its official conversations secret reflected insurmountable public opposition to government policy; Konoye and others would not be able to deliver what they promised.[9]

The president, on even less familiar ground when dealing with the Middle East, reflected a stereotypical concern with poverty in complete disregard of the dissimilarity of conditions in a land five thousand miles away. Talk centered on the fact that an Arab's shirt might cost as much as several days of food for an entire family. Arabia, in the same mind's eye, suffered from a shortage of tea and coffee. Given this level of insight, it should come as no surprise that Iran withdrew its minister in 1936 to protest publication of American articles derogatory to the shah or that Welles could regale the president by telling him how the shah was said to have slapped a member of his cabinet for broaching an unwelcome subject. When Roosevelt reached Teheran in 1943 and reports circulated that he had moved into the Soviet compound out of fear of assassination, his reputation suffered disproportionately: first, he was viewed as cowardly; second, he was a coward who allowed aspersions to be cast upon the Iranian constabulary. More insulting still was his refusal to accept hospitality from the shah. Rarely, in addressing the president, did Hull resort to language such as went out under his name on 23 December 1943. Iranians, he told Roosevelt, were not only "bitterly disappointed," they

> felt humiliated that you were unable to make a return call upon the Shah and receive the hospitality and honor which he was eager to accord to you. The chagrin of the Iranians is all the more poignant because Marshal Stalin took special pains to call upon the Shah with whom he remained in conference for nearly two hours. The Iranians, who are an almost morbidly sensitive people on the matter of courtesies and protocol, felt, furthermore, mortified at the report that there had been a plot against the lives of the three distinguished statesmen meeting in Iran. They feel that this in some manner implied that the Iranians themselves might have some designs.[10]

The next year, after offering to help Iran with reforestation, one of the projects closest to his heart, Roosevelt was informed that though the shah welcomed all offers of aid, Iran's first priority was pipeline irrigation. He made the same proposal to King Ibn Saud of Saudi Arabia, only to be reminded that the United States had already sent two experts on such a mission at Saud's request, that their work had been completed, and that they had departed for Washington with proper salutations and gratitude. Patrick Hurley, dispatched to Teheran to study local conditions, returned home convinced that America could transform Iran into a showcase of capitalism and democracy. Roosevelt agreed, adding only that the United States ought to teach "personal cleanliness." To Churchill, he suggested that Iran needed trustees until such time as it could eliminate graft and the feudal system; the sooner it was taught to westernize, the sooner it would cease to be "a headache" to London, Moscow, and Washington.[11]

Generally speaking, Roosevelt's advisers were more apt to confirm his parochial cast of mind than to modify it. Hull, who became something of a permanent fixture at the State Department, made little effort to familiarize himself with foreign points of view and felt no qualms about admitting it. To the Italian ambassador, he volunteered that he knew nothing of the merits of the Ethiopian question. At one point, Breckinridge Long had made the mistake of trying to familiarize him with the inner workings of fascism and Mussolini's position on Albania. Presidential adviser Louis Howe was soon warning Roosevelt that Long had been hypnotized by the duce and that his reporting was "little short of Italian propaganda." Hull later admitted to having the ambassador "checked on" (twice). One will find Long becoming distinctly more "American" in subsequent correspondence with his superiors. The first order of business was to satisfy a secretary of state whose memoirs reveal a world of ignorance on the subject of Italy, Germany, and Japan. Matter-of-factly, Hull likened the Far East to the Western Hemisphere and dismissed his adversaries as "stupid" (Tōjō), "deceitful" (Kurusu), and "slick" (Wikawa). In the case of Matsuoka, the epithet chosen was "crooked as a basket of fishhooks" (implying that American policy toward Japan had been fairly straight). Just as he took it for granted that the autocratic de Gaulle showed "few signs of political acumen," so did he pass judgment on Konoye for believing in one-party rule.[12]

Bullitt, whom *Newsweek* hailed as "America's diplomatic field marshal," conceived of Hitler as a "neurotic Austrian house-painter" and liked to call attention to Göring's giant girth. He found the latter so repugnant that he "literally could not address a word to him." Bullitt also invented a code for contacting the White House in which countries were called by various parts of a house. Thus Germany assumed the name "porch" and France became "step." England was known as "doormat" and Italy "garbage can," while Japan became "sink" and Russia "toilet." For Bullitt, just as for other trusted presidential counselors, it was difficult to take "those dinky little European states" seriously.[13]

Dodd, in Berlin, retained a feeling for the German language from his days as a student at Heidelberg. On the other hand, he never learned to speak it fluently and had to rely on an official interpreter. One of his first letters home took the form of a warning: "One must remember always that German statesmen and even *gelëhrte männer* are quite adolescent in their analyses of international problems"; they had not learned "the give-and-take group compromises which English and American leaders always apply." Curiously enough, in the same letter he predicted "a more moderate course" for the Hitler regime and, instead of interpreting Hitler's policy of *Ostpolitik* in such a way as to make it intelligible to FDR, stressed that Germany was out to "destroy France" and "break English power."[14]

Josephus Daniels in Mexico and William Eddy in Arabia provide still other cases in point. One will search Daniels's memoirs in vain for any suggestion as to what America might learn from Mexico. The one exception, certain "conditions" in unnamed schools, remains vague, and the reader is warned against Mexican superstition and excessive for-mality. The book abounds in strictures, while the occasional compli-ment is likely to sound patronizing. In referring to a talk given at one of Mexico's top agricultural colleges, Daniels described "a very excellent speech, such as you might expect from any head of an agricultural col-lege in our own country."[15] Eddy was the American soldier who es-corted Ibn Saud to his meeting with FDR aboard a United States de-stroyer in 1945. His familiarity with Middle Eastern culture would lead one to expect tolerance, if not understanding. Instead, the reader of his memoirs is served with a diet of unqualified criticism and misleading generalization: "The Arab is by nature a fatalist and accepts what comes as a matter of course." It strikes Eddy as strange, if not absurd, that after explaining to Saud about the deep-freeze system aboard an American warship, the king, having come along as a guest, insisted on bringing a herd of sheep to be slaughtered on the fantail. Evidently, Saud understood more about refrigeration than his host did about the delicious taste of freshly slaughtered lamb! Eddy includes only one ref-erence to religion, an incident involving Saud's sons, who, though raised as strict Moslems, insisted on being admitted to a sailor's movie showing Lucille Ball "loose in a college men's dormitory late at night barely surviving escapades in which her dress is ripped off." The vis-itors, he is happy to recall, "fully approved of what they saw."[16]

Parochialism, as a state of mind, can be found not only in many of Roosevelt's intimate advisers and hand-picked envoys but also in con-gressional leaders with whom the White House was frequently in touch. Key Pittman, senator from Nevada as well as chairman of the Foreign Relations Committee and an individual with whom the presi-dent worked hand in glove, had managed to avoid virtually every ques-tion concerning foreign policy for almost all of the years since coming to the Senate in 1912. As one biographer puts it, his vision ended at the Nevada border.[17] Another figure upon whom Roosevelt leaned heavily from time to time was Sol Bloom. Acting chairman of the House For-eign Affairs Committee during the Munich crisis and chairman begin-ning in 1940, the New Yorker served as Roosevelt's floor leader during the fruitless neutrality fight of 1939. Along with a number of other leaders, he insisted that the Nazi-Soviet Non-Aggression Pact posed no threat to the West because Hitler was only assuring himself of Russian asylum for a time when he might be overthrown and no other country would accept him. It was second nature for Bloom to mispronounce names of foreign visitors to Congress; indeed, in his *Autobiography* he boasts of his failure to pronounce the name of a Brazilian town where he had stayed as United States delegate to an inter-American conference. Without hesitation, he relates that his Brazilian hosts rendered poor breakfast service and tried to swindle him on the price of a cup of coffee. Nor is he reluctant to suggest that graft might have determined the choice of the conference site, one which offended his sense of good taste: "Architecturally, Gardenia [Quitandinha] is a noble pile of Hollywood Swiss . . . built for display, to impress city yokels. . . . My feet still hurt whenever I think of those icy floors and deep-freeze beds."[18]

A third individual worthy of mention is Senator William Borah, the so-called "Lion of Idaho." Former chairman of Pittman's committee and still its most powerful member, he prided himself on never having left the United States lest he fall prey to a presumed tendency on the part of those who venture abroad to be subverted. As one who felt that Secretary of State Kellogg had been fatally contaminated with British ideas during his sojourn as ambassador to the Court of St. James's, he must have been pleased to see Roosevelt exclude State Department career officers from so many influential posts on the same ground.[19]

This, then, was the American *weltanshauung. Time,* one of the nation's most popular magazines, continued for more than a year and a half to refer to Germany's leader as "Handsome Adolf" (before adopting the title "Realm Leader"). Gandhi of India was "St. Gandhi" and Konoye of Japan "a finicking hypochondriac" who spent each Sunday seated in lotus form meditating on the deeper, incalculable manifestations of nothingness. Emperor Hirohito ("Owl Eyes") was jocularly called by his religious title, "Son of Heaven," and was said to be "purblind and rapidly growing pudgy."[20]

Catering to the ethnocentric taste of its readership, *Time*'s editors depicted the Orient as a fairy-tale place far removed from the pale of reality. China was the "land of the flying horse, of dwarfs and golden monkeys, and of citizens with tails." It was reported that the king of Cambodia retired every year to a floating pavilion next to his palace for thirty days of meditation, "but no sooner has he entered with great pomp than he scoots out the back door, dallies 29 days with 100 wives (in better days he had twice as many), slips back in, and on the 30th day publicly emerges, greatly refreshed from his meditations." Burma's premier, U Saw, "strutted" through the streets of London in a silken toga, and the king of Siam "frolicked" in the sand. Henry Pu-Yi, emperor-designate of Manchukuo, attracted attention for his quaint insistence upon having only one wife, even to the point of refusing to consummate a second marriage forced upon him by law. He rode a bicycle round and round his garden doing such tricks as balancing on one wheel. In similar reportorial style, European-educated Emperor Bao Dai of Annam (Vietnam) was pictured among his jazz records, ping-pong tables, radio, and detective stories.[21]

No region of the world, however remote, escaped caricature. The maharaja of Indore was presented to American readers as passionately interested in two things, hunting and the harem, and the sultan of Johore was introduced as a man who cultivated amours in London. Equally exotic were the potentates of the Middle East. King Faisal of Iraq, aged six, would not object to being kidnapped by fugitives as long as a "reasonable number of playthings went with him." Farouk of Egypt, a kindred spirit, came across editorially as a chubby youth gulping down five pounds of bonbons a day; Haile Selassie of Ethiopia had a "bowlegged little" son-in-law who discommoded the White House kitchen with his Coptic Christian diet while the "chocolate-brown" Ethiopian empress waddled "like an ambulating lump of cocoa butter." For some reason, the editors went out of their way in the case of the empress to explain that for Abyssinians fatness was a mark of aristocratic birth.[22]

We have singled out one periodical, *Time* magazine, but *Time* was not unique. If, for example, one had been reading *Newsweek*, one would have found many of the same features. Typically, a column dealing with foreign affairs would focus on British custom, Argentine disorder, a fire in Greece, a suicide in Czechoslovakia, or a Nicaraguan bomb. Cuba was discussed in terms of a "mob's delight in almost any revolution." One could, if one wished, read about a nonsensical incident in Uruguay, superstition in Bulgaria, or Iraq's twenty-one-year-old monarch, who, when allowed to rule for a day at the age of sixteen, had "ordered the Grand Vizier to buy for him all the available phonograph records in Baghdad." The Japanese were said to be holding air raid drills for the "spiritual education" of their people.[23]

For a variety of reasons, not least of all its geographical position, the United States has never been especially cosmopolitan. There have been times, notably during the history of the early republic and again at the dawn of the twentieth century, when Americans were unusually cognizant of international reality. Plainly, the decade of Franklin Roosevelt was not such a time. If the year 1945 inaugurated a new era in which Roosevelt's countrymen for the first time accepted the responsibility inherent in great power status, then the years spanning the New Deal must be described as belonging to an age of delayed adolescence, one which found a fitting symbol in FDR.

By extension, once one accepts the idea of Roosevelt, indeed of America in general, during the 1930s as parochial, it is only one short step to the realization that foreign policy sprang from a political strategy geared almost exclusively to movement on the home front. One is better able to understand why Roosevelt may have refused to challenge Hiram Johnson on the matter of neutrality and in 1934 allowed Congress to determine American silver policy at the expense of China. The following year, over Hull's protest, the president encouraged Senator Nye to interest his senatorial committee in neutrality legislation. And again, one can understand. State Department records were made so readily available to Nye by order of the White House that Hull proved unable to control the use made of them. On 2 October 1935, Roosevelt was simply echoing isolationist spokesmen when he said at San Diego: "The United States of America shall and must remain . . . unentangled and free."[24]

On more than one occasion, it seems that FDR eschewed greater combativeness in foreign policy because he did not wish to cut into what he thought might be vital support needed for the passage of domestic legislation. This, despite a sharp divergence of opinion on the part of his advisers. Henry Stimson and Joseph Green, in contrast to Secretary Hull and law professor Felix Frankfurter, felt that he stressed domestic issues far more than was necessary or prudent. Green in particular complained that politics pervaded the State Department to a degree unknown in his experience and that this could be ascribed to the orientation of Judge Moore as well as to Hull. Whatever the truth, Roosevelt continued to go his way, calling all of his key ambassadors home to campaign for him in 1936 and again in 1940.[25] His decision not to do more for Haile Selassie or Loyalist Spain and his reluctance to draw closer to the Soviets in 1938 and 1939—all of these were crucial decisions dictated to some degree by his deference to opinion polls and a tendency to back away from any articulate minority. The same was true of his delaying tactics on Argentine trade, Poland's fate, and Stilwell's removal. Only where a way could be found to bypass Congress altogether, as in the last nine months of 1941 on the issue of military intervention, did he extend himself fully. More often, he remained on the defensive, halting before entrenched opposition and moving only upon majority request when the path was reasonably clear. It was in response to congressional pressure that he acted on such matters as Philippine freedom and Indian independence. At the same time, in areas such as economic warfare against Japan, he gave the appearance of responding to congressional pressure.[26]

During 1938 and 1939, British officials thought that he did much to advance interventionist sentiment, and he did indeed wage a clever campaign through surrogates, then and later.[27] Carlson, Baruch, Hull, Messersmith, Harriman, and Hamilton Fish Armstrong were some of the more influential figures he called upon to sound the trumpet. Through Stimson's Committee for Non-Participation in Japanese Aggression and through the voices of Claude Pepper and Walter Judd, he used others to nudge popular opinion in the desired direction.[28] Meanwhile, in private conference with congressmen he spoke of the danger posed by German bases on the Canary Islands, only fifteen hundred miles from Brazil and thus within flying distance of the Mississippi Valley via touchdowns in Yucatan and Texas.[29]

More often he adopted a passive stance. Far from assuming a forward position in 1938–41, in response to the Sino-Japanese war, the *Panay* incident, anti-Semitic violence, and the Czech crisis, he showed himself content to follow the crowd. A list of isolationist utterances along this line would include his Morgantown speech of September 1938 and his press conference of five days later. In certain instances, he dealt the interventionist cause a serious setback, as when he repudiated a statement made the following February to the effect that the Rhine was America's first line of defense. Well could Stimson criticize him for excessive timidity and journalist Arthur Krock maintain that he never really got out in front of public opinion.[30]

Parochialism fostered a number of widely held myths, which, when considered together, may help to give us a more precise picture of New Deal diplomacy. Among these was the idea that dictators are by definition unpopular with their people. Without such a concept in mind, it is difficult to account for Roosevelt's view of the ruling elite of Germany and Japan.[31] Eventually, even Chiang, who merited American support during the 1930s because he was assumed to represent the cause of embattled democracy, landed alongside Hitler, Mussolini, and Tōjō in the class of odious tyrants judged by Roosevelt to be de facto unpopular.[32] Among those who had the ear of the president, most were confident that Hitler's blood purge of 1934 reflected internal weakness and spelled imminent collapse. Americans were thus puzzled when, in 1935, an internationally supervised plebiscite in the Catholic, union-controlled Saar region between France and Germany returned a 90 percent vote for union with Hitler's Third Reich and only 1 percent expressed any desire to go with France.[33] In the case of Austria, not many in or around the White House would have agreed with Brüning and the British that Hitler's claim to majority support was genuine. Among the exceptions were Welles, Cudahy, Bullitt, and Wilson, but most Americans went on believing in the "undemocratic" nature of Anschluss.[34]

As part and parcel of this general line of thought, Stalin's purge trials of 1936–38 were presumed to rule out any likelihood that Soviet armies might be able to stand up to the Wehrmacht. By the same token, it was believed that a German assault on Russia, if successful, would result in massive repudiation of the communist government. History proved otherwise. But again, we are confronted with a positive article of the Roosevelt creed which, however mistaken, could never be shaken. Japan's Prince Konoye, on a visit to the United States in 1934, could see that Americans were drawing a totally false distinction between the Japanese people and their leaders, yet there was nothing he could do to set the record straight. FDR and his advisers never ceased to posit an unpopular and bellicose military clique ruling in defiance of a gentle and pacifistically inclined populace. By strengthening Russia and China, he fancied himself laying the groundwork for Japanese revolt from within.[35]

In the long run, American estimates would have to be revised. Allied victory did not result in a popular uprising against Franco any more than the people of Japan were prone to desert their government during the darkest days of the war.[36] Popular yearning for democracy turned out to be anything but universal, although American ambassadors in Bulgaria and Romania would continue as late as 1946 to operate on the assumption that local citizens desired nothing so much as a Western-style republic.[37]

Allied to the theory of unpopular dictators, and no less mischievous, was the idea that absolutist regimes were so internally divided that one official or group of officials could always be played off against another. In Germany, von Ribbentrop was viewed as the malignant influence, while men such as von Weizsäcker and Göring were regarded as somewhat more reasonable. Davis attributed Germany's moderation in external affairs during 1937 to "internal difficulties," and Weizsäcker, as if to turn the American assumption to his own purposes, advised a credulous Welles to tell Hitler that von Ribbentrop was standing in the way of peace.[38] In the Soviet Union, it was Litvinov who seemed always to strike the sour note, opposing a softer line on debts and so forth. Bullitt thought he had found a genuine friend in General Voroshilov, whom he took considerable pains to cultivate. Before long, he was able to report with evident satisfaction: "Litvinov positively quivered when I brought Voroshilov's name into the conversation." Stalin never appeared to be anything other than sympathetic, and when the leader of the Kremlin named the Narkomindel (Soviet foreign office) as the reason why he could not endorse Bullitt's plan for a new American embassy to be built in a choice location, the American ambassador believed it implicitly. In like manner, Soviet Ambassador Oumansky, thought to be unrepresentative because of his gruff intransigence, was called by Bullitt a "filthy little squirt," and Roosevelt was convinced that all outstanding issues could be resolved if the outwardly more pliant Alexander Troyanovsky had a freer hand.[39] In China, Madame Chiang posed so successfully as an adversary to her husband that FDR told Wallace, on his way to Chungking, he ought to try to restore the Chiangs to domestic harmony. Stilwell meanwhile assumed in like manner that Chiang's authority could be circumvented by dealing with Mme Chiang and even with her sister.[40]

Moderates were often viewed by the White House as in a position to challenge "militants" or "extremists," and it was assumed that their hand would be strengthened by a relatively mild policy on the part of the United States. Germany's former Chancellor Heinrich Brüning could, for example, be sure of a sympathetic hearing when he told Stimson that Werner von Fritsch and other "moderate" leaders of the German army were afraid of developing an air fleet because of possible repercussions in England. Similarly, Schacht and von Trott could count on respectful attention once the war began when they suggested that a moderate American peace plan would consolidate German opinion in such a way as to bring not only peace but a change in leadership.[41]

Nowhere did such analysis do more to affect American policy than in dealings with China and Japan. Down to the bombing of Pearl Harbor, Tokyo council chambers were thought to be dominated by a small military clique. Whether one read the *Chicago Daily News* or another paper, whether one listened to FDR or to one of his officials, the idea was never open to doubt. One reason Hornbeck gave for not negotiating in good faith with Tokyo was that behind Premier Konoye, and more powerful than he, stood the military. Surely, professional soldiers would thwart any moderate plan he might endorse. The same concept discouraged the administration in late 1937 and early 1938 from acting as broker in peace arrangements between Nanking and Tokyo. According to Carlson, those in China who were urging an American role and advocating compromise—such men as H. H. Kung—represented a civilian business class whose promises would inevitably be overridden by soldiers eager to fight. It is not that there were no dissident voices but simply that those closest to the White House espoused the conventional wisdom. There is little difference between what FDR told Arthur Krock about Japan in 1934 and how he briefed congressional leaders in June of 1941.[42]

How different all of this thinking was from Sir George Sansom's eminently well-informed but unheeded advice of April 1941 published in *Foreign Affairs:*

> It is necessary to rid our minds of a number of misconceptions which arise because we think in terms of our own vocabulary when we discuss Far Eastern Affairs. We are inclined to postulate the existence of a numerous class of "liberals" and we are misled . . . into supposing that there is in Japan a school of political thought which approves of democratic institutions.
>
> A further assumption, no less unjustified, allows us to picture this liberal element in Japanese life as a force hostile to what is called the "military party." There is little in Japan's past history to justify such assumptions. It is a mistake to suppose that there is a split between military and civilian opinion in Japan. . . . Totalitarian ways of thinking have for years past been gaining strength in other branches of government. They have strong adherents in the Departments of the Interior and Education.
>
> Even supposing the present rulers of Japan to have imposed their new system on the country against the popular will, it is difficult to imagine how that popular will could have expressed itself in action. Neither the political nor the social tradition of Japan have been such as to encourage ideological revolt. This is not to say that the Japanese people are docile . . . but Liberalism has never secured a firm foothold in Japan.
>
> The mass of the Japanese people have very little knowledge of what democracy means.[43]

The irony is that, for one reason or another, Japanese leaders were involved in promoting a myth that contributed to their own demise. The West was encouraged to believe in two false divisions: one between extremists and moderates, the other between noncombatants and the military. Stimson had it straight from Japan's ambassador that a powerful contest was being waged between soldier and civilian. Perhaps to save face, perhaps with some other end in view, Hirota attributed Tokyo's nationalistic Amau Declaration to militarists even though Ambassador Saito informed Washington otherwise. Very early Otohiko Matsukata fixed in FDR's mind the idea that the war in Manchuria was caused by a group of willful field officers, and in this there may have been some truth. But the notion was misleading, especially when applied across the board and propagated by Elder Statesman Ishii, by the Japanese ambassadors to Britain and the Netherlands, indeed, it would seem, by nearly all Japanese diplomats.[44] Bullitt wrote Moore in December 1937 that "all Japanese diplomats nowadays . . . preface their conversations with the statement that neither they nor their government have any control over the military men in China."[45]

In seeking a satisfactory explanation, one cannot overlook the psychological benefit derived from avoidance of a direct confrontation. At the same time, in practical terms, if the government in power was perceived as moderate or civilian, Roosevelt's aim would be to prolong its life; if it were military or extremist, he would avoid coercive measures which might strengthen its hand against moderates presumably waiting in the wings. Regardless of the situation, American officials would refrain from applying too much pressure. Frederick Moore, Washington lobbyist and counselor to the Japanese government, argued along this line in conversation with Hornbeck as well as in print: FDR should postpone economic sanctions so as to avoid undermining the moderate-civilian government which functioned in 1938. According to Moore, the temples of Tokyo were overflowing with peace-loving citizens praying for a military withdrawal from China, and if the United States declared economic war, it would simply unite the disparate factions. Although Grew did not endorse Moore's entire argument, he did agree that economic sanctions would undermine the moderates. British Ambassador Craigie disagreed, preferring a tougher Anglo-American posture on the order of Theodore Roosevelt's world cruise of the Great White Fleet. But it was Grew, rather than Craigie, who spoke for America. Neither Hull nor Welles, neither Hornbeck nor Roosevelt himself, saw any weakness in Moore's logic.[46]

A second practical reason for Japanese complicity in American misunderstanding, particularly after 1944, was of course the war trials atmosphere. Civilian leaders who wished to divorce themselves from an aggressive China policy found a convenient scapegoat in the military. Tōjō was doomed to execution, and better Tōjō alone than Tōjō in the company of Tōgō. To appreciate the frequency with which Japanese defendants resorted to this tactic, one has only to study the record of the war trials and read the recollections of Konoye, Yoshida, Tōgō, and Saionji.[47]

As for the theory itself, with its tendency to imply that military leaders were alone responsible for inciting Japan to war, it must be weighed against other factors including the subordination of press and media to Japan's political leadership, Japan's instinctive deference to a powerful government, and the respect traditionally enjoyed by army and navy alike. Ambassador Grew noted that even in the highest Japanese intellectual circles it was not generally thought that government policy on Manchuria violated the Nine-Power Treaty. Equally clear to Grew was the fact that war in 1937 had broad cabinet support and that the New Order proclaimed two years later appealed to all elements of the population. *Kokumin Shimbun* insisted in 1939 that Japanese policy was not dictated solely by the military and suggested that Grew might do well to set his countrymen straight on this point. By November of 1941, the Japanese diet sounded more hard-line than the cabinet, and Tōgō could truthfully say, though he later changed his tune, that Japan was united. Had Matsuoka not been cheered on arrival home after leading his country out of the League? And had it not been under a civilian premier, Wakatsuki, backed by a notably "moderate" foreign minister, Shidehara, that the ugly Mukden incident of 1931 had occurred? Impartial observers could not fail to notice that between 1932 and 1936, a time of peace, Japan was ruled by navy cabinets. By contrast, it was under civilian leadership that she subscribed to the Anti-Comintern Pact and decided to recognize the Wang government in China. It was also under a civilian government that she went to war in 1937, signed the Tripartite Pact, moved into southern Indochina, and made those decisions in the early fall of 1941 that led to war with the United States.[48] It can, of course, be argued that civilian leaders were sometimes under the influence of powerful elements within the army. Nevertheless the point stands.

Nothing proved more deleterious to Japanese-American relations in the long run than the renewal of conflict on the Chinese mainland in 1937; yet at the time, Japan was ruled by the liberal civilian government of Prince Konoye, along with a civilian foreign minister, Hirota. As the youngest premier in half a century, Konoye was the overwhelming choice of public opinion and something of a democratic idol. Still, he decided on war with China and did so *against the advice of major elements of the General Staff.* What is more, he had just ousted what Grew described as a "military-controlled" cabinet under General Senjuro Hayashi, a soldier whom Grew thought would be well advised to confine himself to military affairs. Grew does not mention that Hayashi's foreign minister signaled a *milder* approach to China in several conciliatory speeches to the diet. It was the civilian Konoye-Hirota team that coined the expression "We will not treat with Chiang Kaishek" and explained to a cheering diet in January 1938 that such a phrase was meant to be stronger than a declaration of war. By the same token, it was not civilians but the Japanese General Staff that took umbrage at such tactics and contrived to maintain contact with Chiang's associates, causing Wang Ching-wei to split off as leader of a separate movement. Many army officers believed the China issue insoluble except through diplomacy; they preferred German mediation and a number of other expedients to war just as they engaged in maneuvers to dissuade Konoye from leaving the path of diplomacy and tried to persuade the emperor to intercede for a negotiated peace. After the capture of Nanking, General Tada, vice-chief of staff, wanted to offer Chiang a Bismarckian settlement, but Konoye would not hear of it because he assumed Nanking's surrender would bring about Chiang's own downfall. Even though Tada was supported by the service ministries and the naval General Staff, civilian leaders overrode them on a jingo wave of public opinion. Far from being a mere military plot, as implied by Hirota and others, the resumption of war in China can be attributed to the emperor, the premier, and the foreign minister. All three were civilians supported by Home Minister Nobumasa Suetsugu and Education Minister Kōichi Kido.[49]

Those wedded to the theory of a strict dichotomy between military and civilian will have to go even further to explain why it was that when Japan's war minister proposed to send troops into North China in July of 1939, he was not opposed by a single civilian in the cabinet, only by the navy minister. Similarly, when Konoye sought cabinet permission in early 1941 to open talks with the United States, War Minister Tōjō supported him and civilian Matsuoka dissented. While the military opposed plans for an attack on Russia, Matsuoka favored it. At other times, the military was divided, as for example over the question of risking war with the United States as well as over the Tripartite Pact, with the navy opposed and the army in favor.[50] Nor was the army itself entirely free from internal division.

Few myths have been as widely held as that of military warmongering, and few have been as groundless. The case of Japan is only one of many capable of giving it the lie. Dodd wrote Hull in 1935 that "Hitler, Goering, and Goebbels are listening more and more to the generals— and anyone knows a general's attitude toward war." Naturally, this remark was congenial to Roosevelt's way of thinking; it likewise appealed to Bullitt, who shared Dodd's fear that the Reichswehr would overawe Hitler and break loose against France.[51] But neither Dodd, Bullitt, nor Roosevelt had his finger on the facts. The German army opposed Hitler's remilitarization of the Rhineland as unnecessarily risky given the nation's current state of preparedness, just as it disapproved a show of force against Austria and discouraged the sending of additional contingents to Spain. Nor did it approve of Hitler's sudden thrust against Poland in 1939. French military leaders seem to have been equally conservative. When confronted with the Rhineland takeover, it was the politicians of France who wanted to mobilize their army and send an ultimatum to Berlin. One can apply this same rule to any number of situations, including Mussolini's Italy and Roosevelt's America.[52]

Still another characteristic feature of New Deal thought was the deep trust it placed in disarmament and economic policy as a means of safeguarding the peace. The two were interconnected in Roosevelt's mind because he expected that any world conference dealing with one issue would have to deal with the other. During the 1930s, Japan, Germany, and Italy were assumed to be on the brink of economic disaster and attempting to stay afloat through a revival of their war industries. It was further supposed that there would come a point (Bullitt believed that for Hitler it was January 1937) when a choice would have to be made between war and collapse. The arms race was thus no more than a temporary expedient grinding down the poor and leading ineluctably to state bankruptcy. Neither Europe nor Japan was expected to have the wherewithal to support the munitions industry indefinitely. In the case of Italy it was alleged that there was not enough money for the average family to buy spaghetti. Or, as FDR put it to Colonel House, "The patient will die of the 'armament disease' in a few years unless a major operation is performed." Not only were huge monetary benefits expected once the crushing burden of arms was eliminated; it was also taken as axiomatic that any unemployment resulting from disarmament would be remediable by economic appeasement, in particular the freeing of trade.[53]

Nor is this the only link in Roosevelt's chain of reasoning between poverty and war. Poverty, in his opinion, presupposed injustice, injustice implied disharmony, and disharmony, in turn, bred national aggressiveness. The leader of a disadvantaged nation would fabricate foreign threats and, by resorting to aggression, activate the principle of group cohesion under external pressure. Peace advocates commonly spoke of the "have" and "have-not" nations and regarded Bolshevism and its ideological counterparts, fascism and Nazism, as the offspring of economic imbalance.[54] Senator Borah was one of the leading proponents of this idea, insisting that the best cure for Soviet communism was the trade that would flow from American recognition. It was a widely held view. When Frances Perkins returned from Austria in 1936, Roosevelt wanted to know "the degree of poverty and how widely Nazi ideas were in circulation." The reason the Near East was so explosive, he told her, was because the people were poor. They had too little to eat and too little work to keep them occupied. Germany was not poor in quite the same way. Nevertheless, it was felt to be economically unstable, and FDR agreed with Cudahy that Hitler would attempt a dramatic stroke to enhance German prestige and keep the lid on "serious social unrest" at home. Congressman Bloom put it as succinctly as anyone when he insisted that "hunger has been the fundamental cause of all the wars of history. . . . Fill the lack, and the cause is gone. . . . No two men ever willingly fought after eating a hearty meal."[55] Vintage FDR.

History would soon demonstrate the simplistic nature of such a notion, along with a number of other tenets integral to Roosevelt's policy. If the president looked to economics as a way of neutralizing antisocial impulses, he also regarded it as a means of coercion short of war. From his earliest years in public life, he had preached the doctrine that sanctions against an "outlaw" power would succeed in bringing about a peaceful change in that government's policy. As assistant secretary of the navy, he favored the use of warships to pinch off Japanese supply routes, and when Japanese forces landed in Manchuria, he again felt they could be expelled through economic pressure. Belief in trade sanctions not only formed the linchpin of his plan for world government as submitted to the Bok Peace Award Committee in 1923; it foreshadowed his later wish that the League be converted into a body dealing with world problems on a strictly economic basis. After advocating Anglo-American boycotts against Japan in 1933, after vainly attempting to interdict Tokyo's access to Western money markets, and after trying, in addition, to force Berlin into disarmament by throttling her commerce, he continued to feel in 1937 that the threat of punitive trade measures could be used to achieve disarmament. Two years later, Morgenthau was still urging him to use it.[56] When London called for a show of unity during the China crisis of 1937, he considered everything from a freezing of Japanese assets to a ban on salmon fishing and closure of the Panama Canal. The following year, as Morgenthau set up his Division of Economic Warfare and the Department of Commerce discouraged trade with Tokyo, particularly the sale of American aircraft, Roosevelt confidently told a visitor to the White House that Japanese gold reserves, which had totaled 800 million yen in 1937, were down to 300 million and expected to fall as low as 100 million by 1939. It was this simple. In 1939, he asked his treasury secretary what he thought of the idea of asking Americans "to stop selling merchandise to Japan" (Morgenthau answered that he did not think Americans would take it seriously).[57]

We need not dwell upon the consequences that are bound to flow from a profound misreading of events. Clearly, Japan, Germany, and Italy were not on the brink of economic chaos. If anything, they managed to solve their financial problems more expeditiously than did the United States. Six months after Roosevelt predicted the collapse of the German economy, Hugh Wilson reported "boom conditions" in Berlin and a "shortage of labor." Workmen had excellent security and very tolerable living conditions, including paid vacations. They could have built public works as readily as armies if full employment had been their sole aim. They armed, Wilson held, not to put people to work but to assume what they considered their rightful place in the world, to rectify territorial injustice, and to hold their heads high. Mussolini spoke the truth when he said in 1939 that the chief problem in Europe was not economic but political. This was the case everywhere. When Saud was offered a reward reputed to be in the neighborhood of £20 million if he would help in creating a Jewish state, he turned his back. Argentina rejected a similar inducement to abandon its ties with the Axis. And to the surprise of Washington, economic measures were of little use in preventing Poland from falling completely into the Soviet orbit.[58]

Roosevelt's decade offers little evidence that economics alone furnished an answer to the world's most pressing problems. Hull clung tenaciously to the idea that "the political line-up followed the economic line-up," yet political considerations prevented FDR from reaching a commercial détente with Germany, Japan, or Italy. After the Soviet invasion of Finland, Ambassador Steinhardt let it be known that his country was prepared to relax its moral embargo if Moscow would grant a lenient peace. Instead, the Kremlin exacted unusually harsh terms: 10 percent of Finnish territory and 15 percent of her resources. In the case of Italy and Ethiopia, Roosevelt penalized his own countrymen by declaring a moral embargo before other nations had acted. While Americans were being asked to halt their shipments of petroleum, Italy loaded all the oil she needed elsewhere. Nor was the embargo nearly as "moral" as it sounded. Federal subsidies and a lucrative mail contract gave the White House a lockhold on American Export Lines. Ultimately, the United States shipped more oil than ever to Mussolini, and Roosevelt, under pressure from Italian-American voters, retreated behind a policy of "normal" trade. Eight Latin American states, including Brazil, turned out to be hostile to a sanctionist policy and England opposed it out of fear that Mussolini might retaliate with an aerial attack on the British fleet then stationed at Alexandria.[59]

When Schacht warned in 1934 that "those politicians who think they can change the domestic evolution of Germany by exploiting her economic difficulties are indulging in a colossal fallacy," he could have been speaking for the Gaimusho or any other foreign chancellery. Roosevelt convinced Congress to pass an arms embargo applicable to both sides of the Chaco War and, without waiting to see what other nations would do, declared it in effect. Fortunately, the League followed suit. Nevertheless, it proved utterly futile. Bolivia and Paraguay contrived to buy arms from European sources, and the chief loser turned out to be American business. The same thing happened when Roosevelt responded to Mexico's seizure of foreign oil by cutting back on the purchase of Mexican silver. When it was found that this hurt the owners of Mexican mines, 90 percent of whom were American, the measure was quickly dropped. Having prohibited the purchase of Mexican oil, he watched Nazi Germany move in to fill the economic vacuum. In a similar case, he had no sooner ordered a wheat embargo against Spain than Madrid found a new source in Argentina.[60] And what was true of Mexico and Spain was triply true of Germany and Japan. Morgenthau, chief proponent of trade as a weapon, had to admit in 1947 that all his efforts against Tokyo and Berlin had amounted to little more than "yapping at the heels of a world striding inexorably towards war."[61]

Two other components of New Deal philosophy may be introduced at this stage since, in conjunction with Roosevelt's reliance upon economic sanctions, they formed the second and third segments of a much larger scheme of operation. The first of these relates to that most intangible of commodities known as style. One would suppose that FDR's experience on the black leather couch in 1933 might have undermined his faith in the efficacy of atmospherics. But this was not so. In 1933, despite Robert Kelley's admonition to bargain carefully with the Soviet Union and secure a hard-and-fast agreement on paper, we have seen how he dispensed with such advice and engaged Litvinov in a series of cordial tête-à-têtes lasting from one to three hours. Even when he could see that these tactics were going to fail, he again tried to touch the human element, seeking to have himself represented to Soviet authorities as "a very great man" who now felt betrayed. On 1 April 1934, Bullitt wrote that Litvinov's son was expected to visit Washington and might he not be invited to stay at the White House? "Litvinov would appreciate this more than a dozen large concessions—it might pull a lot of chestnuts out of the fire for us." FDR replied, "We should love to have young Litvinov spend the night at the White House. You can tell him I will show him my ships and stamps personally."[62]

Neither the president nor any of his aides ever discarded their trust in stage management. According to one loyal associate, it amounted almost to an "obsession." Seeking at Teheran to create what he called a "family circle," Roosevelt turned a deaf ear to warnings from Standley, Deane, and Harriman that in Moscow substance, and substance only, counted. Winant, his ambassador to Great Britain, thought very much along the same line, turning aside suggestions that Western access to Berlin should be guaranteed on paper and protesting that the agreement reached by the European Advisory Commission would have been impossible had he not succeeded in establishing a close personal relationship with Ambassador Gusev, Russian delegate to the commission.[63] Bullitt, for his part, seems to have had the idea that he could woo Stalin's commissar of war by importing polo equipment and teaching the Red Army to play the game. He also introduced baseball as a means of easing tension between the embassy and the Moscow soviet, until a Soviet catcher got hit in the face by a fast pitch. Nor can one forget presidential envoy Evans Carlson, who spoke of being impressed by a prolonged handshake of several minutes' duration given him by Red Chinese Army Commander Chu Teh.[64]

The third side of Roosevelt's tactical triangle came down to what is popularly known as public opinion or, in his own words, "the marching of the general spirit of things." During a Groton debate at the age of fifteen, he reasoned that no foreign power would dare to seize Hawaii because "the expression of the feelings of the United States would be enough to stop it, just as the feeling of America led Louis Napoleon to withdraw his troops from Mexico, a number of years ago."[65] It never occurred to him that in the absence of a favorable European balance, not to mention a navy powerful enough to control the central Pacific and an army capable of holding Canada to ransom, Hawaii would have been defenseless against imperial aggrandizement. Neither does he seem to have been aware that General Sheridan marched and countermarched along Mexico's northern border in the months following the Civil War with half again as many troops as France deployed. Sheridan's veterans lent much in the way of credibility to President Johnson's "wish" regarding French withdrawal.

"I still believe," Roosevelt confided to Lord Cecil on 6 April 1937, in the "effectiveness of preaching and preaching again." To President Butler of Columbia University he insisted the same year that "much can be accomplished by the iteration of moralities." This was of course the period of his sternest lectures to Japan, talk of a quarantine, and the attempt to humiliate Tokyo at Brussels. When the American gunboat *Panay* came under fire, he again dealt in words—and to the open disgust of advisers Leahy, Davis, and Moore, who remarked that words without action were worse than useless. This was especially true in the

Orient, where an empty gesture or hollow phrase could be fraught with danger. As a confirmed master in the art of mobilizing public opinion at home, FDR doubtless assumed that there was an equally potent force overseas if only it could be tapped. Speaking to world leaders after taking the oath of office, he pointed out with reference to armament that "an overwhelming majority of the nations" faced the danger of "recalcitrant obstruction by a very small minority." Lippmann's claim that 8 percent of the world was thwarting the manifest desire for peace of the remaining 92 percent made such an impression on him that he repeated it at the annual Woodrow Wilson Foundation dinner. The only problem was that his lofty appeals to world opinion drove the Japanese into a corner in 1934 and forced their leaders to wear the dunce cap. Germany, too, was administered a sound pummeling for its alleged unwillingness to disarm.[66]

Over the years, presidential abuse of dictators and dictatorship proceeded apace. Italy made known its pique even as German leaders decried Roosevelt's ceaseless scolding. Still the president continued. His Thirty-one Nations Address, to which he attached a 20 percent chance of success, went to press well before it reached Berlin, thus supplying Hitler with a ready-made excuse to answer in public. Grew's "Horse's Mouth" speech was splashed about in like manner. Other examples of presidential rhetoric would include State of the Union messages delivered in 1936 and 1938, FDR's Buenos Aires speech of 1936, and the one he delivered to a home audience on 26 October 1938. All were slashing attacks on Axis governments with an implied appeal to the people over the heads of their officials. Hull's Eight Pillars of Peace Address, first given at Buenos Aires, was circulated to other countries, and after sixty of them indicated approval, including Germany and Italy, the secretary of state repeated his formula on an international radio hookup. One can see the germ of Radio Free Europe in Frankfurter's suggestion that Americans should broadcast to the German people in their own language. Behind most of these schemes lay the assumption that ordinary citizens of almost any country would be more receptive to peace overtures than their government. Roosevelt continued to find such an idea highly attractive and gave serious thought to the possibility of reaching Hitler's constituency over a radio transmitter in Alsace.[67]

In like manner, he put great stock in documents such as those signed at Yalta. Instinctively, too, he would rely upon organizations like the League and United Nations while looking to the international conference as a forum and sounding board. World opinion was always for him one of the most potent weapons available, and it is this notion which shaped the wording of the Welles Plan, with its mechanism for mobilizing neutral sentiment. Finally, he believed in lecturing foreign representatives. Bill Donovan, on a presidential mission to Spain, treated Foreign Minister Serrano Suñer exactly the way Hull had treated the Spanish ambassador. But of all Roosevelt's men, it was undoubtedly Cordell Hull who turned in the most stellar performance. In 1935, when Hull reproached the Italian ambassador for Italy's decision to spend vast sums on arms and nothing on its debt, Roosevelt described his presentation of the American case as a real "classic." "You did a splendid job of making our position clear," he told the secretary, while "pointing out the very untenable position in which Italy has deliberately placed herself." Phillips agreed that Hull had done a "marvelous" job, and Dodd wrote from Berlin that the secretary's position was "unanswerable from the Italian side"—if only the peoples of Europe could read it. Long after world opinion had failed to sustain Ethiopia or Finland against attack by *force majeure,* and long after Germany's blitzkrieg, with its attendant slaughter of Polish civilians, failed to outrage world opinion, Hull did not hesitate to warn the Soviet Union that if she interfered with other governments after the war she would not have "a friend on earth."[68]

It would be superfluous to add that Roosevelt's reliance upon words had little impact other than to embolden his enemies and demoralize many of America's friends, in particular the British. Portugal objected to "the habit of entrusting the solution of grave external problems to vague formulae," and there were those within the president's own circle who questioned the wisdom of iteration. Welles joked that Hull's "pious remonstrances" were about "as potent" as a "snowball in hell." Norman Davis was no more likely than Welles to mistake the objects of primary concern to a dictator, and Hugh Wilson held that there was nothing to gain from what he called a national "hymn of hate." Both Davis and Moffat issued periodic warnings to the White House, while Long conjured up the picture of a couple of scolds shouting names at each other over the back fence.[69]

Without in any way wishing to excuse Roosevelt, it is probably safe to say that in his attitude toward words and public opinion, as also in his parochial leanings generally, he belonged heart and soul to the American scene. Joseph Conrad once wrote that "the air of the New World seems favourable to the art of declamation." Indeed so. In the heady atmosphere of the Kellogg Pact, Herbert Hoover had never lost his taste for invoking world opinion. Neither can one forget the spectacle of Henry Stimson shaming Japan at one of his press conferences and causing W. Cameron Forbes, American ambassador to Tokyo, to file a formal protest. It was an age in which Stimson could praise Lord Lytton's Report as "one of the most significant steps ever taken under international cooperation in such a crisis." Hoover could speak proudly of his nonrecognition policy and hail Stimson's open letter to the Senate Foreign Relations Committee as "one of the country's great state papers." And if Stimson honestly believed, as he was to state in his *Far Eastern Crisis* (1936), that no nation was more sensitive to world opinion than Japan, Hoover was certain that his secretary had mobilized such opinion.[70]

Had Hoover, Stimson, and Roosevelt leaned less upon the reed of world opinion, had they been more familiar with the general course of world history as it bore upon their growing dilemma, one can only wonder if the outcome might not have been somewhat different. In a manner of speaking, nearly all of the problems affecting America's standing and reputation during this period can be traced to one pervasive quality—that of parochialism—which brings us full circle. Greater sensitivity to foreign attitudes would have implied more of a readiness to arm. It would have counseled less deference to a fickle and often uninformed public opinion. Above all, it would have dictated a broader spirit of understanding, hence of tolerance and compromise. Like all mortals, Roosevelt was a man thrown up by time and place. But it is clear that his options were dictated as much by personal preference as they were by force of circumstance. What is unfortunate about the foundation upon which he based much of his thinking is that it shut so many doors to peace. The ideas upon which he rested his case from 1933 to 1945 proved to be a veritable bed of sand. The rain fell, the floods came, the winds blew and beat against that house, and it fell.

Conclusion

I<small>N</small> the last analysis, statesmanship depends upon the ability to reduce events to an intelligible pattern, to devise long-range strategy, and to settle on appropriate tactics. Just as victory at chess hinges on a series of adjustments adhering to an overall game plan, so too in foreign policy. The diplomatic gambit may vary in accord with challenge and response, but it must be drawn and redrawn from a single harmonious point of view, either the president's or that of a trusted adviser. Because Roosevelt played diplomatic chess by seeking fresh counsel with every new move, ambivalence became the dominant feature of his policy. The observer is confronted with a continual balancing of dissimilar points of view, one against the other, and all of them against public opinion. By having at his side a Morgenthau and a Hull, he virtually ensured cross purposes. His delegation to the Brussels Conference consisted of Moffat and Hornbeck, who stood on opposite sides of the spectrum, with Norman Davis in the middle. Each of the three spoke for a distinct current of opinion, while Davis received two different sets of instructions.[1] Likewise, when Hull played croquet, he often flanked himself with Moffat and Hornbeck, with Dunn situated somewhere in between. From this essentially fragmented center of policy making there came the "two stools" approach to difficult decisions.

Roosevelt could have adopted a clear-cut, well-reasoned policy aimed at bringing peace to the Far East had he followed one of two options. He might, in the first instance, have attempted to come to terms with Japan in order to establish a new balance of power. The Gaimusho never forgot Woodrow Wilson's admission of its "special interests" in China, just as it believed that the principle of the Lansing-Ishii Treaty carried over into the Nine-Power Treaty. In fact, the latter was seen as having nothing whatever to do with Manchuria.[2] A compromise settlement with Japan would therefore have meant recognizing Manchukuo, pressing China for cooperation, and perhaps signing a new Root-Takahira agreement. This was the course recommended by House, Sayre, Moffat, and MacMurray. Others to whom it appealed included Moore, Moley, Tugwell, and the historian Samuel Flagg Bemis, not to mention John Foster Dulles, William R. Castle, and Yale professor Edwin M. Borchard.[3] Lippmann, Vandenberg, Moffat, Wilson, Johnson, and Grew all advocated a trade treaty with Japan in 1940 or, at the very least, a nonconfrontational policy.[4] The major consideration would have been to protect America's economic stake on the mainland, promote naval disarmament, and steer Japan away from Hitler.

A second policy, the one championed by Stimson, would have been to contest Japanese control of Manchuria by bringing maximum diplomatic, moral, and economic pressure to bear. This implied an early effort to educate public opinion to some form of intervention. It also presupposed the building and maintenance of a navy powerful enough to command respect and the forging of whatever diplomatic ties might be needed to make such a plan work. In line with this, there might well have been a naval understanding or tacit entente with Britain as urged by House, Dodd, and the Chinese. Bullitt reported in 1935 that Japan viewed the American navy with something less than awe.

What Roosevelt did was to straddle. On the one hand, he adopted Stimson's moral imperative. On the other, he delayed economic sanctions and declined to build his navy to treaty strength despite clear indications of congressional support and the insistent prodding of his advisers.

Virtually all of his diplomatic counselors, as we have seen, encouraged him to be more active in preparing the nation's defenses. This is a fact which bears repeating. Grew lobbied throughout the decade, emphasizing the particular need to arm if there was to be any thought of invoking economic sanctions.[5] Heartened by the defeat of the Ludlow Amendment, Hull joined Grew by renewing his own call for preparedness. With strong backing from Baruch, Hornbeck, Davis, and Welles, the president's secretary of state urged him to request three battleships and two carriers. It was disappointing, therefore, when the hoped-for response never came.[6] Even if FDR, along with his military observers, felt that Britain and France would be more than equal to a German attack, he was still remiss. He must still be faulted for not fashioning the type of military strength which would have given his voice real cutting power in the diplomatic counsel chambers of Europe and the Far East. Credibility in the exercise of world leadership cannot be purchased on the cheap or without a philosophy capable of supporting sacrifice.

Roosevelt's own view of rearmament was uncomplicated and to the point: arms would not keep. If one had them, one would likely use them. They would also provoke neighboring countries and arouse bellicosity at home. Samuel Fuller was speaking as the president's alter ego when he told Schacht in 1935 that Germany could not continue to make munitions without using them. FDR himself told Norman Davis that "excessive armaments are in themselves conducive to those fears and suspicions which breed war. Competition in armament is a still greater menace."[7] It was perfectly in character for him to discourage French and British military buildups even as Germany forged steadily ahead, and he went a step further when he told Congress that any threat of war was "due in no small measure to the uncontrolled activities of the manufacturers and merchants of [the] engines of destruction."[8]

Politically, of course, this was the path of least resistance. Public pressure to build the navy was not immediately overwhelming, but there were always groups adamantly opposed; and though there was no initial sense of urgency among the people to establish a new relationship with Britain, there was much in the way of ethnic and isolationist hostility. The White House knew of no massive movement for reconciliation with Japan, but there did exist a vigorous China lobby. When FDR embraced Hornbeck's counsel to "let Nature take its course," he was drifting between Scylla and Charybdis. He would strike no compromise and allow none to be struck.[9] Such a strategy seemed to work for a few years; but when opinion boiled up, as it did in 1937, he felt the need to resort to rhetoric. In July of 1939, under pressure from a majority of the Senate Foreign Relations Committee, he was brought to the next step, economic sanctions, and because these were mild enough to satisfy almost everyone, including the U.S. Chamber of Commerce, they were, in the opinion of Morgenthau, too little, too late. At the same time, they caused Roosevelt to lose control.[10] In response to mounting public sentiment, he soon had little choice but to approve sanctions with teeth. This meant that he found himself throwing down the gauntlet to Japan at the worst psychological moment. One ally, France, had been eliminated, while another was stretched to its outermost limit, having been forced to abandon Crete, Greece, Syria, and Libya. Nazi guns were pounding at the heart of Moscovy.

Ultimately, it was the indecisiveness in Roosevelt's style which dominated all else. While Dooman delivered an ultimatum to Tokyo, the president put on a jolly reception for Admiral Nomura, telling him that instead of calling him "ambassador" he would like to use the more familiar title "admiral." At Argentia, Roosevelt promised Churchill he would deliver an explicit warning to Japan. Instead, he conveyed a rather mild message, further diluted by friendly talk of a summit conference. In one instance, he adopted Stimson's interventionist policy; in another, he supported the Tydings-McDuffie Act, which Stimson disapproved and which suggested disengagement. The British urged him to settle with Japan or mobilize all the resources at his command. In other words, he must either fish or cut bait. What he did, in fact, was to substitute words for action, condemnation for policy.[11]

With respect to Europe, one can never be certain that if Roosevelt's tactics and strategy had been different, he might have succeeded in averting World War II, any more than one has a right to assume that different approaches would have produced an acceptable solution to challenges facing the United States in the Far East. Stalin might have found a way of enlarging Russia's sphere of influence without the help of Washington. At the same time, it cannot be denied that FDR carried great weight as head of a nation which had long been a decisive factor on the world scene. He must bear a measure of blame for the outbreak of fighting in Europe if for no other reason than the fact that while he encouraged democratic leaders to count on speedy aid from America, aid that proved wanting when the chips were down, he assured Hitler of his sympathy for revanchist goals and erected little in the way of a credible deterrent.

Such a tendency was already apparent when he sympathized with German grievances on the Versailles settlement while applauding French resistance to pro-German adjustments embodied in the Four Power Pact. Resistance mounted rapidly on both sides and with it the likelihood of bloodshed.[12] There was grave danger in the Atlantic that Britain and France would invite war if they perceived the United States as a reliable partner in case of need. Conversely, there was the risk that

Germany might go to extremes if she assumed too little strength on the side of America. It was Roosevelt's greatest undoing as a peace-maker that he managed to convey both impressions simultaneously.[13] Grooming the image of crusader at home, he acted secretly as an agent of appeasement. In the end, he fueled optimism on both sides of the conflict until a peaceful solution slipped gradually beyond reach.

Elsewhere, he exhibited similar bifurcation, making certain that France experienced difficulty maintaining order in Vietnam, yet not so much difficulty that she had to abandon her colony altogether.[14] He applied damaging pressure on Chiang without forcing substantial change. He raised Indian hopes without furnishing the means of satisfaction.[15]

In more positive language, Roosevelt had alternatives. Neither isolationist sentiment nor the need for domestic reform, neither his subordinates nor the bureaucratic tangle ever prevented him from rearming. No agent inside or outside of his administration compelled him to rush the opening of the London Economic Conference in 1933 and then to torpedo it. He need not have signed a recognition treaty with the Soviet Union without assurance of a satisfactory quid pro quo. He was under no pressure to tilt against de Gaulle or to take sides against the inclusion of Russia in an entente capable of halting Axis growth. Nor did he have to bring down upon his country the heaped-up scorn of the dictators. Nothing obliged him to egg France and Britain on in the ominous years before September 1939, intimating aid far beyond what he could deliver.

When all factors are weighed, it is perhaps the parochial aspect of America, as much as anything else, which frustrated its chance for a more fruitful international exchange. There was no compelling reason why Washington had to select envoys incapable of conducting an official conversation in the tongue of the country to which they were accredited, particularly such nations as Mexico, Italy, Czechoslovakia, Russia, Germany, China, and Japan. The Spanish foreign minister, surprised that FDR would appoint Carlton Hayes to head the American mission in Madrid when the latter could speak neither Spanish nor French, remarked in his memoirs that this was enough in itself to render Hayes unfit for useful service. Roosevelt need not have chosen men to serve as secretary of state and chief of the Division of Western Europe who spoke no language but their own.[16] Although his policy on diplomatic appointments did not differ substantially from that of other presidents, one could wish that it had, for his record in this regard proved to be completely undistinguished.

Apart from the many misconceptions that remained after his death to encumber America in its unaccustomed role as world leader, he must bear additional responsibility for the failure of two international conferences, London and Brussels. It is far from clear that the Four Freedoms were any more prevalent ten years after the war than they had been ten years before. Hopkins let it be known that Roosevelt had no intention of fighting for the freedom of states and territories along the Soviet border; the president believed that Kremlin leaders would have too many internal problems following the war to pose a significant threat. A recent study of Soviet-American relations concludes, not surprisingly, that FDR's "understanding of Stalin and Soviet policy remained superficial." Surely, one can claim no more for his approach to Chungking. Newly published Sino-American correspondence demonstrates more convincingly than ever the personal pressure that Roosevelt brought to bear upon Chiang Kai-shek for a political solution acceptable to Stalin. Chiang was urged to set up meetings with representatives of the Soviet Union and later to include communist leaders in his delegation to the San Francisco Conference. The consistency with which Roosevelt, and later Truman, pursued this line of policy was all the more significant in light of Chiang's caution in eschewing any direct move to counteract it.[17]

Roosevelt cannot be portrayed as misreading the situation on grounds of invincible ignorance. When Nelson Johnson left his embassy in 1941, after eleven years of experience in China, he harbored few illusions about the Red Chinese. Nor was Johnson the only American who found reason to doubt White House logic. Republican spokesman John Foster Dulles had no difficulty recognizing the policy of the USSR in January 1944 as that of Peter the Great, and former President Hoover sensed the Soviet threat so acutely that he opposed the whole notion of supplying Moscow with Lend-Lease. Among Democrats, there were many who shifted to a more realistic interpretation of the Soviet Union as events gave pause. Bullitt, after opening his Moscow embassy on a note of utopian optimism, swung to the other extreme, reducing Stalin to the level of a "Caucasian bandit." Others who came to question the policy of implicit trust, especially after the Warsaw uprising, included Eugene Lyons, George Kennan, James Forrestal, Averell Harriman, Secretary of State Stettinius, and Assistant

Secretary of State Berle, who resigned. Major General John R. Deane, American military attaché in Moscow, warned that "gratitude cannot be banked in the Soviet Union," and Admiral Standley, the American ambassador for whom Deane worked, was fired for expressing a similar view.[18] Roosevelt himself, shortly before his death, began to lock horns with Stalin on such issues as prisoners of war, representation at San Francisco, the Bern talks, and Poland. Still, on the day he died he felt confident enough to write Churchill that "our course thus far is correct" and "I would minimize the general Soviet problem as much as possible."[19]

In addition to the many options open to him during World War II, there were manifold choices within his sphere of action during the Hundred Days. These, as we have seen, included courses of action or inaction with regard to arms talks, the debt controversy, naval talks, and the Four Power Pact. Presidential advisers House, Moley, Tugwell, Moffat, and many others argued that the United States should not hazard war over an issue as morally tenuous as Manchukuo, especially when American trade in the Orient lay predominantly on the side of Tokyo. Nothing doomed Roosevelt to timidity during the 1935 campaign for World Court membership. Nothing was preordained as he suffered successive defeats on the form of neutrality legislation.

Fellow passengers gasped when the president, journeying aboard the USS *Iowa* to his fateful encounter at Teheran, was nearly hit by a torpedo mistakenly fired by one of his own destroyer escorts.[20] In a very real sense, however, the incident was mirror-perfect as a reflection of diplomatic reality. Scholars have praised Roosevelt's "competitive administration" for holding the door open to creativity, but foreign observers regarded it with less tolerance.[21] According to von Weizsäcker, FDR failed to prepare his diplomatic ground.[22] Halifax sat speechless as Norman Davis called Stettinius naive, and Hull took aim at Wallace. Hopkins undercut Hull while Ickes berated both Hull and FDR. "It is a most bewildering country," wrote the British ambassador. The Ickes who confided to Britain's Colonel Wedgwood that the president and Hopkins were sick men was the same Ickes who phoned Senator Johnson to congratulate him on the Senate's defeat of Roosevelt's World Court proposal. The Dodd who blamed Roosevelt and Morgenthau for errors on trade policy also made an offer to Britain's ambassador Phipps in 1934 which was repudiated by the White House. In the same way, and for similar cause, Roosevelt's envoy to India, Louis Johnson, extended himself beyond what the administration proved willing to support. Erratic behavior at the London Economic Conference and the disowning of Morgenthau's plan for postwar Germany are only two of the better-known examples of administrative disarray. The list is long. John Cudahy, American ambassador to Belgium, told the Germans in January 1940 that he was not in accord with Roosevelt's neutrality policy. Later, relieved of his position on account of the Nazi assault, he took a still more critical line, reminding Hitler that he disagreed utterly with American policy, predicting that England was finished, and advising von Ribbentrop on how to counter Roosevelt's tactics.[23]

To be sure, the slack in executive control was partly deliberate. Instead of assigning responsibility for a given area to a single expert, the president would play one adviser against another. Diplomatic decisions were thus floated as trial balloons, and no subordinate was ever in position to make a name for himself. Likewise, persons outside the White House could be held accountable for any move that misfired. Leading with another man's chin is the way one historian has described the technique, and it helps explain the many times FDR ordered his overseas representatives to present an administration proposal "unofficially" or on a strictly "personal" basis.[24] His refusal to be publicly linked with Bullitt's proposals in early 1933, as well as the way he dissociated himself from initiatives forwarded by others are all a part of the whole. This, too, is the background against which he tried to impute linguistic disability to foreign contacts.

We are speaking of a president who upheld the democratic norm and championed the rights of smaller nations yet suggested that the world be governed by Four Policemen and organized according to three regional Monroe Doctrines.[25] Before proposing a system of Four Policemen, he had spoken in terms of three and before that of two (the United States and Britain).[26] Hull may have promised to obliterate spheres of influence, but such thinking did not originate in the mind of FDR.[27] When the British argued the case for world organization at Argentia, and then again a year later, the president demurred, causing Welles to protest that the less powerful nations might at least be given a forum for complaint. It was Churchill, not his American counterpart, who pressed for "a wider and more permanent system of general security." London, not Washington, looked first and most penetratingly at the question of postwar organization.[28] Only after Willkie published *One World* and Churchill's ideas had begun to gain currency in America and England did Roosevelt attempt to propel himself from the rear of the movement to its van. Senator Fulbright told him that unless he moved quickly Republicans would gain a monopoly on plans for world organization. Thus it was that on returning from Teheran, where he had just advocated a four-power condominium, he spoke over the radio of "the rights of every nation, large or small": "The doctrine that the strong shall dominate the weak is the doctrine of our enemies—and we reject it."[29]

He has been called a hero of world order and acclaimed as herald of the destruction of the system of plural state sovereignty.[30] But whatever sacrifices he may have made to obtain Soviet cooperation on behalf of a new league, whatever arrangements he may have made to locate it in New York, he hardly deserves to be placed on a level with the Prophet of Princeton. In the twelve years from 1933 to 1945, the United States did not divest itself of a single imperial possession, notwithstanding its plan for release of the Philippines. It did not abrogate one colonial leasehold. On the contrary, control over foreign peoples grew, alike in terms of population and acreage. The idea of a renascent American imperialism, sometimes referred to as "the American peril" overseas, remained very much alive, as we have had occasion to observe. It was mainly the imperialism of other countries that Roosevelt found despicable, which may help to explain Churchill's remark that "idealism at others' expense and without regard to the consequences of ruin and slaughter which fall upon millions of humble homes cannot be considered as its highest or noblest form."[31]

Actually, FDR passed through three stages of opinion on the subject of imperialism. Before reentering public life in 1928, he envisioned the Caribbean as an American lake and gave wholehearted support to United States protectorates. In an address to the students of Milton Academy, one published only six years before his race for the presidency, he listed imperialism as one of the signs of civilization's progress: "Backward peoples are made wards of those more advanced. Power is exported. Capital is international. Foreign affairs are discussed by the average citizen. Wars and armaments are the concern of more than kings."[32] Needless to say, by the time he entered the White House, he had arrived at a quite different position. During the campaign of 1932 and throughout his first two terms, he spoke disparagingly of imperialism, and though he took little initiative on his own to reduce the size of American holdings, he did preside over a loosening of the national grip. The United States made no move to abandon its fortified position at Guantánamo Bay or to pull up stakes in the Virgin Islands, but San Juan obtained greater autonomy and Manila a timetable for independence. In the third phase of Roosevelt's thinking, he began to confront difficult choices dictated by the national interest. Although he continued to speak out against imperialism and did much to put foreign colonies on the road to ultimate extinction, he expressed a desire to extend American rule over Manus, Noumea, and Clipperton Island.[33] Realizing that it would not be feasible, from the standpoint of hemispheric opinion, to purchase Chile's Easter Island and Ecuador's Galápagos Islands outright, he sought to administer both holdings under the cover of a Pan American trust. This is what transpired in Micronesia, where American forces operated as U.N. auxiliaries in theory but in reality functioned as an auxiliary arm of the White House. Farther to the east, he was anxious to police Dakar. He also encouraged Britain to take over Bizerte, and it seems that he had his eye fixed on the Canary Islands.[34]

FDR had a tendency to substitute such terms as "anti-imperialism," "world opinion," and the "sanctity" of treaties for more traditional concepts of right and wrong. One critic has called it "rendering unto Caesar that which is God's." Churchill referred to it as conformity to "the ethics of the twentieth century." Whatever it was, the pitfalls to which it led in a mind such as the president's were enormous. The United States found it possible to go back on important commitments and to act treacherously in connection with the vital interests of an ally. Wholesale internment of Japanese-Americans could be justified as an act of wartime emergency, while Mexico and Bolivia were able to confiscate foreign property worth millions of dollars in the name of national liberation with little or no concern for the probable reaction of Washington. Roosevelt felt no obligation to support a bill that would have admitted twenty thousand Jewish children, refugees from the Nazi holocaust, nor did he hesitate to urge the French resident general of Morocco to limit the percentage of local Jews eligible to enter professions. Moroccans would do well, he advised, to forestall complaints about unseemly influence such as were heard in Germany.[35]

Inevitably, Roosevelt's position changed from year to year and from one situation to another, regardless of the point at issue. It might be a question of freedom of trade; it might be dictatorship; it might be open covenants openly arrived at or the Versailles Treaty, which he finally waved aside with a deprecatory gesture.[36] Although a staunch opponent of Japanese control of Manchukuo, he urged Chiang to overlook Soviet control of the Chinese province of Outer Mongolia. In 1939, he wrote his friend Murray that if Britain wanted to remain in Egypt and Asia Minor it ought to adopt a firmer line with the native peoples. In the same way, he applied no pressure on Queen Wilhelmina to abandon her East Indian possessions, and the Court of St. James's remained free to stay on in Malaya. The British and the Dutch, as he confided to Halifax, had "done a good job."[37]

Naturally, it is for the reader, and for the reader alone, to judge how much of Roosevelt's record is attributable to circumstance and how much to the man himself. It may be fairly said, however, that no other American administration before 1933 had as many opportunities as the New Deal to avert the coming of war, to settle wars in progress, or to shape the future of peace. Herein lies the disproportion. Not one of FDR's offers of mediation ever succeeded, and most were flatly refused.[38] He made at least thirty unsuccessful protests and appeals, five of them to thwart Italy's occupation of Ethiopia. Four proceeded from a desire for Italian neutrality during the war; three revolved around the Munich Conference; three others sought to avert the outbreak of war.[39] Out of dozens of prewar diplomatic initiatives and schemes emanating from the White House, all but a handful proved fruitless.[40]

The man who presided over American fortunes for more than a decade was not without magic. There was an electricity in his voice, an intuitive brilliance about his style, that made him the salesman par excellence of domestic legislation. One cannot but admire the skill with which he launched Destroyers for Bases and coaxed Lend-Lease through a skittish Congress. Few presidents have been as eloquent in the cause of democracy or breathed as much optimism into a people that needed dearly to be encouraged.

Nonetheless, it is possible to mistake form for substance, magnetism for the man. This holds especially true in the realm of foreign policy where FDR accumulated the largest overseas credibility gap of any president on record. Scores of promises made to leaders of other nations were retracted or broken. Most were to Britain, but they included a great many to China and France.[41] The French, revolted as always by the slightest whiff of cant or humbug, could speak in certain quarters of Roosevelt and "the Missouri winds" while German officials could liken the Western democracies to "shifting sand."[42] In point of fact, there is something close to the heart of New Deal diplomacy which has about it the quality of *both* wind *and* sand.

Notes

Abbreviations

AEU	Amérique, 1918–40: Etats-Unis
BUL	Birmingham University Library
CCC	Churchill College, Cambridge
CUOHC	Columbia University Oral History Collection
DBFP	*Documents on British Foreign Policy*
DDF	*Documents diplomatiques français, 1932–1939*
DGFP	*Documents on German Foreign Policy*
Dodd's Diary	William E. Dodd, Jr., and Martha Dodd, eds., *Ambassador Dodd's Diary, 1933–1938*
FDRL	Franklin D. Roosevelt Library, Hyde Park
FNSP	Fondation Nationale des Sciences Politiques
FO	Foreign Office of Great Britain
FR	*Foreign Relations of the United States*
GP	Grew Papers, Houghton Library, Harvard University
LC	Library of Congress
Letters	Elliott Roosevelt, ed., *F.D.R.: His Personal Letters*, 4 vols.
MRP	Map Room Papers, FDRL
NLS	National Library of Scotland
OF	Official Files, FDRL
PAC	Public Archives of Canada
PDM-ROC	*Principal Documentary Material of the Republic of China in the Period of the Sino-Japanese War: Wartime Diplomacy*, 3 vols.
PPF	President's Personal File, FDRL
PREM	Prime Minister's Files, PRO
PRO	Public Record Office, Kew
PSF	President's Secretary's File, FDRL
Quai d'Orsay	Ministère des Relations Extérieures, Paris

RC   Loewenheim, Langley, and Jonas, eds., *Roosevelt and Chur-*
                   chill: Their Secret Wartime Correspondence
RG, NA   Record Group, National Archives, Washington, D.C.
SCRT   USSR, Ministry of Foreign Affairs, ed., *Stalin's Correspon-*
                   dence with Roosevelt and Truman, 1941–1945
SRO   Scottish Record Office
ULC   Cambridge University Library, Cambridge, England

Preface

1. These sources are untapped, not in the sense of having been previously screened from public view (though certain sources do indeed fall into this category) but rather in the sense of not having been brought to bear on the subject under review.

2. Typical is Robert Dallek, *Franklin D. Roosevelt and American Foreign Policy, 1932–1945* (New York: Oxford University Press, 1979). The most comprehensive and competent single-volume survey on the topic to date, it reflects the advantages and disadvantages inherent in any such summary treatment. Without benefit of archival material in Canada, Scotland, or France, and without utilization of published official French records, one gains the standard impression of a president disinclined initially to move forcefully in foreign affairs, one preoccupied during the Hundred Days with matters of domestic relief. Little is added to Arnold A. Offner's account of the appeasement of Nazi Germany. If anything Dallek hedges on this issue, tending to view FDR as more of an opponent than a supporter of compromise. On the Far East, Roosevelt emerges as a man of vision, who did his best to engage Japan in serious negotiation, at least until September 1941. This is a chief executive who made few, if any, personal errors in foreign policy and whose failure, when apparent, may almost always be traced to forces beyond his control. In short, Dallek's conclusions differ on nearly every score from those contained in the present volume. As regards factual content, Dallek does not clarify Roosevelt's plan to clamp a naval blockade on Japan nor does he explain the Quarantine Address in the context of its causal connection with League of Nations action. We learn virtually nothing about the Brussels Conference of 1937. The Welles Plan is reviewed without indication of its basic orientation, and the reader is left to assume that Roosevelt acted resolutely and consistently in opposition to the Hitler regime. William R. Davis was not, as the author maintains, an emissary acting on German initiative, and though FDR may have "hit the roof" (Dallek's phrase) when publicly portrayed as anxious to mediate, this was the unvarnished truth. There is no mention in Dallek's book of the revealing circumstances surrounding Ambassador Saito's funeral or of a succession of important talks: between Grew and Nomura in 1939, Sayre and Arita in 1940, and Grew and Arita in 1940. The critical role of Maryknoll missionaries James M. Drought

and James E. Walsh is dismissed in a single sentence. Moreover, one will search in vain for any sustained analysis of the Hull-Nomura talks. Dallek gives no inkling of a secret military pact between London and Washington in the fall of 1940. Japan's offer of a modus vivendi in late 1941 finds no place in the narrative either. On the Welles mission to Europe, the author is again ambivalent, at one point indicating that it might well have been serious, at another injecting doubt. There is no detailed description of Roosevelt's relationship with Stalin or Chiang, nor is there any comprehensive treatment of Roosevelt's reputation abroad. The list could be extended. See Dallek, *Roosevelt*, 81, 85, 97, 125, 138, 149, 153, 159, 164, 207, 215–17, 236, 285, 529.

3. The reference here is to talks involving Grew, Nomura, Sayre, and Arita as mentioned in note 2 above.

4. Previous accounts of the period have failed to underscore the coincidence between a shift in American policy during September and October 1940 and an equally dramatic shift in British policy at the same time. There has been no suggestion that Admiral Richardson's instructions or the Grew-Dooman ultimatum may by credited as proof of an earlier policy turnabout. Churchill's cabinet remarks have not been taken into account, nor has mention been made of a suggestive gap in the record of British cabinet minutes. Canadian Prime Minister Mackenzie King's reference to a sudden British decision to guarantee American Far East possessions has not figured in the equation, nor has attention been paid to Roosevelt's war measures accompanied by a series of uncharacteristically bellicose remarks made to Congressmen Rayburn and McCormack, as well as to administration officials—all in or around the first week of October 1940, when Churchill made his decision to reopen the Burma Road. Finally, no satisfying explanation has been offered of why Britain chose to hazard war with Japan by reopening the Burma Road when for years her leaders had ruled out such a course without American military support tantamount to an alliance.

5. Arnold A. Offner, *American Appeasement: United States Foreign Policy and Germany, 1933–1938* (Cambridge, Mass.: Harvard University Press, 1969), is a pioneer work that still furnishes the best general coverage of the subject but passes over all of these key episodes. See also Offner, *The Origins of the Second World War: American Foreign Policy and World Politics, 1917–1941* (New York: Praeger, 1975), and Offner, "Appeasement Revisited: The United States, Great Britain, and Germany, 1933–1940," *Journal of American History* 64 (September 1977): 373–93, both of which take the story down to 1941 without alluding to most of the critical points stressed in the present volume.

Introduction

1. The debate pits such historians as Charles Beard and Robert Divine against Basil Rauch, Victor Albjerg, Robert Accinelli, and others. See, for exam-

ple, Robert A. Divine, "Franklin D. Roosevelt and Collective Security, 1933," *Mississippi Valley Historical Review* 48 (June 1961):42–59; Victor Albjerg, "Isolationism and the Early New Deal, 1932–1937," *Current History* 35 (October 1958):204–10; Charles A. Beard, *American Foreign Policy in the Making, 1932–1940* (New Haven: Yale University Press, 1946), 148; Robert A. Divine, *Roosevelt and World War II* (Baltimore: Johns Hopkins University Press, 1969), 5–7; Robert D. Accinelli, "The Roosevelt Administration and the World Court Defeat, 1935," *The Historian* 40 (May 1978):466. One of the more recent works that portrays FDR as an isolationist is David G. Haglund, *Latin America and the Transformation of U.S. Strategic Thought, 1936–1940* (Albuquerque: University of New Mexico Press, 1984), 27–28.

2. Willard Range, *Franklin D. Roosevelt's World Order* (Athens: University of Georgia Press, 1959), 186–87.

3. Arnold Offner concludes that FDR was all for appeasement. John Haight maintains that he opposed appeasement in principle but felt tactically bound to yield, thereby forcing Bonnet into surrender. William Langer and S. Everett Gleason are not certain what to conclude, while Donald Drummond holds that Roosevelt "dabbled" in appeasement; see William L. Langer and S. Everett Gleason, *The Challenge to Isolation, 1937–1940* (New York: Harper, 1952), 58; Donald F. Drummond, *The Passing of American Neutrality, 1937–1941* (Ann Arbor: University of Michigan Press, 1955), 78ff.; Offner, *Appeasement*, 276–80; John McVickar Haight, Jr., "France, the United States, and the Munich Crisis," *Journal of Modern History* 32 (December 1960):356–58.

4. Compare Range with Daniel M. Smith. Then see John Lewis Gaddis, who alternates between the two views while maintaining a healthy sense of balance: Smith, "Authoritarianism and American Policy Makers in Two World Wars," *Pacific Historical Review* 43 (August 1974):306, 311; Range, *Roosevelt's World Order*, 27; Gaddis, *The United States and the Origins of the Cold War, 1941–1947* (New York: Columbia University Press, 1972), 6, 17, 27, 100, 191; then 6–7, 9, 12, 15–16, 23–31, 35, 42, 64, 79, 82–83, 96, 101–2, 173. James MacGregor Burns believes FDR combined realism with idealism but was essentially an "idealist"; see *Roosevelt: The Soldier of Freedom* (New York: Harcourt Brace Jovanovich, 1970), 298. See also Robert A. Divine's book review in the *Journal of American History* 57 (June 1970):206.

5. Langer and Gleason deny that Roosevelt deliberately involved his country in war on either front. Raymond Esthus agrees, while Thomas A. Bailey and Paul B. Ryan are not certain, saying only that war was not a "major" aim of the administration. Burns, on the other hand, maintains that Roosevelt desired an incident in the Atlantic "to propel the nation toward full intervention." Range cannot fathom Roosevelt's goal in the fall of 1941; Robert Dallek feels he aimed at involvement as of August. A number of older accounts, in particular those by Charles Beard, Frederic Sanborn, and John Flynn, portray him as seeking war

to ensure his hold on the presidency or to divert attention from unresolved domestic issues. More recently, there has been a tendency to see him either as drifting into war through inadvertence and inertia or as stumbling into it on the basis of overconfidence or racial arrogance. See William L. Langer and S. Everett Gleason, *The Undeclared War, 1940–1941* (New York: Harper, 1953), 211–12, 740; Thomas A. Bailey and Paul B. Ryan, *Hitler vs. Roosevelt: The Undeclared Naval War* (New York: Free Press, 1979), 261; Burns, *Soldier of Freedom*, 104–5; Range, *Roosevelt's World Order*, 26; Dallek, *Roosevelt*, 285; Frederic R. Sanborn, *Design for War: A Study of Secret Power Politics, 1937–1941* (New York: Devin-Adair, 1951); John T. Flynn, *While You Slept: Our Tragedy in Asia and Who Made It* (New York: Devin-Adair, 1951); Norman Graebner, "Japan: Unanswered Challenge, 1931–1941," in Margaret F. Morris and Sandra L. Myres, eds., *Essays on American Foreign Policy* (Austin: University of Texas Press, 1974), 118, 142; Christopher G. Thorne, *Allies of a Kind: The United States, Britain, and the War against Japan, 1941–1945* (New York: Oxford University Press, 1978), 3–5.

6. Robert Theobald argued the case for deliberate exposure of the fleet, as did Harry Elmer Barnes (FDR "ordered Marshall to disappear until it would be too late effectively to warn Short and Kimmel"). This kind of conspiracy theory has been rebutted by such research scholars as Roberta Wohlstetter and Arnold Offner, but it is by no means dead. Retired Rear Admiral Husband E. Kimmel, in charge of Pearl Harbor's naval defenses at the time of the attack, told reporters in 1966 that "FDR and the top brass deliberately betrayed the American forces at Pearl Harbor." According to Kimmel, Roosevelt gave orders that no word on Japanese fleet maneuvers was to go to Pearl Harbor except through Marshall, and Marshall was told "not to say anything." Kimmel admitted that he could not substantiate any of his charges, but they were repeated in 1976, when Hamilton Fish, a retired congressman, published his *FDR: The Other Side of the Coin: How We Were Tricked into World War II* (New York: Vantage Press, 1976), 133, 146, 151. See also Richard T. Ruetten, "Harry Elmer Barnes and the 'Historical Blackout.'" *The Historian* 33 (February 1971):203; Theobald, *The Final Secret of Pearl Harbor* (New York: Devin-Adair, 1954), 199–200; *New York Times*, 7 December 1966, p. 22; *Newsweek*, 12 December 1966, p. 40. The most recent resurrection of the thesis is John Toland, *Infamy: Pearl Harbor and Its Aftermath* (Garden City, N.Y.: Doubleday, 1982). Toland argues that Roosevelt had received persuasive evidence indicating an attack on Pearl Harbor but that no official in Washington expected serious damage to the fleet. A recent essay in defense of FDR's innocence is David Kahn, "The United States Views Germany and Japan in 1941," in Ernest R. May, ed., *Knowing One's Enemies: Intelligence Assessment before the Two World Wars* (Princeton: Princeton University Press, 1984). For the most up-to-date critique of New Deal appeasement on the Spanish front, see Douglas Little, *Malevolent Neu-*

trality: The United States, Great Britain, and the Origins of the Spanish Civil War (Ithaca: Cornell University Press, 1985), esp. pp. 10, 17, 265.

7. For a powerful argument affirming such a threat, see Dexter Perkins, "Was Roosevelt Wrong?" in Glyndon G. Van Deusen and Richard C. Wade, eds., Foreign Policy and the American Spirit: Essays by Dexter Perkins (Ithaca: Cornell University Press. 1957).

8. See Ruetten, "Barnes," 204, 206n., 214. Ruetten is excellent on historiography as is Richard E. Welch, Jr., "New Deal Diplomacy and Its Revisionists," Reviews in American History 5 (September 1977):410–17.

9. Alsop to Mrs. Roosevelt, 29 September 1939, PPF 300, FDRL.

10. Arthur Schlesinger once made the claim that Roosevelt's "Good Man" cable to Chamberlain during the Munich crisis of 1938 represented a position of firmness (quoted in Francis L. Loewenheim, "An Illusion That Shaped History: New Light on the History and Historiography of American Peace Efforts before Munich," in Daniel R. Beaver, ed., Some Pathways in Twentieth-Century History: Essays in Honor of Reginald Charles McGrane [Detroit: Wayne State University Press, 1969], 288n.).

11. In Dorothy Borg and Shumpei Okamoto, eds., Pearl Harbor as History: Japanese-American Relations, 1931–1941 (New York: Columbia University Press, 1973), responsibility for the war between Japan and the United States is divided among the fighting in China, the Japanese, Japanese censorship, American reporters, Stanley Hornbeck, the Japanese cabinet, Japanese intellectuals, Joseph Grew, Admiral Nomura, and poor communications. Hornbeck is accorded an entire chapter while FDR is discussed only incidentally in a chapter he must share with former president Hoover. A significant last chapter, which seeks to examine images, policies, and interests of both Japan and the United States, fails to mention Roosevelt at all. FDR is indexed for only 36 out of 604 pages; Hull receives 43, Grew 55, and Hornbeck 56. According to an essay by Mushakōji Kinhide, it was the American image of Japan and Japanese perceptions of the United States which were at fault, never Roosevelt. Thus the Tripartite Pact is portrayed as having triggered an irreversible deterioration in relations.

12. R. J. C. Butow, "The Hull-Nomura Conversations: A Fundamental Misconception," American Historical Review 65 (July 1960):822–36; Butow, The John Doe Associates: Backdoor Diplomacy for Peace, 1941 (Stanford: Stanford University Press, 1974).

13. See Lester H. Brune, "Considerations of Force in Cordell Hull's Diplomacy, July 26 to November 26, 1941," Diplomatic History 2 (Fall 1978):389–405; and Waldo H. Heinrichs, Jr., American Ambassador: Joseph C. Grew and the Development of the United States Diplomatic Tradition (Boston: Little, Brown, 1966).

14. See, for example, Burns, Soldier of Freedom, p. 495.

15. Walter La Feber, "Roosevelt, Churchill, and Indochina, 1942–1945," *American Historical Review* 80 (December 1975):1295; Irvine H. Anderson, Jr., "The 1941 *De Facto* Embargo on Oil to Japan: A Bureaucratic Reflex," *Pacific Historical Review* 44 (May 1975):230; Jonathan G. Utley, "Upstairs, Downstairs at Foggy Bottom: Oil, Exports and Japan, 1940–41," *Prologue* 8 (Spring 1976):17–28; Thomas R. Maddux, "United States–Soviet Naval Relations in the 1930s: The Soviet Union's Efforts to Purchase Naval Vessels," *Naval War College Review* 29 (Fall 1976):28–37; Dick Steward, *Trade and Hemisphere: The Good Neighbor Policy and Reciprocal Trade* (Columbia: University of Missouri Press, 1975), 113; Randall Bennett Woods, *The Roosevelt Foreign Policy Establishment and the "Good Neighbor": The United States and Argentina, 1941–1945* (Lawrence: Regents Press of Kansas, 1979), x (Woods's culprit is "bureaucratic proliferation and competition within the Roosevelt foreign policy establishment").

16. For an interesting discussion along this line, see Alfred B. Rollins, Jr., "Was There Really a Man Named Roosevelt?" in George Athan Billias and Gerald Grob, eds., *American History: Retrospect and Prospect* (New York: Free Press, 1971). Any number of additional examples could be adduced. M. J. J. Smith divides the blame for failure at the 1937 Brussels Conference between Chamberlain and Hull's "clique" at the State Department. Steward exculpates FDR when he attributes grave shortcomings of the Good Neighbor Policy to "forces, not men." An account of U.S. failure to confront the dictators more forcefully lays the blame on domestic opposition and on European policies of appeasement. Still another account, in this instance dealing with Roosevelt's Good Neighbor Policy, apportions blame variously to the Depression, the end of the Depression, the Welles-Hull feud, Welles's sex scandal, intra-administration disputes, the end of World War II, Hull's illness, FDR's death, and ignorance on the part of Stettinius, Truman, Byrnes, and Rockefeller. See M. J. J. Smith, "F.D.R. and the Brussels Conference, 1937," *Michigan Academician* 14 (Fall 1981); Steward, *Trade and Hemisphere*, 241; Howard C. Payne, Raymond Callahan, and Edward M. Bennett, *As the Storm Clouds Gathered: European Perceptions of American Foreign Policy in the 1930s* (Durham: Moore, 1979), 52–53; Irwin F. Gellman, *Good Neighbor Diplomacy: United States Policies in Latin America, 1933–1945* (Baltimore: Johns Hopkins University Press, 1979), 58, 179, 185, 197, 199, 202–4, 210, 225–28.

17. See, for example, William W. Kaufmann, "Two American Ambassadors: Bullitt and Kennedy," in Gordon A. Craig and Felix Gilbert, eds., *The Diplomats, 1919–1939* (Princeton: Princeton University Press, 1953).

18. See, for example, Brune, "Hull's Diplomacy," and Howard Jablon, *Crossroads of Decision: The State Department and Foreign Policy, 1933–1937* (Lexington: University Press of Kentucky, 1983). According to Jablon, FDR is viewed as largely a victim of bad advice (coming mainly from State) while he

was, at the same time, distracted by the rush of domestic events (131–40). According to James MacGregor Burns, who has written one of the most penetrating of all accounts, Stimson prevailed upon Willkie to direct his criticism of the Darlan deal at the State Department, which he refers to as "that battered old punching bag" (Burns, *Soldier of Freedom*, 296). See also James MacGregor Burns, *Roosevelt: The Lion and the Fox* (New York: Harcourt, Brace and World, 1956), 398–99: "When a leader fails to live up to the symbolic role he has come to occupy, his admirers cling to the image they love by imputing mistakes to the leader's advisers. . . . The president's tactics were his own."

19. James B. Crowley, who presents the situation in Tokyo with great clarity, nevertheless concludes with an anomalous reference to Japan's "aggression" and her "obsession with national security" (*Japan's Quest for Autonomy: National Security and Foreign Policy, 1930–1938* [Princeton: Princeton University Press, 1966], 394). After five hundred pages of narrative in which the reader is frequently permitted to observe presidential weakness and drift, Dallek concludes that "too much has been made of Roosevelt's shortcomings and too little of the constraints under which he had to work in foreign affairs." Suddenly, one is asked to see Roosevelt in traditional terms: as chief architect of the basic strategic decisions of World War II, as prudent and wise in selecting Dodd and Kennedy, and as reasonably realistic about the Russians. FDR could not have restrained Soviet expansion, and he had "a good general grasp of Chinese realities" (*Roosevelt*, 529, 532–33, 535, 537).

20. See, for example, on Japan, Peter Herde, *Pearl Harbor, 7 Dezember 1941* . . . (Warmstadt: Wissenschaftliche Buchgesellschaft, 1980); on Anglo-American relations, David Reynolds, *The Creation of the Anglo-American Alliance, 1937–1941* (Chapel Hill: University of North Carolina Press, 1982); on FDR and World War II, Thorne, *Allies*; on Pearl Harbor, Gordon W. Prange, *At Dawn We Slept: The Untold Story of Pearl Harbor* (New York: McGraw-Hill, 1981); on Franco-American relations, Jean-Baptiste Duroselle, *L'abîme, 1939–1945* (Paris: Imprimerie Nationale, 1982).

21. The suggestion appears in Langer and Gleason, *Challenge to Isolation*, p. 81.

22. See, for example, Dorothy Borg, *The United States and the Far Eastern Crisis of 1933–1938* (Cambridge, Mass.: Harvard University Press, 1964); Drummond, *American Neutrality*; Gaddis, *Cold War*; Paul Schroeder, *The Axis Alliance and Japanese-American Relations, 1941* (Ithaca: Cornell University Press, 1958); Range, *Roosevelt's World Order*; William L. Neumann, *After Victory: Churchill, Roosevelt, Stalin and the Making of the Peace* (New York: Harper, 1967); and Gaddis Smith, *American Diplomacy during the Second World War, 1941–1945* (New York: Wiley, 1967). More specifically, see John Morton Blum, ed., *From the Morgenthau Diaries: Years of Crisis, 1928–1938* (Boston: Houghton Mifflin, 1959), 484; Dallek, *Roosevelt*, 78; Burns, *Lion and*

the Fox, 262; Arthur D. Morse, *While Six Million Died: A Chronicle of American Apathy* (New York: Random House, 1968), 309; Albjerg, "Isolationism," 207; Accinelli, "World Court," 464, 474. See also Warren F. Kuehl, "Midwestern Newspapers and Isolationist Sentiment," *Diplomatic History* 3 (Summer 1979):283–306; Offner, *Appeasement;* Crowley, *Japan's Quest;* Bryce Wood, *The United States and Latin American Wars, 1932–1942* (New York: Columbia University Press, 1966); Akira Iriye, *After Imperialism: The Search for a New Order in the Far East, 1921–1931* (Cambridge, Mass.: Harvard University Press, 1965); Payne, Callahan, and Bennett, *As the Storm Clouds Gathered*, 155. Warren F. Kimball sees "remarkable contempt and hubris directed at the aspirations and national pride of smaller nations," and Thomas R. Maddux faults Roosevelt for a "reluctance to be firm," a preoccupation with domestic considerations, and "a tendency to advance proposals without sufficient investigation and reflection" (Kimball, "Churchill and Roosevelt: The Personal Equation," *Prologue* 6 [Fall 1974]:176; Maddux, *Years of Estrangement: American Relations with the Soviet Union, 1933–1941* [Tallahassee: Florida State University Press, 1980], viii). Vojtech Mastny has called FDR "incorrigibly optimistic"; George Kennan has characterized his diplomatic style as "basically histrionic"; and Gerhard L. Weinberg has found his policy "faltering and vague" (Mastny, *Russia's Road to the Cold War: Diplomacy, Warfare, and the Politics of Communism, 1941–1945* [New York: Columbia University Press, 1979], 123–25, 249–52; for Kennan's view, see Hugh de Santis, *The Diplomacy of Silence: The American Foreign Service, the Soviet Union, and the Cold War, 1933–1947* [Chicago: University of Chicago Press, 1980], 25; Weinberg, *The Foreign Policy of Hitler's Germany: Starting World War II, 1937–1939* [Chicago: University of Chicago Press, 1980], 111). Even the Good Neighbor Policy, so highly touted by Samuel Flagg Bemis and Edward O. Guerrant, has come in for sharp reevaluation. Compare Edward O. Guerrant, *Roosevelt's Good Neighbor Policy* (Albuquerque: University of New Mexico Press, 1950), 135, 170, and Samuel Flagg Bemis, *The Latin American Policy of the United States* (1943; paperback, New York: Norton, 1967), 368, 382, with Paul A. Varg, "The Economic Side of the Good Neighbor Policy: The Reciprocal Trade Program and South America," *Pacific Historical Review* 45 (February 1976):47–71, and Robert Freeman Smith, "The Good Neighbor Policy: The Liberal Paradox in United States Relations with Latin America," in Leonard P. Liggio and James J. Martin, eds., *Watershed of Empire: Essays on New Deal Foreign Policy* (Colorado Springs: Ralph Myles, 1976), 65, 67, 81, 88, 90–91. Justus Doenecke and Warren Kuehl have gone far to remove isolationism as an apology for weak leadership in the 1930s; William Widenor has thrown doubt on the realism of New Deal planning for world government (the United Nations); the Red Chinese, whose cause FDR did so much to promote, are increasingly shown to have been more repressive and less democratic than originally supposed, and the Roosevelt treatment of Chiang Kai-shek is occasionally portrayed as insensitive and flimsy. As for FDR's policy vis-à-vis Japan, here too, arguments never before taken seriously are beginning to make their presence felt. The direction of the trend is unmistakable. See Justus D. Doenecke, *When the Wicked Rise: American Opinion-Makers and the Manchurian Crisis of 1931–33* (Lewisburg: Bucknell University Press, 1984); Warren F. Kuehl, "Webs of Common Interests Revisited: Nationalism, Internationalism and Historians of American Foreign Relations," *Diplomatic History* 10 (Spring 1986):107–20; William C. Widenor, "American Planning for the United Nations: Have We Been Asking the Right Questions?" *Diplomatic History* 6 (Summer 1982):245–65; Steven W. Mosher, *Broken Earth: The Rural Chinese* (New York: Free Press, 1983); Patricia Neils, "Henry R. Luce and American Images of China," *Tamkang Journal of American Studies* 2 (Spring 1986):17–39; Michael Hunt, *The Making of a Special Relationship: The United States and China to 1914* (New York: Columbia University Press, 1983), 306; Gerald K. Haines, "American Myopia and the Japanese Monroe Doctrine, 1931–41," *Prologue* 13 (Spring 1981):101–14; Haines, "The Roosevelt Administration Interprets the Monroe Doctrine," *Australian Journal of Politics and History* 24 (December 1978):332–45. For additional material in the same mold of demythologizing, see Dirk Bavendamm, *Roosevelts Weg Zum Krieg: Amerikanische Politik, 1914–1939* (Munich: Herbig, 1983); David S. Wyman, *The Abandonment of the Jews: America and the Holocaust, 1941–1945* (New York: Pantheon, 1984); Monty Noam Penkover, *The Jews Were Expendable: Free World Diplomacy and the Holocaust* (Urbana: University of Illinois Press, 1983).

23. See, for example, the work of Lloyd Gardner and William Appleman Williams as discussed in Welch, "Revisionists," 412–16.

24. Sumner Welles covered his tracks with great skill in a series of publications. In *Seven Decisions That Shaped History* (New York: Harper, 1951), he claimed that Roosevelt's administration would "never need an apology"; yet this is precisely what he attempted to supply (ibid., xviii; Welles, *The Time for Decision* [New York: Harper, 1944], 73–147). Langer and Gleason echo Welles's theme by depicting a noble president inflexibly opposed to any compromise with Hitler. According to them, the secret Davis and Mooney missions were "devious attempts" by the Axis "to interest President Roosevelt in the role of mediator" (*Challenge to Isolation*, 247, 249, 258). A recent article by Stanley E. Hilton, written without benefit of the Lothian and Halifax papers, attempts to buttress Welles further. But little attention has been paid to the weaknesses in Welles's logic. See Hilton, "The Welles Mission to Europe, February–March 1940: Illusion or Realism?" *Journal of American History* 58 (June 1971):93–120.

25. Shigenori Tōgō, *The Cause of Japan*, trans. Fumihiko Tōgō (New York: Simon and Schuster, 1956); Mamoru Shigemitsu, *Japan and Her Destiny: My*

Struggle for Peace (New York: E. P. Dutton, 1958); Nobutaka Ike, trans. and ed., *Japan's Decision for War: Records of the 1941 Policy Conferences* (Stanford: Stanford University Press, 1967). Ike implies that Japan sought "a great empire" rather than strategic and economic conditions that would have made it possible to find common ground with the West (xix). Shigemitsu, who made no effort to present the case for Manchukuo, was appointed foreign minister after the war.

26. See Chin-tung Liang, *General Stilwell in China, 1942–1944: The Full Story* (New York: St. John's University Press, 1972). Herbert Feis, who was commissioned by the State Department to write *The China Tangle*, is prominent among those who have tried to write on China without Chinese sources.

27. Lord Templewood (Samuel Hoare), *Complacent Dictator* (New York: Knopf, 1947), 5, 27, 81; Hoare to Halifax, 8, 19 November 1940, Hoare to Cadogan, 11 November 1940, FO 800/323, PRO. Weddell resigned in April 1942 to be succeeded by Carlton Hayes.

28. In *The Reckoning* (Boston: Houghton Mifflin, 1965), Eden applies words like "feckless," "hysterical," and "conjuror" to FDR (433, 457). Recently, Lord Coleraine spoke candidly in an interview with Thorne (Thorne, *Allies*, 115n.). The Spanish foreign minister, it should be noted, spoke of Weddell as pleasant but lacking in diplomacy and somewhat naive ("un peu enfant") (Ramón Serrano Suñer, *Entre les Pyrénées et Gibraltar* [Geneva: Editions du Cheval Aila, 1947], 236, 238).

29. War Cab. 267, CAB 65/9 PRO.

30. Saint-Quentin to Bonnet, 27 September 1938, *DDF*, ser. 2, 11:588, 588n.

31. *DDF*, ser. 2, 9:847n.

32. James Leutze, "The Secret of the Churchill-Roosevelt Correspondence: September 1939–May 1940," *Journal of Contemporary History* 10 (July 1975): 483; Welles to Bullitt, 22 October 1937, *FR* (1937), 3:632.

33. *DBPF*, ser. 2, 5:574n.

34. *DGPF*, ser. D, 1:707; the president "does not know what he should do; he can hardly . . . (group missing)."

35. Heinrichs points this out in his biography of Grew (*American Ambassador*, 368).

36. Long's comments are available in his diary at the Library of Congress, and the Bullitt letter can be found in the Robert Kelley Papers at Georgetown University.

37. The pages that were missing in the Long Diary were 1–112 (covering 1933–34), 245–54, 261–62, and 297–300. Page 309 had been razored away.

38. Situations that parallel the case of Nomura in 1941 include Roosevelt's exchanges with French labor leader Léon Jouhaux in 1938 and Japanese officials in 1934 (including Konoye).

39. FDR to Krock, 12 November 1936, box 52, Arthur Krock Papers, Prince-

ton University; James H. Drumm, resumé of interview with FDR, 15 August 1933, FR (1933), 4:656; Graham J. White, *FDR and the Press* (Chicago: University of Chicago Press, 1979), 12; Burns, *Lion and the Fox*, 319, 348.

40. See Thomas H. Greer, *What Roosevelt Thought: The Social and Political Ideas of Franklin D. Roosevelt* (East Lansing: Michigan State University Press, 1958), 184 (quotation) and Roosevelt's Annual Message to Congress, 1939.

41. See, for example, MRP, box 12, FDRL.

42. *Time*, 14 March 1938, p. 11.

43. Franklin D. Roosevelt, "Shall We Trust Japan?" *Asia* 23 (July 1923):475–78, 526, 528; FDR editorial, 30 April 1925, in Donald S. Carmichael, ed., *F.D.R. Columnist: The Uncollected Columns of Franklin D. Roosevelt* (Chicago: Pellegrini and Cudahy, 1947), 57–58, 60.

44. Henry L. Stimson Diary, 31 December 1932, 9 January 1933, Yale University. See also Stimson to FDR, 15 November 1937, PPF, FDRL.

45. See *Letters*, 2:510; James Roosevelt, *My Parents: A Differing View* (Chicago: Playboy Press, 1976), 26, 39–40, 54.

46. FDR to Hull, 14 November 1934, *Letters*, 3:431; FDR to Welles, 28 February 1936, ibid., 565; FDR toast to King George VI and Queen Mary, 8 June 1939, OF 48A, FDRL; Julius W. Pratt, *Cordell Hull, 1933–44,* 2 vols. (New York: Cooper Square, 1964), 2:597. Murray was serving as British military attaché in Washington when he first met FDR during World War II.

47. Long Diary, 12 June 1935, box 5, Breckinridge Long Papers, LC.

48. FDR to Sara Roosevelt, 26 October 1902, *Letters*, 1:481; Franklin D. Roosevelt, "Our Foreign Policy: A Democratic View," *Foreign Affairs* 6 (July 1928):575.

49. FDR to George VI, 22 November 1940, *Letters*, 4:1084.

50. Ibid., 2:9.

51. Smith, "Authoritarianism," 305–8; Edward B. Parsons, *Wilsonian Diplomacy: Allied-American Rivalries in War and Peace* (St. Louis: Forum Press, 1978), 15; William L. Neumann, *America Encounters Japan: From Perry to MacArthur* (Baltimore: Johns Hopkins University Press, 1963), 132, 145, 150–51; Neumann, "Franklin D. Roosevelt and Japan, 1913–1933," *Pacific Historical Review* 22 (May 1953):145–46; Neumann, "Franklin Delano Roosevelt: A Disciple of Admiral Mahan," *U.S. Naval Institute Proceedings* 78 (July 1952):716.

52. Neumann, *Japan*, 139–40, 152–54, 157–58; Smith, "Authoritarianism," 308; Crowley, *Japan's Quest*, 17–23, 35.

53. Robert E. Sherwood, *Roosevelt and Hopkins: An Intimate History* (New York: Harper, 1948), 436; Harold L. Ickes, *The Secret Diary of Harold L. Ickes,* 3 vols. (New York: Simon and Schuster, 1953–54), 2:481; John Foster Dulles, draft of foreign policy statement, 26 January 1944, box 23, Dulles Papers, Princeton University; Parsons, *Wilsonian Diplomacy*, 192–93.

Chapter 1

1. For a detailed citation of authors and their works, see Frederick W. Marks III, "Franklin Roosevelt's Diplomatic Debut: The Myth of the Hundred Days," *South Atlantic Quarterly* 84 (Summer 1985):245–46. According to Langer and Gleason, Roosevelt "was so preoccupied with domestic problems that he had little time or energy for the consideration of foreign affairs." Robert Dallek's assessment, advanced as recently as 1979, remains fundamentally the same. Dallek argues that Britain pressured Roosevelt into an early opening of the London Economic Conference when America's domestic crisis "made foreign relations a secondary concern." Inclined "to move slowly in foreign affairs," FDR canceled plans to go to Europe as president-elect owing to the heat of the economic crisis at home, and it was not until 1934 that he felt free "to pay more mind to foreign relations." Dallek makes no reference to the exhaustive series of foreign policy interviews which Roosevelt chose to conduct on his own. Nor is there any indication of Roosevelt's desire to accelerate the pace of international negotiation and expand his personal role; there is likewise nothing to suggest Governor Gore's unhappy experience in Puerto Rico or Roosevelt's campaign against the collection of foreign debts (the author credits him instead with a "nationalistic" policy on debts). Dallek is equally silent on the defeat of the St. Lawrence Waterway Treaty, the Bullitt exposé, the McReynolds broadcast, and Roosevelt's corresponding press conference. Finally, there is no record of the unraveling of Hull's tariff truces or of Roosevelt's opposition to the Four Power Pact (only the claim that he was "happy to support it," which is misleading at best). These are all points which will be introduced in the course of the following chapter. See Dallek, *Roosevelt*, 23, 27, 41, 58–59, 62, 65, 75, 78, 81, 85; Langer and Gleason, *Challenge to Isolation*, 16.

2. Stanley Baldwin, "Notes on a Visit to the United States," November 1933, book 108, Baldwin Papers, ULC.

3. For the common view, see Divine, "1933," 58; A. J. P. Taylor, *The Origins of the Second World War* (1961; rpt. New York: Atheneum, 1964), 128, 191; Borg, *Far Eastern Crisis*, 22; Howard Jablon, "Cordell Hull, His 'Associates,' and Relations with Japan, 1933–1936," *Mid-America* 56 (July 1974):160; Burns, *Lion and the Fox*, 247–48, 262–63; Dallek, *Roosevelt*, 23, 81, 85; Arthur M. Schlesinger, Jr., *The Coming of the New Deal* (Boston: Houghton Mifflin, 1958), 204–5; Schlesinger, *The Crisis of the Old Order* (Boston: Houghton Mifflin, 1957), 441.

4. Beard, *American Foreign Policy*, 148; Divine, "1933," 59. Borg writes that FDR was "inevitably" preoccupied with domestic affairs; Jablon that he had little time for diplomacy before 1936 (Borg, *Far Eastern Crisis*, 22; Jablon, "Hull," 160). For a similar view, see Accinelli, "World Court," 478; Drummond,

American Neutrality, 21, 372–74; Taylor, *Origins,* 128, 191; and Nancy Harvison Hooker, ed., *The Moffat Papers: Selections from the Diplomatic Journals of Jay Pierrepont Moffat, 1919–1943* (Cambridge, Mass.: Harvard University Press, 1956), 77n. In the dissenting column, one will find Daniel Smith, among others. Smith ("Authoritarianism," 313) maintains that FDR showed a deep interest in foreign affairs from the moment he entered the White House.

5. Stimson Diary, 26 February 1933, Yale University; FDR to Murray, 25 August 1932, file 8808, Lord Elibank Papers, NLS; Lord Astor's Notes on the U.S.A., 24 December 1932, bk. 110, Baldwin Papers, ULC; Davis to FDR, 15 October 1932, box 51, Norman Davis Papers, LC; Davis to Hull, 13 April 1933, 550.S1 Washington/359, RG 59, NA; Davis to Hull, 9 April 1933, 862.00/2947, RG, NA. See also memoranda of various conversations in box 9, Davis Papers, LC. Harrison reported from Bucharest, MacVeagh from Athens.

6. Herridge to Bennett, 14 March 1933, box 275, Richard Bennett Papers (microfilm M1024), PAC; Claudel to Quai d'Orsay, 22 February 1933, dossier 303, AEU, Quai d'Orsay, Paris; Lindsay to Simon, 20 January 1933, *DBFP,* ser. 2, 5:744; British Cabinet Meetings, 13, 22 February 1933, CAB 23/75, PRO; Fleuriau to Simon, 24 February 1932, bk. 121, Baldwin Papers, ULC; Edgar Nixon, ed., *Franklin D. Roosevelt and Foreign Affairs,* 3 vols. (Cambridge, Mass.: Belknap Press of Harvard University, 1969), 1:16–17. Nearly all of the published diplomatic correspondence of France, Germany, and Britain is useful for similar insight into the period.

7. FDR press conference, 31 March 1933, Rosso to FDR, 30 May 1933, Nixon, ed., *Roosevelt,* 1:30, 188–89n. See also, for example, Prittwitz to Foreign Ministry, 16 March, 7 April 1933, Schacht's report on his trip to the United States, Luther to Foreign Ministry, 23 May 1933, *DGFP,* ser. C, 1:174, 263, 479, 486; Herriot to Paul-Boncour, 27 April 1933, Laboulaye to Paul-Boncour, 9 April, 7 June 1933, *DDF,* ser. 1, 3:245, 334, 659; Lindsay to Simon, 25 April 1933, Simon Papers, FO 800/288, PRO; Matsuoka to House, 5 April 1934, box 79, Edward M. House Papers, Yale University; House to FDR, 28 March 1933, PPF 222, FDRL; Hornbeck to Robbins, 10 March 1933, OF, FDRL; Joseph Grew, *The Turbulent Era,* 2 vols. (Boston: Houghton Mifflin, 1952), 2:944; Hornbeck memorandum, 14 September 1933, 033.9411/288, RG 59, NA; Fleuriau to Quai d'Orsay, 25 April 1933, Laboulaye to Quai d'Orsay, 17, 19 April 1933, Herriot to Quai d'Orsay, 25 April 1933, Naggiar to Quai d'Orsay, 13 April 1933, dossier 314, AEU, Quai d'Orsay.

8. Raymond Moley, *After Seven Years* (New York: Harper, 1939), 201, 206–7; Pratt, *Hull,* 1:36; Franklin D. Roosevelt, *On Our Way* (New York: John Day, 1934), 114; *News-Week,* 5 August 1933, p. 11; Eleanor Roosevelt, *This I Remember* (New York: Harper, 1949), 110–11; Herbert Feis, *1933: Characters in Crisis* (Boston: Little, Brown, 1966), 132–34, 137.

9. *Time,* 8 May 1933, p. 9, and 29 May 1933, p. 13; Hooker, ed., *Moffat,* 17

April, 3 May 1933, 93–94; Roosevelt's Address to the Heads of Nations Represented at the London and Geneva Conferences, Nixon, ed., *Roosevelt,* 1:126; Minute to FO document by Howard Smith, 17 May 1933, *DBFP,* ser. 2, 5:250; Morgenthau Farm Credit Administration Diary, 22 May 1933, Morgenthau Papers, FDRL; "Morgenthau Diaries," *Collier's,* 11 October 1947, p. 72; Reminiscences of John Campbell White (1953), 82, CUOHC. In his message of instruction, FDR urged international stabilization of currencies, a freeing of the flow of world trade, the elimination of "offensive" weapons, and a nonaggression pact to limit and reduce arms and also to preclude offensive crossing of frontiers.

10. See note 1, as well as Dallek, *Roosevelt,* 26, 41, 62, 65; Schlesinger, *Coming of the New Deal,* 204–5; also Moley, *Seven Years,* 205–6, and Feis, *1933,* 133, 142–43.

11. Wrong to Skelton, 28 January 1933, Herridge to Skelton, 14 March 1933, Hume Wrong Papers, PAC; Lindsay to Simon, 17 March 1933, Simon Papers, FO 800/291, PRO; Murray to FDR, 13 February 1933, file 8808, Elibank Papers, NLS; Chamberlain to Ida Chamberlain, 29 January 1933, to Hilda Chamberlain, 4 February 1933, NC 18, Neville Chamberlain Papers, BUL; draft message to Sir Ronald Lindsay, undated, Fleuriau to Simon, 24 February 1933, and Lord Astor's notes on the U.S.A., Cliveden, 24 December 1932, books 110 and 121, Baldwin Papers, CUL; Lothian to House, 13 February 1933, GD 40/17, file 200, Lothian to Garvin, 16 February 1933, GD 40/17, file 264, Lord Lothian Papers, SRO; Stimson Diary, 3 February 1933, Yale University; Lindsay to Simon, 30 January 1933, *DBFP,* ser. 2, 5:748; Davis to FDR, 15 November 1932, box 51, Davis Papers, LC (Davis wrote from Geneva: "There is no use in trying to have the Economic Conference before next April or May"); Prittwitz to Foreign Ministry, 16 March 1933, Ritter note on conversation with Davis, 10 April 1933, Schacht to Foreign Ministry, 15 May 1933, *DGFP,* ser. C, 1:174, 273–74, 424; Claudel to Paul-Boncour, 21 February, 9 March 1933, *DDF,* ser. 1, 2:671, 767. James Warburg may or may not be correct in assuming that FDR changed his mind on holding the conference in Washington on account of doubt as to its outcome. It is clear, however, that both Warburg and Bullitt supported the president's desire to hold the conference at an earlier date than planned and in Washington rather than London (Reminiscences of James P. Warburg [1951–52], 2:311, CUOHC).

12. Schacht to Foreign Ministry, 6 May 1933, *DGFP,* ser. C, 1:392; Moley, *Seven Years,* 225; Pratt, *Hull,* 1:154; Maddux, *Estrangement,* 19–26.

13. Moley, *Seven Years,* 203, 225; Cordell Hull, *The Memoirs of Cordell Hull,* 2 vols. (New York: Macmillan, 1948), 1:248–49; Borg, *Far Eastern Crisis,* 62.

14. See, for example, Drummond, *American Neutrality,* 372–74; Burns, *Lion and the Fox,* 262; Albjerg, "Isolationism," 207.

15. Kuehl, "Isolationist Sentiment"; Comte Daniel de Martel to Joseph

Paul-Boncour, 17 July 1933, report of French naval attaché in Washington, 23 September 1933, *DDF*, ser. 1, 4:22–23, 289–90; Travis B. Jacobs, "Roosevelt's Quarantine Speech," *The Historian* 24 (August 1962):501n.

16. Marian G. McKenna, *Borah* (Ann Arbor: University of Michigan Press, 1961), 288–89; *Time*, 6 March 1933, p. 19; Strong to Delano, 11 March 1933, Nixon, ed., *Roosevelt*, 1:22–23; Buchan to Baldwin, 20 December 1934, book 121, Baldwin Papers, ULC; Lord Halifax, *Fullness of Days* (New York: Dodd, Mead, 1957), 296.

17. Kuehl, "Isolationist Sentiment." See also Kuehl, "Webs of Common Interests," and Doenecke, *When the Wicked Rise*.

18. Accinelli, "World Court," 464; Beard, *American Foreign Policy*, 145.

19. Hull to Roosevelt, 27 May 1933, Nixon, ed., *Roosevelt*, 1:184, 184n.; Borg, *Far Eastern Crisis*, 23–24, 29–30; Divine, "1933," 56–59; Fred L. Israel, *Nevada's Key Pittman* (Lincoln: University of Nebraska Press, 1963), 133; Hull, *Memoirs*, 1:228–30.

20. Roosevelt, *Looking Forward* (New York: John Day, 1933), 255; Roosevelt, *On Our Way*, 136; Roosevelt press conference of 3 February 1934, as well as speeches 3 January, 18 May 1934, and 9 December 1935, cited in Sanborn, *Design for War*, 9–10, 15; Laboulaye to Daladier, 3 February 1934, *DDF*, ser. 1, 5:603; William C. Bullitt, "How We Won the War and Lost the Peace," *Life*, 30 August 1948, p. 83; Robert A. Divine, *The Illusion of Neutrality* (Chicago: University of Chicago Press, 1962), 67, 103, 158; FDR to Leland Harrison, 1 November 1935, *Letters*, 3:515; FDR speech of 2 October 1935 (San Diego) quoted in Moley, *Seven Years*, 319; FDR press conferences of 19 and 24 July, 28 August 1935, Nixon, ed., *Roosevelt*, 2:572, 579, 623; FDR speech at Chautauqua, 14 August 1936, ibid., 3:377, 380–82; FDR Message to Congress, January 1936, quoted in Offner, *Appeasement*, 134. So much did Roosevelt allow himself to become identified with Nye that when Hitler addressed the Reichstag on 28 April 1939, he told his listeners that Roosevelt had "appointed" the Nye Committee.

21. Quoted by Albjerg, "Isolationism," 209.

22. Orville H. Bullitt, ed., *For the President, Personal and Secret: Correspondence between Franklin D. Roosevelt and William C. Bullitt* (Boston: Houghton Mifflin, 1972), 21–24; *DGFP*, ser. C, 1:174n.; CAB 23/75, 30 January 1933, PRO; *New York Times*, 3 February 1933, p. 10, 4 February 1933, p. 8, and 5 February 1933, p. 1.

23. Bullitt, ed., *For the President*, 24, 29. Senator Joseph Robinson told colleagues that FDR had flatly denied being represented by Bullitt (*New York Times*, 3 February 1933, p. 10). One can pinpoint other presidential falsehoods between 1933 and 1945, again in connection with foreign policy, and mostly in the form of direct statements to the American people. For example, on 2 March 1934, Roosevelt told the press that Norman Davis was going to Europe "purely

and solely in a private capacity" and would not "have anything to do with the Government work" until and unless there occurred a meeting in Geneva. Several days later, Davis was meeting with the British prime minister (FDR press conference, 2 March 1934; Bingham to FDR, 8 March 1934, Nixon, ed., *Roosevelt*, 2:4, 16). Asked by reporters on 9 May whether Moscow had made any offer on the question of debts, Roosevelt replied "no." Asked on 15 August by the press if he had reviewed the Russian debt situation, he responded, "I have not had time to talk about it at all." Both statements were untrue (Maddux, *Estrangement*, 36). On 12 October 1939, two weeks before he ordered the American navy to cooperate with the Royal Navy in the unneutral tracking of German vessels, Roosevelt wrote Robert Wood that although one could not be neutral in thought, this ought not affect "neutrality of action in any shape, manner, or form" (*Letters*, 4:938; James O. Richardson, *On the Treadmill to Pearl Harbor: The Memoirs of Admiral James O. Richardson* [Washington, D.C.: Department of the Navy, 1973], 157). On 16 August 1940, Roosevelt told reporters that negotiations between Washington and London for the use of British bases by the United States were in no way connected with any plan to transfer American destroyers to the Royal Navy—another fabrication. See Langer and Gleason, *Challenge to Isolation*, 761. During the fall campaign, after almost certainly making a secret commitment to defend British possessions in the Far East and with definite plans to embark upon a program of greatly increased aid to Britain, which would almost certainly draw America into the war, FDR assured the American people that "your boys are not going to be sent into any foreign wars" (Madison Square Garden, 30 October); again, in Buffalo on 2 November: "Your president says this country is not going to war" (Langer and Gleason, *Undeclared War*, 207; Charles A. Beard, "Roosevelt Deceived the Public," in Robert Dallek, ed., *The Roosevelt Diplomacy and World War II* [New York: Holt, Rinehart and Winston, 1970], 10). On 21 January 1941, Roosevelt told reporters, when questioned about convoys, that he had never given any thought to the question. A day later, he admitted to Stimson that he had (Warren F. Kimball, *The Most Unsordid Act: Lend Lease, 1939–1941* [Baltimore: Johns Hopkins University Press, 1969], 180). On 18 August, Roosevelt wrote Churchill that a warning he had given the Japanese was "no less vigorous than and was substantially similar to the statement we had discussed." This was not the case (FDR to Churchill, 18 August 1941, FO 371/27909, PRO). On 6 September, Roosevelt grossly misrepresented the facts of the *Greer* incident with obvious intent to foment war sentiment (Dallek, *Roosevelt*, 287). In 1943, he denied to Churchill that he had approached Stalin (through Joseph Davies) with an eye to a personal meeting à deux. In fact, he had done just this (Elizabeth Kimball MacLean, "Joseph E. Davies and Soviet-American Relations, 1941–43," *Diplomatic History* 4 [Winter 1980]:92). In 1944, he assured Polish Prime Minister Mikolajczyk that he had opposed the Curzon Line as Poland's eastern boundary during talks with Stalin at Teheran. In truth, he had not (FR [Malta and Yalta], 204–5). On 1 March 1945, he denied at a joint session of Congress that Far Eastern questions had been discussed at Yalta. The fact is they had (Theoharis, "Byrnes," 584).

24. British Cabinet Meeting Minutes, 30 January 1933, CAB 23/75, PRO.

25. Bullitt to FDR, 13 June 1933, Bullitt, ed., *For the President*, 35; Moley, *Seven Years*, 225, 239n.; *Time*, 26 June 1933, p. 16; Bingham Diary, 19 June 1933, box 1, Robert Bingham Papers, LC. One of the best accounts to date of the London Conference was written by a participant, Herbert Feis. See Feis, *1933*, chaps. 17–20, esp. pp. 144, 341–43.

26. *Time*, 26 June 1933, p. 16; Ickes, *Diary*, 1:76–77; Jeanette P. Nichols, "Roosevelt's Monetary Diplomacy in 1933," *American Historical Review* 56 (January 1951):314–16; Bingham Diary, 1 July 1933, box 1, Bingham Papers, LC; Chamberlain to Hilda Chamberlain, 15 July 1933, NC 18, Chamberlain Papers, BUL; Harold Macmillan, *Winds of Change, 1914–1939* (New York: Harper, 1966), 270; FDR to George V, 16 May 1933, RA GVK2378/1, George V Papers, Royal Archives, Windsor Castle. Bullitt had taken the trouble in January to ascertain from MacDonald and Chamberlain that it would be possible for Britain to return to gold (Bullitt to FDR, 23 January 1933, PPF, 1124, FDRL).

27. All along, French and British newspapers had been representing the American delegation as having no plan or coordination and being out of touch with the president (Bingham Diary, 26 June 1933, box 1, Bingham Papers, LC).

28. *Spectator* 151 (July–December 1933), 7 July, p. 4; Chamberlain to [Ida Chamberlain?], 7 October 1933, to Hilda Chamberlain, 21 October 1933, NC 18, Chamberlain Papers, BUL.

29. Pratt, *Hull*, 1:49, 64–66; Nichols, "Monetary Diplomacy," 316; *Time*, 10 July 1933, p. 15. The stabilization proposal would have been more or less on American terms (Nichols, "Monetary Diplomacy," 301–2, 316).

30. Albjerg, "Isolationism," 205–6; *Contemporary Review*, vol. 144. For additional insight into the difficult question of why FDR might have acted as he did, see Feis, *1933*, 224–25, 232–33; Elliot A. Rosen, *Hoover, Roosevelt, and the Brains Trust* (New York: Columbia University Press, 1977), 362–80.

31. Stimson's report on his trip to Britain, 1933, Stimson Diary, Yale University; Memorandum by Krock of interview with James Cox, 8 August 1933, box 1, Krock Papers, Princeton University. See also Israel, *Pittman*, and Bingham Diary, 12, 26, 29 June 1933, box 1, Bingham Papers, LC; Feis, *1933*, 173, 189.

32. *Time*, 26 June 1933, p. 17, and 3 July 1933, p. 34; Bullitt to FDR, 13 June 1933, Rosenberg to Bullitt, 10 July 1933, Bullitt, ed., *For the President*, 35–36; Krock memorandum of conversation and interview with James Cox, 8 August 1933, box 1, Krock Papers, Princeton University; Bingham Diary, 29 June 1933, box 1, Bingham Papers, LC.

33. Krock memorandum of conversation and interview, 8 August 1933, box 1, Krock Papers, Princeton University; *Time*, 3 July 1933, p. 34.

34. D'Arcy to Vansittart, 24 August 1934, bk. 109, Baldwin Papers, ULC. Bullitt, who clung to the belief that "if all is not right with the world, all is right with the United States," began to enthuse about dealings with the Soviet Union. "Our future," he cabled, "lies in the Americas and the Far East" (Bullitt to FDR [January 1933?], PPF 1124, FDRL; Bullitt, ed., *For the President*, 37).

35. Press conference, 31 May 1933, Nixon, ed., *Roosevelt*, 1:193; Roosevelt press conference, 5 August 1933, *The Complete Presidential Press Conferences of Franklin D. Roosevelt*, 25 vols. (New York: Da Capo Press, 1972), 2:143–45, 147.

36. Long Diary, 28 February, 28 March 1936, box 5, Long Papers, LC; Eden memorandum, 1 September 1937, vol. 29, Avon Papers, BUL. See also Gade to Hull, 3 February 1937 (holding out hope that Belgium might become the first European country to negotiate a debt settlement with the United States), 033.5511 Van Zeeland, Paul/1, RG 59, NA; Dodd to Hull, 9 April 1937, 600.0031 World Program/71, RG 59, NA. Republicans in their campaign platform of 1936 pledged "every effort to collect the war debt."

37. Moley, *Seven Years*, 69–70; Castle to Hoover, 7 January 1933?, box 24, William Castle Papers, Herbert Hoover Library, West Branch, Iowa. The Lausanne Conference of 1932 agreed to cancel all German reparations until better conditions returned to Germany.

38. Sara Roosevelt to FDR, 4 April 1927, 25 November 1932, 27, 30 June 1933, 5 September 1937, boxes 9 and 10, Roosevelt Family Papers, FDRL; Pratt, *Hull*, 2:597–99.

39. Maddux, *Estrangement*, 21, 26, 161.

40. Roosevelt, *Looking Forward*, 249; Nixon, ed., *Roosevelt*, 2:26–27n.; Pratt, *Hull*, 1:273–78.

41. Cabinet Minutes, 30 January 1933, CAB 23/75, PRO; Chamberlain to Ida Chamberlain, 25 February 1933, NC 18, Chamberlain Papers, BUL; Nixon, ed., *Roosevelt*, 1:13n.; Lindsay to Simon, 30 January 1933, *DBFP*, ser. 2, 5:748–49; Davis to Hull, 13 April 1933, 550.S1 Washington/359, RG 59, NA; Fleuriau to Simon, 24 February 1933, bk. 121, Baldwin Papers, ULC; Dallek, *Roosevelt*, 28.

42. Chamberlain to Hilda Chamberlain, 4 October 1933, to Ida Chamberlain, 9 June 1934, NC 18, Chamberlain Papers, BUL; *Time*, 26 June 1933, p. 15; *News-Week*, 7 October 1933, p. 13; Lindsay to Simon, 4 June 1933, *DBFP*, ser. 2, 5:815.

43. Lindsay to Simon, 18 May 1934, *DBFP*, ser. 2, 6:926, 928.

44. Hjalmar Schacht, *Confessions of the "Old Wizard": The Autobiography of Hjalmar Horace Greeley Schacht* (1955; Westport, Conn.: Greenwood Press, 1974), 283; Pratt, *Hull*, 1:183, 186–87. For the views of Herbert Feis and William Bullitt on how FDR should have handled Schacht, see Feis, *1933*, 139.

45. Lord Astor's notes on the U.S.A., 24 December 1932, bk. 110, Baldwin Papers, ULC; Stimson Diary, 20 January 1933, Yale University; John Stevenson to Lord Lothian, 5 January 1933, Lothian to Colonel House, 13 February 1933,

and clipping from *New York Times*, 4 February 1933, GD 40/17, files 199 and 200, Lothian Papers, SRO; Nixon, ed., *Roosevelt*, 1:95n.; FDR memorandum for Hull, 1 April 1933, OF 29, FDRL; Hoover to Stimson, January 1933, PPF 716, FDRL; FO instructions to Lindsay, February 1933, Lindsay to Vansittart, 24 March 1933, to Simon, 17 October 1933, *DBFP*, ser. 2, 5:782, 847; Davis to Hull, 13 April 1933, 550.S1 Washington/359, RG 59, NA.

46. Chamberlain to Buchan, 19 November 1937, box 9, Lord Tweedsmuir Papers, Queens University, Kingston, Canada; Monnet to Daladier, 19 May 1939, Monnet memorandum, 18 May 1939, French memorandum, July 1939 (author unknown), 4 DA 6, dr. 3, sdr. b, Edouard Daladier Papers, FNSP; Monnet to Reynaud, 21 September 1939, 74 AP17, de Beaumont to Daladier, 22 April 1939, Gaucheron to Quai d'Orsay, 4 April 1935, F 60/454, Archives Nationales, Paris; Laboulaye to Barthou, 22 February, 12 April 1934, *DDF*, ser. 1, 5:799; 6:206, 208; Pratt, *Hull*, 1:204−5; Straus to House, 25 September 1934, 8 March 1935; House to Cudahy, 29 January 1934, boxes 32 and 107, House Papers, Yale University; Phipps to Halifax, 26 March 1938, MSS 14, Eric Phipps Papers, CCC; Mallet Memoirs, 56, Victor Mallet Papers, CCC; John W. Wheeler-Bennett, *King George VI* (New York: St. Martin's Press, 1958), 392; Roosevelt to MacVeagh, 16 January 1934, PPF 4083, FDRL.

47. George W. Grayson, Jr., "The Era of the Good Neighbor," *Current History* 56 (June 1969):327; Welles, *Time for Decision*, 202.

48. Stimson Diary, 9 January 1933, Yale University; *News-Week*, 5 August 1933, p. 11; *Time*, 21 August 1933, p. 16; Welles to Hull, 19 August 1933, *FR* (1933), 5:368.

49. Presidential press conference, 27 September 1933, Nixon, ed., *Roosevelt*, 1:409; Welles to Hull, 3 October 1933, OF 470, FDRL; *Time*, 6 November 1933, p. 26, and 5 February 1934, p. 23; Guerrant, *Good Neighbor*, 5; Laboulaye to Paul-Boncour, 20 December 1933, dossier 303, AEU, Quai d'Orsay. A good general account of U.S. relations with Cuba during 1933 is Robert Freeman Smith, *The United States and Cuba: Business and Diplomacy, 1917−1960* (New York: Bookman Associates, 1960), chap. 10.

50. Spruille Braden, *Diplomats and Demagogues* (New York: Arlington House, 1971), 114; *News-Week*, 4 November 1933, p. 7, 23 December 1933, p. 12; *Time*, 6 November 1933, p. 21, and 18 December 1933, p. 15, 22 January 1934, p. 14; Pratt, *Hull*, 1:157. A typical appraisal in the American press is *News-Week*, 30 December 1933, p. 10. Secretary of State Charles Evans Hughes had stood firm against similar pressure at Havana (to thunderous applause), but the Latin American demand for an explicitly noninterventionist policy can be traced at least as far back as 1928 (Lester D. Langley, *The United States and the Caribbean, 1900−1970* [Athens: University of Georgia Press, 1980], 125−27; Haglund, *Latin America*, 46).

51. Acting Secretary of State to Long, 7 June 1933, *FR* (1933), 1:416; La-

boulaye to Paul-Boncour, 19 April, 1933; Herriot to Paul-Boncour, 26 April 1933, *DDF*, ser. 1, 3:246, 327; Moffat memorandum, 24 March 1933, *FR* (1933), 1:397. Italy asked for American support on 31 March (in London), 11 April (in Paris), 12 May (again in London), and 31 May and 3 June (in Rome) (Davis to FDR, 13 April 1933, box 51, Davis Papers, LC; Atherton to Hull, 31 March 1933, Davis memorandum, 13 April 1933, Atherton to Hull, 12 April 1933, Long to Hull, 6 June 1933, *FR* [1933], 1:400, 403–4, 410, 412, 415; James Francis Watts, Jr., "The Public Life of Breckinridge Long, 1916–1944" [Ph.D. dissertation, University of Missouri, 1964], 104; Atherton to Hull, 12 May 1933, Davis to Hull, 21 May 1933, Long to Hull, 31 May, 3 June 1933, 740.0011 Four Power Pact/69, 78, 84, 88, RG 59, NA; Laboulaye to Quai d'Orsay, 25 April 1933, Herriot [to Quai d'Orsay?], received 25 April 1933, AEU, Quai d'Orsay).

52. Davis to Moffat, 18 October 1933, box 41, Davis Papers, LC; Roosevelt-MacDonald conversation, 23 April 1933, Phillips memorandum, 26 April 1933, Atherton to Hull, 12 May 1933, Davis to Hull, 28 September 1933, *FR* (1933), 1:103, 110, 138, 233; Massigli to Paul-Boncour, 18 March 1933, Laboulaye to Paul-Boncour, 25 April 1933, memorandum by French delegates to the disarmament conference, 27 April 1933, *DDF*, ser. 1, 3:21, 316–17, 337; Vansittart to Simon, 5 May 1933, Simon Papers, FO 800/288, PRO; Offner, *Appeasement*, 23–24; memorandum of a conversation between FDR, Herriot, Laboulaye, and Phillips, 26 April 1933, 550.S1 Washington/359, RG 59, NA; Joachim von Ribbentrop, *The Ribbentrop Memoirs* (London: Weidenfeld and Nicolson, 1954), 104.

53. FDR to Davis, 21, 30 August 1933, Davis to FDR, 15 October 1932, memorandum of Roosevelt-Davis phone conversation, 28 April 1933, boxes 9 and 51, Davis Papers, LC; memorandum of Roosevelt-Davis phone conversation, 9 October 1933, 500.A15A4 General Committee/623, RG 59, NA; Davis to Hull, 28 April and 11 October 1933, *FR* (1933), 1:117, 246–47, 252.

54. Laboulaye to Quai d'Orsay, 25 April 1933, Herriot to (Quai d'Orsay?), undated, dossier 314, AEU, Quai d'Orsay; Long to FDR, 15 December 1933, Nixon, ed., *Roosevelt*, 1:534–37; Dallek, *Roosevelt*, 67–68.

55. *News-Week*, 25 November 1933, p. 13.

56. Chamberlain to Hilda Chamberlain, 18 March, 1, 9 April 1933, NC 18, Chamberlain Papers, BUL; Lindsay to Vansittart, 24 March 1933, *DBFP*, ser. 2, 5:781–82, 793 n.1; memorandum of conversation between Davis and MacDonald, 4 May 1933, box 9, Davis Papers, LC; Bullitt to LeHand, 30 or 31 January 1933, Bullitt, ed., *For the President*, 27–28; Pratt, *Hull*, 1:37; Bullitt, "Lost the Peace," 83; Dallek, *Roosevelt*. 23, 27; Divine, "1933," 56–57; memorandum of conversation between Roosevelt, Herriot, Laboulaye, and Phillips, 26 April 1933, 550.S1 Washington/359, RG 59, NA. According to Phillips, Roosevelt had promised to "abandon our rights of neutrality."

57. Nixon, ed., *Roosevelt*, 1:189n.

58. Morris to Hull, 16 November 1933, 550.S1/1304 (see rest of file as well), RG 59, NA. See also *DDF*, ser. 1, vol. 3.

59. For FDR's discussion of this treaty with the press, see Nixon, ed., *Roosevelt*, 1:165. Additional reverses dogged him to his death in 1945.

60. Dallek, *Roosevelt*, 39.

61. Kelley memorandum, 27 July 1933, Kelley to Hull, 26 May 1936, Bullitt to Hull, 16 November 1936, box 3, Robert Kelley Papers, Georgetown University; Keith D. Eagles, "Ambassador Joseph E. Davies and American-Soviet Relations, 1937–1941" (Ph.D. dissertation, University of Washington, 1966), 66–70.

62. Morgenthau Farm Credit Administration Diary, 29 May 1933, 38, Morgenthau Papers, FDRL; British Cabinet Meeting, 17 May 1933, CAB 23/76, PRO; minute on FO document by Howard Smith, 17 May 1933, *DBFP*, ser. 2, 5:250; Israel, *Pittman*, 94.

63. *Time*, 18 December 1933, p. 7.

64. Roosevelt Address to Congress, 3 January 1934, Nixon, ed., *Roosevelt*, 1:573; Bullitt to FDR, 7 April 1935, FDR to Bullitt, 21 April 1935, Bullitt, ed., *For the President*, 103, 106, 113.

65. A. J. P. Taylor has pointed this out in *Origins*, 61.

Chapter 2

1. Seiji Hishida, *Japan among the Great Powers: A Survey of Her International Relations* (London: Longman's Green, 1940), 339; A. E. Hindmarsh, "The Realistic Foreign Policy of Japan," *Foreign Affairs* 13 (January 1935):262; K. K. Kawakami, "Britain's Trade War with Japan," *Foreign Affairs* 12 (April 1934):483–94.

2. Russell D. Buhite, *Nelson T. Johnson and American Policy toward China, 1925–1941* (East Lansing: Michigan State University Press, 1968), 69–70. In 1936, the Soviets had signed a joint defense agreement with Outer Mongolia and were clearly bidding for more (Shigemitsu, *Japan*, 94–95).

3. Shigemitsu, *Japan*, 94; Richard J. Grigg, "Japanese-American Relations, 1931–1937" (Ph.D. dissertation, Georgetown University, 1950), 193, 237–38.

4. Crowley, *Japan's Quest*, 226; Daniel T. J. Liu, "A Study of Diplomatic Relations between China and the United States of America: The Sino-Japanese War, 1937–1941," *Chinese Culture* 15 (December 1974):35n.

5. Hindmarsh, "Japan," 269; Christopher G. Thorne, *The Limits of Foreign Policy: The West, the League, and the Far Eastern Crisis of 1931–1933* (London: Hamish Hamilton, 1972), 32.

6. Henry L. Stimson and McGeorge Bundy, *On Active Service in Peace and War* (New York: Harper, 1947), 225; Walter H. Mallory, "The Permanent Conflict in Manchuria," *Foreign Affairs* 10 (January 1932):222–23. One of the very

best sources for this aspect of the situation is a brilliant 105-page memorandum by John Van A. MacMurray entitled "Developments Affecting American Policy in the Far East," November 1935, vol. 86 (1937), Grew Papers, Houghton Library, Harvard University.

7. William L. Neumann, "Ambiguity and Ambivalence in Ideas of National Interest in Asia," in Alexander DeConde, ed., *Isolation and Security* (Durham: Duke University Press, 1957), 140–44; Mallory, "Permanent Conflict," p. 222.

8. Hishida, *Japan*, 289; Grew to Hull, 24 March 1933, FR (1933), 3:247; Buhite, *Johnson*, 66; MacMurray memorandum, 1 November 1935, vol. 86, Grew Diary (1937), GP; see esp. 2, 4, 55, 58–59, 67, 80, 83, 86, 88, 93ff.

9. Kiyoshi Karl Kawakami, *Manchukuo: Child of Conflict* (New York: Macmillan, 1933), 99; James A. B. Scherer, *Manchukuo: A Bird's Eye View* (Tokyo: Hokuseido Press, 1933), 26–27; Shigemitsu, *Japan*, 98; P. O. O'Hara, *Manchukuo: The World's Newest Nation* (Mukden: Manchuria Daily News, 1932), 63. Obviously, France's presence in British North America never approached Japan's in Manchukuo.

10. Sadao Asada, "Japan's 'Special Interests' and the Washington Conference, 1921–22," *American Historical Review* 67 (October 1961):69–70.

11. Grew to Hull, 8 February 1934, 893.01—Manchuria/1013, RG 59, NA; Grew to Hull, Johnson to Hull, 6 March, Lockhart to Hull, 17, 19 April, Grew to Hull, 22 April 1933, FR (1933), 3:224, 269, 280, 285.

12. Kawakami, *Manchukuo*, 16; M. S. Myers to Johnson, 3 February 1934, Grew to Hull, 8 February 1934, Johnson memorandum of conversation with Chinese vice-minister for foreign affairs, 19 March 1934, Johnson to Hull, 11 April 1934, FR (1934), 3:24–25, 31, 81–82, 107; Hishida, *Japan*, 340–41; James E. Walsh, Visitation Diaries, 10 November 1938, James E. Walsh Papers, Maryknoll Archives.

13. Corbin to Delbos, 23 December 1937, dossier 382, AEU, Quai d'Orsay; Welles memorandum, 24 November 1939, Grew to Hull, 4 December 1939, FR (Japan), 2:36–37; Frederick C. Adams, "The Road to Pearl Harbor: A Reexamination of American Far Eastern Policy, July 1937–December 1938," *Journal of American History* 58 (June 1971):78; Myers to Hull, 31 March 1934, 693.001 Manchuria/21, RG 59, NA; John W. Masland, "Commercial Influence upon American Far Eastern Policy, 1937–1941," *Pacific Historical Review* 11 (September 1942):293–94, 297–99; Reverend James M. Drought, "Working Analysis" (undated, most likely late 1940), box 5, James M. Drought Papers, Maryknoll Archives; Hishida, *Japan*, 343; Grigg, "Japanese-American Relations," 182; Errol MacGregor Clauss, "The Roosevelt Administration and Manchukuo, 1933–1941," *The Historian* 32 (August 1970):608; Heinrichs, *Grew*, 261; Neumann, *Japan*, 226–27.

14. Masland, "Commercial Influence," 282–84. Only 19 percent of American businesses in 1941 favored a policy of economic sanctions against Japan

(ibid., 296). For an excellent breakdown of investment and trade statistics, see Henry to Delbos, 10 September 1937, dossier 381, AEU, Quai d'Orsay.

15. *Contemporary Review* 152 (July–December 1937); Sedgwick to Lothian, 30 November 1934, GD 40/17, file 287, Lothian Papers, SRO; Martel to Paul-Boncour, 17 July 1933, report of French naval attaché, 2 September 1933, *DDF,* ser. 1, 4:22–23, 289–90; *Time,* 3 July 1933, p. 22.

16. Neumann, "Ambiguity," 140; John W. Masland, "Missionary Influence upon American Far Eastern Policy," *Pacific Historical Review* 10 (September 1941):279–80, 287, 290.

17. Moffatt Diplomatic Journal, vol. 39, 29 September, 10 October 1937, J. Pierrepont Moffat Papers, Houghton Library, Harvard University; Hornbeck to Phillips, 2 January 1934, PPF, FDRL; Hornbeck memorandum, 9 May 1933, PSF 37, FDRL; James C. Thomson, Jr., "The Role of the Department of State" in Borg and Okamoto, eds., *Pearl Harbor,* 82, 85; Hornbeck to Hull, 26 February 1934, PSF 60, FDRL.

18. For Bullitt, see Bullitt to FDR, 7 December 1937, Bullitt, ed., *For the President,* 244.

19. House to Lothian, 13 December 1934, GD 40/17, file 282, Lothian Papers, SRO; FDR to House, undated (spring of 1934?), House to FDR, 9 October 1934, Straus to House, 9 April 1934, Straus to House, 25 September 1934, Cudahy to House, 29 December 1933, Long to House, 27 May, 2 November, 17 July 1933, Dodd to House, 22 September 1933, boxes 32, 39, 71, 95, 107, House Papers, Yale University; Bingham file, PPF 716, FDRL; House to FDR, 28 March 1933, PPF 222, FDRL.

20. FDR to House, 10 April 1935, PPF 222, FDRL.

21. See the Elibank Papers, in particular House to Murray, 14 November 1932, 12 January 1933, FDR to Murray, 18 January 1933, file 8808, Elibank Papers, NLS; also Lansbury to Baldwin, 27 August 1936, bk. 129, Baldwin Papers, ULC; Lothian to House, 13 February 1933, House to Lothian, 13 December 1934, GD 40/17, files 200, 282, Lothian Papers, SRO; Murray to House, 12 March 1933, Konoye to House, 9 August 1934 and undated, House to Straus, 9 November 1935, House to Straus, 23 June 1936, Matsuoka to House, 13 April 1933, House to Long, 21 October 1933, Long to House, 27 May 1933, Hull to House, 13 June 1936, Makino to House (1936?), boxes 63, 67, 71, 76, 79, 82a, 107, House Papers, Yale University; Grew to Hull, 27 February 1935, *FR* (1935), 3:853; Hornbeck memorandum, 25 June 1936, *FR* (1936), 4:222.

22. House to Lothian, 13 December 1934, GD 40/17, file 282, Lothian Papers, SRO; Matsuoka to House, 13 April 1933, House to Matsuoka, 25 April 1934, House to FDR, 9 October 1934, Hull to House, 13 June 1936, boxes 63, 79, 95, House Papers, Yale University; Hornbeck memorandum, 25 June 1936, *FR* (1936), 4:222; House to FDR, 28 March 1933, PPF 222, FDRL.

23. House to Yasuo Fuwa, 8 February 1936, Konoye to House, 21 September

1935, Grew to House, 20 January 1938, boxes 47, 52, 67, House Papers, Yale University.

24. Watts, "Breckinridge Long," 76n.; memorandum by Messersmith (undated), file 1980, George S. Messersmith Papers, University of Delaware.

25. Heinrichs, *Grew,* 158, 212–13, 216; Grew to Hull, 27 August 1937, *FR* (1937), 3: 487; Grew to Hull, 11 May 1933, Nixon, ed., *Roosevelt,* 1:178–80; Grew, personal notes, September 1940 (reference to 1934), 101:4510, Grew Diary, GP; Grew to Hull, 27 December 1934, cited in Borg, *Far Eastern Crisis,* 524.

26. Grew, personal note, November 1939, vol. 94, Grew Diary, GP; also Grew Diary, 19–30 May 1939, Grew to FDR, 14 December 1940, 101:4075, ibid.; Grew to FDR, 21 December 1939, OF 594, FDRL; Heinrichs, *Grew,* 189, 211, 221–22. For similar equivocation on Germany, where Grew was stationed before World War I, see ibid., 1–33, 233.

27. Rita Halle Kleeman, *Gracious Lady: The Life of Sara Delano Roosevelt* (New York: D. Appleton-Century, 1935), 1–17; Daniel W. Delano, Jr., *Franklin Roosevelt and the Delano Influence* (Pittsburgh: James S. Nudi Publications, 1946), chaps. 9 and 10; Barbara Tuchman, *Stilwell and the American Experience in China, 1911–1945* (1970; New York: Bantam, 1972, paperback), 220; *Letters,* 1:18n.

28. FDR to Sara and James Roosevelt, 16 May 1899, FDR to Sara Roosevelt, 11 June 1905, FDR to Stephen Early, 19 October 1939, *Letters,* 1:310, 2:7, 4:943; Stimson Diary, 17 May 1934, Yale University; Ross T. McIntire, *White House Physician* (New York: G. P. Putnam's Sons, 1946), 109; MacDonald's report to the British Cabinet, 5 May 1933, CAB 23/76, PRO; Lindsay to Simon, 15 February 1934, Simon Papers, FO 414/272, PRO; Bullitt to LeHand, 22, 26 January 1933, Bullitt, ed., *For the President,* 26–27; Lindsay to Simon, 8 March 1933, *DBFP,* ser. 2, 5:778. Davis at one point asked MacDonald why he was so pro-Japanese (Davis to Hull, 13 April 1933, 550.S1 Washington/359, RG 59, NA).

29. Claudel to Quai d'Orsay, 2 April 1933, dossier 320, AEU, Quai d'Orsay; Heinrichs, *Grew,* 213; FDR to House, 5 April 1933, PPF 222, FDRL; Stimson to Grew, 1 March 1933, 033.9411/282, RG 59, NA; Matsuoka to House, 15 April 1933, box 79, House Papers, Yale University; FDR press conference, 31 March 1933, Nixon, ed., *Roosevelt,* 1:30, 172n.; file 033.9411 Matsuoka, Yosuke/42, RG 59, NA; Borg, *Far Eastern Crisis,* 36; Grew, *Turbulent Era,* 2:944.

30. Phillips to Grew, 15 June 1933, Hornbeck memorandum of conversation with Japanese counselor, 25 July 1933, *FR* (1933), 3:745–47; *Department of State Bulletin,* 10 June 1933; Phillips to Grew, 15 June 1933, 711.9412 B/2 and 3, RG 59, NA; Havas news dispatch, 12 June 1933, dossier 133, Asia-Japon, Quai d'Orsay.

31. Grew, *Turbulent Era,* 2:944; Laboulaye to Quai d'Orsay, 5 November

1933, dossier 320, AEU, Quai d'Orsay; Grew to Hull, 31 August 1933, *FR* (1933), 3:707–8; Laboulaye to Paul-Boncour, 14 October 1933, *DDF*, ser. 1, 4:574; Document File Note (undated) and Grew to Hull, 11 October 1933, 711.9412 B/12 and 13, RG 59, NA. The first American arbitration treaty with Japan was signed by William Howard Taft on 5 May 1908; it was then extended three times and permitted to expire 24 August 1928. According to Hornbeck, Tokyo refused to agree to the format of treaties which the United States had signed with other countries (Hornbeck to Phillips, 21 December 1933, 033.9411 Tokugawa, Iyesato/6½, RG 59, NA).

32. Howell to FDR, 20 January 1934, PPF 604, FDRL; FDR to Howell, 25 January 1934, Nixon, ed., *Roosevelt*, 1:610; State Department draft, 10 February 1934, OF 197, FDRL; Lindsay to Simon, 15 February 1934, Simon Papers, FO 414/272, PRO.

33. Grew to Hull, 5 April, 4 May 1934, *FR* (1934), 3:641, 649–50; Rengo News Agency dispatches, 24, 27 January 1934, dossier 321; Corbin to Quai d'Orsay, 24 February 1934, dossier 385, AEU, Quai d'Orsay.

34. Pila (French ambassador in Tokyo) to Barthou, 4 July 1934, *DDF*, ser. 1, 6:869; Hull, *Memoirs*, 1:278; FDR to Hull, 26 February 1934, Nixon, ed., *Roosevelt*, 1:654; Hornbeck to Phillips, 2 January 1934, PPF 604, FDRL; Quai d'Orsay note on Japanese policy, undated, dossier 385, AEU, Quai d'Orsay.

35. Grew to Hull, 21 February 1934, Hornbeck memorandum, 24 April 1934, Cunningham to Hull, 10 June 1935, *FR* (1934), 3:44–45, 129, *FR* (1935), 3:224. Roosevelt had also encouraged Soong in a scheme to form an international consultative committee to the point of suggesting names of prominent Americans. By 1 November 1933, Soong was out of office and the scheme had died, but the United States accepted a role in the League's technical project for reconstruction of China (Hornbeck to Hull, 28 September 1933, Prentice Gilbert to Hull, 26 September 1933, 893.50A/67 and 68, RG 59, NA).

36. Borg, *Far Eastern Crisis*, 80–81, 523; Buhite, *Johnson*, 96; Hull to Grew, 28 April 1934, *FR* (Japan), 1:231–32; bulletin from Agence Economique et Financiere, 17 April 1934, undated memorandum from the Quai d'Orsay (May?) 1934, dossier 385, AEU, Quai d'Orsay.

37. Borg, *Far Eastern Crisis*, 92–93, 98; Crowley, *Japan's Quest*, 198–99; Saito to Hull, (16?) May 1934, *FR* (Japan), 1:232–33; Hull memorandum, 16 May 1934, 711.94/970½ RG 59, NA; Lindsay to Simon, 31 May 1934, Simon Papers, FO 414/272, PRO.

38. Lindsay to Simon, 31 May 1934, Simon Papers, FO 414/272, PRO; Reuters news dispatch, 13 June 1934, dossier 385, AEU, Quai d'Orsay; Phillips to Grew, 11 June 1934, Grew to Hull, 13 June 1934, *FR* (1934), 3:662; Grew to Hull, 13 June 1934, 811.001 Roosevelt Visit/19, RG 59, NA.

39. Patterson memorandum, 27 February 1934, Satterthwaite to FDR, 27 January 1934, 811.001 Roosevelt Visit/1 and 4, RG 59, NA; Hull to Bullitt, 17

May 1934, FDR to Hull, 15 May 1934, 123 Bullitt, William C./63½ and 64, RG 59, NA.

40. Phillips memorandum of conversation with Roosevelt, 11 June 1934, 033.9411 Konoye, Fuminaro/14, RG 59, NA. For additional data on Saito in 1934, see vol. 95, Grew Diary, GP.

41. Hull to Grew, 6 August 1934, 711.94/974A, RG 59, NA; Henry to Quai d'Orsay, 24 June 1934, dossier 133, Asia-Japon, Havas and Reuters news dispatches, 26–27 June 1934, dossier·385, AEU, Quai d'Orsay. For Roosevelt's denial, as issued by Hull, see Hull to Grew, 15 June 1934, *FR* (1934), 3:663.

42. OF 197, FDRL.

43. Pila to Barthou, 4 July 1934, *DDF*, ser. 1, 6:869.

44. It should be noted that although relations with the United States were undoubtedly a cause of Saito's fall from power in 1934, there were other factors as well, including a succession of scandals and the unsatisfactory outcome to trade conferences with Britain and the Netherlands (Grew to Hull, 2 July 1934, 894.00 PR/79, RG 59, NA).

45. *Time*, 9 October 1933, p. 23.

46. Drought memorandum for the acting secretary of state, 1 November 1934, OF 197, FDRL; Drought to Buell, 28 August 1934, box 2, Drought Papers, Maryknoll; Hornbeck memorandum, 26 June 1934, *FR* (1934), 3:665.

47. Bullitt to Hull, 21 March 1934, 711.6112 (aggressor)/4, RG 59, NA; Chamberlain Diary, 9, 30 October 1934, NC 2/23a, Chamberlain Papers, BUL; note by Mr. Orde of the FO, 28 August 1934, *DBFP*, ser. 2, 13:19.

48. FDR to Davis, 9 November 1934, box 51, Davis Papers, LC; Dallek, *Roosevelt*, 89; Chamberlain Diary, 9 October 1934, NC 2/23a, Chamberlain Papers, BUL; Phipps to Simon, 10 December 1933, *DBFP*, ser. 2, 5:187–88; Grigg, "Japanese-American Relations," 184, 190; Corbin to Doumergue, 12 April 1934, *DDF*, ser. 1, 6:209.

49. Hornbeck to Phillips, 21 December 1933, 033.9411 Tokugawa Iyesato/6½, RG 59, NA; Heinrichs, *Grew,* 216; Grew to Hull, 5 April 1934, *FR* (1934), 3:640; Hornbeck to Robbins, 10 March 1933, Phillips to FDR, 14 December 1933, OF 197, FDRL; Hornbeck to Dunn, 28 March 1934, PSF, box 60, FDRL; Hornbeck to Phillips, 2 January 1934, PPF 604, FDRL; Asano to MacIntyre, 11 May 1934, PPF 719, FDRL. Asano, a leading industrialist, was ostensibly on his way to the Geneva Labor Conference to represent Japanese labor.

50. FDR memorandum for Morgenthau, 6 December 1934, OF 150, FDRL; Bullitt to Hull, 1 November 1934, 123 Bullitt, William C./102, RG 59, NA; House to Lothian, 13 December 1934, GD 40/17, file 282, Lothian Papers, SRO; Pratt, *Hull*, 1:101–2; Stimson and Bundy, *Active Service*, 167; FDR to Davis, 5 October, 9 November 1934, box 51, Davis Papers, LC.

51. Grew to Hull, 27 December 1934, Hornbeck memorandum, 3 January 1935, Hull to FDR, 22 January 1935, *FR* (1935), 3:827, 837, 842–43; Donald

Cameron Watt, *Personalities and Policies: Studies in the Formulation of British Foreign Policy in the Twentieth Century* (London: Longman's, 1965), 91–92; Lothian to House, 20 November 1934, GD 40/17, file 200, Lothian Papers, SRO.

52. Grew to Hull, 19 April 1935, *FR* (1935), 3:116; Borg, *Far Eastern Crisis*, 318–19; *Time*, 28 October 1935, p. 11.

53. Mackenzie King Diary, 5 March 1937, William Lyon MacKenzie King Papers, PAC; *Time*, 16 November 1936, pp. 30–31; Bingham Diary, 6 October 1936, box 1, Bingham Papers, LC; Borg, *Far Eastern Crisis*, 168, 181, 244, 531–32; Davis to Hornbeck, 23 March 1937, box 27, Davis Papers, LC; Ickes, *Ickes*, 2:7, 83. The United States would disarm the Philippines and Samoa (the Aleutians, too, if Japan agreed to include the Kuriles) and pledge not to arm western Alaska. Britain would be expected to do likewise in Hong Kong and Shanghai, the Dutch in North Borneo. Japan would disarm her island mandates. Thus the only remaining fortified outposts would be Japan proper, Singapore, Hawaii, Australia, and New Zealand. None of the neutralized islands were to be used in time of war.

54. Leahy Diary, 1, 14 September 1937, microfilm 17,718, William Leahy Papers, LC; Hamilton memorandum, 12 October 1937, *FR* (1937), 3:598–600; Neumann, "Ambiguity," 151.

55. Grew to Hull, 18 November 1937, *FR* (1937), 3:690–97; Wilson memorandum, 16 November 1937, ibid., 4:195–96; Borg, *Far Eastern Crisis*, 429, 463; FDR to Griscom, 22 October 1937, PPF 4949, FDRL; Heinrichs, *Grew*, 251–52. Lloyd Griscom, who had been active in 1905, suggested a repeat performance, and the idea appealed as much to FDR as it did to Davis. One might also note that when Grew published *Ten Years* and *The Turbulent Era*, he covered up Roosevelt's reversal of course in the Dooman proposal by making it appear that it had come from Tokyo (Grew, *Ten Years in Japan* [New York: Simon and Schuster, 1944], 225; *Turbulent Era*, 2:1201).

56. George Summerlin to McIntyre, 11 November 1937, memorandum by R.B. for McIntyre, 16 November 1937, PPF 1589, FDRL.

57. FDR to Konoye, 16 November 1937, *FR* (1937), 3:683.

58. Matsukata to FDR, 29 December 1937, PPF 1589, FDRL; Moffat memorandum, 2 December 1937, *FR* (1937), 4:234. MacMurray was chairman of the Joint Preparatory Committee on Philippine Affairs.

59. Neumann, "Ambiguity," 144; Masland, "Commercial Influence," 299; Hull, *Memoirs*, 1:540; Chamberlain to Hilda Chamberlain, 12 December 1937, NC 18, Chamberlain Papers, BUL.

60. Donald Watt, "Roosevelt and Neville Chamberlain: Two Appeasers," *International Journal* 28 (Spring 1973):191–95; John McVickar Haight, Jr., "Franklin D. Roosevelt and a Naval Quarantine of Japan," *Pacific Historical Review* 40 (May 1971):209–17; Borg, *Far Eastern Crisis*, 501.

61. Victor Mallet (counselor to the British embassy and chargé) to Eden, 12 October 1937, FO 414/274, PRO; Dieckhoff to Foreign Ministry, 1, 15 October 1937, *DGFP*, ser. D, 1:632, 639; Borg, *Far Eastern Crisis*, 333; Henry to Quai d'Orsay, 8–9 October 1937, dossier 307, AEU, Quai d'Orsay.

62. Henry to Quai d'Orsay, 17 July 1937, dossier 381, AEU, Quai d'Orsay; Pratt, *Hull*, 1:241; Grew memorandum, 10 August 1937, *FR* (Japan), 1:340.

63. The tenth American rejection occurred in response to Britain's request for a naval demonstration. See Welles memoranda, 27 November, 13 December 1937, British Embassy to State Department, 22 January 1938, *FR* (1937), 3:724–25, 798–99, 849–50; Henry to Quai d'Orsay, 20 July 1937, dossier 381, AEU, Corbin to Quai d'Orsay, 14 July 1937, dossier 275, Europe-Grande Bretagne, Quai d'Orsay.

64. Eden to Lindsay, 21 July 1937, Halifax to Eden, 18 September 1942 (citation of older records), vol. 29, Eden Papers, FO 954, PRO; John Harvey, ed., *The Diplomatic Diaries of Oliver Harvey, 1937–1940* (New York: St. Martin's Press, 1970), 2 November 1937, p. 55; FO to Mallet, 30 September 1937, also undated communication sent on the heels of the Quarantine Address, PREM 1/314, PRO; Minutes of the War Cabinet, 13 October 1937, CAB 23/89, PRO; Chamberlain to Hilda Chamberlain, 9 October 1937, to Ida Chamberlain, 16 October 1937, Chamberlain Papers, BUL; Eden memorandum, 21 July 1937, FE 37/2, Avon Papers, BUL; Anthony Eden, *Facing the Dictators* (Boston: Houghton Mifflin, 1962), 603–5; Nicholas R. Clifford, *Retreat from China: British Policy in the Far East, 1937–1941* (Seattle: University of Washington Press, 1967), 26. Bingham had made a similar proposal in 1934 (Bingham Diary, 27 March 1934, box 1, Bingham Papers, LC).

65. Henry L. Stimson, *The Far Eastern Crisis* (New York: Harper, 1936), 251–53; Dallek, *Roosevelt*, 148. See also FDR's letter to his old Groton headmaster in which he explains the logic of quarantining delinquents (FDR to Peabody, 16 October 1937, *Letters*, 3:717).

66. Moffat Diplomatic Journal, 5 October 1937, Moffat Papers, Harvard University.

67. See Hughe Knatchbull-Hugessen, *Diplomat: In Peace and War* (London: John Murray, 1949), 121–22; *Spectator* 159 (July–December 1937), 8 October 1937, p. 569.

68. Daniels, strongly in favor of calling a conference of the nine powers, had consulted Roosevelt on this very question before representing him in Europe as commissioner for the dedication of monuments to Americans serving in World War I. Roosevelt apparently encouraged him to promote the idea, and when he returned, he wrote the president, "I am quite sure you are responsible for calling this duty of the nine powers . . . [to the attention of] our British cousins, but as usual, they came on a slow train, with a month of precious time lost" (Daniels to FDR, 5 October 1937, PPF 86, FDRL).

69. Wilson to Davis, 24 September 1937, box 67, Davis Papers, LC.

70. Austin Chamberlain, notes on the U.S.A., November–December 1935, AC 41/3/2a, Chamberlain Papers, BUL; FO to Mallet, 30 September 1937, Mallet to FO, 5 October 1937, PREM 1/314, PRO. Britain was willing to engage in economic sanctions outside the League if Roosevelt would agree to cooperate on the military as well as economic front, but the United States rejected military measures in preference to economic cooperation under the League umbrella (foreign secretary to Mallet [undated but clearly just after the Quarantine Address], PREM 1/314, PRO).

71. Chamberlain to Ida Chamberlain, 4 July 1937, NC 18, Chamberlain Papers, BUL; FDR to Chamberlain, 28 July 1937, PREM 1/261, PRO; Davis to Chamberlain, 10 June 1937, Chamberlain to Davis, 8 July 1937, Bingham to Davis, 1 July 1937, Davis to Bingham, 14 July 1937, boxes 3 and 8, Davis Papers, LC. Halifax visited Germany during the period 17–21 November and the special French delegation was in London for two days, 29–30 November. See the Halifax Papers (two rolls of microfilm), part of the Hickleton Papers, CCC.

72. For Noyon, see W. N. Medlicott, *British Foreign Policy since Versailles, 1919–1963* (London: Methuen, 1968), 154; Winston Churchill, *The Gathering Storm* (Boston: Houghton Mifflin, 1948), 245ff.; Joseph E. Davies, *Mission to Moscow* (New York: Simon and Schuster, 1941), 221; Buck to Eden, 28 September 1937, FE 37/8, vol. 6, Avon Papers, BUL. References in the Quarantine Address itself point to the influence of Noyon: "In times of so-called peace, ships are being attacked and sunk by submarines without cause or notice . . . nations are fomenting and taking sides in civil warfare."

73. Eden memoranda, 21 July, 1 September 1937, vol. 29, FE 37/2, BUL.

74. The London *Times* had regretted the lack of Anglo-American cooperation in an editorial of 26 August. See Johnson to Hull, 26 August 1937, Hornbeck memorandum, 27 August 1937 (on Belgian pressure for joint Anglo-American-French action), Johnson to Hull, 1 September 1937 (Chinese reproof of the United States for not joining hands with Britain), *FR* (1937), 3:480, 488–89, 504. A note addressed to the State Department by the British embassy on 1 October, and handed to Hull by the chargé, emphasized the "strong feeling" not only in Great Britain but in other countries as well that "a lead should be given by the United Kingdom and the United States in some form of economic boycott on Japan. The British Government would be glad to know what is the attitude of the United States Government to such views" (ibid., 560). By this time, London had begun to desist from its fruitless campaign for joint measures and was beginning to recommend "similar representations" (U.S. chargé in London to Hull, 24 September, 1 October 1937, Grew to Hull, 6 October 1937, ibid., 549, 561, 591; see also Nicholas R. Clifford, "Britain, America, and the Far East, 1937–1940: A Failure in Cooperation," *Journal of British Studies* 3 [November 1963]:139–42).

75. Clifford, "Far East," 142; Borg, *Far Eastern Crisis,* 363; Harrison to Hull, 5 October 1937, *FR* (1937), 4:55. Moffat saw the speech as putting an end to the shilly-shallying in Geneva even as he feared it would "drive us much further than we wish to go" (Diary, 5 October 1937, Diplomatic Journal, Moffat Papers, Harvard University). Britain withdrew its opposition to the Chinese drive for League economic measures, at least in part out of fear of the opposition party accusing it of refusing another American offer (Minutes of the War Cabinet, 13 October 1937, CAB 23/89, PRO; *New York Times,* 6 October 1937, pp. 1, 4; *Chicago Tribune,* 6 October 1937, p. 1; Harrison to Hull, 5, 6 October 1937, *FR* (1937), 4:58, 61; *Spectator* 159 [July–December 1937]:569).

76. Hornbeck to Hull, 11 September 1935, Hull to FDR, 13 October 1935, *FR* (1935), 1:745–46, 773–75; *Letters,* 3:349. See also Long Diary for September and October 1935, box 5, Long Papers, LC.

77. William Phillips Diary, 4 October 1935, vol. 8, William Phillips Papers, Harvard University. Two days after FDR spoke (6 October), the League "followed" his example of declaring a state of war between Italy and Ethiopia.

78. Nevins and Rosenman err in claiming the speech received bad press. Haight is impressed above all with Roosevelt's adherence to a plan for naval blockade, holding that he did not really back down, as claimed by such authorities as Burns, Rauch, Beard, and Welles. Borg and Leuchtenburg also defend him against charges of inconsistency but argue that he had no definite plan in mind from which to back down. Offner and Dallek agree that he had no definite plan; but Jacobs interprets this fact, as well he might, not so much as precluding a backdown as providing the explanation for one. He holds that FDR not only beat a dramatic retreat on 6 October but did so in the face of remarkably friendly public opinion because he was not organized enough to have a definite course of action to pursue. Bryson agrees with Jacobs on the question of backdown but cites the case of Georgian editorial opinion to cast doubt on Jacobs's assumption of a solidly friendly South. See Haight, "Naval Quarantine"; John McVickar Haight, "Roosevelt and the Aftermath of the Quarantine Speech," *Review of Politics* 24 (April 1962):233–59; Jacobs, "Quarantine"; Thomas A. Bryson, "Roosevelt's Quarantine Speech, the Georgia Press and the Borg Thesis: A Note," *Australian Journal of Politics and History* 21 (August 1975):95–98; William E. Leuchtenburg, "Franklin D. Roosevelt, 'Quarantine Address, 1937,'" in Daniel J. Boorstin, ed., *An American Primer* (Chicago: University of Chicago Press, 1968), 871–81; Borg, *Far Eastern Crisis,* 378; Offner, *Appeasement,* 190; Dallek, *Roosevelt,* 148.

79. Moffat Diplomatic Journal, 10 October 1937, Moffat Papers, Harvard University.

80. Roosevelt to Murray, 7 October 1937, Murray memorandum, 10 September 1940 (in retrospect), file 8809, Elibank Papers, NLS; Welles memoranda, 12, 14 October 1937, *FR* (1937), 3:600–601, 609; Chamberlain to Hilda Cham-

berlain, 9 October 1937, NC 18, Chamberlain Papers, BUL; British Embassy to Department of State, 19 October 1937, Bingham to Hull, 28 October 1937, Welles memorandum, 13 November 1937, *FR* (1937), 4:90–91, 115, 155.

81. Haight, "Roosevelt and the Aftermath," 244–49, 251–52; Range, *Roosevelt's World Order,* 172; Borg, *Far Eastern Crisis,* 370, 418–21; Neumann, *Japan,* 285; Sanborn, *Design for War,* 275; Bullitt to FDR, 24 November 1937, Bullitt, ed., *For the President,* 241; Savage to Hull, 1 September 1937, box 15, Walton Moore Papers, FDRL; Welles, *Seven Decisions,* 8, 71–72; Haight, "Naval Quarantine," 222, 225. Haight blames Chamberlain and Eden's resignation for failure of FDR's naval blockade to materialize.

82. *Time,* 18 October 1937, p. 19; Mallet to Eden, 12 October 1937, Eden Papers, FO 414/274, PRO; *Chicago Tribune,* 6 October 1937, pp. 1, 12, 5 November 1937, p. 2; Hull, *Memoirs,* 1:545; Beard, *American Foreign Policy,* 198–207; Borg, *Far Eastern Crisis,* 388–89, 630n., 631n. See also the *New York Times* survey of editorial opinion, 6 October 1937, p. 17.

83. Pratt, *Hull,* 1:364; Sherwood, *Roosevelt and Hopkins,* 298; Raoul Jean Jacques de Roussy de Sales, *The Making of Yesterday: The Diaries of Raoul de Roussy de Sales* (New York: Reynal and Hitchcock, 1947), 29; Georges Bonnet, *De Munich à la Guerre: Défense de la paix* (Paris: Librairie Plon, 1967), 123, 278. One could cite Roosevelt's implied assurance of American military backing for French Indochina, which he withdrew when pressed; also his secret modification of a warning to Japan in August 1941 (contrary to pledges made at Argentia). See Chapter 3.

84. Borg, *Far Eastern Crisis,* 422; MacDonald's report on Brussels to the British War Cabinet, 24 November 1937, CAB 23/90, PRO; John McVickar Haight, Jr., "France and the Aftermath of Roosevelt's 'Quarantine Speech,'" *World Politics* 14 (January 1962):303; Moffat Diplomatic Journal, 2, 8, 15 November 1937, Moffat Papers, Harvard University; Eden, *Facing the Dictators,* 611; Davis to Hull, 14 November 1937, *FR* (1937), 4:184.

85. Hooker, ed., *Moffat,* 1, 2 November 1937, 161, 165; Haight, "France and the Aftermath," 295–96; Charles E. Bohlen, *Witness to History, 1929–1969* (New York: Norton, 1973), 44.

86. Confidential note on Brussels sent by the Quai d'Orsay to all French ambassadors, 31 December 1937, dossier 362, SDN (Societé des Nations): Conflit Sino-Japonais, Quai d'Orsay; Haight, "France and the Aftermath," 301, 304; Haight, "Roosevelt and the Aftermath," 253–55; Borg, *Far Eastern Crisis,* 433; Moffat Diplomatic Journal, 30 October 1937, Moffat Papers, Harvard University; MacDonald's report on Brussels to the British War Cabinet, 24 November 1937, CAB 23/90, PRO.

87. Welles to Bullitt, 9 November 1937, *FR* (1937), 4:170; Henry to Delbos, 7 November 1937, *DDF,* ser. 2, 7:355–56: "D'ailleurs, ne se rend-on pas compte en France qu'une attaque japonaise contre Hong Kong, ou l'Indochine ou les

Indes néerlandaises constituerait également une attaque contre les Philippines?" Hull apparently told Henry the same thing (Davis to Hull, 14 November 1937 [11 P.M.], *FR* [1937], 4:185).

88. Bullitt to Hull, 8 November 1937, *FR* (1937), 3:667; Welles to Bullitt, 9 November 1937, ibid., 4:170; Delbos to Henry, 9 November 1937, Henry to Delbos, 10 November 1937, *DDF*, ser. 2, 7:364–65, 369–70; Bullitt to Hull, 8 November 1937, 793.9411/89, RG 59, NA; Hooker, ed., *Moffat*, 3 November 1937, p. 169.

89. Bullitt to Hull, 13 January, 9 May 1938, Wilson to Hull, 13, 29 October 1938, Johnson to Hull, 4 November 1938, *FR* (1938), 3:20–21, 164, 319, 364; Bingham to Hull, 4 November 1937, *FR* (1937), 3:658; Bullitt to Hull, 10 November 1937, ibid., 4:173; Henry to Delbos, 10 November 1937, *DDF*, ser. 2, 7:370.

90. Borg, *Far Eastern Crisis*, 436, 438; Haight, "France and the Aftermath," 305; *Time*, 6 December 1937, p. 20; Watt, "Appeasers," 191; Chamberlain to Hilda Chamberlain, 28 July 1934, NC 18, Chamberlain Papers, BUL.

91. Hugh R. Wilson, Jr., *A Career Diplomat* (New York: Vantage Press, 1960), 62; Pratt, *Hull*, 1:265–67; Grew to Hull, 18 November 1937, *FR* (1937), 3:693; Borg, *Far Eastern Crisis*, 459, 480; Hull, *Memoirs*, 1:554–55.

92. For British demands, see Davis to Hull, 14 November 1937, *FR* (1937), 4:184.

93. See Hull to Gibson, 8 October 1937, Gibson to Hull, 13 October 1937, Welles memorandum, 1 November 1937, *FR* (1937), 4:68, 72, 140; Henry to Quai d'Orsay, 2 November 1937, dossier 361, SDN: Conflit Sino-Japonais, Quai d'Orsay.

94. See Grew to Hull, 18 November 1937, Hamilton memorandum, 20 November 1937, *FR* (1937), 4:137ff., 211–12, 216–17; Pratt, *Hull*, 1:265–67.

Chapter 3

1. FDR saw the Matsukata brothers on 10 December. See Borg, *Far Eastern Crisis*, 465–66, 480; Saito to Hull, 8 November 1937, Spruks memorandum, 15 November 1937, Hull to Grew, 14 March 1938, 811.4611 Japan/89, 90, 93, RG 59, NA; Grew to Hull, 18 November 1937; Wilson memorandum, 16 November 1937, *FR* (1937), 3:691, 4:195–96; Castle to Wilson, 23 December 1937, box 1, Hugh Wilson Papers, Hoover Library; Grew to House, 20 January 1938 (with *Nichi Nichi* enclosure), box 52, House Papers, Yale University; Hornbeck memorandum, 21 January 1938, *FR* (1938), 3:46. The initial indication of Tokyo's strategy came on the same day as the Quarantine Address. Grew wrote Hull that Matsukata, now planning to visit Washington, was saying that Japanese sentiment had turned increasingly away from Great Britain and toward the United States. If, therefore, FDR wished to offer his good of-

fices, it should not be in connection with Britain (Grew to Hull, 5 October 1937, 033.9411/307, RG 59, NA).

2. Leahy Diary, 13, 29 January 1938, Leahy Papers, LC; Hornbeck memorandum and Hull memorandum, 14 November 1938, *FR* (1938), 3:573−75; Adams, "Road," 89.

3. Neumann, *Japan*, 252.

4. Ibid., 241; Sanborn, *Design for War*, 40, 43; Jonathan G. Utley, "Diplomacy in a Democracy: The United States and Japan, 1937−1941," *World Affairs* 139 (Fall 1976):132; Hornbeck memorandum, 13 January 1939, *FR* (1939), 3:482; *Time*, 8 May 1939, p. 12.

5. Fred E. Israel, ed., *The War Diary of Breckinridge Long: Selections from the Years 1939−1944* (Lincoln: University of Nebraska Press, 1966), 16 June 1940, p. 107; Hornbeck memorandum, 11 May 1939, *FR* (1939), 3:34; Hornbeck, "State Department Reflections on Certain Features of the Far Eastern Situation," 4 July 1940 (in retrospect), Stimson letter to *New York Times* (clipping), 11 January 1940, OF 150, FDRL; Berle Diary, 16, 23 January 1940, FDRL.

6. Lindsay to Simon, 15 February 1934, Simon Papers, FO 414/272, PRO; *Time*, 17 October 1938, p. 24; *Japan Times*, 20 April 1939 (clipping) in vol. 95, Grew Diary, GP. Saito's real name was Hirosi, but he romanized it to Hiroshi. After resigning in October of 1938 because of ill health, he died 26 February 1939. For an excellent summary of Washington's role in the Saito funeral, see Roger Dingman, "Farewell to Friendship: The USS *Astoria*'s Visit to Japan, April 1939," *Diplomatic History* 10 (Spring 1986):121−39.

7. Welles actually made light of Japan's seizure of Hainan (Saint-Quentin to Quai d'Orsay, 15 February 1939, dossier 321, AEU, Quai d'Orsay). See also a report by the French naval attaché in Tokyo, "L'Annexation des Iles Spratley par le Japon," C.R.R. 5, Archives de la Mer, Chateau Vincennes, Paris; Pratt, *Hull*, 2:457; Hull, *Memoirs*, 1:628; Herbert Feis, *The Road to Pearl Harbor: The Coming of the War between the United States and Japan* (New York: Atheneum, 1966), 18; Grew Diary, 19−30 May 1939, vol. 94, GP. Finally, see an unidentified document in ibid., vol. 95.

8. *Japan Advertiser*, 19 April 1939; *Japan Times*, 20 April 1939; unidentified document as cited in note 7, vol. 95, Grew Diary, GP; Grew to Hull, 4 March 1939, 701.9411/1103, RG 59, NA; Hull to Grew, 25 March 1939, *FR* (1939), 4:457.

9. Heinrichs, *Grew*, 279−80; Grew to Hull, 27, 30 March, 6 April 1939, Hull to Grew, 28, 31 March, 3 April 1939, 701.9411/1126, 1135, 1136, 1138, 1141A, RG 59, NA.

10. *Japan Times*, 11 April 1939, in vol. 95, Grew Diary, along with unidentified document, GP; Hull to Grew, 28 March, 14 April 1939, Grew to Hull, 30 March, 6, 26 April 1939, 701.9411/1126, 1138, 1145, 1163A, 1174, RG 59, NA.

11. Hull, *Memoirs,* 1:629–30; Saint-Quentin to Quai d'Orsay, 12 April 1939, dossier 321, AEU, Quai d'Orsay.

12. Pratt, *Hull,* 2:457; Grew Diary, vol. 94, 21 October 1939, GP; communication de la direction politique à l'ambassade de Grande-Bretagne à Paris, 29 April, *DDF,* ser. 2, 15:864. Wang, closest of Sun's disciples, had served in the highest echelons of the Kuomintang.

13. Hull to Hiranuma, 8 July 1939, *FR* (Japan), 2:7; Kawakami, "Far Eastern Triangle," 640; Pratt, *Hull,* 2:458; British Embassy to Department of State, 20 October 1939, *FR* (1939), 3:292; Hull, *Memoirs,* 1:717–24, 727; Grew Diary, vol. 94, 19 October 1939, GP; Halifax to Cecil, 30 January 1940, A51084, vol. 14, Lord Cecil Papers, British National Library; Lothian to Halifax, 3 November 1939, FO 800/317, PRO.

14. Asada, "Japan's 'Special Interests,'" 63; MacMurray memorandum, 1 November 1935, Grew Diary, vol. 86, GP. The entire memorandum is of great importance, but see esp. 55, 59, 67, 80, 83, 88, 93, 97.

15. Grew Diary, vol. 94, Personal Note 127, June–September 1939, GP; Heinrichs, *Grew,* 290; Grew to Ballantine, 5 August 1939, 711.94/8539, RG 59, NA.

16. Quoting MacMurray, he pointed out that "patient efforts of Japan for nearly ten years tried to preserve the letter and spirit of the Washington Treaties in the face of Chinese intransigence and the selfishness of the signatory powers . . . the effect of our attitude was to condone the high-handed behavior of the Chinese. . . . The Chinese had been willful in their scorn of the legal obligations." For Grew's set speech to various groups, see Grew Diary, vol. 94, June–September 1939, GP.

17. Grew Diary, vol. 94, October 1939, GP; Grew to Hull, 1 December 1939, 711.94/1396, RG 59, NA; Heinrichs, *Grew,* 293, 296; Winston Churchill, *The Grand Alliance* (Boston: Houghton Mifflin, 1950), 583–84.

18. Heinrichs, *Grew,* 295–308, esp. 298; Matsukata to FDR, 20 December 1939, PPF 1589, FDRL; Grew to Hull, 1, 4, 7, 11 December 1939; Hull to Grew, 14 December 1939, 711.94/1373, 1375, 1380, 1383, 1386, 1396, RG 59, NA.

19. Grew to Hull, 27 December 1940, *FR* (1940), 4:474; Grew memorandum, 21 October 1939, *FR* (1939), 3:299–300; Kawakami, "Far Eastern Triangle," 643; Brian Crozier, *The Man Who Lost China* (New York: Scribner's, 1976), 223–24. Sayre was a cousin of State Department counselor Judge Moore as well as Woodrow Wilson's son-in-law. MacMurray had been chairman of the Joint Preparatory Committee on Philippine Affairs since 2 December 1937, and Sayre owed his original appointment under Roosevelt to the influence of Colonel House. For House's letter of recommendation, see House to FDR, 8 August 1933, box 95, House Papers, Yale University. For Dulles's letter to Sayre, enclosing a copy of his speech on "peaceful change," see the Dulles Papers at Princeton University.

20. Sayre's correspondence with FDR from 1 November 1939 to 2 July 1940 (some eleven messages) is in box 7, Francis B. Sayre Papers, LC.

21. Saionji-Harada Memoirs, film 3:2817–20, 2985, Princeton University; Eugene Ott (German ambassador to Tokyo) to German Foreign Ministry, 10 May 1940, *DGFP*, ser. D, 9:323–24; Grew memorandum, 10 June 1940, *FR* (Japan), 2:70; Grew to Hull, 3, 6 May 1940, Welles to Grew, 4 May 1940, *FR* (1940), 4:322–24, 327–29.

22. Hull to Grew, 8 May 1940, *FR* (1940), 4:330; Heinrichs, *Grew*, 308–9; Francis B. Sayre, *Glad Adventure* (New York: Macmillan, 1957), 205–6; Tōgō, *Cause of Japan*, 46.

23. Heinrichs, *Grew*, 309–11; Hull to Grew, 7, 11 July 1940, Grew to Hull, 11 July 1940, *FR* (1940), 4:389, 397, 400–401; *New York Times*, 7 July 1940, pp. 1, 16.

24. Bernard B. Fall, *The Two Viet-Nams* (New York: Praeger, 1968), 41–44, 466n.; Grew to Hull, 28 June 1938, *FR* (1938), 3:207. When war came on 7 December, it was their control of southern Indochina that enabled the Japanese to sink the British battleships *Repulse* and *Prince of Wales* (Churchill, *Grand Alliance*, 617, 619).

25. Clifford, *Retreat from China*, 142–43. On tungsten, see *Letters*, 4:1249.

26. Clifford, "Far East," 148–49; Drummond, *American Neutrality*, 156; British Embassy to Department of State, 27 June 1940, Hull memorandum, 28 June 1940, *FR* (1940), 4:365–66, 369–70.

27. Lothian to Hoare, 3 November 1939, Lord Templewood Papers, 11:5, ULC; Chamberlain to Hilda Chamberlain, 14 July 1940, NC 18, Chamberlain Papers, BUL; Hornbeck memorandum, 19 June 1940, *FR* (1940), 4:359; Drummond, *American Neutrality*, 156–57. The interpretation is further confirmed by Halifax's statement to cabinet ministers on 29 July 1940 that Britain could not reopen the Burma Road due to a lack of American military backing (Minutes of Cabinet, 29 July 1940, FO 800/321, PRO).

28. Hornbeck memorandum, 13 July 1940, *FR* (1940), 4:584.

29. When a flight of dive bombers struck Pearl Harbor on the morning of 7 December 1941, few were aware that President Roosevelt had already vouchsafed American belligerency in the event that Thai, Dutch, or British territory should come under attack by Japan. Partial evidence for such a commitment was first uncovered during a congressional investigation in 1945–46. Since then, scholars have agreed that FDR did in fact give an explicit pledge to Halifax during the first week of December 1941 and that this capped a period of gradually increased verbal assurance beginning in late July, but all accounts are vague as to why Britain risked war by reopening the Burma Road in October 1940. Robert Dallek skirts the issue altogether, while David Reynolds suggests that closure was merely a temporary and "tactical withdrawal" on the part of a country that in the long run "could not afford to offend the U.S.A." Reynolds

refers to American economic sanctions as well as the U.S. loan to China as possible inducements to British action, but he does not argue that either had a decisive influence on Churchill. See Dallek, *Roosevelt*, 239–42; Reynolds, *Anglo-American Alliance*, 135, 140; also Burns, *Soldier of Freedom*, 159–61, and Raymond A. Esthus, "President Roosevelt's Commitment to Britain to Intervene in a Pacific War," *Mississippi Valley Historical Review* 50 (June 1963):28–38. According to Esthus, Halifax urged Hull in April 1941 to approve an Anglo-American ultimatum threatening Japan with American intervention in the event of an attack on British or Dutch possessions in the Pacific. There are two ways, however, in which British requests, particularly those of Halifax, may be misleading. First, they may have reflected Whitehall's desire to formulate certain guarantees on the embassy level which had already been negotiated at the summit. Second, Halifax may not have known, or may have chosen to ignore, various forms of support that Washington had already provided, including a unilateral ultimatum to Tokyo.

30. On 31 July 1941, according to British War Cabinet minutes, the discussion touched upon a plan to approach the United States for a promise of military backing if British *or* Dutch possessions were attacked and the desirability of a concerted warning to Japan along this line by Britain, the United States, the Netherlands, and the dominions (CAB 65/23, PRO). Various precedents can be cited for executive resort to secrecy in the formation of an entente. Kenneth Waltz, discussing British ties with France and Russia (forged in 1904 and 1907 respectively), has pointed out that "arrangements were made that were kept secret not only from people and Parliament but until 1912 from the cabinet itself"—arrangements that "effectively, if informally, bound England to fight a future war against the Central Powers" (*Foreign Policy and Democratic Politics: The American and British Experience* [Boston: Little, Brown, 1967], 9, 68).

31. Lothian to House, 20 November 1934, GD 40/17, file 200, Lothian Papers, SRO; Lothian to Halifax, 3 November 1939, FO 800/317, PRO; Harvey, ed., *Harvey*, 2 November 1937, p. 55. The British, noted Harvey, would not engage in sanctions with the United States unless they were backed by force. See also Lothian's speech to the Council on Foreign Relations, as recapped by Stimson in 1934: the British felt they could do nothing about Japanese expansion unless they were prepared to go to war, and this would be possible only with a definite American commitment (Stimson Diary, 5 October 1934, Stimson Papers, Yale University).

32. British consulate general to FO, 12 November 1937, FO 371/21041, PRO.

33. Bonnet to Saint-Quentin, 16 June 1939, Saint-Quentin to Bonnet, 17 June 1939, Papiers 1940: Fouques Duparc, Quai d'Orsay; Article by P. E. Flandin in *L'Europe*, 25 June 1939, carton 116, P. E. Flandin Papers, Bibliothèque Nationale, Paris; summary of report of French naval attaché in Tokyo, 1 June

1939, C.R.R. #6, Archives de la Mer, Chateau Vincennes, Paris; Henry to Quai d'Orsay, 10 May 1939, dossier 366, SDN: Conflit Sino-Japonais, Quai d'Orsay; Mackenzie King Diary, 19 October 1937, 30 January 1939, PAC.

34. Mackenzie King Diary, 28–29 April, 27 September 1940, PAC; Mackenzie King to Churchill, 30 May 1940, vol. 286, Mackenzie King Papers, PAC.

35. Since August, a group consisting of Admiral Robert L. Ghormley, Major General George Strong, and Major General Delos Emmons had been in London on a secret mission foreshadowing the historic Anglo-American staff conversations of early 1941 in Washington (Frazier Hunt, *The Untold Story of Douglas MacArthur* [New York: Devon-Adair, 1954], 199).

36. Long Diary, 14 September 1940, box 5, Long Papers, LC. See also his telling entries for 28 September and 7 October in Israel, ed., *Long*, 132–33, 136, as well as an undated memorandum by Reverend James M. Drought, box 1, Drought Papers, Maryknoll.

37. British War Cabinet Minutes, 2 October 1940, War Cab 264, CAB 65/9, PRO; High commissioner in Great Britain to Canadian secretary of state for external affairs, 2 October 1940, Department of External Affairs, *Documents on Canadian External Relations*, 8 vols. (Ottawa, 1909–41), 8:1315.

38. *New York Times*, 14 January 1982, p. B4. This is an article on the 1978 discovery of a secret used by FDR to record news conferences in the Oval Office.

39. Mackenzie King Diary, 8 October 1940, PAC.

40. Israel, ed., *Long*, 7 October 1940, pp. 136–37; British War Cabinet Minutes, 2, 7 October 1940, War Cab 264, CAB 65/9, PRO.

41. British high commissioner to Canadian prime minister, 10 October 1940, Department of External Relations memorandum, 10 October 1940, in *Documents on Canadian External Relations*, 8:1179–80. The section in that volume entitled "Allied Military Conversations on Pacific Defense" begins with an entry not surprisingly dated 10 October 1940. See also Robert J. Quinlan, "The United States Fleet: Diplomacy, Strategy and the Allocation of Ships (1940–1941)," in Harold Stein, ed., *American Civil-Military Decisions: A Book of Case Studies* (Birmingham: University of Alabama Press, 1963), 157–61; Langer and Gleason, *Challenge to Isolation*, 588; Neumann, "Ambiguity and Ambivalence," 151; Richardson, *On the Treadmill*, 387, 399–400, 435. Richardson was relieved of his command in January 1941.

42. Halifax to Linlithgow, 12 October 1940, Halifax Papers, CCC; *Time*, 21 October 1940, pp. 24–25; Hull, *Memoirs*, 1:868.

43. Grew, *Turbulent Era*, 2:927; Grew Diary, October 1940 (mailed to the State Department in November), 101:4556, Grew Diary, Personal Notes, December 1940, 101:4673–75, GP; Heinrichs, *Grew*, 315–18.

44. Butow, *John Doe Associates*, 112; FDR to Sayre, 31 December 1940,

Sayre to FDR, 13 November 1940, box 7, Sayre Papers, LC; Sayre, *Glad Adventure,* 214.

45. Charles A. Lindbergh, *The Wartime Journals of Charles A. Lindbergh* (New York: Harcourt Brace Jovanovich, 1970), 7 December 1940, pp. 422–23.

46. Dooman memorandum, 14 February 1941, Grew to Hull, 26 February 1941, *FR* (Japan), 2:137–42.

47. Grew to Hull, 26, 27 February 1941, ibid., 138, 143.

48. Langer and Gleason, *Undeclared War,* 325–26; U.S. Congress, Joint Committee on the Investigation of the Pearl Harbor Attack, *Hearings on the Pearl Harbor Attack,* 79th Cong., 2d sess., 39 parts (Washington, D.C., 1946), pt. 2:671–72, 727. Butow is another authority who doubts that the Dooman warning on 14 February was official, even though he notes that Dooman had conferred with both Hull and members of the Far Eastern Division before delivering it (*John Doe Associates,* 128–29).

49. Kimball, *Unsordid Act,* 99.

50. Hull memorandum, 8 March 1941, *FR* (Japan), 2:389; memorandum handed to FDR by Bishop Walsh, 23 January 1941, *FR* (1941), 4:14–16.

51. Wikawa to Drought, 23 January 1941, Drought memorandum, 10 March 1941, Wikawa to Henderson, 1 October 1945, box 1, Drought Papers, Maryknoll. Wikawa's daughter was a student at Columbia University, where he had earlier delivered a series of lectures (*Japan Times,* 20 April 1939, clipping contained in Grew Diary, vol. 95 [1939], GP; Donald W. Smith [U.S. assistant commercial attaché] to Hull, 25 February 1941, Grew to Hull, 27 February 1941, Walker to FDR, 28 February 1941, Walker to Hull [11 March 1941?], Ballantine memorandum, 28 March 1941, *FR* [1941], 4:51, 53–54, 69–70, 115). For Chinese interest in involving the Catholic Church as early as 1939, see Hamilton memorandum, 25 October 1939, *FR* (1939), 3:302.

52. Hull, *Memoirs,* 2:995; "Proposal Presented to the Department of State through the Medium of Private American and Japanese Individuals on 9 April 1941," Hull memorandum, 16 April 1941, *FR* (Japan), 2:398–402, 407.

53. See Drought Papers, box 1, Maryknoll.

54. Walsh memorandum on the 1940–41 negotiations, 15 September 1971, Walsh confidential memorandum, 11 December 1945, Walsh to Drought, 25 September 1941, Walsh memorandum, 15 December 1941, Walsh Visitation Diary, 28 September 1941, Walsh Papers, Maryknoll.

55. British Embassy in Washington to Foreign Office, undated, FO 371/27910, PRO. Hull was saying that if the United States could reach a satisfactory China settlement, "they would not quarrel about Manchukuo," although he would deny the latter if made public. See also Eugene Ott to Foreign Ministry, 5 May 1941 (on the U.S. position), *DGFP,* ser. D, 12:715; Hull memorandum, 16 April 1941, *FR* (Japan), 2:409.

56. Minutes, 13 September 1941, FO 371/27910, PRO; Ribbentrop, *Memoirs*, 153; Ernst von Weizsäcker, *Memoirs of Ernst von Weizsäcker* (London: Victor Gollancz, 1951), 261; Drought memorandum, undated (1941 or 1942?), box 1, Drought Papers, Maryknoll; Walker to Hull, 7 March 1941, *FR* (1941), 4:63. See also Johanna M. Meskill, *Hitler and Japan: The Hollow Alliance* (New York, Atherton, 1966). For a dissenting opinion, see Butow, *John Doe Associates*, 143.

57. James E. Walsh memorandum, 18 October 1941, *FR* (1941), 4:536–37; Drought to Walker, 4 June 1941, box 1, Drought Papers, Maryknoll; Ballantine memoranda, 21, 30 May 1941, Toyoda to Nomura, 13 September 1941, *FR* (Japan), 2:437–38, 444, 454, 623.

58. Tōgō, *Cause of Japan*, 71, 174–77; Ike, trans. and ed., *Japan's Decision*, 263; Paul Schroeder's contribution in Dallek, ed., *Roosevelt Diplomacy*; Hull memoranda, 16 April, 2, 11, 16 May 1941, *FR* (Japan), 2:406–11, 417–18, 431–32.

59. Drought to Walker, 4 June, 7 July 1941, Drought to Walsh, 18 June 1941, box 1, Drought Papers, Maryknoll; "Informal and Unofficial Oral Statement Handed by the Secretary of State to the Japanese Ambassador," 16 May 1941, *FR* (Japan), 2:433. See also, for Wakasugi's indication of Japanese willingness to pull *all* of its troops out of China, Welles memorandum, 13 October 1941, *FR* (Japan), 2:685.

60. James MacGregor Burns, for example, insists that Roosevelt did not want war and that he tried to avoid a showdown; the basic problem was that both Japan and the United States misunderstood each other (*Soldier of Freedom*, 145–46, 149–51).

61. Drought to Walker, 7 July 1941, box 1, Drought Papers, Maryknoll; Ballantine memorandum, 1 September 1941, Grew memoranda, 3, 4 September 1941, Hull memoranda, 28 August, 3 September 1941, FDR to Konoye, 3 September 1941, *FR* (Japan), 2:571–72, 584–94; Tōgō, *Cause of Japan*, 90–92; R. J. C. Butow, "Backdoor Diplomacy in the Pacific: The Proposal for a Konoye-Roosevelt Meeting, 1941," *Journal of American History* 59 (June 1972):48–72; Hull, *Memoirs*, 2:1019–27; Ike, trans. and ed., *Japan's Decision*, 146; Konoye memoir in *Pearl Harbor Attack*, pt. 20:4001–2.

62. Nomura to Hull, 20 November 1941, Ballantine memorandum, 22 November 1941, Grew to Hull, 24 November 1941, *FR* (Japan), 2:755–62.

63. Anderson, "Embargo," 230–31.

64. For use of the term "Indochina," see Hull memorandum, 27 November 1941, Ballantine memorandum, 1 December 1941, *FR* (Japan), 2:770, 775. For an example of Hull's vagueness, see his *Memoirs*, 2:1034ff. See also Grew memoranda, 7, 8 October 1941, *FR* (Japan), 2:446, 665–68; FDR to Hull, 28 September 1941, Walsh memorandum for Hull, 15 November 1941, *FR* (1941), 4:483, 527–28.

65. Jonathan Utley has argued that Roosevelt's policy was undermined by hawkish subordinates, that the president himself did not intend to make such a sharp and final break in trade ties with Japan—in other words, that he was not spoiling for war but was drawn in willy-nilly. The thesis is interesting although hard to square with Roosevelt's personal hatred and suspicion of Tokyo coupled with his complete lack of understanding and sympathy for the Japanese position. There is FDR's consistently anti-Japanese rhetoric, his initiation and long history of personal support for economic sanctions, and his provocative transfer of the fleet to Hawaii. In addition, he systematically eliminated soft-line officials from positions of power within the government—men such as Sayre and Moffat, who were far more even-handed than he. Nor does the theory take sufficient account of Roosevelt's consistent opposition to compromise on the part of Britain and his deliberate stalling in the Hull-Nomura exchange. See Utley, *Going to War with Japan, 1937–1941* (Knoxville: University of Tennessee Press, 1985), 177–82. Utley raises some very good questions, even if his text contains some apparent contradictions (xi–xii, 16, 21, 66–67, 151). If anything, the narrative tends to paint the picture of a president very much in control of the ultimate direction his administration was taking (46, 98–100). There is no evidence that Roosevelt ever regretted any of the key decisions taken by his government during 1941.

66. Hull, *Memoirs*, 2:984, 1015; Butow, *John Doe Associates*, 156; memorandum by Far East Division for Hull, 10 April 1941, Hornbeck memorandum, 11 April 1941, *FR* (1941), 4:136–37, 142–44.

67. See, for example, Hull memoranda, 14 April, 2, 11, 16 May 1941, *FR* (Japan), 2:402–6, 411, 417–18, 431–32.

68. See, for example, Hull memorandum, 14 March 1941, *FR* (Japan), 2:397.

69. Butow, *John Doe Associates*, 212–13; Wikawa to Drought, 18 June 1941, box 1, Drought Papers, Maryknoll; Ballantine memorandum, 14 July 1941, Turner to Stark, 21 July 1941, *FR* (Japan), 2:505, 516.

70. Walsh to Drought, 25 September 1941, Walsh Papers, Maryknoll; Welles memorandum, 24 October 1941, Ballantine memoranda, 7, 15 November 1941, *FR* (Japan), 2:693, 708, 731. Ballantine held talks with Colonel Iwakuro.

71. Welles memorandum, 9 August 1941, *FR* (1941), 1:348; James A. Farley, *Jim Farley's Story: The Roosevelt Years* (New York: McGraw-Hill, 1948), 345. See also Minutes of British War Cabinet Meeting, 19 August 1941, Confidential Annex B, CAB 65/23, PRO; Drought memorandum for the acting secretary of state, 1 November 1934, Official File 197, FDRL; Drought to Buell, 28 August 1934, box 2, Drought Papers, Maryknoll.

72. Heinrichs, *Grew*, 348. Hiranuma was shot on 16 August 1941.

73. Butow, "Hull-Nomura Conversations," 835; Hull, *Memoirs*, 2:996; Lewis L. Strauss, *Men and Decisions* (Garden City, N.Y.: Doubleday, 1962), 124–25. But compare Butow, "Hull-Nomura Conversations," with Butow,

330 · NOTES TO PAGES 102–106

"Backdoor Diplomacy," written twelve years later, in which the author continues to criticize the Maryknoll priests but drops his attack on Nomura.

74. Hull, *Memoirs*, 2:994–95; Butow, "Backdoor Diplomacy," 56; Strauss, *Men and Decisions*, 125. This is a fair sampling of interpretation.

75. Drought memorandum, 28 February 1941, box 1, Drought Papers, Maryknoll; Walker to FDR, 28 February 1941, FR (1941), 4:54. For evidence of Drought's prior consultation with Hull, see Walker to Hull, 17 March 1941, containing Drought's "Preliminary Draft of an 'Agreement in Principle' " (ibid., 4:98–102). Hull was not, in other words, faced with a fait accompli on 9 April.

76. Ballantine memorandum, 7 April 1941, FR (1941), 4:127.

77. Walker to Hull, 17 March 1941, ibid., 97. Drought's memoranda for 17 and 18 March record the danger of assassination as perceived by Japanese envoys and statesmen. Wikawa and Iwakuro were fully aware of the risk to their lives, and Wikawa's mother had expressed herself ready for any eventuality (box 1, Drought Papers, Maryknoll).

78. Walker to Hull, 18 March 1941, Walker to Hull, undated, FR (1941), 4:112, 119; Hull memorandum, 16 April 1941, FR (Japan), 2:407.

79. Hull, *Memoirs*, 2:996; Drought, "Private Explanation," 12 May 1941, box 1, Drought Papers, Maryknoll; Tōgō, *Cause of Japan*, 67; Walker to Hull, 12 May 1941, FR (1941), 4:184, 186; Konoye memoir in *Pearl Harbor Attack*, pt. 20:3985.

80. Hornbeck to Hull, 7 March 1941, memorandum by Far Eastern Division for Hull, 10 April 1941, memorandum prepared for the secretary of state, 15 April 1941, Hornbeck to Hull, 10 June 1941, FR (1941), 4:62–63, 136–37, 153, 263; Wikawa to Drought, 18 June 1941, Drought to Walker, 20 June 1941, box 1, Drought Papers, Maryknoll.

81. Pratt, *Hull*, 2:480; John H. Boyle, "The Drought-Walsh Mission to Japan," *Pacific Historical Review* 34 (May 1965):141–61; Ike, trans. and ed., *Japan's Decision*, xxi; Butow, *John Doe Associates*, 140. Compare Walker to Hull, 17 March 1941 (containing Drought's "Preliminary Draft of an 'Agreement in Principle' ") with the Draft Understanding submitted by Drought, 9 April 1941, FR (1941), 4:98–102, FR (Japan), 2:398–402.

82. Walsh to Drought, 17 May 1941, Walsh confidential memorandum, 11 December 1945, Walsh Visitation Diary, 26–27, 30 November, 3, 5, 10, 17, 23, 27, 28 December 1940, Walsh Papers, Maryknoll; Drought to Walsh, 3 June 1941, Drought memorandum, undated, box 1, Drought to Walker, 27 January 1941, box 2, Drought Papers, Maryknoll; Hamilton memorandum, 25 October 1939, FR (1939), 3:302; Boyle, "Drought-Walsh Mission," 154.

83. The same scholar who speaks of Drought's innocence and naiveté attributes his failure in 1941 to the fact that he was highly emotional and vindictive, still suffering from moods of shyness, melancholy, and high scruple that

attended his induction into the priesthood. For this and other negative commentary on Drought, see Butow, *John Doe Associates*, 49, 103, 110, 150, 315, 341, 343; Strauss, *Men and Decisions*, 123–25. Butow implies that Drought's reasons for entering the priesthood led to disillusionment, frustration, and a Messiah complex.

84. Drought to Horinouchi, 7 March 1938, box 2, Drought Papers, Maryknoll.

85. Walsh Visitation Diary, 16, 24 August, 3 September 1940, Paul Le Veness, "Bishop Walsh's China: The Life and Thought of an American Missionary in China," Walsh Papers, Maryknoll.

86. Drought memorandum, 17 March 1941, box 1, Drought Papers, Maryknoll; Walsh memorandum, 18 October 1941, *FR* (1941), 4:531.

87. Le Veness, "Bishop Walsh's China," Walsh Papers, Maryknoll; Drought to Buell, 28 August 1934, box 2, Drought, "Preliminary Draft of an 'Agreement in Principle' between the United States and Japan," undated, box 5, Drought memorandum, January 1941, box 1, Drought Papers, Maryknoll.

88. Drought, "Working Analysis of Our [Japan's] Position and Policy in the Far East with Particular Reference to the United States," box 5, Drought Papers, Maryknoll.

89. Boyle, "Drought-Walsh Mission," 147–48; Drought, "Working Analysis of Our Position and Policy in the Far East with Particular Reference to the United States," box 5, Drought memorandum "Exclusively from the Japanese Viewpoint," 29 March 1941, box 1, Drought Papers, Maryknoll.

90. Drought, "Preliminary Draft of an 'Agreement in Principle' between the United States and Japan," box 5, Drought Papers, Maryknoll; Butow, *John Doe Associates*, 150.

91. Hull oral statement to Nomura, 21 June 1941, Ballantine memorandum, 14 July 1941, Turner to Stark, 21 July 1941, *FR* (Japan), 2:485, 505, 516; Ike, trans. and ed., *Japan's Decision*, 96–97, 263, 282.

92. Craigie to FO, 1 November 1941, Cadogan to Craigie, 8 November 1941 (draft), FO 371/27911, PRO; Lothian to Halifax, 1 February 1940, FO 800/324, PRO; Churchill, *Grand Alliance*, 595; Reynolds, *Anglo-American Alliance*, 134, 142–43.

93. Minute by C. E. Scott, 7 October 1941, Halifax to the British Embassy in Washington, 17 October 1941, FO 371/27910, PRO; Craigie to FO, 1 November 1941, FO 371/27911, PRO; Hull memorandum, 6 May 1941 (re: Lothian), *FR* (1941), 4:198; FO to Washington Embassy, 18 October 1941, CAB 65/23, PRO ("we should prefer, if possible, to keep Japan out of the world conflict and to detach her from the Axis" though we have been content thus far to follow the United States in its policy of "maximum economic pressure").

94. Drought to Walker, 13 August 1941, box 1, Drought Papers, Maryknoll;

Tōgō, *Cause of Japan,* 187; Halifax to Eden, 3 June 1942, in Thomas E. Hachey, ed., *Confidential Dispatches: Analyses of America by the British Ambassador, 1939–1945* (Evanston, Ill.: New University Press, 1974), 33.

95. Hamilton memorandum, 13 November 1938, *FR* (1938), 3:571–72; Leahy Diary, 24 August 1937, Leahy Papers, LC; FDR to Sara and James Roosevelt, 10 April 1898, FDR to Babs, 7 July 1916, *Letters,* 1:194, 2:304; Jablon, "Hull," 164; Range, *Roosevelt's World Order,* 81; James Roosevelt, *My Parents,* 159–60, 257; "Reminiscences of Arthur Krock" (1950), 76, CUOHC; Sol Bloom, *The Autobiography of Sol Bloom* (New York: G. P. Putnam's, 1948), 245; Stimson and Bundy, *On Active Service,* 366. Litvinov wrote in his diary for 1937: "Roosevelt has already made up his mind on the issue of war with Japan" (Maxim Litvinov, *Notes for a Journal* [New York: Morrow, 1955], 231).

96. FDR press conference, 12 December 1934, Nixon, ed., *Roosevelt,* 2:313. By 1936, Japan had built up to the 10-10-6 ratio allowed by treaty. The United States had not (Fred Greene, "The Military View of American National Policy, 1904–1940," *American Historical Review* 66 [January 1961]:360).

97. Stimson and Bundy, *On Active Service,* 173; British Embassy in Washington, Annual Report on the United States, 21 January 1937, FO 371/20670; John F. Kennedy, *Why England Slept* (New York: Wilfred Funk, 1940), 18, 234 (gives total national defense expenditures on a year-by-year basis); Kaufmann, "Bullitt and Kennedy," 653; William R. Emerson, "F.D.R. (1941–1945)" in Ernest R. May, ed., *The Ultimate Decision: The President as Commander-in-Chief* (New York: Braziller, 1960), 142–44; Tuchman, *Stilwell,* 219, 259; Brune, "Hull's Diplomacy," 393; Thomsen and Bötticher to German Foreign Ministry and Wehrmacht Headquarters, 24 September 1938, *DGFP,* ser. D, 2:923; Pershing to FDR, 25 November 1938, *Letters,* 4:837–38. As late as the end of 1939, Roosevelt continued to refuse to bring army and navy personnel figures up to what Congress had authorized—280,000 for the army and 180,000 for the navy (Haglund, *Latin America,* 142).

98. Langer and Gleason, *Challenge to Isolation,* 130, 469–75, 505, 680–81; Bullitt, "Lost the Peace," 88; Reminiscences of Arthur Krock (1950), 77, CUOHC; George Morgenstern, *Pearl Harbor: The Story of the Secret War* (New York: Devin-Adair, 1947), 53. Soon after FDR called for an annual productive capacity of fifty thousand planes in the spring of 1940, one hundred representatives of airplane manufacturers were called to Washington. Secretary of the Treasury Morgenthau made a welcoming speech to be sent with pictures all over the country, presumably to show that the administration was on the job. The assembled manufacturers were also addressed by the secretary and assistant secretary of war, the acting secretary of the navy, and others. However, when the aircraft makers asked what they could do to help, they received no information (Dewey Address, 8th draft, box 281, Dulles Papers, Princeton University).

99. Saint-Quentin to Quai d'Orsay, 19 January 1939, dossier 321, AEU, Quai d'Orsay; Sherwood, *Roosevelt and Hopkins*, 493; FDR to Bell, 13 May 1938, *Letters*, 4:784; Borg, *Far Eastern Crisis*, 249–50. A Guam fortification bill finally passed Congress in February 1941 (Hachey, ed., *Confidential Dispatches*, 33).

100. Beard, *American Foreign Policy*, 148; Louis Morton, "National Policy and Military Strategy," *Virginia Quarterly Review* 36 (Winter 1960):6; Dulles to Hamilton Fish Armstrong, 18 March 1940, box 19, Dulles Papers, Princeton University; Lothian interview with FDR, 11 October 1934, GD 40/17, file 285, Lothian Papers, SRO. Dissenting Republicans included Dulles, Stimson, Hurley, and Johnson (Russell D. Buhite, *Patrick J. Hurley and American Foreign Policy* [Ithaca: Cornell University Press, 1973], 74; Buhite, *Johnson*, 79–80, 93; Pratt, *Hull*, 1:232).

101. Hooker, ed., *Moffat*, 129; Vansittart to Lindsay, September 1934, bk. 109, Baldwin Papers, ULC; Borg, *Far Eastern Crisis*, 605–8n.; Sayre, *Glad Adventure*, 201, 231; Naggiar to Paul-Boncour, 22 March 1938, *DDF*, ser. 2, 9:23; Emerson, "F.D.R.," 143, 146–47; Neumann, "Ambiguity," 154–55; Langer and Gleason, *Undeclared War*, 900; Dwight D. Eisenhower, *At Ease* (Garden City, N.Y.: Doubleday, 1967), 247.

102. Grew to Hull, 29 December 1934, *FR* (1934), 3:689–90.

103. William R. Castle article in the *Washington Star*, 18 October 1936, in box 8, Moore Papers, FDRL; Sanborn, *Design for War*, 39; Dilks, ed., *Cadogan*, 172; Langer and Gleason, *Undeclared War*, 471; Quinlan, "United States Fleet," 160–61, 171; Leutze, *Bargaining for Supremacy*, 181–83; Richardson, *Memoirs*, 19, 163, 332; Neumann, "Ambiguity," 150–51.

104. Neumann, "Mahan," 713–14; Dilks, ed., *Cadogan*, 375; Quinlan, "United States Fleet," 184; Neumann, *Japan*, 289; Stimson and Bundy, *On Active Service*, 366, 386; Kennedy to Hull, 24 June 1940, *FR* (1940), 4:582n. Once the United States became a full-fledged combatant in the Atlantic, beginning with the *Greer* incident in September, the British changed their specifications as to where they wanted Roosevelt's naval strength to be concentrated (Leutze, *Bargaining for Supremacy*, 156, 259).

105. Bailey and Ryan, *Hitler vs. Roosevelt*, 134–35; Ike, trans. and ed., *Japan's Decision*, 233, 280. Oddly enough, Ike argues against the theory of deterrence through strength, submitting that Japan decided to risk war because it perceived the United States as a threat (xiii, xxiv, xxv). For British views, see Leutze, *Bargaining for Supremacy*, 201, 205–6, 232, 246.

106. Moffat Diplomatic Journal, 4, 5 October 1937, Moffat Papers, Harvard University.

107. Israel, ed., *Long*, 20 November 1941, pp. 223–24. Typical in the same way is an article by Arthur Krock written for the *New York Times*, November 1941, box 397, Herbert Hoover Papers, Hoover Library.

108. Israel, ed., *Long*, 31 August 1941, p. 215; Frederick Moore, *With Japan's*

Leaders: An Intimate Record of Fourteen Years as Counsellor to the Japanese Government, Ending December 7, 1941 (New York: Scribner's, 1942), 243–44; Langer and Gleason, *Undeclared War,* 920; Neumann, *Japan,* 276–77; Rear Admiral Kemp Tolley, "The Strange Assignment of USS *Lanikai,*" *U.S. Naval Institute Proceedings* 88 (September 1962):71–83. The move was not needed for surveillance. For a cogent challenge to the Tolley thesis, see Stanley Falk, *Seven Days to Singapore* (New York: G. P. Putnam's Sons, 1975), 62n.

109. Churchill, *Grand Alliance,* 605.

110. Neumann, *Japan,* 129; Paul H. Clyde, "Historical Reflections on American Relations with the Far East," *South Atlantic Quarterly* 61 (Autumn 1962):446; Moore, *With Japan's Leaders,* 296, 303; Russell Weigley, "The Role of the War Department," in Borg and Okamoto, eds., *Pearl Harbor,* 186; Hornbeck memorandum, 16 May 1933, 550.S1 Washington/505, RG 59, NA; Long Diary, 27 July 1939, box 5, Long Papers, LC; *Time,* 14 October 1940, p. 40, 21 October 1940, pp. 25, 30–31, 23 December 1940, p. 30, 7 April 1941, p. 44, 17 November 1941, p. 27, 8 December 1941, pp. 14, 28. Bingham recorded in his diary for 12 April 1934 that the Russians were building an air force at Valdosta capable of destroying "the inflammable Japanese cities" (box 1, Bingham Papers, LC).

111. Neumann, *Japan,* 24; Grew, speech to American groups, summer of 1939, Grew Diary, vol. 94, GP; Thorne, *Allies,* 3.

112. Thorne, *Allies,* 158–59; Murray to FDR, 21 June 1939, Elibank Papers, file 8809, NLS; Krock memorandum of talk with FDR, 13 September 1934, box 52, Krock Papers, Princeton University; Burns, *Soldier of Freedom,* 57.

113. Wayne S. Cole, *America First: The Battle against Intervention, 1940– 1941* (Madison: University of Wisconsin Press, 1953), 189–90; Hornbeck memorandum, 30 August 1941, *FR* (1941), 4:412; Robert F. Smylie, "John Leighton Stuart: A Missionary Diplomat in the Sino-Japanese Conflict, 1937–1941," *Journal of Presbyterian History* 53 (Fall 1975):272; London *Times Literary Supplement,* 13 June 1975 (article on Hornbeck); Lothian to FO, 30 August 1939, FO 371/22815, PRO; Lothian to Halifax, 14 December 1939, FO 800/324; Grew, *Turbulent Era,* 2:1212; Langer and Gleason, *Challenge to Isolation,* 588; Neumann, "Ambiguity," 151; Richardson, *Memoirs,* 333, 387, 399–400, 435; Quinlan, "United States Fleet," 161; Halifax to Churchill, 11 October 1941, Halifax Papers, CCC; E. Stanley Jones, "An Adventure in Failure," *Asia and the Americas* 45 (December 1945):612; Neumann, *Japan,* 287–88. The western approaches to Pearl Harbor were well covered by patrol planes (Walter Millis, *This Is Pearl!* [New York: Morrow, 1947], 269; see also Offner, *Origins,* 243–44). For a definitive account of how and why United States forces were surprised at Pearl Harbor, see Prange, *At Dawn We Slept,* esp. 725–38. In recent years, evidence has been brought to light that Roosevelt, in the company of a handful of high officials such as Marshall and Knox, *may* have had sufficient information

in the final hours to anticipate confidently a blow aimed specifically at Pearl Harbor; but even in this instance, the presumption would have been that Pearl Harbor's defenses were adequate to beat off serious damage. See Toland, *Infamy*, chap. 16.

Chapter 4

1. Both Daladier and Bonnett fought the Versailles Treaty and wrecked their careers temporarily by telling the truth about it (Bullitt to Hull, 15 September 1938, *FR* [1938], 1:601). The Left in Britain, as well as much of the press, championed equality of status for Germany (Lord Templewood, *Nine Troubled Years* [London: Collins, 1954], 113). Typical was the *Times* of London in 1934: "There is more reason to fear for Germany than to fear Germany" (quoted in Taylor, *Origins*, 76; see also Samuel Flagg Bemis, "First Gun of a Revisionist Historiography for the Second World War," *Journal of Modern History* 19 [March 1947]:55; McKenna, *Borah*, 275, 346, 352, 355, 357). For American opinion generally, see articles by Allen Dulles and Arnold Toynbee in the January and April issues of *Foreign Affairs* (1934).

2. Stimson Diary, 9 November 1932, Stimson Papers, Yale University. Both Stresemann and Brüning pleaded for German equality and it was denied. Hitler made the same futile plea but proceeded unilaterally.

3. The Allies claimed they were fighting only against the kaiser and his Junker backers, but the Allied blockade was maintained long after he surrendered while many starved to death. Impossible demands were made on the German economy and hundreds of thousands of Germans were turned over to Czech and Polish jurisdiction.

4. Thomas Johnston, "Kismet—or Real Appeasement?" *Fortnightly Review* (May 1939):501–9.

5. Bonnet, *De Munich*, 19. Except during the brief period 1919–39, Moravia had always been a part of either Germany or Austria, and the Bohemian crownlands, as they were formerly known, had been as much a part of Germany as Wales was of England (Borchers speech, box 19, Dulles Papers, Princeton University; see also Churchill, *Gathering Storm*, 342; Taylor, *Origins*, 202).

6. Giselher Wirsing, *Roosevelt et l'Europe*, trans. Jean Carrère (Paris: Bernard Grasset, 1942), 268–72; Keith Feiling, *The Life of Neville Chamberlain* (London: Macmillan, 1946), 343–44, 391, 399; John Simon, *Retrospect* (London: Hutchinson, 1952), 239–40; Taylor, *Origins*, 158, 201, 205; von Ribbentrop, *Memoirs*, 93–96; Saul Friedländer, *Prelude to Downfall: Hitler and the United States, 1939–1941* (New York: Knopf, 1967), 6.

7. Lord Cecil to Gilbert Murray, 22 November 1932, vol. 16B, Gilbert Murray Papers, Oxford University; Stimson and Bundy, *On Active Service*, 272; Kennedy to Hull, 12 October 1938, *FR* (1938), 1:86; Welles report, 13 March

1940, *FR* (1940), 1:86; Borchers speech, box 19, Dulles Papers, Princeton University; Manfred Jonas, *Isolationism in America, 1935−1941* (Ithaca: Cornell University Press, 1966), 226; Feiling, *Chamberlain*, 413; Taylor, *Origins*, 195, 215; von Ribbentrop, *Memoirs*, 96−99; *Time*, 8 May 1939, p. 18.

8. W. Roberts (FO Egyptian Department) minute, 5 July 1935; London *Times*, 8 July 1935 (clipping), FO 371/19115, PRO. See also Luigi Villari, *Italian Foreign Policy under Mussolini* (New York: Devin-Adair, 1956).

9. Long to FDR, 16 September 1935, box 58, PSF, FDRL; Lothian to Dulles, 26 December 1939, GD 40/17, file 400, Lothian Papers, SRO. Italy was offered southern portions of Turkey but wisely declined; nationalist forces under Mustafa Kemal were growing too strong to be denied. Orlando's disappointment was compounded by the sealing off of Italian emigration to North and South America.

10. London *Times*, 8 July 1935 (clipping); foreign secretary memorandum, 9 July 1935, FO 371/19115, PRO; SEC report on Ethiopia, undated, PPF 207, FDRL; Medlicott, *British Foreign Policy*, 143n.

11. M. Lampson to FO, 5 July 1935, British consul at Turin to FO, 1 July 1935; Hoare to Drummond, 6 July 1935, FO 371/19115, PRO; Villari, *Mussolini*, 140; Churchill, *Gathering Storm* (tongue well in cheek), 165−66; Jonas, *Isolationism*, 110; SEC report, PPF 207, FDRL; Hull to Bingham, 11 July 1935, *FR* (1935), 1:730. When Long sent Hull his recommendation for a compromise regarding the Italian position in Ethiopia, Hull replied (14 September 1935): "Your plan . . . is exceedingly interesting . . . of course we ourselves could not take any steps" (the implication was that Geneva, instead of Washington, would have to offer the compromise—something which it proceeded to do and which Mussolini hastened to reject). Long, in fact, urged such a plan on Mussolini "personally," and the duce demurred. His mind was "closed" (Long to Hull, 12, 17, 19 September, Hull to Long, 14 September 1935, 765.84/1134, 1152, 1205, 1265, RG 59, NA).

12. Moley, *Seven Years*, 222; Stimson and Bundy, *On Active Service*, 171, 207.

13. Morgenthau Farm Credit Administration Diary, 29 May 1933, p. 38, Morgenthau Papers, FDRL; Laboulaye to Paul-Boncour, 11 October 1933, Laboulaye to Louis Barthou, 22 February 1934, *DDF*, ser. 1, 4:546−47; 5:797; Bullitt to FDR, 8 July 1933, Bullitt, ed., *For the President*, 37. For Havas in Latin America, see Gellman, *Good Neighbor*, 151.

14. FDR debate speech, 19 January 1898, FDR to Sara Roosevelt, 22 April 1912, Eleanor Roosevelt to Sara Roosevelt, 11 February 1919, *Letters*, 1:164; 2:185, 468; Sir Arthur Willert, *Washington and Other Memories* (Boston: Houghton Mifflin, 1972), 59; Phipps to Cooper, 8 December 1938, Knatchbull-Hugessen Papers, CCC; Margaret Coit, *Mr. Baruch* (Boston: Houghton Mifflin, 1957), 466; Hull to FDR, 7 February 1934, Wilson to FDR, 12 March 1938,

boxes 41, 45, PSF, FDRL; Charles de Gaulle, *The Complete War Memoirs of Charles de Gaulle, 1940–1946,* trans. Jonathan Griffin and Richard Howard (New York: Simon and Schuster, 1964), 968–69; Robert Murphy, *Diplomat among Warriors* (Garden City, N.Y.: Doubleday, 1964), 52.

15. Drummond, *American Neutrality,* 76–77; Long to FDR, 7 February 1934, box 58, PSF, FDRL; Lord Astor's "Notes on the United States," 24 December 1932, bk. 110, Baldwin Papers, ULC; *Time,* 17 April 1933, p. 15, and 26 June 1933, p. 15; FDR to Hull, 4 April 1938, *Letters,* 4:770 (see also ibid., 3:437n.); Bowers to FDR, 2 August 1933, FDR to Straus, 8 June 1936, boxes 730, 4714, PPF, FDRL; Blum, ed., *Morgenthau Diaries, 1928–1938,* 459–61; Frances Perkins, *The Roosevelt I Knew* (New York: Viking, 1946), 352; Moley, *Seven Years,* 72, 222; *New York Times,* 6 October 1937, p. 16; Lindsay to Simon, 10 May 1933, *DBFP,* ser. 2, 5:796; Straus to FDR, 20 January 1936, FDR to Bowers, 22 August 1933, Nixon, ed., *Roosevelt,* 1:372, 3:166–68; FDR, editorial in *Macon Daily Telegraph,* 5 May 1925, in Carmichael, ed., *F.D.R. Columnist,* 69; Bullitt to Moore, 18 April 1940, box 3, Moore Papers, FDRL; Morgenthau to FDR, 7 October 1938, Morgenthau Presidential Diaries, vol. 1, FDRL; Robert Dallek, *Democrat and Diplomat: The Life of William E. Dodd* (New York: Oxford University Press, 1968), 277; *FR* (Cairo and Teheran), 530.

16. FDR to Churchill, 11 November 1942, *RC,* 279; Bullitt to FDR, 10 January 1937, 1 February 1939, Bullitt, ed., *For the President,* 206, 306; Biddle memorandum, 1 July 1940, box 41, PSF, FDRL; Dallek, *Roosevelt,* 229–30; de Gaulle, *Memoirs,* 60–61.

17. Robinson to Lothian, 24 December 1934, GD 40/17, file 285, Lothian Papers, SRO; Atherton to Hornbeck, 29 January 1935, *FR* (1935), 3:28; Dallek, *Dodd,* 243, 250 (a major theme).

18. Vansittart to Lindsay, September 1934, John Buchan, "Notes on My Visit to America," in a letter to Baldwin, 20 December 1934, bks. 109, 122, Baldwin Papers, ULC; Lothian to FO, 30 August 1939, FO 371/22815, PRO; Lindsay to Simon, 13 February 1935, FO 414/272, PRO; James M. Witherow to Lothian, 23 February 1938, GD 40/17, file 358, Lothian Papers, SRO; McKenna, *Borah,* 283; Eden to Cadogan, 21 August 1943, Eden Papers, vol. 2, FO 954, PRO; Austen Chamberlain, "Notes on the USA, November to December, 1935," AC 41/3/2a, Austen Chamberlain Papers, BUL; King George to FDR, 13 March 1945, Halifax Papers, CCC; *RC,* 295 (see also ibid., 125n.); *Time,* 17 November 1941, p. 14. Very useful on Lothian is David Reynolds, "Lord Lothian and Anglo-American Relations, 1939–1940," *Transactions of the American Philosophical Society* 73, pt. 2 (1983).

19. Kleeman, *Gracious Lady,* 156; *Letters,* 1:39n.; FDR to Sara Roosevelt, 12 August 1903, Eleanor Roosevelt to Sara Roosevelt, 19 June 1905, ibid., 1:499, 501n., 2:12–13; Sara Roosevelt to FDR, 27 May 1899, box 7, Family Papers, FDRL; Thorne, *Allies,* 98; FDR to Bingham, 11 July 1935, Nixon, ed., *Roose-*

velt, 2:553–54; Frankfurter to FDR, 24 January 1935, box 98, Felix Frankfurter Papers, LC. Perhaps the best account of the Anglo-American relationship, when it comes to summary judgment as well as specific matters such as American "chip-on-the shoulder" attitudes, is again by David Reynolds: *Creation of the Anglo-American Alliance* (see pp. 25, 28). Reynolds is very astute on finance and global responsibility, and he includes a brilliant section on the Welles mission. For British criticism of FDR and the United States in general, see pp. 11–13, 56–57. For FDR's inflated promises, see pp. 61–62, 67, 102ff., 120. For American ignorance of Britain and her empire, see pp. 24–25.

20. Moffat Diplomatic Journal, 17 May 1939, Moffat Papers, Harvard University; Grace Tully, *F.D.R. My Boss* (New York, Scribner's, 1949), 318–20; Eleanor Roosevelt, *This I Remember*, 184–86; James Roosevelt, *My Parents*, 207; Blum, ed., *Morgenthau Diaries, 1928–1938*, 498; FDR to Bingham, 11 July 1935, Nixon, ed., *Roosevelt*, 2:554; Berle Diary, 22 September 1939, Berle Papers, FDRL.

21. Subsequently, Roosevelt continued to correspond with Murray and on several occasions with Mrs. Murray, whose photograph he solicited and whose return to America he tried to induce. Her death in 1942 effectively ended the Roosevelt-Murray correspondence (boxes 8809–11, Elibank Papers, NLS; also box 53, PSF, FDRL, esp. FDR to Faith Murray, 17 April 1940, and Faith to FDR, 22 November 1939, 4 August 1940).

22. MacDonald press conference, 26 April 1933, Nixon, ed., *Roosevelt*, 1:71; D'Arcy to Vansittart, 24 August 1934, Vansittart to Lindsay, September 1934, bk. 109, Baldwin Papers, ULC; Hull, *Memoirs*, 1:380; Bingham to Hull, 10 September 1934, carton 11, Green Papers, Princeton University; Pratt, *Hull*, 1:93–94; Offner, *Appeasement*, 106. The British wished to extradite one of their nationals, a Mr. Factor, from Chicago, where he was being held as a star witness for a federal court procedure that had convicted several kidnappers. His continued testimony was required to complete the case for the prosecution (Bingham Diary, 11 April 1934, box 1, Bingham Papers, LC).

23. Phillips Diary, 9 November 1935, Phillips Papers, Harvard University; Lindsay to Eden, 17 March 1937, vol. 29, Avon Papers, BUL; Murray to Tweedsmuir, 20 November 1936, file 8808, Elibank Papers, NLS; Leo Amery to Neville Chamberlain, 19 November 1937, NC 7/2, Chamberlain Papers, BUL.

24. Lawrence W. Pratt, "The Anglo-American Naval Conversations on the Far East of January 1938," *International Affairs* 47 (October 1971):756; Lockart Report, 15 April 1939, FO 371/22829, PRO; Chamberlain to Amery, 27 July 1939, NC 7/2; "Palestine Policy and American Zionists: Paper to be Circulated to the War Cabinet by the First Lord" (undated), NC 7/9/71, Chamberlain Papers, BUL; Murray to FDR, 16 December 1938, box 53, PSF, FDRL. See also note of a conversation between President Roosevelt and Colonel Hon. Arthur Murray at Hyde Park, 23 October 1938, file 8809, Elibank Papers, NLS. The

British did in fact select their Lincoln copy of the Magna Carta as the highly publicized centerpiece of a 1939 World's Fair exhibit in New York (Reynolds, *Creation of the Anglo-American Alliance*, 23).

25. Levinson to Lothian, 26 December 1939, GD 40/17, file 402, Lothian Papers, SRO; FDR to Hull, 26 July 1937, *Letters*, 3:695; Moore, *With Japan's Leaders*, 100–101; FDR toast to George VI, 8 June 1939, OF 48A, FDRL; Moore memorandum, 24 August 1937, dispatch dated 9 March 1938, Moore to FDR, 13 October 1937, Moore to Hull, 22 October 1937, Moffatt memorandum of meeting on Pacific islands, 29 December 1937, boxes 4, 15, Moore Papers, FDRL; *FR* (1937), 2:125–33; *Time*, 16 November 1936, p. 30, 14 March 1938, p. 12.

26. FDR to Hull and Ickes, 10 January 1944, box 60, PSF, FDRL; Churchill, *Their Finest Hour*, 573; FDR to Edgar Smith, 5 August 1942, 18 December 1944, FDR to Wigglesworth, 26 August 1942, in *A Baker Street Folio: Five Letters about Sherlock Holmes from Franklin Delano Roosevelt* (Summit, N.J.: Pamphlet House, 1945). Most likely, FDR borrowed his theory on Holmes from Christopher Morley, who proposed it in a 1934 column written for the *Saturday Review*.

27. FDR to Muriel and Warren Robbins, 30 May 1891, Eleanor Roosevelt to Sara Roosevelt, 25 July 1905, FDR to Sara Roosevelt, 4 March 1897, 30 July 1905, *Letters*, 1:20, 69, 2:46, 51; Diary of European trip, summer 1918, ibid., 2:391, 413, 419, 451, 462; James Roosevelt to FDR, 9 June 1897, box 3, Roosevelt Family Papers, FDRL; Kleeman, *Gracious Lady*, 216.

28. See, for example, Heinrichs, *Grew*, 233.

29. Dodd to Hull, 23 August 1933, *FR* (1933), 2:259; Hull, *Memoirs*, 1:233, 240, 472, 597–98; *Time*, 19 June 1933, p. 12; *Dodd's Diary*, 4–5, 86; Henry Morgenthau, "The Morgenthau Diaries," *Collier's*, 11 October 1947, p. 72; Offner, *Appeasement*, 234; Nixon, ed., *Roosevelt*, 1:337; FDR press conferences, 7 September 1934, 12 March 1936, ibid., 2:207–8, 3:249; FDR, *On Our Way*, 115, 136; Pratt, *Hull*, 1:90; Corbin to Doubergue, 12 April 1934, *DDF*, ser. 1, 6:209; Dallek, *Roosevelt*, 102; William Phillips, *Ventures in Diplomacy* (Boston: Beacon Press, 1952), 165–66.

30. Hull, *Memoirs*, 1:472, 597–98; Friedländer, *Prelude*, 11; Drummond, *American Neutrality*, 85; memorandum by acting secretary of state, 8 August 1936, *DGFP*, ser. C, 5:800, 800n., 888; Thomsen to Foreign Ministry, 17, 27 March 1939, ibid., ser. D, 6:14, 130; memorandum by Ambassador Dieckhoff, 29 July 1940, ibid., 10:351–52. This is not to say that American and German firms did not invent ways of circumventing official restrictions even as their respective governments looked the other way. For this side of the story, see Offner, "Appeasement Revisited," 374–76.

31. Lindsay to Simon, 30 January 1933. *DBFP*, ser. 2, 5:750–51; Prittwitz to Foreign Ministry, 16 March, 7 April 1933, Schacht to Foreign Ministry, 6 May

1933, *DGFP*, ser. C, 1:175, 263, 264n., 393; Davis to Hull, 16 April 1933, 500.A15A4 General Committee/297, RG 59, NA; Laboulaye to Paul-Boncour, 16 May 1933, *DDF*, ser. 1, 3:492.

32. Dodd Memorandum, March 1934, *FR* (1934), 2:219; House to Cudahy, 2 April 1934, box 32, House Papers, Yale University; Dodd to FDR, 15 August 1934, PPF 1043, FDRL; Pratt, *Hull*, 1:186–87; memorandum by State Secretary Bülow, 23 November 1934, *DGFP*, ser. C, 3:664.

33. *Dodd's Diary*, 342; Offner, *Appeasement*, 206–9; Martha Dodd, *Through Embassy Eyes* (New York: Harcourt Brace, 1939), 359–60; Dieckhoff to German Foreign Ministry, 5 August 1937, *DGFP*, ser. D, 1:627; Hull conversation with Dieckhoff, 5 August 1937, 14 January 1938, microfilm roll 29, Hull Papers, LC; Robert Dallek, "Beyond Tradition: The Diplomatic Careers of William E. Dodd and George S. Messersmith, 1933–1938," *South Atlantic Quarterly* 66 (Spring 1967):241n. A German ultimatum produced a cable dated 23 November and addressed to Dodd in Berlin ordering him out of Germany by 31 December. Returning to the United States, he made numerous speeches calling for concerted action against the dictators. Three times he tried to see the president. Once he asked to talk with Hull. In every instance, the answer was a polite no (*Dodd's Diary*, 3, 23, 30 November, 14 December 1937, pp. 430, 434–35, 445). For Bullitt's opinion, see Bullitt to FDR, 23 November 1937, Bullitt, ed., *For the President*, 235; Offner, *Appeasement*, 206–9; Dallek, *Dodd*, 313–14.

34. *Dodd's Diary*, 240; S. R. Fuller to Roosevelt, 11 May 1933, Nixon, ed., *Roosevelt*, 1:175; Fuller memorandum of conversation with Schacht, 23 September 1935, *FR* (1935), 2:282–86; Fuller to Hull, 14 October 1935, 862.00/3558, RG 59, NA; McKenna, *Borah*, 349–50. Borah continued to sympathize with the Hitler regime. He had no problem with Berlin's takeover of Prague in 1939, and he toyed with the idea of visiting Hitler all through the year 1938, having been assured that his reception in Germany would be excellent (ibid., 359–60).

35. Dallek, *Roosevelt*, 124; François-Poncet to Flandin, 12 March 1936, Laboulaye to Flandin, 19 March 1936, *DDF*, ser. 2, 1:517, 609–10; 600.0031 World Program, RG 59, NA; Stafford Little Foundation lecture at Princeton University, 19 March 1936, box 15, Dulles Papers, Princeton University; Bingham Diary, 30 June 1934, 20 March, 15 April 1936, box 1, Bingham Papers, LC; FDR to Dodd, 5 August 1936, Dodd to FDR, 19 October 1936, box 49, Dodd Papers, LC; Leith-Ross to Phipps, 4 February 1937, Phipps Papers, CCC; Lothian memorandum, 11 May 1937, Halifax Papers, CCC.

36. Davis to Astor, 20 May 1936, box 2, Davis Papers, LC; Bingham Diary, 10 March 1936, box 1, Bingham Papers, LC; Bullitt to Hull, 20 April 1936, file 8, box 3, Kelley Papers, Georgetown University. The outcome of the general effort in this direction was the rather meaningless Franco-German Pact of 1938

(E. Monick's note on Bullitt interview, 22 December 1936, *DDF*, ser. 2, 4:324; *Time*, 19 December 1938, p. 16).

37. Cudahy to FDR, 26 December 1936, FDR to Cudahy, 15 January 1937, Cudahy to Hull, 27 January 1937, *FR* (1937), 1:25–27, 35; Bingham Diary, 20 October 1936, box 1, Bingham Papers, LC; *Dodd's Diary*, 18 August, 5 December 1936, pp. 344, 369.

38. Loewenheim, "Illusion," 178–79, 183, 207, 210–11; Krock to FDR, 9 November 1936, FDR to Krock, 12 November 1936, Krock, "Reminiscences," 230, box 52, Krock Papers, Princeton University; Blum, ed., *Morgenthau Diaries, 1928–1938*, 458–59; Mackenzie King Diary, 31 July 1936, 5 March 1937, PAC.

39. Lindsay Annual Report on the United States to Eden, 21 January 1937, Lindsay to Vansittart, 8 March 1937, FO 371/20670; Dorothy Borg, "Notes on Roosevelt's 'Quarantine' Speech," *Political Science Quarterly* 72 (September 1957):408–10; Watt, "Appeasers," 187–90; *Dodd's Diary*, 377, 380, 389, 401; FDR to Dodd, 5 August 1936, FDR to Phillips, 17 May 1937, *Letters*, 3:606n., 680; Bullitt to FDR, 17 January 1937, Bullitt, ed., *For the President*, 207; memorandum by Acting Secretary of State Dieckhoff, 17 September 1936, Foreign Minister von Neurath memorandum, 16 October 1936, Luther to Foreign Ministry, 24 November 1936, *DGFP*, ser. C, 5:979, 1103, 1142.

40. Vansittart to Lindsay, 17 November 1936, Phipps Papers, CCC; Lansbury to Baldwin, 27 August 1936, bk. 129, Baldwin Papers, ULC; Smuts to Lothian, 24 March 1936, GD 40/17, file 445, Lothian Papers, SRO; Biddle memorandum, 19 February 1937, Bullitt to Hull, 20 February 1937, *FR* (1937), 1:46, 48; *Dodd's Diary*, 29 December 1936, 27 January, 20 April 1937, pp. 376–77, 380, 401.

41. Davies to FDR and Hull, January 1937, box 3, Davies Papers, LC; Levinson to Lothian, 29 April 1937, Lothian to Levinson, 9 June 1937, GD 40/17, file 341, Lothian Papers, SRO; Morris to Hull, 15 April 1937, Dodd to Hull, 9 April 1937, 600.0031 World Program/66 and 71; RG 59, NA; Morgenthau to FDR, 15 January 1937, Nixon, ed., *Roosevelt*, 3:586–87.

42. Feis to MacMurray, 17 February 1937, box 21, Feis Papers, LC; Loewenheim, "Illusion," 179–80; Mackenzie King to FDR, 6 March 1937, *Letters*, 3:666; *Dodd's Diary*, 20 April 1937, p. 401; Davies to FDR and Hull, January 1937, box 3, Davies Papers, LC; Nixon, ed., *Roosevelt*, 3:588n.

43. Welles memorandum to FDR, 10 January 1938, *FR* (1938), 1:116; Langer and Gleason, *Challenge to Isolation*, 23; *Letters*, 4:1460; Bullitt to Hull, 23 November 1937, box 24, PSF, FDRL.

44. François-Poncet to Quai d'Orsay, 19 November 1937, dossier 307, AEU, Quai d'Orsay; Lamarle to Paul-Boncour, 5 April 1938 (recounting events of the previous fall), *DDF*, ser. 2, 9:221. See also ibid., 112n.; Bullitt to Hull, 13 January, 23 November 1937, PSF, box 24, FDRL; Offner, *Appeasement*, 190; Dieck-

hoff to Foreign Ministry, 27 September, 20 December 1937, *DGFP*, ser. D, 1:630, 658; Bullitt to Hull, 23 November 1937 (a thirty-two-page letter), Bullitt, ed., *For the President*, 239.

45. *Time*, 29 November 1937, p. 19, and 13 December 1937, pp. 19—20; Bullitt to Hull, 4 December 1937, Johnson to Hull, 3 December 1937, *FR* (1937), 1:184—86.

46. Wilson, *Career Diplomat*, 28; Stimson, *Far Eastern Crisis*, 248—49; McKenna, *Borah*, 349—68; speech by German consul general, 30 January 1940, box 19, Dulles Papers, Princeton University; Bullitt to Moore, 7 April 1935, to FDR, 8 November 1936, Bullitt, ed., *For the President*, 108, 180; Davies, *Mission to Moscow*, 140, 142—43; Bingham to FDR, 26 March 1935, PPF 716, FDRL; Biddle to Hull, 12 July 1939, 760.62/702, RG 59, NA; Kirk to Hull, 8 December 1939, 760D.61/688, RG 59, NA; Frankfurter to FDR, 11 July 1936, Feis to Frankfurter, 18 January 1938, boxes 33 and 98, Herbert Feis Papers, LC.

47. Moffat Diplomatic Journal, 3 November 1937, Moffat Papers, Harvard University; Davis to Hull, 15 April 1933, 500.A15A4 General Committee/297, RG 59, NA; Beatrice Bishop Berle and Travis Beal Jacobs, eds., *Navigating the Rapids, 1918—1971: From the Papers of Adolf A. Berle* (New York: Harcourt Brace Jovanovich, 1973), 164, 183—84; speech by German consul general, 30 January 1940, box 19, Dulles Papers, Princeton University; *Time*, 29 November 1937, pp. 18—19, and 24 January 1938, p. 15; Hooker, ed., *Moffat*, 21 October 1938, pp. 220—21. In addition to the Quarantine Address of 5 October 1937, one can cite in this same connection FDR's Armistice Day Address of 11 November 1935, his Annual Message of 3 January 1936 (which contained no less than four cutting references to "autocracy"), his Address at Chautauqua of 14 August 1936 (which condemned violation of international agreements and "new born fanaticisms"), his Radio Greeting to Twenty-one American Republics of 7 November 1936 ("democratic institutions are so seriously threatened"); major addresses at Rio and Buenos Aires in December of 1936 (in which he again condemned aggression and "new fanaticisms"), all in Samuel I. Rosenman, ed., *The Public Papers and Addresses of Franklin D. Roosevelt*, 13 vols. (New York: Russell and Russell, 1938—50), 4:442, 5:9—12, 289, 583, 599, 605—7.

48. Offner, "Appeasement," 376—77; Bullitt to FDR, 8 November 1936, 7 December 1937, Bullitt, ed., *For the President*, 180—82, 242; Bullitt to FDR, 10 May 1937, PSF box 43, FDRL; Feis to MacMurray, 17 February 1937, box 21, Feis Papers, LC.

49. Eden memorandum, 21 January 1938, vol. 29, FO 954, PRO; Langer and Gleason, *Challenge to Isolation*, 21—26; Welles to FDR, 26 October 1937, box 23, PSF, FDRL. Welles's first memorandum was issued 6 October. There followed additional plans dated 9 October, 26 October, and 10 January, 1938.

50. Langer and Gleason, *Challenge to Isolation*, 22; FO to Lindsay, February 1938, Lindsay to FO, 22 January, 16 February 1938, FO to Lindsay, 13 January

1938, FO 371/21526, PRO; Eden memorandum (17 January?) 1938, vol. 29; un-dated précis by Michael Wright, based on the Halifax files, vol. 30, FO 954; FO to Lindsay, 4 February 1938, Lindsay to FO, 6, 12 February 1938, PREM 1/259, PRO; Stephen Roskill, *Hankey: Man of Secrets*, 3 vols. (London: Collins, 1970–74), 3:301; Maurice Cowling, *The Impact of Hitler: British Politics and British Policy, 1933–1940* (Cambridge: Cambridge University Press, 1975), 176; Dilks, ed., *Cadogan*, 12 January 1938, p. 36; Offner, *Appeasement*, 229–34; Bullitt to FDR, 20 January 1938, Bullitt, ed., *For the President*, 252.

51. Henry to Delbos, 24 February 1938, *DDF*, ser. 2, 8:517; Welles memoran-dum, 1 February 1938, *FR* (1938), 1:11; Davis to Astor, 17 February 1938, box 2, Davis Papers, LC; Long Diary, 6 February, 2 March 1938, box 5, Long Pa-pers, LC.

52. Lindsay to FO, 22 January, 25 February 1938, FO 371/21526, PRO; Lindsay to FO, 6 February 1938, PREM 1/259, PRO; Undated précis by Michael Wright based on Halifax files, vol. 30, FO 954, PRO; Arthur Murray, ed., *The Diary of Faith Murray* (Edinburgh: R. and R. Clark, 1944), 6 April 1938, p. 94; Drummond, *American Neutrality*, 76; Saint-Quentin to Bonnet, 19, 20 April 1938, *DDF*, ser. 2, 9:411, 429.

53. Welles memorandum, 22 March 1939, *FR* (1939), 2:622–23; Long Diary, 6 February 1935 (State Department ideas on Ethiopia "coincide entirely" with my own), 5 August, 12 September 1935, 18 February 1938, Long Papers, LC; Long to Hull, 12, 17, 19 September 1935, Hull to Long, 14, 20 September 1935, 765.84/1134, 1152, 1205, 1265, RG 59, NA; Saint-Quentin to Bonnet, 8 De-cember 1938, *DDF*, ser. 2, 13:125.

54. Saint-Quentin to Quai d'Orsay, 22 March 1938, dossier 308, AEU, Quai d'Orsay; Saint-Quentin to Paul-Boncour, 26 March, 1 April 1938, Bonnet to Saint-Quentin, 23 May 1938, *DDF*, ser. 2, 9:111, 194–95, 857.

55. Saint-Quentin to Bonnet, 11 June 1938, *DDF*, ser. 2, 10:39–40; Haight, "Munich Crisis," 340; Dallek, *Roosevelt*, 163; Dieckhoff to State Secretary Weizsäcker, 31 May 1938, Chargé Thomsen to German Foreign Ministry, 10 September 1938, Chargé Kordt to German Foreign Ministry, 12 September 1938, ibid., 2:371, 736, 743–44. The April 1936 issue of *Foreign Affairs* carried three anti-Nazi articles; but not until July 1938 did the journal become irre-vocably committed.

56. Dirksen to Weizsäcker, 13 June, 20 July 1938, *DGFP*, ser. D, 1:714–15, 717–18, 721, 723; Offner, *Appeasement*, 251–53.

57. François-Poncet to Bonnet, 15 August 1938, *DDF*, ser. 2, 10:678; Hender-son to Halifax, 26 July 1938, *DBFP*, ser. 3, 2:12; memorandum by State Secre-tary von Weizsäcker, 8 July 1938, *DGFP*, ser. D, 2:481; Wilson, *Career Diplo-mat*, 45; Wilson Diary, 5 August 1938, Carr to Hull, 6 August 1938, Wilson to Biddle, 6 October 1938, boxes 1, 4, Wilson Papers, Hoover Library.

58. Bonnet, *De Munich*, 119–20, 123–24; Hooker, ed., *Moffat*, 199; Offner,

Appeasement, 258; Haight, "Munich Crisis," 340–41, 343; Watt, "Appeasers," 200.

59. *DDF*, ser. 2, 11:57n.; Truelle to Bonnet, 1 September 1938, ibid., 10:915; Georges Bonnet, *Défense do la paix: De Washington au Quai d'Orsay*, 2 vols. (Geneva: Constant Bourquin, 1948), 1:24; Green memorandum, 12 February 1937, box 12, Green Papers, Princeton University; Bullitt to FDR, 8 December 1936, Bullitt, ed., *For the President*, 198; Janet Adam Smith, *John Buchan* (London: Rupert Hart-Davis, 1965), 444–45; Harvey, ed., *Harvey*, 6 September 1938, p. 170.

60. Phipps to Halifax, 2 September 1938, *DBFP*, ser. 3, 2:218–19; Saint-Quentin to Bonnet, 27 September 1938, Bonnet to Saint-Quentin, 27 November 1938, *DDF*, ser. 2, 11:588, 588n., 12:814; Bonnet, *De Munich*, 124–25; Lindbergh, *Journals*, 19, 29 September 1938, pp. 71, 79; Bullitt to Hull, 15 September 1938, memorandum of conversation between Kennedy and Welles, 27 September 1938, Kennedy to Hull, 28 September 1938, Kennedy conversation with Hull, 24 September 1938, 760F.62/827, 1117⁷⁄10, 1248, 1333 (see also the rest of the file).

61. Moffat memorandum, 20 September 1938, Hull memorandum, 23 September 1938, *FR* (1938), 1:625–26, 638–39; Lindsay to FO, 19 September 1938, FO 371/21527; Berle, *Rapids*, 26 September 1938, p. 186.

62. Blum, ed., *Morgenthau Diaries, 1928–1938*, 522; Phillips to Hull, 29 September 1938, *FR* (1938), 1:699; Loewenheim, "Illusion," 288n.; Edward L. Henson, Jr., "Britain, America and the Month of Munich," *International Relations* 2 (April 1962):299–300.

63. Krock, "Reminiscences," *New York Times*, 19 June 1945 (clipping), box 52, Krock Papers, Princeton University. See also FDR to Prince Louis Ferdinand, 14 January 1935, FDR to Hitler, 11 July 1935, Gilbert to Hull, 9 January 1939, Summerlin to McIntyre, 10 January 1938, Prince Ferdinand to FDR, 31 December 1936, 811.458 Germany/18, 23, 25, 27, 30, RG 59, NA.

64. Saint-Quentin to Bonnet, 28 September, 2 October 1938, *DDF*, ser. 2, 11:656, 759–60; Hull to Wilson, 18 October 1938, Wilson to Hull, 21 October 1938, *FR* (1938), 1:724, 727; Loewenheim, "Illusion," 288n.; Lord Templewood, *Nine Troubled Years*, 325; Kaufmann, "Bullitt and Kennedy," 661; Wilson, *Career Diplomat*, 70–71. For other indications of Roosevelt's attitude, see Bullitt to Hull, 28 September 1938, and Phillips to Hull, 29 September 1938, *FR* (1938), 1:692, 699.

65. Halifax to Chamberlain, undated, and memorandum of conversations between FDR and Colonel Murray, PREM 1/367, PRO; Murray to FDR, 16 December 1938, Murray to LeHand, 20 May 1939, box 53, PSF, FDRL; note of conversation between Roosevelt and Murray, 23 October 1938, Murray to Halifax, 20 November 1938, file 8809, Elibank Papers, NLS; Coit, *Baruch*, 469–

71, 474; Ickes, *Ickes*, 2:533; Summerlin to McIntyre, 16 January 1939, OF 463, FDRL; Saint-Quentin to Bonnet, 28 January 1939, *DDF*, ser. 2, 13:809.

66. Saint-Quentin to Bonnet, 10, 11 April 1939, *DDF*, ser. 2, 15:532–33, 543.

67. Tweedsmuir to Baldwin, 8 April 1937, box 8, Tweedsmuir to his sister Anna, 20 February 1939, box 10, Tweedsmuir Papers, Queens University, Kingston, Canada; Eduard Beneš, *The Memoirs of Dr. Eduard Beneš* (London: Allen & Unwin, 1954), 79; Phipps to Halifax, 6 February, 20 April 1939, Phipps Papers, CCC; notes on a conversation between Roosevelt and Sir Arthur Willert, 25–26 March 1939, Cooper to Halifax, 22 March 1939, Lockhard report, 15 April 1939, FO 371/22829, PRO; Gordon Wright, "Ambassador Bullitt and the Fall of France," *World Politics* 10 (October 1957):72; Murray to FDR, 16 December 1938, box 53, PSF, FDRL; Halifax to Lindsay, 18 March, 11 April 1939, Campbell to Halifax, 23 August 1939, *DBFP*, ser. 3, 4:380, 5:169, 7:165; Leutze, *Bargaining for Supremacy*, 43; Wheeler-Bennett, *George VI*, 391, 511, 515; Waclaw Jedrzejewicz, ed., *Diplomat in Paris, 1936–1939: Papers and Memoirs of Julius Lukasiewicz, Ambassador of Poland* (New York: Columbia University Press, 1970), 168, 183; von Ribbentrop, *Memoirs*, 105–8; Saint-Quentin to Bonnet, 11 June 1938, *DDF*, ser. 2, 10:39–40.

68. Bullitt, ed., *For the President*, 304; von Ribbentrop, *Memoirs*, 101n.; Compton, *Swastika*, 74; record of Anglo-French conversations held in the prime minister's room, House of Commons, 22 March 1939, *DBFP*, ser. 3, 4:463; Chamberlain to Hilda Chamberlain, 5 February 1939, NC 18, Chamberlain Papers, BUL; Biddle memorandum, 1 July 1940, PSF, box 41, FDRL; Wirsing, *Roosevelt et l'Europe*, 268–69; Fish, *FDR*, 59–60, 62; *Journal Officiel de la République Française Débats Parlementaires*, 8 February 1939 (session of 7 February), carton 126, p. 104, Pierre Etienne Flandin Papers, Bibliothèque Nationale, Paris; Jean Montigny, *La France: Devra-t-elle faire la guerre pour la Tchécoslovaquie?* (Paris: Le Mans, 1938), carton 127, Flandin Papers, Bibliothèque Nationale, Paris; Noel to Quai d'Orsay, 31 May 1938, dossier 308, Corbin to Bonnet, 28 July 1938, dossier 309, Corbin to Quai d'Orsay, 25 July 1939, dossier 318, AEU, Quai d'Orsay; report by French naval attaché in Tokyo, 1 June 1939, C.R.R. 6, Archives de la Mer, Chateau Vincennes, Paris; Duroselle, *L'abîme*, 31.

69. Bonnet, *De Munich*, 279; German ambassador in Rome to German Foreign Ministry, 1 June 1940, *DGFP*, ser. D, 9:367; Bullitt, ed., *For the President*, 342–43; Davies, *Mission to Moscow*, 301; Bullitt to Hull, 8 January 1935, 123 Bullitt, William C./179, RG 59, NA. For Churchill, see *Hinge of Fate*, 111. De Gaulle and Churchill were both critical of FDR after the fact. For France's wishful thinking on an American bail-out, see Payne, Callahan, and Bennett, *Storm Clouds*, 3.

70. *Dodd's Diary*, 4 January 1936, p. 293. On 23 November 1939, Hitler was

still assuring his colleagues that America posed no threat on account of her neutrality laws (Compton, *Swastika*, 31).

71. Sherwood, *Roosevelt and Hopkins*, 167; Willi A. Boelcke, ed., *The Secret Conferences of Dr. Goebbels: The Nazi Propaganda War, 1939–43* (New York: Dutton, 1970), 4 September 1940, p. 85; Langer and Gleason, *Undeclared War*, 346; Friedländer, *Prelude*, 267; Gerhard L. Weinberg, "Hitler's Image of the United States," *American Historical Review* 69 (July 1964):1015; Compton, *Swastika*, 26, 31, 131–32; Dewitt C. Poole, "Light on Nazi Foreign Policy," *Foreign Affairs* 25 (October 1946):146.

72. François-Poncet to Bonnet, 5 September 1938, *DDF*, ser. 2, 11:12; Hugh Gibson, ed., *The Ciano Diaries, 1939–1943* (Garden City, N.Y.: Doubleday, 1946), 241; Sanborn, *Design for War*, 65; Hull memorandum, 16 May 1934, *FR* (1934), 3:651–52; Chargé Kirk to Hull, 11 July 1935, *FR* (1935), 1:730–31; Phillips to Hull, 30 August 1938, *FR* (1938), 1:562; Welles memorandum, 2 May 1940, Hull to Phillips, 30 May 1940, *FR* (1940), 2:696, 713.

73. Offner, *Appeasement*, 273; *News-Week*, 24 April 1939, p. 1. Hitler's speech, which came to eighteen pages single-spaced, is contained among other documents in Papiers 1940: Fouques Duparc, Quai d'Orsay.

74. Biddle to Hull, 12 July, 13 August 1939, 760C.62/702, 807, RG 59, NA; Pratt, *Hull*, 1:317.

75. Saint-Quentin to Bonnet, 28 May 1939, Papiers 1940: Fouques Duparc, Quai d'Orsay; Telford Taylor, *Munich: The Price of Peace* (Garden City, N.Y.: Doubleday, 1979), 518; Eagles, "Davies," 76–77; Wheeler-Bennett, *George VI*, 391; Bonnet to Saint-Quentin, 27 November 1938, *DDF*, ser. 2, 12:816; Carr to Hull, 6 August 1938, box 1, Wilson Papers, Hoover Library; Maddux, *Estrangement*, 99.

76. Eagles, "Davies," 270; Churchill, *Gathering Storm*, 389; Albjerg, *Churchill*, 108; Payne, Callahan, and Bennett, *Storm Clouds*, 98. For the anti-Soviet slant of the State Department generally, and in particular the embassy secretaries, Loy Henderson and George Kennan, see Eagles, "Davies," 201–2, 204, 224–26, 232–33, 267, 274–75, 283, 288, 349; Henry to Quai d'Orsay, 8 October 1937, dossier 361, SDN: Conflit Sino-Japonais, Interior Department memorandum, 3 February 1939, AEU, Saint-Quentin to Quai d'Orsay, 30 August 1939, dossier 123, Asia:Japon, Quai d'Orsay.

77. Lindbergh, *Journals*, 27 September 1938, p. 78; Hoover Address to Council on Foreign Relations, 31 March 1938, box 2, Wilson Papers, Hoover Library; Hoover to Castle, 11 December 1939, box 24, Castle Papers, Hoover Library; Thomas R. Maddux, "Red Fascism, Brown Bolshevism: The American Image of Totalitarianism in the 1930s," *The Historian* 40 (May 1978):102.

78. Saint-Quentin to Quai d'Orsay, 9 February 1940, dossier 319ter, AEU, Quai d'Orsay; Offner, *Origins*, 168; Mooney to FDR, 12, 14 March 1940,

740.0011 EW 39/1824½, RG 59, NA; memorandum of conversation at FO, 14 September 1933, box 9, Davis Papers, LC; Bingham Diary, 25 June 1934, box 1, Bingham Papers, LC; Friedländer, *Prelude*, 37. Reber is apparently Sam Reber, who became Truman's acting head of the American mission in Bonn (Eleanor Dulles, *Chances of a Lifetime* [Englewood Cliffs: Prentice-Hall, 1980], 245).

79. Friedländer, *Prelude*, 37–38; Offner, *Origins*, 168; Hull to Kirk, 13 October 1939, Harrison to Hull, 31 October 1939, Berle memorandum, 31 October 1939, 740.00119 European War 1939/78, 112, 117, RG 59, NA.

80. Gunther to Hull, 2 October 1939, Kirk to Hull, 7, 9 October, 5 November 1939, Schoenfeld to Hull, 8 October 1939, Davies to Hull, 7 October, 8 November 1939, Berggrav to Roosevelt, 7 October 1939, Hull to Kirk, 13 October 1939, Johnson to Hull, 16 December 1939, Steinhardt to Hull, 10 October 1939, Messersmith memorandum, 12 December 1939, 740.00119 European War 1939/17, 52, 54, 55, 66, 67, 78, 122, 172, 188½, 209, 254, 729, RG 59, NA; Bullitt to Hull, 8 December 1939, 760.61/687, RG 59, NA; Langer and Gleason, *Challenge to Isolation*, 256–59.

81. Mooney to Roosevelt, 15 March 1940, box 4, PSF, FDRL; Berle Diary, 16 October 1939, Berle Papers, FDRL; Drummond, *American Neutrality*, 133; Messersmith to Swanson, 8 October 1938, 093.622/43, RG 59, NA; Messersmith memorandum, 25 January, 13 February 1940, Bullitt to Hull, 23 October 1939, Harrison to Hull, 31 October 1939, 740.00119 European War 1939/104, 112, RG 59, NA; Messersmith to Phillips, 16 November 1934, item 442, Messersmith Papers, University of Delaware.

82. Mooney to FDR, 13, 14, 15 March 1940, box 4, PSF, FDRL; Mooney to FDR, 12 March (as well as 13, 14, and 15) 1940, 740.0011 European War 39/1824½, RG 59, NA; Hull to American Embassy, Berlin, 12 February 1940, 121.840 Welles, Sumner/7, RG 59, NA.

83. For Welles's itinerary, see Welles to FDR, 2 March 1940, Welles to Hull, 17 March 1940, box 4, PSF, FDRL; Schmidt (Foreign Ministry interpreter) memorandums, 1, 2, 4 March 1940, *DGFP*, ser. D, 8:821, 839, 850–62.

84. Messersmith memorandum, 13 February 1940, 740.00119 European War 1939/104, RG 59, NA (see also ibid., file 1824½).

85. Lothian to Smuts, 14 September 1939, GD 40/17, file 445, Lothian Papers, SRO; Berle Diary, 10 February 1940, Berle Papers, FDRL; Dallek, *Roosevelt*, 216; Thomsen to Foreign Ministry, 10 February 1940, Hull to Caffery, 8 February 1940, Berle to FDR, 18, 26 March 1940, FDR to Berle, 27 March 1940, *FR* (1940), 1:117–18, 129–31; Davies to Hull, 8 November 1939, Atherton to Hull, 13 February 1940, 740.00119 European War 1939/172 and 254, RG 59, NA.

86. For example, Hilton, "Welles Mission."

87. Ulrich von Hassell, *The von Hassell Diaries, 1938–1944* (Garden City,

N.Y.: Doubleday, 1947), 120; Hilton, "Welles Mission," 104–5, 117; Welles, *Time for Decision*, 111, 113, 119, 145; Welles's report on his special mission, 26 February, 1 March 1940, *FR* (1940), 1:28, 34; Bullitt, ed., *For the President*, 404, British ambassador in Chile to Halifax, undated, FO 371/24406, PRO; Chamberlain to Lothian, 4 February 1940, Halifax Papers, FO 800/324.

88. De Sales, *Diaries*, 108; German Embassy to German Foreign Ministry, 16 May 1940, *DGFP*, ser. D, 9:354; Thomsen to Foreign Ministry, 7, 18 March 1940, ibid., 8:868, 934; Friedländer, *Prelude*, 40; Hans Rothfels, *The German Opposition to Hitler* (Hinsdale, Ill.: Regnery, 1948), 135ff.

89. Halifax to Lothian, 11 March 1940, extract from War Cabinet conclusions, 13 March 1940, Vansittart minute on prime minister's account of talks with Welles, 18 March 1940, Halifax minute, 20 March 1940, minutes by Vansittart on Halifax report, undated, FO 371/24406, PRO; Chamberlain to Lothian, 4 February 1940, Halifax Papers, FO 800/324, PRO; Welles reports, 11 March 1940, *FR* (1940), 1:77; Levinson to Lothian, 29 April 1937, 7 January 1940, GD 40/17, files 341, 402, Lothian Papers, SRO; Cowling, *Hitler*, 358.

90. Welles report on his special mission, 11, 12, 13 March 1940, *FR* (1940), 1:77, 80, 84, 88–89; Hilton, "Welles," 116.

91. De Sales, *Diaries*, 106; von Hassell, *Diaries*, 14–17 February, 11 March 1940, pp. 112–13, 120; Thomsen to Foreign Ministry, 10 February 1940, Dieckhoff memorandum, 4 March 1940, *DGFP*, ser. D, 8:757–58, 864, 864n.; Langer and Gleason, *Challenge to Isolation*, 247–48; Welles to FDR, 2 March 1940, box 4, PSF, FDRL.

92. "Origine du Voyage Sumner Welles," author unknown, 24 February 1940, 3DA5, dr. 7, sdr. b, Beneš memoire, 2DA3, dr. 6, sdr. d, Daladier Papers, Fondation Nationale des Sciences Politiques, Paris; Saint-Quentin to Quai d'Orsay, 10 February 1940, Daladier to Saint-Quentin, 16 February 1940, dossier 319ter, Saint-Quentin to Quai d'Orsay, 1 October 1938, dossier 310, AEU, Quai d'Orsay; Bullitt, ed., *For the President*, 403–4. Bullitt presented FDR with evidence assembled by Assistant Secretary of State Judge Moore purporting to prove that Welles made homosexual advances to a train porter. Roosevelt said he knew about this but preferred to retain a valued aide, despite the danger of blackmail. Threat of exposure in September 1943 in the form of a Senate probe finally rang down the curtain on an illustrious career (ibid., 513–18; Israel, ed., *Long*, 29 August 1943, p. 324; see also Irwin Gellman's paper delivered at the American Historical Association convention of 29 December 1979, summarized in the Society for Historians of American Foreign Relations, *Newsletter* [March 1980]).

93. Daladier notes on conversations with Welles, undated, 3DA5, dr. 7, sdr. b, Daladier Papers, Fondation Nationale des Sciences Politiques, Paris; Bullitt to FDR, 18 April 1940, Bullitt, ed., *For the President*, 410; Hilton, "Welles," 115; Bullitt to Moore, 18 April 1940, box 3, Moore Papers, FDRL. For further details in connection with Welles's visit to Paris, see Duroselle, *L'abîme*, 95–97.

94. Welles memorandum, 22 March 1939, *FR* (1939), 2:622–23. For administration thinking on the diplomatic importance of the Vatican connection, see Levinson to Lothian, 26 December 1939, GD 40/17, file 402, Lothian Papers, SRO; Berle, *Rapids*, 26 December 1939, p. 279.

95. Phillips to Hull, 1 March 1940, box 46, Hull Papers, LC; Phillips to Hull, 28 February 1940, box 4, PSF, FDRL; Hilton, "Welles Mission," 99, 108, 120; Welles report, 26 February 1940, *FR* (1940), 1:22.

96. Welles to Hull, 27 February, 17 March 1940, box 4, PSF, FDRL.

97. Bullitt to Hull, 14 May 1940, Welles report, 19 March 1940, *FR* (1940), 1:115, 2:703, 703n. See also ibid., 2:687.

98. Corbin to Quai d'Orsay, 24, 27 May 1940, Papiers 1940: Fouques Duparc, Quai d'Orsay; note by French undersecretary for Europe, 3 June 1940, Churchill to Reynaud, 27 May 1940, Daladier to Saint-Quentin, 25 May 1940, Papiers 1940: Reynaud, Quai d'Orsay; Taylor to FDR, 3, 11 May 1940, Lothian to Hull, 25 May 1940, Lothian to FDR, 26 May 1940, Hull to Phillips, 26 May 1940, Hull memorandum, 26 May 1940, *FR* (1940), 2:701–2, 709–12.

99. Hull, *Memoirs*, 1:783–84; Phillips to Hull, 27 May, 1 June 1940, *FR* (1940), 2:712, 715.

100. *New York Times*, 7 July 1940, p. 1; *Time*, 25 October 1937, p. 22; Colonna to Hull, 11 June 1940, *FR* (1940), 2:716; Thomsen to Foreign Ministry, 8 September 1940, *DGFP*, ser. D, 11:42.

101. Harvey, ed., *Harvey*, 15 June 1940, p. 391; Churchill, *Their Finest Hour*, 115, 118.

102. Churchill, *Their Finest Hour*, 226.

103. Dallek, *Roosevelt*, 8, 10; Morgenthau, "Morgenthau Diaries," *Collier's*, 11 October 1947, p. 77; Morgenthau Farm Credit Administration Diary, 15 May 1933, Morgenthau Papers, FDRL; Phillips, *Ventures in Diplomacy*, 219; Drummond, *American Neutrality*, 80, 97; "State Department Reflections," 4 July 1940, OF 150, FDRL; Davies, *Mission to Moscow*, 146 (diary entry for 28 April 1937).

104. Leutze, *Bargaining for Supremacy*, 43, 256; Richardson, *Memoirs*, 157–58; *RC*, 79, 83; Bullitt memorandum, 23 April 1941, Bullitt, ed., *For the President*, 512.

105. Halifax to Eden, 7 July 1941, vol. 29, FO 954, PRO; Sherwood, *Roosevelt and Hopkins*, 290–91; Friedländer, *Prelude*, 254; Stimson Diary, 21 July 1941, Stimson Papers, Yale University.

106. *Pearl Harbor Attack*, pt. 26:265.

107. Halifax to Eden, 13 June 1941, Halifax Papers, CCC; Quinlan, "United States Fleet," 191ff.; War Cabinet Minutes, 19, 25 August 1941, CAB 65/19, 23, PRO; Burns, *Soldier of Freedom*, 127. See also Mackenzie King's opinion, dated 22 August 1941, that Roosevelt wanted immediate American entry into the war (MacKenzie King Diary, 22 August 1941, PAC); also Sir Robert Gordon Menzies's

impression as recorded in his memoir, *Afternoon Light* (London: Cassell, 1967), 135.

108. War Cabinet Minutes, 8 September 1941, 5 P.M., CAB 65/23; FDR to Churchill, 8 October 1941, vol. 29, Eden Papers, FO 954, PRO; Churchill to Roosevelt, 12 December 1941, *RC*, 171. Secondary accounts of this episode, as given by Sherwood, as well as Langer and Gleason, are misleading in that they do not mention Roosevelt's offer of American *crews* as well as American ships or the fact that he went back on his word (Sherwood, *Roosevelt and Hopkins*, 375–76; Langer and Gleason, *Undeclared War*, 779). Although the evidence is not conclusive that Churchill knew of Roosevelt's *volte-face* before he spoke in Commons, there can be little doubt of it. In any other context, the reference to Gallup polls would appear inexplicably harsh.

109. Friedländer, *Prelude*, 290; *RC*, 157n.; Bailey and Ryan, *Hitler vs. Roosevelt*, 199–200; Compton, *Swastika*, 88; *Time*, 3 November 1941, p. 13.

110. Divine, *Illusion*; Accinelli, "World Court."

Chapter 5

1. Madame Chiang to Chiang, 24 December 1942, *PDM-ROC*, vol. 1, pt. 1, p. 785; *FR* (Cairo and Teheran), 323; FDR to Currie, 12 September 1942, OF 4341, FDRL; Milton Viorst, *Hostile Allies: FDR and Charles de Gaulle* (New York: Macmillan, 1965), 223–24.

2. Jan Ciechanowski, *Defeat in Victory* (Garden City, N.Y.: Doubleday, 1947), 247, 249. Juho K. Passikivi had formerly served as Finnish envoy to Sweden as well as in the national government of Finland.

3. John C. Campbell, "Negotiating with the Soviets: Some Lessons of the War Period," *Foreign Affairs* 34 (January 1956):305–19; Thomas M. Campbell and George C. Herring, Jr., eds., *The Diaries of Edward R. Stettinius, Jr., 1943–1946* (New York: New Viewpoints, 1975), 80, 263; Bullitt, "Lost the Peace," 94; Roosevelt to Churchill, 18 March 1942, *RC*, 196.

4. See de Gaulle, *Memoirs*, 538, 574; Dilks, ed., *Cadogan*, 715; Eden, *Reckoning*, 590–91; *FR* (Malta and Yalta), 501.

5. Stalin to Roosevelt and Churchill, 26, 29 February, 17 March 1944, Roosevelt and Churchill to Stalin (9 March?) 1944, *SCRT*, 117, 126, 129, 131; minutes of Roosevelt-Stalin meeting, 8 February 1945, *FR* (Malta and Yalta), 768–69; minutes of conference on USS *Iowa* between FDR and the Joint Chiefs of Staff, 19 November 1943, Minutes of Roosevelt-Stalin Meeting, 28 November 1943, *FR* (Cairo and Teheran), 261, 483; Bohlen, *Witness*, 207; Sherwood, *Roosevelt and Hopkins*, 777.

6. John P. Vloyantes, "The Significance of Pre-Yalta Policies Regarding Liberated Countries in Europe," *Western Political Quarterly* 11 (June 1958):216; Thomas G. Paterson, "The Abortive American Loan to Russia and the Origins of

the Cold War, 1943–1946," *Journal of American History* 56 (June 1969):73–76; Harriman to Stettinius, 6 January 1945, *FR* (Malta and Yalta), 313–14; George C. Herring, Jr., "Lend Lease to Russia and the Origins of the Cold War, 1944–1945," *Journal of American History* 66 (June 1969):95–99; Halifax to Eden, 26 August, Eden to Halifax, 13 September 1944, Halifax Papers, CCC. See also public opinion polls in Ernest R. May, *"Lessons" of the Past: The Use and Misuse of History in American Foreign Policy* (New York: Oxford University Press, 1973), 6; Maddux, *Estrangement*, 152; FDR to Bullitt, 7 January 1934, Bullitt, ed., *For the President*, 74–75; FDR to Churchill, 11 November 1942, *RC*, 278, 701n.; minutes of FDR meeting with Joint Chiefs of Staff, 28 November 1945, minutes of the First and Third Plenary Meetings at Teheran, 28, 30 November 1943, *FR* (Cairo and Teheran), 478, 494–95, 576; Burns, *Soldier of Freedom*, 408; Churchill to FDR, 1 April 1945, vol. 30, Eden Papers, FO 954, PRO; Winston Churchill, *Triumph and Tragedy* (Boston: Houghton Mifflin, 1953), 512. On one occasion, Madame Chiang wrote her husband: "Hopkins says that in Roosevelt's mind there are two ways to give Stalin a second front (Stalin does not care where it is), Turkey or Italy, and Roosevelt thinks Turkey because it is easier to bribe" (Madame Chiang to Chiang, 24 December 1942, *PDM-ROC*, vol. 1, pt. 1, pp. 784–85). Stalin got nearly everything he wanted at Teheran: OVERLORD on time as planned at Quebec, along with a pincer invasion of southern France to accompany it; assurance that there would not be any diversionary activity in the Mediterranean to delay OVERLORD; assurance on the Curzon Line and freedom to do with Poland pretty much as he pleased; assurance on similar freedom of action in the Baltic states; a promise of Dairen; agreement with FDR to divide Germany and keep France weak; promise of a liberal share of the Italian fleet. See *FR* (Cairo and Teheran), 576; Harriman to Hopkins, 9 September 1944, *FR* (Quebec 1944), 198–99, 200n.

7. Schoenfeld to Hull, 2 September 1944, Bohlen to Hull, 4 September 1944, Ciechanowski memorandum, 4 September 1944, Churchill to Roosevelt, 4 September 1944, minutes of Roosevelt conversation with Archduke Otto, 15 September 1944, *FR* (Quebec 1944), 185–87, 189–90, 200n., 368; FDR to Churchill, 26 August 1944, Churchill to Roosevelt, 4 September 1944, *RC*, 568, 571. British pressure on the White House did result in one delayed American flight operation over Warsaw, but it was too little, too late (Eden, *The Reckoning*, 549; Churchill, *Triumph and Tragedy*, chap. 6).

8. Mikolajczyk to Harriman and Harriman memorandum, 16 October 1944, minutes of the Third Plenary Meeting at Yalta, 6 February 1945, *FR* (Malta and Yalta), 204–5, 667; minutes of Roosevelt-Stalin meeting at Teheran, 1 December 1943, *FR* (Cairo and Teheran), 594, 599–600. See also Robert L. Messer, *The End of an Alliance: James F. Byrnes, Roosevelt, Truman, and the Origins of the Cold War* (Chapel Hill: University of North Carolina Press, 1982), 50.

9. Dilks, ed., *Cadogan*, 607, 719; Kimball, "Churchill and Roosevelt," 171;

Vojtech Mastny, "Soviet War Aims at the Moscow and Teheran Conferences of 1943," *Journal of Modern History* 47 (September 1975):501–2; minutes of tripartite dinner meeting, 28 November 1943, *FR* (Cairo and Teheran), 512.

10. Eden War Cabinet memorandum, 22 November 1943, CAB 66/43 W. P. (43) 528, PRO; Eden report (on Roosevelt's views), 13 April 1943, War Cabinet 53, Conclusions, Confidential Annex, CAB 65/38, PRO; Mastny, *Russia's Road*, 250–51; Churchill to Roosevelt, 16 December 1944, 8, 10, 13, 27 March 1945, Roosevelt to Churchill, 16, 30 December 1944, 11, 15, 29 March 1945, *RC*, 632–34, 640, 645n., 665–67, 669–71, 674, 687, 690; Churchill, *Triumph and Tragedy*, 382–83; FDR to Stalin, 30 December 1944, *FR* (Malta and Yalta), 224 (included only for the sake of thoroughness, not because it is typical of the Roosevelt approach); minutes of the Third and Sixth Plenary Meetings, 6, 9 February 1945, ibid., 668, 847; Ciechanowski, *Defeat in Victory*, 272–73; Kimball, "Churchill and Roosevelt." Churchill's sense of obligation stemmed from many factors, not all of them strategic. Mikolajczyk lived in England. Twenty percent of the RAF pilots who defended London during the blitz were Polish. Thousands more were manning destroyers for the Royal Navy; and Polish infantry was fighting under British generals in the Middle East.

11. Stanislaw Mikolajczyk, *The Rape of Poland* (New York: Whittlesey House, 1948), 56; Ciechanowski, *Defeat in Victory*, 272–73, 314, 343; Roosevelt to Churchill, 7 February 1944, *RC*, 430; Roosevelt to Stalin, 26 April 1943, *SCRT*, 61; Campbell and Herring, eds., *Stettinius*, 84; Dallek, *Roosevelt*, 453; Hull *Memoirs*, 2:1442, 1444–45; Summerlin to McIntyre, 16 January 1939, OF 463, FDRL; Eden, *The Reckoning*, 539; minutes of the Third Plenary Meeting, 6 February 1945, *FR* (Malta and Yalta), 667. Mikolajczyk resigned on 24 November 1944, three weeks after Roosevelt's reelection. For FDR's fiercely hostile reference while at boarding school (Groton) in 1897 to Ignacy Jan Paderewski as a "long-haired Polish Jew," see *Letters*, 1:138.

12. Mikolajczyk, *Rape of Poland*, viii; Dallek, *Roosevelt*, 454–55; Mastny, "Soviet War Aims," 501; minutes of the Fourth and Sixth Plenary Meetings, 7, 9 February 1945, *FR* (Malta and Yalta), 709, 846–48, 853; Churchill, *Triumph and Tragedy*, 372, 382–83. See also Keith Eubank, *Summit at Teheran* (New York: Morrow, 1985).

13. See, for example, Stalin to Roosevelt and Churchill, 29 January 1944, *SCRT*, 117–18.

14. See, for example, Roosevelt to Stalin (messages) received on 12 April and 8 June 1942, Roosevelt to Stalin, 9 July 1942, ibid., 23, 25, 29; OF 4770, FDRL.

15. MacLean, "Davies," 88–89.

16. William Standley and Arthur Ageton, *Admiral Ambassador to Russia* (Chicago: Regnery, 1955), 152–53; Sherwood, *Roosevelt and Hopkins*, 621, 734; FDR to Stalin (messages) received on 6 and 11 September 1943, FDR to Stalin, 27 September 1943, Stalin to FDR, 8, 28 September 1943, *SCRT*, 88–95.

17. Churchill to FDR, 12 June 1943, Eden to Churchill, 26 October 1943, Eden Papers, FO 954, PRO; Hull, *Memoirs*, 2:1309; Bohlen, *Witness*, 136; Stalin to FDR, 17, 19 October 1943, FDR to Stalin, 14, 25 October 1943, *SCRT*, 99–103.

18. FDR to Stalin, 8 November 1943, FDR to Stalin, 24 (message received) November 1943, Stalin to FDR, 5, 25 November, 20 December 1943, *SCRT*, 104–5, 108, 114.

19. Sherwood, *Roosevelt and Hopkins*, 778, 804; *RC*, 12. Only once, and at the end of the conference, did FDR consent to meet Churchill alone.

20. Sherwood, *Roosevelt and Hopkins*, 846.

21. Ibid., 777, 911; MacLean, "Davies," 89; Bullitt to Hull, 9 November 1935, Bullitt, ed., *For the President*, 140; minutes of tripartite dinner meeting, 28 November 1943, minutes of Roosevelt-Stalin meeting, 29 November 1943, *FR* (Cairo and Teheran), 513, 531; Halifax to Churchill, 11 January 1942, vol. 29, Eden Papers, FO 954, PRO; Churchill, *Triumph and Tragedy*, 393; Lord Moran, *Churchill Taken from the Diaries of Lord Moran* (Boston: Houghton Mifflin, 1966), 240; Walter R. Roberts, *Tito, Mihailović and the Allies, 1941–1945* (New Brunswick: Rutgers University Press, 1973), 265. Churchill may have been the first to use the name "Joe" in reference to Stalin (*RC*, 231n.).

22. Tully, *F.D.R.*, 332–33; Liang, *Stilwell*, 56–59, 232n.; Charles F. Romanus and Riley Sunderland, *Stilwell's Mission to China* (Washington, D.C.: Department of the Army, 1953), 169; Stilwell Diary, 25–26 June 1942, in Theodore H. White, ed., *The Stilwell Papers* (New York: William Sloane, 1948), 119; Theodore H. White and Annalee Jacoby, *Thunder Out of China* (New York: William Sloane, 1946), 155.

23. Tuchman, *Stilwell*, 514; Hull, *Memoirs*, 2:1583; Sherwood, *Roosevelt and Hopkins*, 404; minutes of Roosevelt-Chiang dinner meeting, 23 November 1943, minutes of the Pacific War Council, 12 January 1944, *FR* (Cairo and Teheran), 325, 869. The Pacific War Council consisted of ambassadors from China, Australia, New Zealand, the Dutch East Indies, the Philippines, and Britain, in addition to Roosevelt.

24. Sherwood, *Roosevelt and Hopkins*, 512; Liang, *Stilwell*, 255. It has long been conventional, and still is in many quarters, to view FDR as doing all in his power to save "face" for Chiang. See, for example, Cohen, *America's Response*, 162, and Thomas G. Paterson, J. Garry Clifford, and Kenneth Hagan, *American Foreign Policy: A History since 1900* (Lexington, Mass.: D.C. Heath, 1983), 396. Doubtless, too, China would never have been classed as one of the "Big Four" had it not been for U.S. insistence; see Alan C. J. Feng, "The Strange Alliance: Political Implications of Soviet-American Wartime Collaboration," in Thomas B. Lee, ed., *Ideology and Practice: The Evolution of U.S. Foreign Policy* (Taipei: Tamkang University Press, 1985), 44on.

25. Chiang to Mme Chiang, undated letter, January 1943, Chiang to Mme

Chiang, 29 January 1943, *PDM-ROC*, vol. 1, pt. 1, pp. 787–88; Pratt, *Hull*, 2:737; Romanus and Sunderland, *Stilwell's Mission*, 163; Daniel Whitford Fitz-Simons, "Henry A. Wallace: Diplomat, Ideologue, and Administrator, 1940–1945" (Ph.D. dissertation, St. John's University, 1977), 194; Sherwood, *Roosevelt and Hopkins*, 406; Tuchman, *Stilwell*, 368, 398–99; Chiang to FDR, 9 October 1944, box 10, MRP, FDRL; Paul K. T. Sih, "The Failure of a Mission," *Modern Age* 17 (Winter 1973):101.

26. Minutes of Roosevelt-Chiang dinner meeting, 23 November 1943, *FR* (Cairo and Teheran), 324. See also ibid., 367; Sherwood, *Roosevelt and Hopkins*, 792; White and Jacoby, *Thunder Out of China*, 291; FDR memorandum for Hull, 7 April 1944, box 10, MRP, FDRL; minutes of Roosevelt-Stalin meeting, Yalta, 8 February 1945, *FR* (Malta and Yalta), 771. Stalin desired full control of both Dairen and Port Arthur (according to Feng) but compromised by accepting Dairen as a free port. He likewise pressed for full ownership of the Manchurian railways but agreed to joint control with China (Feng, "Strange Alliance," 442n.). Nevertheless, Chiang did not emerge from the Soviet-American horsetrade without serious political injury. There is no better expression of Chiang's intense concern over the future disposition of Dairen and Port Arthur than his cable to Mme Chiang, 18 June 1943, *PDM-ROC*, vol. 1, pt. 1, p. 853.

27. Michael Schaller, *The U.S. Crusade in China, 1938–1945* (New York: Columbia University Press, 1979), 152–53; Frank Dorn, *Walkout with Stilwell in Burma* (New York: Crowell, 1971), 75–79; FDR to Hurley, 17 November 1944, Hurley to FDR, 15 January 1945, George Elsey memorandum, 18 November 1944, boxes 11, 165, MRP, FDRL; White and Jacoby, *Thunder Out of China*, 251–52; John Morton Blum, ed., *The Price of Vision: The Diary of Henry A. Wallace, 1942–1946* (Boston: Houghton Mifflin, 1973), 18 May 1944, p. 333; Welles, *Seven Decisions*, 217; Feis, *China Tangle*, 205–6, 286, 316; Currie to FDR, 15 March 1941, box 37, PSF, FDRL; Thorne, *Allies*, 435; Fitz-Simons, "Wallace," 214.

28. Chiang was dubbed a reactionary and pictured in alliance with the landlord class while as many as five hundred thousand of his troops were said to be involved in a military blockade of the Red Chinese. For this and other charges against the KMT, see Schaller, *U.S. Crusade*, 115–18, 125–27; Tuchman, *Stilwell*, 166–68, 186–88, 677; Paterson, Clifford, and Hagan, *American Foreign Policy*, 396, 398–99. Equally vital for an appreciation of conventional historiography is the fact that by 1944 a good many critical reports on the China situation were being printed and broadcast by writers and journalists of the caliber of Pearl Buck, Theodore White, Brooks Atkinson, Edgar Snow, and Agnes Smedley. *Time* magazine, hitherto generally supportive of Chiang and his government, published a harsh statement by Mme Sun Yat-sen detailing rampant inflation, official corruption, details of the Honan famine disaster, and the Soong family feud. *Time* also brought out favorable reports of Mao's village

setup, along with his land reform and guerrilla tactics (Neils, "American Images," 22−30). In fairness to Chiang, however, it can and has been argued (1) that China made more progress, socially as well as economically, under KMT inspiration and leadership during the decade 1927−37 than ever before in its history—this, in fact, was called the "golden decade." Pearl Buck's husband showed that the United States had a higher percentage of tenant farmers than did China. (2) When Chiang lost control of Manchuria, pursuant to the terms of Yalta, he lost his richest and most industrially productive province. (3) Mao made false promises. Like the Bolsheviks, he promised private landownership but confiscated such land once in power. (4) Chiang placed his trust in the United States and turned down nearly a dozen Japanese offers of a separate peace, which would have permitted him to turn his undivided attention to domestic dissidents. (5) Corruption was common to many postwar regimes, including those of Germany, France, Italy, and especially Greece. For that matter, no less an American hero than Abraham Lincoln was accused of corruption, nepotism, and brutal repression during the American Civil War, and not without reason. Jefferson Davis was clean as a whistle by comparison. Inevitability is hard for any historian to prove. In recent years, there has been a mounting awareness that the Chinese communists were more truly communist, more closely affiliated with the Soviet Union (their 1959 divorce notwithstanding), less democratic, and more repressive than scholars were once inclined to believe. White soon repudiated the basic thesis of his *Thunder Out of China*. But for more recent examples of revisionism, see Kenneth Shewmaker, *Americans and the Chinese Communists, 1927−1945* (Ithaca: Cornell University Press, 1971); Neils, "American Images"; Moore, *Land and Peasant* (which argues that the Chinese communists were never successful politically prior to the Japanese occupation of North China in 1937); Mosher, *Broken Earth*, 301−2, 305. On the basis of scores of interviews with villagers, former tenant farmers, and peasants, Mosher also denies that Mao and his organization ever won the hearts and minds of the people. See, in addition, Walter Robertson, Oral History Interview, pp. 10, 14, 24, Eisenhower Library, Abilene, Kansas; Neils, "American Images," 35−36.

29. Wallace Diary, 12 May 1944, Blum, ed., *Wallace*, 331; Tuchman, *Stilwell*, 612; Fitz-Simons, "Wallace," 192, 194, 205; *Letters*, 4:1530; Buhite, *Hurley*, 150. It should be noted that Willkie went to China in October 1942 as FDR's personal representative (Romanus and Sunderland, *Stilwell's Mission*, 252); Tuchman suggests that Hurley might have been useful during an election year as a "tame Republican" (*Stilwell*, 509).

30. White and Jacoby, *Thunder Out of China*, 246−47, 253; Buhite, *Hurley*, 200−201.

31. *Time*, 26 June 1939, p. 32, 14 April 1941, p. 38; Tuchman, *Stilwell*, 408−9; Thorne, *Allies*, 173, 425; Crozier, *Man Who Lost China*, 253−54; Currie

report to FDR, 15 March 1941, box 37, PSF, FDRL. See also OF 3719, FDRL (on Currie). Strongly supportive of communist ideals, Lattimore, who left the United States after the war to teach in Leeds, England, was denounced as a communist spy by Louis Budenz, former head of the Communist party in America. Currie was later named by the FBI as a source of information passed to the USSR. In 1956, he came under investigation by a Senate Judiciary Subcommittee and at the same time lost his citizenship for residing out of the United States for more than five years.

32. Romanus and Sunderland, *Stilwell's Mission*, 73–74. Chiang had a second chief of staff responsible for Chinese armies fighting independently.

33. Tuchman, *Stilwell*, 4, 62, 109, 164, 320, 492, 509; Liang, *Stilwell*, 237; White, ed., *Stilwell Papers*, 36, 49, 277; Thorne, *Allies*, 6, 324, 453.

34. Sherwood, *Roosevelt and Hopkins*, 739; White, ed., *Stilwell Papers*, 245; Romanus and Sunderland, *Stilwell's Mission*, 378n.; Charles F. Romanus and Riley Sunderland, *Stilwell's Command Problems* (Washington, D.C.: Department of the Army, 1956), 383; Tuchman, *Stilwell*, 194–95, 362, 364; Alsop, "Why We Lost China," 38.

35. Liang, *Stilwell*, xiii, 3–5, 280n.; Alsop, "Why We Lost China," 26–27, 46; Romanus and Sunderland, *Stilwell's Mission*, 151, 318; Tuchman, *Stilwell*, 369.

36. Chiang to Mme Chiang, 18 June 1943, *PDM-ROC*, vol. 1, pt. 1, p. 852; Liang, *Stilwell*, 4, 42–44, 267–69, 276–77; White, ed., *Stilwell Papers*, 56; Romanus and Sunderland, *Stilwell's Mission*, 139, 230.

37. Liang, *Stilwell*, 236, 239, 268, 279n.; White, ed., *Stilwell Papers*, 333–34.

38. White, ed., *Stilwell Papers*, x; Joseph Alsop, "Why We Lost China," 17; Liang, *Stilwell*, 235, 273–74; Tuchman, *Stilwell*, 200, 233, 370, 410.

39. Feis, *China Tangle*, 260. This is the group that included Davies, Service, Emmerson, and Ludden. It may be noted that the China hands were not only correct in assessing Mao's chances as a potential winner—however much this may have been a form of self-fulfilling prophecy—they were also right in assuming that Mao's party would not have to remain allied with the Soviet Union (though such a tie was in fact sustained until 1959 and with repercussions which have been traced as far as Korea and Vietnam). One should perhaps be careful, in this connection, not to assume that increased solicitude for Mao during the war would have precluded his eventual enmity toward the United States.

40. See PPF 4951, FDRL; Tuchman, *Stilwell*, 513–14. Some years later, Carlson ran for Congress as a Communist. For the best account of public relations techniques as used by Mao and Chou, see Shewmaker, *Americans and the Communist Chinese*.

41. Tully, *F.D.R.*, 331–32, 335; William D. Hassett, *Off the Record with F.D.R., 1942–1945* (New Brunswick: Rutgers University Press, 1958), 181, 288;

transcript of presidential press conference, 19 February 1943, PPF 7308; Eleanor Roosevelt, *This I Remember*, 283.

42. Interestingly enough, while there is evidence for this idea, it has never been proven. Generals Wedemeyer and Chennault would have disagreed; and common sense alone suggests that Chiang's seven-year campaign against a million Japanese troops on a poor man's budget would not have succeeded without considerable willingness on the part of the people to sacrifice. Japan was no mean opponent. After crushing China in 1895, the Land of the Rising Sun had driven Russia to the peace table and delivered the karate chop to another potentially powerful adversary at Pearl Harbor. Is one to suppose that China's three-month defense of Shanghai (1937) and month-and-a-half-long defense of Hengyang (1944) could have occurred without a high degree of organization and commitment? The capital city of Chungking, with virtually no defense against aerial assault, withstood the barrage of an estimated 1,290 Japanese bombers during a single three-month period in 1939. Moreover, those who observed the local populace turn out en masse to build airfields with nothing but straw baskets slung on poles over their shoulders were not likely to doubt Chiang's standing with his own people. The stone for this work was hauled from riverbeds in wheelbarrows while women and children sat for entire days pounding mud over a bed of crushed rock. Nine airfields were completed in record time, four of them with nine thousand feet of runway to accommodate B-29s. Without a single steam shovel, truck, or bag of cement, the Chinese finished the task in ninety days. Surely, Mao's men had no monopoly on esprit de corps. Typically, Herbert Feis, in *China Tangle*, does not outline the actual Sino-Japanese military situation, or even the Chinese Nationalist position as against the Chinese communists. We do not learn how many were killed on opposing sides. We are not told how many troops Chiang used against Japan; only how many were not used (Feis, *China Tangle*, 136, 260–61; see also Liang, *Stilwell*, 234n., 239; Tuchman, *Stilwell*, 530; Buhite, *Johnson*, 145; Sih, "Failure of a Mission," 102; Crozier, *Man Who Lost China*, 218–19). Warren I. Cohen saw no conclusive answer to such questions on the basis of the available evidence, although he doubted that the Chinese general in charge of the defense of Hengyang was loyal enough to Chungking to be seen as an intregal part of Chiang's war effort ("Who Fought the Japanese in Hunan? Some Views of China's War Effort," *Journal of Asian Studies* 27 [November 1967]:111–15).

43. Alsop, "Why We Lost China," 16; Liang, *Stilwell*, 276. In light of FDR's relationship with China, it is doubly interesting to recall Truman's record. Although Chiang received American aid to airlift his troops into Manchuria and a considerable number of American troops helped occupy key Chinese cities in 1945, these same troops left in 1946 *when their presence was most sorely needed*, and the ranking American general in China (Wedemeyer) was denied permission to send seven United States divisions into Manchuria.

Although a thousand American military advisers took up their station at Chiang's side in 1946, they constituted a smaller group than Wedemeyer had requested and were never permitted by the White House to go to the fighting front. Wedemeyer's detailed blueprint for American aid was first ignored, then suppressed. Chiang received a billion dollars during the four years after V-J Day, but this was less on balance than went to Japan or even to the Philippines, and most of it was used to disarm the Japanese in 1945 or facilitate Chiang's 1949 retreat to Formosa. *Desperately needed financial aid was withheld during the critical period from the late summer of 1945 to the summer of 1947.* Furthermore, when, in 1948, Congress voted $128 million in additional military aid, Truman delayed its delivery until the end of the year. The White House thus halted on a Chinese Vistula, leaving Chiang to perish in a Warsaw of American making. China received no Marshall Plan aid despite inflation and unemployment worse than Germany's, and the Marshall truce mission of 1946 dealt Mao a veritable death blow by cutting off American military aid for just long enough to reinvigorate his forces (not until May of 1947 did Marshall end the arms embargo affecting KMT troops). Where Churchill had insisted on no peace without victory in Greece, Marshall forced Chiang to pretend interest in a coalition and to cancel a number of victory drives, much the way Stilwell had done earlier. North of Hankow, two hundred thousand of Chiang's men had trapped seventy thousand communists when the Marshall truce allowed a Red escape to Shantung Province. Near Canton, an additional hundred thousand Reds escaped on junks to Shantung for the same reason. Chiang was also forced by Marshall to give up control of the vital Kalgan Pass, which guarded the entrance to Manchuria and through which hundreds of thousands of communists subsequently poured en route to their homes and Russian aid. Before the truce expired, they fortified the pass and necessitated a bloody campaign by Chiang to regain control. In January 1947, Red armies, which had been well armed and well supplied by Soviet Russia, marched effortlessly through Kalgan Pass on their way to a southern victory. Once more, American intervention deprived the Kuomintang of a valuable hard-earned tempo. One might add that General Wedemeyer's recommendations cannot be judged unreasonable or far-fetched given his prior experience as Stilwell's second in command and the added fact that he was altogether capable of viewing China's internal condition with alarm. No blind partisan of the generalissimo, he sent home reports of spiritual insolvency on the part of the KMT, coupled with a lack of popular confidence. By Wedemeyer's estimate, there was widespread corruption and disillusionment, accompanied by growing disaffection and a corresponding increase in attraction by the Left. Wedemeyer did not hesitate to advocate an immediate end to favoritism of the rich, a merit system for military promotion, and an improvement in relations between KMT army officers and rank and file. In similar vein, Chiang's bleeding of Formosa was regarded as a cause of continued unrest. Smuggling, repression, and other charges all contributed to his overall negative impression. At the same time, it is only fair to assume that a general whose initial impression could be so critical and stated in such damaging terms must have had strong countervailing grounds for believing in the ability of the Kuomintang to survive—and not only to survive but eventually to flourish, with the help of generous American aid. Despite all of Chiang's obvious problems and deficiencies, Wedemeyer concluded that the Chinese leader had been treated unrealistically, indeed disgracefully, by Washington. And as part of said "disgraceful" treatment, he included the U.S. arms embargo, along with the Marshall mission. See Stueck, *Wedemeyer Mission*, 3, 11, 35–36, 40, 42, 44–45; Claire Lee Chennault, *Way of a Fighter* (New York: Putnam, 1949), xi–xvii; John Foster Dulles, *War or Peace* (New York: Macmillan, 1950), 226–27. See, in addition, two very well-informed oral histories at the Eisenhower Library, Abilene, Kansas: those of Walter Judd and Walter Robertson. Stueck, in defense of Truman's policy, has held that corruption within the Kuomintang was even more pronounced after 1945 than before. In Stueck's judgment, not only were the American people unwilling to support "the action necessary to sustain the Nationalist government" but such action would have been "the height of folly" because of the need to concentrate on European recovery. Above all, Stueck cannot believe, as Wedemeyer did, that "just a bit more aid . . . could have stymied one of the great revolutions of modern times" (*Wedemeyer Mission*, 1, 117–18). Plainly, there is room here for renewed debate along the lines of what was heard in and out of Congress during the actual period under review. To cite just two of the better-known examples of post-mortem opinion, Eisenhower was happy to quote James Forrestal's warning of 1945 to the effect that withdrawal of American forces from China, especially the marines, would "invite a vacuum of anarchy in Manchuria" into which "the Russians will flow" (Dwight D. Eisenhower, *Mandate for Change* [Garden City, N.Y.: Doubleday, 1963], 79). American chargé Walter Robertson, head of the U.S. mission in China during the interval between Hurley's departure and Stuart's arrival and also Marshall's truce negotiator, later claimed that "we stood by and watched the Republic of China drift into economic collapse without making any effort to stop it." He felt all the more strongly about this since the U.S. military record in China struck him as equally derelict. The Soviet Union, only five days in the war against Japan, had occupied Manchuria and, after refusing to allow the United States to transport Chiang's troops thither to accept Tokyo's surrender, it began turning over enormous quantities of Japanese equipment to Mao's forces in patent violation of the terms of its "friendship" pact with China. Chiang, who now appealed for a loan of $500 million, needed this aid more than any other ally, having been at war for eight years. Washington, however, procrastinated. Eventually, Marshall (in December) gave the loan his blessing, but only on the basis of unacceptable terms

360 · NOTES TO PAGES 188–194

involving coalition government and currency reform. There followed the American arms embargo, affecting only Chiang's side of the conflict while Soviet generals continued their arming of Mao. Robertson's conclusion was bitter: "We refused to give the [KMT] government aid at the only time which, in my opinion, it ever had any chance of saving the situation." Thereafter, Chiang had to pay his soldiers in "completely worthless money." It is interesting to note Robertson's recollection of the San Francisco Conference, which was held preparatory to an agreement on the United Nations (in April 1945): Soong had asked Dulles if he knew of any secret deal on China. Dulles then went to Stettinius and, after hearing Stettinius's denial, passed the false information on to Soong (Robertson, Oral History Interview, pp. 13, 17–20; J. F. Dulles Address to UN Association of Japan, 23 April 1951, box 107, Dulles Papers, Princeton University).

44. See, for example, Feis, *China Tangle*, 347.

45. Ibid., 279, 306, 342–45; Thorne, *Allies*, 576–78; Robertson, Oral History Interview, pp. 14–16, Eisenhower Library. For a different view, see Warren I. Cohen, "American Observers and the Sino-Soviet Friendship Treaty of August, 1945," *Pacific Historical Review* 35 (August 1966):347–49.

46. Feis, *China Tangle*, 278, 314, 346–47; Thorne, *Allies*, 576; Dulles, *War or Peace*, 146.

47. Clifford, *Retreat from China*, ix.

48. Thorne, *Allies*, 423, 560–62. Seymour began at his new post on 7 February 1942.

49. Thorne, *Allies*, 5, 423, 441, 562; Eden, *The Reckoning*, 492; RC, 656; Winston Churchill, *Closing the Ring* (Boston: Houghton Mifflin, 1951), 328–29; Campbell and Herring, eds., *Stettinius*, 15 April 1944, p. 53.

50. Churchill to Roosevelt, 11, 23 June 1944, RC, 528, 540; Churchill, *Triumph and Tragedy*, chap. 18.

51. Churchill to Roosevelt, 15 December 1944, RC, 516, 630; FDR to Churchill, 13 December 1944, Churchill to Leeper, 5, 9 December 1944, to Scobie, 8 December 1944, to Roosevelt, 14 December 1944, to Smuts, 14 December 1944, Hopkins to Churchill, 16 December 1944, Churchill to Alexander, 24 December 1944; all quoted in Churchill, *Triumph and Tragedy*, 289–91, 295–96, 300–302, 310–11, 315, 324.

52. Churchill, *Triumph and Tragedy*, 396.

53. Churchill to Leeper, 5 December 1944, to Scobie, 8 December 1944, ibid., 290, 292–94.

54. Taylor, *Origins*, 190; Bloom, *Autobiography*, 232–33; William Strang, *Britain in World Affairs: The Fluctuation in Power and Influence from Henry VIII to Elizabeth II* (New York: Praeger, 1961), 337–38; Thorne, *Allies*, 562; Bullitt to Hull, 22 September 1938, 760.62/998, RG 59, NA; Churchill,

Gathering Storm, chap. 1 and p. 328; Churchill, *Closing the Ring*, 328; Dallek, *Roosevelt*, 6.

55. Mackenzie King Diary, 12 June 1939, 23, 24, 29 April 1940, PAC; François-Poncet to Quai d'Orsay, 8 October 1937, dossier 307, AEU, Quai d'Orsay; Wirsing, *Roosevelt et l'Europe*, 272; Coit, *Baruch*, 438; Pratt, *Hull*, 1:62; *Time*, 27 December 1937, pp. 14–15; Murray to FDR, 11 June 1933, file 8808, Murray to Halifax, 22 October 1938, file 8809, Elibank Papers, NLS; *Newsweek*, 24 April 1939, p. 12; Bullitt to Hull, 22 September 1938, 760F.62/998, RG 59, NA; Murray to FDR, 20 December 1938, box 53, PSF, FDRL; George C. Herring, Jr., "The United States and British Bankruptcy, 1944–1945: Responsibilities Deferred," *Political Science Quarterly* 86 (June 1971):271; Hassett, *Off the Record*, 314; Eleanor Roosevelt, *This I Remember*, 242–43, 253, 260, 275.

56. Sherwood, *Roosevelt and Hopkins*, 444 (Roosevelt and Churchill never became chums, 363); Moran, *Churchill*, 247, 249–50, 791, 837; Thorne, *Allies*, 120; Louis P. Lochner, ed., *The Goebbels Diaries, 1942–1943* (Garden City, N.Y.: Doubleday, 1948), 73; undated memorandum by Messersmith, file 2013, Messersmith Papers, University of Delaware.

57. Although he never wished to emulate such figures as Laval, Franco, and Mussolini, his criticism was invariably balanced. And just as he was compelled to admire Japan for her "many gifts and qualities," he could also say of the infamous fuehrer (whose policies he loathed): "I admire men who stand up for their country in defeat, even though I am on the other side" (Churchill, *Gathering Storm*, 83; *Grand Alliance*, 594).

58. Sherwood, *Roosevelt and Hopkins*, 617; Churchill, *Gathering Storm*, 107, 165–66; Churchill, *Their Finest Hour* (Boston: Houghton Mifflin, 1949), 49, 520, 579; Churchill, *Grand Alliance*, 200; Churchill, *Closing the Ring*, 51.

59. Annex to memorandum, 15 March 1945, box 52, Charles Taussig Papers, FDRL; Morgenthau Presidential Diary, vol. 6, 19 August 1944, p. 1387, Morgenthau Papers, FDRL; Roosevelt to Churchill, 16 April 1942, *RC*, 206.

60. Bohlen, *Witness*, 188; Burns, *Soldier of Freedom*, 366; Pratt, *Hull*, 2:1278, 1288–89; Elliott Roosevelt, *As He Saw It*, 188–91; Churchill, *Closing the Ring*, 373–74; Churchill, *Triumph and Tragedy*, 241; Franz von Papen, *Memoirs* (London: André Deutsch, 1952), 570–71.

61. George Earle interview with *Philadelphia Enquirer*, 30 January 1949, quoted in von Papen, *Memoirs*, 523. For Churchill's warnings on the future of Romania, see Churchill to Roosevelt, 8 March 1945, *RC*, 662.

62. Conversations at Teheran, 28 November 1943, CAB 66/45 W.P. (44) 8, PRO; Dallek, *Roosevelt*, 438; minutes of Roosevelt-Churchill dinner meeting, 13 September 1944, *FR* (Quebec 1944), 325–26; minutes of the Second and Seventh Plenary Meetings at Yalta, 5, 10 February 1945, *FR* (Malta and Yalta), 614, 618, 621, 902; Churchill, *Closing the Ring*, 401; Albjerg, *Churchill*, 136–37;

Ernest Llewellyn Woodward, *British Foreign Policy in the Second World War*, 5 vols. (London: Her Majesty's Stationery Office, 1970–76), 1:lvi; Melvin Small, "How We Learned to Love the Russians: American Media and the Soviet Union during World War II," *The Historian* 36 (May 1974):471; Churchill to Roosevelt, 15 January 1945, *RC*, 650–51; Eleanor Roosevelt to Arthur Murray, 10 October 1946, file 8810, Elibank Papers, NLS.

63. See, for example, *Contemporary Review* 144 (July–December 1933):16, 22; *New Statesman* 5 (January–June 1933):312, 618, 620, 750; *Fortnightly Review* 132 (July–December 1932):303–14, 423–31, 558–68, 735–43; 143 (January–June 1938):641ff. See also Simon, *Retrospect*, 189, 239–40; Halifax Papers, 800/316, PRO; Harding to Cadogan, 22 May 1935, Cadogan Papers, FO 800/293, PRO; Chamberlain to Hilda Chamberlain, 15 July 1939, NC 18, Chamberlain memorandum on British relations with Japan, September 1934, NC 8/19/1, Chamberlain Papers, BUL.

64. Alfred Zimmern, "Disarmament: The Decisive Phase," *Fortnightly Review* 132 (July–December 1932):681–91; [London] *Morning Post*, 21 January 1937, in FO 371/21040, PRO. For other examples, see *Spectator* 149 (July–December 1932).

65. White, ed., *Stilwell Papers*, 15–16. Roosevelt's susceptibility to British influence had been evident for some time; see Dieckhoff to Weizsäcker, 22 March 1938 ("the key to the American attitude is in London"), *DGFP*, ser. D, 1:697; Henry to Delbos, 13 July 1936 ("the attitude of the United States will depend largely on British politics"), *DDF*, ser. 2, 2:677.

66. Sherwood, *Roosevelt and Hopkins*, 308; Churchill to Roosevelt, 4 August 1942, FDR to Churchill, 11 December 1942, *RC*, 231n., 294; Moran, *Churchill*, 243 (on FDR's following of the Churchill lead re: Soviet votes in the United Nations); Hornbeck memorandum, 19 June 1940, *FR* (1940), 4:359; William H. McNeill, *America, Britain, and Russia: Their Co-operation and Conflict, 1941–1946* (Oxford: Oxford University Press, 1953), 52; Leutze, *Bargaining for Supremacy*, 98–99, 156; Langer and Gleason, *Undeclared War*, 423; Bullitt, ed., *For the President*, 558.

67. Kimball, "Churchill and Roosevelt," 170.

68. Eden to Halifax, 28 January 1944, Halifax to Eden, 13 February 1944, Halifax to FO, 8 October 1943, vol. 30, Eden Papers, FO 954, PRO.

69. Dallek, *Roosevelt*, 259–60; Tully, *F.D.R.*, 300, 305; Burns, *Soldier of Freedom*, 178; Halifax to Eden, 5 January 1942, vol. 29, Churchill to Roosevelt, 18 March 1945, vol. 30, Eden Papers, FO 954, PRO; Sherwood, *Roosevelt and Hopkins*, 442; Churchill to Roosevelt, 23, 27 June 1944, Roosevelt to Churchill, 26 June 1944, *RC*, 541, 542, 544; Bullitt, ed., *For the President*, 558. The story lends itself to retelling, of course, and has been embroidered by Tully, Hopkins, and others. Of its essential truth, however, there can be little doubt.

70. La Feber, "Indochina," 1286.

71. Churchill, *The Hinge of Fate* (Boston: Houghton Mifflin, 1950), 383.

72. Herring, "British Bankruptcy," 266–67.

73. Churchill told the House of Commons after Yalta that he assumed Stalin would wish to live in "honorable friendship and equality with the western democracies. I feel also that their word is their bond" (*RC*, 517). He seems no more sincere here, however, than at a somewhat later date: "I felt bound to proclaim my confidence in Soviet good faith in the hope of procuring it" (Hanson Baldwin, "Churchill Was Right," *Atlantic* 194 [July 1954]:25). Such logic was not a part of his intellectual baggage.

74. Churchill, *Closing the Ring*, 454; Churchill to Roosevelt, 18 March 1945, vol. 30, Eden Papers, FO 954, PRO.

75. Churchill, *Their Finest Hour*, 553.

76. Churchill, *Gathering Storm*, 190; *Their Finest Hour*, 256; *Grand Alliance*, 663; *Hinge of Fate*, 695; *Triumph and Tragedy*, 473–78. Other British leaders with blood ties include Lindsay, who was twice married to an American; Chamberlain, son of an American stepmother (Mary Endicott, daughter of President Cleveland's secretary of war); and Harold Macmillan, whom Churchill sent to North Africa as his liaison with the U.S. Army and avowedly for his American background (Murphy, *Diplomat*, 164).

77. Halifax to Anne Chamberlain, 13 May 1948, Halifax Papers, CCC; Churchill, *Their Finest Hour*, 7–8; Maurice Ashley, *Churchill as Historian* (London: Seckers and Warburg, 1968), 10.

78. Guerrant, *Good Neighbor*, 43; Churchill, *Their Finest Hour*, 530; Churchill to Eden, 30 March 1941, quoted in Churchill, *Grand Alliance*, 357; ibid., 603; Churchill, *Hinge of Fate*, 209; *Closing the Ring*, 329.

79. Eden, *The Reckoning*, 491; de Gaulle, *Memoirs*, 233; Moran, *Churchill*, 243; Thorne, *Allies*, 120n.

80. Churchill, *Grand Alliance*, 55; *Hinge of Fate*, 5, 219, 377, 465, 477, 482, 682, 813; *Closing the Ring*, 346, 363, 452; Moran, *Churchill*, 244; Eden, *The Reckoning*, 632; Dallek, *Roosevelt*, 351.

81. Faulkner to Halifax, 24 June 1943, Eden Papers, vol. 30, FO 954, PRO.

82. Phipps to Eden, 2 May 1937, 1 January 1938, Phipps to Halifax, 1 November 1938, 28 March 1939, Lindsay to Phipps, 9 November 1937, Phipps Papers, CCC; British Embassy in Washington, "Notes on Personalities," FO 371/20665; Halifax to Eden, 25 August 1944, Henderson to Colville, 17 March 1945, FO minute by Eden, 26 January 1945, vol. 30, Eden Papers, FO 954, PRO; Hoare to Halifax, 8 November 1940, box 13, item 20, Templewood Papers, ULC; Bullitt, ed., *For the President*, 160. Vansittart called Kennedy a "foul specimen of double crosser and defeatest" (ibid., 437).

83. MacDonald to Tweedsmuir, 7 December 1936, Earl of Crawford to Tweedsmuir, 23 September, 3 November 1936, box 8, George VI to Tweedsmuir, 5 July 1939, box 11, Tweedsmuir Papers, Queens University, Kingston,

Canada; Sherwood, *Roosevelt and Hopkins*, 351; Halifax, *Fullness*, 262, 277; Thorne, *Allies*, 143; Wheeler-Bennett, *George VI*, 619–20; Arthur C. Murray, *At Close Quarters: A Sidelight on Anglo-American Diplomatic Relations* (London: John Murray, 1946), 98; Milner to Lothian, 4 May 1939, GD 40/17, file 398, Lothian Papers, SRO.

84. A. J. P. Taylor, *Beaverbrook* (London: Hamish Hamilton, 1972), 366.

85. For FDR's warm welcome in Quebec, Canada, see PPF 1710, FDRL. For Wilson's hostility, see Dilks, ed., *Cadogan*, 36, 53; Chamberlain to Ida Chamberlain, 24 September, 7 October (on Baldwin's opinion), 28 October 1933, 4 July 1937, 20 July 1940, NC 18, Chamberlain Papers, BUL; Lord Vansittart, *The Mist Procession* (London: Hutchinson, 1958), 465; Bullitt to FDR, 5 May 1937, Bullitt, ed., *For the President*, 213; *Time*, 16 November 1936, p. 30; Eden to Lindsay, 14 February 1936, FO 414/273, PRO; Davis to Chamberlain, 10 June 1937, Chamberlain to Davis, July 1937, PREM 1/261, PRO; Wheeler-Bennett, *George VI*, 371; Bingham to Davis, 1 July 1937, box 3, Davis Papers, LC.

86. Lothian to Churchill, 28 November 1940, vol. 29, Eden Papers, FO 954, PRO; Baldwin, "Notes on a Visit to the USA November 1933," bk. 108, Baldwin Papers, ULC; Chamberlain to Hilda Chamberlain, 28 July 1934, to Ida, 6 February 1937 (on Runciman's visit), NC 18, Chamberlain Papers, BUL; La Feber, "Indochina," 1285; Moran, *Churchill*, 242–43; Dilks, ed., *Cadogan*, 693; Eden, *The Reckoning*, 431; Craigie FO minute, 7 August 1934, *DBFP*, ser. 2, 13:11; ibid., 13–14n. (on Vansittart). On this point, British, French, and German observers were as one (Millet to Eden, 12 October 1937, FO 414/274, PRO; Bonnet, *De Munich*, 125 ["préoccupations de politique intérieure dominaient toutes les autres"]; Dieckhoff to Foreign Ministry, 15 October 1937, *DGFP*, ser. D, 1:639–40).

87. George VI to FDR, 3 June 1941, quoted in Wheeler-Bennett, *George VI*, 525; Chamberlain memorandum to cabinet, September 1934, NC 8/19/1, BUL. In *David Copperfield*, Spenlow and Jorkins is a firm of proctors to whom Copperfield is articled. Jorkins, a gentle, retiring man, seldom appears, but Spenlow makes Jorkins's supposed intractable character the ground for refusing inconvenient requests.

88. Lindsay to Simon, 27 July 1933, FO 414/272, PRO; Halifax to Eden, 29 October 1942, vol. 29, Eden Papers, FO 954, PRO; Dilks, ed., *Cadogan*, 512, 579, 585–87; Lindsay to Simon, 30 January 1933, 18 May 1934, *DBFP*, ser. 2, 5:750, 6:926; Thorne, *Allies*, 245 (on Eden); Cadogan to Halifax, 10 January 1945, Halifax Papers, CCC ("I am rather appalled at the haphazard amateurish surroundings of the President. How do these people carry on? At Teheran, I was invited to discuss a draft of the communiqué with major Boettiger. Major Boettiger may be an excellent fellow—even an excellent son-in-law [to Roosevelt] but I don't know what qualifications he has for communiqué drafting. I found

him sitting on an untidy camp bed in a rather squalid pavilion in the Russian compound").

89. Chamberlain to Ida Chamberlain, 27 October 1934, to Hilda, 9 October, 12 December 1937, NC 18, Chamberlain Papers, BUL; Roskill, *Hankey*, 3:302; Milner to Lothian, 4 May 1939, GD 40/17, file 398, Lothian Papers, SRO; Loewenheim, "Illusion," 287n.; Moran, *Churchill*, 245 ("the President has changed his mind again. But nobody appears in the least surprised").

90. Cadogan to Halifax, 10 January 1944, Halifax Papers, CCC; Eden, *The Reckoning*, 290, 431, 447, 457, 495, 520, 595; Eden to Baldwin, 19 December 1938, bk. 124, Baldwin Papers, ULC; Gary R. Hess, "Franklin Roosevelt and Indochina," *Journal of American History* 59 (September 1972):356; Dilks, ed., *Cadogan*, 693 (on Eden). See also Lyttelton's opinion that FDR became "intensely jealous of Winston" (Thorne, *Allies*, 120).

91. Eden to Chamberlain, 17 January 1938, Halifax to Eden, 26 November 1941, vol. 29, Halifax to Eden, 2 January 1944, vol. 30, Eden Papers, FO 954, PRO; Dilks, ed., *Cadogan*, 401 (on Halifax's opinion); Earl of Birkenhead, *Halifax: The Life of Lord Halifax* (London: Hamish Hamilton, 1965), 477, 479, 502–3, 514, 520, 525; Moran, *Churchill*, 791; Halifax, *Fullness*, 261–62, 296.

92. See note 39 for the conclusion of the present volume, as well as Mastny, *Russia's Road*, 48, 239–40; also Churchill, *Gathering Storm*, 449; Milovan Djilas, *Conversations with Stalin* (New York: Harcourt Brace, 1962), 73; Davies, *Mission to Moscow*, 346.

93. Sherwood, *Roosevelt and Hopkins*, 861, 893; Nikita Khrushchev, *Khrushchev Remembers: The Last Testament*, trans. and ed. Strobe Talbott (Boston: Little, Brown, 1974), 349–50, 356, 363, 411; Admiral Nicholas Horthy, *Memoirs* (London: Hutchinson, 1956), 192–93, 255.

94. Borg, *Far Eastern Crisis*, 436; *Time*, 1 December 1941, p. 14; Shigemitsu, *Japan and Her Destiny*; Ike, trans. and ed., *Japan's Decision*, 101; Grew to Hull, 29 December 1934, *FR* (1934), 3:688.

95. Langer and Gleason, *Undeclared War*, 462; Weinberg, "Hitler's Image," 1011–13; Compton, *Swastika*, 21–23; Mussolini speech at Campidoglio World Fair Grounds, 20 April 1939, box 58, PSF, FDRL; German ambassador in Rome to Foreign Ministry, 1 June 1940, *DGFP*, ser. D, 9:492. See also the conclusion of the present volume, note 39.

96. Friedländer, *Prelude*, 4, 13; Italian newspaper clippings, box 58, PSF, FDRL; Osborne to Halifax, 9 May 1939, *DBFP*, ser. 3, 5:489; *Time*, 8 May 1939, p. 11; Weinberg, "Hitler's Image," 1010; Compton, *Swastika*, 21–22.

97. Von Ribbentrop, *Memoirs*, 103–8; Friedländer, *Prelude*, 74–77, 266; *The German White Paper* (New York, 1940), 10–11, 16, 19, 32–33, 43; Biddle to FDR, 20 May 1939, OF 1667, FDRL; Lochner, ed., *Goebbels Diaries*, 45; Compton, *Swastika*, 51, 72–73; Warren F. Kimball, "Dieckhoff and America: A German's

View of German-American Relations, 1937–1941," *The Historian* 27 (February 1965):225–26; Dieckhoff memoranda, 29 July, 2 November 1940, *DGFP*, ser. D, 10:357–59; 11:458; Weizsäcker, *Memoirs*, 179, 260; William L. Shirer, *The Rise and Fall of the Third Reich* (New York: Crest, 1963 paperback), 517, 1329n.; von Hassell, *Diaries*, 36–37, 153.

98. Von Ribbentrop, *Memoirs*, 113, 169–70; Hugh R. Trevor-Roper, ed., *Hitler's Table-Talk, 1941–1944* (London: Weidenfeld and Nicolson, 1953), 8, 587, 624, 657; Luther to German Foreign Ministry, 18 August 1936, *DGFP*, ser. C, 5:916; Thomsen to Foreign Ministry, 17 May 1939, Dieckhoff Memoranda, 29 July, 2 November 1940, ibid., ser. D, 6:532–33, 10:360–62, 11:458; Henderson to FO, 18 August 1938, FO 371/21709, PRO (report on the German press); Compton, *Swastika*, 45; Schacht report on trip to the United States, 1933, *DGFP*, ser. C, 1:486; Serrano Suñer, *Entre les Pyrénées et Gibraltar*, 162 (Hitler stressed the need for an Afro-European defense against American imperialism).

99. Stimson Diary, 14 March 1935, Stimson Papers, Yale University; Smith, *Buchan*, 404–5; Tweedsmuir to Carruthers, 4 August 1936, Tweedsmuir to Murray, 8 October 1937, Tweedsmuir to Gillon, 26 March 1938, 19 January 1940, boxes 7–9, 11, Tweedsmuir Papers, Queens University, Kingston, Canada; FDR to Mackenzie King, 16 April 1936, Mackenzie King to FDR, 8, 17 March, 23 April 1937, Tweedsmuir to Mackenzie King, 27 May 1937, vols. 225, 241, 243, Mackenzie King Papers, PAC; Mackenzie King Diary, 7, 8, 15 November 1935, 6 March, 29–30 June, 10 September 1937, 15–16, 18 August 1940, 17, 20 April 1941, PAC; Wrong to Skelton, 26 February 1936, Wrong Papers, PAC.

100. Leon Blum editorial in *Le Populaire*, 26 August 1939; Kaufmann, "Bullitt and Kennedy," 653; Green memorandum, 12 February 1937, carton 12, Green Papers, Princeton University; Bonnet, *Défense de la Paix: De Washington au Quai d'Orsay*, 12–13; Henry to Delbos, 10 November 1937, *DDF*, ser. 2, 7:370; Jean Monnet, *Memoirs*, trans. Richard Mayne (London: Collins, 1978), 471. See also Bonnet, *De Munich*, and (for the Havas line in Latin America) Gellman, *Good Neighbor*, 151.

101. Pratt, *Hull*, 2:566.

102. Murphy, *Diplomat*, 171.

103. De Gaulle, *Memoirs*, 210, 233, 544, 573–74, 768–69; Viorst, *Hostile Allies*, 153, 155, 172, 190–91. De Gaulle, in one of his books, had expressed doubt about the future of parliamentary democracy in France, and Roosevelt wrote his son Elliott that the general was "out to achieve one-man government in France" (Edward R. Drachman, *United States Policy toward Vietnam, 1940–1945* [Rutherford, N.J.: Fairleigh Dickinson University Press, 1970], 10).

104. Pratt, *Hull*, 2:590; Hull, *Memoirs*, 2:1223. See also the index to Hull's memoirs, in which more space is given to de Gaulle and the Free French issue than to either Japan, Germany, or the Soviet Union.

105. Hassett, *Off the Record*, 259; Pratt, *Hull*, 2:chap. 7, 576; FDR to Churchill, 7 September 1943, *Letters*, 4:1453–54; Viorst, *Hostile Allies*, 151–52.

106. Murphy, *Diplomat*, 180–81; Viorst, *Hostile Allies*, 156, 171, 173.

107. Murphy, *Diplomat*, 168, 172–73; Dwight D. Eisenhower, *Crusade in Europe* (Garden City, N.Y.: Doubleday, 1948), 137; Pratt, *Hull*, 2:554, 573–74; Drachman, *Vietnam*, 60–61, 76; de Gaulle, *Memoirs*, 576, 767, 769; FDR to John A. Roosevelt, 13 February 1943, FDR to Churchill, 7 September 1943, *Letters*, 4:1400, 1453; Dallek, *Roosevelt*, 459; Hull, *Memoirs*, 2:1208; Sherwood, *Roosevelt and Hopkins*, 686; Viorst, *Hostile Allies*, 172–73, 225–26.

108. Fall, *Two Viet-Nams*, 41n., 42–43, 56–58; FDR to Donovan, 17 November 1944, FDR memorandum for Stettinius, 1 January 1945, box 55, PSF, FDRL; Thorne, *Allies*, 629; Oliver Lyttelton, notes on discussion with FDR, 24 November 1942, vol. 29, Eden Papers, FO 954, PRO; Viorst, *Hostile Allies*, 223–24.

109. De Gaulle, *Memoirs*, 911; Viorst, *Hostile Allies*, 225–26; minutes of Roosevelt-Stalin meeting, 28 November 1943, *FR* (Cairo and Teheran), 484–85.

110. Raymond Cartier, *Roosevelt* (Lyon: Gutenberg, 1945); Firmin Roz, *Roosevelt* (Paris: Dunod, 1948). According to Roz, the similarities between T.R. and FDR were far more striking than the differences; FDR was not partisan in the sense of being a Democrat or a Republican—he was first, last, and always an American; he was free of personal egotism or chauvinism; and so forth (see 6, 117, 217, 220).

111. Pierre Gosset and Renée Gosset, "Les secrets de la Paix Manquée: Le déclin de Roosevelt," *Realités Littéraires*, ser. 3 (1949):3–5, 13–14, 33, 37, 40, 52; Georges Ollivier, *Franklin Roosevelt: L'homme de Yalta* (Paris: La Libraire Français, 1955), 5–7, 149, 161, 184, 194, 197, 200, 203–4, 219–21, 235–37, 240–41; Arthur Conte, *Yalta ou le partage du monde* (Paris: Laffont, 1974), 372–75.

112. Admiral Jean Decoux, *A la Barre de l'Indochine* (Paris: Plon, 1949), 343; Fall, *Two Viet-Nams*, 40–41n.; James Roosevelt, *My Parents*, 206; Mussolini speech, 20 April 1939, box 58, PSF, FDRL; Viorst, *Hostile Allies*, 155; Murphy, *Diplomat*, 114–15; de Gaulle, *Memoirs*, 393; Willkie address, 7 April 1944, Omaha, Wallace Diary, vol. 18, p. 3270, CUOHC.

113. Straus to House, 9 April 1934, box 107, House Papers, Yale University; *Letters*, 3:437n.; Laboulaye to Paul-Boncour, 15 December 1933, *DDF*, ser. 1, 5:276; Saint-Quentin to Paul-Boncour, 26 March 1938, ibid., ser. 2, 9:112; Hull memorandum, 13 September 1941, *FR* (1941), 2:914; Serrano Suñer, *Entre les Pyrénées et Gibraltar*, 133, 138, 321–22, 324, 328–30, 336; David Ben Gurion, *Ben Gurion Looks Back: In Talks with Moshe Pearlman* (New York: Simon and Schuster, 1965), 106–8; Burns, *Soldier of Freedom*, 380; Gary R. Hess,

America Encounters India, 1941–1947 (Baltimore: Johns Hopkins University Press, 1971), 150–51, 156–57, 163–64, 167–69, 183–87.

114. Menzies, *Afternoon Light,* 136. Nicholas Halasz, *Roosevelt through Foreign Eyes* (New York: Van Nostrand, 1961), the only book to appear thus far on Roosevelt's overseas reputation, has fallen far short of the mark, confusing popularity at home with popularity abroad, virtually ignoring the abuse heaped upon FDR for his spoiler role in the London Economic Conference, exaggerating the significance of eulogies, and representing even German and Japanese leaders as admirers. We are told that Berlin hailed Roosevelt for his neutrality "because it ran counter to . . . large segments of the American people," and we are invited to accept at face value the praise Tokyo bestowed upon its conquerer in 1945. As sources, Halasz frequently cites "an Englishman" or "a Swiss newspaper," and when a specific title is supplied, there is generally no indication of page; see, for example, 33, 35, 69, 312–13.

115. George Kennan, *Memoirs, 1925–1950* (New York: Bantam, 1969), 369.

Chapter 6

1. Langer and Gleason, *Undeclared War,* 624; Howard F. Cline, *The United States and Mexico* (Cambridge, Mass.: Harvard University Press, 1953), 251; Guerrant, *Good Neighbor,* 1; Gellman, *Good Neighbor,* 227–28 (see also 1–2, 73, 127, 171, 198). For a similar appraisal, see the following influential school texts: Thomas A. Bailey, *A Diplomatic History of the American People,* 9th ed. (Englewood Cliffs: Prentice-Hall, 1970), 689; Samuel Flagg Bemis, *A Short History of American Foreign Policy and Diplomacy* (New York: Henry Holt, 1959), 515. For a more recent text, see Paterson, Clifford, and Hagan, *American Foreign Policy,* 350, 360, 362, 364–65, 367. Although the Paterson coverage includes FDR's heavy-handed approach to Machado's Cuba, it is generally enthusiastic about the Good Neighbor, particularly with regard to the administration's abjuring of military force. Lloyd Gardner's *Imperial America* renders a fairly bland account with surprisingly little on the subversive effect of American foreign aid. On this score, Gardner and Paterson are alike. Neither compares the mediation record and overall reputation of the second Roosevelt with that of the first (T.R.); nor do they compare the World War II record of Latin American wartime cooperation with that of World War I under Wilson. See Lloyd C. Gardner, *Imperial America: American Foreign Policy since 1898* (New York: Harcourt Brace Jovanovich, 1976), 135–42. For another positive picture of the Good Neighbor, see Samuel L. Baily, ed., *Nationalism in Latin America* (New York: Knopf, 1971), 22. Several recent monographs portray FDR's policy in a more critical light, but mainly regarding its failure to do more on the economic plane. Dick Steward, for instance, finds beneath FDR's "rhetoric of idealism" the "diplomacy of imperialism" (*Trade and Hemisphere,* viii).

See also ibid., vii, 2, 196–97, 204, 207–8, 240–41, 280; Steward, *Money, Marines, and Mission: Recent U.S.–Latin American Policy* (Lanham, Md.: University Press of America, 1980), 29, 34–35. For some time, the trend in economic analysis has been to view Roosevelt's Good Neighbor as "United States hemispheric hegemony pursued by other means" and therefore as nothing new. Nevertheless, economics has remained the sole yardstick or criterion for such negative evaluation (as opposed to Roosevelt's reputation relative to other presidents, his relative lack of success as a mediator, or his relative failure at achieving wartime cooperation). See Jablon, *Crossroads of Decision*, 133; Koppes, "Good Neighbor," 81; Smith, "Good Neighbor," 65, 67–68, 81, 90–91; Varg, "Good Neighbor." For accounts that tend to be ambivalent, see Haglund, *Latin America*, 3, 34, 46, 48–49, 51–52; David Green, *The Containment of Latin America* (Chicago: University of Chicago Press, 1971), vii, ix, 59–60, 83–85, 101, 187, 201, 295; Lester D. Langley, *The Cuban Policy of the United States: A Brief History* (New York: Wiley, 1968), 153–61; Langley, *United States and the Caribbean*, 115, 137–62. Haglund outlines deep Axis inroads but regards New Deal policy as a definite improvement over that of Hoover. Steward has a familiar tendency to shift the blame away from Roosevelt personally; thus, "Forces, not men, were in the saddle of state. No horseman could have reached the stirrup" (*Trade and Hemisphere*, 241). Green subscribes to the conventional view of FDR's reputation (alleging an unprecedented personal following along with "almost unanimous" Latin American support for the United States in World War II). While downplaying Roosevelt's pressure on Cuba in 1933 and taking a favorable view of New Deal responses to expropriation in Bolivia and Mexico, he offers a damning indictment of New Deal economic initiatives. Langley, in his *Cuban Policy*, likewise takes a generally critical line, especially on financial initiatives, yet minimizes the element of political coercion (with FDR dispatching only two warships and Welles asking for only three). By the same token, *United States and the Caribbean* presents a Republican policy without serious problems yet with introductory remarks which prepare the reader for something else. In the same manner, Steward presents a somber record of action and inaction on the part of the New Deal while concluding on an incongruously roseate note.

2. FDR to Dodd, 9 November 1936, *Letters*, 3:625; Luther to the German Foreign Ministry, 18 August 1936, *DGFP*, ser. C, 5:917.

3. Grayson, "Good Neighbor," 327; Pratt, *Hull*, 1:165; Harold F. Peterson, *Argentina and the United States, 1810–1960* (Albany: State University of New York Press, 1964), 391; Carleton Beals, Bryce Oliver, Herschel Brickell, and Samuel Guy Inman, *What the South Americans Think of Us* (New York: McBride and Co., 1945), 305, 377; James C. Carey, *Peru and the United States, 1900–1962* (South Bend: Notre Dame University Press, 1964), 107; *New York Times*, 28 November 1936, pp. 1, 3, 1 December 1936, p. 1, 2 December 1936, p.

1, 3 December 1936, p. 1; *Chicago Tribune*, 1 December 1936, p. 1. One of the key elements of the Roosevelt policy consisted of the limitation or elimination of controls by the U.S. government over the finances of Latin American nations, especially in the case of Haiti and the Dominican Republic (Guerrant, *Good Neighbor*, 168-69). On the other hand, as will soon be seen, the overall financial dependency of Latin America upon Washington increased substantially as a result of enormous infusions of U.S. government aid.

4. E. Bradford Burns, *The Unwritten Alliance: Rio Branco and Brazilian-American Relations* (New York: Columbia University Press, 1966), ix-x; Burns, *A History of Brazil* (New York: Columbia University Press, 1970), 237; Frederick W. Marks III, *Velvet on Iron: The Diplomacy of Theodore Roosevelt* (Lincoln: University of Nebraska Press, 1979), 180-90; Welles to FDR, 17 October 1940, OF 11, FDRL; Varg, "Good Neighbor," 48.

5. Memorandum from France's Department of the Interior, 11 February 1939, Saint-Quentin to Quai d'Orsay, dossier 374, AEU, Quai d'Orsay; Langer and Gleason, *Undeclared War*, 601-2; Compton, *Swastika*, 252; Charles R. Whittlesey, "Five Years of the Export-Import Bank," *American Economic Review* 29 (September 1939):494-95; John Morton Blum, ed., *From the Morgenthau Diaries: Years of Urgency, 1938-1941* (Boston: Houghton Mifflin, 1965), 55; Blum, ed., *Morgenthau Diaries, 1928-1938*, 493; Smith, "Good Neighbor," 83; *World Almanac*, 1939, p. 219, 1940, p. 219; Lothian to Halifax, 3 September 1940, Hachey, ed., *Confidential Dispatches*, 7; Division of the American Republics memorandum, 8 November 1940, box 8, Moore Papers, FDRL; *Time*, 7 October 1940, p. 30; Mellett to FDR, 8 January 1941, box 69, PSF, FDRL; Beals et al., *South Americans*, 93.

6. Guerrant, *Good Neighbor*, 187; Beals et al., *South Americans*, 136; Wallace to FDR, 26 August 1942, OF 11C, FDRL.

7. Josephus Daniels, *Shirt-Sleeve Diplomat* (Chapel Hill: University of North Carolina Press, 1947), 25, 51, 107, 287-88, 292, 298; Cline, *Mexico*, 271-72.

8. *Time*, 10 November 1941, p. 22; Daniels, *Shirt-Sleeve Diplomat*, 108, 224, 227, 233-37.

9. Brand to Lothian, 5 December 1939, GD 40/17, Lothian Papers, SRO; Daniels, *Shirt-Sleeve Diplomat*, 230, 267; Blum, ed., *Morgenthau Diaries, 1928-1938*, 494-97; Green, *Containment*, 7-9.

10. Pratt, *Hull*, 2:686; Berle and Jacobs, eds., *Navigating the Rapids*, 186; Brand to Lothian, 5 December 1939, GD 40/17, Lothian Papers, SRO; Betty Kirk, *Covering the Mexican Front* (Norman: University of Oklahoma Press, 1942), 200-201; Anthony Sampson, *The Seven Sisters: The Great Oil Companies and the World They Shaped* (New York: Viking, 1975), 109; Steward, *Trade and Hemisphere*, 204.

11. Blum, ed., *Morgenthau Diaries, 1928–1938*, 493, 495; Kirk, *Mexican Front*, 310, 317–18. Cárdenas, among other things, obliged American business to become involved in education and to construct schools for this purpose (Steward, *Trade and Hemisphere*, 199).

12. Kirk, *Mexican Front*, 258, 280, 298; Thomsen to German Foreign Ministry, 4 May 1940, *DGFP*, ser. C, 1:283. For the best and most up-to-date treatment of the massive cracks made by the Axis in hemispheric solidarity, see Haglund, *Latin America*, esp. 3, 133, 161, 166 (from 1938 on, FDR received from observers in Latin America "an almost continual stream of bad tidings," ibid., 77).

13. Cline, *Mexico*, 295–99; Fitz-Simons, "Wallace," 97, 103; Campbell and Herring, eds., *Stettinius*, 263; *Time*, 7 December 1936, p. 13; Robert Payne, *The Life and Death of Trotsky* (New York: McGraw-Hill, 1977), 391–92; Robert D. Warth, *Leon Trotsky* (Boston: Twayne, 1977), 172. Warth observes that President Vargas, after being urged by Stettinius to open diplomatic relations with Moscow, asked if it would be possible "for the United States to give us assurance that if we did do this that there would not be trouble in the future." Stettinius replied: "There was no question that the President of the United States would be delighted to sponsor such a relationship."

14. Fitz-Simons, "Wallace," 25, 66; Kirk, *Mexican Front*, 254–55, 262; *Time*, 9 December 1940, pp. 28–29.

15. Langer and Gleason, *Undeclared War*, 158–62, 608–10; *Time*, 20 October 1941, p. 20, 1 December 1941, p. 15; Cline, *Mexico*, 268, 277–78; Kirk, *Mexican Front*, 327.

16. Welles to Armstrong (Standard Oil representative), 15 November 1937, *FR* (1937), 5:304. See also ibid., 277–311 and ibid. (1938), 5:537ff.; Green, *Containment*, 27; *Time*, 22 May 1939, p. 28. Standard Oil lost 2.5 million acres on a fifty-five-year lease.

17. F. P. Walters, *A History of the League of Nations* (London: Oxford University Press, 1960), 534; Castle memorandum, 3 January 1933, *FR* (1933), 1:351; Wood, *Latin American Wars*, 116, 118, 120–21; *Time*, 22 May 1939, p. 28; Beals et al., *South Americans*, 35–36, 38; Fitz-Simons, "Wallace," 108, 110–11; Steward, *Money*, 50. Wallace had apparently weakened Peñaranda further by intervening in a domestic labor dispute involving striking miners (Fitz-Simons, "Wallace," 84–86).

18. Guerrant, *Good Neighbor*, 34–36; Beals et al., *South Americans*, 44.

19. Argentina did three-quarters of the world's trade in beef and veal; two-thirds in linseed. It was also the world's leading exporter of corn and second biggest exporter of wheat, wool, lamb, and mutton (*Time*, 5 May 1941, p. 38).

20. Bemis, *Latin American Policy*, 335; Peterson, *Argentina*, 427.

21. Phillips memorandum, 12 July 1933, James Drumm resumé of interview

with FDR, 15 August 1933, *FR* (1933), 4:646, 656; Bemis, *Latin American Policy*, 286–87; Hull, *Memoirs*, 1:323; *Time*, 23 November 1936, p. 24; Berle and Jacobs, eds., *Navigating the Rapids*, 119; Wood, *Latin American Wars*, 369–70.

22. *New York Times*, 3 December 1936, p. 19; *Chicago Tribune*, 3 December 1936, p. 11; *Time*, 14 December 1936, p. 13, 5 May 1941, p. 40; Wallace to McIntyre, 13 March 1937, FDR memorandum for Wallace, 29 March 1939, Hull to FDR, 14 March 1941, Welles to FDR, 21 July 1941, OF 366, FDRL.

23. Mellett to FDR, 8 January 1941, box 69, PSF; Hull to FDR, 14 March 1941, OF 366, FDRL; *New York Times*, 21 March 1941, p. 42; Langer and Gleason, *Undeclared War*, 620; Peterson, *Argentina*, 407–8.

24. FDR to Vargas, 6 July 1936, *FR* (1936), 5:300; Hull to Weddell, 19 March 1936, Prado to Hull, 16 January 1937, Welles to Leahy, 24 February 1937, Welles press conference, 26 June 1937, Hull to Hannah Clothier Hull, 20 July 1937, 832.34/264, 271, 271A, 282, 283, RG 59, NA.

25. See 832.34/290, RG 59, NA; also Welles to FDR, 16 August 1937, OF 11, FDRL; Weddell to Hull, 10 August 1937, Hull memorandum, 12 August 1937, *FR* (1937), 5:154, 156; Bryce Wood, "External Restraints on the Good Neighbor Policy," *Inter-American Economic Affairs* 16 (Autumn 1962):6–10, 15. *O Jornal*, as Rio's most influential paper, was a reliable guide to official thinking (Haglund, *Latin America*, 68).

26. Langer and Gleason, *Undeclared War*, 623; Peterson, *Argentina*, 427; *RC*, 420; Guerrant, *Good Neighbor*, 16, 36, 41–42, 182; Steward, *Trade and Hemisphere*, 176.

27. Hull, *Memoirs*, 2:1391, 1398, 1402–8; Guerrant, *Good Neighbor*, 48–53. For a crushing indictment of the Roosevelt policy vis à vis Argentina, see Steward, *Trade and Hemisphere*, 189; Woods, *Roosevelt Foreign Policy*, x.

28. Braden to Welles, 27 November 1942, Spruille Braden Papers, Columbia University; Langer and Gleason, *Undeclared War*, 618; Guerrant, *Good Neighbor*, 103; Bowers to FDR, 10 January 1940, PPF 730, FDRL; White to Morgenthau, 31 March 1939, box 6, Harry Dexter White Papers, Princeton University; Long Diary, 6 January 1939, box 5, Long Papers, LC; Chargé Thomsen to Foreign Ministry, *DGFP*, ser. D, 6:130; Carey, *Peru*, 104; Claude G. Bowers, *Chile through Embassy Windows: 1939–1953* (New York: Simon and Schuster, 1958), 59–60, 100; Bowers, *My Life* (New York: Simon and Schuster, 1962), 304, 307–9. Chilean President Arturo Alessandri, who had to put down a Nazi coup attempt in September 1938, proceeded to execute sixty-two young Nazi sympathizers. The U.S. reputation also suffered serious damage at the start in 1933 when FDR appointed as his ambassador Hall Sevier, a former member of the Texas legislature who had to be removed after a year and a half for alcoholism (Haglund, *Latin America*, 87–88; Gellman, *Good Neighbor*, 72).

29. Guerrant, *Good Neighbor*, 101, 167–68, 190, 200; Berle Diary, 5 December 1939, Berle Papers, FDRL; Adams, *Economic Diplomacy*, 251–52;

Time, 14 October 1940, p. 26. Bemis cited a figure of $500 million in Lend-Lease for military equipment and economic support of the war (*A Short History,* 516).

30. Hugh Butler, "Expenditures and Commitments by the United States Government in or for Latin America," Senate Document 132, 78th Cong., 1st sess. (Washington, D.C.: U.S. Government Printing Office, 1943), viii–ix, 37, 62, 78–80. Butler subsequently employed an accounting firm which confirmed his original estimate to within a margin of only 5 percent error (Justus F. Paul, "Senator Hugh Butler and Aid to Latin America, 1943–44," *South Dakota History* 8 [Winter 1977]:34–45). Butler pointed out, in particular, that "wages paid to Latin American workers on U.S. projects run from three to seven times as high as the prevailing wages. In the Dominican Republic, the prevailing wage is 70 cents a day. We pay the Dominicans $3 to $5 a day. In Paraguay, the prevailing wage is 60 cents a day. We paid the Paraguayans $3 to $5 a day. Bolivia's average is 90 cents a day. We pay the Bolivians from $6 to $8. Brazil has an average of $1.80. We pay from $5 to $10. As a result, the laborer is getting a week's pay for a day's work . . . [and he] lays off for a week. Labor turnover is tremendous." Needless to say, the problem this created for native employers could be devastating (Hugh Butler, "Our Deep Dark Secrets in Latin America," *Reader's Digest* 43 [December 1943]:23).

31. Butler, "Latin America," 21; Beals *et al., South Americans,* 14, 24; Guerrant, *Good Neighbor,* 124–25. The country was Guatemala.

32. Interview with Claude Bowers by Louis M. Starr, 30 August 1954, p. 133, Reminiscences of John Campbell White (interview by Wendell Link, March 1953), 114, 119, CUOHC. See also statistics given by *World Almanac,* 1939; ibid., 1940; Butler, "Latin America," 21.

33. Fitz-Simons, "Wallace," 120; *Letters,* 4:842; *Time,* 5 June 1939, p. 15, 26 June 1939, p. 20.

34. *Time,* 7 October 1940, pp. 29–30; Smith, "Good Neighbor," 79, 83.

35. See Cardenas's tactics as described by *Time,* 4 November 1940, p. 39.

36. Hornibrook to Hull, 28 October 1937, *FR* (1937), 5:193; Fitz-Simons, "Wallace," 96–97.

37. Reminiscences of John Campbell White, 116–17, CUOHC; Fitz-Simons, "Wallace," 95; Wallace to Hull, 14 August 1937, *FR* (1937), 5:189. Nicaragua received a loan of $2 million for construction equipment (Guerrant, *Good Neighbor,* 103).

38. Braden to FDR, 27 March 1939, Braden to Welles, 27 December 1941, Spruille Braden Papers, Rare Book and Manuscript Library, Columbia University; Saint-Quentin to Bonnet, 9 December 1938, notes from the French Ministry of Colonies, 7 March 1940, dossier 374, AEU, Quai d'Orsay; Steward, *Trade and Hemisphere,* 70, 79.

39. Braden to Welles, 27 November 1942, 19 March, 29 April 1943, tran-

script from H. U. Kaltenborn broadcast, 13 March 1944 (NBC), Braden memorandum, 22 July 1944, Lee to Braden, 4 April 1945, boxes 14, 16, Braden Papers, Columbia University; Smith, "Good Neighbor," 78; Lindsay to Simon, 31 May 1934, Watson to Simon, 9 January 1935, FO 414/272, PRO; FDR press conference, 9 March 1934, Nixon, ed., *Roosevelt*, 2:21; Guerrant, *Good Neighbor*, 103; Butler, "Expenditures," 79; Adams, *Economic Diplomacy*, 138-39; Langley, *United States and the Caribbean*, 150; Steward, *Trade and Hemisphere*, 120; Gellman, *Good Neighbor*, 176. Senator Butler pointed out that the United States purchased all of Cuba's 1942 sugar crop and that Mexico's ambassador to Argentina had likened Roosevelt's good neighborism to the exploits of Don Quixote ("Latin America," 24-25). In Steward's judgment, "monoculture, not viability," was the chief outgrowth of Cuba's trade treaty with the United States—"with no other nation in the western hemisphere did the U.S. trade program border so closely on economic nationalism" (*Trade and Hemisphere*, 89-90, 111).

40. Le Saulnier de Saint-Jouan to Quai d'Orsay, 5 March, 26 April 1938, dossier 374, AEU, Quai d'Orsay; Ickes, *Ickes*, 1:547; Fitz-Simons, "Wallace," 118, 122; Beals et al., *South Americans*, 10-12, 58-59, 177, 212-13; Moore to FDR, 10 January 1935, Roosevelt to Moore, 4 February 1935, Nixon, ed., *Roosevelt*, 2:349-50, 390; Guerrant, *Good Neighbor*, 157-58; *Time*, 23 December 1940, p. 30; Long Diary, 6 January 1939, box 5, Long Papers, LC; Carey, *Peru*, 107. Langley concludes that Puerto Rico, by 1940, had "experienced seven years of hectic planning and erratic administration" with "little to show." These were "violent years" in a land which by 1945 was still termed "an unsolved problem" (*United States and the Caribbean*, 159-60).

41. Welles, *Time for Decision*, 202; Lester D. Langley, "Negotiating New Treaties with Panama, 1936," *Hispanic American Historical Review* 48 (May 1968):229-30; Welles to FDR, 14 June 1938, 14 March 1939, OF 110, FDRL; Langer and Gleason, *Undeclared War*, 150, 611-15; Mellett to FDR, 8 January 1941, box 69, PSF, FDRL; *Time*, 20 October 1941, p. 20.

42. For this side of the story, see Pratt, *Hull*, 2:683; Gibson to Hull, 23 October 1933, Hull to Gibson, 24 October 1933, acting secretary of state to Dawson, 12, 24 June, 13, 23 November 1933, Dawson to acting secretary of state, 19, 21, 26 June, 11, 13, 14, 16, 20, 23 November, Dawson to Hull, 28 October, 5 November 1933, Hull to Dawson, 31 October 1933, Whitehouse to acting secretary of state, 30 November, 5 December 1933, *FR* (1933), 5:82-87, 254-65; *Time*, 10 November 1941, p. 22.

43. Goiran to Quai d'Orsay, 15 February 1934, dossier 375, AEU, Quai d'Orsay; Brand to Lothian, 5 December 1939, GD 40/17, Lothian Papers, SRO. Upon the resumption of relations between Mexico and the United Kingdom, British firms were awarded $130 million in compensation as compared with an American figure of $42 million (Cline, *Mexico*, 242-43, 250-51).

44. Nelson Rockefeller's Office for the Coordination of Commercial and Cultural Relations between the American Republics (*Time*, 9 June 1941, p. 33).

45. See OF 11, FDRL; also Randall B. Woods, "Hull and Argentina: Wilsonian Diplomacy in the Age of Roosevelt," *Journal of Interamerican Studies and World Affairs* 16 (August 1974):360; *Time*, 28 February 1938, p. 24, 7 October 1940, p. 30; Wallace Diary, 3 March 1944, vol. 18, 3133, Wallace Papers, CUOHC. See also d' Aumele (French minister to Colombia) to Quai d'Orsay, 21 March 1939, dossier 374, AEU, Quai d'Orsay; Braden to Welles, 29 June 1943, Braden Papers, Columbia University.

46. Wood, *Latin American Wars*, 15, 365, 369-70.

47. Ibid., 14.

48. Ibid., 362-63, 368; Pratt, *Hull*, 1:164.

49. Wood, *Latin American Wars*, 5, 266, 345-46, 386; *Time*, 12 October 1936, p. 25, 24 October 1938, p. 17; Walters, *History of the League*, chap. 43; Phillips to Wilson, 27 June 1933, *FR* (1933), 4:343. FDR could not even persuade Lescot of Haiti to shake hands with Trujillo of the Dominican Republic in the interest of pacifying their troubled border (Reminiscences of John Campbell White, 119-22, CUOHC).

50. Hull, *Memoirs*, 1:332; Moore to FDR, 25 November 1936, Nixon, ed., *Roosevelt*, 3:509. As it turned out, he did not sign the decree until March of 1938. By this time, Bolivia had already resorted to expropriation (March 1937) and Ecuador had subjected the South American Development Company (an American firm) to considerable harassment (December 1937). For the latter, see consul general at Guayaquil to secretary of state, 13 January 1938, *FR* (1938), 5:537ff. The U.S. nonintervention pledge, given at Montevideo and formalized three years later at Buenos Aires, proved to be more apparent than real, even under Roosevelt's stewardship. Laurence Duggan, chief of State's Latin American Division in 1940, made it clear that Washington retained its unilateral freedom of action (as indeed proved to be the case under Presidents Kennedy and Johnson). See Haines, "Roosevelt Administration."

51. Borg, *Far Eastern Crisis*, 370-72; Bemis, *Latin American Policy*, 286-87; Hull, *Memoirs*, 1:499; Guerrant, *Good Neighbor*, 117; Wood, *Latin American Wars*, 363; Peterson, *Argentina*, 394, 396; Pratt, *Hull*, 1:164, 175-76; Castle to Hoover, 28 January 1939, box 297, Hoover Papers, Hoover Library (based on firsthand reports from former Princeton University professor Philip Marshall Brown). According to Langley, the Buenos Aires Conference of 1936 was a disappointment while Haglund calls it a singular failure for New Deal diplomacy (Langley, *United States and the Caribbean*, 162; Haglund, *Latin America*, 39). Recent verdicts on the Lima meeting range from "fine phraseology" and "good intentions" (Haglund, 108-9) and "little positive response" (Steward, *Money*, 61) to Gellman's slightly more optimistic "solidarity . . . inched forward" (*Latin*

America, 79). Langley is another student of the subject who emphasizes that Lima left much to be desired (*United States and the Caribbean*, 163).

52. Hull, *Memoirs*, 1:690; Gellman, *Good Neighbor*, 91; Haglund, *Latin America*, 149—52.

53. Dallek, *Roosevelt*, 235; Pratt, *Hull*, 2:699, 701.

54. Hull, *Memoirs*, 2:1150; Berle and Jacobs, eds., *Navigating the Rapids*, 398—99.

55. Halifax to Eden, 26 June 1943, Hachey, ed., *Confidential Dispatches*, 73; Welles, *Seven Decisions*, 98.

56. Guerrant, *Good Neighbor*, 3, 189—90; Bemis, *Latin American Policy*, 264.

57. Francis Bertie to Lord Grey, 3 October 1906, FO 115/1394; FO to Durand, September 1906, FO 115/1393, PRO; Offner, *Appeasement*, 92; *Time*, 9 June 1941, p. 22; Guerrant, *Good Neighbor*, 80, 204; Pratt, *Hull*, 2:677—79.

58. Varg, "Good Neighbor," 48—49; Adams, *Economic Diplomacy*, 190—91; Smith, "Good Neighbor," 88—89; Steward, *Trade and Hemisphere*, 32—33, 45, 53—55, 70, 84, 176, 197, 279, 284. In addition to barter, Peek also wanted export subsidies, overseas dumping of surplus agricultural products, and loans to such nations as Germany to purchase American farm products. When a Peek-supported deal to sell U.S. cotton to Germany on a barter basis was blocked by Hull, Peek launched an all-out attack on the Reciprocal Trade Program with much of the press on his side. In the end, though, Hull had the last word. For an excellent contemporary critique of Hull's program, see William Castle's address to the Inter-American Forum at George Washington University, 7 December 1938, *Vital Speeches*, vol. 5, 1 January 1939.

59. See Smith, "Good Neighbor"; also, Welles to Hull, 19 August 1933, *FR* (1933), 5:368—69; Adams, *Economic Diplomacy*, 190—91; Bowers, *Chile*, 290; Bowers, *My Life*, 310; Campbell and Herring, eds., *Stettinius*, 260—63; Saint-Quentin to Bonnet, 10 December 1938, *DDF*, ser. 2, 13:169; Lindsay to Eden, 22 March 1937, FO 414/274, PRO.

60. Wirsing, *Roosevelt et l'Europe*, 12, 32, 228, and all of chapter 8; also, and especially, 31, 37, 199, 224, 226, 265, 268—70, 272, 274, 282, 304—5, 314, 319, 361, 384, 392, 401, 415, 419, 435, 470—71, 474—75, 477ff., 482—84, 489; Brian Crozier, *Franco: A Biographical History* (London: Eyre and Spottiswoode, 1967), 356; Georges du Breuil, *Roosevelt le responsable* (Marseilles: Editions de la Boussole, 1942), 13—14; Ollivier, *Roosevelt*, 234, 237; *Izvestia* clipping, 1 March 1934, dossier 387, AEU, Quai d'Orsay; report by the French naval attaché in Tokyo, 1 May 1940, C.R.R. 5, Archives de la Mer, Chateau Vincennes, Paris. See also two books by Ameury de Riencourt, *L'Amerique impériale* (Paris: Gallimard, 1970) and *L'ere des nouveaux Césars* (Paris: Laffont, 1959).

61. *Time*, 9 June 1941, p. 22; Wood, *Latin American Wars*, 5, 7—8; Smith, "Good Neighbor," 66—67; Gellman, *Good Neighbor*, 54, 59.

62. Grayson, "Good Neighbor," 328; Smith, "Good Neighbor," 67. As Langley

has stated, the United States "greatly expanded its cultural programs for the hemisphere, including a tour of Latin America by Yale's glee club. Committees on agricultural education, foreign students, and exchange fellowships and professorships promoted cultural togetherness. The Office of Coordinator of Inter-American Affairs, under the leadership of Nelson Rockefeller, beamed anti-Axis radio broadcasts, distributed free magazines (*En Guardia* was the best known), and hired Walt Disney to produce cartoons with Latin American themes" (*United States and the Caribbean*, 178). This was probably the nation's first notable venture in the field of psychological warfare.

63. Smith, "Good Neighbor," 79.

64. Le Saulnier de Saint-Jouan to Quai d'Orsay, 5 March, 26 April 1938, dossier 374, AEU, Quai d'Orsay; Bowers, *Chile*, 128–29; Beals et al., *South Americans*, 112; *New York Times*, 28 November 1936, p. 3, 4 December 1936, p. 1; Roosevelt speech at Buenos Aires, 1 December 1936, Nixon, ed., *Roosevelt*, 3:518; Green, *Containment*, 38.

65. Campbell and Herring, eds., *Stettinius*, 260–63; Green, *Containment*, ix, 166, 183; Gellman, *Good Neighbor*, 215. Latin Americans resented the great power veto as designed for use at the United Nations, wishing instead for an autonomous inter-American system that could be used to restrain the United States (Green, *Containment*, 187). Irwin Gellman recognizes a serious deterioration in hemispheric harmony, but the reasons he adduces for this parlous state are not convincing (see pp. 179, 185, 197–98; also note 16 of the introduction to this volume). Among other things, Gellman traces the origin of this decline in American harmony to 1943—when the United States was just beginning to realize the greatest military victory of its history. In any case, by 1945 (for whatever reason), Wallace noted that Latin America felt "ignored—worse exploited" (ibid., 198). For one of the best assessments of the spirit prevailing in early 1945 at Chapultepec (Mexico City), see Green, *Containment*, 201, 207, 295: "Latin America was rife with economic discontent and with distrust of the economic policies of the United States in Latin America. Far from signalling the 'end of Latin American distrust of the United States' (in Senator Austin's classic phrase), the Chapultepec Conference showed clearly the distance between Americans and Latin Americans on economic questions. The split emerged clearly on such subjects as tariff protection, foreign capital participation in Latin American enterprises, government intervention in economic affairs, and the problem of multilateral finance mechanisms . . . the splits could be seen quite starkly by noting the nature of a number of draft resolutions introduced by the Latin Americans but never acted upon because of a lack of United States support or encouragement." Agreement at Chapultepec was "imposed by unanswerable economic power rather than by conversion of the Latin American dissenters. Disagreements were sharp and frequent. . . . The Good Neighbor Policy had assumed that political stability in Latin America was a prerequisite for 'healthy'

economic development under United States supervision. But by the mid-1950s it was clear that the economic dependency which the United States had fostered in Latin America was seriously undermining political stability." One might add that when the U.S. delegation reached San Francisco, it was confronted, once again, with the embarrassing subject of Argentina (Campbell and Herring, eds., *Stettinius*, 290–91).

66. Hooker, ed., *Moffat*, 113, 115; Gibson to Hull, 12 September 1934, Sevier to Hull, 14 September 1934, Desportes to Hull, 16 September 1934, Hull to U.S. Embassy, Argentina, 19 September 1934, Dreyfus to Hull, 26 September 1934, Foreign Policy Association, "The Munitions Industry: An Analysis of the Senate Investigation," p. 255, carton 11, Green Papers, Princeton University; Wood, *Latin American Wars*, 116, 365; Wood, "External Restraints," 24; Beals et al., *South Americans*, 122.

67. Smith, "Good Neighbor," 78; *Time*, 15 May 1939, p. 15, 22 May 1939, p. 29, 26 June 1939, p. 20.

68. Smith, "Good Neighbor," 65, 67–68, 81, 90–91. According to Smith, Roosevelt's policy suffered from an overdose of paternalism and the questionable assumption that Washington had all the answers to all the world's ills (ibid., 91).

69. Raymond Kerrison, *Bishop Walsh of Maryknoll* (New York: Putnam's, 1962), 283.

70. Hugh Gibson, "Diary of Hoover Good Will Mission, Latin America, May–June 1946," 64–65, Gibson Papers, Hoover Library. Mrs. Berle's only comment at the time was that sentiment against artificial birth control was nothing but superstition and the people needed to be civilized. Apparently, she also gave a series of lectures at the embassy to which she sold tickets. The subject: "How Not to Lose Your Man" (ibid.).

Chapter 7

1. *Letters*, 1:199; 2:451; Tully to Early, 11 December 1941, ibid., 4:1255–56; Dallek, *Roosevelt*, 3; Leutze, "Roosevelt-Churchill Correspondence," 480; Smith, *Buchan*, 389; Delano, *Delano*; Bemis, *Latin American Policy*, 256–57; Perkins, *Roosevelt*, 19–20; Kleeman, *Gracious Lady*, 216, 267.

2. Delano, *Delano*, chap. 10; Phillips, *Ventures*, 219; FDR to Muriel and Warren Robbins, 30 May 1891, Eleanor to Sara Roosevelt, 25 July 1905, FDR to Sara Roosevelt, 30 July, 1 August 1905, 22 April 1912, 25 August 1915, FDR Diary of European trip, summer of 1918, *Letters*, 1:20; 2:46, 51, 55, 185, 287, 391, 413, 419, 433–34, 451. FDR's reference to a "dusky gentleman" with a "duskier wife and daughter" indicates his adherence to the prevailing racial stereotypes of the time (ibid., 287).

3. *Time*, 21 October 1940, p. 27; Adam Ulam, *Stalin* (New York: Viking, 1973), 17, 78–79, 110, 116–17, 320, 338–39.

4. Delano, *Delano*, chaps. 9 and 10; Roosevelt Family Papers, box 7, Sara Roosevelt to FDR, 6 February 1925, box 8, Roosevelt Family Papers, FDRL; Dallek, *Roosevelt*, 15; Dieckhoff memorandum, 29 July 1940, *DGFP*, ser. D, 10:360.

5. Offner, *Appeasement*, 28; Morgenthau, "Morgenthau Diaries," Collier's, 11 October 1947, p. 72; Dallek, *Roosevelt*, 436; FDR to Murray, 13 May 1938, box 53, PSF, FDRL; Roosevelt Address to Congress, 4 January 1935, Nixon, ed., *Roosevelt*, 2:334; FDR to Long, 19 September 1935, box 58, PSF, FDRL; Morgenthau Farm Credit Administration Diary, 9 May 1933, Morgenthau Papers, FDRL.

6. FDR editorials in the *Macon Daily Telegraph*, 21, 30 April 1925, in Carmichael, ed., *F.D.R. Columnist*, 37–38, 59; FDR to Bowers, 22 August 1933, Nixon, ed., *Roosevelt*, 1:372; Sherwood, *Roosevelt and Hopkins*, 63.

7. Long Diary, 30 September 1938, Long Papers, LC; FDR address at Chicago, 9 December 1935, FDR address at Morgantown, Maryland, 4 September 1938, both quoted in Sanborn, *Design for War*, 15, 42; FDR to John F. Montgomery, 29 August 1934, Dearing to FDR, 2 December 1935, FDR to Dearing, 20 December 1935, Nixon, ed., *Roosevelt*, 2:192, 3:109–10, 130; Faith Murray to FDR, 29 October 1938, FDR to Arthur Murray, 24 July 1939, box 53, PSF, FDRL; Saint-Quentin to Paul-Boncour, 26 March 1938, *DDF*, ser. 2, 9:113; FDR to Bullitt, 16 March 1936, Bullitt, ed., *For the President*, 150; FDR to MacVeagh, 1 December 1939, *Letters*, 4:961; FDR to Churchill, 17 April 1944, *RC*, 489–90; Roberts, *Tito*, 166; Hess, *India*, 52.

8. Elliott Roosevelt, *As He Saw It*, 156; FDR to Churchill, 16 April 1942, *RC*, 206; FDR to Welles, 7 January 1938, box 95, PSF, FDRL; Neumann, *After Victory*, 69.

9. Hess, "Indochina," 363; Hull memorandum, 14 February 1941, State Department memorandum, 19 May 1942, *FR* (Japan), 351, 388–89; Romanus and Sunderland, *Stilwell's Command Problems*, 447.

10. Perkins, *Roosevelt*, 82; Welles to FDR, 11 March, 28 November 1938, OF 134, FDRL; Hull to FDR, 23 December 1943, FDR to Hurley, 10 January 1944, box 55, PSF, FDRL. Roosevelt apologized, but the damage had been done.

11. FDR to the shah of Iran, 2 September 1944, *Letters*, 4:1538; shah of Iran to FDR, 4 October 1944, box 55, PSF, FDRL; FDR to King Saud, 10 February 1944, PPF 7960, FDRL; Ickes to Hull, 21 May 1941, *FR* (1941), 3:653; Buhite, *Hurley*, 129–31; FDR to Churchill, 29 February 1944, *RC*, 499n.

12. Henderson B. Braddick, "A New Look at American Policy during the Italo-Ethiopian Crisis, 1935–36," *Journal of Modern History* 34 (March 1962):66; Hull to Bingham, 11 July 1935, *FR* (1935), 1:730; Long to FDR, 7 July 1933, Nixon, ed., *Roosevelt*, 1:284–87; Long to FDR, 14 September 1933, box 58, PSF, FDRL; Hull, *Memoirs*, 1:414, 423, 902, 2:961, 995, 1005, 1054, 1062.

13. Bullitt, ed., *For the President*, 66; Bullitt to FDR, 3 June 1935, 23 Novem-

ber 1937, 1 February 1939, ibid., 123, 232, 306; *Newsweek*, 24 April 1939, p. 12; Wilson, *Career Diplomat*, 75–76; Bullitt to FDR, 24 November 1936, box 41, PSF, FDRL.

14. Dodd to FDR, 30 July 1933, Nixon, ed., *Roosevelt*, 1:337; Dallek, *Dodd*, 246; Dodd to FDR, 27 February 1937, box 51, Dodd Papers, LC.

15. Daniels, *Shirt-Sleeve Diplomat*, 25, 128, 165–66, 171, 292, 301–2, 356–57.

16. William A. Eddy, *FDR Meets Ibn Saud* (New York: American Friends of the Middle East, 1954), 20, 23–26.

17. Langer and Gleason, *Challenge to Isolation*, 137, 146; Wayne S. Cole, "Senator Key Pittman and American Neutrality Policies, 1933–1940," *Mississippi Valley Historical Review* 46 (March 1960):648, 662; Israel, *Pittman*, 92, 135, 148, 162; Hull, *Memoirs*, 1:412, 642; *Time*, 24 February 1936, p. 23, 18 November 1940, p. 20; Drought to Gorman, 25 March 1936, box 1, Drought Papers, Maryknoll; British Embassy in Washington, "Notes on Personalities," FO 371/20665, PRO.

18. Langer and Gleason, *Challenge to Isolation*, 146; Moffat Diplomatic Journal, 25 August 1939, Moffat Papers, Harvard University; *Time*, 19 June 1939, p. 16; Bloom, *Autobiography*, 283–85. For Drew Pearson's story of how provincially Mrs. Bloom conducted herself in conversation with Mrs. Vargas, see Dawson to Gibson, 28 April 1936, box 5, Gibson Papers, Hoover Library.

19. British Embassy in Washington, "Notes on Personalities," FO 371/20665; Lindsay to FO, 12 December 1935, FO 371/19169, PRO; McKenna, *Borah*, 220–22; Robert D. Schulzinger, *The Making of the Diplomatic Mind*, 143; Tully, *F.D.R.*, 175; Campbell and Herring, eds., *Stettinius*, 2 October 1943, p. 8; Castle to Wilson, 10 February 1933, box 1, Wilson Papers, Hoover Library; Witherow to Lothian, 23 February 1938, GD 40/17, file 358, Lothian Papers, SRO.

20. *Time*, 4 September 1933, pp. 15, 17, 2 October 1933, p. 18, 6 November 1933, p. 26, 5 March 1934, p. 15, 19 March 1934, p. 17, 9 December 1935, p. 25, 2 November 1936, p. 15, 16 November 1936, p. 35, 13 December 1937, p. 23, 20 December 1937, p. 15, 7 March 1938, p. 19, 26 June 1939, p. 32, 4 November 1940, p. 27, 7 April 1941, p. 44, 28 April 1941, p. 28.

21. *Time*, 5 March 1933, p. 20, 26 June 1933, p. 20, 3 July 1933, p. 22, 19 March 1934, p. 17, 14 November 1938, p. 24, 21 October 1940, p. 40, 28 October 1940, p. 24, 5 May 1941, p. 33, 26 May 1941, p. 17, 3 November 1941, p. 27.

22. *Time*, 31 July 1933, p. 9, 9 October 1933, p. 22, 23 November 1936, p. 22, 10 April 1939, p. 24, 7 October 1940, p. 39, 18 November 1940, p. 36, 9 June 1941, p. 40. According to *News-Week*, the Abyssinian empress was "swarthy, short, and so fat she can hardly walk" (7 October 1933, p. 13). For similar treatment of other regions of the world, see *Time*, 10 April 1933, p. 25, 26 June 1933, p. 20, 14 August 1933, p. 20, 28 August 1933, p. 15, 9 October 1933, p. 23, 27 November

1933, p. 16, 26 March 1934, p. 18, 23 November 1936, p. 24, 22 November 1937, pp. 21, 26, 7 February 1938, p. 18, 28 February 1938, p. 24.

23. *News-Week,* 5 August 1933, pp. 12, 14, 12 August 1933, pp. 12, 15, 19 August 1933, pp. 3, 5, 12, 15–16, 16 September 1933, pp. 14, 16, 23 September 1933, p. 14.

24. *New York Times,* 3 February 1933, p. 10, 4 February 1933, p. 8, 5 February 1933, p. 1; *New York Times* clipping, 6 February 1933, in GD 40/17, file 199, Lothian Papers, SRO; Offner, *Appeasement,* 36; Borg, *Far Eastern Crisis,* 123–24; Hooker, ed., *Moffat,* 113; Hull, *Memoirs,* 1:398, 400–403, 405; Pratt, *Hull,* 1:191, 193–94; FDR address at San Diego, 2 October 1935, Rosenman, ed., *Public Papers,* 4 (1935):410. See also Templewood, *Nine Troubled Years,* 264.

25. Duggan to Gilbert Murray, 28 February 1935, vol. 69, Murray Papers, Oxford University; Hull to FDR, 11 April 1935, Nixon, ed., *Roosevelt,* 2:471; Stimson Diary, 2 November 1935, Yale University; Green to Moffat, 9 January, 22 April, 12 September 1936, Moffat Diplomatic Journal, Moffat Papers, Harvard University; FDR to Straus, 8 June 1936, *Letters,* 3:593. Long questioned if it was wise for the president to call so many key men home at the most dangerous moment since 1918. Bingham said he felt it would be unwise to leave London and he stayed on (to die in harness, as it happened). At the same moment, Ambassador Straus was dying of a stomach ailment and Long, who also suffered from intestinal symptoms, came home to undergo successful surgery.

26. Richard P. Traina, *American Diplomacy and the Spanish Civil War* (Bloomington: Indiana University Press, 1968); Bullitt, "Lost the Peace," 86; Richardson, *Memoirs,* 434; Liang, *Stilwell,* 266; Farley, *Farley's Story,* 342; Wallace to McIntyre, 13 March 1937, OF 366, FDRL; Maddux, *Estrangement,* 84; Hess, *India,* 36, 93; Pratt, *Hull,* 1:232; Dallek, *Roosevelt,* 195. On congressional pressure for economic sanctions in 1939, see Lothian to Scott, 31 March 1939, FO 371/22815, PRO; Langer and Gleason, *Challenge to Isolation,* 157–58; Utley, "Diplomacy," 133.

27. Lindsay to Eden, 8 February 1938, FO to Lindsay, 18 February 1938, FO 371/21526, PRO; Lockhard Report, 15 April 1939, FO 371/22829; Erwin Canham, "The President's Diplomacy," *Spectator,* 5 May 1939; Lindsay to Eden, 7 February 1938, vol. 29, Eden Papers, FO 954, PRO. See also *Spectator,* 6 January 1939, p. 2.

28. Harriman address at Yale University, 4 February 1941, PPF 6207, FDRL; Jones, "Adventure in Failure," 612; Masland, "Missionary Influence," 293, 295. Hamilton Fish Armstrong (editor of *Foreign Affairs*) wrote FDR in 1934 that he was writing articles and a book and would like to "have the advantage of being 'steered' by you before expressing any opinion" (Armstrong to FDR, 8 May 1934, PPF 6011, FDRL).

29. Willert, *Washington,* 216; record of Willert interview, 25, 26 March 1939, FO 371/22829, PRO.

30. Sanborn, *Design for War*, 42–43; Stimson Diary, 24 October 1938, Yale University; Krock, "Reminiscences," p. 228, box 52, Krock Papers, Princeton University.

31. Sherwood, *Roosevelt and Hopkins*, 702; Smith, "Authoritarianism," 323. The same tended to be true of left-wing thought in Britain (Clifford, *Retreat from China*, 4).

32. Range, *Roosevelt's World Order*, 190–91. According to German chargé Thomsen, Roosevelt's "pathological hatred" of the leaders of Germany and Italy had led him "to declare (before the members of the Senate Committee on Military Affairs who had previously been bound to secrecy) that it would be a good thing if they were assassinated" (Thomsen to Foreign Ministry, 17 May 1939, *DGFP*, ser. D, 6:533). For contingency plans to assassinate Chiang, see Schaller, *Crusade in China*, 153–54. For a tendency on the part of Americans to judge Chinese leaders by American standards and thereby to misjudge them, owing in part to communist deftness at public relations, see Shewmaker, *Americans and the Communist Chinese*; David D. Barrett, *Dixie Mission: The United States Army Observer Group in Yenan* (Berkeley and Los Angeles: University of California Press, 1970), 82.

33. Offner, *Appeasement*, 97–98, 104, 107–8.

34. Wiley to Hull, 19 March 1938, *FR* (1938), 1:458; Stimson Diary, 2 November 1935, Stimson Papers, Yale University; Cudahy to House, 29 December 1933, box 32, House Papers, Yale University; Bullitt to Moore, 7 April 1935, Bullitt, ed., *For the President*, 108; Cudahy to FDR, 27 December 1933, PPF 1193, FDRL; Welles, *Time for Decision*, 22–23, 81; Taylor, *Origins*, 26; Lord Cushendun to Phipps, 24 September 1928, Knatchbull-Hugessen Papers, CCC. Brüning told Stimson in late 1935 that at least 70 percent of the Austrian people were behind Hitler (Stimson Diary, 2 November 1935, Stimson Papers, Yale University). See the *Spectator* for an example of how positive the British press could be on Anschluss as compared with Italian and Japanese operations in Ethiopia and Manchuria.

35. Imai Seiichi, "Cabinet, Emperor and Senior Statesmen," in Borg and Okamoto, eds., *Pearl Harbor*, 68; *Time*, 9 June 1941, p. 20; Vincent to Hornbeck, 23 July 1938, *FR* (1938), 3:234–35; Blum, ed., *Morgenthau Diaries, 1928–1938*, 481.

36. Carlton J. H. Hayes, *Wartime Mission in Spain, 1942–1945* (New York: Macmillan, 1945), 304. Clyde, "Far East," is excellent on American misperceptions of China—see especially 444. See also Shewmaker, *Americans and the Communist Chinese*.

37. May, "Lessons," 28–29.

38. Welles, *Time for Decision*, 135; Lady Astor to Norman Davis, 31 October 1938, box 2, Davis Papers, LC; Weizsäcker, *Memoirs*, 223; Eden to Lindsay, 5 May 1937, FO 371/20704, PRO.

39. FDR to Bullitt, 29 August 1934, Bullitt to Moore, 6 October 1934, Bullitt to FDR, 4 March 1936, Bullitt, ed., *For the President*, 95, 98–99, 148; Bohlen, *Witness*, 33; Eagles, "Davies," 53, 103; *RC*, 645n.

40. Blum, ed., *Wallace*, 8 May 1944, p. 329; Alsop, "Lost China," 46; White, ed., *Stilwell Papers*, 233, 237.

41. Stimson Diary, 5 March 1936, Stimson Papers, Yale University; Friedländer, *Prelude*, 39–40; Kirk to Hull, 5 November 1939, 740.00119 European War 1939/122, RG 59, NA.

42. Krock memorandum of talk with Roosevelt, 13 September 1934, box 52, Arthur Krock Papers, Princeton University; *Time*, 9 June 1941, p. 20; Lothian to Halifax, 3 November 1939, FO 800/317, PRO; Graebner, "Japan," 125; Laboulaye to Paul-Boncour, 14 October 1933, *DDF*, ser. 1, 4:575; Buhite, *Johnson*, 100; Eden, *Facing the Dictators*, 603; Hornbeck memorandum, 10 December 1938, *FR* (1938), 3:416; Hornbeck memorandum, 11 May 1939, *FR* (1939), 2:34; Carlson to FDR, 16 October 1938, PPF 4951, FDRL. For accounts that assume a clear division in Japanese leadership, see Langer and Gleason, *Challenge to Isolation*, 156; *Undeclared War*, 892; Borg, *Far Eastern Crisis*, 443; Robert J. C. Butow, *Tōjō and the Coming of the War* (Princeton: Princeton University Press, 1961), 30–33, 36, 47, 86, 88, 91, 137, 153, 165–66, 211, 223, 228, 240–41, 243, 255–56, 283, 296, 308, 348–49; Neumann, *Japan*, 186; Joseph W. Ballantine, "Mukden to Pearl Harbor: The Foreign Policies of Japan," *Foreign Affairs* 27 (July 1949):651. For a more accurate view, see Clauss, "Roosevelt Administration"; Crowley, *Japan's Quest*, xvii, 126, 129, 135, 141–42, 172–73, 231, 246–49, 276ff., 350–51, 358–62, 367–69, 372–74, 376, 378, 393, 395; James William Morley, ed., *Deterrent Diplomacy: Japan, Germany and the USSR, 1935–1940* (New York: Columbia University Press, 1976), 185–86. Heinrichs, in his biography of Grew, alternates between the two views, adhering mainly to the older view; while Clifford, *Retreat from China*, takes middle ground (see p. 4).

43. Sir George Sansom, "Liberalism in Japan," *Foreign Affairs* 19 (April 1941):551–55, 559.

44. Stimson Diary, 31 December 1932, 5, 12 January 1933, Stimson Papers, Yale University; Borg, *Far Eastern Crisis*, 77, 147ff., 157–58, 457; Otohiko Matsukata to Roosevelt, 20 February 1934, Nixon, ed., *Roosevelt*, 1:656–57; Bullitt to Hull, 16 April 1934, *FR* (1934), 3:111.

45. Bullitt to Moore, 17 December 1937, box 3, Moore Papers, FDRL. See also Castle to Wilson, 23 December 1937, box 1, Wilson Papers, Hoover Library. A French observer traced this myth to Russian slander at the time of Theodore Roosevelt. Count Witte, during the Portsmouth Peace Conference, in an alleged effort to set class against class, pretended to differentiate between the Japanese people and their military leaders (report of French naval attaché in Tokyo, 1 May 1940, C.R.R. 5, Archives de la Mer, Chateau Vincennes, Paris).

46. See Moore, *With Japan's Leaders*, esp. chap. 2 ("The Japanese Army Takes

Control"); also Vincent to Hornbeck, 23 July 1938, Grew to Hull, 2 August 1938, *FR* (1938), 3:234–35, 250; Clifford, *Retreat from China*, 50–51.

47. Langer and Gleason, *Undeclared War*, 698; Shigeru Yoshida, *The Yoshida Memoirs: The Story of Japan in Crisis* (London: Heinemann, 1961), 9, 13, 16, 20; Tōgō, *Cause of Japan*, 15, 116–19. The Saionji-Harada memoirs features unit titles such as "Fears of Right-Wing Grow" and "Coping with Right-Wingers"; see especially pp. 2593 and 2998 on the film published by the Japanese Ministry of Foreign Affairs. The theme of the entire account is rampant militarism. See also a typical explanation by Takehiko Yoshihashi, *Conspiracy at Mukden: The Rise of the Japanese Military* (New Haven: Yale University Press, 1963).

48. Grew, *Turbulent Era*, 2:934, 1038; personal note, November 1939, Grew Diary, *Kokumin Shimbun*, 18 May 1939 (clipping) in vol. 94, Grew Diary, 19–30 May 1939, GP; Butow, *Tōjō*, 332–33; Tōgō, *Cause of Japan*, 184; Kakegawa Tomiko, "The Press and Public Opinion in Japan, 1931–1941," in Borg and Okamoto, eds., *Pearl Harbor*, 541; Heinrichs, *Grew*, 175–77; Shigemitsu, *Japan and Her Destiny*, 85–88, 139, 144; Hull, *Memoirs*, 1:286.

49. Grew to Hull, 18 February, 1, 4 June 1937, *FR* (1937), 4:712, 716, 718 (on Konoye's popularity); Shigemitsu, *Japan and Her Destiny*, 144, 146–47; Clifford, *Retreat from China*, 11; Crowley, *Japan's Quest*, 350–51, 358–62, 367–69, 372–74, 376, 378, 380, 393.

50. Butow, *John Doe Associates*, 224; Grew to Hull, 2 July 1934, *FR* (1934), 3:205; Churchill, *Grand Alliance*, 585; Shigemitsu, *Japan and Her Destiny*, 170; Sadao Asada review of Stephen E. Pelz, *Race to Pearl Harbor* in the *Journal of American History* 62 (December 1975):758.

51. Dodd to Hull, 5 April 1935, *FR* (1935), 2:320–21; Bullitt to Moore, 7 April 1935, Bullitt, ed., *For the President*, 107.

52. Italy's army never warmed to the Ethiopian venture. Again, it was a civilian, Mussolini, who lashed his generals on. Likewise, in England, it was the brass who advised steadily against military intervention on the side of Ethiopia. Later, when Churchill, another civilian, ordered armed intervention in the Greek civil war, his military advisers preferred another approach. In the United States, the situation was much the same. If generals had made policy, they would have withdrawn American forces from China and the Philippines in 1935. Two years later, with hostilities in progress between Tokyo and Nanking, they were adamant about the need to reduce America's military presence in China, appealing over Hull's head to the White House. Only reluctantly did FDR agree. The same year, when he proposed a naval blockade of Japan, it was admirals who stood in his way. German observers were not far wrong when they called the military the most potent force for peace in the United States. Neither the army nor the navy endorsed the policies that led to war with Japan in 1941. As best they could, they counseled forbearance, and in the face of prickly issues they

urged postponement to allow more time for preparation. This was the same advice, of course, that Japanese admirals were giving Konoye. See Messersmith to Hull, 18 February 1938, FR (1938), 1:20; Taylor, Origins, 93, 95, 98, 105; Churchill, Gathering Storm, 194, 250–51; Churchill, Triumph and Tragedy, 75, 310; Greene, "Military View," 370–71; Louis Morton, "Army and Marines on the China Station: A Study in Military and Political Rivalry," Pacific Historical Review 29 (February 1960):70–71; Haight, "Naval Quarantine," 210–11; Leutze, Bargaining for Supremacy, 10; Emerson, "F.D.R.," 144–46; German Embassy in Washington to Foreign Ministry, 26 February, 11 March 1941, DGFP, ser. D, 12:162, 267; Grew Diary, personal notes, December 1940, vol. 101 GP (on General Johnson).

53. Dodd to FDR, 19 August 1936, Nixon, ed., Roosevelt, 3:391; SEC Study of Germany (late 1935?), PPF 207, FDRL; Krock memorandum of talk with FDR, 13 February 1937, box 52, Krock Papers, Princeton University; Henry to Delbos, 7 November 1937, DDF, ser. 2, 7:356; Blum, ed., Morgenthau Diaries, 1928–1938, 458–59; FDR to Davis, 9 November 1934, box 51, Davis Papers, LC; FDR to House, 16 June 1937, PPF 222, FDRL; Bullitt to Moore, 8 January 1937, box 3, Moore Papers, FDRL. This was reflected in a Time essay, "Background for War," 22 May 1939, pp. 30–35. For Stimson's view, see Stimson and Bundy, On Active Service, 306.

54. FDR speech at Buenos Aires, 1 December 1936, Nixon, ed., Roosevelt, 3:518; Taylor, Origins, 104–6; Jonas, Isolationism, 107; Dallek, Dodd, 276; Lothian to Dulles, 26 December 1939, box 18, Dulles Papers, Princeton University. Dodd referred to the "haves" as "possession" powers.

55. Perkins, Roosevelt, 88, 349; FDR to Cudahy, 15 January 1937, Letters, 3:652–53; FDR to Bloom, undated, quoted in Bloom, Autobiography, 331; Leroy Ashby, The Spearless Leader (Urbana: University of Illinois Press, 1972), 114.

56. Bullitt to FDR, 23, 26 January 1933, PPF 1124, FDRL; Bullitt to FDR, 1 January 1934, Bullitt, ed., For the President, 71; memorandum of Davis talks with FDR, 26 January 1933, and with Lindsay, 19 March 1935, box 9, Davis Papers, LC; FDR to House, 10 April 1935, Letters, 3:472–73; FDR to House, 10 April 1935, PPF 222, FDRL; Bingham Diary, 11 April 1934, box 1, Bingham Papers, LC; Morgenthau Presidential Diary, 11, 15 April 1939, vol. 1, pp. 59, 81, Morgenthau Papers, FDRL; memorandums by the director of Department III of the German Foreign Ministry, 11, 12 December 1934, DGFP, ser. C, 3:735–36; Blum, ed., Morgenthau Diaries, 1928–1938, 459; Eleanor Roosevelt, This I Remember, 360; Watt, "Appeasers," 190; Neumann, Japan, 285; Stimson Diary, 9 January 1933 (on FDR opinion), 17 May 1934, Stimson Papers, Yale University; Offner, Appeasement, 105.

57. Neumann, Japan, 252; Benjamin H. Williams, "The Coming of Economic Sanctions into American Practice," American Journal of International Law 37

(July 1943):390–91, 394n.; Welles, *Seven Decisions*, 76–77; Halifax to Kerr, 17 October 1938, *DBFP*, ser. 3, 8:146; Morgenthau Presidential Diary, 19 June 1939, vol. 1, p. 126, Morgenthau Papers, FDRL.

58. Wilson to Hull, 24 May 1938, quoted in Wilson, *Career Diplomat*, 34; Wilson to Davis, 2 April 1938, box 67, Davis Papers, LC; Taylor, *Origins*, 104–6; Selig Adler, "The United States and the Holocaust," *American Jewish Historical Quarterly* 64 (September 1974):16; Hoskins memorandum, 31 August 1943, box 60, PSF, FDRL; Richard C. Lukas, *The Strange Allies: The United States and Poland, 1941–1945* (Knoxville: University of Tennessee Press, 1978), 171.

59. Langer and Gleason, *Challenge to Isolation*, 401–2; Long Diary, November 1935 (esp. 22, 26, 27 November), box 5, Long Papers, LC; Wilson to Castle, 20 December 1939, box 1, Wilson Papers, Hoover Library; Steward, *Trade and Hemisphere*, 283. Brazil was not even a member of the League.

60. Hjalmar Schacht, "German Trade and German Debts," *Foreign Affairs* 13 (October 1934):4; Walters, *History of the League*, 534; Wood, *Latin American Wars*, 63–64; Daniels, *Shirt-Sleeve Diplomat*, 250–52; Fitz-Simons, "Wallace," 26–27.

61. Morgenthau, "Morgenthau Diaries," *Collier's*, 11 October 1947, p. 74.

62. Eagles, "Davies," 101; Claudel to Paul-Boncour, 31 March 1933, *DDF*, ser. 1, 3:125; Maddux, *Estrangement*, 19; Dallek, *Roosevelt*, 80; Bullitt to FDR, 1 April 1934, Nixon, ed., *Roosevelt*, 2:47; FDR to Bullitt, 23 April 1934, Bullitt, ed., *For the President*, 84.

63. Messersmith memorandum, undated, item 2013, Messersmith Papers, University of Delaware; Walter Millis, ed., *The Forrestal Diaries* (New York: Viking, 1951), 41 (on Harriman); Neumann, *After Victory*, 117; Deane to Marshall, 2 December 1944, *FR* (Malta and Yalta), 448. According to Winant, Americans ought to be satisfied with "implicit" rights and not arouse omnipresent Soviet suspicion (Murphy, *Diplomat*, 232).

64. *Letters*, 3:417; Bohlen, *Witness*, 25; Hassett, *Off the Record*, 287–88; FDR to Currie, 12 September 1942, OF 3719, FDRL.

65. FDR to Cudahy, 8 January 1934, PPF 1193, FDRL; FDR speech, 19 January 1898, *Letters*, 1:163.

66. FDR to Lord Cecil, 6 April 1937, *Letters*, 3:672; FDR to Butler, 20 October 1937, PPF 445, FDRL; Leahy Diary, 13, 16 December 1937, Leahy Papers (microfilm 17,718), LC; FDR to Congress, 16 May 1933, FDR speech to Woodrow Wilson Foundation, 28 December 1933, Nixon, ed., *Roosevelt*, 1:124, 561; Laboulaye to Paul-Boncour, 16 May 1933, *DDF*, ser. 1, 3:496; FDR to Bingham, 13 November 1933, PPF 716, FDRL; Lothian to T. J., 29 November 1934; House to Lothian, 13 December 1934, GD 40/17, files 282–83, Lothian Papers, SRO; Hull, *Memoirs*, 1:230; FDR, *On Our Way*, 115, 136.

67. Bailey and Ryan, *Hitler vs. Roosevelt*, 23; Heinrichs, *Grew*, 293, 296;

Time, 26 June 1933, p. 15; Hull, *Memoirs*, 1:583; Churchill, *Gathering Storm*, 329; Welles memorandum, 1 February 1938, *FR* (1938), 1:9; Templewood, *Nine Troubled Years*, 267; Pratt, *Hull*, 1:287–88; Frankfurter to FDR, 17 October 1933, quoted in Max Freedman, ed., *Frankfurter and Roosevelt: Their Correspondence, 1928–1945* (Boston: Little, Brown, 1967), 164; Frankfurter to FDR, 9 May 1933, FDR speeches, 3 January, 1 December 1936, Nixon, ed., *Roosevelt*, 1:102, 3:154–56, 518; FDR to Dodd, 6 January 1936, *Letters*, 3:543; Bullitt to FDR, 1 June 1939, Bullitt, ed., *For the President*, 355; Saint-Quentin to Paul-Boncour, 26 March 1938, *DDF*, ser. 2, 9:113; Dallek, *Roosevelt*, 183.

68. Hull, *Memoirs*, 2:1465–66; Pratt, *Hull*, 1:204–5; Templewood, *Complacent Dictator*, 97. For Brussels, see Hooker, ed., *Moffat*, 160; Moffat Diplomatic Journal, 2, 15 November 1937, Moffat Papers, Harvard University. See also Welles, "Thwarted Peace Plan," *Washington Post*, 4 May 1948, p. 15; Welles memorandum, 10 January 1938, *FR* (1938), 1:117.

69. Hull, *Memoirs*, 1:535–36; British Library of Information to FO, 11 January 1938, FO 371/21526, PRO; Moffat Diplomatic Journal, 5 January 1939, vol. 42, Moffat Papers, Harvard University; Welles, *Seven Decisions*, 70; Davies, *Mission to Moscow*, 434; Wilson, *Career Diplomat*, 28, 52–53; Long Diary, 3 February 1939, box 5, Long Papers, LC.

70. Thorne, *Limits*, 414 (quotation from Conrad's *Nostromo*); Hoover Address to Council on Foreign Relations, 31 March 1938, box 2, Wilson Papers, Hoover Library; Crowley, *Japan's Quest*, 144–45; Graebner, "Japan," 125; Stimson, *Far Eastern Crisis*, 239; Henry L. Stimson, "Bases of American Foreign Policy during the Past Four Years," *Foreign Affairs* 11 (April 1933):390.

Conclusion

1. Hooker, ed., *Moffat*, 183.

2. Long Diary, 22 January 1938, box 5, Breckinridge Long Papers, LC; Crowley, *Japan's Quest*, 17–23; Watts, "Breckinridge Long," 26.

3. Borg and Okamoto, eds., *Pearl Harbor*, 7; *Newsweek*, 17 April 1939, p. 1; "State Department Reflections on Certain Features of the Far Eastern Situation," 4 July 1940, OF 150, FDRL (on Lippmann's position in 1940); Neumann, *Japan*, 239 (on Bemis); Dulles to Lothian, 3 January 1940, box 18, Dulles Papers, Princeton University; Moore, "An Appeal to Reason," 577–78; Edwin Borchard to William Borah, 16 February 1939, container 513, Borah Papers, LC.

4. See OF 150, FDRL (on Lippmann and Vandenberg); also Mary G. Hubert, "The Role of Nelson Trusler Johnson in Sino-American Diplomatic Relations, 1930–1935," (Ph.D. dissertation, Catholic University, 1964); Heinrichs, *Grew*, 268–70; Thorne, *Limits*, 386 (on Lippmann's position in 1934).

5. Grew, *Turbulent Era*, 2:1168n., 1206, 1211, 1229; Grew to Hull, 27 De-

cember 1934, Hornbeck memorandum, 3 January 1935, Hull to FDR, 22 January 1935, *FR* (1935), 3:827, 837.

6. Langer and Gleason, *Challenge to Isolation*, 469; Sherwood, *Roosevelt and Hopkins*, 113; Standley and Ageton, *Admiral Ambassador*, 30; Hull, *Memoirs*, 1:457, 459; Davis to Hull, 10 November 1937, *FR* (1937), 4:177; Stimson account of a trip to Great Britain, 1933, Stimson Diary, Stimson Papers, Yale University; Hornbeck memorandum, 24 May 1934, 711.94/970A, RG 59, NA; Davis-Roosevelt phone conversation, 28 April 1934, box 9, Davis Papers, LC.

7. Fuller memorandum, 23 September 1935, *FR* (1935), 2:284; FDR to Davis, 5 October 1934, box 51, Davis Papers, LC. For another sample of such thought, see Cudahy to Moore, 20 March 1937, box 4, Moore Papers, FDRL.

8. John E. Wiltz, *In Search of Peace: The Senate Munitions Inquiry, 1934–36* (Baton Rouge: Louisiana State University Press, 1963), 40.

9. Carruthers to Murray, 6 December 1935, vol. 68, Murray Papers, Oxford; Halifax to Cecil, 30 January 1940, A51084, vol. 14, Cecil Papers, British National Library; Chamberlain to Ida Chamberlain, 27 October 1934, NC 18, Chamberlain Diary, 30 October 1934, NC 2/23a, Chamberlain memorandum on British relations with Japan circulated to the cabinet, September 1934, NC 8/19/1, Chamberlain Papers, BUL; Watt, *Personalities*, 43, 95; Drummond, *American Neutrality*, 135; Drought memorandum, undated, box 1, Drought Papers, Maryknoll; Dallek, *Roosevelt*, 89, 239; Cadogan to Hornbeck, 14 February 1938, Hornbeck to Cadogan, 13 April 1938, Cadogan to Hornbeck, 23 May 1938, Biddle to Hull, 7 December 1938, *FR* (1938), 3:89–93, 141–53, 173, 411–12.

10. Langer and Gleason, *Undeclared War*, 21; "State Department Reflections on Certain Features of the Far Eastern Situation," OF 150, FDRL.

11. Israel, ed., *Long*, 17 February 1941, 181; Cadogan minute, 25 August 1941, FO 371/27909; Langer and Gleason, *Undeclared War*, 676–77, 695–97. True to form, Roosevelt wrote Churchill on 18 August: "The statement I made to him was no less vigorous than and was substantially similar to the statement we had discussed" (FO 371/27909, PRO).

12. See Chapter 1.

13. One diplomat who saw this clearly was the Latvian minister to the United States (Moffat Diplomatic Journal, 28 April 1939, Moffat Papers, Harvard University).

14. Hess, "Indochina," and La Feber, "Indochina," both suggest that FDR could have prevailed on the question of an Indochina trusteeship if he had pressed harder. For FDR's decision to release American pressure, see FDR memorandum for Stettinius, 1 January 1945, PSF, box 55, FDRL. See also Thorne, *Allies*, 630; Drachman, *Vietnam*, 80–88, 160–62.

15. Phillips went off to New Delhi without even a briefing by the State Department (Hess, *India*, 96).

16. *Dodd's Diary*, 2 May 1935, p. 240; Willard L. Beaulac, *Career Ambassador*

(New York: Macmillan, 1951), 185; Serrano Suñer, *Entre les Pyrénées et Gibraltar*, 239 ("et que déja cette anomalie accusait son insuffisance diplomatique"). In China, neither Gauss, who lived there for more than twenty years, nor Hurley, spoke Chinese. Johnson spoke it well but could not read or write it. Carr knew nothing of the politics or language of Czechoslovakia. Dodd could not converse officially in German. Neither Bullitt, Davies, nor Standley understood Russian. Phillips had to communicate with Mussolini and the king of Italy in English, though he tried to learn Italian. Daniels, in Mexico, was content to rely upon English. See also Standley and Ageton, *Admiral Ambassador*, 114; Blum, ed., *Wallace*, 125 (on Gauss); Phillips, *Ventures in Diplomacy*, 190, 202; Butow, *John Doe Associates*, 293; Offner, *Appeasement*, 246; Barrett, *Dixie Mission*, 27. A great many more cases could be cited. James Dunn, who served as chief of the Division of Western Europe before Moffat took over, spoke only English; yet Roosevelt named him in 1944 to be assistant secretary of state in charge of western Europe, the Near East, Africa, and the Far East. Nelson T. Johnson, to his great credit, learned to speak Chinese, but it took him two years to do so and, as mentioned above, he never learned to read or write it (Buhite, *Johnson*, 7).

17. Maddux, *Estrangement*, viii; Mme Chiang to Chiang, 24 December 1942, Roosevelt to Chiang, 17 July 1944, 15 March 1945, *PDM-ROC*, vol. 1, pt. 1, pp. 784–85, 877, vol 3, pt. 8, p. 906. For Chiang's extreme reluctance to confront FDR on the issue of Stilwell and coalition government, see Mme Chiang to Mrs. Kung, 26 May 1943, Chiang to Mme Chiang, 21 June 1943, ibid., vol. 1, pt. 1, pp. 842, 854; Chiang to T. V. Soong, 18 June, 9 July 1942, ibid., vol. 3, pt. 6, pp. 603–611.

18. Buhite, *Johnson*, 143–44; Dulles draft of foreign policy statement, 26 January 1944, box 23, Dulles Papers, Princeton University; Burns, *Soldier of Freedom*, 111; Lisle A. Rose, *After Yalta* (New York: Scribner's 1973), 11; Harriman to Hopkins, 9 September 1944, *FR* (Quebec 1944), 198–99; Athan Theoharis, "Roosevelt and Truman on Yalta: The Origins of the Cold War," *Political Science Quarterly* 87 (June 1972):218; John Lukacs, *The Great Powers and Eastern Europe* (New York: American Book Company, 1953), 624; Standley and Ageton, *Admiral Ambassador*, 308, 344–45; John R. Deane, *The Strange Alliance* (New York: Viking, 1947), 84–86. On the British side, there was of course Churchill, as well as the newly converted Eden (War Cabinet 53 Conclusions, Confidential Annex, 13 April 1943, CAB 65/38, PRO [shows that Eden earlier agreed with Roosevelt]).

19. FDR to Stalin, 25 March (date of receipt of two letters), 29 March 1945, *SCRT*, 197–99, 202–3; FDR to Churchill, 12 April 1945, quoted in Churchill, *Triumph and Tragedy*, 454.

20. Sherwood, *Roosevelt and Hopkins*, 768. On the first day out from Hampton Roads, Virginia, Roosevelt's battleship was almost torpedoed by an escorting destroyer, the *William D. Porter*. The president was on deck watching

the *Iowa*'s five-inch guns thumping away when his ship made a sharp twenty-nine-knot turn to avoid a deadly missile that exploded harmlessly to starboard. FDR ordered that no disciplinary action be taken against the captain of the *Porter*, and details of the incident were still classified in 1981 (*Christian Science Monitor*, 27 May 1981, p. 13).

21. Julius Pratt and Arthur Schlesinger have been among Roosevelt's supporters on this score; see Pratt, "The Ordeal of Cordell Hull," *Review of Politics* 28 (January 1966):76, 98.

22. Weizsäcker, *Memoirs*, 181.

23. Halifax to Eden, 30, 31 March, 14 April, 22 May 1943, 19 June, 25 August 1944, vol. 30, Eden Papers, FO 954, PRO; Wedgwood to Churchill, 14 June 1941, PREM 4/25/6, PRO; Ickes, *Ickes*, 1:284–85; *Dodd's Diary*, 344; Dallek, *Dodd*, 217–18; Hess, *India*, 56–59, 184; Compton, *Swastika*, 15–16; Friedländer, *Prelude*, 210–11; German ambassador in Belgium to German Foreign Ministry, 24 January 1940, *DGFP*, ser. D, 8:693. For still other examples involving Bullitt and Welles, Norman Davis and FDR, see Saint-Quentin to Quai d'Orsay, 10 February 1940, dossier 319ter, Henry to Quai d'Orsay, 12 August 1937, dossier 374, AEU, Quai d'Orsay. Saint-Quentin, who admitted to being confused on occasion, guessed that FDR's aides were attempting to cover up presidential indiscretion by accusing each other.

24. For "leading with another man's chin," see Kimball, *Lend-Lease*, 99.

25. The "Four" would have been China, the Soviet Union, Britain, and the United States. The three regions suitable in his mind for a Monroe Doctrine application were the Western Hemisphere, eastern Europe, and the Far East.

26. British War Cabinet 53 Conclusions, Confidential Annex, 13 April 1943, CAB 65/38, PRO; Lyttelton Notes on Discussion with FDR, 24 November 1942, vol. 29, Eden Papers, FO 954, PRO; Range, *Roosevelt's World Order*, 172; Neumann, *After Victory*, 102.

27. Hull spoke along these lines when he addressed Congress on his return from Moscow in 1943.

28. Welles, *Seven Decisions*, 188; Welles memoranda, 11 August 1941, *FR* (1941), 1:363, 366; Minutes of British War Cabinet, 23 November 1942, War Cab. 157, CAB 65/28, PRO; Langer and Gleason, *Undeclared War*, 685; Sherwood, *Roosevelt and Hopkins*, 359–60; Dulles, *War or Peace*, 77–78. For a dissenting opinion, see Greer, *What Roosevelt Thought*, 196. See also Robert A. Divine, *Second Chance: The Triumph of Internationalism in America during World War II* (New York: Atheneum, 1967), 43–44, 83.

29. Dallek, *Roosevelt*, 419, 440; Neumann, *After Victory*, 124; Andrew Berding, ed., *Dulles on Diplomacy* (Princeton: Van Nostrand, 1965), 9.

30. See, for example, McNeill, *America, Britain and Russia*, 762.

31. Serrano Suñer, *Entre les Pyrénées et Gibraltar*, 159; Churchill, *Hinge of Fate*, 219. The Philippines received their independence in 1946. One of the best

accounts of how the United States reacted to the issue of colonialism as it affected the national interest on the aftermath of World War II is to be found in Dulles, *War or Peace*, 77ff.

32. Dulles and Ridinger, "Anti-Colonial Policies"; Lowell T. Young, "Franklin D. Roosevelt and America's Islets: Acquisition of Territory in the Caribbean and in the Pacific," *Historian* 35 (February 1973):205–6; Dallek, *Roosevelt*, 18; Franklin Roosevelt, *Whither Bound?* (Boston: Houghton Mifflin, 1926), 27.

33. Manus Island was an Australian mandate and Noumea was situated in New Caledonia. See Thorne, *Allies*, 665–67; also Bullitt to FDR, 22 February, 4 April 1939, Bullitt, ed., *For the President*, 316–17, 334–36. John Gunther quotes FDR as saying he would like to colonize Argentina (Burns, *Soldier of Freedom*, 57). For his effectiveness in pressuring Britain and other imperial powers to set timetables for independence, see William Roger Louis, *Imperialism at Bay: The United States and the Decolonization of the British Empire, 1941–1945* (Oxford: Oxford University Press, 1978).

34. Louis, *Imperialism*, 354; FDR to Welles, 25 March 1939, *Letters*, 4:871–72; Range, *Roosevelt's World Order*, 110; Gellman, *Good Neighbor*, 96; Moore to Roosevelt, 10 January 1935, Roosevelt to Moore, 4 February 1935, Nixon, ed., *Roosevelt*, 2:349–50, 390; Eden to Churchill, 28 March 1943, W.P. (43) 130, CAB 66/35, PRO (on Dakar and Bizerte); Serrano Suñer, *Entre les Pyrénées et Gibraltar*, 162.

35. FDR's friend Emil Ludwig recalled in one of his books that once when Mrs. Roosevelt asked her husband if it was not time to begin introducing the children to their Christian faith, he replied that he had never given it any thought—it was better not to think about those things (*Roosevelt* [Paris: Plon, 1938], 343). See also, Burns, *Soldier of Freedom*, 549, 552; John Foster Dulles, *War, Peace, and Change* (New York: Harper, 1939), 117; Churchill, *Gathering Storm*, 165–66; RC, 308; Morse, *While Six Million Died*, 262–66; FDR press statement, 17 January 1933, Nixon, ed., *Roosevelt*, 1:4. When, on the night of 9–10 November 1938, there occurred the most savage anti-Semitic pogrom yet to be recorded in the history of the Third Reich, Roosevelt told the press with apparent indignation that he could "scarcely believe that such things could occur in a twentieth-century civilization." A week later, however, after recalling his ambassador from Berlin, he felt free to amuse Mackenzie King with a joke about a Jew crossing himself. Welles told Saint-Quentin that the United States wanted to avoid a complete rupture with Hitler, but the administration did not feel it could send Hugh Wilson back to his post without losing face domestically—unless of course Germany were to give some "satisfaction": the Jewish emigrés "must at least be allowed to take their shirts with them" (Mackenzie King Diary, 17 November 1938, PAC; Saint-Quentin to Bonnet, 30 November 1938, Papiers 1940: Fouques Duparc, Quai d'Orsay; Dallek, *Roosevelt*, 167–68).

36. In 1933, Roosevelt sided with barter advocate George Peek against re-

ciprocal trade advocate Cordell Hull. Only later did he become known as a champion of free trade (Laboulaye to Paul-Boncour, 19 April 1933, *DDF*, ser. 1, 3:246; see also Laboulaye to Flandin, 19 March 1936, ibid., 1:610; Dieckhoff memorandum, 29 July 1940, *DGFP*, ser. D, 10:361; Lindsay to Simon, 30 January 1933, *DBFP*, ser. 2, 5:750–51; FDR, "Our Foreign Policy," 577, for his pro-League stance; Dallek, *Roosevelt*, 12). For FDR's early lip service to open diplomacy, see FDR, "Shall We Trust Japan?" 478.

37. La Feber, "Indochina," 1285; William L. Neumann, "Roosevelt's Options and Evasions in Foreign Policy Decisions, 1940–1945," in Leonard P. Liggio and James J. Martin, eds., *Watershed of Empire: Essays on New Deal Foreign Policy* (Colorado Springs: Ralph Myles, 1976), 173; FDR to Murray, 19 January 1939, file 8809, Elibank Papers, NLS; FDR memorandum for Hull, 7 April 1944, box 10 MRC, FDRL; Serrano Suñer, *Entre les Pyrénées et Gibraltar*, 159, 162.

38. Among the offers that come readily to mind are the following: in 1937, the United States repeatedly offered its good offices to Tokyo to end the war in China. In 1940, Roosevelt again offered such offices through the Sayre mission (Hornbeck memorandum, 21 January 1938, *FR* [1938], 3:45; see also Chapter 3 of the present volume). During the years 1935–40, FDR repeatedly offered his personal intervention to settle issues outstanding between Germany and the states of Europe (see Chapter 4). In 1939, Roosevelt offered his good offices to resolve the conflict between Moscow and Helsinki (Langer and Gleason, *Challenge to Isolation*, 328).

39. The following instances are cited without reference to the futility of various presidential appeals to Latin American countries or to Roosevelt's numerous pleas to Stalin with reference to sites of proposed meetings.

1933: On 16 May, Roosevelt issued his message to fifty-four heads of state calling for action to prevent a breakdown in the disarmament talks at Geneva and for balanced budgets. On 19 May, he issued a joint statement with T. V. Soong appealing for peace in China.

1935: On 25 August, a stern warning was issued to Moscow with regard to the Comintern: "Most serious consequences" would follow if the Soviet Union was "unwilling or unable" to cooperate (Hull, *Memoirs*, 1:305). In July, the Italian ambassador was warned that the United States would regard with "extreme misgivings" any step by Italy which would bring about war in Ethiopia (Kirk to Hull, 11 July 1935, 765.84/490, RG 59, NA). The same month, a press release issued by Hull appealed to Italy for peace on the basis of the Kellogg Pact (Hull, *Memoirs*, 1:421). On 1 August, a Roosevelt press release appealed once again for peace between Rome and Addis Ababa (Hull to Bingham, 31 July 1935, *FR* [1935], 1:733). On 18 August, FDR sent a personal appeal to Mussolini via Hull and Kirk, saying that the consequences of war "would adversely affect the interests of all nations." According to Long, Mussolini returned an insolent reply (Hull to Kirk, 18 August 1935, *FR* [1935], 1:739; Long Diary, 4 September

1935, box 5, Long Papers, LC). On 12 September, Hull again called for peace on the basis of the Kellogg Pact (Hull press statement, *FR* [1935], 1:746–49). At the time that Italy invaded Ethiopia, Roosevelt begged France personally to close the Suez Canal (minutes of Roosevelt-Stalin meeting, 29 November 1943, *FR* [Cairo and Teheran], 530 [FDR recalling 1935]).

1936: In December at Buenos Aires, Hull enunciated his "Eight Pillars of Peace" as a platform upon which the nations of the world might stand in peace, prosperity, and security.

1937: On 16 July, Hull reiterated his Eight Pillars and subsequently, in a message to all governments of the world, he asked for universal support. Some sixty states, including Germany, Italy, and Japan, gave a positive response. But Portugal, in an expression of dissent, made pointed reference to Roosevelt's misplaced trust in "vague formulae" (Borg, *Far Eastern Crisis*, 290). On 23 August, the date of a second bombing disaster in China, Hull proclaimed anew his Pillars of Peace (ibid., 307–8).

1938: On 26 September, FDR urged a peaceful solution of the Czech crisis with a proviso that the United States had "no political involvements" and would assume "no obligations." He then appealed to Mussolini and Hitler for an immediate conference of all interested parties at some neutral spot in Europe. Mussolini responded, but it was owing to British rather than American pressure (Langer and Gleason, *Challenge to Isolation*, 33; Phillips, *Ventures*, 222; *Letters*, 4:819; Feiling, *Chamberlain*, 373). On 28 September, Roosevelt urged Stalin to appeal to both the Czechs and Germans for a rational solution to the issues dividing them (Lukacs, *Great Powers*, 160). In early October, the day after he appealed to Polish Foreign Minister Beck not to seize Czech territory by force, the Poles seized Teschen (Biddle, *Poland*, 23). In December, he appealed to Mussolini to persuade Hitler to treat his Jewish population more humanely (Alexander DeConde, *Half Bitter, Half Sweet: An Excursion into Italian-American History* [New York: Scribner's 1971], 231).

1939: In January, Mussolini turned down Roosevelt's proposal to let Jewish emigrants go to Ethiopia (ibid.). On 8 April, Roosevelt lodged a protest with Italy with reference to her takeover of Albania. His message contained a veiled appeal to the Italian people over the head of their government, prompting Moffat to remark: "There was a rather general feeling that we had been issuing too many statements of late" (Moffat Diplomatic Journal, 8, 9 April 1939, Moffat Papers, Harvard). On 14 April, FDR issued his Thirty-one Nations appeal to Hitler (the same day that he told Henry Wallace that there was no sense "delivering a sermon to a mad dog") (Moffat Diplomatic Journal, 15, 16 April 1939, ibid.; Langer and Gleason, *Challenge to Isolation*, 88). When Hitler returned a withering reply in his Reichstag speech two weeks later, Senator Borah observed that in the fuehrer Roosevelt had met his match (Sherwood, *Roosevelt and Hopkins*, 116). On 13 August, Roosevelt appealed to Colonel

Beck to strike some form of compromise with Germany (Biddle to Hull, 13 August 1939, 760 C.62/807, RG 59, NA). On 23 August, Phillips was ordered to deliver a Roosevelt message to the king of Italy suggesting that Mussolini should try to avert war by presenting a plan for a conference on arms reduction and trade cooperation. Ambassador Kennedy reported from London that the appeal to the king was regarded as "lousy and a complete flop" (Phillips, Ventures, 231–32; Dallek, Roosevelt, 196; Welles to Phillips [containing message of Roosevelt to the king of Italy], 23 August 1939, FR [1939], 1:352). On 24 August, FDR sent an appeal to Hitler and to President Moscicki of Poland, urging negotiation, arbitration, or conciliation. When Moscicki agreed to negotiation or conciliation, Roosevelt forwarded the reply to Berlin. Berle likened the White House initiative to the sending of a valentine to one's mother-in-law out of season (Roosevelt to Hitler and Moscicki, 24 August 1939, Moscicki to Roosevelt, 25 August 1939, Roosevelt to Hitler, 25 August 1939, FR [1939], 1:360–62, 368–69; Pratt, Hull, 1:317ff.; Langer and Gleason, Challenge to Isolation, 189–90). On 1 September, Roosevelt sent an appeal to Berlin, Rome, Warsaw, Paris, and London that open cities be spared from bombing. All agreed, but almost immediately the residence of the American ambassador to Poland was damaged by bombing (Weinberg, "Hitler's Image," 1013; Jedrzejewicz, ed., Diplomat in Paris, 302–8). On 11 October, Roosevelt appealed to President Kalinin of the Soviet Union to respect Finnish independence and offered American mediation. Molotov replied sarcastically in an interview with Ambassador Steinhardt (Hooker, ed., Moffat, 271n.; Langer and Gleason, Challenge to Isolation, 323). On 20 October, he appealed to Hitler to respect Dutch and Belgian neutrality (Dallek, Roosevelt, 208). On 29 November, he offered his good offices in the Finnish-Soviet dispute. An hour and a half later came news of the Russian decision to break relations with Helsinki. He then appealed vainly to Finland and the Soviet Union to refrain from bombing open cities (Langer and Gleason, Challenge to Isolation, 328–30).

1940: On 13 March, Roosevelt issued a statement in support of Finnish integrity and independence. Helsinki nevertheless had to yield to a humiliating treaty imposed by Moscow (ibid., 403). On 29 April, he appealed to Mussolini to remain neutral in the war and exert influence for peace. The answer he received was a cold one (ibid., 441–43). On 14 May, he sent a second appeal to Mussolini for the continued neutrality of Italy (ibid., 451–52). On 26 May, he lodged a third appeal, offering to communicate Italian desiderata to France and Britain and act as monitor of any agreement that might be reached (Hull to Phillips, 26 May 1940, FR [1940], 2:711). On 30 May, he sent a fourth appeal to Mussolini threatening in the event of Italian belligerency to double the size of the American effort to supply the Allies and hinting at the possibility of American entry into the war (Hull to Phillips, 30 May 1940, FR [1940], 2:713). Mussolini's replies became more insulting with each appeal, and this time the duce responded with a statement that he did not wish to receive any more American pressure. During the same month, Bullitt demanded that Pope Pius XII excommunicate Mussolini if he brought Italy into the war. Maintaining that such action would look ridiculous and have positively no effect, the Vatican refused even to consider it (DeConde, *Half Bitter*, 235). On 7 June, Roosevelt wished to send Mussolini a fifth appeal, but he was dissuaded by Hull and Welles (Hull, *Memoirs*, 1:784). It should be noted that during this period, 1940–41, FDR lodged repeated protests and appeals in Tokyo connected with Japanese expansion into Indochina, and the Japanese replied with thinly veiled insults (Langer and Gleason, *Undeclared War*, 14).

1941: In January, Colonel Donovan was sent by Roosevelt to appeal to Bulgarian and Yugoslav leaders to resist Hitler's offer of alliance. On 1 March, Bulgaria joined the Axis and on 25 March, so did Yugoslavia. An American-inspired revolt on 27 March did not prevent the Germans from forcing Belgrade to surrender within a month, and Donovan made a poor showing in Bulgaria (record of a conversation with the king of Bulgaria by Fritz von Twardowski, 31 January 1941, *DGFP*, ser. D, 11:1202; Friedländer, *Prelude*, 188–91).

1942: During the Allied landing in North Africa, Roosevelt broadcast a vain appeal in French for the Vichy commanders to surrender on the spot without bloodshed (Burns, *Soldier of Freedom*, 292, 298).

1944: Roosevelt made two fruitless appeals to Stalin to refrain from recognizing the Lublin government of Poland, one on 16 December, the other 30 December (Theoharis, "Cold War," 218; FDR to Stalin, 16, 30 December 1944 [messages received on 20 and 31 December], *SCRT*, 175, 182–83).

40. Notable among the prewar diplomatic initiatives and schemes that enjoyed a partial measure of success were Roosevelt's Reciprocal Trade Program and the Anglo-American Trade Treaty. For the limitations of the former, see Guerrant, *Good Neighbor*, 96–99; Bemis, *Latin American Policy*, 308, 310; Varg, "Good Neighbor." Eminently debatable would be "unconditional surrender" as a wartime formula and the Soviet-American treaty of recognition. See Maddux, *Estrangement*, chaps. 2 and 3, for the inadequacy of the latter. Roosevelt's trade pact with Canada began as a Canadian initiative with which the president did not immediately cooperate (Richard N. Kottman, "The Canadian-American Trade Agreement of 1935," *Journal of American History* 52 [September 1965]:275–96). Destroyers for Bases and Lend-Lease, which originated largely as requests from abroad, belong properly in the category of foreign aid. There is also the United Nations, which, as indicated above, owed little to FDR in terms of prewar impetus (before 1942). If, then, we exclude Roosevelt's dubious record in Latin America, as set forth in Chapter 6, this leaves the great majority of his initiatives stillborn or fruitless. What follows is an incomplete sampling:

1933: Codification of American law (hemispheric) (Guerrant, *Good Neigh-*

bor, 80–81); arms limitation and nonproliferation treaties (FDR speech at Chautauqua, 14 August 1936, Nixon, ed., *Roosevelt*, 3:379; Pratt, *Hull*, 1:93–94); St. Lawrence Waterway Treaty with Canada (FDR to the Senate, 10 January 1934, Nixon, ed., *Roosevelt*, 1:583–85; Pittman to Howe, 10 March 1934, ibid., 2:23; Dwight D. Eisenhower, *Mandate for Change* [Garden City, N.Y.: Doubleday, 1963], 574); World Non-Aggression Pact (Bemis, *Latin American Policy*, 270); tariff truce (see Chapter 1); World Economic Conference to be held in Washington (notes on Ritter-Davis conversation, 10 April 1933, *DGFP*, ser. C, 1:273–74); world currency stabilization (see Chapter 1); "Root and Branch" economic plan presented to Britain and Italy in the fall (House to Long, 21 October 1933, Bingham to Hull, 23 October 1933, boxes 15, 71, House Papers, Yale University).

1934: Plan to force German cooperation on arms limitation (memorandum of Davis-Roosevelt talk, 28 April 1934, box 9, Davis Papers, LC); comprehensive effort to reach a settlement on the Far East with Japan (see Chapter 2); arms embargo against Bolivia and Paraguay (Wood, *Latin American Wars*, 63–65); London naval talks (Watt, *Personalities*, 91–92, 95).

1935: Proposal to Italy through Long for a settlement of the Ethiopian war (Long to Hull, 12, 17 September 1935, *FR* [1935], 1:749–51, 754–57); attempt through Samuel Fuller to reach a settlement with Germany (Samuel Fuller, memorandum of conversation with Schacht, 23 September 1935, *FR* [1935], 2:282–86); proposal to Britain through Bingham for a meeting of the Kellogg Pact signatories (Hoare to Eden, 9 October 1935, section 8:3, Templewood Papers, ULC).

1936: Second attempt through Fuller to reach common ground with Germany (Dallek, *Roosevelt*, 124); world peace conference planned for the summer, to meet at sea, possibly in the Canary Islands or Azores (Lindsay to Eden, Annual Report, 21 January 1937, Lindsay to Vansittart, 8 March 1937, FO 371/20670, PRO; Borg, "Quarantine," 408–10; *Letters*, 3:541; George Lansbury to Baldwin, 27 August 1936, bk. 129, Baldwin Papers, ULC).

1937: World peace conference planned for Washington in the spring (Ian Colvin, *None So Blind* [New York: Harcourt, Brace and World, 1965], 181; Eden, *Facing the Dictators*, 595–96; *Dodd's Diary*, 369, 377, 380, 386, 388–89; Laboulaye to Delbos, 8 September 1936, *DDF*, ser. 2, 3:346); world conference for revision of the Versailles settlement (Lindsay to Vansittart, 8 March 1939, FO 371/20670, PRO); mediation proposal on the order of Theodore Roosevelt's Portsmouth Conference proposed to Japan through Dooman on 8 November (see Chapter 2); Quarantine Address, Brussels Conference, naval quarantine of Japan (Haight, "Naval Quarantine," 210, 216–17); neutralization plan for the Pacific (Eden to Lindsay, 5 May 1937, FO 371/20704, PRO; Borg, *Far Eastern Crisis*, 244–48).

1938: Welles Plan, Frontiers Conference (Lindsay to Foreign Office, 19 September 1938, FO 371/21527, PRO).

1940: Welles mission (see Chapter 4); invitation to forty-six neutrals to exchange views on arms control and free trade as a means of arriving at a peace settlement (Dallek, *Roosevelt*, 216).

1941: Effort to bring Ireland actively into the war on the side of the Allies (Willkie and Donovan trips) (Friedländer, *Prelude*, 214–15); various proposals to Tokyo, including a possible Japanese withdrawal from Indochina in return for simultaneous withdrawal by the British, Dutch, and French (Welles memorandums, 24, 28 July 1941, *FR* [Japan], 2:529, 538–39); multiple partition of Germany (Roosevelt advocated three German states after the war, possibly five) (William M. Franklin, "Zonal Boundaries and Access to Berlin," *World Politics* 16 [October 1963]:10); Palestine trusteeship (Herbert Parzen, "The Roosevelt Palestine Policy, 1943–1945: An Exercise in Dual Diplomacy," *American Jewish Archives* 26 [April 1974]:39; Wallace Diary, 6 March 1944, vol. 18, p. 3151, CUOHC); United States of Africa (Henry L. Feingold, "Roosevelt and the Holocaust: Reflections on New Deal Humanitarianism," *Judaism* 18 [Summer 1969]:265); Morgenthau Plan for Germany, Korean trusteeship (Louis, *Imperialism*, 355); Indochina trusteeship (ibid., 9, 38–39); partition of Yugoslavia (Welles, *Seven Decisions*, 136; Burns, *Soldier of Freedom*, 365); four policemen scheme of world order; plan to raise Iran to the status of a "modern nation" (Buhite, *Hurley*, 129–31); a new state (Wallonia) to be formed out of parts of Belgium, Luxembourg, Alsace-Lorraine, and France (Lyttelton notes on discussion with FDR, 24 November 1942, Eden Papers, vol. 29, FO 954, PRO).

41. China: At Cairo, Roosevelt promised Chiang a loan of a billion dollars. It was never delivered (Liang, *Stilwell*, 232n.). Repeatedly, he promised that the Hump tonnage would be increased to meet Chinese demands. It never was (White and Jacoby, *Thunder Out of China*, 155). Chiang complained on 26 June 1942 that 90 percent of the aid promised by Roosevelt had never been delivered, and he had good reason for concern (Sherwood, *Roosevelt and Hopkins*, 404–7; Liang, *Stilwell*, 55–59; Romanus and Sunderland, *Stilwell's Mission*, 169–71; White, ed., *Stilwell Papers*, 119; Langer and Gleason, *Undeclared War*, 490). At Cairo, Roosevelt promised Chiang that China would remain in control of Dairen and Port Arthur. This promise was broken at Yalta. For the promise, see minutes of Roosevelt-Chiang dinner meeting, 23 November 1943, *FR* (Cairo and Teheran), 324. At Cairo, Roosevelt promised Chiang an amphibious invasion to coordinate with the invasion of Burma, but it was never delivered (Welles, *Seven Decisions*, 155; Romanus and Sunderland, *Stilwell's Command Problems*, 297). Roosevelt subsequently promised Chiang that the Burma campaign would be delayed by one year. It was not (Liang, *Stilwell*, 9). On 4 October 1944, FDR assured Dr. Kung that General Stilwell's recall was imminent. Two days later, he sent Chiang an entirely different message (Liang, *Stilwell*, 264).

Britain: In 1933, FDR told Prime Minister MacDonald that he would seek congressional support on the debt question, which he never did (MacDonald report, 5 May 1933, CAB 23/76, PRO; *DBFP*, ser. 2, 5:793n.). Later, on 22 May,

Roosevelt indicated to the British that he would send a message to Congress proposing that British refusal to pay should be regarded as deferment instead of default. He did not do so (Lindsay to Simon, 4 June 1933, *DBFP*, ser. 2, 5:815). At the same time, Roosevelt promised foreign leaders that he would work for currency stabilization. He never did. For the promise, see Pratt, *Hull*, 1:37. During the London Economic Conference, Roosevelt vetoed an offer made by his delegates, Warburg, Harrison, and Sprague, even though he had approved Warburg's memorandum on the question, reading it to his delegation before departure and incorporating it into a statement of aims. FDR also repudiated a compromise stabilization proposal made later on his behalf by Raymond Moley (Nichols, "Monetary Diplomacy"). In 1937, he repudiated specific offers made by Norman Davis at the Brussels Conference (MacDonald's report to the British War Cabinet, 24 November 1937, War Cab. 43, CAB 23/90, PRO; Haight, "Roosevelt and the Aftermath," 254–55). In the spring of 1939, Roosevelt told King George VI that he deemed war virtually inevitable and that the United States would enter after the first bombing of London (Wheeler-Bennett, *George VI*, 388, 391). In the summer of 1939, he agreed to deliver a strong note of warning to Japan, but this was never sent (Clifford, "Far East," 147). Early in the war, Roosevelt and Churchill entered into a compact whereby the prime minister agreed to abandon major nuclear research in England and to transfer his distinguished scientists to the United States, where they would cooperate with American research in developing the atomic bomb. This was to be on the basis of a full flow of information between the two countries. Late in 1942, however, the flow from Washington ceased. FDR chided his scientists, but when they revealed their suspicion of British leaks, their position was sustained and an angry Britain had no recourse (Albjerg, *Churchill*, 219–20). In addition to 50 destroyers, Roosevelt originally promised 20 motor torpedo boats, 10 large flying boats, 250,000 rifles, and 150 to 200 aircraft supplied with Swedish engines. In the actual exchange of letters that consummated the deal, Roosevelt mentioned only the destroyers. Lothian protested, but the president excused himself on grounds of domestic politics. After that, the ambassador did everything but sit on the doorstep of the White House, all in vain. Some items were not granted until after Lothian's death (Butler, *Lothian*, 298–99; War Cab. 230, CAB 65/8, PRO). In September 1941, Roosevelt promised Churchill to supply enough U.S. naval transports, manned by American crews, to ship twenty thousand British troops from England to the Middle East. A month later, the president retracted his offer in its original form, saying that he could not allow American ships and crews to load British troops in England. Churchill had to change his plans (Minutes of British Cabinet Meetings, 8 September, 9 October 1941, CAB 65/23, PRO). On Christmas Eve 1941, Roosevelt promised Churchill that American reinforcements on their way to the relief of the Philippines would go on to aid the British if they could not reach their intended destination. The promise was rescinded in the face of a stiff protest by Stimson (*RC*, 173). In April 1943, Roosevelt promised Churchill that the United States would not send an OSS mission to Chetnik headquarters in Yugoslavia, but the mission went (Roosevelt to Churchill, 3 September 1944, ibid., 571).

Argentina: In 1936, while in Buenos Aires, FDR promised the Argentines that he would use his influence in Congress to expedite the import of Argentine meat into the United States (previously barred on account of alleged hoof and mouth disease). He never did (Hull, *Memoirs*, 1:497–98; *Time*, 14 December 1936, p. 13).

Greece: He made repeated promises to Greece in 1940 and 1941 to supply aircraft needed in the fight against the Axis. These promises were never kept (Langer and Gleason, *Undeclared War*, 118; G. E. Patrick Murray, "Under Urgent Consideration: American Planes for Greece, 1940–1941," *Aerospace Historian* 24 [Summer/June 1977]:61–69; Friedländer, *Prelude*, 192; Berle and Jacobs, eds., *Navigating the Rapids*, 356, 367; Berle Diary, 6 February 1941, FDRL [supplements the published version]; *FR* [1940], 3:593–610; *FR* [1941], 2:669–70, 673–74, 703, 712, 720).

Germany: In 1938, he reneged on an offer to sell helium to the Germans even though they had already paid for it (Wilson to Hull, 29 April 1938, *FR* [1938], 2:459–60; Wilson, *Career Diplomat*, 30–31; Hull, *Memoirs*, 1:597–98).

Belgium: At a press conference held 25 August 1939, FDR promised to support King Leopold's peace message. When Brussels later called to complain that nothing came of the offer, it was found that the president had forgotten about it (Moffat Diplomatic Journal, 25 August 1939, Moffat Papers, Harvard University).

Japan: In 1933, Roosevelt let it be known that he would welcome a nonaggression pact with Japan, but when Tokyo showed interest, he declined (see Chapter 2; also Howell to FDR, 20 January 1934, PPF 604, FDRL). In both 1934 and 1941, Roosevelt proposed to meet personally with Japanese leaders in the Pacific and then retracted his offer when it was taken up by Tokyo (see Chapters 2 and 3; also Heinrichs, *Grew*, 360; Phillips memorandum of conversation with Roosevelt, 11 June 1934, 033.9411, Konoye, Fuminaro/14, RG 59, NA; Phillips to Grew, 11 June 1934, *FR* [1934], 3:662). In 1941, he proposed a modus vivendi with Japan, which he withdrew upon Tokyo's expression of interest (see Chapter 3).

France: Prior to inauguration day, Bullitt, on Roosevelt's behalf, suggested that the president intended to insert a special passage in his inaugural address warmly positive toward France, saying that debt talks with her would resume and take into account the desiderata formulated by the French Chamber. This never happened (Paul-Boncour to Claudel, 28 March 1933, *DDF*, ser. 1, 3:99). On 7 November 1937, French chargé Henry reported Roosevelt as saying that an attack on Hong Kong, Indochina, or the Dutch Indies would be regarded in the same way as an attack on the Philippines. But on 9 November, Norman Davis suggested to the French at Brussels that they ought to pull out of Indochina, and on 10 November, Welles replied to French demands for clarification by rephrasing Roosevelt's statement in such a way as to make it appear ambiguous (Henry to Delbos, 7, 10 November 1937, Delbos to Henry, 9 November 1937, *DDF*, ser. 2, 7:355–56, 364–65, 369–70). Roosevelt made a number of reassuring statements to France, either directly or through one of his envoys, to the effect that Paris could count on substantial American support in case of war with Germany. On 11 June 1938, for example, Ambassador Saint-Quentin reported him as saying that "if France goes down, quite obviously we shall go down with her" (Saint-Quentin to Bonnet, 11 June 1938, *DDF*, ser. 2, 10:39). This, doubtless, is one reason why Anthony Biddle concluded in his official report on the causes of French surrender that the Quai d'Orsay "overestimated the mood and capacity of the United States to arm and prepare itself adequately and in sufficient time to come to the aid of the Allies" (Biddle memorandum, 1 July 1940, PSF, Box 41, FDRL). Roosevelt was reported as assuring Léon Jouhaux, president of the French equivalent of the American Federation of Labor, that if Britain and France called a conference on Czechoslovakia and the United States were invited, it was prepared to accept. But when the French inquired further, Hull denied it (Moffat memorandum, 20 September 1938, and Hull memorandum 23 September 1938, *FR* [1938], 1:625–26, 638–39 [Lindsay also reported FDR as saying that if a frontiers conference were held, he would attend as long as it was held outside Europe—Lindsay to FO, 19 September 1938, FO 371/21527, PRO]). Roosevelt assured the French on many occasions during the war that he would work for the complete restoration of their empire. In fact, he did the opposite (Halifax to Churchill, 5 February 1941, Halifax Papers, CCC; Langer and Gleason, *Undeclared War*, 87; La Feber, "Indochina," 1278; Murphy, *Diplomat*, 168; FDR to Leahy, 20 January 1942, *Letters*, 4:1275). Roosevelt made promises to General Giraud at Casablanca involving delivery by the United States of large amounts of military hardware which never arrived (Viorst, *Hostile Allies*, 145, 151–52).

The Soviet Union: FDR offered Moscow a loan in 1933 when he intended to extend only a credit (Maddux, *Estrangement*, 22–23). At various times, he assured Stalin that the USSR might purchase a disassembled battleship in the United States as well as an assembled battleship, a submarine, and two destroyers. None of these promises was ever kept (ibid., 86–88, 101; Ickes, *Ickes*, 2:111; Leahy Diary, 9 December 1937, Leahy Papers, LC). According to Litvinov, Roosevelt offered the Soviet Union a nonaggression pact along with a Pacific pact, and in neither case did the United States prove willing to follow through (Maddux, *Estrangement*, 23, 31–32). In 1938, Roosevelt proposed to Stalin that the United States and Russia establish a military liaison in the Far

East, but he quickly abandoned the idea (ibid., 98; Maddux, "United States–Soviet Naval Relations," 30). In 1942, he promised the Soviet Union that a second military front would be opened in western Europe that year. The pledge was broken (Dallek, *Roosevelt,* 343–44; *RC,* 29; Maurice Matloff, "Franklin Delano Roosevelt as War Leader," in Harry L. Coles, ed., *Total War and Cold War: Problems in Civilian Control of the Military* [Columbus: Ohio State University Press, 1962], 51).

42. See, for example, Haight, "Munich Crisis," 351; Compton, *Swastika,* 26; Davies Diary, 17 January 1937 (Berlin), box 3, Davies Papers, LC; Kaufmann, "Bullitt and Kennedy," 653.

Bibliography

Primary Sources

Unpublished Official Records

FRANCE
Archives de la Mer, Chateau Vincennes, Paris
    Dossiers C.R.R. 5 and 6.
Archives Nationales, Paris
    Dossier F60/454.
Ministère des Relations Extérieures, Paris
    Record Groups:
    Amerique, 1918–40: Etats-Unis
    Asia-Oceanie: Japon
    Europe: Grande Bretagne
    Europe: Italie
    Papiers 1940—Etats-Unis: Fouques Duparc
    SDN: Conflit Sino-Japonais

GREAT BRITAIN
Public Record Office, Kew
    Record Groups:
    FO 371; FO 414; FO 800; FO 954; CAB 23; CAB 65; CAB 66; PREM 1; PREM
        3; PREM 4.

UNITED STATES
National Archives, Washington, D.C.
    Record Group 59 (Department of State)

Published Official Records

BELGIUM

Ministère des Affaires Etrangères. *Documents diplomatiques belges, 1920–1940; La politique de sécurité extérieure.* 5 vols. Brussels, 1964–66.

CANADA

Department of External Affairs. *Documents on Canadian External Relations.* 8 vols. Ottawa, 1909–41.

FRANCE

Ministère des Affaires Etrangères. *Documents diplomatiques français, 1932–1939.* Paris, 1964–.

The French Yellow Book: Diplomatic Documents Concerning the Events and Negotiations Which Preceded the Opening of Hostilities between Germany on the One Hand, and Poland, Great Britain, and France on the Other. London, 1939.

GERMANY

Auswärtiges Amt. *Documents on the Events Preceding the Outbreak of the War.* Berlin and New York, 1940.

German White Book: Documents Concerning the Last Phase of the German-Polish Crisis. New York, 1939.

The German White Paper. New York, 1940.

See also Kent, George, under collected works.

GREAT BRITAIN

Woodward, E. L. and Rohan Butler, eds. *Documents on British Foreign Policy, 1919–1939,* Series 2, Vols. 5, 6, 13; Series 3, Vols. 1–9. London: H. M. Stationery Office, Series 2, 1946–79; Series 3, 1949–55.

JAPAN

Ike, Nobutaka, trans. and ed. *Japan's Decision for War: Records of the 1941 Policy Conferences.* Stanford, 1967.

Gen in Kenkyūbu [the Japan Association of International Relations Committee to Study the Origins of the Pacific War], ed. *Taiheiyō sensō e no michi: Kaisen gaikō-shi* [The road to the Pacific war: A diplomatic history of the prewar years]. Tokyo, 1962–63.

POLAND

Ministry of Foreign Affairs. *Official Documents Concerning Polish-German and Polish-Soviet Relations, 1933–1939.* London, 1939.

REPUBLIC OF CHINA

Committee for the Study of Party History, ed. *Principal Documentary Material of the Republic of China in the Period of the Sino-Japanese War: Wartime Diplomacy.* 3 vols. Taipei, 1981.

UNITED STATES

Congress. Joint Committee on the Investigation of the Pearl Harbor Attack. *Hearings on the Pearl Harbor Attack.* 79th Cong., 2d sess., 39 parts. Washington, D.C., 1946.

Department of State. *Documents on German Foreign Policy, 1918–1945.*

Series C (1933–37), Washington, D.C., 1959–66; Series D (1937–41), Washington, D.C., 1959–64.

Foreign Relations of the United States: Japan, 1931–1941, 2 vols. Washington, D.C., 1943.

Foreign Relations of the United States: Conferences at Cairo and Teheran, 1943. Washington, D.C., 1961.

Foreign Relations of the United States: The Conferences at Malta and Yalta, 1945. Washington, D.C., 1955.

Foreign Relations of the United States: The Conference at Quebec, 1944. Washington, D.C., 1972.

Papers Relating to the Foreign Relations of the United States, 1933–1941. Washington, D.C., 1950–69.

House of Representatives. *American Neutrality Policy.* Washington, D.C., 1936.

International Military Tribunal for the Far East. *Record of the Proceedings, Documents, Exhibits, Judgment, Dissenting Judgments, Preliminary Interrogations, Miscellaneous Documents.* Tokyo, 1946–49.

Senate. *Neutrality.* Hearings. 74th Cong. 2d sess. Washington, D.C., 1936.

USSR

Ministry of Foreign Affairs. *Stalin's Correspondence with Roosevelt and Truman, 1941–1945.* New York, 1965. Taken from *Correspondence between the Chairman of the Council of Ministers of the U.S.S.R. and the Presidents of the U.S.A. and the Prime Ministers of Great Britain during the Great Patriotic War of 1941–1945.* New York: Capricorn, 1965, paperback.

Manuscript Collections

Archives Nationales, Paris
  René Cassin Papers 382 AP
  Coffinger Papers AB XIX 3059

Louis Marin Papers 317 AP
René Mayer Papers 363 AP
Joseph Paul-Boncour Papers Entrée 6299
Paul Reynaud Papers 74 AP
André Tardieu Papers 324 AP
Bibliothèque Nationale, Paris
  Pierre Etienne Flandin Papers
Birmingham University, Birmingham, England
  Avon Papers
  Austen Chamberlain Papers
  Neville Chamberlain Papers
British National Library
  Lord Cecil Papers
Cambridge University Library, Cambridge, England
  Stanley Baldwin Papers
  Lord Templewood (Samuel Hoare) Papers
Churchill College, Cambridge University, Cambridge, England
  Halifax Papers
  Knatchbull-Hugessen Papers
  Victor Mallet Papers
  Eric Phipps Papers
Columbia University Archives
  Spruille Braden Papers
Columbia University Oral History Project
  Reminiscences of:
  Adolf Berle
  Claude Bowers
  Spruille Braden
  Ellis Briggs
  Loy Henderson
  Nelson T. Johnson
  Arthur Krock
  Herbert Lehman
  Frances Perkins
  William Phillips
  Samuel Rosenman
  Norman Thomas
  Henry C. Wallace
  James P. Warburg
  John C. White
Dwight D. Eisenhower Library, Abilene, Kansas
  Walter Judd Oral History
  Walter Robertson Oral History

Fondation Nationale des Sciences Politiques, Paris
    Léon Blum Papers
    Edouard Daladier Papers
Franklin Delano Roosevelt Library, Hyde Park, New York
    Adolf Berle Diary
    Stephen Early Papers
    Harry Hopkins Papers
    Henry Morgenthau Farm Credit Administration Diaries
    Henry Morgenthau Presidential Diaries
    Map Room Papers
    Walton Moore Papers
    Official File Papers
    President's Personal File Papers
    President's Secretary's File Papers
    Roosevelt Family Papers
    Charles Taussig Papers
    Henry A. Wallace Papers
Georgetown University Library, Washington, D.C.
    Robert Kelley Papers
Harvard University, Cambridge, Massachusetts (Houghton Library)
    Joseph Grew Papers
    J. Pierrepont Moffat Papers
    William Phillips Papers
    Oswald Garrison Villard Papers
Hoover Institute, Stanford University, Palo Alto, California
    Joseph W. Ballantine Papers
    Hugh Gibson Papers
    Stanley K. Hornbeck Papers
    Joseph Stilwell Papers
Herbert Hoover Library, West Branch, Iowa
    William Castle Papers
    Hugh Gibson Papers
    Herbert Hoover Papers
    Hugh Wilson Papers
House of Lords Library, London
    Lord Samuel Papers
Library of Congress, Washington, D.C.
    Joseph and Stewart Alsop Papers
    Robert Bingham Papers
    Charles Bohlen Papers
    William Borah Papers
    Harold Burton Papers
    Wilbur J. Carr Papers

Raymond Clapper Papers
Tom Connally Papers
Josephus Daniels Papers
Joseph Davies Papers
Norman Davis Papers
William Dodd Papers
Herbert Feis Papers
Felix Frankfurter Papers
Cordell Hull Papers
Harold Ickes Papers
Nelson Johnson Papers
Frank Knox Papers
William Leahy Papers
Breckinridge Long Papers
Key Pittman Papers
Francis B. Sayre Papers
Lawrence Steinhardt Papers
Henry Wallace Papers
Wendell Willkie Papers
Maryknoll Archives, Maryknoll, New York
James M. Drought Papers
James E. Walsh Papers
Ministère des Relations Extérieures, Paris
Pierre Laval Papers
Paul Reynaud Papers
National Library of Scotland, Edinburgh
Lord Elibank Papers
Oxford University, Oxford, England (Bodleian Library)
Gilbert Murray Papers
Princeton University, Princeton, New Jersey (Mudd Library)
John Foster Dulles Papers (Firestone Library)
Joseph C. Green Papers
Saionji Harada Memoirs (film)
Arthur Krock Papers
John Van Antwerp MacMurray Papers
Harry Dexter White Papers
Public Archives of Canada, Ottawa
Richard B. Bennett Papers (microfilm from University of New Brunswick)
William Lyon Mackenzie King Papers
Hume Wrong Papers
Public Record Office, Kew, England
Alexander Cadogan Papers FO 800/293
Lord Simon Papers FO 800/287-91

Queens University, Kingston, Canada
  Lord Tweedsmuir (John Buchan) Papers
Royal Archives, Windsor Castle, England
  George V Papers
Scottish Record Office, Edinburgh, Scotland
  Lord Lothian (Phillip Kerr) Papers
University of Chicago, Chicago, Illinois
  Salmon O. Levinson Papers
University of Delaware, Newark, Delaware
  George S. Messersmith Papers
University of Iowa, Iowa City, Iowa
  Henry A. Wallace Papers
Yale University, New Haven, Connecticut
  Edward M. House Papers
  Henry L. Stimson Papers

Periodicals

Chicago Tribune
Contemporary Review
Foreign Affairs
Fortnightly
New Statesman and Nation
Newsweek
New York Times
Review of Reviews
Spectator
Time
Times (London)
U.S. News

Collected Works

Baily, Samuel L., ed. *Nationalism in Latin America*. New York: Knopf, 1971.
A Baker Street Folio: Five Letters about Sherlock Holmes from Franklin Delano Roosevelt. Summit, N.J.: Pamphlet House, 1945.
Berle, Beatrice, and Travis Beal Jacobs, eds. *Navigating the Rapids, 1918–1971: The Papers of Adolf A. Berle*. New York: Harcourt Brace Jovanovich, 1973.
Blum, John Morton, ed. *From the Morgenthau Diaries: Years of Crisis, 1928–1938*. Boston: Houghton Mifflin, 1959.

————. *From the Morgenthau Diaries: Years of Urgency, 1938–1941.* Boston: Houghton Mifflin, 1965.

————. *From the Morgenthau Diaries: Years of War, 1941–1945.* Boston: Houghton Mifflin, 1967.

————. *The Price of Vision: The Diary of Henry A. Wallace, 1942–1946.* Boston: Houghton Mifflin, 1973.

Boelcke, Willi A., ed. *The Secret Conferences of Dr. Goebbels: The Nazi Propaganda War, 1939–43.* New York: Dutton, 1970.

Bullitt, Orville H., ed. *For the President, Personal and Secret: Correspondence between Franklin D. Roosevelt and William C. Bullitt.* Boston: Houghton Mifflin, 1972.

Campbell, Thomas M., and George C. Herring, Jr., eds. *The Diaries of Edward R. Stettinius, Jr., 1943–1946.* New York: New Viewpoints, 1975.

Cannistraro, Philip V., Edward D. Wynot, Jr., and Theodore P. Kovaleff, eds. *Poland and the Coming of the Second World War: The Diplomatic Papers of A. J. Drexel Biddle, Jr., the United States Ambassador to Poland, 1937–1939.* Columbus: Ohio State University Press, 1976.

Carmichael, Donald S., ed. *F.D.R. Columnist: The Uncollected Columns of Franklin D. Roosevelt.* Chicago: Pellegrini and Cudahy, 1947.

Dilks, David, ed. *The Diaries of Sir Alexander Cadogan, 1938–1945.* London: Cassell, 1971.

Dodd, William E., Jr., and Martha Dodd, eds. *Ambassador Dodd's Diary, 1933–1938.* New York: Harcourt Brace, 1941.

Freedman, Max, ed. *Frankfurter and Roosevelt: Their Correspondence, 1928–1945.* Boston: Little, Brown, 1967.

Gibson, Hugh, ed. *The Ciano Diaries, 1939–1943.* Garden City, N.Y.: Doubleday, 1946.

Hachey, Thomas E., ed. *Confidential Dispatches: Analyses of America by the British Ambassador, 1939–1945.* Evanston, Ill.: New University Press, 1974.

Harvey, John, ed. *The Diplomatic Diaries of Oliver Harvey, 1937–1940.* New York: St. Martin's, 1970.

Hooker, Nancy Harvison, ed. *The Moffat Papers: Selections from the Diplomatic Journals of Jay Pierrepont Moffat, 1919–1943.* Cambridge, Mass.: Harvard University Press, 1956.

Israel, Fred L., ed. *The War Diary of Breckinridge Long: Selections from the Years 1939–1944.* Lincoln: University of Nebraska Press, 1966.

Jedrzejewicz, Waclaw, ed. *Diplomat in Paris, 1936–1939: Papers and Memoirs of Julius Lukasiewicz, Ambassador of Poland.* New York: Columbia University Press, 1970.

Kimball, Warren F., ed. *Churchill and Roosevelt: The Complete Correspondence.* 3 vols. Princeton: Princeton University Press, 1984.

Lash, Joseph, ed. *From the Diaries of Felix Frankfurter.* New York: Norton, 1975.

Lissance, Arnold, ed. *The Halder Diaries: The Private War Journals of Colonel General Franz Halder.* 2 vols. Boulder, Colo.: Westview Press, 1976.

Lochner, Louis P., ed. *The Goebbels Diaries, 1942–1943.* Garden City, N.Y.: Doubleday, 1948.

Loewenheim, Francis L., Harold D. Langley, and Manfred Jonas, eds. *Roosevelt and Churchill: Their Secret Wartime Correspondence.* New York: Dutton, 1975.

May, Ernest R., ed. *Knowing One's Enemies: Intelligence Assessment before the Two World Wars.* Princeton: Princeton University Press, 1984.

Millis, Walter, ed. *The Forrestal Diaries.* New York: Viking, 1951.

Murray, Arthur, ed. *The Diary of Faith Murray.* Edinburgh: R. and R. Clark, 1944.

Nixon, Edgar, ed. *Franklin D. Roosevelt and Foreign Affairs.* 3 vols. Cambridge, Mass.: Belknap Press of Harvard University Press, 1969.

Roosevelt, Elliott, ed. *F.D.R.: His Personal Letters.* 4 vols. New York: Duell, Sloane and Pearce, 1947–50.

Rosenman, Samuel I., ed. *The Public Papers and Addresses of Franklin D. Roosevelt.* 13 vols. New York: Russell and Russell, 1938–50.

Schewe, Donald B., ed. *Franklin D. Roosevelt and Foreign Affairs, Second Series: January 1, 1937–August 31, 1939.* 13 vols. New York: Clearwater, 1979.

Trevor-Roper, Hugh R., ed. *Hitler's Table Talk, 1941–1944.* London: Weidenfeld and Nicolson, 1953.

White, Theodore H., ed. *The Stilwell Papers.* New York: William Sloane, 1948.

Woodward, E. L., and Rohan Butler, eds. *Documents on British Foreign Policy, 1919–1939.* Series 2, London, 1946–79; Series 3, London, 1949–55.

Memoirs and Other Works by Contemporaries

Anders, Wladyslaw. *An Army in Exile: The Story of the Second Polish Corps.* London: Macmillan, 1949.

Ashley, Maurice. *Churchill as Historian.* London: Seckers and Warburg, 1968.

Ba Maw, U. *Breakthrough in Burma: Memoirs of a Revolution, 1939–1946.* New Haven: Yale University Press, 1968.

Barrett, David. D. *Dixie Mission: The United States Army Observer Group in Yenan, 1944.* Berkeley and Los Angeles: University of California Press, 1970.

Baudouin, Paul. *The Private Diaries of Paul Baudouin.* London: Eyre and Spottiswoode, 1948.

Beaulac, Willard L. *Career Ambassador.* New York: Macmillan, 1951.

———. *The Fractured Continent: Latin America in Close-Up.* Stanford: Hoover Institution Press, 1980.

Beneš, Eduard. *The Memoirs of Dr. Eduard Beneš.* London: Allen & Unwin, 1954.

————. "Memoirs of Eduard Beneš." *Nation,* 3 July 1948.

Bloom, Sol. *The Autobiography of Sol Bloom.* New York: G. P. Putnam's, 1948.

Bohlen, Charles E. *The Transformation of American Foreign Policy.* New York: Norton, 1969.

————. *Witness to History, 1929–1969.* New York: Norton, 1973.

Bonnet, Georges. *Défense de la Paix: De Washington au Quai d'Orsay.* Geneva: Constant Bourquin, 1948.

————. *De Munich à la guerre: Défense de la paix.* Paris: Librairie Plon, 1967.

Borah, William. *Bedrock Views on Basic National Problems.* Washington, D.C.: National Home Library, 1936.

Bowers, Claude G. *Chile through Embassy Windows, 1939–1953.* New York: Simon and Schuster, 1958.

————. *My Life.* New York: Simon and Schuster, 1962.

————. *My Mission to Spain.* New York: Simon and Schuster, 1954.

Briggs, Ellis. *Farewell to Foggy Bottom.* New York: David McKay, 1964.

Butler, Hugh. *Expenditures and Commitments by the United States Government in or for Latin America.* Senate Document 132, 78th Cong., 1st sess. Washington, D.C.: U.S. Government Printing Office, 1943.

Byrnes, James F. *Speaking Frankly.* New York: Harper, 1947.

Carton de Wiart, Adrian. *Happy Odyssey.* London: Cape, 1950.

Chennault, Claire Lee. *Way of a Fighter.* New York: Putnam, 1949.

Churchill, Winston S. *Closing the Ring.* Boston: Houghton Mifflin, 1951.

————. *The Gathering Storm.* Boston: Houghton Mifflin, 1948.

————. *The Grand Alliance.* Boston: Houghton Mifflin, 1950.

————. *The Hinge of Fate.* Boston: Houghton Mifflin, 1950.

————. *Their Finest Hour.* Boston: Houghton Mifflin, 1949.

————. *Triumph and Tragedy.* Boston: Houghton Mifflin, 1953.

Ciechanowski, Jan. *Defeat in Victory.* Garden City, N.Y.: Doubleday, 1947.

Craigie, Robert. *Behind the Japanese Mask.* London: Hutchinson, 1946.

Daniels, Josephus. *Shirt-Sleeve Diplomat.* Chapel Hill: University of North Carolina Press, 1947.

Davies, Joseph E. *Mission to Moscow.* New York: Simon and Schuster, 1941.

Deane, John R. *The Strange Alliance.* New York: Viking, 1947.

Decoux, Admiral Jean. *A la Barre de l'Indochine.* Paris: Plon, 1949.

De Gaulle, Charles. *The Complete War Memoirs of Charles de Gaulle, 1940–1946.* Translated by Jonathan Griffin and Richard Howard. New York: Simon and Schuster, 1964.

De Roussy de Sales, Raoul Jean Jacques. *The Making of Yesterday: The Diaries of Raoul de Roussy de Sales.* New York: Reynal and Hitchcock, 1947.

Dirksen, Herbert von. *Moscow, Tokyo, London: Twenty Years of German Foreign Policy.* Norman: University of Oklahoma Press, 1952.

Djilas, Milovan. *Conversations with Stalin.* New York: Harcourt Brace, 1962.

Dodd, Martha. *Through Embassy Eyes.* New York: Harcourt Brace, 1939.

Dorn, Frank. *Walkout with Stilwell in China.* New York: Crowell, 1971.

Dulles, Allen. *The Secret Surrender.* New York: Harper, 1966.

Dulles, John Foster. *War or Peace.* New York: Macmillan, 1950.

———. *War, Peace, and Change.* New York: Harper, 1939.

Eddy, William A. *FDR Meets Ibn Saud.* New York: American Friends of the Middle East, Inc., 1954.

Eden, Anthony. *Facing the Dictators.* Boston: Houghton Mifflin, 1962.

———. *The Reckoning.* Boston: Houghton Mifflin, 1965.

Eisenhower, Dwight D. *Crusade in Europe.* Garden City, N.Y.: Doubleday, 1948.

Farley, James A. *Jim Farley's Story: The Roosevelt Years.* New York: McGraw-Hill, 1948.

Fish, Hamilton. *FDR, The Other Side of the Coin: How We Were Tricked into World War II.* New York: Vantage Press, 1976.

Fotitch, Constantin. *The War We Lost: Yugoslavia's Tragedy and the Failure of the West.* New York: Viking, 1948.

François-Poncet, André. *The Fateful Years: The Memoirs of a French Ambassador in Berlin, 1931–1938.* New York: Harcourt Brace, 1949.

Grew, Edward. *Twenty-five Years, 1892–1916.* 2 vols. New York: Frederick A. Stokes Co., 1925.

Grew, Joseph. *Report from Tokyo.* New York: Simon and Schuster, 1942.

———. *Ten Years in Japan.* New York: Simon and Schuster, 1944.

———. *The Turbulent Era.* 2 vols. Boston: Houghton Mifflin, 1952.

Lord Halifax. *Fullness of Days.* New York: Dodd, Mead, 1957.

Hanfstaengl, Ernest. *Hitler, the Missing Years.* London: Eyre and Spottiswoode, 1957.

Harriman, W. Averell, and Elie Abel. *Special Envoy to Churchill and Stalin, 1941–1946.* New York: Random House, 1975.

Hassell, Ulrich von. *The von Hassell Diaries, 1938–1944.* Garden City, N.Y.: Doubleday, 1947.

Hassett, William D. *Off the Record with F.D.R., 1942–1945.* New Brunswick: Rutgers University Press, 1958.

Hayes, Carlton J. H. *Wartime Mission in Spain, 1942–1945.* New York: Macmillan, 1945.

Henderson, Neville. *Failure of a Mission.* New York: G. P. Putnam's Sons, 1940.

Hitler, Adolf. *Mein Kampf.* New York: Stackpole Sons, 1939.

Hoover, Herbert. *The Memoirs of Herbert Hoover: The Great Depression, 1929–1941.* New York: Macmillan, 1952.

Hoover, Herbert, and Hugh Gibson. *The Problems of Lasting Peace.* Garden City, N.Y.: Doubleday, Doran, 1943.

Hornbeck, Stanley H. *The United States and The Far East: Certain Fundamentals of Policy.* Boston: World Peace Foundation, 1942.

Horthy, Admiral Nicholas. *Memoirs.* London: Hutchinson, 1956.

Hull, Cordell. *The Memoirs of Cordell Hull.* 2 vols. New York: Macmillan, 1948.

Ickes, Harold L. *The Secret Diary of Harold L. Ickes.* 3 vols. New York: Simon and Schuster, 1953–54.

Kennan, George. *Memoirs, 1925–1950.* New York: Bantam, 1969.

Kerr, Phillip (Lord Lothian). *Liberalism in the Modern World.* London: Lovat Dickson, 1933.

Khrushchev, Nikita. *Khrushchev Remembers: The Last Testament.* Translated and edited by Strobe Talbott. Boston: Little, Brown, 1974.

Knatchbull-Hugessen, Hughe. *Diplomat: In Peace and War.* London: John Murray, 1949.

Krock, Arthur. *Memoirs: Sixty Years on the Firing Line.* New York: Funk and Wagnalls, 1968.

Lane, Arthur Bliss. *I Saw Poland Betrayed.* Indianapolis: Bobbs, 1948.

Leahy, William D. *I Was There.* New York: Whittlesey House, 1950.

Leeper, Reginald. *When Greek Meets Greek.* London: Chatto and Windus, 1950.

Lindbergh, Charles A. *The Wartime Journals of Charles A. Lindbergh.* New York: Harcourt Brace Jovanovich, 1970.

Litvinov, Maxim. *Notes for a Journal.* New York: Morrow, 1955.

McIntire, Ross T. *White House Physician.* New York: G. P. Putnam's Sons, 1946.

Macmillan, Harold. *Winds of Change, 1914–1939.* New York: Harper, 1966.

Maisky, Ivan. *Memoirs of a Soviet Ambassador: The War, 1939–43.* London: Hutchinson, 1967.

Menzies, Robert Gordon. *Afternoon Light.* London: Cassell, 1967.

Mikolajczyk, Stanislaw. *The Rape of Poland.* New York: Whittlesey House, 1948.

Moley, Raymond. *After Seven Years.* New York: Harper, 1939.

Monnet, Jean. *Memoirs.* Translated by Richard Mayne. London: Collins, 1978.

Moore, Frederick. *With Japan's Leaders: An Intimate Record of Fourteen Years as Counsellor to the Japanese Government, Ending December 7, 1941.* New York: Scribner's, 1942.

Lord Moran. *Churchill Taken from the Diaries of Lord Moran.* Boston: Houghton Mifflin, 1966.

Morgenthau, Henry. "The Morgenthau Diaries." *Collier's,* 11 October 1947.

Murphy, Robert. *Diplomat among Warriors.* Garden City, N.Y.: Doubleday, 1964.

Murray, Arthur (Viscount Elibank). *At Close Quarters: A Sidelight on Anglo-American Diplomatic Relations.* London: John Murray, 1946.

———. *Master and Brother: Murrays of Elibank*. London: John Murray, 1945.

Papen, Franz von. *Memoirs*. London: André Deutsch, 1952.

Perkins, Frances. *The Roosevelt I Knew*. New York: Viking, 1946.

Phillips, William. *Ventures in Diplomacy*. Boston: Beacon Press, 1952.

Reynaud, Paul. *In the Thick of the Fight, 1930–1945*. New York: Simon and Schuster, 1955.

———. *Mémoires*. 2 vols. Paris: Flamarion, 1963.

Ribbentrop, Joachim von. *The Ribbentrop Memoirs*. London: Weidenfeld and Nicolson, 1954.

Richardson, James O. *On the Treadmill to Pearl Harbor: The Memoirs of Admiral James O. Richardson*. Washington, D.C.: Department of the Navy, 1973.

Roosevelt, Eleanor. *This I Remember*. New York: Harper, 1949.

Roosevelt, Elliott. *As He Saw It*. New York: Duell, Sloane and Pearce, 1946.

Roosevelt, Franklin D. *Complete Presidential Press Conferences of Franklin D. Roosevelt*. 25 vols. New York: Da Capo Press, 1972.

———. *Looking Forward*. New York: John Day, 1933.

———. *On Our Way*. New York: John Day, 1934.

———. "Our Foreign Policy: A Democratic View." *Foreign Affairs* 6 (July 1928): 573–86.

———. "Shall We Trust Japan?" *Asia* 23 (July 1923): 475–78, 526, 528.

———. *Whither Bound?* Boston: Houghton Mifflin, 1926.

Roper, Daniel. *Fifty Years of Public Life*. Durham: Duke University Press, 1941.

Rosenman, Samuel I. *Working with Roosevelt*. New York: Harper, 1952.

Sayre, Francis Bowes. *Glad Adventure*. New York: Macmillan, 1957.

Schacht, Hjalmar. *Account Settled*. London: Weidenfield and Nicolson, 1948.

———. *Confessions of the "Old Wizard": The Autobiography of Hjalmar Horace Greeley Schacht*. 1955. Reprint. Westport, Conn.: Greenwood Press, 1974.

Serrano Suñer, Ramón. *Entre les Pyrénées et Gibraltar*. Geneva: Editions du Cheval Aila, 1947.

Shigemitsu, Mamoru. *Japan and Her Destiny: My Struggle for Peace*. New York: E. P. Dutton, 1958.

Shirer, William L. *Rise and Fall of the Third Reich*. New York: Crest, 1963.

Simon, John. *Retrospect*. London: Hutchinson, 1952.

Standley, William, and Arthur Ageton. *Admiral Ambassador to Russia*. Chicago: Regnery, 1955.

Stettinius, Edward R. *Roosevelt and the Russians*. Garden City, N.Y.: Doubleday, 1949.

Stimson, Henry L. *The Far Eastern Crisis*. New York: Harper, 1936.

Stimson, Henry L., and McGeorge Bundy. *On Active Service in Peace and War*. New York: Harper, 1947.

Strauss, Lewis L. *Men and Decisions.* Garden City, N.Y.: Doubleday, 1962.

Lord Templewood (Samuel Hoare). *Complacent Dictator.* New York: Knopf, 1947.

―――. *Nine Troubled Years.* London: Collins, 1954.

Tōgō, Shigenori. *The Cause of Japan.* Translated by Fumihiko Tōgō. New York: Simon and Schuster, 1956.

Tully, Grace. *F.D.R. My Boss.* New York: Scribner's, 1949.

Lord Vansittart. *The Mist Procession.* London: Hutchinson, 1958.

Wallace, Henry A. *Toward World Peace.* New York: Reynal and Hitchcock, 1948.

Wehle, Louis B. *Hidden Threads of History.* New York: Macmillan, 1953.

Weizsäcker, Ernst von. *Memoirs of Ernst von Weizsäcker.* London: Victor Gollancz, 1951.

Welles, Sumner. *Seven Decisions That Shaped History.* New York: Harper, 1951.

―――. "Thwarted Peace Plan." *Washington Post,* 4 May 1948, p. 15.

―――. *The Time for Decision.* New York: Harper, 1944.

Wheeler, Post, and Hallie Erminie Rives. *Dome of Many Coloured Glass.* Garden City, N.Y.: Doubleday, 1955.

Willert, Sir Arthur. *Washington and Other Memories.* Boston: Houghton Mifflin, 1972.

Wilson, Hugh R. *Diplomat between Wars.* New York: Longman's Green, 1941.

Wilson, Hugh R., Jr. *A Career Diplomat.* New York: Vantage Press, 1960.

Yoshida, Shigeru. *The Yoshida Memoirs: The Story of Japan in Crisis.* London: Heinemann, 1962.

Secondary Works

Ph.D. Dissertations

Burns, Richard Dean. "Cordell Hull: A Study in Diplomacy, 1933–1941." University of Illinois, 1960.

Eagles, Keith D. "Ambassador Joseph E. Davies and American-Soviet Relations, 1937–1941." University of Washington, 1966.

Fitz-Simons, Daniel Whitford. "Henry A. Wallace: Diplomat, Ideologue, and Administrator, 1940–1945." St. John's University, 1977.

Grigg, Richard J. "Japanese-American Relations, 1931–1937." Georgetown University, 1950.

Harrison, Richard Arnold. "Appeasement and Isolation: The Relationship of

British and American Foreign Policies, 1935–1938." Princeton University, 1974.

Hubert, Mary G. "The Role of Nelson Trusler Johnson in Sino-American Diplomatic Relations, 1930–1935." Catholic University, 1964.

Manning, Donald J. "Soviet-American Relations, 1929–1941: The Impact of Domestic Considerations on Foreign Policy Decision-Making." Michigan State University, 1978.

Miner, Deborah N. "United States Policy toward Japan 1941: The Assumption That Southeast Asia Was Vital to the British War Effort." Columbia University, 1976.

Renter, Paul H., Jr. "William Phillips and the Development of American Foreign Policy, 1933–1947." University of Southern Mississippi, 1979.

Starr, Daniel P. "Nelson Trusler Johnson: The United States and the Rise of Nationalist China, 1925–1937." Rutgers University, 1967.

Watts, James Francis, Jr. "The Public Life of Breckinridge Long, 1916–1944." University of Missouri, 1964.

Articles

Accinelli, Robert D. "The Roosevelt Administration and the World Court Defeat, 1935." *The Historian* 40 (May 1978): 463–78.

Acheson, Dean. "Morality, Moralism, and Diplomacy." *Yale Review* 47 (June 1958): 481–93.

Adams, Frederick C. "The Road to Pearl Harbor: A Reexamination of American Far Eastern Policy, July 1937–December 1938." *Journal of American History* 58 (June 1971): 73–92.

Adler, Les K., and Thomas G. Paterson. "Red Fascism: The Merger of Nazi Germany and Soviet Russia in the American Image of Totalitarianism, 1930s–1950s." *American Historical Review* 75 (April 1970): 1046–64.

Adler, Selig. "The United States and the Holocaust." *American Jewish Historical Quarterly* 64 (September 1974): 14–23.

Albjerg, Victor. "Isolationism and the Early New Deal, 1932–1937." *Current History* 35 (October 1958): 204–10.

Allen, William R. "The International Trade Philosophy of Cordell Hull, 1907–1933." *American Economic Review* 43 (March 1953): 101–16.

Alsop, Joseph. "Why We Lost China." *Saturday Evening Post*, 7 January 1950, pp. 16–17, 38–41, 46–48; 14 January 1950, pp. 26–27, 87–90; 21 January 1950, pp. 30, 111–14.

Alvarez, David J. "The Embassy of Laurence A. Steinhardt: Aspects of Allied-Turkish Relations, 1942–1945." *East European Quarterly* 9 (Spring 1975): 39–52.

Anderson, Irvine H., Jr. "The 1941 *De Facto* Embargo on Oil to Japan: A Bureaucratic Reflex." *Pacific Historical Review* 44 (May 1975):201–31.

Armstrong, Hamilton Fish. "Armistice at Munich." *Foreign Affairs* 17 (January 1939): 197–290.

Asada, Sadao. "Japan's 'Special Interests' and the Washington Conference, 1921–22." *American Historical Review* 67 (October 1961): 62–70.

Baldwin, Hanson. "Churchill Was Right." *Atlantic* 194 (July 1954): 23–32.

Ballantine, Joseph W. "Mukden to Pearl Harbor: The Foreign Policies of Japan." *Foreign Affairs* 27 (July 1949): 651–64.

Barclay, G. St. J. "Australia Looks to America: The Wartime Relationship, 1939–1942." *Pacific Historical Review* 46 (May 1977): 251–71.

Baumont, Maurice. "French Critics and Apologists Debate Munich." *Foreign Affairs* 25 (July 1947): 685–90.

Beloff, Max. "Soviet Foreign Policy, 1929–1941: Some Notes." *Soviet Studies* (October 1950): 123–37.

Bemis, Samuel Flagg. "First Gun of a Revisionist Historiography for the Second World War." *Journal of Modern History* 19 (March 1947): 55–59.

Benda, Julien. "Pacifism and Democracy." *Foreign Affairs* 19 (July 1941): 693–701.

Bergman, Alexander. "The Soviet Version of World War Two." *East Europe* 12 (April 1963): 23–28.

Blakeslee, George H. "The Japanese Monroe Doctrine." *Foreign Affairs* 11 (July 1933): 671–81.

Borg, Dorothy. "Notes on Roosevelt's 'Quarantine' Speech." *Political Science Quarterly* 72 (September 1957): 405–33.

Bowers, Robert E. "Hull, Russian Subversion in Cuba, and Recognition of the USSR." *Journal of American History* 53 (December 1966): 542–54.

Boyle, John H. "The Drought-Walsh Mission to Japan." *Pacific Historical Review* 34 (May 1965): 141–61.

Braddick, Henderson B. "A New Look at American Policy during the Italo-Ethiopian Crisis, 1935–36." *Journal of Modern History* 34 (March 1962): 64–73.

Bruenn, Howard G. "Clinical Notes on the Illness and Death of President Franklin D. Roosevelt." *Annals of International Medicine* 72 (1970): 579–91.

Brune, Lester H. "Considerations of Force in Cordell Hull's Diplomacy, July 26 to November 26, 1941." *Diplomatic History* 2 (Fall 1978): 389–405.

Bryson, Thomas A. "Roosevelt's Quarantine Speech, the Georgia Press, and the Borg Thesis: A Note." *Australian Journal of Politics and History* 21 (August 1975): 95–98.

Buhite, Russell D. "Patrick J. Hurley and the Yalta Far Eastern Agreement." *Pacific Historical Review* 37 (August 1968): 343–53.

―――. "Soviet-American Relations and the Repatriation of Prisoners of War, 1945." *The Historian* 35 (May 1973): 384–97.

Bullitt, William C. "How We Won the War and Lost the Peace." *Life* 25 (30 August 1948): 83–97; (16 September 1948): 86–103.

Burns, Richard Dean, and W. Addams Dixon. "Foreign Policy and the 'Democratic Myth': The Debate on the Ludlow Amendment." *Mid-America* 47 (October 1965): 288–306.

Butler, Hugh. "Our Deep Dark Secrets in Latin America." *Reader's Digest* 43 (December 1943): 21–25.

Butow, R. J. C. "Backdoor Diplomacy in the Pacific: The Proposal for a Konoye-Roosevelt Meeting, 1941." *Journal of American History* 59 (June 1972): 48–72.

―――. "The Hull-Nomura Conversations: A Fundamental Misconception." *American Historical Review* 65 (July 1960): 822–36.

Campbell, John C. "Negotiating with the Soviets: Some Lessons of the War Period." *Foreign Affairs* 34 (January 1956): 305–19.

Castle, Alfred L. "William R. Castle and Opposition to U.S. Involvement in an Asian War, 1939–1941." *Pacific Historical Review* 54 (August 1985): 337–51.

Chase, John L. "Unconditional Surrender Reconsidered." *Political Science Quarterly* 70 (June 1955): 258–79.

Clauss, Errol MacGregor. "The Roosevelt Administration and Manchukuo, 1933–1941." *The Historian* 32 (August 1970): 595–611.

Clifford, Nicholas R. "Britain, America, and the Far East, 1937–1940: A Failure in Cooperation." *Journal of British Studies* 3 (November 1963): 137–54.

Clyde, Paul H. "Historical Reflections on American Relations with the Far East." *South Atlantic Quarterly* 61 (Autumn 1962): 437–49.

Cohen, Michael J. "American Influence on British Policy in the Middle East during World War Two: First Attempts at Coordinating Allied Policy on Palestine." *American Jewish Historical Quarterly* 57 (September 1977): 50–70.

Cohen, Warren I. "American Observers and the Sino-Soviet Friendship Treaty of August, 1945." *Pacific Historical Review* 35 (August 1966): 347–49.

―――. "Who Fought the Japanese in Hunan? Some Views of China's War Effort." *Journal of Asian Studies* 27 (November 1967): 111–15.

Cole, Wayne S. "American Entry in World War II: A Historiographical Appraisal." *Mississippi Valley Historical Review* 43 (March 1957): 595–617.

―――. "Senator Key Pittman and American Neutrality Policies, 1933–1940." *Mississippi Valley Historical Review* 46 (March 1960): 644–62.

Conroy, Hilary. "The Strange Diplomacy of Admiral Nomura." *Proceedings of the American Philosophical Society* 114 (June 1970): 205–16.

Craig, Gordon A. "High Tide of Appeasement: The Road to Munich 1937–38." *Political Science Quarterly* 65 (March 1950): 20–37.

Cronon, E. David. "Interpreting the New Good Neighbor Policy: The Cuban

Crisis of 1933." *Hispanic American Historical Review* 39 (November 1959): 538–67.

Crowley, James B. "Japanese Army Factionalism in the Early 1930s." *Journal of Asian Studies* 21 (May 1962): 309–26.

———. "A Reconsideration of the Marco Polo Bridge Incident." *Journal of Asian Studies* 22 (May 1963): 277–91.

Current, R. N. "How Stimson Meant to 'Maneuver' the Japanese." *Mississippi Valley Historical Review* 40 (June 1953): 67–74.

Dallek, Robert. "Beyond Tradition: The Diplomatic Careers of William E. Dodd and George S. Messersmith, 1933–1938." *South Atlantic Quarterly* 66 (Spring 1967): 233–44.

———. "Franklin Roosevelt as World Leader." *American Historical Review* 76 (December 1971): 1503–13.

Dennett, Tyler. "America's Far Eastern Diplomacy." *Current History* 37 (October 1932): 15–19, 125.

DeNovo, John A. "The Culbertson Economic Mission and Anglo-American Tensions in the Middle East, 1944–1945." *Journal of American History* 63 (March 1977): 913–36.

Diggins, John P. "Flirtation with Fascism: American Pragmatic Liberals and Mussolini's Italy." *American Historical Review* 71 (January 1966): 487–506.

———. "The Italo-American Anti-Fascist Opposition." *Journal of American History* 54 (December 1967): 579–98.

———. "Mussolini and America: Hero Worship, Charisma, and the 'Vulgar Talent.'" *The Historian* 28 (August 1966): 559–85.

Dingman, Roger. "Farewell to Friendship: The USS *Astoria*'s Visit to Japan, April 1939." *Diplomatic History* 10 (Spring 1986): 121–39.

Divine, Robert A. "Franklin D. Roosevelt and Collective Security, 1933." *Mississippi Valley Historical Review* 48 (June 1961): 42–59.

Dorn, W. L. "The Debate over American Occupation Policy in Germany in 1944–1945." *Political Science Quarterly* 72 (December 1957): 481–501.

Doyle, Michael K. "The United States Navy—Strategy and Far Eastern Foreign Policy, 1931–1941." *Naval War College Review* 29 (Winter 1977): 52–60.

Dulles, Eleanor Lansing. "The Export-Import Bank of Washington: The First Ten Years." Department of State Commercial Policy Series, No. 75 (Washington, D.C., 1944).

Dulles, Foster Rhea, and Gerald E. Ridinger. "The Anti-Colonial Policies of Franklin D. Roosevelt." *Political Science Quarterly* 70 (March 1955): 1–18.

Lord Elibank (Arthur Murray). "Franklin Roosevelt: Friend of Britain." *Contemporary Review* 1074 (June 1955): 362–68.

Emerson, William R. "F.D.R. (1941–1945)." In Ernest R. May, ed., *The Ultimate Decision: The President as Commander-in-Chief*, pp. 135–77. New York: Braziller, 1960.

————. "Franklin Roosevelt as Commander-in-Chief in World War II." *Military Affairs* 22 (Winter 1958–59): 181–207.

Esthus, Raymond A. "President Roosevelt's Commitment to Britain to Intervene in a Pacific War." *Mississippi Valley Historical Review* 50 (June 1963): 28–38.

Fagan, George Vincent. "F.D.R. and Naval Limitation." *U.S. Naval Institute Proceedings* 81 (April 1955): 411–18.

Feingold, Henry L. "Roosevelt and the Holocaust: Reflections on New Deal Humanitarianism." *Judaism* 18 (Summer 1969): 259–76.

Feis, Herbert. "War Came at Pearl Harbor: Suspicions Considered." *Yale Review* 45 (March 1956): 378–90.

Ferrell, R. H. "Pearl Harbor and the Revisionists." *The Historian* 17 (February 1955): 215–33.

Field, Henry. "How F.D.R. Did His Homework." *Saturday Review,* 8 July 1961, 8–10, 46.

Franklin, William M. "Yalta Viewed from Tehran." In Daniel R. Beaver, ed., *Some Pathways in Twentieth-Century History: Essays in Honor of Reginald Charles McGrane,* pp. 253–61, 300–301. Detroit: Wayne State University Press, 1969.

————. "Zonal Boundaries and Access to Berlin." *World Politics* 16 (October 1963): 1–31.

Friedlander, Robert A. "New Light on the Anglo-American Reaction to the Ethiopian War, 1935–1936." *Mid-America* 45 (April 1963): 115–25.

Gibbs, Norman. "The Naval Conferences of the Interwar Years: A Study in Anglo-American Relations." *U.S. Naval War College Review* 30 (Summer 1977): 50–63.

Gosset, Pierre, and Renée Gosset. "Les secrets de la paix manquée: Le déclin de Roosevelt." *Realités Litteraires,* ser. 3, (1949): 3–76.

Gottschalk, Louis. "Our Vichy Fumble." *Journal of Modern History* 22 (March 1948): 47–56.

Grace, Richard. "Whitehall and the Ghost of Appeasement: November 1941." *Diplomatic History* 3 (Spring 1979): 173–91.

Graebner, Norman. "Japan: Unanswered Challenge, 1931–1941." In Margaret F. Morris and Sandra L. Myres, eds., *Essays on American Foreign Policy.* Austin, Texas: University of Texas Press, 1974.

Green, O. M. "Realities in the Far East." *Fortnightly* 132 (July–December 1932): 303–14.

Greene, Fred. "The Military View of American National Policy, 1904–1940." *American Historical Review* 66 (January 1961): 354–77.

Gunther, John. "Siam the Incredible Kingdom." *Foreign Affairs* 17 (January 1939): 417–25.

Hachey, Thomas E. "American Profiles on Capitol Hill: A Confidential Study for the British Foreign Office in 1943." *Wisconsin Magazine of History* 57 (Winter 1973–74): 141–53.

Haight, John McVickar, Jr. "France and the Aftermath of Roosevelt's 'Quarantine Speech.' " *World Politics* 14 (January 1962): 283–306.

———. "France, the United States, and the Munich Crisis." *Journal of Modern History* 32 (December 1960): 340–58.

———. "Franklin D. Roosevelt and a Naval Quarantine of Japan." *Pacific Historical Review* 40 (May 1971): 203–26.

———. "Roosevelt and the Aftermath of the Quarantine Speech." *Review of Politics* 24 (April 1962): 233–59.

Haines, Gerald K. "American Myopia and the Japanese Monroe Doctrine, 1931–41." *Prologue* 13 (Spring 1981): 101–14.

———. "The Roosevelt Administration Interprets the Monroe Doctrine." *Australian Journal of Politics and History* 24 (December 1978): 332–45.

Halperin, Samuel, and Irvin Oder. "The United States in Search of a Policy: Franklin D. Roosevelt and Palestine." *Review of Politics* 24 (July 1962): 320–41.

Halperin, Samuel, and Irvin Oder. "The United States in Search of a Policy: Franklin D. Roosevelt and Palestine." *Review of Politics* 24 (July 1962): 320–41.

———. "The Runciman Visit to Washington in January 1937: Presidential Diplomacy and the Non-Commercial Implications of Anglo-American Trade Negotiations." *Canadian Journal of History/Annales Canadiennes d'Histoire* (August 1984): 317–39.

———. "Testing the Water: A Secret Probe towards Anglo-American Military Co-operation in 1936." *International History Review* 7 (May 1985): 214–34.

Hecht, Robert A. "Great Britain and the Stimson Note of January 7, 1932." *Pacific Historical Review* 38 (June 1969): 177–91.

Henson, Edward L., Jr. "Britain, America and the Month of Munich." *International Relations* 2 (April 1962): 291–301.

Herring, George C., Jr. "Lend Lease to Russia and the Origins of the Cold War, 1944–1945." *Journal of American History* 66 (June 1969): 93–114.

———. "The United States and British Bankruptcy, 1944–1945: Responsibilities Deferred." *Political Science Quarterly* 86 (June 1971): 260–80.

Herzog, James H. "Influence of the United States Navy in the Embargo of Oil to Japan, 1940–41." *Pacific Historical Review* 35 (August 1966): 317–28.

Hess, Gary R. "Franklin Roosevelt and Indochina." *Journal of American History* 59 (September 1972): 353–68.

Hilton, Stanley E. "The Welles Mission to Europe, February–March 1940: Illusion or Realism?" *Journal of American History* 58 (June 1971): 93–120.

Hindmarsh, A. E. "The Realistic Foreign Policy of Japan." *Foreign Affairs* 13 (January 1935): 262–70.

Iriye, Akira. "Chang Hsüeh-liang and the Japanese." *Journal of Asian Studies* 20 (November 1960): 33–43.

Israel, Jerry. "'Mao's Mr. America': Edgar Snow's Images of China." *Pacific Historical Review* 47 (February 1978): 107–22.

Jablon, Howard. "Cordell Hull, His 'Associates,' and Relations with Japan, 1933–1936." *Mid-America* 56 (July 1974): 160–74.

Jacobs, Travis Beal. "Roosevelt's Quarantine Speech." *The Historian* 24 (August 1962): 483–502.

Jones, E. Stanley. "An Adventure in Failure." *Asia and the Americas* 45 (December 1945): 609–16.

Kaufmann, William W. "Two American Ambassadors: Bullitt and Kennedy." In Gordon A. Craig and Felix Gilbert, eds., *The Diplomats, 1919–1939*, pp. 649–81. Princeton: Princeton University Press, 1953.

Kawakami, K. K. "Britain's Trade War with Japan." *Foreign Affairs* 12 (April 1934): 483–94.

———. "Far Eastern Triangle." *Foreign Affairs* 18 (July 1940): 632–45.

Kimball, Warren F. "Churchill and Roosevelt: The Personal Equation." *Prologue* 6 (Fall 1974): 169–82.

———. "Dieckhoff and America: A German's View of German-American Relations, 1937–1941." *The Historian* 27 (February 1965): 218–43.

———. "Lend Lease and the Open Door: The Temptation of British Opulence, 1937–1942." *Political Science Quarterly* 86 (June 1971): 232–59.

———. "Naked Reverse Right: Roosevelt, Churchill, and Eastern Europe from TOLSTOY to Yalta—and a Little Beyond." *Diplomatic History* 9 (Winter 1985): 1–24.

Koch, H. W. "The Spectre of a Separate Peace in the East: Russo-German 'Peace Feelers,' 1942–1944." *Journal of Contemporary History* 10 (July 1975): 531–49.

Koppes, Clayton R. "The Good Neighbor Policy and the Nationalization of Mexican Oil: A Reinterpretation." *Journal of American History* 69 (June 1982): 62–81.

Kottman, Richard N. "The Canadian-American Trade Agreement of 1935." *Journal of American History* 52 (September 1965): 275–96.

Kuehl, Warren F. "Midwestern Newspapers and Isolationist Sentiment." *Diplomatic History* 3 (Summer 1979): 283–306.

———. "Webs of Common Interests Revisited: Nationalism, Internationalism, and Historians of American Foreign Relations." *Diplomatic History* 10 (Spring 1986): 107–20.

Kuklick, Bruce. "The Division of Germany and American Policy on Reparations." *Western Political Quarterly* 23 (June 1970): 276–93.

———. "A Historian's Perspective: American Appeasement of Germany, 1941–1951." *Prologue* 8 (Winter 1976): 237–42.

La Feber, Walter. "Roosevelt, Churchill, and Indochina, 1942–1945." *American Historical Review* 80 (December 1975): 1277–95.

Langer, John Daniel. "The 'Red General': Philip R. Faymonville and the Soviet Union, 1917–52." *Prologue* 8 (Winter 1976): 208–21.

Langley, Lester D. "Negotiating New Treaties with Panama, 1936." *Hispanic American Historical Review* 48 (May 1968): 220–33.

———. "The World Crisis and the Good Neighbor Policy in Panama, 1936–41." *Americas* 24 (October 1967): 137–52.

Leighton, Richard M. "Overlord Revisited: An Interpretation of American Strategy in the European War, 1942–1944." *American Historical Review* 68 (July 1963): 919–37.

Leuchtenburg, William E. "Franklin D. Roosevelt, 'Quarantine Address, 1937.'" In Daniel J. Boorstin, ed., *An American Primer*, pp. 871–81. Chicago: University of Chicago Press, 1968.

Leutze, James. "The Secret of the Churchill-Roosevelt Correspondence: September 1939–May 1940." *Journal of Contemporary History* 10 (July 1975): 465–92.

Little, Douglas. "Antibolshevism and American Foreign Policy, 1919–1939: The Diplomacy of Self-Delusion." *American Quarterly* 35 (Fall 1983): 376–90.

Liu, Daniel T. J. "A Review of Diplomatic Relations between the Republic of China and the United States of America: The Sino-Japanese Conflicts, 1931–1936." *Chinese Culture* 15 (September 1974): 43–75.

———. "A Study of Diplomatic Relations between China and the United States of America: The Sino-Japanese War, 1937–1941." *Chinese Culture* 15 (December 1974): 11–38.

Loewenheim, Francis L. "An Illusion That Shaped History: New Light on the History and Historiography of American Peace Efforts before Munich." In Daniel R. Beaver, ed., *Some Pathways in Twentieth-Century History: Essays in Honor of Reginald Charles McGrane*, pp. 177–220, 286–95. Detroit: Wayne State University Press, 1969.

MacLean, Elizabeth Kimball. "Joseph E. Davies and Soviet-American Relations, 1941–43." *Diplomatic History* 4 (Winter 1980): 73–93.

McNeal, Robert H. "Roosevelt through Stalin's Spectacles." *International Journal* 18 (Spring 1963): 194–206.

Maddux, Thomas R. "American Diplomats and the Soviet Experiment: The View from the Moscow Embassy, 1934–1939." *South Atlantic Quarterly* 74 (Autumn 1975): 468–87.

———. "Red Fascism, Brown Bolshevism: The American Image of Totalitarianism in the 1930s." *The Historian* 40 (May 1978): 85–103.

———. "United States–Soviet Naval Relations in the 1930s: The Soviet Union's Efforts to Purchase Naval Vessels." *Naval War College Review* 29 (Fall 1976): 28–37.

Major, John. "F.D.R. and Panama." *Historical Journal* 28 (June 1985): 357–77.

Mallory, Walter H. "The Permanent Conflict in Manchuria." *Foreign Affairs* 10 (January 1932): 220–29.

Mark, Eduard M. "Allied Relations in Iran, 1941–1947: The Origins of a Cold War Crisis." *Wisconsin Magazine of History* 59 (Autumn 1975): 51–63.

Marks, Frederick W. III. "Facade and Failure: The Hull-Nomura Talks of 1941." *Presidential Studies Quarterly* 15 (Winter 1985): 99–112.

———. "Franklin Roosevelt's Diplomatic Debut: The Myth of the Hundred Days." *South Atlantic Quarterly* 84 (Summer 1985): 245–63.

———. "The Origin of FDR's Promise to Support Britain Militarily in the Far East—A New Look." *Pacific Historical Review* 53 (November 1984): 447–62.

———. "Six between Roosevelt and Hitler: America's Role in the Appeasement of Nazi Germany." *Historical Journal* 28 (December 1985): 969–82.

Masland, John W. "Commercial Influence upon American Far Eastern Policy, 1937–1941." *Pacific Historical Review* 11 (September 1942): 281–99.

———. "Missionary Influence upon American Far Eastern Policy." *Pacific Historical Review* 10 (September 1941): 279–96.

Mastny, Vojtech. "Soviet War Aims at the Moscow and Teheran Conferences of 1943." *Journal of Modern History* 47 (September 1975): 481–504.

———. "Stalin and the Prospects of a Separate Peace in World War II." *American Historical Review* 77 (December 1972): 1365–88.

Matloff, Maurice. "Franklin Delano Roosevelt as War Leader." In Harry L. Coles, ed., *Total War and Cold War: Problems in Civilian Control of the Military*, pp. 42–65. Columbus: Ohio State University Press, 1962.

May, Ernest. "The Development of Political-Military Consultation in the United States." *Political Science Quarterly* 70 (June 1955): 161–80.

———. "The United States, the Soviet Union, and the Far Eastern War." *Pacific Historical Review* 24 (May 1955): 153–74.

Moore, James R. "Sources of New Deal Economic Policy: The International Dimension." *Journal of American History* 61 (December 1974): 728–44.

Moore, John Basset. "An Appeal to Reason." *Foreign Affairs* 11 (July 1933): 547–88.

Morton, Louis. "Army and Marines on the China Station: A Study in Military and Political Rivalry." *Pacific Historical Review* 29 (February 1960): 51–73.

———. "The Decision to Use the Atomic Bomb." *Foreign Affairs* 35 (January 1957): 334–53.

———. "National Policy and Military Strategy." *Virginia Quarterly Review* 36 (Winter 1960): 1–17.

———. "Pearl Harbor in Perspective: A Bibliographical Survey." *U.S. Naval Institute Proceedings* 81 (December 1955): 461–68.

———. "Soviet Intervention in the War with Japan." *Foreign Affairs* 40 (July 1962): 653–62.

————. "World War II: A Survey of Recent Writings." *American Historical Review* 75 (December 1970): 1987–2007.

Mosely, Philip E. "Dismemberment of Germany." *Foreign Affairs* 28 (April 1950): 487–98.

————. "Hopes and Failures: American Policy toward East Central Europe, 1941–1947." *Review of Politics* 17 (October 1955): 461–85.

————. "The Occupation of Germany: New Light on How the Zones Were Drawn." *Foreign Affairs* 28 (July 1950); 580–604.

Muir, Ramsay. "Civilization and Liberty." *Nineteenth Century and After* 116 (September 1934): 213–25.

Murray, G. E. Patrick. "'Under Urgent Consideration': American Planes for Greece, 1940–1941." *Aerospace Historian* 24 (Summer/June 1977): 61–69.

Neils, Patricia. "Henry R. Luce and American Images of China." *Tamkang Journal of American Studies* 2 (Spring 1986): 17–39.

Neumann, William L. "Ambiguity and Ambivalence in Ideas of National Interest in Asia." In Alexander DeConde, ed., *Isolation and Security*, pp. 133–58. Durham: Duke University Press, 1957.

————. "Franklin Delano Roosevelt: A Disciple of Admiral Mahan." *U.S. Naval Institute Proceedings* 78 (July 1952): 712–19.

————. "Franklin D. Roosevelt and Japan, 1913–1933." *Pacific Historical Review* 22 (May 1953): 143–53.

————. "Roosevelt's Options and Evasions in Foreign Policy Decisions, 1940–1945." In Leonard P. Liggio and James J. Martin, eds., *Watershed of Empire: Essays on New Deal Foreign Policy*, pp. 162–82. Colorado Springs: Ralph Myles, 1976.

Nichols, Jeannette P. "Roosevelt's Monetary Diplomacy in 1933." *American Historical Review* 56 (January 1951): 295–317.

Nomura, Kichisaburo. "Japan's Demand for Naval Equality." *Foreign Affairs* 13 (October 1934): 196–203.

————. "Stepping-Stones to War." *U.S. Naval Institute Proceedings* 77 (September 1951): 927–31.

Norman, John. "The Influence of Pro-Fascist Propaganda on American Neutrality, 1935–1936." In Dwight E. Lee and George E. McReynolds, eds., *Essays in History and International Relations*, pp. 193–214. Worcester, Mass.: Clark University Press, 1949.

Offner, Arnold A. "Appeasement Revisited: The United States, Great Britain, and Germany, 1933–1940." *Journal of American History* 64 (September 1977): 373–93.

Orzell, Laurence J. "A 'Painful Problem': Poland in Allied Diplomacy, February—July 1945." *Mid-America* 59 (October 1977): 147–70.

Parzen, Herbert. "The Roosevelt Palestine Policy, 1943–1945: An Exercise in Dual Diplomacy." *American Jewish Archives* 26 (April 1974): 31–65.

Paterson, Thomas G. "The Abortive American Loan to Russia and the Origins of the Cold War, 1943–1946." *Journal of American History* 56 (June 1969): 70–92.

Paul, Justus F. "Senator Hugh Butler and Aid to Latin America, 1943–1944." *South Dakota History* 8 (Winter 1977): 34–45.

Perkins, Dexter. "Was Roosevelt Wrong?" In Glyndon G. Van Deusen and Richard C. Wade, eds., *Foreign Policy and the American Spirit: Essays by Dexter Perkins*, pp. 107–25. Ithaca: Cornell University Press, 1957.

Plesur, Milton. "The Relations between the United States and Palestine." *Judaism* 3 (Fall 1954): 469–79.

Poole, Dewitt, C. "Light on Nazi Foreign Policy." *Foreign Affairs* 25 (October 1946): 130–54.

Pratt, Julius W. "The Ordeal of Cordell Hull." *Review of Politics* 28 (January 1966): 76–98.

Pratt, Lawrence W. "The Anglo-American Naval Conversations on the Far East of January 1938." *International Affairs* 47 (October 1971): 745–63.

Quinlan, Robert J. "The United States Fleet: Diplomacy, Strategy and the Allocation of Ships (1940–1941)." In Harold Stein, ed., *American Civil-Military Decisions: A Book of Case Studies*, pp. 153–202. Birmingham: University of Alabama Press, 1963.

Ray, Deborah Wing. "The Takoradi Route: Roosevelt's Prewar Venture beyond the Western Hemisphere." *Journal of American History* 62 (September 1975): 340–58.

Repko, Allen F. "The Failure of Reciprocal Trade: United States–Germany Commercial Rivalry in Brazil, 1934–1940." *Mid-America* 60 (January 1978): 3–20.

Reynolds, David. "FDR's Foreign Policy and the British Royal Visit to the U.S.A., 1939." *The Historian* 45 (August 1983): 461–72.

———. "Lord Lothian and Anglo-American Relations, 1939–1940." *Transactions of the American Philosophical Society* 73, pt. 2 (1983).

Rhodes, Benjamin D. "The Origins of Finnish-American Friendship, 1919–1941." *Mid-America* 54 (January 1972): 3–19.

———. "The Royal Visit of 1939 and the 'Psychological Approach' to the United States." *Diplomatic History* 2 (Spring 1978): 197–211.

Ruetten, Richard T. "Harry Elmer Barnes and the 'Historical Blackout.'" *The Historian* 33 (February 1971): 202–14.

Sansom, Sir George. "Liberalism in Japan." *Foreign Affairs* 19 (April 1941): 551–60.

Schacht, Hjalmar. "German Trade and German Debts." *Foreign Affairs* 13 (October 1934): 1–5.

———. "Germany's Colonial Demands." *Foreign Affairs* 15 (October 1936): 223–34.

Schatz, Arthur W. "The Anglo-American Trade Agreement and Cordell Hull's

Search for Peace, 1936–1938." *Journal of American History* 57 (June 1970): 85–103.

Sessions, Gene A. "The Clark Memorandum Myth." *Americas* 34 (July 1977): 40–58.

Sewall, Arthur F. "Key Pittman and the Quest for the China Market, 1933–1940." *Pacific Historical Review* 44 (August 1975): 351–71.

Sharp, Tony. "The Origins of the 'Teheran Formula' on Polish Frontiers." *Journal of Contemporary History* 12 (April 1977): 381–93.

Sih, Paul K. T. "The Failure of a Mission." *Modern Age* 17 (Winter 1973): 100–102.

Small, Melvin. "How We Learned to Love the Russians: American Media and the Soviet Union during World War II." *The Historian* 36 (May 1974): 455–78.

Smith, Daniel M. "Authoritarianism and American Policy Makers in Two World Wars." *Pacific Historical Review* 43 (August 1974): 303–23.

Smith, M. J. J. "F.D.R. and the Brussels Conference, 1937." *Michigan Academician* 14 (Fall 1981): 109–22.

Smith, Robert Freeman. "The Good Neighbor Policy: The Liberal Paradox in United States Relations with Latin America." In Leonard P. Liggio and James J. Martin, eds., *Watershed of Empire: Essays on New Deal Foreign Policy*, pp. 65–94. Colorado Springs: Ralph Myles, 1976.

Smylie, Robert F. "John Leighton Stuart: A Missionary Diplomat in the Sino-Japanese Conflict, 1937–1941." *Journal of Presbyterian History* 53 (Fall 1975): 256–76.

Sontag, Raymond J. "Reflections on the Yalta Papers." *Foreign Affairs* 33 (July 1955): 615–23.

Steele, Richard. "Franklin D. Roosevelt and His Foreign Policy Critics." *Political Science Quarterly* 94 (Spring 1979): 15–32.

———. "The Pulse of the People: Franklin D. Roosevelt and the Gauging of American Public Opinion." *Journal of Contemporary History* 9 (October 1974): 195–216.

Sternsher, Bernard. "The Stimson Doctrine: FDR versus Moley and Tugwell." *Pacific Historical Review* 31 (August 1962): 281–89.

Stimson, Henry L. "Bases of American Foreign Policy during the Past Four Years." *Foreign Affairs* 11 (April 1933): 383–96.

Stoler, Mark A. "The 'Second Front' and American Fear of Soviet Expansion." *Military Affairs* 39 (October 1975): 136–41.

Stromberg, Roland N. "American Business and the Approach of War, 1935–1941." *Journal of Economic History* 13 (Winter 1953): 58–78.

Taborsky, Edward. "Beneš and the Soviets." *Foreign Affairs* 27 (January 1949): 302–14.

———. "The Triumph and Disaster of Eduard Beneš." *Foreign Affairs* 36 (July 1958): 669–84.

Theoharis, Athan. "James F. Byrnes: Unwitting Yalta Myth-Maker." *Political Science Quarterly* 81 (December 1966): 581–92.

———. "Roosevelt and Truman on Yalta: The Origins of the Cold War." *Political Science Quarterly* 87 (June 1972): 210–41.

Thorne, Christopher. "Indochina and Anglo-American Relations, 1942–1945." *Pacific Historical Review* 45 (February 1976): 73–96.

Tolley, Rear Admiral Kemp. "The Strange Assignment of USS *Lanikai*." *U.S. Naval Institute Proceedings* 88 (September 1962): 71–83.

Trask, Roger R. "The 'Terrible Turk' and Turkish-American Relations in the Interwar Period." *The Historian* 33 (November 1970): 40–53.

Ullman, Richard H. "The Davies Mission and United States–Soviet Relations, 1937–1941." *World Politics* 9 (January 1957): 220–39.

Utley, Jonathan G. "Diplomacy in a Democracy: The United States and Japan, 1937–1941." *World Affairs* 139 (Fall 1976): 130–40.

———. "Upstairs, Downstairs at Foggy Bottom: Oil, Exports and Japan, 1940–41." *Prologue* 8 (Spring 1976): 17–28.

Valaik, J. David. "Catholics, Neutrality, and the Spanish Embargo, 1937–1939." *Journal of American History* 54 (June 1967): 73–85.

Varg, Paul A. "The Economic Side of the Good Neighbor Policy: The Reciprocal Trade Program and South America." *Pacific Historical Review* 45 (February 1976): 47–71.

Villa, Brian L. "The U.S. Army, Unconditional Surrender, and the Potsdam Proclamation." *Journal of American History* 63 (June 1976): 66–92.

Vloyantes, John P. "The Significance of Pre-Yalta Policies Regarding Liberated Countries in Europe." *Western Political Quarterly* 11 (June 1958): 209–28.

Watt, Donald. "Roosevelt and Neville Chamberlain: Two Appeasers." *International Journal* 28 (Spring 1973): 185–204.

Wegerer, Alfred von. "The Origins of This War: A German View." *Foreign Affairs* 18 (July 1940): 700–718.

Weinberg, Gerhard L. "Hitler's Image of the United States." *American Historical Review* 69 (July 1964): 1006–21.

———. "The May Crisis, 1938." *Journal of Modern History* 29 (September 1957): 213–25.

Welch, Richard E., Jr. "New Deal Diplomacy and Its Revisionists." *Reviews in American History* 5 (September 1977): 410–17.

Whittlesey, Charles R. "Five Years of the Export-Import Bank." *American Economic Review* 29 (September 1939): 487–502.

Widenor, William C. "American Planning for the United Nations: Have We Been Asking the Right Questions?" *Diplomatic History* 6 (Summer 1982): 245–65.

Wilcox, Francis O. "The Neutrality Fight in Congress, 1939." *American Political Science Review* 33 (October 1939): 811–25.

Williams, Benjamin H. "The Coming of Economic Sanctions into American Practice." *American Journal of International Law* 37 (July 1943): 386–96.

Wiltz, John Edward. "The Nye Committee Revisited." *The Historian* 23 (February 1961): 211–33.

Wood, Bryce. "External Restraints on the Good Neighbor Policy." *Inter-American Economic Affairs* 16 (Autumn 1962): 3–24.

Woods, Randall B. "Conflict or Community? The United States and Argentina's Admission to the United Nations." *Pacific Historical Review* 46 (August 1977): 361–86.

———. "Hull and Argentina: Wilsonian Diplomacy in the Age of Roosevelt." *Journal of Interamerican Studies and World Affairs* 16 (August 1974): 350–71.

Wright, Gordon. "Ambassador Bullitt and the Fall of France." *World Politics* 10 (October 1957): 63–90.

Wright, Quincy. "The Transfer of Destroyers to Great Britain." *American Journal of International Law* 34 (October 1940): 680–89.

Wright, Theodore P., Jr. "The Origins of the Free Elections Dispute in the Cold War." *Western Political Quarterly* 14 (December 1961): 850–64.

Young, Lowell T. "Franklin D. Roosevelt and America's Islets: Acquisition of Territory in the Caribbean and in the Pacific." *The Historian* 35 (February 1973): 205–20.

Books

Abbazia, Patrick. *Mr. Roosevelt's Navy.* Annapolis, Md.: Naval Institute Press, 1975.

Adams, Frederick C. *Economic Diplomacy: The Export-Import Bank and American Foreign Policy, 1934–1939.* Columbia: University of Missouri Press, 1976.

Akagi, Roy Hidemichi. *Japan's Foreign Relations.* Tokyo: Hokuseido Press, 1936.

Albjerg, Victor L. *Winston Churchill.* New York: Twayne, 1973.

Allen, H. C. *Great Britain and the United States.* New York: St. Martin's Press, 1955.

Alsop, Joseph, and Robert Kintner. *American White Paper.* New York: Simon and Schuster, 1940.

Ambrose, Stephen. *Eisenhower and Berlin, 1945: The Decision to Halt at the Elbe.* New York: Norton, 1967.

Anglin, Douglas C. *The St. Pierre and Miquelon Affair of 1941: A Study in Diplomacy in the North Atlantic Quadrangle.* Toronto: University of Toronto Press, 1966.

Armstrong, Anne. *Unconditional Surrender: The Impact of the Casablanca Policy upon World War II*. New Brunswick: Rutgers University Press, 1961.

Ashby, Leroy. *The Spearless Leader*. Urbana: University of Illinois Press, 1972.

Backer, John H. *The Decision to Divide Germany: American Foreign Policy in Transition*. Durham: Duke University Press, 1978.

Bailey, Thomas A. *A Diplomatic History of the American People*. 9th ed. Englewood Cliffs, N.J.: Prentice-Hall, 1970.

Bailey, Thomas A., and Paul B. Ryan. *Hitler vs. Roosevelt: The Undeclared Naval War*. New York: Free Press, 1979.

Bartlett, Bruce R. *Cover-Up: The Politics of Pearl Harbor, 1941–1946*. New Rochelle: Arlington House, 1978.

Bavendamm, Dirk. *Roosevelts weg Zum Krieg: Amerikanische Politik, 1914–1939*. Munich: Herbig, 1983.

Beals, Carleton, Bryce Oliver, Herschel Brickell, and Samuel Guy Inman. *What the South Americans Think of Us*. New York: McBride and Co., 1945.

Beard, Charles A. *American Foreign Policy in the Making, 1932–1940*. New Haven: Yale University Press, 1946.

—––. *President Roosevelt and the Coming of the War, 1941: A Study in Appearances and Realities*. New Haven: Yale University Press, 1948.

Beitzell, Robert. *The Uneasy Alliance: America, Britain, and Russia, 1941–1943*. New York: Knopf, 1972.

Bemis, Samuel Flagg. *The Latin-American Policy of the United States*. 1943; paperback, New York: Norton, 1967.

—––. *A Short History of American Foreign Policy and Diplomacy*. New York: Henry Holt, 1959.

Bennet, Edward M. *Franklin D. Roosevelt and the Search for Security: American-Soviet Relations, 1933–1939*. Wilmington: Scholarly Resources, 1985.

Bergamini, David. *Japan's Imperial Conspiracy*. New York: Morrow, 1971.

Birkenhead, Earl of. *Halifax: The Life of Lord Halifax*. London: Hamish Hamilton, 1965.

Bishop, Donald G. *The Roosevelt-Litvinov Agreements: The American View*. Syracuse, N.Y.: Syracuse University Press, 1965.

Blum, John Morton. *Roosevelt and Morgenthau*. Boston: Houghton Mifflin, 1970.

Borg, Dorothy. *The United States and the Far Eastern Crisis of 1933–1938*. Cambridge, Mass.: Harvard University Press, 1964.

Borg, Dorothy, and Shumpei Okamoto, eds. *Pearl Harbor as History: Japanese-American Relations, 1931–1941*. New York: Columbia University Press, 1973.

Buhite, Russell D. *Nelson T. Johnson and American Policy toward China, 1925–1941*. East Lansing: Michigan State University Press, 1968.

———. *Patrick J. Hurley and American Foreign Policy.* Ithaca: Cornell University Press, 1973.

Burns, E. Bradford. *A History of Brazil.* New York: Columbia University Press, 1970.

———. *The Unwritten Alliance: Rio Branco and Brazilian-American Relations.* New York: Columbia University Press, 1966.

Burns, James MacGregor. *Roosevelt: The Lion and the Fox.* New York: Harcourt, Brace and World, 1956.

———. *Roosevelt: The Soldier of Freedom.* New York: Harcourt Brace Jovanovich, 1970.

Busch, Noel F. *What Manner of Man?* New York: Harcourt, 1944.

Buss, Claude A. *The Far East.* New York: Macmillan, 1955.

Butler, J. R. M. *Lord Lothian (Philip Kerr), 1882–1940.* London: St. Martin's, 1960.

Butow, Robert J. C. *The John Doe Associates: Backdoor Diplomacy for Peace, 1941.* Stanford: Stanford University Press, 1974.

———. *Tojo and the Coming of the War.* Princeton: Princeton University Press, 1961.

Campbell, Thomas M. *Masquerade Peace: America's UN Policy, 1944–1945.* Tallahassee: Florida State University Press, 1973.

Carey, James C. *Peru and the United States, 1900–1962.* South Bend, Ind.: Notre Dame University Press, 1964.

Cartier, Raymond. *Roosevelt.* Lyon: Gutenberg, 1945.

Charlton, Michael. *The Eagle and the Small Birds.* Chicago: University of Chicago Press, 1984.

Clifford, Nicholas R. *Retreat from China: British Policy in the Far East, 1937–1941.* Seattle: University of Washington Press, 1967.

Cline, Howard F. *The United States and Mexico.* Cambridge, Mass.: Harvard University Press, 1953.

Coit, Margaret. *Mr. Baruch.* Boston: Houghton Mifflin, 1957.

Cole, Wayne S. *America First: The Battle against Intervention, 1940–1941.* Madison: University of Wisconsin Press, 1953.

———. *Roosevelt and the Isolationists, 1932–1945.* Lincoln: University of Nebraska Press, 1983.

———. *Senator Gerald P. Nye and American Foreign Relations.* Minneapolis: University of Minnesota Press, 1962.

Colville, John. *The Fringes of Power.* New York: Norton, 1985.

———. *Winston Churchill and His Inner Circle.* New York: Windham Books, 1981.

Colvin, Ian. *None So Blind.* New York: Harcourt, Brace and World, 1965.

Compton, James V. *The Swastika and the Eagle: Hitler, the United States, and the Origins of World War II.* Boston: Houghton Mifflin, 1967.

Conte, Arthur. *Yalta ou la partage du monde.* Paris: Laffont, 1974.

Cowling, Maurice. *The Impact of Hitler: British Politics and British Policy, 1933–1940.* Cambridge: Cambridge University Press, 1975.

Craig, Gordon A., and Felix Gilbert, eds. *The Diplomats, 1919–1939.* Princeton: Princeton University Press, 1953.

Cronon, E. David. *Josephus Daniels in Mexico.* Madison: University of Wisconsin Press, 1960.

Crowley, James B. *Japan's Quest for Autonomy: National Security and Foreign Policy, 1930–1938.* Princeton: Princeton University Press, 1966.

Crozier, Brian. *Franco: A Biographical History.* London: Eyre and Spottiswoode, 1967.

———. *The Man Who Lost China.* New York: Scribner's, 1976.

Dallek, Robert. *Democrat and Diplomat: The Life of William E. Dodd.* New York: Oxford University Press, 1968.

———. *Franklin D. Roosevelt and American Foreign Policy, 1932–1945.* New York: Oxford University Press, 1979.

———, ed. *The Roosevelt Diplomacy and World War II.* New York: Holt, Rinehart and Winston, 1970.

Davis, Lynn Etheridge. *The Cold War Begins: Soviet-American Conflict over Eastern Europe.* Princeton: Princeton University Press, 1974.

Dawson, Raymond H. *The Decision to Aid Russia, 1941.* Chapel Hill: University of North Carolina Press, 1959.

DeConde, Alexander. *Half Bitter, Half Sweet: An Excursion into Italian-American History.* New York: Scribner's, 1971.

De Goutel, Eric, Francis Mercury, and Michel Honorin. *Roosevelt du New Deal à Yalta.* Geneva: Famot, 1974.

Delano, Daniel W., Jr. *Franklin Roosevelt and the Delano Influence.* Pittsburgh: James S. Nudi Publications, 1946.

De Riencourt, Ameury. *L'Amerique imperiale.* Translated by Magdeleine Paz. Paris: Gallimard, 1970.

———. *L'Ère des nouveaux Césars.* Paris: Laffont, 1959.

De Santis, Hugh. *The Diplomacy of Silence: The American Foreign Service, the Soviet Union, and the Cold War, 1933–1947.* Chicago: University of Chicago Press, 1980.

Divine, Robert A. *The Illusion of Neutrality.* Chicago: University of Chicago Press, 1962.

———. *The Reluctant Belligerent: American Entry into World War II.* New York: Wiley, 1965.

———. *Roosevelt and World War II.* Baltimore: Johns Hopkins University Press, 1969.

———. *Second Chance: The Triumph of Internationalism in America during World War II.* New York: Atheneum, 1967.

Doenecke, Justus D. *When the Wicked Rise: American Opinion-Makers and the Manchurian Crisis of 1931–33*. Lewisburg: Bucknell University Press, 1984.

Dorn, Frank. *Walkout with Stilwell in Burma*. New York: Crowell, 1971.

Drachman, Edward R. *United States Policy toward Vietnam, 1940–1945*. Rutherford, N.J.: Fairleigh Dickinson University Press, 1970.

Drummond, Donald F. *The Passing of American Neutrality, 1937–1941*. Ann Arbor: University of Michigan Press, 1955.

Du Breuil, Georges. *Roosevelt la responsable*. Marseilles: Editions de la Boussole, 1942.

Duroselle, Jean-Baptiste. *From Wilson to Roosevelt*. Cambridge, Mass.: Harvard University Press, 1963.

———. *L'abîme, 1939–1945*. Paris: Imprimerie Nationale, 1982.

———. *La décadence, 1932–1939*. Paris: Imprimerie Nationale, 1979.

Eubank, Keith. *Summit at Teheran*. New York: Morrow, 1985.

Fall, Bernard B. *The Two Viet-Nams*. New York: Praeger, 1968.

Feiling, Keith. *The Life of Neville Chamberlain*. London: Macmillan, 1946.

Feingold, Henry. *The Politics of Rescue: The Roosevelt Administration and the Holocaust, 1938–1945*. New Brunswick: Rutgers University Press, 1970.

Feis, Herbert. *The China Tangle*. Princeton: Princeton University Press, 1953.

———. *Churchill-Roosevelt-Stalin: The War They Waged and the Peace They Sought*. Princeton: Princeton University Press, 1957.

———. *1933: Characters in Crisis*. Boston: Little, Brown, 1966.

———. *The Road to Pearl Harbor: The Coming of the War between the United States and Japan*. 1950. Reprint. New York: Atheneum, 1966.

———. *The Spanish Story: Franco and the Nations at War*. New York: Knopf, 1948.

Flynn, John T. *The Roosevelt Myth*. New York: Devin-Adair, 1956.

———. *While You Slept: Our Tragedy in Asia and Who Made It*. New York: Devin-Adair, 1951.

Freidel, Frank. *Franklin D. Roosevelt: The Apprenticeship*. Boston: Little, Brown, 1952.

———. *Franklin D. Roosevelt: The Ordeal*. Boston: Little, Brown, 1954.

———. *Franklin D. Roosevelt: The Triumph*. Boston: Little, Brown, 1956.

———. *Franklin D. Roosevelt: Launching the New Deal*. Boston: Little, Brown, 1973.

Friedländer, Saul. *Prelude to Downfall: Hitler and the United States, 1939–1941*. New York: Knopf, 1967.

Friedman, Saul S. *No Haven for the Oppressed: United States Policy toward Jewish Refugees, 1938–1945*. Detroit: Wayne State University Press, 1973.

Furuya, Keiji. *Chiang Kai-shek: His Life and Times*. New York: St. John's University Press, 1981.

Gaddis, John Lewis. *The United States and the Origins of the Cold War, 1941–1947.* New York: Columbia University Press, 1972.

Gardner, Lloyd C. *Architects of Illusion: Men and Ideas in American Foreign Policy, 1941–1949.* Chicago: Quadrangle Books, 1970.

———. *Economic Aspects of New Deal Diplomacy.* Madison: University of Wisconsin Press, 1964.

———. *Imperial America: American Foreign Policy since 1898.* New York: Harcourt Brace Jovanovich, 1976.

Gellman, Irwin F. *Good Neighbor Diplomacy: United States Policies in Latin America, 1933–1945.* Baltimore: Johns Hopkins University Press, 1979.

———. *Roosevelt and Batista: Good Neighbor Diplomacy in Cuba, 1933–1945.* Albuquerque: University of New Mexico Press, 1973.

Goodhart, Philip. *Fifty Ships That Saved the World: The Foundation of the Anglo-American Alliance.* New York: Doubleday, 1965.

Graebner, Norman. *Roosevelt and the Search for a European Policy, 1937–1939.* Oxford: Oxford University Press, 1980.

Green, David. *The Containment of Latin America.* Chicago: University of Chicago Press, 1971.

Greer, Thomas H. *What Roosevelt Thought: The Social and Political Ideas of Franklin D. Roosevelt.* East Lansing: Michigan State University Press, 1958.

Grosser, Alfred. *Foreign Policy under de Gaulle.* Boston: Little, Brown, 1967.

Guerrant, Edward O. *Roosevelt's Good Neighbor Policy.* Albuquerque: University of New Mexico Press, 1950.

Haglund, David G. *Latin America and the Transformation of U.S. Strategic Thought, 1936–1940.* Albuquerque: University of New Mexico Press, 1984.

Haight, John McVickar, Jr. *American Aid to France, 1938–1940.* New York: Atheneum, 1970.

Halasz, Nicholas. *Roosevelt through Foreign Eyes.* New York: Van Nostrand, 1961.

Heinrichs, Waldo H., Jr. *American Ambassador: Joseph C. Grew and the Development of the United States Diplomatic Tradition.* Boston: Little, Brown, 1966.

Herde, Peter. *Pearl Harbor, 7 Dezember 1941: Der Ausbruch des Krieges zwischen Japan und den vereinigten Staaten und die Ausweitung des Europäischen Krieges zum Zweiten Weltkrieg.* Warmstadt: Wissenschaftliche Buchgesellschaft, 1980.

Herring, George. *Aid to Russia, 1941–1946.* New York: Columbia University Press, 1973.

Hess, Gary R. *America Encounters India, 1941–1947.* Baltimore: Johns Hopkins University Press, 1971.

Higgins, Trumbull. *Soft Underbelly: The Anglo-American Controversy over the Italian Campaign, 1939–1945.* New York: Macmillan, 1968.

———. *Winston Churchill and the Second Front, 1940–1943.* New York: Oxford University Press, 1957.

Hishida, Seiji. *Japan among the Great Powers: A Survey of Her International Relations.* London: Longman's, 1940.

Howard, Michael. *The Mediterranean Strategy in the Second World War.* New York: Praeger, 1968.

Hyde, Hartford Montgomery. *Room 3603.* New York: Farrar Straus and Giroux, 1963.

Ienaga, Saburō. *The Pacific War: World War II and the Japanese, 1931–1945.* Translated by Frank Baldwin. New York: Pantheon, 1978.

Iriye, Akira. *After Imperialism: The Search for a New Order in the Far East, 1921–1931.* Cambridge, Mass.: Harvard University Press, 1965.

———. *Mutual Images: Essays in American-Japanese Relations.* Cambridge, Mass.: Harvard University Press, 1975.

Israel, Fred L. *Nevada's Key Pittman.* Lincoln: University of Nebraska Press, 1963.

Jablon, Howard. *Crossroads of Decision: The State Department and Foreign Policy, 1933–1937.* Lexington: University Press of Kentucky, 1983.

Jakobson, Max. *Diplomacy of the Winter War, 1939–1940.* Cambridge, Mass.: Harvard University Press, 1961.

Johnson, Claudius O. *Borah of Idaho.* New York: Longman's Green, 1936.

Jonas, Manfred. *Isolationism in America, 1935–1941.* Ithaca: Cornell University Press, 1966.

Jones, Kenneth Paul, ed. *U.S. Diplomats in Europe, 1919–1941.* Santa Barbara, Calif.: ABC-Clio, 1981.

Kawakami, K. K. *Japan in China.* London: John Murray, 1938.

———. *Manchukuo: Child of Conflict.* New York: Macmillan, 1933.

Kecskemeti, Paul. *Strategic Surrender: The Politics of Victory and Defeat.* Stanford: Stanford University Press, 1958.

Kennedy, John F. *Why England Slept.* New York: Wilfred Funk, 1940.

Kent, George O. *A Catalogue of Files and Microfilms of the German Foreign Ministry Archives, 1920–1945.* 4 vols. Stanford: Hoover Institution Press, 1962–72.

Kerrison, Raymond. *Bishop Walsh of Maryknoll.* New York: Putnam's, 1962.

Kimball, Warren F. *The Most Unsordid Act: Lend Lease, 1939–1941.* Baltimore: Johns Hopkins University Press, 1969.

———. *Swords into Plowshares? The Morgenthau Plan for Defeated Nazi Germany, 1943–1946.* Philadelphia: Lippincott, 1976.

Kirk, Betty. *Covering the Mexican Front.* Norman: University of Oklahoma Press, 1942.

Kirkpatrick, Ivone. *Mussolini: A Study in Power.* New York: Hawthorne Books, 1964.

Kleeman, Rita Halle. *Gracious Lady: The Life of Sara Delano Roosevelt.* New York: D. Appleton-Century, 1935.

Koskoff, David E. *Joseph P. Kennedy: A Life and Times.* Englewood Cliffs, N.J.: Prentice-Hall, 1974.

Kottman, Richard N. *Reciprocity and the North American Triangle.* Ithaca: Cornell University Press, 1968.

Kubek, Anthony. *How the Far East Was Lost: American Policy and the Creation of Communist China, 1941–1949.* Chicago: Regnery, 1963.

Kuklick, Bruce. *American Policy and the Division of Germany: The Clash with Russia over Reparations.* Ithaca: Cornell University Press, 1972.

Langer, William L., and S. Everett Gleason. *The Challenge to Isolation, 1937–1940.* New York: Harper, 1952.

———. *The Undeclared War, 1940–1941.* New York: Harper, 1953.

Langley, Lester D. *The Cuban Policy of the United States: A Brief History.* New York: Wiley, 1968.

———. *The United States and the Caribbean, 1900–1970.* Athens: University of Georgia Press, 1980.

Lash, Joseph P. *Roosevelt and Churchill, 1939–1941: The Partnership That Saved the West.* New York: Norton, 1976.

Las Vergnas, Raymond. *F. D. Roosevelt ou la dictature de la liberté.* Paris: Éditions Universelles, 1944.

Lee, Bradford A. *Britain and the Sino-Japanese War, 1937–1939: A Study in the Dilemmas of British Decline.* Stanford: Stanford University Press, 1973.

Leigh, Michael. *Mobilizing Consent: Public Opinion and American Foreign Policy, 1937–1947.* Westport, Conn.: Greenwood Press, 1976.

Leutze, James R. *Bargaining for Supremacy: Anglo-American Naval Collaboration, 1937–1941.* Chapel Hill: University of North Carolina Press, 1977.

Liang, Chin-tung. *General Stilwell in China, 1942–1944: The Full Story.* New York: St. John's University Press, 1972.

Liggio, Leonard P., and James J. Martin, eds. *Watershed of Empire: Essays on New Deal Foreign Policy.* Colorado Springs: Ralph Myles, 1976.

Little, Douglas. *Malevolent Neutrality: The United States, Great Britain, and the Origins of the Spanish Civil War.* Ithaca: Cornell University Press, 1985.

Lloyd, Alan. *Franco.* Garden City, N.Y.: Doubleday, 1969.

Louis, William Roger. *British Strategy in the Far East, 1919–1939.* Oxford: Clarendon Press, 1971.

———. *Imperialism at Bay: The United States and the Decolonization of the British Empire, 1941–1945.* Oxford: Oxford University Press, 1978.

Lu, David J. *From the Marco Polo Bridge to Pearl Harbor: Japan's Entry into World War II.* Washington, D.C.: Public Affairs Press, 1961.

Ludwig, Emil. *Roosevelt.* Paris: Plon, 1938.

Lukacs, John. *The Great Powers and Eastern Europe*. New York: American Book Company, 1953.

Lukas, Richard C. *The Strange Allies: The United States and Poland, 1941–1945*. Knoxville: University of Tennessee Press, 1978.

Lundestad, Geir. *The American Non-Policy towards Eastern Europe, 1943–1947: Universalism in an Area Not of Essential Interest to the United States*. New York: Humanities Press, 1975.

Macartney, C. A. *October Fifteenth: A History of Modern Hungary, 1929–1945*. Edinburgh: University of Edinburgh, 1957.

McCagg, William O. *Stalin Embattled, 1943–1948*. Detroit: Wayne State University Press, 1978.

MacDonald, C. A. *The United States, Britain, and Appeasement, 1936–1939*. New York: St. Martin's Press, 1981.

McKenna, Marian G. *Borah*. Ann Arbor: University of Michigan Press, 1961.

McNeill, William H. *America, Britain and Russia: Their Co-operation and Conflict, 1941–1946*. Oxford: Oxford University Press, 1953.

Maddox, Robert James. *William E. Borah and American Foreign Policy*. Baton Rouge: Louisiana State University Press, 1969.

Maddux, Thomas R. *Years of Estrangement: American Relations with the Soviet Union, 1933–1941*. Tallahassee: Florida State University Press, 1980.

Marks, Frederick W. III. *Velvet on Iron: The Diplomacy of Theodore Roosevelt*. Lincoln: University of Nebraska Press, 1979.

Marquand, David. *Ramsay MacDonald*. London: Jonathan Cape, 1977.

Martin, Gilbert. *Winston S. Churchill: Finest Hour, 1939–1941*. Boston: Houghton Mifflin, 1983.

Mastny, Vojtech. *Russia's Road to the Cold War: Diplomacy, Warfare, and the Politics of Communism, 1941–1945*. New York: Columbia University Press, 1979.

Maxon, Yale C. *Control of Japanese Foreign Policy: A Study of Civil-Military Rivalry, 1930–1945*. Berkeley and Los Angeles: University of California Press, 1957.

May, Ernest R. *"Lessons" of the Past: The Use and Misuse of History in American Foreign Policy*. New York: Oxford University Press, 1973.

Medlicott, W. N. *British Foreign Policy since Versailles, 1919–1963*. London: Methuen, 1968.

Meskill, Johanna M. *Hitler and Japan: The Hollow Alliance*. New York: Atherton, 1966.

Messer, Robert L. *The End of an Alliance: James F. Byrnes, Roosevelt, Truman, and the Origins of the Cold War*. Chapel Hill: University of North Carolina Press, 1982.

Millis, Walter. *This Is Pearl!* New York: Morrow, 1947.

Montague, L. L. *Haiti and the United States, 1714–1938*. Durham: Duke University Press, 1940.

Moore, Barrington, Jr. *Social Origins of Dictatorship and Democracy: Land and Peasant in the Making of the Modern World*. Boston: Beacon Press, 1966.

Morgenstern, George. *Pearl Harbor: The Story of the Secret War*. New York: Devin-Adair, 1947.

Morison, Elting. *Turmoil and Tradition: A Study of the Life and Times of Henry L. Stimson*. New York: Atheneum, 1964.

Morley, James William, ed. *Deterrent Diplomacy: Japan, Germany and the USSR, 1935–1940*. New York: Columbia University Press, 1976.

Morse, Arthur D. *While Six Million Died: A Chronicle of American Apathy*. New York: Random House, 1968.

Mosher, Steven W. *Broken Earth: The Rural Chinese*. New York: Free Press, 1983.

Neumann, William L. *After Victory: Churchill, Roosevelt, Stalin and the Making of the Peace*. New York: Harper, 1967.

———. *America Encounters Japan: From Perry to MacArthur*. Baltimore: Johns Hopkins University Press, 1963.

O'Connor, Raymond G. *Diplomacy for Victory: FDR and Unconditional Surrender*. New York: Norton, 1971.

Offner, Arnold A. *American Appeasement: United States Foreign Policy and Germany, 1933–1938*. Cambridge, Mass.: Harvard University Press, 1969.

———. *The Origins of the Second World War: American Foreign Policy and World Politics, 1917–1941*. New York: Praeger, 1975.

O'Hara, P. O. *Manchukuo: The World's Newest Nation*. Mukden: Manchuria Daily News, 1932.

Ollivier, Georges. *Franklin Roosevelt: L'homme de Yalta*. Paris: La Libraire Français, 1955.

Parsons, Edward B. *Wilsonian Diplomacy: Allied-American Rivalries in War and Peace*. St. Louis, Mo.: Forum Press, 1978.

Paterson, Thomas G., J. Garry Clifford, and Kenneth Hagan. *American Foreign Policy: A History since 1900*. 2d ed. Lexington, Mass.: D. C. Heath, 1983.

Payne, Howard C., Raymond Callahan, and Edward M. Bennett. *As the Storm Clouds Gathered: European Perceptions of American Foreign Policy in the 1930s*. Durham: Moore, 1979.

Payne, Robert. *The Life and Death of Trotsky*. New York: McGraw-Hill, 1977.

Pelz, Stephen E. *Race to Pearl Harbor: The Failure of the Second London Naval Conference and the Onset of World War II*. Cambridge, Mass.: Harvard University Press, 1974.

Penkover, Monty Noam. *The Jews Were Expendable: Free World Diplomacy and the Holocaust*. Urbana: University of Illinois Press, 1983.

Peterson, Harold F. *Argentina and the United States, 1810–1960.* Albany: State University of New York, 1964.

Pike, F. B. *Chile and the United States, 1880–1962.* South Bend, Ind.: Notre Dame University Press, 1963.

Poole, Peter A. *The United States and Indochina: From FDR to Nixon.* Hinsdale, Ill.: Dryden Press, 1973.

Prange, Gordon W. *At Dawn We Slept: The Untold Story of Pearl Harbor.* New York: McGraw-Hill, 1981.

Pratt, Julius W. *Cordell Hull, 1933–44.* 2 vols. New York: Cooper Square, 1964.

Range, Willard. *Franklin D. Roosevelt's World Order.* Athens: University of Georgia Press, 1959.

Rappaport, Armin. *Henry L. Stimson and Japan, 1931–33.* Chicago: University of Chicago Press, 1963.

Rémond, René, and Janine Bourdin. *Édouard Daladier, chef de gouvernment, avril 1938–septembre 1939.* Paris: Fondation Nationale des Sciences Politiques, 1977.

Reynolds, David. *The Creation of the Anglo-American Alliance, 1937–1941.* Chapel Hill: University of North Carolina Press, 1982.

Roberts, Walter R. *Tito, Mihailović and the Allies, 1941–1945.* New Brunswick: Rutgers University Press, 1973.

Romanus, Charles F., and Riley Sunderland. *Stilwell's Command Problems.* Washington, D.C.: Department of the Army, 1956.

———. *Stilwell's Mission to China.* Washington, D.C.: Department of the Army, 1953.

———. *Time Runs Out in CBI.* Washington, D.C.: Department of the Army, 1959.

Rose, Lisle A. *After Yalta.* New York: Scribner's, 1973.

———. *Dubious Victory: The United States and the End of World War II.* Kent, Ohio: Kent State University Press, 1973.

———. *Roots of Tragedy: The United States and the Struggle for Asia, 1945–1953.* Westport, Conn.: Greenwood Press, 1976.

Rosen, Elliot A. *Hoover, Roosevelt, and the Brains Trust.* New York: Columbia University Press, 1977.

Roskill, Stephen. *Hankey: Man of Secrets.* 3 vols. London: Collins, 1970–74.

Rothfels, Hans. *The German Opposition to Hitler.* Hinsdale, Ill.: Regnery, 1948.

Royama, Masamichi. *Foreign Policy of Japan, 1914–1939.* Tokyo: Institute of Pacific Relations, 1941.

Roz, Firmin. *Roosevelt.* Paris: Dunod, 1948.

Rozek, Edward J. *Allied Wartime Diplomacy: A Pattern in Poland.* New York: Wiley, 1958.

Russett, Bruce M. *No Clear and Present Danger: A Skeptical View of the U.S. Entry into World War II.* New York: Harper, 1972.

Sainsbury, Keith. *The Turning Point: Roosevelt, Stalin, Churchill, and Chiang Kai-shek, 1943: The Moscow, Cairo, and Teheran Conferences.* Oxford: Oxford University Press, 1985.

Sampson, Anthony. *The Seven Sisters: The Great Oil Companies and the World They Shaped.* New York: Viking, 1975.

Sanborn, Frederic R. *Design for War: A Study of Secret Power Politics, 1937–1941.* New York: Devin-Adair, 1951.

Sbrega, John J. *Anglo-American Relations and Colonialism in East Asia, 1941–1945.* New York: Garland, 1983.

Schaller, Michael. *The U.S. Crusade in China, 1938–1945.* New York: Columbia University Press, 1979.

Scherer, James A. B. *Manchukuo: A Bird's Eye View.* Tokyo: Hokuseido Press, 1933.

Schlesinger, Arthur M., Jr. *The Crisis of the Old Order, 1919–1933.* Boston: Houghton Mifflin, 1957.

———. *The Coming of the New Deal.* Boston: Houghton Mifflin, 1958.

———. *The Politics of Upheaval.* Boston: Houghton Mifflin, 1960.

Schroeder, Paul. *The Axis Alliance and Japanese-American Relations, 1941.* Ithaca: Cornell University Press, 1958.

Sharp, Tony. *The Wartime Alliance and the Zonal Division of Germany.* Oxford: Clarendon Press, 1975.

Sherwood, Robert E. *Roosevelt and Hopkins: An Intimate History.* New York: Harper, 1948.

Shewmaker, Kenneth. *Americans and the Communist Chinese, 1927–1945.* Ithaca: Cornell University Press, 1971.

Shirer, William L. *The Rise and Fall of the Third Reich.* 1959. Reprint. New York: Crest, 1963.

Sivachev, Nikolai V., and Nikolai N. Yakovlev. *Russia and the United States.* Translated by Olga Adler Titelbaum. Chicago: University of Chicago Press, 1979.

Smith, Gaddis. *American Diplomacy during the Second World War, 1941–1945.* New York: Wiley, 1967.

Smith, Janet Adam. *John Buchan.* London: Rupert Hart-Davis, 1965.

Smith, Robert F. *The United States and Cuba: Business and Diplomacy, 1917–1960.* New York: Bookman Associates, 1960.

Steward, Dick. *Money, Marines, and Mission: Recent U.S.–Latin American Policy.* Lanham, Md.: University Press of America, 1980.

———. *Trade and Hemisphere: The Good Neighbor Policy and Reciprocal Trade.* Columbia: University of Missouri Press, 1975.

Stoler, Mark A. *The Politics of the Second Front: American Military Planning and Diplomacy in Coalition Warfare, 1941–1943*. Westport, Conn.: Greenwood, 1976.

Strang, William. *Britain in World Affairs: The Fluctuation in Power and Influence from Henry VIII to Elizabeth II*. New York: Praeger, 1961.

Stueck, William W. *The Wedemeyer Mission: American Politics and Foreign Policy during the Cold War*. Athens: University of Georgia Press, 1984.

Tansill, Charles C. *Back Door to War: The Roosevelt Foreign Policy, 1933–1941*. Chicago: Regnery, 1952.

Taylor, A. J. P. *Beaverbrook*. London: Hamish Hamilton, 1972.

———. *The Origins of the Second World War*. 1961. Reprint. New York: Atheneum, 1964.

Taylor, Telford. *Munich: The Price of Peace*. Garden City, N.Y.: Doubleday, 1979.

Theobald, Robert A. *The Final Secret of Pearl Harbor*. New York: Devin-Adair, 1954.

Thorne, Christopher G. *Allies of a Kind: The United States, Britain, and the War against Japan, 1941–1945*. New York: Oxford University Press, 1978. Paperback.

———. *The Approach of War, 1938–1939*. New York: St. Martin's Press, 1967.

———. *The Limits of Foreign Policy: The West, the League, and the Far Eastern Crisis of 1931–1933*. London: Hamish Hamilton, 1972.

Toland, John. *Infamy: Pearl Harbor and Its Aftermath*. Garden City, N.Y.: Doubleday, 1982.

Traina, Richard P. *American Diplomacy and the Spanish Civil War*. Bloomington: Indiana University Press, 1968.

Trefouse, Hans L. *Germany and American Neutrality, 1939–1941*. New York: Bookman Associates, 1951.

Tuchman, Barbara. *Stilwell and the American Experience in China, 1911–1945*. New York: Bantam, 1972.

Ulam, Adam. *Expansion and Coexistence: The History of Soviet Foreign Policy, 1917–67*. New York: Praeger, 1968.

———. *Stalin*. New York: Viking, 1973.

Utley, Freda. *The China Story*. Chicago: Regnery, 1951.

Utley, Jonathan. *Going to War with Japan, 1937–1941*. Knoxville: University of Tennessee Press, 1985.

Varg, Paul A. *The Closing of the Door: Sino-American Relations, 1936–1946*. East Lansing: Michigan State University Press, 1973.

Villari, Luigi. *Italian Foreign Policy under Mussolini*. New York: Devin-Adair, 1956.

Viorst, Milton. *Hostile Allies: FDR and Charles de Gaulle*. New York: Macmillan, 1965.

Walters, F. P. *A History of the League of Nations.* London: Oxford University Press, 1960.

Walton, Richard J. *Henry Wallace, Harry Truman, and the Cold War.* New York: Viking, 1976.

Waltz, Kenneth Neal. *Foreign Policy and Democratic Politics: The American and British Experience.* Boston: Little, Brown, 1967.

Warth, Robert D. *Leon Trotsky.* Boston: Twayne, 1977.

Watt, Donald Cameron. *Personalities and Policies: Studies in the Formulation of British Foreign Policy in the Twentieth Century.* London: Longman's, 1965.

Weinberg, Gerhard L. *The Foreign Policy of Hitler's Germany: Diplomatic Revolution in Europe, 1933–1936.* Chicago: University of Chicago Press, 1970.

———. *The Foreign Policy of Hitler's Germany: Starting World War II, 1937–1939.* Chicago: University of Chicago Press, 1980.

Whalen, Richard J. *The Founding Father: The Story of Joseph P. Kennedy.* New York: New American Library, 1964.

Wheeler-Bennett, John W. *King George VI.* New York: St. Martin's Press, 1958.

White, Graham J. *FDR and the Press.* Chicago: University of Chicago Press, 1979.

White, Theodore H., and Annalee Jacoby. *Thunder Out of China.* New York: William Sloane, 1946.

Williams, Keith, and John Barnes. *Baldwin: A Biography.* London: Macmillan, 1969.

Wilson, Theodore A. *The First Summit: Roosevelt and Churchill at Placentia Bay, 1941.* Boston: Houghton Mifflin, 1969.

Wiltz, John E. *In Search of Peace: The Senate Munitions Inquiry, 1934–36.* Baton Rouge: Louisiana State University Press, 1963.

Wirsing, Giselher. *Roosevelt et l'Europe.* Translated by Jean Carrère. Paris: Bernard Grasset, 1942.

Wittner, Lawrence S. *American Intervention in Greece, 1943–1949.* New York: Columbia University Press, 1982.

Wohlstetter, Roberta. *Pearl Harbor: Warning and Decision.* Stanford: Stanford University Press, 1962.

Wood, Bryce. *The Making of the Good Neighbor Policy.* New York: Columbia University Press, 1954.

———. *The United States and Latin American Wars, 1932–1942.* New York: Columbia University Press, 1966.

Woods, Randall Bennett. *The Roosevelt Foreign Policy Establishment and the "Good Neighbor": The United States and Argentina, 1941–1945.* Lawrence: University of Kansas Press, 1979.

Woodward, Ernest Llewellyn. *British Foreign Policy in the Second World War.* 5 vols. London: Her Majesty's Stationery Office, 1970–76.

Wright, William. *Heiress*. Washington, D.C.: New Republic Books, 1978.

Wyman, David S. *The Abandonment of the Jews: America and the Holocaust, 1941–1945*. New York: Pantheon, 1984.

———. *Paper Walls: America and the Refugee Crisis, 1938–1941*. Amherst: University of Massachusetts Press, 1968.

Yoshihashi, Takehiko. *Conspiracy at Mukden: The Rise of the Japanese Military*. New Haven: Yale University Press, 1963.

Zawodny, Janusz K. *Death in the Forest: The Story of the Katyn Forest Massacre*. South Bend, Ind.: University of Notre Dame Press, 1962.

Index